MORAL RESPONSIBILITY

LIBRARY OF ETHICS AND APPLIED PHILOSOPHY

VOLUME 27

For further volumes:
http://www.springer.com/series/6230

MORAL RESPONSIBILITY

Beyond Free Will and Determinism

Edited by

NICOLE A VINCENT
Delft University of Technology, Delft, The Netherlands
Macquarie University, Sydney, Australia

IBO VAN DE POEL
Delft University of Technology, Delft, The Netherlands

and

JEROEN VAN DEN HOVEN
Delft University of Technology, Delft, The Netherlands

Springer

Editors
Nicole A Vincent
Delft University of Technology
Department of Philosophy
Faculty of Technology,
Policy & Management
Jaffalaan 5
2628 BX Delft
The Netherlands
n.a.vincent@tudelft.nl

Department of Philosophy
Faculty of Arts
Macquarie University
Sydney NSW 2109
Australia
nicole.vincent@mq.edu.au

Prof. Dr. Jeroen van den Hoven
Delft University of Technology
Department of Philosophy
Faculty of Technology,
Policy & Management
Jaffalaan 5
2628 BX Delft
The Netherlands
m.j.vandenhoven@tudelft.nl

Ibo van de Poel
Delft University of Technology
Department of Philosophy
Faculty of Technology,
Policy & Management
Jaffalaan 5
2628 BX Delft
The Netherlands
I.R.vandePoel@tudelft.nl

ISSN 1387-6678
ISBN 978-94-007-1877-7 e-ISBN 978-94-007-1878-4
DOI 10.1007/978-94-007-1878-4
Springer Dordrecht Heidelberg London New York

Library of Congress Control Number: 2011934879

Printed on acid-free paper

Springer is part of Springer Science+Business Media (www.springer.com)

Contents

Contributors

Diana Abad Department of Philosophy, University of Potsdam, Potsdam, Germany, diana.abad@uni-potsdam.de

Jason Benchimol Department of Philosophy, University of Washington, Seattle, WA, USA, jdbench@uw.edu

Gunnar Björnsson Linköping University, Linköping, Sweden; University of Gothenburg, Gothenburg, Sweden, gunnar.bjornsson@liu.se

Lene Bomann-Larsen Department of Philosophy, Classics, History of Art and Ideas, University of Oslo, Oslo, Norway, lene.bomann-larsen@hf.uio.no

Alexander Brown School of Political, Social and International Studies, University of East Anglia, Norwich, UK, alexander.c.brown@uea.ac.uk

Susan Dimock York University, Toronto, Canada, ON, dimock@yorku.ca

Rosemary Lowry Department of Philosophy, Eindhoven University of Technology, Eindhoven, The Netherlands, r.j.lowry@tue.nl

Seumas Miller Centre for Applied Philosophy and Public Ethics, Australian National University, Canberra, ACT, Australia; Charles Sturt University, Canberra, NSW, Australia; Department of Philosophy, Delft University of Technology, Delft, The Netherlands, seumas.miller@anu.edu.au

Ibo van de Poel Department of Philosophy, Delft University of Technology, 2600 GA Delft, The Netherlands, I.R.vandePoel@tudelft.nl

Michael Smith Department of Philosophy, 1879 Hall, Princeton University, Princeton, NJ 08544, USA, msmith@princeton.edu

Steve Vanderheiden Department of Political Science, University of Colorado, Boulder, CO, USA; Centre for Applied Philosophy and Public Ethics (CAPPE), Canberra, ACT, Australia, vanders@colorado.edu

Nicole A Vincent Department of Philosophy, Delft University of Technology, 2600 GA Delft, The Netherlands; Department of Philosophy, Faculty of Arts, Macquarie University, Sydney, NSW 2109, Australia, n.a.vincent@tudelft.nl; nicole.vincent@mq.edu.au

Chapter 1
Introduction

Nicole A Vincent and Ibo van de Poel

1.1 Beyond Free Will and Determinism

It is now well over a decade since John Fischer and Mark Ravizza (1998) – and before them, Jay Wallace (1994) and Daniel Dennett (1984) – defended responsibility from the threat of determinism. What these authors' compatibilist theories have in common is the idea that responsible agents are not those agents whose actions are un-caused, but rather those agents who possess certain competences or capacities. But defending responsibility from determinism is a potentially endless and largely negative enterprise – it can go on for as long as dissenting voices remain (i.e. indefinitely), and although such work strengthens the theoretical foundations of these theories, it won't necessarily build anything on top of those foundations, nor will it move these theories into new territory or explain how to apply them to practical contexts. To this end, instead of devoting more effort to the negative enterprise of building up even stronger fortifications against the ever-present threat of determinism, the papers in this volume address these more positive challenges by exploring ways in which compatibilist responsibility theory can be extended and/or applied in a range of practical contexts.

This book begins with two chapters that set out a finer-grained understanding of the rich and multi-faceted notion of responsibility found in contemporary debates, situated within a broadly compatibilist framework.

In philosophical discussions, responsibility is often talked about as if it were a single, unitary and generic concept, or at least that is the impression that such discussions can create. For instance, in the compatibilist literature, the topic seems to be whether determinism rules out *responsibility*. In political philosophy, luck egalitarians and their opponents debate whether people's entitlements should track their *responsibility*. And in the area of neurolaw, some people claim that "a truly scientific mechanistic view of the nervous system make[s] nonsense of the very idea

N.A Vincent (✉)
Department of Philosophy, Delft University of Technology, 2600 GA Delft, The Netherlands

Department of Philosophy, Faculty of Arts, Macquarie University, Sydney NSW 2109, Australia
e-mail: n.a.vincent@tudelft.nl; nicole.vincent@mq.edu.au

N.A Vincent et al. (eds.), *Moral Responsibility*, Library of Ethics and Applied Philosophy 27, DOI 10.1007/978-94-007-1878-4_1,

of *responsibility*" (Dawkins 2006, emphasis added; also Greene and Cohen 2004), while others deny that neuroscience challenges *responsibility* (e.g. Gazzaniga 2006; Morse 2006). If confronted head on, most philosophers would probably acknowledge as Fischer and Ravizza do that the term "'responsibility' admits of a variety of uses" (1998:2, note 1), but somehow this variety seldom comes across in anything other than footnotes and its implications are seldom drawn out.

To this end, **Nicole Vincent**'s paper "A Structured Taxonomy of Responsibility Concepts" aims to remedy this situation by saying something more substantial about this variety of uses of the term "responsibility", about how these uses relate to one another, and by explaining how we are better off for knowing about these things. First, Vincent distinguishes six different responsibility concepts which, drawing inspiration from H. L. A. Hart's terminology, she calls capacity responsibility, virtue responsibility, causal responsibility, outcome responsibility, role responsibility and liability responsibility. Sometimes "responsible" describes a kind of person, either in terms of their *capacities* ("a fully responsible person"), or in terms of their *character* virtues or lack thereof ("an irresponsible person"). At other times it describes relations between events, either in *causal* terms ("his depression was responsible for his behaviour"), or in *moral* terms ("he is responsible for that accident"). And finally, it can also refer to a person's *duties* ("these are your responsibilities"), or to how they should be *treated* ("you will be held responsible for that accident"). Second, Vincent argues that these six responsibility concepts relate to one another via justificatory relations that obtain between claims which employ them, and she explains the nature of these justificatory relations. For instance, she points out that people are normally expected to take *liability* responsibility precisely because of and usually only for those things for which they are *outcome* responsible; it is precisely because a person had certain *role* responsibilities which they subsequently violated that we tend to attribute *outcome* responsibility to them but not to others who did not have those role responsibilities; and we normally impose fewer and less weighty *role* responsibilities onto people whose *capacity* responsibility was reduced. Finally, she also argues that not only can an awareness of this rich complexity help us to systematically resolve a range of problems in scholarly as well as public debates, but that it also suggests a new set of problems that compatibilists should address. Namely, she suggests that since "responsibility" refers to a range of different ideas, compatibilists must explain in what way determinism is meant to pose a threat to each of these different ideas, and then spell out how compatibilism addresses these different challenges.

On Vincent's account, claims about what states of affairs can be legitimately attributed to a given person as things of their doing and for which they can be blamed (in her terminology, things for which they are outcome responsible) hinge crucially on whether those people acted in a way that transgressed how they ought to have acted (in her terminology, whether they breached their role responsibilities). This feature of Vincent's analysis suggests that there exists a relationship between *backward*-looking responsibility claims (claims about who is outcome responsible for the things that happened in the past) and *forward*-looking responsibility claims (claims about who had- and subsequently violated what role responsibilities), and the explicit aim of **Ibo van de Poel**'s paper "The Relation Between Forward-Looking and Backward-Looking Responsibility" is to shed further light on this relationship. In this regard, van de Poel distinguishes two varieties of backward-looking responsibility: accountability and blameworthiness. He argues that accountability implies having to account for one's actions, but if the account given is insufficient then one will be blameworthy. Furthermore, he also argues that although accountability is sometimes based on an improperly discharged forward-looking responsibility, it may also be based on the breach of a moral duty. This is important because although the duty to account for one's actions presupposes at least three conditions – a capacity condition, a causality condition and a wrongdoing condition – van de Poel argues that the exact formulation of these conditions is different for these two routes to accountability.

However, van de Poel's paper does a lot more than just shed light on the nature of the relationship between backward and forward-looking responsibility concepts. He begins by distinguishing nine different responsibility concepts from one another – namely, responsibility as cause, as task, as authority, as capacity, as virtue, as obligation, as accountability, as blameworthiness and as liability. Although a number of these concepts map straight-forwardly onto the six concepts distinguished by Vincent, some important differences and discrepancies remain. For instance, van de Poel's concept of responsibility as *authority* has no counterpart in Vincent's analysis, but yet we often say that something is someone's responsibility, meaning that they are in charge of it (in Hohfeld's terms, that they have some kind of *privilege/liberty* or perhaps a *power* with respect to it) and not just that it is their burden to carry (in Hohfeld's terms, that it is their *duty* or *liability*) (Hohfeld 1975). Secondly, van de Poel's responsibility as *accountability* also finds no direct counterpart in Vincent's taxonomy, but yet, as he argues, it is only when a person fails to provide a satisfactory account for what has happened that we would even start thinking of blaming them if what happened was untoward. Finally, although both cite wrongdoing as a condition of (outcome- or blame-) responsibility for untoward states of affairs, while van de Poel distinguishes two different ways in which this condition can be satisfied – one via a consequentialist route that is traversed when a forward-looking responsibility is not (properly) discharged, and another via a deontic route that occurs in the face of a duty transgression – Vincent's analysis does not distinguish between these two routes since on her account this condition is satisfied simply when an agent breaches their role responsibility. Thus, in addition to offering an in-depth discussion of the relationship between backward and forward-looking responsibility concepts, van de Poel's analysis also further enriches our understanding of the subtle differences and relationships between this range of different responsibility concepts.

These first two chapters develop the idea that the word "responsibility" refers to a range of subtly different and inter-related concepts, they provide examples of how this affects a range of important practical debates, and they offer suggestions about how this bears on compatibilist responsibility theory. The discussion that follows in the next six chapters can be fruitfully understood as addressing these different facets of the notion of responsibility.

Michael Smith's paper "Beyond Belief and Desire: or, How to Be Orthonomous" provides a detailed account of an important capacity which on his account is required for responsible moral agency – namely, the capacity to be orthonomous. On Smith's account, the standard belief-desire account of action explanation is attractive in part because it explains two crucial distinctions: (i) the distinction, among the things that we do, between the active and the passive, and (ii) the distinction, among the things that we do with respect to which we are active, between those that we do intentionally and those that we do not do intentionally. However, on his account there is a crucial flaw in this standard belief-desire account of action explanation. The account is normally taken to posit four basic elements – two psychological (a desire for an end and a means-end belief), one non-psychological (a bodily movement), and a relation that holds between them (a causal relation of the right kind) – whereas in reality there are five basic elements. Namely, he argues that our being rational to the extent that we are plays a distinct explanatory role. On this account, once we acknowledge the presence of this extra psychological element in every action explanation, we put ourselves in a position to explain a third crucial distinction, one which crosscuts the second: (iii) the distinction between the things that we do rationally and those that we do not do rationally. More generally, we open the door to an understanding of ourselves as orthonomous agents – that is, as agents who have the distinctive capacity to be ruled by the right (to be rational) as opposed to the wrong (to be irrational) – and of the ways in which, when faced with temptations, we may exercise the distinctive capacity we have to be orthonomous. On Smith's account, it is our capacity to be orthonomous that explains when and why we are appropriately held responsible.

A central component in compatibilist thinking is *capacitarianism* – i.e. the idea that *responsibility tracks capacity*. But precisely how is it that changes in capacity (e.g. in a person's *mental* capacities) are meant to result in changes to responsibility (e.g. in what that person can be blamed for doing)? Furthermore, responsibility is also often viewed as something that comes in *degrees* – i.e. people's responsibility is said to be *diminished* by various mental conditions, and the *severity* of punishments imposed onto wrongdoers is also said to co-vary with (among other things) the degree of their responsibility – but exactly why does responsibility come in degrees rather than being an all-or-nothing concept? Also, is there any *relationship* between the former two observations – i.e. that responsibility comes in degrees and that it tracks capacity – and if so then what is it?

Rosemary Lowry's paper "Blame, Reasons and Capacities" answers these questions in two stages. At the first stage, Lowry argues that a person is *blameworthy* when they fail to do what they have most *reason* to do, and that what they have *reason* to do is in turn constrained by what they *can* do (i.e. by what capacities they possess and by what opportunities are available to them). This first stage sets up a chain of justificatory relations between claims about *capacity*, claims about *reasons*, and claims about *blame* (and thus about responsibility, at least for blameworthy states of affairs). At the second stage, Lowry extends Michael Smith's procedure for determining whether an agent possesses certain rational capacities, so that it can be used to measure the degree to which a person *can* do something – i.e. to measure the degree to which they have certain capacities and opportunities. According to this procedure, a person who can perform a given act – the act for which the capacity of interest is said to be a pre-condition – in a *wide range* of possible worlds, has the requisite capacity to a *larger degree* than a person who can only perform that act in a *narrower range* of possible worlds. Thus, on Lowry's account, blame comes in degrees because reasons come in degrees, reasons come in degrees because capacities come in degrees, and the procedure which she develops helps us to measure these degrees of capacity and thus the degrees of responsibility.

Normally, and in line with Lowry's discussion, reductions in relevant mental capacities (e.g. a reduced ability to control one's conduct) result in judgments of diminished responsibility (e.g. diminished or even completely extinguished blame). This is a straight forward consequence of the above-mentioned capacitarian idea that responsibility tracks capacity. However, although reduced capacity can often be cited as an exculpating factor, sometimes it can not. For instance, under many jurisdictions, drink-drivers and other self-intoxicated parties are not permitted to cite their subsequently reduced mental capacities as a defense to an accusation of criminal responsibility. This feature of the criminal law seems like a practical manifestation of John Fischer and Mark Ravizza's *tracing principle*, according to which the exculpatory value of capacity reductions for which agents are responsible should either be *discounted* or even completely *extinguished* (Fischer and Ravizza 1998:49–51).

However, in "Please Drink Responsibly: Can the Responsibility of Intoxicated Offenders be Justified by the Tracing Principle?" **Susan Dimock** argues that the tracing principle does not in fact support the policy of disallowing self-intoxicated parties from citing their diminished mental capacities as an excuse to the accusation of criminal responsibility. On Dimock's account, there is nothing inherently culpable in the choices that are made by most defendants who eventually become intoxicated, and this is especially so in light of the fact that instead of prohibition, the state rather urges the public to "drink responsibly", and it even happily – almost complicitly – collects substantial revenues from taxation on alcohol sales. Hence, Dimock continues, there is no reason to suppose that such people are blameworthy for becoming intoxicated, and thus no plausible ground for alleging that they are responsible for their subsequent loss of capacities. Put a different way, on Dimock's account there is no culpable action to which self-intoxicated people's diminished capacities can usually be traced back, and thus the discounting function of the tracing principle should not as a general rule be applied to these cases. If Dimock is right, then what is so often taken as a textbook example of the tracing principle (i.e. self-intoxication) is not an example of it at all, and so urgent legal reform is needed in jurisdictions which currently disallow self-intoxicated people to cite their diminished capacities as a defense to the accusation of criminal responsibility, or which (as in Canada) even allow evidence of self-intoxication to be substituted for evidence of fault or *mens rea*.

The tracing principle is sometimes also cited to explain what justifies blaming people for their unintended omissions and for other instances of negligence. Negligence presents a problem because the blamed parties did not realize what they ought to have done – this lack of knowledge is precisely what distinguishes negligence from recklessness – which means that they lacked the capacity to guide their actions by the appropriate knowledge since that knowledge was not available to them, and this lack of capacity seems in turn to undermine the attribution of blame. However, the tracing retort to this worry is that negligent parties should have realized what they ought to have done – i.e. that they are responsible for their current incapacity – because their incapacity was an outcome of some earlier instance of *non*-negligent blameworthy actions on their part – i.e. it was allegedly a consequence of their earlier *choices*. Blame for negligence is thus meant to derive on this account from blame for an earlier exercise of choice.

However, **Jason Benchimol**'s paper "The Moral Significance of Unintentional Omission: Comparing Will-Centered and Non-Will-Centered Accounts of Moral Responsibility" argues that this use of the tracing principle is deeply problematic, and moreover, that it is not even needed to explain what justifies blame for negligence. On the first point, Benchimol draws attention to four problems. First, even if we can't trace back the current negligent action to an earlier blameworthy exercise of choice, intuitively that does not seem to undermine the claim that the negligent action was itself blameworthy. Second, the search for a prior choice to which the current negligent action can be traced may in fact lead us so far back in time that any blame for the negligent action will be diluted almost to the point of extinction, since only a person with incredible powers of foresight would have recognized that their earlier choice was fraught with danger, but yet some of the most systematic examples of inattention, forgetfulness and other forms of negligence are the most worthy candidates for attracting blame. Third, this view seriously distorts the substantive content for which negligent parties are meant to be blamed and for which they are supposed to atone, since attention is drawn away from their negligence to some temporally (and possibly extremely remote) prior choice which is blameworthy on account of substantively different features. And fourth, the view that *all* blame for negligence derives from prior blameworthy choice can not make sense of why someone who *does* make a prior blameworthy choice but later *does not* act negligently is intuitively less blameworthy than someone whose prior choice is the same but who later *does* act negligently, because *ex hypothesi* all blame must attach to the earlier choice which was the same in both cases. On the second point, Benchimol argues that nothing is gained by insisting that only prior blameworthy choices can ground blame for negligence, because it is not the fact of a choice being a choice per se that makes it a proper target of moral criticism, but the fact that the evaluative attitudes which it expresses are reprehensible, and this component is already present in negligence anyway. Thus, like Dimock, though for different reasons, Benchimol too draws attention to what he believes is a common misapplication of the tracing principle.

While the previous four papers focus on the relationship between mental capacity, role responsibilities, and outcome responsibility, as well as on two instances of alleged misapplication of the tracing strategy that is often cited to explain why not all mental incapacities exculpate, the next two papers focus on the relationship between claims about what a person is outcome responsible for and their liability responsibility, and on how recalcitrant incompatibilist doubts about the legitimacy of holding people liability responsible for what they do (i.e. legal punishment) can be overcome by drawing on contractualist ideas.

Given the distinction and the relationship that obtains between backward- and forward-looking responsibility claims which Vincent and van de Poel discuss, one way to understand the debate about luck egalitarianism in political philosophy is that it is a debate about how to justify the connection between facts about outcome responsibility (or responsibility as blame in van de Poel's terminology) and conclusions about liability responsibility (or responsibility as liability in van de Poel's terminology). Put more precisely, this debate can be understood as addressing the following two questions: (1) do conclusions about people's liability responsibility (i.e. about how specific individuals may be treated) really follow purely from facts about their outcome responsibility (i.e. about what states of affairs those individuals are responsible for bringing about); and if so, then (2) how do we determine precisely what consequences one must take liability responsibility for (i.e. how one should take responsibility) given the sort of thing for which one is allegedly outcome responsible? Serena Olsaretti (2009) and Nicole Vincent (2009) have both recently described the luck egalitarian debate in this way, and a common feature of their arguments is their insistence that to justify this transition from outcome responsibility to liability responsibility we need to draw upon further substantive normative premises – what Olsaretti calls "a principle of stakes" and what Vincent calls "reactive norms".

However, **Diana Abad**'s paper "Desert, Responsibility and Luck Egalitarianism" argues that the connection between claims about outcome responsibility and conclusions about liability responsibility can be substantially (though not completely) bridged simply by the concept of *desert*. On Abad's account, desert is a three-place relation – X deserves Y in virtue of Z – where X is the desert *subject*, Y is the desert *object*, and Z is the desert *base*. Furthermore, she also suggests that to deserve something means that it is *appropriate* to get it, where *propriety* in turn means that it is both *fitting* and *required* that the desert subject get the desert object in virtue of the desert base. Given this conceptual analysis of desert, Abad then argues that question (2) above (i.e. *how* people should take responsibility) is addressed by the *fittingness* component of the notion of propriety, while question (1) above (i.e. *whether* people should take responsibility for the things for which they are responsible) is addressed by the *requirement* component of the notion of propriety. Put another way, on Abad's account, the concept of desert provides a formal framework within which we can addresses both of these questions in a single move, since what desert entails is that it is *required* that *fitting* treatment be visited onto outcome responsible parties. However, Abad also admits that there are limits to desert as a bridging principle between outcome and liability responsibility – namely, that the *concept* of desert does not itself specify *who* deserves *what* in virtue of *what*, and nor is responsibility the *only base* upon which subjects can deserve various objects. The practical upshot of this is that the same subject can deserve different and incompatible objects (i.e. treatments or liability responsibility) in virtue of different bases, and so substantive normative premises will indeed need to be considered in the process of reconciling these different desert claims with one another. In effect, Abad's argument entails that although desert can provide a formal link between claims about outcome responsibility and conclusions about liability responsibility, the substantive normative premises at which Olsaretti and Vincent gesture will still be needed to turn these formal links into substantive conclusions about how people may be treated.

Despite many compatibilists' confidence that compatibilism can successfully reconcile legal responsibility with a scientific world view, various authors still worry that although scientific evidence of causation may not undermine responsibility attributions, it may still never the less undermine the law's distinctly backward-looking justifications for its punitive practices. For instance, although Joshua Greene and Jonathan Cohen praise the compatibilist approach, saying that "[c]ompatibilists make some compelling arguments" (2004:1777), never the less they believe that the law's retributive practices can only be defended under libertarianism (which they find wanting). Consequently, they recommend that the law's backward-looking punitive aims should be replaced with such forward-looking punitive aims as deterrence, prevention and treatment. The worry here is not just that the law's actual punitive practices may turn out to be too lenient or too harsh, but that compatibilism simply can't provide the right kind of normative justification to warrant genuinely backward-looking punishment.

Within this context, accepting this incompatibilist challenge **Lene Bomann-Larsen**'s paper "Communicative Revisionism" explores whether contractualism can provide the needed normative foundation for a genuinely backward-looking form of punishment within a broadly compatibilist framework. Echoing the concerns of Greene and Cohen, Bomann-Larsen argues that although free will may not be relevant to legal determinations of guilt and responsibility, it does never the less seem relevant to backward-looking desert-based practices like punishment. However, instead of accepting the revisionist recommendations of authors like Greene and Cohen, who would have us abandon the search for such backward-looking justifications for punishment, Bomann-Larsen suggests that contractualism can provide the right sorts of justifications while remaining consistent with compatibilist commitments. However, although on her account this move fits well with a communicative theory of punishment which is thoroughly backward-looking, some revision to the law's actual punitive practices will still be needed because although it is plausible that contracting parties may accept some forms of hard treatment to communicate censure, most would likely reject "extreme punishment . . . which either makes reconciliation with community impossible [e.g. life imprisonment], or which imposes irreparable damage" on the offender (e.g. capital punishment). Thus, although she argues that genuinely backward-looking punitive practices can be justified in a way that respects compatibilist commitments, what must still never the less be revised is the kind and severity of some current legal punitive practices.

Finally, since much compatibilist thinking focuses on the topic of individual responsibility, this book's remaining four chapters investigate theoretical and applied problems in the area of collective responsibility. Although collective responsibility has attracted a lot of philosophical discussion, the compatibilist literature on responsibility has tended to focus on individual responsibility. It is therefore an interesting question whether, and to what extent, compatibilist notions of responsibility can account for cases of collective or joint responsibility.

A good starting point for such a discussion is **Alex Brown**'s contribution on "Moral Responsibility and Jointly Determined Consequences". Brown offers a critical examination of some aspects of Fischer and Ravizza's compatibilist theory of responsibility. Fischer and Ravizza offer both a negative argument for compatibilism – i.e. that the inevitability of certain events or consequences does not rule out the possibility of an agent's moral responsibility for those consequences – and a positive argument – i.e. that moral responsibility for consequences depends on action-responsiveness. With respect to the first, Brown highlights a flaw in Fischer and Ravizza's account of simultaneous over-determination of consequence-universals. With respect to the second, he points out that if, as Fischer and Ravizza propose, action-responsiveness were a necessary condition of an agent's being morally responsible for certain consequences, then an act or omission that only jointly determines a consequence could not attract moral responsibility. Given these problems, Brown argues that in addition to an account of moral responsibility for cases of individual action, we also need accounts of moral responsibility and action-responsiveness which are designed specifically to handle cases of joint action.

In his contribution Brown discusses three types of cases of joint determination of consequences:

- *Cumulative*: The case Brown discusses is *Revolutionaries*, where two revolutionaries independently and unaware of each other try to kill the same governmental official by shooting him. Since both are not trained shooters, only the combined, cumulative effect of their shootings kills the mayor.
- *Joint enterprise*: For example, two *Fundamentalists* cooperate to kill a country leader. Although only one of them pulls the trigger, we are inclined to hold them both responsible for the leader's death.
- *Probabilistic*: Brown's example is a *Firing Squad*, consisting of six good shooters, but only one of the six rifles being loaded. The deserter who is executed is sure to be killed, but the soldier who actually killed the deserter is selected randomly. We are inclined to hold the six soldiers jointly responsible.

In none of these examples is Fischer and Ravizza's condition of action-responsiveness met. As Brown points out, this condition, among other things, requires that the action of the person held responsible is *sufficient* to bring about the consequence, but yet in none of the above cases does this obtain. To deal with this problem, Brown proposes an alternative notion of action-responsiveness for cases of joint responsibility: "An individual's act or omission is jointly action-responsive with respect to a consequence C if and only if it along with the acts or omissions of at least one other individual is part of a process of type P which is sufficient for C to obtain and a different consequence would have obtained if it along with the other acts or omissions had not occurred and all other triggering events that would have been sufficient to cause C are not in play."

In his paper "Joint Responsibility without Individual Control: Applying the Explanation Hypothesis", **Gunnar Björnsson** further explores cases of what Brown calls cumulative determination of consequences. The example he discusses is, however, in one respect distinguishably different from Brown's *Revolutionaries*. In *Revolutionaries*, the individual contributions are not sufficient for the overall effect, but they are necessary. In Björnsson's example, *The Lake*, they are neither sufficient nor necessary. In *The Lake*, three people pour an equal amount of solvent into a lake with the consequence that the fish are killed. In this example, two amounts of solvents are enough to kill the fish. Björnsson argues that in cases like this most people have a strong intuition that the individuals are responsible, but it is not clear how this intuition is to be explained. In cases like *The Lake*, individuals jointly cause a detrimental effect without being individually in control of the effect. Since the individual contributions are neither necessary nor sufficient for the effect, accounts of responsibility in terms of "difference making" do not work in cases like this. By working through a number of variations on *The Lake* example, Björnsson also points out that accounts in terms of causal involvement or causal facilitation do not work either. Existing accounts of joint responsibility in terms of joint actions, joint intentions or social ties fail due to another feature of *The Lake* example – namely, that the individuals are unaware of each other's existence, and hence we can't even plausibly claim that their responsibility stems from their membership in a relevant social group.

To address these problems, Björnsson offers a reconstruction and explanation of our intuitions in cases of cumulative actions or omissions. To this end, he employs his own "explanation hypothesis", which he developed in an earlier paper. This hypothesis states that the motivational structure of an agent should be an integral part of the explanation for why the (undesirable) outcome occurred, for that agent to be responsible for the outcome. Björnsson argues that in cases like *The Lake* we consider the three individuals individually responsible "because their motivational structures are part of a significant explanans only taken together with the motivational structures of the other two." Focusing on only one of them is not only unsatisfactory because the individual contributions do not make a difference to the outcome, but also because it neglects the role of the other two, who, from an explanatory point of view, played exactly the same role.

Steven Vanderheiden focuses on still further kinds of cases of joint responsibility. Vanderheiden asks whether persons can reasonably be held morally responsible for harmful consequences that result from the acts or omissions of their nation or society, even if they as individuals try to avoid contributing toward those consequences. The example he discusses is global climate change. The 1992 UN Framework Convention on Climate Change holds nations responsible for the climate-related harm that they cause through their greenhouse gas emissions. Vanderheiden argues that this implies holding citizens of those nations responsible (in the liability responsibility sense) even if some of them did not contribute to the harm (i.e. even though they were apparently not outcome responsible), which makes this responsibility attribution seem unreasonable. Vanderheiden argues that the attribution is nevertheless just because all citizens participate in a culture that permits or even encourages consumption patterns that directly contribute to global warming. Moreover, all citizens – even those who actively oppose current government policies – benefit from the consumption patterns, and hence on his account all citizens are therefore responsible although not necessarily to the same degree.

The example of climate change that Vanderheiden discusses is somewhat similar to the pattern of joint enterprise discussed by Brown. It has, however, some features that are distinctively different from cases like *Fundamentalists*. In *Fundamentalists*, all participants actively and willingly cooperate to attain the effect, whereas Vanderheiden is also interested in those participants that do not actively or willingly cooperate. The key question for Vanderheiden is thus what would be required to "extricat[e] oneself from responsibility for harm caused by group actions." One option he considers is voting for candidates or policies that aim at avoiding contributing to global warming, but he replies that such voting alone is not sufficient to avoid responsibility. This is especially not sufficient if this voting is likely to be ineffective in terms of overall policies, and if the dissenting voters continue to profit from the collective benefits of the harmful practices. If ineffective voting would be enough to generate an excuse, then it would invite moral free riding: enjoying the collective benefits while bearing none of the responsibility for creating these benefits through ineffective "resistance". Thus, following David Miller, Vanderheiden suggests that the only sincere opposition is to refuse to partake in the benefits of society's harmful practices. But entirely refusing such benefits may be practically impossible for citizens of affluent societies as some of the benefits are public goods and one is born and raised in affluent circumstances that are themselves the result of those unjust practices. This is not to deny that one can extricate oneself from some responsibility, but, if we follow Vanderheiden, not from *all* responsibility for the negative consequences of climate change. Interestingly, Vanderheiden's conclusion has a distinct compatibilist flavor: one can be responsible for consequences even if these consequences are inevitable.

The final paper by **Seumas Miller** provides a methodologically-individualistic theoretical framework for reasoning about collective responsibility – and in particular, about collective responsibility for epistemic actions – and it demonstrates this framework's usefulness by investigating the topic of our collective responsibility for harms due to human-induced global warming and climate change. Miller begins by outlining a theory of *joint action* as the action of individuals within stratified organizational frameworks that define specific role responsibilities for constituent individuals, or what he calls "multi-layered structures of joint action characteristic of organizational action". His stated explicit aim throughout this chapter is "to display the continuity between individual and institutional moral responsibility for actions: the continuity between, for example, the moral responsibility for harmful climate change of individual citizens and that of governments". However, on Miller's account many important issues in the debate about collective responsibility for harms due to human-induced climate change hinge on *epistemic* factors that in his view have received insufficient attention in the literature, and so to this end he adapts the previously-developed theory to take account of *joint epistemic action*. An account of *collective moral responsibility* for joint (epistemic and behavioural) action (and omissions) is then developed, and it is subsequently put to use to explain who has, and in what degrees, "both retrospective responsibility for causing harm and also prospective responsibility for addressing the problem in terms of mitigation and/or adaptation".

This book's chapters deal with a range of theoretical problems discussed in classic compatibilist literature – e.g. the relationship between responsibility and capacity, the role of historical tracing in discounting the exculpatory value of incapacities, and the justifiability of retributive punishment. But instead of motivating their discussions by focusing on the alleged threat that determinism poses to responsibility, these chapters' authors have animated their discussions by tackling practical problems which crop up in contemporary debates about responsibility in the hope of both applying and extending compatibilist thought. For instance, how is the narrow philosophical concept of responsibility that was defended from the threat of determinism related to the plural notions of responsibility present in everyday discourse, and how might this more fine-grained understanding of responsibility open up new vistas and challenges for compatibilist theory? What light might compatibilism shed, and what light might be shed upon it, by political debates about access to public welfare in the context of responsibility for one's own health, and by legal debates about the impact of self-intoxication on responsibility. Finally, and perhaps most importantly, does compatibilist theory, which was originally designed to cater for analysis of individual actions, scale to scenarios that involve group action and collective responsibility – for instance, for harms due to human-induced climate change – or must compatibilism be modified in some way to handle collective responsibility scenarios and problems? Although the range of topics covered by the papers in this volume is broad, what ties them together is their authors' commitment to using the foundations of compatibilist theory to address important moral, political and legal questions about responsibility, and to develop this otherwise largely-negative branch of philosophy in a distinctly positive and practical direction.

Acknowledgments The papers in this volume are a selection of papers presented at the international conference *Moral Responsibility: Neuroscience, Organization & Engineering*, that was held in Delft, The Netherlands, on August 24–27, 2009, as well as some invited contributions. This volume was composed as part of the research programs "The Brain and The Law" and "Moral Responsibility in R&D Networks", both supported by the Netherlands Organization for Scientific Research (NWO). The editors express their gratitude to Malik Aleem Ahmed for helping them to prepare this manuscript for publication despite our constantly-shifting deadlines and a never-ending stream of "another thing please" requests. Special thanks also go to Antony Duff, Walter Glannon and Neil Levy for providing timely, insightful and helpful feedback – often on successive drafts of the same papers – as well as to Maja de Keijzer and Nicoline Ris from Springer and Springer's anonymous referees. Ibo van de Poel is grateful to the Netherlands Institute for Advanced Study (NIAS), for providing him with the opportunity, as a Fellow-in-Residence, to work on this volume during his stay in the academic year 2009–2010. And Nicole Vincent is grateful for the generous financial and moral support of the Philosophy Department at Delft University of Technology, as well as the 3TU Centre for Ethics and Technology (3TU.Ethics), but also to Saskia Polder-Verkiel for helping her to plan the aforementioned conference, for making things happen when the pressure was on, and for her feedback on oral presentations of many of the papers contained in this volume.

References

Dawkins, Richard. 2006. "Let's all Stop Beating Basil's Car." Accessed February 12, 2007. http://www.edge.org/q2006/q06_9.html#dawkins.

Dennett, Daniel Clement. 1984. *Elbow Room: The Varieties of Free Will Worth Wanting*. Cambridge, MA: MIT Press.

Fischer, John Martin and Mark Ravizza. 1998. *Responsibility and Control: A Theory of Moral Responsibility*. Cambridge, UK: CUP.

Gazzaniga, Michael S. 2006. "Facts, Fictions and the Future of Neuroethics." In *Neuroethics: Defining the Issues in Theory, Practice, and Policy*, edited by Judy Illes, 141–48. New York, NY: Oxford University Press.

Greene, Joshua and Jonathan Cohen. 2004. "For the Law, Neuroscience Changes Nothing and Everything." *Philosophical Transactions of the Royal Society of London* 359:1775–85.

Hohfeld, Wesley Newcomb. 1975. "Rights and Jural Relations." In *Philosophy of Law*, edited by Joel Feinberg and Hyman Gross, 357–67. Belmont, CA: Wadsworth Publishing Company.

Morse, Stephen J. 2006. "Moral and Legal Responsibility and the New Neuroscience." In *Neuroethics: Defining the Issues in Theory, Practice, and Policy*, edited by Judy Illes, 33–50. New York, NY: Oxford University Press.

Olsaretti, Serena. 2009. "Responsibility and the Consequences of Choice." *Proceedings of the Aristotelian Society* (Hardback) 109(1pt2):165–88.

Vincent, Nicole. 2009. "What Do You Mean I Should Take Responsibility for My Own Ill Health?" *Journal of Applied Ethics and Philosophy* 1:39–51.

Wallace, R. Jay. 1994. *Responsibility and the Moral Sentiments*. Cambridge, MA: Harvard University Press.

Chapter 2
A Structured Taxonomy of Responsibility Concepts

Nicole A Vincent

Abstract This paper distinguishes six different responsibility concepts from one another, and it explains how those concepts relate to each other. The resulting "structured taxonomy of responsibility concepts" identifies several common sources of disputes about responsibility, and it suggests a procedure for resolving such disputes. To demonstrate their utility, this taxonomy and procedure are then used to illuminate debates in two familiar contexts.

2.1 Introduction

In philosophical discussions, responsibility is often talked about as if it were a single, unitary and generic concept, or at least that is the impression that such discussions can create. For instance, the compatibilist literature considers whether determinism rules out *responsibility* (Wallace 1994; Fischer and Ravizza 1998; Pereboom 2001; Dennett 2003). In political philosophy, luck egalitarians and their opponents argue about the extent to which people's entitlements should track their *responsibility* (Dworkin 1981; Cohen 1989; Rakowski 1991; Anderson 1999; Arneson 2000). And in the area of neurolaw, some people claim that "a truly scientific mechanistic view of the nervous system make[s] nonsense of the very idea of *responsibility*" (Dawkins 2006, emphasis added; also Greene and Cohen 2004), while others deny that neuroscience challenges *responsibility* (e.g. Morse 2006; Gazzaniga 2006). If confronted head on, most philosophers would probably acknowledge that the term "'responsibility' admits of a variety of uses" (Fischer and Ravizza 1998:2, note 1), but somehow this variety seldom comes across in anything other than footnotes.

This paper aims to remedy this situation by saying something more substantial about this variety of uses of the term "responsibility" and by explaining how we are better off for knowing about it. Section 2.2 distinguishes six different senses of the term "responsibility" – six different responsibility concepts – and it introduces some terminology to keep these concepts disambiguated. Section 2.3 explains how these

N.A Vincent (✉)
Department of Philosophy, Delft University of Technology, 2600 GA Delft, The Netherlands

Department of Philosophy, Faculty of Arts, Macquarie University, Sydney NSW 2109, Australia
e-mail: nicole.vincent@mq.edu.au; n.a.vincent@tudelft.nl

N.A Vincent et al. (eds.), *Moral Responsibility*, Library of Ethics and Applied Philosophy 27, DOI 10.1007/978-94-007-1878-4_2,

responsibility concepts relate to each other – namely, via justificatory relations that obtain between claims which employ them. Together, the first two sections describe what I call a *structured taxonomy of responsibility concepts* (STRC), and the following two sections explain why this taxonomy is useful and not just theoretically neat. Section 2.4 argues that the STRC helps us to identify fifteen distinct sources of disputes about responsibility as well as a corresponding procedure for resolving such disputes, while Section 2.5 demonstrates the utility of this taxonomy and procedure by applying them to two familiar contexts in political philosophy and in tort law.

2.2 Six Concepts[1]

A close examination of ordinary language use reveals that the word "responsibility" refers to a number of different though related ideas. To see this, consider the following parable about Smith the ship captain, originally developed by H.L.A. Hart[2]:

> (1) Smith had always been an exceedingly *responsible* person, (2) and as captain of the ship he was *responsible* for the safety of his passengers and crew. But on his last voyage he drank himself into a stupor, (3) and he was *responsible* for the loss of his ship and many lives. (4) Smith's defense attorney argued that the alcohol and his transient depression were *responsible* for his misconduct, (5) but the prosecution's medical experts confirmed that he was fully *responsible* when he started drinking since he was not suffering from depression at that time. (6) Smith should take *responsibility* for his victims' families' losses, but his employer will probably be held *responsible* for them as Smith is insolvent and uninsured.

The word "responsibility" is used here in at least six different ways, each of which suggests a subtly different responsibility concept, and I will now give each of these concepts a name so that the upcoming discussion can proceed without the ambiguity inherent in using the generic term "responsibility".[3]

First, there is a claim about his *virtue responsibility* – Smith was normally a dependable person who took his duties seriously and did the right thing. To call somebody "responsible" in this sense is to say something good about their character, reputation or intentions, as exemplified by their history which testifies to their manifest commitment to doing what they take to be right. The opposite of calling someone "responsible" in this sense is to call them "irresponsible" (Vincent 2009).[4]

---

[1] The material contained in this section is an elaboration of Vincent (2010:80–82).

[2] This parable is an adapted version of Kutz (2004:549), who in turn derived his version from Hart (1968:211). Hart did not give the captain a name, but I find it helpful to do so.

[3] Although I use H.L.A. Hart's terminology to preserve continuity with his work, there are differences between my and his terminology. Also compare to Chapters 1 and 3 by van de Poel, this volume.

[4] Gary Watson's *aretaic* sense of responsibility is very similar (2004). Also compare (e.g. Haydon 1978; Williams 1995; Bovens 1998; Duff 1998:291; Williams 2008).

Second, there is a claim about Smith's *role responsibility* – as the ship's captain Smith had certain duties to various parties, both on and off his ship. I do not mean to imply, by using the word "role", that we only have role responsibilities in virtue of our institutional, social or conventional roles, nor that we can settle who has which responsibilities simply by examining their roles. As Garrath Williams (2008) points out, duties can arise from plural sources and not just from formal roles. Furthermore, it is also conceivable that a single individual may be subject to a range of conflicting demands at the same time – some related to their various roles (we all wear many hats), and others to "the imperatives of basic human decency" (Williams 2008:467) – and that a conscientious person must find the right way to balance them (Williams 2008:459). Used in this second sense, "responsibilities" refers to duties – to what a person should (not) or ought (not) to do.[5]

Third, there is a claim about his *outcome responsibility* – it is alleged that various states of affairs, such as the loss of the ship and many of its passengers and crew, are rightfully attributable to him as something that he did, and perhaps even as something for which he is blameworthy. Normally, only agents are responsible for things in this sense – for instance, a chair or table can't be outcome responsible for anything – but sometimes legal entities (e.g. corporations) are also treated as agents and are claimed to be responsible for things in this sense. Furthermore, the word "outcome" should not be taken to imply that agents can only be responsible for outcomes, since they are also responsible in this same sense for their actions. I take this to be the sense which philosophers usually have in mind when they talk about responsibility.[6]

---

[5] Unlike Robert Goodin (1986; or 1987) who distinguishes "task responsibilities" from other duties, I use "responsibilities", "role responsibility" and "duties" interchangeably to refer to the various things which we should or ought to do.

[6] I use Stephen Perry's term "outcome responsibility" (2000:555) because it captures the idea of a form of responsibility which looks backwards in time to states of affairs (outcomes or actions) that occurred in the past, and for which the person in question is blameworthy (if what they are responsible for is bad) or perhaps praiseworthy (if it is good), but others have given this concept different names. For instance, Hart calls it "causal responsibility" (1968:212), though I find this name unhelpful since it runs together at least two distinct ideas – i.e. the *normative* concept of responsibility (e.g. see Kutz (2004:555); citing Wallace (2002)) and what I take to be its causal component. Fischer and Ravizza call it "moral responsibility" (1998), and they too distinguish between moral responsibility for actions and for outcomes; though I am not fond of this name either since although it captures the inherently *normative* nature of responsibility, it fails to adequately differentiate between our *forward*-looking moral responsibilities (our "role responsibilities" comprise some of these, and what I will shortly call "liability responsibility" comprises the rest of them) and the *backward*-looking moral responsibility which I am presently calling "outcome responsibility". Also, Peter Cane calls this concept "historical responsibility" (2004:162); Thomas Scanlon calls it "responsibility as attributability" (1998:248); Gary Watson calls it the "attributability" sense of responsibility (2004:263–65); and Garrath Williams and Antony Duff call it "retrospective responsibility" (Williams 2008:457, 459, 460 and 467; Duff 1998). Finally, although Herbert Honoré also uses the label "outcome responsibility" (e.g. Honoré 1999), he uses it to refer to the concept which below I call "liability responsibility".

Fourth, there are two claims about *causal responsibility* – Smith's defense lawyer alleged that Smith's aberrant behaviour was caused by the alcohol and/or by his depression. Used in this way, the word "responsibility" is a synonym for words like "cause" and "condition", and we could re-phrase what the defense lawyer said without loss of meaning as the claim that the alcohol and depression caused (or that they were conditions of) Smith's aberrant behaviour. However, people's *actions* are also very often cited as causes or conditions of various outcomes, and although in doing this we pick out that person's actions as particularly significant in the production of those outcomes, this is not yet the same as the full moral allegation that they are (in the terminology introduced in the previous paragraph) outcome responsible. Hence, we might say that causal responsibility is a thinner and less morally imbued concept than outcome responsibility.

Fifth, there is a claim about his *capacity* responsibility – since Smith was not suffering from depression at that time, the prosecution alleged that his mental capacities were fully intact, which meant that his moral agency was unimpaired. The capacities in question are usually conceived of as the so-called "cognitive" and "volitional" capacities of folk psychology – as Hart describes them, "the capacity to understand what [we are] required . . . to do or not to do, to deliberate and to decide what to do, and to control [our] conduct in the light of such decisions" (1968:218) – and typical cases of agents who lack responsibility in this sense (i.e. who are not (yet) fully responsible) are children and the mentally ill. When capacity responsibility is conceptualized in this mentalistic way, it can be usefully contrasted with the concept of virtue responsibility introduced first above, since a fully (capacity) responsible person may at the same time be a very (virtue) irresponsible person, and someone who is not yet a fully (capacity) responsible person may still be a very (virtue) responsible person (Vincent 2009). Although capacities can come in degrees – for instance, one might be more or less intelligent, or have more or less strength of will to resist temptation – we often set thresholds that must be reached before a person is considered fully responsible. However, although this example cites a *mental* kind of capacity, it is plausible that non-mental factors – e.g. a person's physical strength or the tools at their disposal – may also affect their capacity responsibility. When a person's non-mental capacities are diminished though, we would not usually say that they are not fully responsible, but rather we might simply acknowledge that they lack the corresponding capacity.

And finally, the parable ends with comments about *liability* responsibility – about who will now be held responsible (and how) for what has happened. In this case, financial liability is cited – that is apparently one way to take responsibility – but perhaps Smith should also apologise to the bereaved families and go to prison to properly take due personal responsibility for what happened. When "responsibility" is used in this way, it is usually coupled with another word – i.e. *take* responsibility or *hold* responsible – and it refers to the things that someone must do, or how they should be treated, to set things right.

I take the fact that "responsibility" can be used in so many different ways, to show that this word refers to a "syndrome" of concepts – i.e. to multiple concepts that share a common word – rather than to a single, unitary or generic concept. Furthermore, to my mind at least all of these uses of "responsibility" are equally legitimate – none of them seems merely metaphorical, or like a misuse of the word – and I think that very little if anything is gained by claiming that some of these senses of "responsibility" are more primary while others are more derivative.

2.3 Relations Between These Six Responsibility Concepts[7]

Hart's parable also suggests that claims which employ these concepts stand in certain justificatory relations with respect to one another. Here are three examples: Smith should now do certain things (i.e. take liability responsibility) precisely because of his outcome responsibility; it is precisely because he had certain role responsibilities (which he subsequently violated) that we attribute outcome responsibility to him for the ship's loss, but not to (e.g.) the ship's chef since he did not have them; and the parable also hints that Smith's outcome responsibility may have been reduced had he been suffering from depression at the time, as that would have reduced his capacity responsibility. In fact, moving beyond Hart's parable, it is plausible that a number of other relations also obtain between claims that employ these different responsibility concepts, and these relations can be expressed using a structure diagram of the sort that is sometimes used to chart relations that obtain between premises and the conclusions which they are intended to support in philosophical arguments:

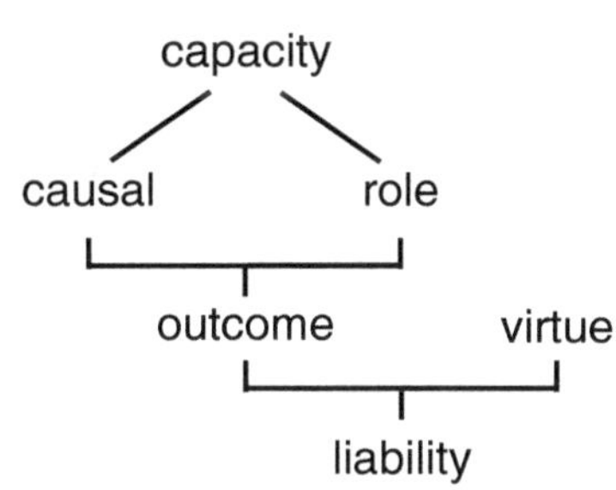

Fig. 2.1 Lines represent justificatory relations between connected responsibility concepts

Three groups of justificatory relations are expressed in this diagram – (1) that claims about outcome responsibility are derived from claims about causal and role responsibility, (2) that claims about capacity responsibility bear on claims about causal and role responsibility, and (3) that claims about liability responsibility are derived from claims about outcome and virtue responsibility – and in what follows I will explain why I think that these relations obtain, as well as characterise the nature of these relations in some detail.

[7] The material in this section combines parts of Vincent (2010:82–85, 2011:80–82, Forthcoming: Section 3.8.). Diagram originally from Vincent (2010:82).

2.3.1 Outcome Responsibility from Causal and Role Responsibility

First, claims about a person's *outcome* responsibility seem to depend on prior claims about their *causal* responsibility and their *role* responsibility.

To see why this might be so, imagine that you stumble upon Jones' dead body while strolling through a forest. It seems that Jones died of a gunshot wound to the head, and that his body was then hastily concealed beneath the bush where you found him. Consider now what processes we might engage in to determine who is responsible (in the outcome responsibility sense) for Jones' death.

Our first question would probably be "Who dunnit?", and so in the beginning our inquiry would focus on discovering such things as who was where at the time of the crime, how they behaved, and what consequences their behaviour brought about. If insufficient information was available then we would probably gather up witnesses and suspects, conduct a line-up to identify prime suspects, and then interrogate some people; in court, both witnesses and suspects might eventually testify, and physical evidence such as finger prints, spent bullet cartridges, DNA samples and so on might also be collected, examined and presented. Many epistemic barriers may stand in the way of answering the *who dunnit* question, but once these puzzle pieces are put together we may discover that Brown is the one who shot Jones dead – or put another way, that Brown is causally responsible for Jones' demise.

But to establish that Brown is outcome responsible for Jones' death, we need to show more than just that she "dunnit". Rather, given causal indeterminacy – i.e. the fact that any outcome is a result of many causal contributions – we must also show that her causal contributions were of particular significance, and the way that we commonly do this is by looking at whether Brown acted contrary to how she should have acted – or put another way, whether she violated her role responsibilities. For instance, Brown might have shot Jones in *self-defence* when he ambushed her on her stroll through the forest, and as long as what she did is viewed as a reasonable response – e.g. not an unwarranted use of extreme force – then this should suffice to establish that Jones was at fault for his own death (because he should not have attacked her), and thus Brown's causal responsibility would not translate into a finding that she was outcome responsible for his death. Alternatively, suppose that Brown was out hunting in a well-known, sign-posted and cordoned-off area of the woods which was only supposed to have other hunters in it, all of whom wore brightly coloured clothing and who knew each others' locations through GPS devices, and that there was simply no way for her to know (nor any reason to suspect) that Jones – a thrill-seeking prankster who liked to frustrate hunters by hiding in bushes and scaring away their game – was hiding in those bushes. In this case it is again likely that Jones' rather than Brown's actions will be viewed as the salient causes of his own demise, and hence that despite Brown's causal responsibility, Jones again would be picked out as the person who is outcome responsible for his own death, because Brown acted *reasonably* (her actions were not unduly risky) whereas Jones did not (his actions were too risky).[8]

The point of these examples is that to turn a finding of causal responsibility into the fully-fledged moral accusation of outcome responsibility, the party whose actions causally contributed to the said outcome must also have violated their role responsibilities in acting like that. As Joel Feinberg puts it, "blame-fixing" requires both a *genuine causal relationship* between the thing that does the causing and the thing that is allegedly caused, as well as a relevant *moral element* (1970:207). Hence, this is why I suggest that claims about a person's *outcome* responsibility gain support from claims about their *causal* responsibility and their *role* responsibility.[9]

2.3.2 Capacity Responsibility to Causal and Role Responsibility

Second, claims about a person's *capacity* responsibility seem to bear on what may legitimately be said about their *causal* responsibility and *role* responsibility.

Regarding the relationship between capacity responsibility and causal responsibility, suppose that Brown's defense had been that she shot Jones while sleepwalking. If this "automatism" defense were accepted as a truthful account of what happened, then the way in which it might work in her favour is by denying that her body movements even count as instances of her actions. Such body movements would be conceptualized as something that *happened to* Brown rather than as something that *she did* – her body movements would not be conceptualized as genuine instances of actions, let alone as her actions – and that in turn would undermine the claim that her actions were causally responsible for Jones' death.

On the other hand, suppose that Brown's defense had been that she shot Jones because God commanded it – a symptom of her severe mental illness. This defense would attempt to get her off the hook by alleging that she can not be blamed because due to her delusion she lacked the pertinent cognitive or volitional capacities – e.g. that she lacked the capacity to know what she was doing, that what she was doing was wrong, or to control her conduct. This is also how we think about children and others whose mental capacity falls below the minimum threshold of fully responsible moral agency – i.e. their reduced capacity is taken as a reason to excuse them, or to simply expect less of them in the first place, and thus subsequently to morally blame them for less. Put another way, this sort of defense presupposes that people are blameworthy when their actions breach their role responsibilities (this is just

[8] My point is not that we would necessarily make this particular evaluation about the risks involved, but rather that *if* we made that evaluation *then* Smith would be deemed responsible.

[9] Gary Watson also argues that we would not usually say that someone was responsible for a bad outcome unless their actions were "contrary to one of [their] responsibilities" (2004:274)

conceptual analysis), and that what role responsibilities a person is subject to is something that depends at least in part on what capacities they (ought to) possess.[10]

In broad terms, people with greater capacities are usually expected to conform to higher standards – i.e. we are *capacitarian* in the sense that we generally hold that *responsibility tracks capacity* – and this expectation can be explained in either a *positive* or a *negative* way. In the positive explanation capacity *generates* duties. The idea is that we ought to do what we have most reason to do, and what we can and can't do (presumably along with a range of many other things) generates the reasons that we have to do various things. An inference is thus first made from what *capacities* I have to what I have *reason* to do, and then another inference is made from what I have most *reason* to do to what I *ought* to do – i.e. we move from *capacity* claims via *reasons* claims to *ought* claims.[11] On this account, if I can not save a child from drowning – perhaps because I do not know that they are drowning, or because I can not swim, or because I do not have a rope to throw to them – then it is simply not true that I ought to save them (unless I am responsible for the fact that I can not do this – see note 10 above). The reason why I would not be blameworthy for not saving them is because I was not in the first place even subject to that saving duty. On the other hand, in the negative explanation capacity *regulates* duties. The idea here is that regardless of the source of our duties, on this second view our *in*capacities can excuse departures from those duties. On this latter account, the three cited considerations – i.e. I don't know that the child is drowning, I can't swim, or I have no rope – do not extinguish the saving duty, but rather they provide an excuse for departing from it. The reason why I would not be blameworthy on this second account is because although I did have the saving duty, my incapacity provided an excuse for departing from it.

Two advantages of the negative explanation are that only it has an explicit place for excuses (and perhaps justifications) which play a prominent role in much ordinary and legal thinking about responsibility, and arguably it also more adequately captures the rich structure of practical reasoning in which some considerations *discount*, *undermine* and *invalidate* (rather than just *outweigh* or *extinguish*) other considerations. Never the less, I suspect that both views of the relationship between capacity responsibility and role responsibility will generate the same conclusions about when someone is outcome responsible for some state of affairs, and since I find the positive explanation simpler, in what follows my discussion will be framed

[10] The "ought to" clause captures the idea, expressed for instance in Fischer and Ravizza's *tracing* principle (1998:48–51), that diminished capacities for which a person is responsible have at most only a discounted exculpatory value – people who cause accidents while voluntarily intoxicated are typically not excused for what they did despite their reduced capacities. For contrast, see Chapters 6 and 7 by Dymock and Benchimol, this volume.

[11] There is room in both inferences for other considerations too: my capacity (e.g. to swim) may be a reason to do various things (e.g. save the drowning child, join the swimming team, etc.), and other reasons (e.g. that I am running late for work) may compete with the capacity-based reasons for determination of what I ought to do. See Chapter 5 by Lowry, this volume, for a discussion of the relationship between *can* claims and *ought* claims via *reasons* claims.

in terms of it rather than in terms of the negative explanation.[12] Thus, the relationship which I think obtains between capacity responsibility and role responsibility, and which is expressed in the above diagram, can be stated as follows. The idea is not that we can read off a person's responsibilities simply from an assessment of their capacities (this would be an instance of *can implies ought*), but it is rather that in determining what responsibilities a person has we should, among other things, consider what capacities they (ought to) possesses – i.e. the idea is that *can*, taken together with a range of other considerations, implies *ought*.

2.3.3 Liability Responsibility from Outcome and Virtue Responsibility

Finally, claims about *liability* responsibility – that is, about who should be held responsible, and about how (the kind and extent) they should be held responsible – seem to be affected by claims about that person's *outcome* responsibility and by the degree of their *virtue* responsibility or lack thereof.

This is particularly easy to see in the criminal law where punishment (one form of liability responsibility) is normally only imposed onto those parties who were previously established as outcome responsible for the corresponding offence, and the kind and extent of their punishment normally depends at least in part on the seriousness of the sort of thing for which they were outcome responsible (e.g. homicide, arson, theft, etc.) and on the degree of their outcome responsibility for it. But we find similar thinking beyond the criminal law too. For instance, whoever broke the vase is normally expected to make up for it; if two people were responsible for breaking it (suppose it fell to the floor when they knocked the table as they chased each other down the hall) then the extent of each one's liability responsibility will usually track the degree of each one's outcome responsibility; and if the vase was a precious antique then their liability will undoubtedly be greater than if it had been a mass-produced IKEA flower pot.[13]

But another consideration that also seems to play a role is what the person has previously been like – i.e. whether they have previously had a "clean slate" and been virtue responsible individuals, or whether this is merely another example of their

---

[12] Peter B. M. Vranas (2007:181) argues that the positive or generative account of the relationship between capacity and obligation is more plausible than the second or regulative account, because there are good reasons to suppose that if I really could not have done something, then I really can not legitimately be expected to have done that thing in the first place.

[13] The main exception to this is vicarious liability – i.e. when one person is held responsible for what another person did – but this can either be explained away and criticized as a departure from an otherwise legitimate moral norm, or we could check whether the specific instance might perhaps be justified. For instance, we might check whether the party that will be held vicariously responsible failed to supervise the other party as they ought to have, and that they are after all outcome responsible for what the other person did which means that no injustice is done *qua* holding them liability responsible. This is presumably one reason why parents are held responsible for their children's actions.

generally irresponsible character as testified to by their history of similar actions. Nicola Lacey (2007:240, 245–47) notes that within the criminal law considerations of what a person's character is like can play a mitigating (good character) or an aggravating (bad character) role at sentencing.[14] And similarly, beyond the criminal law it is again a common enough practice to treat more harshly those people who should have learned from their past actions but didn't (i.e. those who have a history of being irresponsible), and to treat less harshly and maybe even to forgive those for whom this was their first infraction or who have even been model citizens. In other words, a person's *virtue* responsibility can be a mitigating factor, and its lack can be an aggravating factor, by modulating the kind and degree of treatment that we impose upon them in order to hold them (liability) responsible for what they did.

2.3.4 Norm Setting and Substantive Evaluations

Lastly, something which isn't depicted in the diagram at the top of Section 2.3 is that norm setting, substantive evaluations and our aims also play important roles in relating different kinds of responsibility claims to one another, and in this subsection I will offer a brief discussion of the role that such considerations play.

Firstly, just how much and what kind of mental capacity it takes to be a fully capacity responsible person, is at least in part a norm setting exercise. In some places a person is deemed to be fully responsible by the time they turn 18 years of age – the assumption being that by then people have matured and possess a *sufficient* degree of the right kinds of mental capacities – but the sufficiency threshold could also be set at a lower or a higher age. Admittedly, we do not have complete freedom to set this threshold wherever we like, because how much and what kind of capacity it takes to be fully responsible depends at least in part on what sorts of expectations will later be thrust onto those who fall into the "fully responsible" category – "fully responsible" is relative to a context. But given that (as I am about to argue) the expectations that we have of one another are themselves informed by further instances of norm setting and ultimately-contestable substantive evaluations, this might in the end only weakly constrain the norms that we choose in regards to capacity responsibility.

Secondly, just how much care a person must take to avoid being deemed negligent in the event of an accident – i.e. to avoid the claim that they breached their role responsibility – is also a norm setting task. Whether this or that amount of care is *sufficient* is something that is up to us to determine – i.e. it is a norm that we must set. Admittedly, the norms that we set in this regard are not arbitrary either, since they arguably reflect our commitment to (e.g.) efficiency. For instance, whether A is negligent for causing B's losses depends on whether A took *reasonable* precautions, and according to the Learned Hand test what is reasonable in turn depends on the costs involved in taking those precautions weighed against the risk-depreciated savings

[14] The so-called "three strikes laws" demonstrate how a judgment that someone lacks virtue responsibility can be an aggravating factor at sentencing.

that those precautions were intended to yield – i.e. the cheapest cost avoider is the one who should have taken the precautions, and that could just as well be B as A (e.g. Landes and Posner 1987; Posner 1996). However, such comparisons presuppose ultimately-contestable substantive evaluations of people's different interests – i.e. reasonable people can disagree about whether my interest in safety (depreciated by the unlikelihood of me being harmed in our interaction) is more or less valuable than the resources that you would have to forego to take the aforementioned precautions. Thus, whether a person will be seen to be in breach of their role responsibilities or not, is also something that depends on the norms that we set and on the evaluations that we make.

Finally, conclusions about liability responsibility – i.e. about how someone should be treated in order to take due responsibility (or, put another way, to be properly held responsible) for what they have done – are also significantly affected by the norms that we choose. For instance, whether the appropriate kind and degree of punishment for theft is a fine, incarceration, ten lashes of the whip, twenty lashes, amputation of the hand that stole the item, or execution of the offender, is not something that can be read off straight forwardly from a consideration of what they are outcome responsible for, from the degree of their outcome responsibility, and from the degree to which they are a virtue (ir)responsible person. Rather, this too is a thoroughly norm setting exercise since we must decide for ourselves what treatment is appropriate or fitting for a given offence. Admittedly, this norm setting exercise is also not completely unconstrained – for instance, how a person should be treated on account of what they have done depends in part on what we take to be our aims in treating them in that way (e.g. retribution, deterrence, reform or even something else)[15] – and so we do not have completely free reign on what norms we may set. Furthermore, in order for a person to intelligibly be a legitimate subject of retribution, deterrence or reform, they must possess certain mental capacities – that is for instance why some people who do not oppose capital punishment never the less express qualms about executing the mentally ill (e.g. Latzer 2003; Eisenberg 2004), and it may simply be futile to attempt to deter or to reform people that lack certain mental capacities – and so this too is another constraint on how we might eventually hold someone (liability) responsible[16] – i.e. as with all of the other instances of norm setting mentioned in this section, this norm setting exercise also can not be an expression of our pure whim. However, once we do settle on a particular aim[17] – for instance, retribution – and once we confirm that the party slated for punishment possesses a sufficient measure of the right kinds of mental capacities to be a legitimate

[15] I discuss these points in greater depth in Vincent (2010:91–93).

[16] This suggests that there exists a more direct relationship between capacity responsibility and liability responsibility than what is depicted in the diagram at the top of Section 2.3. However, since this relationship is mediated via our aims, and our aims are not themselves depicted in the above diagram (the diagram after all only sets out to depict the relations that obtain between different responsibility concepts), I have therefore chosen to only describe the relationship between capacity responsibility and liability responsibility here.

[17] ... or a collection of aims, since we might after all be pluralists in this regard ...

subject of retribution, *we* will still have to make the difficult decision about what kind of punishment is fitting or appropriate – this is something that we will have to determine and not something that we can discover.[18] Thus, none of these constraints eliminate the fact that conclusions about liability responsibility will also be affected in important ways by the norms which we *choose* or set.

The norms that we set, the evaluations that we make, and the aims that we have also play important roles in relating different kinds of responsibility claims to one another – i.e. they also affect the justificatory relations that obtain between claims that employ different responsibility concepts. But since these relations were not depicted in the diagram at the top of Section 2.3, this sub-section therefore described some of the more prominent roles that they play in our thinking about responsibility.

2.4 The Utility of the STRC

Taken together, the six responsibility concepts and the justificatory relations that obtain between them constitute the core elements of the STRC. The STRC aims to be a "one stop shop" that catalogues, characterizes, distinguishes and relates to one another six different senses of the term "responsibility", and it also suggests some terminology to help us avoid ambiguity in debates about responsibility.

For a simple example of how the STRC helps us to avoid ambiguity, consider the text of a notice that hangs in Café Doerak, my favourite bar in the Dutch city of Delft:

> The management of this establishment is not responsible.

This notice is terribly ambiguous, and one might imagine two people engaged in a frustrating argument about it, simply because each understands it differently, though neither realizes that this is so. But the text of this notice could be helpfully re-written, replacing the generic "responsibility" with the terminology of the STRC, and then something like the following six distinct messages would emerge:

> CAPACITY: The management of this establishment are not (yet) psychologically mature.
> VIRTUE: The management of this establishment are not dependable and might be reckless.
> ROLE: The management of this establishment have no responsibilities towards its clients.
> CAUSAL: The management didn't causally contribute to losses suffered on these premises.
> OUTCOME: The management can't be blamed for whatever happens on these premises.
> LIABILITY: The management won't pay for any losses suffered on these premises.

But is this practically useful? To the extent that at least some responsibility disputes arise through misunderstanding borne out of ambiguity – i.e. because the disputants are not actually using the word "responsibility" in the same way, and hence they are not really even engaged in a genuine dispute but are instead talking

---

18 Abad (Chapter 8, this volume) disagrees – she argues that only some kinds of responses (i.e. liability responsibility) are fitting or appropriate given what someone has done (i.e. given their outcome responsibility).

past one another – the STRC can be useful by helping us to avoid such ambiguity and thus to avoid such misunderstandings.

However, in what follows I will also argue that the STRC can help us to identify fifteen distinct sources of disputes about responsibility, and that it also suggests a handy procedure for systematically resolving such disputes.

2.4.1 Fifteen Sources of Disputes About Responsibility

I have argued that responsibility is not a single, unitary and generic concept, but that it is rather a syndrome of at least six different concepts. However, if this is right then there must be at least six different kinds of responsibility questions that we might ask – i.e. one for each of the STRC's responsibility concepts (in what follows, *P* stands for "person" and *O* stands for their action or an outcome of that action):

(1) Is *P* (outcome) responsible for *O*?
(2) Were *P*'s actions (causally) responsible for *O*?
(3) What were *P*'s (role) responsibilities, and were they breached?
(4) Is *P* a fully (capacity) responsible person?
(5) Is *P* a (virtue) responsible or an (virtue) irresponsible person?
(6) How should *P* be held (liability) responsible for *O*?

Thus, a responsibility dispute might arise whenever people give diverging answers to any of these six responsibility questions. Put another way, for each of the concepts in the STRC diagram shown at the top of Section 2.3, there exists an opportunity for a responsibility dispute to arise, and this gives rise to the first six possible sources of disputes about responsibility. Furthermore, given that justificatory relations obtain between these six responsibility concepts – i.e. that different kinds of responsibility claims stand in relations of justification with respect to one another – if two people give diverging answers to one responsibility question, then they may also give diverging answers to responsibility questions related to connected concepts that are depicted either below or above the corresponding concept in the STRC diagram.

However, disputes about responsibility can also arise because in a pluralistic society reasonable people may disagree about what norms we ought to adopt, about the absolute or relative value of different interests, or about our aims. As I explained in Section 2.3.4. above, norm setting, substantive evaluations and the aims that we pursue play a crucial role in several places within the STRC, and for each of these places there exist multiple opportunities for disagreements to arise.

First, in regards to capacity responsibility, just how much or what kind of mental capacity is required for "full" responsibility, is at least partly a norm-setting issue. Thus, parties might disagree about someone's status as a fully responsible person because (7) they have different views about what kinds of capacities are required for responsible moral agency, (8) they disagree about how much of that capacity a person must have to be fully responsible, or (9) there might be a factual disagreement about just how much of a given capacity that person actually has.

Second, given my account of the relationship between capacity responsibility and role responsibility – i.e. that the capacities which we (ought to) have are among the grounds of the reasons that we have to do various things, and that what we have most reason to do is what we have a role responsibility to do – a dispute might also arise because (10) disputants disagree about what reasons the possession of a particular capacity gives rise to, and thus about what role responsibility that party might have, or (11) they might believe that the person in question had a role responsibility to not jeopardize, or perhaps to develop, a particular capacity, which they failed to fulfil. Furthermore, to the extent that claims about role responsibility are subject to norm setting and substantive evaluations, people may also have diverging opinions about (12) just how much care a person must take to avoid being assessed as negligent in the event of an accident, and about (13) the value of the competing security and liberty interests that were at stake in the given situation (i.e. about the value of what the victim stood to lose and what the injurer had to forego to take sufficient care).

Finally, in regards to liability responsibility, further disagreements may also arise depending on (14) what disputants take to be the aim(s) of holding people responsible,[19] and (15) what they take to be appropriate or fitting treatment for a given transgression.

Reasonable people can disagree about the matters that are raised in points (7–15) above, and such disagreements (either tacit or explicit) can also result in a broader responsibility dispute.

2.4.2 *A Procedure for Resolving Disputes About Responsibility*

The previous section's observations suggest a two-step procedure for resolving disputes about responsibility. First, for a given dispute, we should *identify its subject matter*, which is another way of saying that we should ascertain which of the six responsibility questions – i.e. points (1–6) – the disputants answer differently. Second, for each of the identified disagreements, we should *examine the norms and evaluations – i.e. points (7–15) – related to the corresponding responsibility concept, and the connected concepts – i.e. points (1–6) above – depicted above that difference in the STRC diagram (as well as the related norms and evaluations)*, since that is where we will find the differences from which the dispute ultimately springs and which must therefore be reconciled to resolve that dispute. Rather than mechanically spelling out how this procedure is meant to be used, I will now proceed to the next section which provides an example of this.

2.5 The STRC in Action

This last section will demonstrate the utility of the STRC and the two-step procedure that was described above. Section 2.5.1 will demonstrate how the STRC can make it easier to discern the role which different responsibility claims play in luck

[19] . . . or, if we have plural aims, about the relative importance of our different aims . . .

egalitarian debates; and Section 2.5.2 will demonstrate how this two-step procedure can suggest argumentative strategies in courtroom debates about responsibility.

2.5.1 Luck Egalitarianism

Take two groups of people. In the first group are alcoholics who develop liver cirrhosis and need a liver transplant, heavy smokers who develop emphysema and need a lung transplant, and those with an unhealthy diet and a sedentary lifestyle who develop diabetes and need a range of ongoing medical treatments. In the second group are those whose livers were destroyed through hepatitis contracted by ingesting accidentally contaminated food, those whose lungs were destroyed through hereditary conditions like cystic fibrosis, and those who were born diabetic – and all of them also need identical transplants and medical treatments.

Because livers, lungs and the public health budget are limited resources, some people miss out on the transplants and medical treatments which they need. And many arguments have been offered both *in support of* and *against* the view that we may, or even that we ought to, give preferential treatment to people in the second group since allegedly they are not as responsible for their own ill health (they are allegedly merely unfortunate) as those in the first group (they are allegedly imprudent) – i.e. that if we must choose between two otherwise-identical candidates, one from each group, then we should favour a person from the second group. But rather than attempting to summarize this rich debate in the next few paragraphs, with undoubtedly unsatisfactory results, let me instead cite just three examples of the sorts of considerations which are sometimes raised (some better than others), and then comment on how the STRC helps us to better understand the role which they are intended to play in this debate:

(A) The addictive nature of alcohol and tobacco, and the proliferation of unhealthy eating options, as well as a lack of public parks in cities where people could exercise, are often cited to protect the first group's interests.
(B) The harshness of discriminating between people on this basis, and the fact that our interest in health is in some way different and deserving of special consideration, are also sometimes cited to support the first group's interests.
(C) But others claim that the first group's bad health is due to their own shortcomings as people – i.e. because they are weak and have bad habits like gluttony and over-indulgence – and that since such character faults should not be condoned, we may therefore give preferential treatment to the moral innocents in the second group.

Consider now where, within the STRC diagram shown at the top of Section 2.3, and within the related norm setting, substantive evaluations and aims – i.e. points (1–15) that were listed above – these different sets of considerations are meant to have an impact.

The considerations raised by example (A) address the top-left-hand quadrant of the STRC diagram. Presumably, those who cite the addictive nature of alcohol and tobacco do this to establish that alcoholics' and smokers' outcome responsibility for their own ill health is diminished because addictive substances have detrimental effects on people's capacity responsibility. On this view, people lack the capacity to stop drinking excessively once they are addicted, and thus their resultant liver cirrhosis is not truly a consequences of their own free choice – i.e. it is not something for which they are fully outcome responsible. But a different argumentative strategy is employed by those who cite the proliferation of fast food chains, and the relative difficulty of maintaining a healthy diet and getting sufficient exercise in modern crowded cities. Here, the aim is to show either that people do not in fact have as great a role responsibility to eat a healthy diet and to exercise as what we presumed, or at least that they have legitimate excuses for eating unhealthy food and getting insufficient exercise (because it is allegedly more difficult to eat a healthy diet and to exercise in modern crowded cities), or to shift at least some of the blame for this group's ill health onto another group (perhaps those who advertise and sell unhealthy food, and to urban planners who design such health-unfriendly cities).

Second, the considerations raised by example (B) map onto the middle of the bottom-most part of the STRC diagram. People who raise such considerations do not deny that the first group might be more outcome responsible for their own ill health, but rather they allege that a range of normative considerations also bears on what conclusions about this group's liability responsibility may be derived from claims about their outcome responsibility. For instance, the "harshness" objection suggests that norms of common decency rile against deriving these sorts of conclusions about how people may be treated (about their liability responsibility) from facts about what they are allegedly responsible for (about their outcome responsibility); while the other consideration draws attention to the exceptional value of people's health in an attempt to justify departing from the default rule which stipulates that distributive decisions should normally track people's outcome responsibility. The STRC thus helps us to notice that people who raise considerations like those at (B) do not necessarily take the mere fact that someone *is responsible* for their own ill health as a sufficient reason to conclude that they should therefore *take responsibility* for it, or that they should take responsibility for it *in some specific way*, since in their view a range of normative considerations (e.g. a range of those mentioned in Section 2.3.4 above) also bears on whether and how they should take this responsibility.[20]

Finally, the considerations raised by example (C) map onto the bottom-right part of the STRC diagram. People who raise such considerations attempt to stigmatize

[20] Since different responsibility concepts appear in claims about *taking* responsibility as opposed to claims about the things for which someone allegedly *is* responsible – the former are *forward*-looking while the latter are *backward*-looking – claims about the former can't be derived through mere logical entailment from claims about the latter. Put another way, the fact that someone *is* responsible for some state of affairs (e.g. their bad health) does not yet tell us how that person should take responsibility for it. Abad (Chapter 8, this volume) however disagrees with me on this point.

alcoholics, smokers and the obese, by characterizing them as lacking in moral rectitude, and they insinuate that their bad character (a legitimate target of our criticism) rather than their incapacity (something for which we may not be able to criticize them, unless perhaps via tracing they are outcome responsible for that incapacity) is the true cause of their ill health. On their account, people in the first group lack virtue responsibility rather than having diminished capacity responsibility – they view the alcoholic, the smoker and the obese person as someone with character flaws not as someone with capacity deficits – and they maintain that on account of their character flaws we may legitimately treat them in a less privileged manner.

Viewed through the lens of the STRC, these three sets of considerations play very different roles in this debate. The first set of considerations informs a debate about whether people in the first group are more outcome responsible for their own ill health than people in the second group. The second set of considerations informs a debate about whether we might be able to block the transition from claims about outcome responsibility to claims about liability responsibility. While the third set of considerations informs a debate about whether the correct way to characterize people in the first group is that they have capacity deficits or character flaws, and whether the latter characterization could justify treating these people in a less privileged way. The STRC is, among other things, a theoretical framework, and viewing the debate about luck egalitarianism through the lens of this framework can make it easier to discern precisely how the many different claims that are made in such debates are supposed to bear on the broader issues.

Thus, an important reason why the STRC is useful is because it can help us to navigate our way around such complex debates, but also because it can help us to introduce these debates to novices (e.g. students) in a more structured manner.

2.5.2 Law Suits

Consider now another example, this time aimed at demonstrating the utility of the two-step procedure outlined above:

> You drive to a popular shopping centre but the car park is very busy. After driving around for what seems like ages you finally find an empty spot, but a Porsche parked in the next spot over is straddling the dividing line and partially hanging over into your spot. Resolute to get your shopping done, you carefully maneuver your car into the empty spot, but alas the fit is so tight that you can't even open your door to get out. Annoyed at the Porsche driver's inconsiderateness, you reverse out just a dash too quickly and leave a dinted and scratched Porsche in your wake. Distraught by the prospect of a hefty repair bill you flee the scene, though an anonymous witness jots down your number plate and leaves a note for the Porsche owner, and you are now in court being sued for the cost of repairs.

Suppose that you have no scruples, and that you are quite prepared to lie to avoid being landed with the hefty bill for repairs. Given your aim of avoiding liability responsibility, which is located at the bottom of the STRC diagram, a number of defense strategies are encountered as we work our way up this diagram's branches.

First, traveling one level up the left branch of the STRC diagram, we reach the suggestion that you could deny your outcome responsibility for the damage to the Porsche. After all, if you were not outcome responsible for it, then that would be an effective defense to the claim that you should now accept liability responsibility for it. But how might you support your denial of outcome responsibility?

Second, traveling another level up the left branch of the STRC diagram, we reach the suggestion that you could say "It wasn't me!" – i.e. you could deny your causal responsibility for the damage. If you were not causally responsible for that damage then that would undermine the claim that you were outcome responsible for it, and there are at least two ways of denying your causal responsibility. On the one hand, you could deny that you ever even acted like that – i.e. that you maneuvered your car into that parking spot. On the other hand, you could admit that you acted like that, but then deny that in the process you dinted and scratched the Porsche. In both cases you would be pitching your word against the witness' word, and presumably you have more of an incentive to lie than the witness does, and perhaps your lies might come undone if the security cameras in the car park are suitably positioned to capture footage of you dinting and scratching the Porsche. But never the less, this is still an argumentative strategy that is open to you.

Third, instead of denying your causal responsibility, you could also travel up the right branch of the STRC diagram from outcome responsibility, and try to avoid at least some of the outcome responsibility for those dints and scratches by shifting some of the blame onto others – i.e. by arguing that others also violated their role responsibility. For instance, you could try to shift some of the blame onto the Porsche owner by pointing out that had they not parked their car in such an *inconsiderate way* – in a blameworthy way – then the accident might not have occurred. Alternatively, you could argue that the Porsche owner is outcome responsible for the *excessive portion* of the cost of repairs, because it was after all their folly to put such an extravagantly expensive car in a dangerous public place. Finally, you might even try to shift some of the blame onto the shopping centre management, by arguing that they are at least partially at fault since they made the car parking spaces *too tight*. The broad aim of this argumentative strategy would be to show that although your faulty actions might indeed be among the causes of the dints and scratches, so too are others' faulty actions – i.e. the Porsche owner's inconsiderateness, their folly in leaving such an expensive and fragile item in a dangerous public place, and the shopping centre's stingyness with space – and hence that those others are at least partially outcome responsible (and should thus bear a proportionate amount of liability responsibility) for the accident.

Admittedly, it is not clear that any of these arguments would ultimately work. But facts differ from case to case, and it is plausible that in other cases a judge might rule in your favour. For instance, if the reason why the cost of repairs to the other car was so great was because its owner paid millions to Pablo Picasso to paint their last masterpiece on the duco of their car (and the masterpiece is now scratched), then the judge might indeed make the substantive evaluation that this is pure folly on their part and award them damages consistent only with how much the repairs to a reasonably-priced car would have cost.

The point of this example is not that any of these strategies would necessarily work, but it is rather to demonstrate how the two step procedure outlined above can provide hints about the sort of arguments that you might be able to use in a debate about responsibility.

2.6 Conclusion

As I suggested in the opening paragraph, responsibility is often talked about as if it were a single, unitary and generic concept. However, in this paper I have argued that there are at least six different responsibility concepts, that certain justificatory relations obtain between them, and that knowing about these distinctions and relations is not only interesting but also useful. But although Section 2.5.1 explained how this understanding of responsibility sheds new light on the luck egalitarian debate, and elsewhere (Vincent 2010) I have written about how this understanding illuminates the neurolaw debate which was also cited above in the opening paragraph,[21] I have not yet said anything about how compatibilist responsibility theory might be illuminated by it. Thus, in closing, I will now briefly comment on how the understanding of responsibility developed in this paper bears on compatibilist responsibility theory.

Philosophical compatibilism aims to reconcile moral responsibility with determinism – i.e. to show how responsibility might still be possible even if everything that happens, including everything that we do, is completely caused by prior events. For instance, on John Martin Fischer and Mark Ravizza's account, whether a person is responsible for what they do depends not on whether they could have done otherwise – i.e. freedom from causation is not needed for moral responsibility – but on whether their actions issued from their own moderately reasons-responsive mechanisms.[22] However, if moral responsibility is indeed not a single thing but it is rather a collection of at least six different things, then a question that should now be asked is how compatibilism reconciles each of these six different kinds of responsibility with determinism? For instance, how is determinism meant to pose a threat to the idea that some people have capacity responsibility while others do not, or that some people are responsible in the virtue sense while others are irresponsible? Alternatively, what light might compatibilism shed on what role responsibilities people can be legitimately expected to discharge, or on how people should be held liability responsible for what they do? Such questions have not been explicitly addressed in the compatibilist literature because that literature has all too often treated responsibility as a single thing, but if responsibility is indeed more of a syndrome of things than a single thing then attention should now be paid to these different questions.

---

[21] In that paper I argue that rather than asking whether *neuroscience* is relevant to *responsibility*, we should ask how the *range of different neuroscientific techniques and technologies* can help us to address the *six different kinds of responsibility questions* that we might ask – i.e. the first six questions listed at the top of Section 2.4.1. above.

[22] It also depends on a range of historical factors discussed by Fischer and Ravizza under the heading of the "tracing approach" (1998:48–51).

In a recent paper, John Fischer and Neal Tognazzini argue that many of the long-standing responsibility disputes in philosophy are plausibly due to the fact that the disputants actually have different things in mind when they utter the word "responsibility", and hence they suggest that:

> Clarity now demands that compatibilists and incompatibilists about determinism and moral responsibility specify which face of moral responsibility is at issue in their theses[, since s]omeone may well think that determinism is compatible with [one sense of "responsibility"] even though it is not compatible with [another sense]. (2011:398)

What compatibilists must now do, given that "responsibility" refers to a range of different ideas, is to explain in what way determinism is meant to pose a threat to each of these different ideas, and to spell out how compatibilism addresses these different challenges. To the extent that in ordinary discourse the term "responsibility" refers to a range of different concepts, this would be useful since it would explain how compatibilist responsibility theory can be applied in a range of practical contexts that use the term "responsibility" in these different ways – i.e. to help us resolve the sorts of problems that are encountered in public policy, in courtrooms and in other non-philosophical contexts.

References

Anderson, Elizabeth. 1999. "What Is the Point of Equality?" *Ethics* 10(2):287–337.

Arneson, Richard J. 2000. "Luck Egalitarianism and Prioritarianism." *Ethics* 110(2):339–49.

Bovens, Mark. 1998. "Two Concepts of Responsibility." In *The Quest for Responsibility: Accountability and Citizenship in Complex Organisations*, 22–42. Cambridge: Cambridge University Press.

Cane, Peter. 2004. "Responsibility in Law and Morality: Book Symposium, Author's Introduction." *Australian Journal of Legal Philosophy* 29:160–63.

Cohen, G.A. 1989. "On the Currency of Egalitarian Justice." *Ethics* 99(4):906–44.

Dawkins, Richard. 2006. "Let's All Stop Beating Basil's Car." Accessed February 12, 2007. http://www.edge.org/q2006/q06_9.html#dawkins.

Dennett, Daniel C. 2003. *Freedom Evolves*. New York, NY: Viking.

Duff, R.A. 1998. "Responsibility." In *Routledge Encyclopedia of Philosophy*, edited by Edward Craig, Vol. 9, 290–94. New York, NY: Routledge.

Dworkin, Ronald. 1981. "What Is Equality? Part 2: Equality of Resources." *Philosophy & Public Affairs* 10(4):283–345.

Eisenberg, Leah. 2004. "Medicating Death Row Inmates so They Qualify for Execution." *Virtual Mentor* 6(9).

Feinberg, Joel. 1970. "Sua Culpa." In *Doing & Deserving: Essays in the Theory of Responsibility*, edited by Joel Feinberg, 187–221. Princeton, NJ: Princeton University Press.

Fischer, John Martin and Mark Ravizza. 1998. *Responsibility and Control: A Theory of Moral Responsibility*. Cambridge: Cambridge University Press.

Fischer, John Martin and Neal A. Tognazzini. 2011. "The Physiognomy of Responsibility." *Philosophy and Phenomenological Research* 82(2):381–417.

Gazzaniga, Micheal. S. 2006. "Facts, Fictions and the Future of Neuroethics." In *Neuroethics: Defining the Issues inTheory, Practice, and Policy*, edited by Judy Illes, 141–48. Oxford: Oxford University Press.

Goodin, Robert E. 1986. "Responsibilities." *Philosophical Quarterly* 36:50–56.

Goodin, Robert E. 1987. "Apportioning Responsibilities." *Law and Philosophy* 6:167–85.

Greene, Joshua and Jonathan Cohen. 2004. "For the Law, Neuroscience Changes Nothing and Everything." In *Law & the Brain*, edited by Semir Zeki and Oliver Goodenough, 207–26. New York, NY: Oxford University Press.
Hart, H.L.A. 1968. "IX. Postscript: Responsibility and Retribution." In *Punishment and Responsibility*, 210–37. Oxford: Clarendon Press.
Haydon, Graham. 1978. "On Being Responsible." *The Philosophical Quarterly* 28(110):46–57.
Honoré, Tony. 1999. "4. The Morality of Tort Law: Questions and Answers." In *Responsibility and Fault*, edited by T. Honoré, 67–93. Portland, OR: Hart Publishing.
Kutz, Christopher. 2004. "Chapter 14: Responsibility." In *Jurisprudence and Philosophy of Law*, edited by Jules Coleman and S. Shapiro, 548–87. Oxford, UK: Oxford University Press.
Lacey, Nicola. 2007. "Space, Time and Function: Intersecting Principles of Responsibility Across the Terrain of Criminal Justice." *Criminal Law and Philosophy* 1(3):233–50.
Landes, William M., and Richard A. Posner 1987. *The Economic Structure of Tort Law*. Cambridge, MA: Harvard University Press.
Latzer, Barry. 2003. "Between Madness and Death: The Medicate-to-Execute Controversy." *Criminal Justice Ethics* 22(2):3–14.
Morse, S.J. 2006. "Moral and Legal Responsibility and the New Neuroscience." In *Neuroethics: Defining the Issues in Theory, Practice, and Policy*, edited by Judy Illes, 33–50. Oxford, UK: Oxford University Press.
Pereboom, Derk. 2001. *Living Without Free Will*. Cambridge: Cambridge University Press.
Perry, Stephen R. 2000. "Loss, Agency, and Responsibility for Outcomes: Three Conceptions of Corrective Justice." In *Philosophy of Law* (6th Edition), edited by Joel Feinberg and Jules Coleman, 546–59. Belmont, CA: Wadsworth/Thompson Learning.
Posner, Richard A. 1996. "Lecture Two: The Common Law." In *Law and Legal Theory in England and America*, edited by Richard A. Posner, 39–67. Oxford: Oxford University Press.
Rakowski, Eric. 1991. *Equal Justice*. New York, NY: Oxford University Press.
Scanlon, Thomas. 1998. "Chapter 6: Responsibility." In *What We Owe to Each Other*, 248–94. Cambridge, MA: The Belknap Press of Harvard University Press.
Vincent, Nicole. 2009. "Responsibility: Distinguishing Virtue from Capacity." *Polish Journal of Philosophy* 3(1):111–26.
Vincent, Nicole. 2010. "On the Relevance of Neuroscience to Criminal Responsibility." *Criminal Law and Philosophy* 4(1):77–98.
Vincent, Nicole. 2011. "Madness, Badness and Neuroimaging-Based Responsibility Assessments." In *Law and Neuroscience, Current Legal Issues, Volume 13*, edited by Michael Freeman, 79–95. Oxford: Oxford University Press.
Vincent, Nicole. Forthcoming. "Enhancing Responsibility." In *Legal Responsibility and Neuroscience*, edited by N. Vincent. Oxford: Oxford University Press.
Vranas, Peter B.M. 2007. "I Ought, Therefore I Can." *Philosophical Studies* 136(2):167–216.
Wallace, R. Jay. 1994. *Responsibility and the Moral Sentiments*. Cambridge, MA: Harvard University Press.
Wallace, R. Jay. 2002. "Précis of Responsibility and the Moral Sentiments." *Philosophy and Phenomenological Research* 64(3):680–81.
Watson, Gary. 2004. "Two Faces of Responsibility." In *Agency and Answerability*, edited by Gary Watson, 260–88. Oxford: Oxford University Press.
Williams, Bernard. 1995. "Voluntary Acts and Responsible Agents." In *Making Sense of Humanity*, edited by Bernard Williams, 22–34. Cambridge, UK: Cambridge University Press.
Williams, Garrath. 2008. "Responsibility as a Virtue." *Ethical Theory and Moral Practice* 11(4):455–70.

Chapter 3
The Relation Between Forward-Looking and Backward-Looking Responsibility

Ibo van de Poel

Abstract This contribution discusses the relation between forward-looking and backward-looking responsibility. The notion of forward-looking responsibility I focus on is, following Robert Goodin, that of seeing to it that a certain state of affairs obtains. In addition, I focus on two types of backward-looking responsibility: accountability and blameworthiness. I argue that accountability only entails blameworthiness if the agent cannot cite certain reasonable excuses like ignorance and compulsion (which were already mentioned by Aristotle). It is further argued that accountability can both be based on not properly discharging a forward-looking responsibility and on the breach of a duty that caused a certain negative consequence. I show that in both cases three general conditions need to apply in order to hold an agent reasonably accountable: a capacity condition, a causality condition and a wrongdoing condition. The exact content of these conditions, however, depends on whether accountability is based on a forward-looking responsibility that is not properly discharged or on the breach of a duty.

3.1 Introduction

Traditionally much of the philosophical literature on responsibility has focused on backward-looking responsibility. The main question has been: when, under what conditions, is it proper to blame someone for a certain action or a certain outcome? More recently, a number of authors have discussed forward-looking notions of responsibility, either on consequentialist grounds (e.g. Goodin 1995) or on the basis of virtue ethics or care ethics (e.g. Ladd 1991; Williams 2008). In this contribution, I will explore the relations between forward- and backward-looking notions of responsibility. My focus will be on notions of *moral* responsibility, i.e. responsibility that is grounded in moral considerations, rather than legal or organizational notions of responsibility. Moreover, I will focus on responsibility for consequences (states of affairs) rather than responsibility for actions, although I will understand the notion of "consequence" broadly, as also encompassing for example a person possessing certain virtues.

I. van de Poel (✉)
Department of Philosophy, Delft University of Technology, 2600 GA Delft, The Netherlands
e-mail: I.R.vandePoel@tudelft.nl

N.A Vincent et al. (eds.), *Moral Responsibility*, Library of Ethics and Applied Philosophy 27, DOI 10.1007/978-94-007-1878-4_3,

My approach in this paper is largely conceptual in nature, i.e. I will proceed by conceptually distinguishing and clarifying different notions of responsibility and their relations. In doing so, I will build on accounts of responsibility that are offered by other thinkers and as they can be found in daily language. At some points, I will make choices with respect to how I understand the relevant terms and their relations that are not strictly conceptual but imply a substantial normative choice. Such choices are at some points inevitable if one wants to sketch a coherent picture. Nevertheless, I have tried to provide an account that is general and abstract enough to accommodate different substantive notions of responsibility.

This paper is structured as follows. I start with an overview of different meanings of responsibility, suggesting five major normative notions of responsibility, three of which are primarily backward-looking (accountability, blameworthiness and liability), and two which are primarily forward-looking (responsibility as virtue and as the moral obligation to see to it that something is the case). I will then restrict my analysis to three of the notions: accountability, blameworthiness and the moral obligation to see to it that something is the case. After suggesting a relation between these three that makes sense prima facie, I will add further complexities.

3.2 Notions of Responsibility

The term "responsibility" comes in different meanings and senses. It is therefore useful to distinguish some of the main meanings so that we know what we are talking about. We might to this end distinguish the following meanings of responsibility[1]:

1. *Responsibility-as-cause*. As in: the earth quake is responsible for the death of 100 people.
2. *Responsibility-as-task*.[2] As in: the train driver is responsible for driving the train.
3. *Responsibility-as-authority*.[3] As in he is responsible for the project, meaning he is in charge of the project.

---

[1] Hart (1968:210–37) was probably the first to distinguish four main senses of responsibility: role-responsibility, causal-responsibility, liability-responsibility and capacity-responsibility. The additional senses I distinguish in addition are related to these, but have in certain respects an (importantly) different meaning as explained. All the additional senses can indeed also be found in the literature on responsibility (e.g. Casey 1971; Baier 1972; Ladd 1982; Zimmerman 1988; Lucas 1993; Bovens 1998; Cane 2002; Duff 2007; Williams 2008; Davis forthcoming). Hart discusses blameworthiness as a component of moral liability, but I think that it is conceptually clearer to distinguish both notions.

[2] This is what Hart calls role-responsibility.

[3] This may also be called responsibility-as-office or responsibility-as-jurisdiction. It refers to a realm in which one has the authority to make decisions or is in charge and for which one can be held accountable.

4. *Responsibility-as-capacity*, i.e. as the ability to act in a responsible way. This includes for example the ability to reflect on the consequences of one's actions, to form intentions, to deliberately choose an action and act upon it.
5. *Responsibility-as-virtue*, i.e. as the disposition (character trait) to act responsibly. As in: he is a responsible person.
6. *Responsibility-as-(moral)-obligation*, to see to it that something is the case. As in: he is responsible for the safety of the passengers, meaning he is responsible to see to it that the passengers are transported safely.
7. *Responsibility-as-accountability*, i.e. as the (moral) obligation to account for what you did or what happened (and your role in it happening).
8. *Responsibility-as-blameworthiness*. As in: he is responsible for the car accident, meaning he can be blamed for the car accident happening.
9. *Responsibility-as-liability*. As in: he is liable to pay damages.

The first four meanings are more or less descriptive: responsibility-as-cause, role, authority and capacity describe something that is the case or not. The other five are normative. They imply a normative evaluation, as in responsibility-as-virtue and responsibility-as-blameworthiness, or a prescription, as in responsibility-as-obligation to see to it that something is the case and in responsibility-as-liability (to pay damages, offer excuses, put the situation right, etcetera). Responsibility-as-accountability seems to imply both an evaluation as well as a prescription; the agent is supposed to account for something because an action or outcome can be laid at her feet.[4]

Some of the normative meanings are related to, or rely on the descriptive meanings of responsibility. Responsibility-as-virtue is closely related to responsibility-as-capacity. But whereas the latter only refers to the ability to act responsibly, responsibility-as-virtue refers to the actual disposition, also surfacing in actions, to be a responsible person. Similarly responsibility-as-obligation to see to it that something is the case is closely related to responsibility-as-task.[5] Tasks are typically often formulated in terms of seeing to it that something is the case. The difference is that not every task or role defines a moral obligation. So, while it might be said that Nazi engineer Eichmann had the task (responsibility) that the Jews were effectively transported to the concentration camps, it does not follow that he had a (moral) obligation to see to it that they were effectively transported. In fact, since the transport was part of an immoral plan, aiming at the extinction of the Jews, he might even have had a moral obligation to see to it that they were not effectively transported.

Although responsibility-as-accountability, responsibility-as-blameworthiness and responsibility-as-liability are in meaning not directly related to one of

[4] Sometimes responsibility-as-accountability may be understood in a descriptive sense, as in cases in which one is accountable on the basis of certain organizational or legal rules. In such cases, responsibility-as-accountability seems often closely related to responsibility-as-task.

[5] Goodin (1995) in fact calls such responsibilities task-responsibilities, but – as pointed out in the text – I think there is an essential difference between task-responsibility in the sense I use the term and a (moral) obligation to see to something.

the descriptive notions, it is often assumed that responsibility-as-cause and responsibility-as-capacity are preconditions for holding someone accountable or liable or for blaming someone. Blameworthiness, in turn, is sometimes seen as a condition for moral liability. It is also often believed that responsibility-as-task or responsibility-as-authority may lead to responsibility-as-accountability, especially if the former responsibilities are not properly discharged.

The first two normative meanings are primarily forward-looking (prospective) in nature. This is most obvious for responsibility as the obligation to see to it that something is the case; it relates to something that is, usually, not yet the case. Responsibility-as-virtue is often primarily understood as being forward-looking (e.g. Ladd 1991; Bovens 1998); it relates to responsibilities an agent actively assumes and to a certain attitude rather than to blame (or praise). Nevertheless, one could well argue that a responsible person is one who is willing to account for his actions and who accepts blame and liability where that is due (Williams 2008).

Responsibility-as-accountability, blameworthiness and liability are backward-looking in the sense that they usually apply to something that has occurred. Nevertheless accountability and liability have a forward-looking (prescriptive) element in the sense that the agent is supposed to do something (in the future): to account for his actions, to pay damages and the like.

Now that we have distinguished different meanings of responsibility, it is possible to be a bit more precise about the main question of this paper, i.e. the relation between forward-looking and backward-looking responsibility. I am mainly interested in the relation between the various normative notions of responsibility. As we have seen two of these notions are primarily forward-looking, i.e. responsibility-as-virtue and as the obligation to see to it, and three are primarily backward-looking, i.e. accountability, blameworthiness and liability. Below, I will focus on the forward-looking notion of having to see to it that something is the case. This notion is more directly related to concrete actions and state of affairs than responsibility-as-virtue and therefore more obviously related to the backward-looking notions of responsibility. When I talk below of forward-looking responsibility I mean to refer to responsibility as the (moral) obligation to see to it that something is the case rather than to the virtue notion unless stated otherwise. With respect to the backward-looking notions I will focus on accountability and blameworthiness. Before saying more on the relation between these three notions, it is useful to say a bit more on the relational nature of the concept of responsibility.

3.3 Responsibility as a Relational Concept

In most of its meanings, the notion of responsibility refers to a relation between at least two entities. The most basic form this relation takes is:

(1) *A is responsible for X*

In which A is some agent and X can refer to actions, state of affairs (outcomes), tasks or realms of authority. Two meanings of responsibility, however, seem to resist this conceptualization, namely responsibility-as-capacity and responsibility-as-virtue.[6] Capacity and virtue are better understood as a "property" or characteristic of the agent A rather than as a relation between an agent A and some X. This is not to say that it never makes sense to particularize responsibility-as-capacity or responsibility-as-virtue to a particular X. We might, for example, say that someone is a responsible parent but an irresponsible engineer (both in the virtue sense). However, for both responsibility-as-capacity and responsibility-as-virtue it makes sense to say that A is responsible full stop, while that appears impossible for all other meanings.

Responsibility can also be understood as a triadic relational concept. Duff (2007:23–30) argues that normative notions of responsibility are best understood according to the following scheme[7]:

(2) *A is responsible for X to B*

In which B is some agent, usually different from A. In cases of forward-looking responsibility, (2) reflects the fact that we may have specific responsibilities to different people. Professionals like engineers, for example, have different responsibilities to their employer, to their colleagues, to their clients and to the public.[8] What they owe to their clients is different from what they owe to their employer or to the public; their responsibilities to these different groups of agents may even conflict.

More generally (2) may be seen as a reflection of the fact that forward-looking responsibilities may arise from the specific relations we have with specific people (cf. Scheffler 1997). This is not to deny that we may also have responsibilities to ourselves or general responsibilities. These may be seen as special cases in which B = A, or in which B is humanity (or morality or God if one wishes). In the case of forward-looking responsibility (2) might then be understood as follows:

(3) *A is forward-looking responsible for X to B means that A owes it to B to see to it that X*

How is (2) to be understood for backward-looking notions of responsibility like accountability and blameworthiness? Duff (2007:23) suggests that B is "a person or body who has the standing to call me to answer for X." More generally, B may be any agent who can fittingly, i.e. fairly or reasonably, hold A responsible for X. This may be expressed as follows:

---

[6] According to Duff (2007:23), responsibility-as-capacity can be explained in relational terms as "the capacities that are necessary if one is to answer for one's actions." However, this conflates the conceptual nature of responsibility-as-capacity with its being a precondition for other relational concepts of responsibility.

[7] In fact, responsibility-as-task is also usually understood as a triadic relation.

[8] In fact, we may also have different responsibilities in the different roles we have, for example as teacher, as colleague and as parent, and also these responsibilities may conflict.

(4) *A is backward-looking responsible for X to B means that it is fitting for B to hold A responsible for X*

Holding responsible here includes holding accountable or blaming. Duff suggests that the ones to which I owe something (the agent B in (3)) is the same as the one for whom it would be appropriate to hold me backward-looking responsible (the agent B in (4)). This suggestion, however, seems to me false. I may have a forward-looking responsibility to future generations to limit my emissions of greenhouse gases with an eye to global warming, but it does not follow that they are the only ones who can hold me accountable (or blameworthy) for not limiting my emissions of greenhouse gases. In fact they may never be able to hold me accountable because future generations do not exist yet, and when they (hopefully) exist in the future I may no longer exist. There may nevertheless be others, including I myself, who can properly hold me accountable for my emissions of greenhouse gases.

It has indeed been suggested that in cases of moral backward-looking responsibility, in contrast to legal, organizational or social responsibility, it is in principle appropriate for anyone to hold me accountable (or blameworthy) under certain conditions. The reference to B in other words is superfluous for moral responsibility. In fact, Strawson's conceptualization of backward-looking responsibility as the fittingness of certain reactive attitudes can be understood along the following lines (Zimmerman 2009; Strawson 1962):

(5) *A is responsible for X means it is fitting to adopt some reactive attitude toward A in respect of X*

Or in a formulation that closely resembles a proposal by Wallace (1994:92):

(6) *A is responsible for X if and only if it is fitting to hold A responsible for X*

Formulations (5) and (6) suggest that the fittingness of reactive attitudes is independent from the specific agent B, so that the reference to B becomes superfluous. An interesting criticism of formulations like (5) and (6) is offered by Kutz (2000: 17–65). He admits that in cases of moral responsibility, it might be appropriate for anyone to hold me accountable or to express certain reactive attitudes. However, what reactive attitudes are appropriate or under what conditions it is fitting to hold some agent A responsible may well depend on the specific relation between A and B, so that the reference to B is not superfluous.

A specific case is the situation when B = A. Consider the following example.[9] During a departmental meeting I make a statement or an argument that turns out

[9] This is my example. Kutz provides other examples, including examples in which it seems appropriate for the agent A to assume responsibility rather than, as in my example, there being a degree of freedom in taking responsibility or not. My suggestion is then not that the phenomenon of taking responsibility, to which I draw attention below, exhausts the relational nature of responsibility. Rather it draws attention to an aspect of responsibility that is also not fully grasped by formulations like (4).

to be insulting for one of the other participants in the meeting. Let's suppose that my statement cannot in general be considered insulting or inappropriate nor could I have known that my words would be insulting. Because of this excusable ignorance, it seems inappropriate for other participants in the meeting to hold me responsible (blameworthy) for what turned out to be an insult. For the same reasons I am morally allowed not to blame myself nor should I feel guilty. Nevertheless, it would not be inappropriate if I felt guilty and would offer her excuses. In fact doing so might, depending on the exact circumstances, be laudable or virtuous. This example suggests two things. First, I can appropriately take responsibility for some X even if it would be inappropriate for others to hold me responsible for that X. Second, I have a degree of choice in taking responsibility. Of course, I cannot reasonably take responsibility for everything nor can I reasonably escape responsibility for some things. However, within the bounds of reason and morality, I have some freedom for taking responsibility for certain things or not.

The possibility of taking responsibility seems to undermine formulations (5) and (6). In fact, it is also not fully captured by (4) because, as the example suggests, there may be situations in which it would be both appropriate, i.e. rationally and morally allowable, not to take responsibility and to take responsibility. Whether an agent is, or rather becomes, responsible in such situations depends on the volitional choice of that agent.

Although the phenomenon of taking responsibility is interesting and important, I will neglect it in the rest of this paper. I will focus below on conditions under which it is appropriate to hold A backward-looking responsible (in the different senses of the term) independent from characteristics of B or the relation between A and B. The reason is that I am interested here mainly in the relation between forward-looking and backward-looking responsibility and that I think that it is better not to burden a first-order characterization of that relation with having to account for the relation between A and B as well. Another way of characterizing the account that I will offer is to say that the account that I shall offer will presuppose a standard or default relationship between A and B (cf. Kutz 2000:30) in which A and B are both members of the moral community while abstracting from any further specific relations between A and B, so that the reference to B becomes superfluous because B stands for any member of the moral community.

3.4 The Relation Between Forward-Looking and Backward-Looking Responsibility: A Suggestion

Let me now turn to the main question of this paper: the relation between forward-looking and backward-looking responsibility. The previous sections make it possible to be more precise about what I mean with that. I will be focusing on accountability and blameworthiness as backward-looking notions of responsibility and on the forward-looking notion as the obligation to see to it that. In all these cases the focus will be on responsibility for consequences. I will further understand accountability and blameworthiness in line with (6). This means that I will be focusing on conditions under which it is fitting (appropriate, reasonable) to hold an agent A responsible (accountable, blameworthy) for an outcome X. I will neither pay attention to agents taking accountability or blame nor to the relation between the agent being held responsible (agent A) and the agent holding responsible (agent B). With respect to forward-looking responsibility I will assume that agents (can) have such responsibilities, whatever their exact source or ground, and will inquire what that means for their backward-looking responsibilities.

For a first order answer to the question of the relation between forward-looking and backward-looking responsibility, I turn to a real-life example. The answer is a brief account that Leslie Robertson, the structural engineer who designed the Twin Towers in New York, provided when he was asked whether he felt guilty about the fact that the towers did not stand longer after they had been hit by two planes in a terrorist attack on September, 11 2002:

> The responsibility for arriving at the ultimate strength of the towers was mine. The fact that they did not stand longer could be laid at my feet. Do I feel guilty about . . . the fact that they collapsed? The circumstances on September, 11 were outside of what we considered in the design. . . .. If I knew then what I know now they would have stood longer, of course.[10]

I think that the different elements of his account can be interpreted as follows:

- "The responsibility for arriving at the ultimate strength of the towers was mine." This refers to responsibility as the obligation to see to it that.
- "The fact that they did not stand longer could be laid at my feet." This can be interpreted as: It would be proper (for others) to hold me accountable for that fact.
- "Do I feel guilty about . . . the fact that they collapsed?" This could be interpreted as: "Would it be proper to blame me for it?"
- "The circumstances on September, 11 were outside of what we considered in the design. . . .. If I knew then what I know now they would have stood longer, of course." This can be interpreted as giving an account (invoking certain excuses like nonculpable ignorance) that shows why it would not be proper to blame him.[11]

This example then suggests a first order answer to my question along the following lines:

> If A has the obligation to see to it that some state of affairs X is the case and X happens not to be the case, A is accountable for "not X". If A is not able to give a satisfactory account for "not X", A is also blameworthy.

---

[10] Excerpt from documentary "Why the Twin Towers collapsed" broadcasted by Discovery Channel.

[11] It is very interesting and indeed impressive that on the video of the interview Robertson starts nodding when he poses himself the question "Do I feel guilty?" One interpretation would be that in his non-verbal expressions (the nodding) he answers the question "Do I take the blame?" (He obviously feels very bad about what happened if not guilty), while in his verbal expressions he answers the question "Would it be proper for others to blame me?" His answer to the first question seems affirmative and to the second not.

Below, I will further explore this account, try to make it more precise and adjust it where that might turn out to be necessary. In doing so, I will start at the end of the chain and then work backwards from there.

3.5 Blameworthiness

As indicated earlier, much of the traditional literature on responsibility focuses on responsibility-as-blameworthiness. A range of authors have suggested a set of conditions that need to be satisfied in order for an agent A to be blameworthy for a state of affairs X (e.g. Feinberg 1970; Thompson 1980; Wallace 1994; Bovens 1998; Fischer and Ravizza 1998; Corlett 2001; Swierstra and Jelsma 2006). Conditions that are often mentioned include[12]:

- *Moral Agency*: the agent A is a moral agent, i.e. has the capacity to act responsibly. (responsibility-as-capacity)
- *Causality*: the agent A is somehow causally involved in X. This can be because A causally contributed to X. (responsibility-as-cause)
- *Wrongdoing*: The agent A did something wrong. (On some accounts, the occurrence of X *simpliciter* may constitute the wrongdoing).
- *Freedom*: The agent A was not compelled to bring about X.
- *Knowledge*: A knew, or at least could have known, that X would occur and that this was undesirable.

Although these general conditions can be found in many accounts, there is much debate about at least two issues. One is the exact content and formulation of each of the conditions. For example, does the freedom condition imply that the agent could have acted otherwise? The other is whether these conditions are individually necessary and together sufficient in order for an agent A to be blameworthy for X. One way to deal with the latter issue is to conceive of the mentioned conditions as arguments or reasons for holding someone responsible (blameworthy) for something rather than as a strict set of conditions (Davis forthcoming).

Despite these debates, the above list of conditions is helpful to distinguish between blameworthiness and accountability. My suggestion is that some of the above mentioned conditions are possible excuses (reasons) that can be used by an agent that is accountable for something in order to show that she is not blameworthy.[13] Others are rather preconditions for being accountable.

---

[12] Also control is sometimes mentioned as condition, but see Sher (2006).

[13] A similar suggestion can be found in Hart (1968), Wallace (1994) and Duff (2007). Although Hart and Duff do not distinguish between blameworthiness and liability, they suggest a similar relation between accountability (or answerability) and liability as I do between accountability and blameworthiness. Wallace makes a distinction between A- and B-conditions for responsibility: "B-conditions make it fair to hold people morally to blame ... while A-conditions make it fair to hold people morally accountability" (Wallace 1994:118) His A-conditions focus on when it is in general

The freedom and knowledge condition are both arguments that can be used in an account to excuse oneself.[14] Typically, both are already mentioned by Aristotle as possible reasons why someone is not to be blamed for her actions or the consequences of these (Aristotle, *The Nicomachean Ethics*, book III, chapters 1–5).[15] The capacity and causality condition on the other hand are typically conditions for holding someone accountable. We do not hold people, or other entities, accountable if we do not have reason to believe that they have the capacity to act responsibly[16]; without this capacity they would in fact not be able to provide an account at all, or so it seems. We also do not hold people accountable if we believe that they are completely causally disconnected from the state of affairs X we are concerned about. There should be at least a suspicion of causal involvement or the ability to causally influence the outcome X by the agent A. Although capacity and causality are conditions for holding someone accountable, they may also function as arguments in the account given. We might suspect a causal connection, but the agent might be able to show in her account that we are wrong. Similarly, the agent might argue that she temporarily lacked, for circumstances beyond her control, the capacity to act responsibly and therefore is not to be blamed.

How does the wrongdoing condition fit into this picture? In general it seems that we hold people not only accountable for bad things, but also for neutral things, like a reimbursement, and even for good outcomes, for example to judge whether a certain price would be deserved. What is common to these cases of accountability is that a judgment is made whether a certain treatment is deserved. In the case, we are interested in here, the question is whether blame is deserved. Such accountability for blame is sometimes called answerability. In the words of Hart:

> The original meaning of the word "answer", like that of the Greek "αποχρινέσθαι" and the Latin *respondere*, was not that of answering questions, but that of answering or rebutting accusations or charges, which, if established, carried liability to punishment or blame or other adverse treatment (see O.E.D., *sub. tit. "answer"*). ... a person who fails to rebut a charge is liable to punishment or blame for what he has done, and a person who is liable to punishment or blame has had a charge to rebut and failed to rebut. (Hart 1968:265)

In as far as wrongdoing is a condition for blameworthiness, at least a reasonable suspicion of wrongdoing is a precondition for reasonably holding someone

---

fair to hold people accountable (cf. Wallace 1994:154), this is my first condition (moral agency); his account seems to assume wrongdoing implicitly (e.g. Wallace 1994:156). My conditions for accountability also include conditions for when it is fair to hold someone accountable for a *specific outcome*.

[14] Wallace (1994:136–47) mentions four types of excuses: (1) inadvertence, mistake or accident, (2) unintentional bodily movements, (3) physical constraint and (4) coercion, necessity and duress. The first is a case of non-culpable ignorance (referring to the knowledge condition), the others of compulsion (referring to the freedom condition).

[15] Typically many other authors have treated those two conditions as the conditions for being at fault, suggesting that these are conditions for blameworthiness rather than for accountability.

[16] This capacity might be understood in terms of reason-responsiveness (Fischer and Ravizza 1998) or reflective self-control (Wallace 1994).

Table 3.1 Conditions for accountability and blameworthiness

Conditions for accountability	Possible excuses to avoid blameworthiness (if held accountable)
Capacity	Ignorance (knowledge)
Causality	Compulsion (freedom)
Wrongdoing	(capacity, causality, wrongdoing)

accountable. The reason for this is that accountability shifts the burden of proof for blameworthiness: the agent is now to show – by giving an account – that she is not blameworthy. Such a shift in the burden of proof seems only reasonable if there is a reasonable suspicion of wrongdoing.

To summarize: the suggestion is that an agent A is accountable for X if A has the capacity to act responsibly (has moral agency), is somehow causally connected to the outcome X (by an action or omission) and there is a reasonable suspicion that agent A did somehow something wrong. A may then provide an account that she is not blameworthy. In this account she can refer to the knowledge and freedom conditions, but possibly also to the other three conditions. Table 3.1 summarizes this result.

3.6 Accountability

We now have two suggestions for when an agent A is accountable for X. One was given at the end of the previous section: A is accountable if A has the capacity to act responsibly, is causally involved in X and did something wrong. The other was given earlier: A is accountable for X if A had to see to it that "not X" (i.e. A was forward-looking responsible for "not X") and X happens to be the case. It might well be possible to combine these accounts. We could try to argue that in order for an agent to be forward-looking responsible for X that agent needs to posses moral agency (i.e. the capacity to act responsibly) and A needs to be able to causally influence the occurrence of X. In addition, we could try to argue that the occurrence of X constitutes wrongdoing given A's responsibility to bring about "not X".

Nevertheless, I think it is better not to merge the two suggestions completely. The reason for this is that I think it would tie accountability too closely to the notion of forward-looking responsibility as the obligation to see to it that. Typically, we do not only hold people accountable for not discharging their forward-looking responsibilities but also for not meeting other moral obligations, preeminently for not discharging their duties. One could deal with this by arguing that doing our duty is part of our forward-looking responsibilities. This would, however, eventually stretch forward-looking responsibility such as to include all of our moral obligations. I think this would water down the notion of forward-looking responsibility too much. It is therefore better to distinguish between moral obligations that refer to actions (duties) and ones that refer to outcomes (forward-looking responsibilities).

To do so, I will follow Goodin's characterization of forward-looking responsibility. He conceives of both duties and responsibilities as prescriptions of the general form (Goodin 1995:82):

A ought to see to it that X

Where A is some agent, and X is some state of affairs. For duties, X takes the form:

A does or refrains from doing ϕ

Where ϕ is some specific action. For responsibilities, X does not refer to specific actions of A. X can refer to states-of-the-world, to states-of-mind of A, to A possessing certain virtues, to actions of other agents, as long as it does not include specified actions of A. Goodin suggests that the exercising of forward-looking responsibility:

> ... require[s] certain activities of a self-supervisory nature from A. The standard form of responsibility is that A *see to it* that X. It is not enough that X occurs. A must also have "seen to it" that X occurs. "Seeing to it that X" requires, minimally, that A satisfy himself that there is some process (mechanism or activity) at work whereby X will be brought about; that A check from time to time to make sure that that process is still at work, and is performing as expected; and that A take steps as necessary to alter or replace processes that no longer seem likely to bring about X. (Goodin 1995:83)

According to Goodin these self-supervisory activities are "genuine responsibilities" because "they are injunctions that mandate goals and very general classes of activities, rather than specific actions" (Goodin 1995:83). For Goodin the crucial distinction between duties and responsibilities is the discretionary component built into the latter (Goodin 1995:84). However, also most duties have a discretionary component. Such duties do not prescribe specific actions but rather forbid general classes of actions or prescribe actions with certain properties. There are usually several ways in which one can abide by duties like "tell the truth" or "do not lie". Duties are therefore often best seen as constraints on actions rather than as strict prescriptions.

Nevertheless, there is a sense in which responsibilities are different from duties and it is related to the presence of a discretionary component. The difference is that responsibilities do not require the agent to achieve the outcome X by her own actions. Responsibilities can be delegated whereas duties cannot. If I have the duty to tell the truth it is not enough that somebody else tells the truth or that the truth surfaces in some other way. Each of these does not count as fulfilling the duty; the duty can only be fulfilled by an action of mine. This is different in the case of responsibilities. Consider the following example. Suppose that I have a forward-looking responsibility to see to it that the door of the classroom is closed before my lecture commences. Initially, I can just wait and see whether somebody closes it. If so, my responsibility has been discharged and I can start my lecture. If not, I can ask one of my students to close the door. If he indeed closes the door my responsibility has been discharged. If not, I can decide to close the door myself in order to discharge my responsibility.

The example illustrates two points. One is that fulfilling my responsibility does not require that X is achieved by an action of mine. The other point is that responsibility requires, as also suggested by Goodin, some action on my part of a supervisory nature: I have to see to it that X is achieved. This supervisory activity refers, contrary to what Goodin believes, not to a responsibility but to a duty. This is so because the supervision is to be done by me and cannot be delegated.[17]

The above is helpful in further specifying what it means to say that A did or did not discharge her forward-looking responsibility to see to it that X. Although this responsibility is aimed at realizing X, the occurrence of X is not the main criterion whether A actually fulfilled her forward-looking responsibility. The reason is that X may occur even if A did not see to it that X because X may be caused by something else. So even if A did not discharge her responsibility X may be the case. Moreover, X may not be realized even if A saw to it that X; X may for example not come about due to circumstances that A could neither foresee nor control. Discharging responsibility thus basically means exercising one's (self-) supervisory duties to see to it that X.

As Goodin suggests, both forward-looking responsibilities and duties can lead to what he calls blame-responsibility (and to accountability I would add). Here we can make sense I think of the two suggestions made earlier. There is not one route to accountability and blameworthiness but rather two. One route, call it the consequentialist one, is rooted in A's forward-looking responsibility for X; the other, call it the deontic one, is rooted in some moral duty that is transgressed. On the consequentialist route, an agent is basically accountable for a state of affairs X if that agent was forward-looking responsible for "not X" but did not see to it that "not X". On the deontic route, an agent may said to be accountable if she transgressed a duty D (and blameworthy if she was not acting under compulsion or ignorance). The latter is however accountability for actions rather than for consequences. But suppose that the transgression of D results in X, where X is an undesirable state of affairs; here it might be said that A is accountable for X if A is a moral agent who performed an action that transgressed D, and this action caused or causally contributed to X.

It seems then that the two suggestions with which we started this section are actually two routes to accountability for consequences. Although it is important to see the differences between the routes, I think it can be argued that both routes are based on the same general conditions for accountability, i.e. capacity, causality and wrongdoing, although the latter two conditions have a different meaning in the different routes (see Table 3.2). In the deontic route, wrongdoing consists in the breach of a duty D; the causality conditions boils down to this breach of D (rather than something else) causing a state of affairs X (Feinberg 1970:222). For the consequentialist route, the wrongdoing consists in the not discharging of one's supervisory duties to see to it that "not X."

[17] It might in specific circumstances be possible to delegate some supervision, but the agent cannot delegate away all responsibility and still has a duty to supervise the supervision, et cetera.

Table 3.2 Two routes for accountability

Accountability for X	Consequentialist route	Deontic route
Capacity	Ability to act responsibly	Ability to act responsibly
Wrongdoing	Forward-looking responsibility for "not X" not discharged	Transgression of duty D
Causality	Ability to causally influence the occurrence of X	Transgression of D caused X

How does the causality condition fit into the consequentialist route? My suggestion is that it is a precondition for A's forward-looking responsibility for X (which in turn, in this route, is a precondition for accountability).[18] I do not think it makes sense to ascribe forward-looking responsibility for X to agents who are not able to exercise some causal influence over the occurrence of X.[19]

3.7 Conclusions

The account that I have developed in this paper suggests a number of things. First, it suggests, contrary to what some other authors have suggested (e.g. Vedder 2001; Duff 2007:30–31), that one can be backward-looking responsible (accountable or blameworthy) for a state of affairs without having been forward-looking responsible for preventing that state of affairs. Second, it suggests that it may be useful to distinguish between accountability and blameworthiness. Accountability refers to what some see as a primary meaning of responsibility as answerability and as being able to provide a justification for one's action. Such answerability or justification do not, however, yet imply blameworthiness, which is also often seen as a main connotation of responsibility. Distinguishing between accountability and blameworthiness therefore avoids conceptual confusion. In addition, I have suggested a relation between the two in terms of the traditional conditions for responsibility. Third, I have suggested that accountability may both be rooted in a duty transgressed as well as in a forward-looking responsibility not discharged. Although there are two routes to accountability, both seem to share the basic conditions for accountability: capacity, causality and wrongdoing, even if these conditions have a different content in the two routes.

[18] An alternative would be to require, in analogy with the deontological route, that the transgression of the supervisory duties implied by A's responsibility for "not X" caused X rather than that something else. Apart from that this implies a counterfactual that may be difficult to establish ("what if A had lived by her responsibility?"), this seems me intuitively implausible. If A had to see to it that "not X" and did not fulfill her responsibility, this seems enough reasons to hold A accountable if X occurs. This is different in the deontological route because there the duty D does not contain a direct reference to X.

[19] Note that this causality condition is much weaker than the one in the deontic route.

There are various ways in which the account that I have proposed can be extended. One is by including the notion of moral liability. It has been suggested that one can be liable without being blameworthy (Davis forthcoming). My framework suggests the further question whether one can also be liable without being accountable. Another direction in which the account can be extended is conceiving of responsibility as a triadic rather than as a dyadic relation and by incorporating the role of responsibility-as-virtue and the phenomenon of "taking responsibility".

Acknowledgments This paper was written as part of the research program "Moral Responsibility in R&D Networks", which is supported by the Netherlands Organization for Scientific Research (NWO) under grant number 360-20-160. An earlier version of this paper was presented at the International Conference on Moral Responsibility: Neuroscience, Organization & Engineering, Delft, August 24–27, 2009. I would like to thank the conference participants, my co-workers in the project Moral Responsibility in R&D networks, Sven Ove Hansson, and Michael Davis for comments on earlier versions. I am grateful to NIAS, the Netherlands Institute for Advanced Study, for providing me with the opportunity, as a Fellow-in-Residence, to rewrite and finish this paper during my stay in the academic year 2009–2010.

References

Baier, Kurt. 1972. "Guilt and Responsibility." In *Individual and Collective Responsibility: Massacre at My Lai*, edited by Peter A. French, 35–61. Cambridge, MA: Schenkman.

Bovens, Mark. 1998. *The Quest for Responsibility. Accountability and Citizenship in Complex Organisations*. Cambridge: Cambridge University Press.

Cane, Peter. 2002. *Responsibility in Law and Morality*. Oxford: Hart Publishing.

Casey, John. 1971. "Action and Consequences." In *Morality and Moral Reasoning: Five Essays in Ethics*, edited by John Casey, 155–205. London: Methuen.

Corlett, J. Angelo. 2001. "Collective Moral Responsibility." *Journal of Social Philosophy* 32: 573–84.

Davis, Michael. forthcoming. ""Ain't No One Here But Us Social Forces": Constructing the Professional Responsibility of Engineers." *Science and Engineering Ethics*. Online first. doi: 10.1007/s11948-010-9225-3.

Duff, Antony. 2007. *Answering for Crime: Responsibility and Liability in the Criminal Law*. Oxford: Hart Publishing.

Feinberg, Joel. 1970. *Doing & Deserving: Essays in the Theory of Responsibility*. Princeton, NJ: Princeton University Press.

Fischer, John Martin, and Mark Ravizza. 1998. *Responsibility and Control: A Theory of Moral Responsibility*. Cambridge: Cambridge University Press.

Goodin, Robert E. 1995. *Utilitarianism as a Public Philosophy*. Cambridge: Cambridge University Press.

Hart, H.L.A. 1968. *Punishment and Responsibility: Essays in the Philosophy of Law*. Oxford: Clarendon Press.

Kutz, Christopher. 2000. *Complicity: Ethics and Law for a Collective Age*. Cambridge; New York: Cambridge University Press.

Ladd, John. 1982. "Philosophical Remarks on Professional Responsibility in Organizations." *International Journal of Applied Philosophy* 1:58–70.

Ladd, John. 1991. "Bhopal: An Essay on Moral Responsibility and Civic Virtue." *Journal of Social Philosophy* 32:73–91.

Lucas, J.R. 1993. *Responsibility*. Oxford: Oxford University Press.

Scheffler, Samuel. 1997. "Relationships and Responsibilities." *Philosophy and Public Affairs* 26:189–209.

Sher, George. 2006. "Out of Control." *Ethics* 116:285–301.

Strawson, Peter. 1962. "Freedom and Resentment." *Proceedings of the British Academy* 48: 187–211.

Swierstra, Tsjalling and Jaap Jelsma. 2006. "Responsibility Without Moralism in Techno-Scienctific Design Practice." *Science, Technology & Human Values* 31:309–32.

Thompson, Dennis F. 1980. "Moral Responsibility and Public Officials: The Problem of Many Hands." *American Political Science Review* 74:905–16.

Vedder, Anton. 2001. "Accountability of Internet Access and Service Providers: Strict Liability Entering Ethics?" *Ethics and Information Technology* 3:67–74.

Wallace, R. Jay. 1994. *Responsibility and the Moral Sentiments*. Cambridge, MA: Harvard University Press.

Williams, Garrath. 2008. "Responsibility as a Virtue." *Ethical Theory and Moral Practice* 11: 455–70.

Zimmerman, Michael J. 1988. *An Essay on Moral Responsibility*. Totowa, NJ: Rowman & Littlefield.

Zimmerman, Michael J. 2009. "Responsibility, Reaction and Value." Paper read at International Conference on Moral Responsibility: Neuroscience, Organization & Engineering, August 24–27, 2009, at Delft University of Technology, the Netherlands.

Chapter 4
Beyond Belief and Desire: or, How to Be Orthonomous

Michael Smith

Abstract The standard belief-desire account of the explanation of action is inadequate to the task of explaining even the very simplest actions. We must suppose instead that three psychological states are in play when we explain action, not just two: desire, belief, and the exercise of the capacity to be instrumentally rational. Once we enrich our understanding of action explanation to acknowledge the causal role played by an agent's exercise of his rational capacities, much richer accounts of action explanation come into view, accounts that highlight the many different ways in which agents' actions can be explained by their rational capacities. Of special interest are cases in which agents' actions are explained by their failure to exercise their rational capacities, where these are capacities that they possess, and cases in which their actions are explained by their failure to exercise their rational capacities, where these are capacities that they do not possess. Richer accounts of action explanation such as these suggest a distinctive story about the conditions under which people are responsible for wrongdoing, a story with surprising implications for our understanding of what it is for an agent's moral beliefs to be justified.

4.1 Introduction

The standard belief-desire account of the explanation of action, at least in the form in which that account was put forward by Donald Davidson, is inadequate to the task of explaining even the very simplest actions (Davidson 1963). If some version of the standard account is correct, then we must suppose that it is a variation on the version put forward by Carl G. Hempel (1961) prior to Davidson. According to Hempel, three psychological states are in play when we explain action, not just two as Davidson supposes. Desire and belief are part of the explanation of every action, but so too is the capacity to be instrumentally rational, a capacity that is but one among many capacities rational agents possess (Smith 2009).

Once we enrich our understanding of action explanation to acknowledge the causal role played by an agent's exercise of his rational capacities, much richer accounts of action explanation come into view, accounts that highlight the many

M. Smith (✉)
Department of Philosophy, 1879 Hall, Princeton University, Princeton, NJ 08544, USA
e-mail: msmith@princeton.edu

N.A Vincent et al. (eds.), *Moral Responsibility*, Library of Ethics and Applied Philosophy 27, DOI 10.1007/978-94-007-1878-4_4,

different ways in which agents' actions can be explained by their rational capacities. Of special interest are cases in which agents' actions are explained by their failure to exercise their rational capacities, where these are capacities that they possess, and cases in which their actions are explained by their failure to exercise their rational capacities, where these are capacities that they do not possess (Smith 2003). Richer accounts of action explanation such as these suggest a distinctive story about the conditions under which people are responsible for wrongdoing, a story with surprising implications for our understanding of what it is for an agent's moral beliefs to be justified.

In the first section of the paper I explain why, and in what way, we need to go beyond the standard belief-desire account of action explanation. In the second section I outline the much richer kinds of explanation of action that come into view once we go beyond the standard account in the way suggested, and I describe the conditions of moral responsibility that they suggest. I also provide further support for this story about the conditions of responsibility by bringing out the similarities between it and the conception of responsibility found in the criminal law. And then in the third and final section I outline some of the surprising implications of this conception of responsibility.

4.2 Beyond the Standard Belief-Desire Account of the Explanation of Action

Consider a very simple case of action. Suppose that John non-instrumentally desires more than anything else to get muscly and believes with as much certainty as he believes anything that he can get muscly by exercising. Does it follow that he will exercise, if he does anything at all intentionally?

According to a principle that Donald Davidson accepts, this does follow. The principle is this:

> P1: If an agent wants to do x more than he wants to do y and believes himself free to do either x or y, then he will intentionally do x if he does either x or y intentionally. (Davidson 1970)

In our example, John satisfies this condition, so by Davidson's lights it follows that he will exercise if he does anything intentionally at all. I take it that this is why Davidson thinks that just two psychological states figure in the explanation of action. All we need to know in order to know what John will do intentionally, if he does anything intentionally, is what he desires and believes, or so Davidson seems to think. However a moment's reflection makes it clear that this isn't so.

Given P1, what should we say about the case in which an agent wants x exactly as much as he wants y, but wants each of these more than he wants anything else, and believes himself free to do various things, including either x or y? If P1 tells us everything we need to know, then all we could say is that he will do either x or y, if he does anything intentionally. But as we know from reflection on Buridan's Ass type cases, this isn't all that we can say. When a rational agent goes to the supermarket and is confronted by three identical boxes of cereal, desires most to take one or another box, but desires to take each box exactly as much as he desires to take the others, he may still take (say) the one in the middle intentionally. This is because rational agents possess the capacity to just *pick* an alternative when their antecedent desires and beliefs leave them indifferent. They choose one intentionally despite the fact that they don't antecedently desire it more (Raz 1999:100).

To tell us everything we need to know in order to know what an agent will do intentionally, if he does anything intentionally, P1 would therefore need to be supplemented with an account of the role of this distinctive capacity that rational agents possess to pick or chose, a capacity whose exercise explains why they are not flummoxed, suffering the counterpart of starving to death in Buridan's Ass cases. This is therefore a psychological state of great normative significance, and it is also one whose exercise turns out to be empirically tractable. According to one study, for example, when the choice is between three or four or five identical items, as in the case of choosing a box of cereal in a supermarket, rational agents tend to avoid the endpoints, opting for the item in the middle (Christenfeld 1995).

It might be objected that this is all confused. If rational agents in supermarkets intentionally choose items in the middle of a row of identical items, then it follows that they must have at least some non-instrumental desire for things in the middle, a non-instrumental desire that breaks the alleged tie among agents' non-instrumental desires for objects in middle, those on the right, and those on the left. It might be thought that this follows from what it is to desire something. If a desire is just a disposition to choose, then there is no conceptual space for the idea of an additional capacity to choose. The agents in question might not desire the one in the middle more *antecedently*, but they do when they act.

But a little reflection suggests that this is not really an objection to what's been proposed. If the so-called desire for things in the middle only manifests itself in circumstances in which a tie needs to be broken between alternatives that can't be discriminated between by an agent's other non-instrumental desires – if it is the non-instrumental desire, when an agent's other non-instrumental desires leave a choice underdetermined, for those things in the middle, and if it is constitutive of being rational that agents have some such non-instrumental desire when a tie needs to be broken – then there is only a verbal difference between the suggestion that agents have such desires, and the suggestion that they have the capacity to choose an alternative when their desires leave them indifferent between alternatives, a capacity that they tend to exercise by going for the thing in the middle. The reply to the objection thus concedes everything that is at issue.

Once we allow that an additional role may be played in intentional action by the exercise of an agent's rational capacities, as in Buridan's Ass cases, the question immediately arises whether there are other situations in which a role is played by an agent's exercise of his rational capacities. And the answer is that there are. Almost ten years prior to Davidson, Hempel had put forward his own version of the standard account of action explanation. In the course of doing so, he had pointed out that whenever an agent acts on his desires and beliefs, he must also exercise a distinctive rational capacity to put his desires and beliefs together.

Consider once again our example. Suppose that John does non-instrumentally desire to get muscly more than he desires anything else and believes that he can get muscly by exercising with more certainty than he believes anything else. If he is instrumentally irrational he will not form the instrumental desire to exercise, and, absent the formation of that instrumental desire, he won't exercise (Hempel 1961:266–67). For desire and belief even to begin to play the role that Davidson describes in P1, we therefore need to suppose that a ubiquitous role is played by yet another psychological state. Hempel himself calls this state the agent's being rational, but in fact the psychological state in question is both more specific than this, and we have to understand the role that it plays in a certain way.

If an agent with non-instrumental desires and beliefs is to act at all, he must *have and exercise* the capacity to be *instrumentally rational*. It would not be enough for him merely to have the capacity to be rational, where this is a capacity that he may or may not exercise. To return to our example, even if John does have the capacity to be instrumentally rational, if he does not exercise it on the occasion, then he still will not form the instrumental desire to exercise, and, absent the formation of that desire, he will not exercise. Moreover, not just any old rational capacity will do the job. It wouldn't be enough if the agent exercised his capacity to form his beliefs in the light of the available evidence, for example. Indeed, the exercise of that capacity isn't even necessary for an agent to act. Having means-end beliefs is enough. How he came by his means-end beliefs is neither here nor there.

To see more precisely what the distinctive causal role is that's played by an agent's possession and exercise of his capacity to be instrumentally rational, we need to consider a slightly less simple case of action explanation, a variation on the case that we have discussed thus far. Suppose that John has a non-instrumental desire to get muscly and that he believes there are two ways in which he could do so. He believes that he could get muscly by exercising a lot, and he also believes that he could get muscly by exercising less, but taking pills as well. If he does it by exercising a lot, then it will take longer to get muscly, whereas if he does it by using the combination strategy, then he will get muscly sooner, but once the musculature is achieved, it will last equally long either way.

If John is as confident about one of these causal claims as he is about the other – equally confident that exercising a lot will cause him to get muscly and that exercising less and taking pills will cause him to get muscly – then, assuming that he doesn't care whether he gets muscly sooner or later, it follows that, if he were fully instrumentally rational, he would be indifferent between these options. His instrumental desire to exercise a lot and his instrumental desire to exercise less and take pills would be equally strong. He would be in a Buridan's Ass situation, and would therefore need to just pick an option.

But now suppose that John is equally confident about both strategies and that he opts for the combination strategy. If John's possession and exercise of the capacity to be fully instrumentally rational is part of the explanation of his pursuit of the combination strategy, then we already know something about what he would have done if the option of exercising and taking pills hadn't been available to him. John would have exercised, notwithstanding the fact that it would take him longer to get muscly because, being fully instrumentally rational, he has an instrumental desire just to exercise waiting in the wings to produce action should it turn out that the combination strategy isn't available.

If, however, John is less than fully instrumentally rational – if, say, he has a tendency not to form instrumental desires when gratification is significantly delayed – then we have no grounds for supposing that he would have exercised if the option of taking pills hadn't been available to him. For though it follows from the fact that he exercises and takes pills intentionally that he is at least somewhat instrumentally rational, there is no reason at all to suppose that he is sufficiently instrumentally rational to have formed the desire simply to exercise as well and have it on standby. Indeed, if he has a tendency not to form instrumental desires when gratification is significantly delayed, there is every reason to suppose that he isn't sufficiently instrumentally rational to have formed that desire. Which counterfactuals are true of John thus depends on which explanatory hypothesis is correct.

Here, then, are the questions we must ask. Does John exercise and take pills because he is fully instrumentally rational and picks? Or does he exercise and take pills because, though he is less than fully instrumentally rational, since he had the option of exercising and taking pills, he didn't have to delay gratification? This is an empirical question, one whose answer is fixed by whatever psychological states are the causal antecedents of John's action. If John's action is caused by his possession and exercise of the capacity to be fully instrumentally rational, then he would have just exercised if the combination strategy hadn't been available. But if John's action is caused by his possession and exercise of a diminished capacity to be instrumentally rational, then he wouldn't have just exercised if the combination strategy hadn't been available.

Let's sum up the discussion thus far. We have seen that the standard belief-desire account of the explanation of action, at least in the form proposed by Davidson, is inadequate. We must suppose, with Hempel, that agents possess not only desires and beliefs, but also the capacity to be instrumentally rational to some extent. Moreover we must also suppose that their possession and exercise of this capacity plays its own distinctive explanatory role, complementary to the role played by their desires and beliefs, whenever agents act. We must also suppose that agents possess other rational capacities as well, capacities like the capacity to pick an alternative when antecedent desires and beliefs leave them otherwise indifferent.

I take this to be sufficient reason to move to a Hempelian, rather than a Davidsonian, conception of the standard account of action explanation. An agent's actions are explained by psychological states of three kinds, not just two: his desires, his beliefs, and the exercise of his rational capacities. But once we acknowledge that an agent's possession and exercise of rational capacities plays a distinctive role in the explanation of his actions, our eyes are opened to the possibility of much richer accounts of action explanation. These richer accounts in turn suggest a way in which we might begin to flesh out the conditions of responsibility.

4.3 The Nature of Responsibility

Consider once again the case in which John exercises and takes pills because, though he is less than fully instrumentally rational, he didn't have to delay gratification. It turns out that there are two possibilities here, depending on whether we suppose that John has a diminished capacity to be instrumentally rational which he fully exercises, or an undiminished capacity to be fully instrumentally rational that he fails to exercise on the occasion. There are therefore two corresponding further explanations of John's behaviour, depending on which of these possibilities is realized. In the first, John exercises and takes pills because he lacks the capacity to be fully instrumentally rational. In the second, he exercises and takes pills because, though he has that capacity, he fails to exercise it.

What's especially striking about these two further explanations is that they bear their relationship to ascriptions of responsibility more or less on their face. It follows from the very nature of responsibility that an agent who fails to act permissibly because he lacks the rational capacities required to act in that way is not responsible for failing to act permissibly. He is not responsible because his incapacity serves as an excuse. This is why children, those who are deranged, and those with volitional deficiencies like Obsessive Compulsive Disorder (OCD) are so often excused when they act wrongly. Children, the deranged, and those with OCD lack certain rational capacities, so when they act wrongly because they lack these capacities – and note that this needn't be true every time they act wrongly – they are thereby excused. Ascriptions of responsibility for wrongdoing are assignments of fault and these agents are not at fault.

By contrast, an agent who acts impermissibly because he fails to exercise rational capacities that he possesses is responsible for failing to act in that way. He is responsible precisely because he has no excuse. This is why someone who suffers from (say) weakness of will isn't treated like a child, someone who is deranged, or someone with OCD. Those who suffer from weakness of will have the capacity to will otherwise, but fail to exercise it. When they act impermissibly they are therefore liable to be held responsible because they are expected to exercise their capacity to will otherwise. The fact that they don't exercise their capacities is the problem, not an excuse. Fault is properly assigned to them.

Just to be clear, note I do not intend these claims to express a substantive moral view. They are meant to express conceptual claims, or, if you prefer, metaphysical claims, about what it is for an agent to be responsible. It is a priori that an agent is responsible for wrongdoing just in case he acts impermissibly without justification or excuse, and it is similarly a priori that when an agent's wrongdoing is explained by his lacking certain rational capacities, he has an excuse. This is why I said earlier that I took myself to be spelling out the nature of responsibility. These claims spell out *internal* correctness conditions of responsibility ascriptions, not substantive moral commitments.

There is, of course, a substantive moral view according to which we should treat agents in the way we typically treat responsible agents – we should, for example, punish them – only if they are responsible. In the theory of punishment, this is the view held by retributivists. Others disagree. They hold that we should sometimes treat agents in the way we typically treat responsible agents even when they aren't responsible. In the theory of punishment, this is the view held by utilitarians. They believe that the fact that it would maximize happiness to punish someone (say) is always a good reason to do so, whether he is responsible or not.

Moreover, again just to be clear, the claim that an agent is excused of a wrong that he has done isn't a substantive moral claim either. In particular, it is not, and does not imply, the claim that the agent in question should be left free to do whatever he pleases. To say that an agent is excused of wrongdoing is simply to say that the wrong he did was not his fault. But even when the wrong that someone does is not his fault, his acting wrongly in the circumstances in which he did might still provide others with grounds for coercing him. Those who hold different substantive moral views can and should agree with this.

For example, retributivists and utilitarians can and should agree that someone who does wrong, but who is excused of that wrongdoing because he is deranged, may not be someone who should be left free to do what he pleases. There may be a justification for using coercive means to restrain him if he won't listen to reason. The crucial point is simply that the justification for coercing him could not be that he did something that was his fault. The justification would have to be that (say) what he did, together with his being deranged, shows that he is a danger to himself and others (this is the sort of justification that might be given by those attracted to retributivism on Kantian grounds, though of course this is no part of retributivism itself), or that coercing him would maximize happiness (this is the sort of justification that might be given by a utilitarian).

If what has been said so far is along the right lines, then this suggests a way in which we might proceed in order to fully spell out the conditions of responsibility. We might proceed by coming up with an exhaustive list of the rational capacities whose possession and exercise would be necessary for agents to be responsible when they act impermissibly. We have already seen that at least two such capacities would be required: the capacity to pick an alternative when our non-instrumental desires and means-end beliefs underdetermine the choice between alternatives and the capacity to put our non-instrumental desires together with our means-end beliefs. Are there any others?

A capacity suggested by the foregoing discussion is the capacity to form beliefs in the light of the evidence available to us. Someone who harms another in the course of satisfying some instrumental desire he has is not excused of wrongdoing merely because he had no idea that harm would result. Ignorance is no excuse because we are expected to exercise such capacities as we have to access relevant evidence, and then to form our beliefs on the basis of that evidence. But an agent who was literally *incapable* of forming the belief that harm would result from something that he does would be excused. If he lacks the capacity to access the relevant evidence, or the capacity to form beliefs in the light of that evidence, then the harm that he causes is not his fault. If he has, but simply fails to exercise, these capacities, however, then the harm he causes is his fault.

What about an agent's non-instrumental desires? Are there capacities to form non-instrumental desires that agents must possess if they are to be responsible when they act impermissibly? This is an issue on which there are deep divisions within philosophical psychology. Some theorists line up behind Hume who thinks that the non-instrumental desires that move us to action are "original existences" (Hume 1740). They think that the answer therefore has to be "No". Others line up behind Kant who thinks that we have the capacity to allow only those non-instrumental desires that accord with universal laws of reasons to motivate us (Kant 1786). They think that the answer has to be "Yes". But without addressing the issue that divides these theorists head-on, note that there is at least one reason for supposing that the answer must be "Yes", a reason that can be appreciated by followers of both Hume and Kant alike.

According to the doctrine in meta-ethics known as *Judgement Internalism*, if an agent believes that he ought to φ, then is motivated to φ, at least insofar as he is rational (Smith 1994:63–84). Given that an agent's motivations are constituted by his non-instrumental desires and means-end beliefs, *Judgement Internalism* implies that if an agent believes that his φ-ing is a basic wrong – that is, if he believes that it is a wrong simply in virtue of its being a φ –ing – then, insofar as he is rational, he will have a non-instrumental aversion to φ-ing. The capacity to be rational thus mediates between an agent's beliefs about the things that would be basic wrongs to do and his non-instrumental aversions. For an agent to fail to have a non-instrumental aversion to doing what he believes it would be a basic wrong to do therefore implies irrationality on his behalf, where, as above, this irrationality might therefore be grounded in two quite different sorts of fact about him.

On the one hand, the agent's irrationality might be grounded in an incapacity to acquire non-instrumental aversions that accord with his beliefs about basic wrongs. In commonsense terms, this would be for him to do wrong because he has no capacity for self-control. He knows what he should do, but he can't get himself to want to do it. If this is the form that his irrationality takes, then, as before, if he acts wrongly, he has an excuse, for his inability to control himself constitutes his excuse. His acting wrongly is not his fault. Alternatively, though the agent possesses the capacity to control himself, his irrationality might be grounded in his failure to exercise this capacity. If this is the form that his irrationality takes, then, as before, he has no excuse, for his wrongdoing is his fault.

Moreover, note that there will evidently be complicated mixed cases. If an agent does something wrong because he is (say) crazed on drugs, but he didn't lack the capacity for self-control when he took the drugs, and he knew at that earlier time that taking drugs would cause him to become deranged and do something wrong, then though there is a sense in which he does wrong because he lacks the capacity for self-control – when he was crazed, he couldn't control himself – his doing wrong isn't grounded in his lack of self-control in the way it would have to be to constitute an excuse. This is because his doing wrong can be traced to his earlier failure to exercise the capacity that he possessed for self-control when he took the drugs. His wrongdoing may therefore still be his fault.

So far we have focused on rational capacities that mediate between an agents' beliefs about basic wrongs and their non-instrumental desires. But *Judgement Internalism* implies that additional *cognitive* capacities will also be required if agents are to be responsible for acting impermissibly. We have already seen that when it comes to belief formation, agents who have capacities to access relevant evidence, and then to form their beliefs on the basis of that evidence, are expected to do so. When it comes to exercises of self-control, what is especially important is therefore that agents exercise their capacity to access relevant evidence about which acts are wrong, and that they exercise their capacity to form beliefs on the basis of that evidence. The upshot is thus that even those who do have the capacity for self-control, and who exercise that capacity, may still not be responsible for wrongdoing if they are not responsible for the moral beliefs on which they act.

For example someone who doesn't know that what he is doing is wrong will be excused for his wrong-doing if his ignorance results from an inability to know that what he is doing is wrong: that is to say, he will be excused if he is ignorant because he lacks either the capacity to access the available evidence, or the capacity to form beliefs in the light of that evidence. However if he doesn't know that what he is doing is wrong because he has, but fails to exercise, his capacities to access available evidence, or to form beliefs in the light of that evidence, then he has no excuse. His wrongdoing is his fault because he could and should have exercised his capacity to know what's right and wrong.

Let's step back for a moment. What's remarkable about this account of the internal correctness conditions of ascriptions of responsibility isn't just that it can be derived entirely a priori by reflection on what the rational capacities are whose exercise might play a role when an agent acts, but also that it bears a striking similarity to conceptions of criminal responsibility that we find in the law. This shouldn't really be surprising, given that legal conceptions of criminal responsibility have a distinctively retributivist flavour. But the fact that it is so adds additional credence to the account of responsibility I have been sketching. Here are some examples, just to drive the point home.

The minimum age at which someone can be held criminally responsible in Australia is ten, as younger children are deemed to be incapable of knowing the difference between right and wrong (Australian Government 2005). Australian law also includes the doctrine of *Doli Incapax*. According to this doctrine, though children between the ages of ten and fourteen may possess the capacity to know the difference between right and wrong, they are presumed not to. The presumption therefore has to be proved mistaken before a criminal case can proceed. Both of these ideas fit very smoothly with the idea that agents who are incapable of knowing that what they are doing is wrong, children being a prime example, are excused when they act wrongly.

The law on insanity as a defence in criminal cases builds on a related idea. The law on insanity was developed in *Queen v M'Naghten* in 1843 when Daniel M'Naghten approached a man who he believed to be Sir Robert Peel, the then Prime Minister of England, and shot him in the back, so killing him. When M'Naghten was tried for the man's murder it emerged that he firmly believed that Peel was out to kill him. After testimony from medical experts, M'Naghten was found not guilty by reason of insanity. The decision caused such a controversy that the House of Lords asked the Lords of Justice to formulate a strict definition of when insanity could be used as a defence against criminal charges. According to the definition, now known as the "M'Naghten Rule", insanity is a defence only if:

1. At the time that the act was committed
2. the defendant was suffering from a defect of reason, from a disease of the mind, which caused
3. the defendant to not know
   a. the nature and quality of the act taken or
   b. that the act was wrong. (Hall 2008:226–27)

The M'Naghten Rule is widely accepted in jurisdictions influenced by English law. In crucial respects, the idea behind the M'Naghten Rule is much the same as before. An agent who has lived for long enough to develop the capacity to know what's right and wrong, but who suffers from some "disease of the mind" that destroys that capacity, is excused of wrongdoing if his wrongdoing is the result of his incapacity to know either what he is doing or that what he is doing is wrong.

Critics of the M'Naghten Rule insist that its exclusive focus on cognitive incapacities results in too narrow a conception of the insanity defence. In some jurisdictions, it is therefore supplemented with what is known as the "Irresistible Impulse Test". The Irresistible Impulse Test, developed in a decision by the Alabama Supreme Court in the USA in *Parsons v State* in 1887, holds that even if an accused party could tell right from wrong, he may still be excused by reason of insanity:

A. if mental disease caused the defendant to so far lose the power to choose between right and wrong and to avoid doing the alleged act that the disease destroyed the defendant's free will, and
B. if the mental disease was the sole cause of the act. (Lippman 2009:279)

The Irresistible Impulse Test thus also fits very smoothly with the account of the conditions of responsibility sketched in the previous section. What's relevant to the Irresistible Impulse Test is the capacity for self-control: that is, an agent's capacity to form non-instrumental aversions to doing those things he believes to be basic wrongs. If an agent lacks the capacity for self-control, and acts because he lacks that capacity, then he is excused because his act is not his fault.

Let's sum up. Not only are actions are always explained, inter alia, by agents' exercise of their capacity to be instrumentally rational, a capacity they might possess to a greater or a lesser extent, but many actions are also explained by agents' other rational capacities, sometimes by their exercise of these capacities, and sometimes by their failure to exercise them. These other rational capacities include the capacity to access available evidence; the capacity to form beliefs in the light of that evidence, both beliefs about means to ends and also beliefs about what's right and wrong; and the capacity to exercise self-control, that is, the capacity to form non-instrumental desires and aversions in the light of beliefs about which acts are right and wrong.

Cases in which actions are explained by agents' failure to exercise their rational capacities are in turn of two types. There are those in which their actions are explained by a failure to exercise rational capacities that they possess, and there are those in which their actions are explained by the fact that they do not possess those capacities in the first place. This is important when it comes to ascriptions of responsibility, because it is part of the internal correctness conditions of such ascriptions that when agents act wrongly because they lack some relevant rational capacity, they are excused, whereas when they act wrongly because they have, but fail to exercise, some relevant rational capacity, they are not excused. Distinctions widely made within the criminal law give some support to these ideas.

4.4 Implications

At the very beginning I said that we need to move beyond Davidson's version of the standard story of action explanation, and that, when we do, a distinctive story emerges about the conditions under which people are responsible for wrongdoing, a story with surprising implications about the justification of an agent's moral beliefs. Let me now spell out some of these implications.

In "Sanity and the Metaphysics of Responsibility", Susan Wolf describes an agent whose responsibility is seriously in doubt.

> JoJo is the favourite son of Jo the First, an evil and sadistic dictator of a small, undeveloped country. Because of his father's special feelings for the boy, JoJo is given a special education and is allowed to accompany his father and observe his daily routine. In light of this treatment, it is not surprising that JoJo takes his father as a role model and develops values very much like Dad's. As an adult, he does many of the same sorts of things his father did, including sending people to prison or to death or to torture chambers on the basis of whim. He is not coerced to do these things, he acts according to his own desires. Moreover these are desires he wholly wants to have. When he steps back and asks 'Do I really want to be this sort of person?' his answer is resoundingly 'Yes,' for this way of life expresses a crazy sort of power that forms part of his deepest ideal. . .In light of JoJo's heritage and upbringing — both of which he was powerless to control — it is dubious at best that he should be regarded as responsible for what he does. It is unclear whether anyone with a childhood such as his could have developed into anything but the twisted and perverse person that he has become. (Wolf 1987:53–54)

Wolf doesn't explicitly describe JoJo in the detailed terms that we have seen are crucial for understanding his responsibility. It is, however, easy to see how different ways of filling in the details of his story would affect his responsibility, and while certain of these ways of filling the story deliver unsurprising results, others deliver results that are much more surprising.

Here is one way in which JoJo's story might be filled in. JoJo's father, Jo the First, developed a talent for the manipulation of other people for his own purposes when he was a young boy. It was this talent for manipulation that enabled him to become ruler of the small, undeveloped country, in which he grew up. Once he became leader, Jo the First saw to it, sometimes by manipulation, but when manipulation failed, by whatever means were necessary, that all of those who lived in the country did exactly what he wanted. No one spoke ill of him, not even in private, for fear of dire consequences.

When JoJo was born, Jo the First fixated on him. He saw in JoJo someone who could see to it that no one would speak ill of him even after he died. He therefore gave JoJo a special education which consisted of humiliating him and then building him back up by making him believe that the only way he could have any worth at all was by getting his father's approval, something that he could do by emulating his father's behaviour, singing his praises, and generally seeing to it that others did nothing that his father wouldn't like. When people criticized his decision to homeschool his son, he had them silenced. JoJo too therefore developed a talent for the manipulation of other people for his own purposes – many of which were of course Jo the First's purposes – when he was a young boy.

After Jo the First died, JoJo took over as ruler of the country, doing many of the same sorts of things his father had done, including sending people to prison or to death or to torture chambers on the basis of whim. He did all of this willingly, constantly singing the praises of his father and seeing to it that no one ever said anything to challenge the official view of his father as a great man. Since he was following in his father's footsteps, this meant that he had to see to it that people treated him as a great man as well. When he had a son, he saw in him exactly what his father had seen in him, and decided to give him the same education that he had received. When people criticized his decision to homeschool his son, he had them silenced. Brutally.

If we fill in the details of JoJo's story in this way, then Wolf is surely right that his responsibility is seriously in doubt, as JoJo seems to have been brainwashed to do his father's bidding. His belief that his father is a great man, the belief which sustains his desire to emulate his father's actions, is kept in place not by his assessment of the evidence available to him for his father's greatness, but rather by his need for his father's approval. JoJo seems to lack the capacity to form beliefs about whether his father's, and hence his own, actions are right or wrong in the light of the evidence available to him. He therefore seems not to be responsible for reasons similar to the reasons why children and the insane are not responsible.

Wolf herself points out that JoJo is similar to those who fall under the M'Naghten Rule (Wolf 1987:55). Indeed, she suggests that we should suppose that JoJo is "insane" in an "admittedly specialized sense":

> [A]lthough like us, JoJo's actions flow from desires that flow from his deep self, unlike us, JoJo's deep self is itself insane. Sanity, remember, involves the ability to know the difference between right and wrong, and a person who, even on reflection, cannot see that having someone tortured because he failed to salute you is wrong plainly lacks the requisite ability. (Wolf 1987:56)

There are, of course, differences between JoJo and those who are criminally insane. To return to the M'Naghten Rule, JoJo's brainwashing doesn't seem to have caused a "disease of the mind", unless, of course, we are using the term "disease" in a highly metaphorical sense. (I note in passing that the M'Naghten Rule itself doesn't define what a disease of the mind is, and that in some jurisdictions it is interpreted very broadly.)

On the other hand, however, JoJo's brainwashing plainly has caused him to have a mental problem, a problem whose upshot is a lot like the upshot of M'Naghten's disease of the mind. M'Naghten's disease of the mind caused him to be insensitive to evidence as to whether or not Peel was out to kill him in his formation of his belief that this is what Peel was out to do. JoJo's belief that his father's actions are not wrong is insensitive to evidence as to whether or not his actions are right or wrong because his brainwashing has caused his desire for his father's approval to sustain his belief independently of evidence. Perhaps this similarity is all Wolf needs to be right that JoJo is insane "in a specialized sense". We will return to this point below.

It might be helpful if we think in terms of diagrammatic representations. The responsible agent's actions can be represented as in Fig. 4.1.

In Fig. 4.1, the "→"s represent either a relation that is knowledge conducive (1, 2), or the exercise of some relevant rational capacity (3, 4, 5, 6), or causation of a kind that sustains differential explanation (7, 8) (for more on this, see Smith 2004, 2009). In these terms, what's crucial about JoJo, at least when we fill in the details of his story as we did above, is that he lacks a crucial rational capacity that the responsible agent possesses and exercises: specifically, he lacks the capacity at junction 4. This suffices to excuse him from wrongdoing when his wrongdoing is explained by his lack of this capacity. He is excused, in such cases, because his wrongdoing is not his fault.

There is, however, the following rather different way in which the details of JoJo's story might be filled in. As he grew up, JoJo was given a special education, both formal and informal, by his father, Jo the First. Jo the First was brutal, but also articulate and larger than life, much like one of the main characters in a Quentin

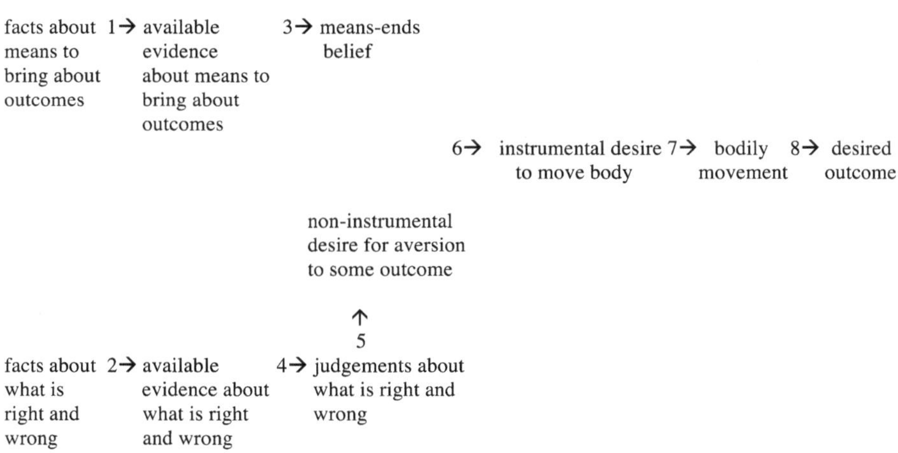

Fig. 4.1 The responsible agent

Tarantino movie. As a result, JoJo came to have the rather idiosyncratic belief that someone who has the sort of power his father has, exercised in the stylish way in which he exercised it, thereby has the right to do whatever he has to do in order to maintain that power, no matter what the consequences are for those he doesn't really care about. JoJo read widely, something his father encouraged, so he realised that his view about his father's entitlements was idiosyncratic. Though this was initially a cause of some cognitive dissonance, one day JoJo came across some books by a German philosopher that contained an elaborate statement and defence of ideas that imply that something like what he had come to believe about his father was in fact true. After reading the German philosopher's work for himself, he concluded that, idiosyncratic though his ideas were, there was also something deeply intuitive about them.

JoJo's interest in philosophy led him to apply to graduate school at an Ivy League university in the USA where the world's leading expert on the German philosopher taught. JoJo's admission file was so strong that he was given a special scholarship. He eventually wrote a dissertation defending his own unusual moral views, drawing on their similarities to those of the German philosopher's, via a wide reflective equilibrium argument, a dissertation that eventually became a celebrated monograph. JoJo's monograph was much discussed by academic philosophers, and also much discussed in the pages of the New York Review of Books and on NPR.

While many reviewers thought that the arguments JoJo gave were spot on, others thought that the position itself, though internally consistent, and though consistent with everything else JoJo believed, depended on basic premises that were themselves manifestly implausible. JoJo's conclusions could be true only if some of the things that they themselves believed were true were false, but they did not think that anything JoJo said had provided them with sufficient reason to reject the truth of what they believed. Some of these reviewers, ignorant of JoJo's history, went so far as to say that it just as well that JoJo was a harmless academic, as by this time he had secured a professorship of his own at a prestigious left-wing university in northern California.

JoJo saw nothing unusual in the fact that his colleagues had such starkly different opinions about his work. He had come to the view years earlier that there are no philosophical theories on any subject matter that command universal assent. As he saw things, all philosophical theories are defended via wide reflective equilibrium arguments of the kind he had given, and this meant that the very deepest philosophical disagreements amounted to disagreements about fundamental premises: that is, they were disagreements about which beliefs are, and which are not, supposed to survive such an argument. He went on to become something of an academic celebrity, universally admired for his charm and wit and intelligence and loyalty to his graduate students and close colleagues, but also feared by those who experienced how ruthlessly dismissive he could be of those with whom he saw no profit to engage.

After Jo the First died, JoJo seized the opportunity to put his ideas into practice on a much larger scale. He returned home to take over as ruler of his country. He did many of the same sorts of things his father had done, including sending people to prison or to death or to torture chambers on the basis of whim. He did all of this willingly, constantly singing the praises of his father and seeing to it that no one ever got away with challenging the official view of his father as a great man. When people criticized his father, or him, he would send them a copy of his monograph and a long list of references to papers in academic journals in which philosophers wrote at length defending the essentials of his views. When he eventually had a son, and people criticized his decision to homeschool him, he would remind them of that one of their heroes, John Stuart Mill, was himself homeschooled by his father. If they persisted with their criticisms, and became disruptive or unpleasant, he had them silenced. Brutally, but stylishly.

If we tell JoJo's story in this way, is it plausible to suppose that he is not responsible for his wrongdoing? By contrast with the earlier telling of his story, it doesn't seem that JoJo's beliefs are the product of brainwashing or wish fulfilment. They are rather the product of deep thought and rational assessment. Indeed, when we tell the story in this way, JoJo *seems* to be at least as rational as anyone we are likely to meet, more rational than most. Moreover he seems to be exceptionally diligent in his exercise of his rational capacities. Given his education and his dedication to the academic enterprise, we might even be tempted to suppose that JoJo's moral beliefs, though false, are as justified as anyone's could be. JoJo thus doesn't seem to lack any rational capacities. But if he lacks no rational capacities, then how could he not be responsible?

What this way of telling JoJo's story teaches us, I think, is that we need to get much clearer about what's happening at both junctions 2 and 4 in Fig. 4.1. In order to do this, it will be helpful if we first of all think about junctions 1 and 3. Imagine someone who lacks peripheral vision, and to whom it therefore seems that there are no objects in his immediate environment when in fact there are. He therefore regularly acquires beliefs about things he can do that are false: for example, he regularly acquires the belief that it is safe to cross the road, when in fact crossing the road would cause him to be hit by a car. Is such a person responsible for his false beliefs? This question would not be easy to answer in practice, but we know how to answer it in theory.

Assuming that the person we are imagining didn't cause his own lack of peripheral vision, he certainly isn't responsible for its seeming to him that there are no dangerous objects in his environment when there are, because he can't help how things seem to him. That is just a given, a function of his perceptual system. Of course, since experience has presumably taught him that he shouldn't trust how things look to him in forming his beliefs about how things are, he may well be responsible for not pausing to ask whether things really are, in every detail, the way they look to him to be. But it is an empirical question whether human beings really do have the capacity to resist the natural inclination to form perceptual beliefs on the basis of perceptual appearances during the hustle and bustle of daily life. Perhaps the connection between perceptual appearances and perceptual beliefs at such times is so immediate that that kind of second-guessing simply isn't realistic. Either human beings don't have such a capacity, or, if they do, it is a capacity that it would be very difficult for them to exercise.

If this is right, then the person we are imagining may not be responsible for his false beliefs at all, or his responsibility might be seriously mitigated. He is not responsible if he is incapable of having the world seem to him to be the way it really is and he non-culpably finds himself unable to resist the natural tendency to believe that things are how they seem to him to be on the basis of the indirect evidence available to him. His responsibility is mitigated if, though he has the latter capacity, it would be very difficult for him to exercise it during (say) the hustle and bustle of daily life. We might put the same points more explicitly in terms of the language of Fig. 4.1 as follows. Focus on the case in which he isn't responsible at all. The person who lacks peripheral vision has two problems. First, perceptual evidence about how things are in certain regions of his immediate environment isn't available to him because things don't seem to him to be the way that they are. And second, indirect evidence about how things are in those regions – for example, indirect evidence that, for all he knows, there is something in those regions of his immediate environment – though available to him, isn't evidence to which he has the capacity to be sensitive during the hustle and bustle of daily life. He therefore isn't responsible for (say) his false belief that it is safe to cross the road because his false belief isn't his fault.

Let's now consider what to say about JoJo in the light of this. Focus on junctions 2 and 4. JoJo acquired the false belief that Jo the First was within his rights to do the brutal things he did in the way in which children usually acquire their moral beliefs, that is, by an informal process of socialization. When he became an adult, however, he questioned whether his beliefs were true, and he concluded that they were. He reached this conclusion in two ways. It both seemed to him that they were true – that is, what he believed was, he thought, deeply intuitive – and, furthermore, after thinking long and hard about questions in moral philosophy, he came up with a reflective equilibrium argument for a theory that entailed the truth of the things that he believed. So is JoJo responsible for his false belief? The answer to this question bears certain similarities to the answer we just gave about the person who lacks peripheral vision.

JoJo also has two sorts of problems. First, direct evidence of his father's wrongdoing isn't available to him, because the things that seem permissible to him aren't permissible. His father seems to JoJo to have the right to brutalize people, when in fact he has no such right. This is strictly analogous to what we said about the person who lacks peripheral vision. Second – and this is a difference between JoJo's case and that of the person who lacks peripheral vision – indirect evidence of his father's wrongdoing isn't available to him either. For in order to access indirect evidence of the wrongness of his father's actions, JoJo would have to be able to construct a theory that entailed that his father's acts were wrong via an attempt to get his beliefs into a wide reflective equilibrium. But he can't. When he succeeds in his attempt to get his beliefs into a wide reflective equilibrium, the theory that he comes up with entails that his father's acts are not wrong.

We can put the same point more simply as follows. For JoJo to be able to access evidence of his father's wrongdoing, there would have to be something that he believes, or something that he feels, or some way that things seem to him to be, that doesn't square with his father's having a right to brutalize people. Absent some such psychological hook, JoJo will be unable to reason himself to the conclusion that his belief that his father has a right to brutalize people is false because there will be nothing for him to reason from. But there are no such psychological hooks in JoJo. His beliefs, his feelings, the ways things seem to him to be, all of these things square with his belief that his father has a right to brutalize people. The upshot is that JoJo isn't responsible for his false belief that his father has a right to brutalize people. He isn't responsible because he cannot access evidence to the contrary. His false belief isn't his fault.

I said at the beginning that the distinctive story we've told about the conditions under which people are responsible for wrongdoing has surprising implications for the justification of an agent's moral beliefs. These implications are implicit in the conclusions we have just drawn from the second way of filling in the details of JoJo's story. As we have seen, even though JoJo succeeds in getting his beliefs into a wide reflective equilibrium, his moral beliefs are false. Should we suppose that his moral beliefs are justified? There are two ways we could go in answering this question. On the one had, we might suppose that the description of the wide reflective equilibrium procedure itself just is an account of the conditions under which an agent's moral beliefs are justified, so that the answer has to be that JoJo's moral beliefs are justified. On the other, we might wonder whether basic moral beliefs that an agent holds only because he is irrational could ever be justified. Since this seems to be so in JoJo's case, we might conclude that the answer has to be that his basic moral beliefs are not justified. I won't decide between these two ways in which we might answer the question in what follows. I will simply spell out the second way of answering the question in a little more detail.

Think again about the difference between the person who lacks peripheral vision and JoJo. In both cases, the world seems to them to be a certain way when it isn't that way. But in the case of the person who lacks peripheral vision, this fact about him doesn't suggest irrationality of any kind. The defect lies in his perceptual system, not in the capacities he possesses insofar as he is a reasoner. In JoJo's case, by contrast, the fact that the world seem to him to be a certain way when it isn't that way does suggest irrationality of some kind. It suggests irrationality because it entails a limitation on his abilities as a reasoner. There is, of course, an assumption that I'm making here, namely, that knowledge of basic moral truths is a priori accessible. But if this assumption is correct, as I think it is (Smith 1994, Chapters 5 and 6), then given that the fact that the world seems to JoJo to be a certain way in basic moral respects when it isn't that way is what explains his inability to know basic moral truths, it follows that that fact is also what explains why he isn't an ideal reasoner. An ideal reasoner is, after all, someone with the ability to know a priori truths.

If this way of thinking about the justification of JoJo's beliefs is correct, then it follows that we need to radically rethink the epistemic significance of the reflective equilibrium procedure (compare Scanlon 2002). Though JoJo succeeds in getting his beliefs into a wide reflective equilibrium, given that he achieves that wide reflective equilibrium only because he isn't an ideal reasoner, we should conclude that the beliefs he comes up with are not justified. To be justified, an agent's moral beliefs mustn't just be such that they would survive his attempts to get his beliefs into a wide reflective equilibrium. That wide reflective equilibrium itself mustn't be sustained by the agent's inability to know certain a priori truths. We are therefore led to the conclusion, which may well come as a surprise to some, that whether or not we think that an agent's moral beliefs are justified will depend crucially on what we take the moral truth to be, as this will in turn affect which reasoning capacities we take the justification of an agent's moral beliefs to depend upon.[1]

References

Australian Government. 2005. "The Age of Criminal Responsibility, Australian Institute of Criminology." Accessed 21 January 2011. http://www.aic.gov.au/publications/current%20series/cfi/101-120/cfi106.aspx.

Christenfeld, N. 1995. "Choices from Identical Options." *Psychological Science* 6:50–55.

Davidson, Donald. 1963. "Actions, Reasons and Causes." Reprinted in *Essays on Actions and Events*, edited by Donal Davidson, 3–20.Oxford: Oxford University Press, 1980.

Davidson, Donald. 1970. "How Is Weakness of the Will Possible?" Reprinted in *Essays on Actions and Events*, edited by Donal Davidson, 21–42. Oxford: Oxford University Press, 1980.

Hall, Daniel. 2008. *Criminal Law and Procedure*. New York, NY: Cengage.

Hempel, Carl G. 1961. "Rational Action." Reprinted in *Readings in the Theory of Action*, edited by Norman S. Care and Charles Landesman, 285–86. Bloomington, IN: Indiana University Press, 1968.

Hume, David. 1740. *A Treatise of Human Nature*. Oxford: Clarendon Press, 1968.

Kant, Immanuel. 1786. *Groundwork of the Metaphysics of Morals*. London: Hutchinson and Company, 1948.

Lippman, Matthew. 2009. *Contemporary Criminal Law: Concepts, Cases, and Controversies*. Thousand Oaks, CA: Sage Publications.

Raz, Joseph. 1999. "Explaining Normativity: Reason and the Will." In *Engaging Reason: On the Theory of Value and Action*, 90–117. Oxford: Oxford University Press.

Scanlon, Thomas M. 2002. "Rawls on Justification." In *The Cambridge Companion to Rawls*, edited by Samuel Freeman, 139–67. New York, NY: Cambridge University Press.

Smith, Michael. 1994. *The Moral Problem*. Oxford: Wiley-Blackwell.

Smith, Michael. 2003. "Rational Capacities." In *Weakness of Will and Varieties of Practical Irrationality*, edited by Sarah Stroud and Christine Tappolet, 17–38. Oxford: Oxford University Press.

Smith, Michael. 2004. "The Structure of Orthonomy." In *Action and Agency*, edited by John Hyman and Helen Steward, 165–93. Cambridge: Cambridge University Press.

Smith, Michael. 2009. "The Explanatory Role of Being Rational." In *Reasons for Action*, edited by David Sobel and Steven Wall, 58–80. New York, NY: Cambridge University Press.

Wolf, Susan. 1987. "Sanity and the Metaphysics of Responsibility." In *Responsibility, Character, and the Emotions: New Essays in Moral Psychology*, edited by Ferdinand Schoeman, 46–62. New York, NY: Cambridge University Press.

[1] Earlier versions of this paper were presented *at Moral Responsibility: Neuroscience, Organization, and Engineering*, a conference held at Technical University Delft in August 2009; at *Workshop on Reasons and Rational Choice* held at the London School of Economics in January 2011; and at the Philosophy Departments at Lingnan University and Monash University in March 2011. Thanks are due to the many people who gave me comments on these occasions. Special thanks are owed to Jay Wallace for the conversations we had while I was writing up the penultimate version and to Nicole Vincent for her written comments. Work on this paper was completed while I visiting the Humboldt University in Berlin, enjoying the benefits of a Forschungspreis from the Alexander von Humboldt Foundation.

Chapter 5
Blame, Reasons and Capacities

Rosemary Lowry

Abstract It is usually agreed that we must recognise that responsibility (in the sense of blameworthiness) comes in degrees if we are to accurately reflect the moral landscape of people's actions. In this paper I develop this view by constructing a framework which will allow us to determine the degree to which an agent is blameworthy for failing to act. This framework accommodates the close connection between an agent's blameworthiness and her reasons, which I argue should lead us to see reasons as coming in degrees. The view that reasons come in degrees is justified on the basis of two claims: first, reasons are constrained by what it is possible for the agent to do, and second, it may be possible *to some degree* for an agent to do something. I conclude the paper by demonstrating how this framework can be used to justify claims about the degree to which an agent has a reason, and the degree to which an agent can be blameworthy in a given case.

5.1 Introduction

While our legal system often requires us to find someone to be guilty or not guilty, it is usually recognised that in reality varying degrees of punishment and censure are appropriate.[1] In order to accommodate varying degrees of punishment and censure, we need an account of responsibility that comes in degrees. The term "responsibility" can be attached to different meanings. In this paper I will be concerned with the sense of responsibility that is associated with the notion of blame. I will be particularly concerned with the occasions when an agent is responsible for failing to act, in the sense of the agent being blameworthy for this failure.

Recognising that responsibility (in the sense of blameworthiness) comes in degrees is important if we are to accurately reflect the moral landscape of people's actions. This recognition helps us to avoid "a social and political picture which simplistically divides people into sheep and shepherds: those who just can't attain responsibility and those who have it absolutely." (Skorupski 2007:101). We must avoid such a picture, because in reality, responsibility is not an "all-or-nothing" concept; in Skorupski's words, "it is not a package deal".

---

[1] Honoré (1998) discusses this issue.

R. Lowry (✉)
Department of Philosophy, Eindhoven University of Technology, Eindhoven, The Netherlands
e-mail: r.j.lowry@tue.nl

N.A Vincent et al. (eds.), *Moral Responsibility*, Library of Ethics and Applied Philosophy 27, DOI 10.1007/978-94-007-1878-4_5,

My specific concern in this paper is to develop a framework which will allow us to determine the degree to which an agent is responsible for failing to act (in the sense of being blameworthy for this failure). If a framework for determining blameworthiness is to be adequate however, it must also accommodate the close connection between an agent's blameworthiness and her reasons. Heuer formulates this connection. In her words, "it is a necessary condition of justified blame that we can blame a person only for (not) doing something that she has a reason to do (or not to do)." (Heuer 2010:237) Following Heuer, I will call this the "reason condition of blame".[2]

The reason condition of blame implies that in order for an agent to be blameworthy for failing to perform some act (ϕ) in a given circumstance, it must be true that the agent has a reason to ϕ in this circumstance. Consequently, if we are to maintain the view that blameworthiness comes in degrees and also accommodate the reason condition of blame, it seems that our account should also allow reasons to come in degrees. That is, if an agent can only be blameworthy to some degree in a given case, then given the reason condition of blame, it is natural that this degree of blameworthiness should be explained by reference to the degree to which the agent has a reason in that case. (Note that I am not referring here to the commonly accepted idea that the *strength* of reasons may vary. Rather, I am suggesting that we reject the view that reasons are an "all or nothing" concept. Consequently, an agent may, for example, have a strong reason to ϕ, but only have this reason to a small degree.) The framework for determining blameworthiness should thus accommodate agents being blameworthy to *some degree*, and also having a reason *to some degree.*

What would justify the claim that reasons come in degrees? There might be different explanations (or arguments) that can be offered for this claim.[3] In this paper I will explore what I consider to be a promising explanation.[4] This explanation is based on two claims: first, reasons are constrained by what it is possible for the agent to do, and second, it may be possible *to some degree* for an agent to do something. The first claim is related to the well-known "ought implies can" principle, though this principle is usually taken to be solely concerned with an agent's capacities.

---

[2] The connection between reasons and blame can be explained by a more fundamental connection: If X has most reason to ϕ, then we tend to think (at least when X has the opportunity and access to information etc.) that X *ought to* ϕ (where "ought" is understood as an all-things-considered notion and a "reason" is understood as a pro tanto term). This connection between what we have reason to do and what we ought to do, offers a connection between reasons and blame. As Williams points out, blame operates in the mode of "ought to have" (1989:40). So if we can say, given certain external conditions such as opportunity and access to information, *X ought to* ϕ, we can also say, given these same conditions, *X will be blameworthy for failing to* ϕ.

[3] While they do not discuss the idea of reasons coming in degrees, Espinoza and Peterson (2011) offer some arguments for why we should think that moral duties and obligations come in degrees. These arguments might also support the idea that reasons come in degrees.

[4] I believe it is promising because of its explanatory power, its preservation of our moral conceptual world and its coherence with the plausible view that blameworthiness is closely related to our capacities. I will return to these virtues in Section 5.4.

There are however two senses in which A's possibilities constrain A's reasons. The first is related to A's capacities, the second is related to A's opportunities. Thus when assessing whether A has a reason to ϕ, we must investigate both her capacities and her opportunities. I will refer to the claim that in order for an agent to have a reason to ϕ, an agent must have certain capacities and opportunities, as the "CO condition on reasons". I will discuss this condition in detail in the next section.

Once we have accepted the CO condition on reasons, the claim that an agent may have a capacity or opportunity to some degree completes the explanation for why reasons come in degrees. That is, if an agent has the capacities or opportunities relevant to the CO condition *to some degree*, we should conclude that she may only have the associated reason to that degree. The claim that capacities come in degrees can be supported by Smith's account of rational capacities. According to Smith, the degree to which an agent has a (rational) capacity is determined by the degree of similarity between the actual world and certain possible worlds in which an agent systematically exercises this capacity. His view therefore provides a framework for understanding those cases where agents appear to have partial capacities. While Smith doesn't accept the CO condition on reasons[5] (and thus the view that reasons come in degrees), I extend his picture in order to produce a framework which allows us to assess whether, and to what degree, an agent has the capacities required for the satisfaction of the CO condition.

I also demonstrate how this same framework can be used to assess the extent of opportunity an agent has. As I shall explain, the distance between the actual world and certain worlds in which an agent systematically ϕ's, also informs us about the extent to which an agent has the opportunities required for the satisfaction of the CO condition. In this way, I provide a framework for understanding reasons as phenomena that come in degrees (and a related procedure for measuring this degree). Moreover, given the reason condition of blame, this framework also provides us with a non-arbitrary way of determining the degree to which an agent can be blameworthy in a given case.

This paper is devoted to developing the framework described above. To do this I begin by arguing for the CO condition on reasons. In Section 5.3 I outline Smith's discussion of rational capacities, and extend this discussion to account for the capacities and opportunities required for the satisfaction of the CO condition. In Section 5.4 I demonstrate how this framework can be used to justify claims about the degree to which an agent has a reason, and the degree to which an agent can be responsible (in the blameworthiness sense) in a given case.

---

5 Smith at least denies the formulation of the CO condition that I will specify in this paper. He and Pettit claim that we should understand reasons in terms of what an idealised version of oneself (Å) would desire the unidealised self (A) to do. Though they claim that we should think of Å as an *advisor* rather than an *exemplar*, their view does not imply that reasons are sensitive to individual capacities. Rather, they claim that "it certainly seems possible that Å could desire that A ϕ in C and yet, due to A's own incapacities – remember, we are not supposing that A herself has and exercises all of the capacities that ensure that her desires conform to the principles of reason, only that Å has and exercises these capacities – A might actually be . . . incapable of coming to believe that this is so" (2006:150).

5.2 The CO Condition

Roughly speaking, the CO condition on reasons implies that in order for an agent to have a reason to perform some act (ϕ), it must be possible for the agent to ϕ. I claimed above that there are two relevant senses in which it must be possible for an agent to ϕ, if she is to have a reason to ϕ: the first relates to her capacities, and the second relates to her opportunities. It is a common claim that reasons are constrained by one's capacities. Streumer (2007), for example, asks us to consider Fred, who is completely and irreversibly paralysed. Fred hears someone screaming for help outside his house. As Streumer concludes, the idea that Fred has a reason to go outside and help this person is implausible because Fred *cannot* help the person.

The CO condition must be concerned with more than mere physical capacities if it is to be plausible however. If it merely implied that an agent must be physically capable of ϕ-ing in order to have a reason to ϕ, a bird physically capable of tapping on the window with its beak in order to warn me of danger, may have a reason to do so. A theory ascribing such reasons would be implausible however. In order for the CO condition to be plausible it should claim that in order for an agent to have a reason to ϕ, it must be possible that the agent ϕ *from the motive of her reason*. Specifying the CO condition in this way avoids the implausible implication that agents who can physically ϕ but cannot grasp the considerations that count in favour of ϕ-ing, have reasons to ϕ nonetheless. Interpreting the condition in this way also ensures that reasons are able to influence and guide those for whom they are reasons, and thus serve a *practical* purpose. And a practical purpose seems to be the appropriate purpose for a theory of reasons to serve.[6]

In addition to being capable of ϕ-ing from the motive of one's reason, one will need to have the opportunity to utilise this capacity, if the CO condition is to be satisfied. This is because if I have the capacity to apply first aid, but find myself stuck in a traffic jam, it is not in any real sense possible for me to apply first aid to the child who has fallen off his bike ten blocks away.[7] It is not possible because I have no opportunity to utilise my capacity to apply first aid. Consequently, the CO condition implies that I do not have a reason to apply first aid to this child. I must have the opportunity and capacity to ϕ from the motive of my putative reason[8] if it is to be genuinely possible that I ϕ from the motive of my reason and the CO condition is to be satisfied.[9]

One further point here is that if someone cannot currently ϕ, but has the opportunity and capacity to get themselves into a state where they can (and have the

[6] For the view that our moral concepts ought to serve a practical purpose, see Dennett (1984:155); Skorupski (2007:89–90).

[7] I am assuming here that by the time I could get there, the child would no longer need first aid.

[8] I say "putative reason" because if an agent lacks the relevant capacities or opportunities, she will, ipso facto, not have this "reason".

[9] Specifying that an agent must have these opportunities also helps to ensure that a theory of reasons serves a practical purpose (because an agent will only have reasons on which her opportunities allow her to act).

opportunity to) ϕ, then it seems that there *is* a real sense in which it is possible for them to ϕ. For instance, suppose a mother is currently incapacitated by depression, and so cannot presently care for her child. Suppose also however, that she is capable of taking medication (and that she has access to this medication, i.e. she has the opportunity to take it) and that this medication will remove her depression and reinstate her capacity to care for her child. It seems that in such a case, despite the woman's present incapacity, it is still possible for her to care for her child because if she would only take the medication (that she has, and is capable of taking) then she would be capable of caring for her child. We should thus interpret the CO condition in a way which allows agents who are currently incapable of ϕ-ing – but who have the opportunity and capacity to get into a state where they have the opportunity and capacity to ϕ – to have reasons to ϕ.

Given these clarifications, we are now in a position to formulate the CO condition with more precision. It is the claim that: if A is to have a reason to ϕ, then A must have the opportunity and capacity to ϕ from the motive of her putative reason, or she must have the opportunity and capacity to get herself into a state where she has the opportunity and capacity to ϕ from the motive of her putative reason.

An important aspect of the CO condition is that it can be satisfied to some degree, which will result in the agent having a reason to that degree. For an example where an agent's limited opportunity results in her having a reason to some degree, consider again the mother who is capable of taking medication which will remove her depression and reinstate her capacity to care for her child. If there is limited opportunity for the mother to get hold of the required medication, she will have a reason to care for her child to a smaller degree than if she could easily access the medication. For an example where an agent's limited capacity results in her having a reason to some degree, consider an acrophobe whose fear of heights cripples her in such a way that it is very difficult for her to think clearly or respond to important considerations when exposed to great heights. Suppose also that she is locked in a room on the tenth story of a building with her co-worker, who is contemplating suicide on the room's balcony. As the agent's acrophobia diminishes the degree to which she has the capacity to venture onto the balcony and dissuade her co-worker from jumping, she will only have a reason to help save her co-worker to *some degree*. Moreover, due to the reason condition of blame, blaming the agent for failing to act on this reason can be appropriate just to the degree that the agent has this reason. In the next section I will construct a framework for determining this degree. In Section 5.4 I will return to this last example in order to demonstrate how the framework I have constructed yields information about particular cases.

5.3 Capacities and Possible Worlds

Smith (2004) notes that a rational capacity manifests itself in a whole raft of possibilities, rather than single possibilities. This is because a capacity consists in intrinsic qualities which will cause the agent to exercise this capacity in a whole raft of circumstances very similar to the agent's actual circumstances. Consequently, when determining whether an agent has a rational capacity to, for example, answer a certain scientific question in circumstances C, we must investigate whether she answers in a raft of circumstances very similar to C. However, the similar circumstances or possible worlds which we need to investigate are ones which share a similarity of a certain kind. In Smith's terminology, we need to "zero in" on what makes it true that an agent has the capacity to answer the scientific question. Consequently, the possible worlds we need to investigate are those where we hold constant the qualities that are both intrinsic to the agent and relevant to her answering the scientific question. For the sake of the example, let's suppose that these intrinsic qualities consist in a person's possession of a particular scientific knowledge base. If the agent answers in a raft of those possible worlds where we hold constant her knowledge base, this will establish that the agent has the *particular* scientific knowledge base which constitutes the capacity to answer the question.

Note that on the notion of capacity presented here, an agent may answer the question in the actual world, through luck, say, despite the absence of her capacity to do so. For instance, suppose I have no idea of the answer to the scientific question, but the answer somehow pops into my head shortly after I am asked. As my answering was a matter of luck, I do not have the particular scientific knowledge base which will cause me to systematically answer in those possible worlds where we hold constant my knowledge base. The fact that I do not systematically answer in these worlds is evidence that I lack the particular scientific knowledge base which constitutes the capacity to answer the question, regardless of whether I answer in the actual world. (While it may sound odd in ordinary English to claim that an agent who answered correctly lacked the capacity to answer correctly, I am using "capacity" in the technical sense outlined above, where the notion of a capacity is attached to a whole raft of possibilities, rather than single possibilities.)

We can extend Smith's method for determining whether an agent has certain rational capacities to those capacities required for the satisfaction of the CO condition on reasons. I argued above that in order for the CO condition to be satisfied, the agent must have both the opportunity and the capacity (i) to ϕ from the motive of her putative reason, or alternatively (ii) to get herself into a state where she has the opportunity and capacity to ϕ from the motive of her putative reason. The following three steps provide a procedure for determining whether an agent has the capacity specified by (i), i.e. the capacity to ϕ from the motive of her putative reason. For the remainder of this section I will refer to this capacity merely as "the capacity to ϕ", but note that this should be understood as: "the capacity to ϕ from the motive of her putative reason".

1. First identify which particular intrinsic qualities constitute the capacity to ϕ. This will be determined by examining the features of people who reliably ϕ.[10]

[10] The features I suggest here should by no means be taken as a definitive list. The features that appear intuitively to constitute a capacity may not be the features which do in fact constitute this capacity. In order to reach a more definitive conclusion, empirical research about the causal factors involved in motivated action would need to be consulted.

Intuitively, it appears that the possession of particular information and particular states of physical, motivational and rational functioning are causal factors involved in an agent's ϕ-ing.[11]

2. Then, hold constant those qualities that are intrinsic to the agent and relevant to the agent's capacity to ϕ. If the suggestion in the previous step is plausible, then we should hold constant the agent's possession of information and her states of physical, motivational and rational functioning. While holding constant the agent's possession of information and her states of physical, motivational and rational functioning, examine close possible worlds.
3. If an agent ϕ-s in a whole raft of these possible worlds, then this will demonstrate that she has the *particular* intrinsic qualities which constitute the capacity to ϕ (i.e. the particular information and particular states of physical, motivational and rational functioning).

These three steps spell out how we can determine whether an agent has the capacities required for the first way in which the CO condition can be satisfied. Note also that this framework allows for an agent to have a capacity to some degree. Step 2 specifies the possible worlds we must examine when determining whether an agent has a capacity to ϕ. While the qualities that are both intrinsic to the agent and relevant to her ϕ-ing are held constant in these possible worlds, other intrinsic features of the agent may be altered. If the agent only systematically ϕ's (and thus demonstrates

[11] We can demonstrate the plausibility of this claim by considering an agent who has a reason to save a drowning child (because this will save the child's life). In order for the agent to ϕ from the motive of her reason in such a case, the agent must possess certain information. More particularly, the agent must know about her reason. The agent could not rescue a child from the motive of her reason without the belief that the child is drowning (note here that such knowledge need not be knowledge that the agent could articulate. Instinctive knowledge about one's reasons may be sufficient for an agent to ϕ from the motive of her reason). Secondly, in order for an agent to ϕ from the motive of her reason, the agent must possess a certain state of physical functioning. More particularly, the agent must be physically able to ϕ. One cannot rescue a drowning child from the motive of her reason without the physical ability to swim or carry the child. Thirdly, in order for an agent to ϕ from the motive of her reason, the agent must have a certain state of motivational functioning. That is, the agent must be able to be motivated by this reason. One cannot rescue a child from the motive of one's reason, if the recognition of this reason cannot motivate the agent. Lastly, in order for the agent to ϕ from the motive of her reason, the agent must have a certain state of rational functioning. More particularly, the agent must recognise the relevant consideration *as* a reason. We should note here that there is a sense in which the agent could rescue the child *because* "the child is drowning", without the agent recognising that "the child is drowning" is, or provides, a reason to rescue the child. This may occur if the consideration "the child is drowning" connects with an agent's motivations through different means, e.g. through conditioning, or because it satisfies another of the agent's desires, such as a desire for praise. In such cases, the rescue mission may be caused by the agent's recognition of the consideration "the child is drowning". Such cases do not however constitute acting from the motive of one's *reason* (they at least do not constitute acting from the motive of the reason "the child is drowning"). To act from the motive of one's reason, the agent must be motivated by the consideration because of its believed status as a reason. Consequently, one cannot rescue a child from the motive of her reason without recognising that "the child is drowning" is, or provides, a reason to rescue the child.

her capacity to ϕ) in possible worlds where her other intrinsic features have been substantially altered, then she may only have the capacity to ϕ to a small degree. This is because the more the actual world has to be altered – in this first way – in order for the agent to systematically ϕ, the less the agent has a capacity to ϕ.

There is also a second way in which the actual world may have to be altered if the agent is to systematically ϕ. The more that *non-intrinsic* features of an agent must be altered in order for her to systematically ϕ, such as perhaps the experiences she has or the people she meets, the more distant the worlds where the agent systematically ϕ's become to the actual world. If these worlds are very distant in this second way to the actual world, then the agent will have only a small degree of *opportunity* to ϕ. The second way in which the actual world may need to be altered in order for the agent to systematically ϕ thus concerns the degree of opportunity that an agent has to ϕ. In summary, the degree to which we have to alter the actual world in order for the agent to systematically ϕ (while holding constant qualities that are both intrinsic to the agent and relevant to her ϕ–ing), reflects both the degree of capacity and the degree of opportunity an agent has to ϕ.

The degree of similarity shared by the closest worlds in which the agent systematically ϕ-s (i.e. closest to the actual world) and the actual world, will determine the degree to which the CO condition is satisfied, and thus the degree to which the agent has the associated reason. As discussed above, if these worlds are very dissimilar or distant to the actual world, the degree to which the agent has the capacity and/or opportunity to ϕ may be small. Moreover, this implies that the degree to which the CO condition is satisfied, and the degree to which the agent has a reason to ϕ, may also be small.

As was also stated above, there is a second way in which the CO condition can be satisfied: when an agent has the capacity and opportunity *to get herself into a state* where she has the opportunity and capacity to ϕ from the motive of her putative reason.[12] As I have already spelled out the three-step method for determining whether an agent has such a capacity and opportunity, I will not repeat these steps here. Instead I will return now to my earlier example in order to further explore what this framework tells us about an agent's reasons and blameworthiness in a given case.

5.4 An Example

If we reject the standard view of reasons as an "all or nothing" concept and accept the account outlined above, an agent will have a reason to ϕ to a degree which is proportional to the degree of her *opportunity* and *capacity* to ϕ from the motive

[12] Note that In order to assess whether the CO condition is satisfied in this second way, we will already have to know which epistemic, physical, motivational and rational states count as states in which an agent's ϕ-ing can be motivated by her putative reason. If we are unsure whether a given state (that an agent has the capacity to get herself into) is a state in which an agent's ϕ-ing can be motivated by her putative reason, then we will need to follow the method outlined above for assessing the first way in which the CO condition is satisfied, before concluding that the CO condition is (or is not) satisfied.

of her reason (or alternatively, to the degree to which she has the opportunity and capacity to get herself into a state where she has the opportunity and capacity to ϕ from the motive of her reason). That is, we now have a framework which allows us to determine whether, and to what degree, an agent has a reason. If an agent has a reason to ϕ, she must either (i) systematically ϕ from the motive of her putative reason in a whole raft of close possible worlds where we hold constant certain qualities, or alternatively (ii) there must be an array of close possible worlds (where we hold constant different qualities) in which the agent has got herself into a state where she has the opportunity and capacity to ϕ from the motive of her putative reason. The degree of similarity that the worlds specified in (i) or (ii) share with the actual world will determine the degree to which the agent has the reason.

To see how this account provides an adequate explanation of those cases where agents have partial capacities, I will return to an earlier example. Consider again the acrophobe who is locked in a room with her co-worker. Suppose that when we hold constant those features which are intrinsic to the agent and relevant to her helping her co-worker (from the motive of her reason), we discover that she only systematically helps her co-worker in those possible worlds where her attitudes and levels of fear have been substantially altered.[13] In this case, the closest worlds in which she systematically helps her co-worker (i.e. closest to the actual world) are very dissimilar to the actual world, and thus the degree to which she has a reason to help her co-worker will be small. This will also imply that the degree to which she can be blameworthy for failing to help her co-worker will be small. On the other hand, suppose that the closest worlds in which the acrophobe systematically helps her co-worker are worlds which are almost unchanged, but the acrophobe has practised her relaxation techniques or has taken the anti-anxiety medicine that she has in her purse. In this case, the degree to which she has a reason to help her co-worker will be higher. Moreover, the degree to which she can be blameworthy for failing to help her co-worker will also be higher.

As this example demonstrates, the framework spelt out in this paper allows us to properly explain cases where there seems to be a sense in which an agent has a reason, but due to the agent's partial incapacity there also seems to be a sense in which she does *not* have this reason. To say that such an agent has a reason to some degree seems preferable to stipulating some arbitrary level of capacity, above which the agent has a reason and below which she lacks this reason. This framework thus provides greater explanatory power than the view that reasons are an "all or nothing" concept.

Another virtue of this framework is that it supports an account of blameworthiness which can track individual capacities. This is a particularly important feature of the framework, given the close connection between blame and capacities. As Honoré explains:

[13] Where we assume that the acrophobe's attitudes and levels of fear are not part of the intrinsic properties which constitute the capacity to help her co-worker from the motive of her reason (and thus have to be held constant when determining if the acrobphobe has this capacity).

> Before imposing sanctions or attaching blame, law and morality require... that in the circumstances the agent had the capacity to reach a rational decision about what to do. When this capacity is present, blame for bad behaviour is appropriate and criminal liability may, depending on the state of the law, be imposed... different degrees of blame, punishment and censure correspond to the extent to which the agent's capacity is impaired. (Honoré 1998:138)

In addition to accommodating the connection between blame and capacities, and degrees of blameworthiness, the framework supports a plausible relationship between reasons and blame. In this way, the framework also preserves our "moral conceptual world".

5.5 Conclusion

In conclusion, I have offered a framework for determining blameworthiness which accommodates agents being blameworthy to *some degree*, and also having a reason *to some degree.* A crucial claim in the paper is that we should reject the standard way of understanding reasons as an "all or nothing" concept. The rejection of the standard view allows the framework to support a plausible relationship between reasons and blame, while also preserving a concept of blame that accommodates degrees of blameworthiness. Understanding reasons as coming in degrees also provides greater explanatory power than the standard view in cases where an agent's partial incapacity makes it unclear whether or not the agent has a reason. The framework outlined in this paper can explain such cases in a non-arbitrary way because it need not imply that an agent either has or lacks a reason. Rather, a partial incapacity may imply that an agent has a reason to some degree. As there is a reason condition on blame, the framework also informs us about the degree to which an agent can be blameworthy in a given case. Finally, the framework accounts for the complexity and variability of our capacities when attributing both reasons and blameworthiness to agents.

References

Dennett, Daniel. 1984. *Elbow Room: The Varieties of Free Will Worth Wanting*. Cambridge, MA: MIT Press.

Espinoza, Nicolas, and Martin Peterson. 2011. "Some Versions of the Number Problems Have No Solution." *Ethical Theory and Moral Practice* 13(4):439–51.

Heuer, Ulrike. 2010. "Reasons and Impossibility." *Philosophical Studies* 147(2):235–46.

Honoré, Tony. 1998. "Being Responsible and Being a Victim of Circumstance." Reprinted in 1999, *Responsibility and Fault*, 121–42. Oxford: Hart Publishing.

Pettit, Philip, and Michael Smith. 2006. "External Reasons." In *McDowell and His Critics*, edited by Cynthia Macdonald and Graham Macdonald, 140–68. Oxford: Blackwell.

Skorupski, John. 2007. "Internal Reasons and the Scope of Blame." In *Bernard Williams*, edited by Alan Thomas, 73–103. New York, NY: Cambridge University Press.

Smith, Michael. 2004. "Rational Capacities." In *Ethics and the A Priori: Selected Essays on Moral Psychology and Meta-Ethics*, edited by Micheal Smith, 114–35. New York, NY: Cambridge University Press.
Streumer, Bart. 2007. "Reasons and Impossibility." *Philosophical Studies* 136:351–84.
Williams, Bernard. 1989. "Internal Reasons and the Obscurity of Blame." Reprinted in 1995, *Making Sense of Humanity: And Other Philosophical Papers*, edited by Bernard Williams, 35–45. Cambridge: Cambridge University Press.

Chapter 6
Please Drink Responsibly: Can the Responsibility of Intoxicated Offenders Be Justified by the Tracing Principle?

Susan Dimock

Abstract Normally, reduced mental capacities are thought to reduce responsibility. This is how, for example, the criminal defences of insanity/mental defect and automatism work. Persons who lack the capacity, due to a disease of the mind, to understand the nature of their actions or that they are wrong, and persons who lack the capacity for voluntary control of their bodily movements, are thought to lack essential capacities for criminal responsibility. These criminal law practices exemplify the intuition that responsibility tracks capacity, a view sometimes called "capacitarianism". An equally widely held view, however, operates to restrict the commitment to capacitarianism: the intuition that when a person is responsible for his own reduced mental capacities, the exculpatory value of those reduced capacities is discounted or even extinguished. The paradigmatic case of such reduced capacities involves persons who have reduced their capacities (of understanding, foresight, knowledge, advertence or self-control) through voluntary intoxication. This intuition is also reflected in the criminal law practices of most jurisdictions. Whether such practices can be justified is the topic of this paper. My conclusion will be that, even if we accept the capacitarian intuition and its limited application to those who are responsible for their own reduced capacities, the legal instantiation of them in criminal practice is unjustified. My argument is that our treatment of intoxicated offenders is not, in fact, supported by these commitments, contrary to what many theorists and jurists think.

6.1 Introduction

Normally, reduced mental capacities are thought to reduce responsibility. This is how, for example, the criminal defences of insanity/mental defect and automatism work. Persons who lack the capacity, due to a disease of the mind, to understand the nature of their actions or that they are wrong (the two pronged McNaughten rule of insanity), and persons who lack the capacity for voluntary control of their

S. Dimock (✉)
York University, Toronto, Canada, ON
e-mail: dimock@yorku.ca

N.A Vincent et al. (eds.), *Moral Responsibility*, Library of Ethics and Applied Philosophy 27, DOI 10.1007/978-94-007-1878-4_6,

bodily movements, whether because they are suffering from a disassociative state caused by a blow to the head, a severe emotional trauma, being swarmed by bees, or sleep-walking, and so who satisfy the legal definition of automatism, are thought to lack essential capacities for criminal responsibility. These criminal law practices exemplify the intuition that responsibility tracks capacity, a view sometimes called "capacitarianism".

An equally widely held view, however, operates to restrict the commitment to capacitarianism: the intuition that when a person is responsible for his own reduced mental capacities, the exculpatory value of those reduced capacities is discounted or even extinguished. The paradigmatic case of such reduced capacities involves persons who have reduced their capacities (of understanding, foresight, knowledge, advertence or self-control) through voluntary intoxication. Even if a person lacks the capacity to understand the nature or consequences of his actions, the capacity to know that his actions are wrong, or the capacity to exercise voluntary control over his bodily movements, if that lack of capacity can be traced to his own voluntary intoxication, the lack of capacity will not exonerate. This intuition is also reflected in the criminal law practices of most jurisdictions (common law as well as civil law systems). Whether such practices can be justified is the topic of this paper. My conclusion will be that, even if we accept the capacitarian intuition and its limited application to those who are responsible for their own reduced capacities, the legal instantiation of them in criminal practice is unjustified. I am not arguing that capacitarianism and its intuitive exception in cases involving the destruction of one's own capacities is itself unjustified: I think them quite correct. Rather, my argument is that our treatment of intoxicated offenders is not, in fact, supported by these commitments, contrary to what many theorists and jurists think. Although I will use Canadian legal practice as my example in what follows, the problems identified here should apply equally to other legal jurisdictions as well.

6.2 Components of Criminal Liability: Elements of a Crime

I am interested in the criminal responsibility of intoxicated offenders. In order to understand for what intoxicated offenders are responsible, let's remind ourselves of the basic elements of criminal offences. First, offences consist of an *actus reus*, a prohibited act, omission, or result. Persons are responsible only for committing or bringing about the *actus reus* of a crime. In order to commit the *actus reus* of an offence, the person's conduct must be voluntary and conscious. There must be an acting agent whose conduct is under her voluntary and conscious control. The voluntariness component of the *actus reus* is well summed up by Vertes J. in R. v. Brenton (R. v. Brenton 1999:para. 42).

> The concept of voluntariness... represents the fundamental principle of our criminal law that no act can be regarded as criminal unless it is a voluntary act: R. v. Stone (1999) 134 C.C.C.(3d) 353 (S.C.C.) (at 421). Thus it is an aspect of the *actus reus*. It is the minimal requirement that acts must be conscious acts. There must be a mind capable of exercising the will-power to do the physical act that represents the crime. There must be a state of

> awareness on the part of the actor that he or she is doing the act. One can phrase this principle in numerous ways but the point is that voluntariness is an aspect of all crimes since all crimes must have an *actus reus* [case references omitted].

Larry Alexander calls this The Voluntary Act Principle: "there can be no criminal liability in the absence of a voluntary act", and says that "it is the law in all Anglo-American jurisdictions that no person is guilty of a crime unless she commits a voluntary act" (Alexander 1990:85).[1] This requirement has been incorporated in the Model Penal Code (Model Penal Code §2.01).

Second, all criminal offences have as an essential component some mental element known as the *mens rea* of the offence. To commit a crime a person must have the required "guilty mind" or fault element. The mental element required for different offences varies. Sometimes a person must act with intention, knowledge, foresight, or wilful blindness to commit a particular crime. These are all subjective mental states, concerning what the actual defendant knew, foresaw, or intended at the time of committing the *actus reus*. When no particular *mens rea* condition is specified, recklessness typically suffices. Recklessness is a subjective awareness of or advertence to the risk that one's conduct might constitute or bring about the *actus reus* of the offence charged, and continuing despite that risk. Many criminal law theorists, as well as some judges, have insisted that all crimes must have a subjective *mens rea* requirement. Indeed, many theorists think that what distinguishes true crimes from regulatory offences or torts is just that the latter can be committed without subjective fault, whereas criminal conduct can only be committed with subjective awareness of the harm one does. But no criminal jurisdiction has operationalized such a blanket requirement, and all legal systems allow that some crimes might be committed with only the objective fault of (gross or criminal) negligence. Negligence does not concern what was in the mind of the accused at the time of action, but rather is determined by a standard of what a reasonable person in the same circumstances would have known, foreseen, intended or appreciated, and gross negligence is a marked departure from what a reasonable person would have done in the circumstances. A person can bring about a prohibited result without any subjective fault, being unaware of the risk that his conduct may produce that result, negligently; here fault is based on the fact that he did not know or attend to facts that a reasonable person in the same circumstances would have attended to, and criminal fault consists of precisely this negligent failure to attend to relevant features of his circumstances, where that leads to a prohibited outcome.

Voluntariness is also a component of *mens rea*. Again Justice Vertes sums up the law well.

> Voluntariness is also linked to the *mens rea* component. It is a principle of fundamental justice that every criminal offence punishable by imprisonment must have a *mens rea* component. There must be at least some minimal mental state as an essential element of the crime.... This requirement of *mens rea* may be satisfied in different ways. There may be a subjective or an objective approach. An offence could require proof of a state of mind

[1] Alexander (1990), quoting Dressler (1987:65).

> such as intent, recklessness or wilful blindness. The *mens rea* requirement could, on the other hand, be satisfied by evidence of negligent conduct (a "marked departure") measured against an objective standard (what should have been in the accused's mind had he or she proceeded reasonably) [case references omitted]. But there must be some *mens rea* element, as there must be an *actus reus*, since otherwise the offence would be one of absolute liability, something that in criminal law violates both s. 7 and s. 11(d) of the Charter: R. v. Hess, [1990] 2 S.C.R. 906. [Section 7 of the Canadian Charter of Rights and Freedoms guarantees the right to life, liberty and security of the person, and the right not to be deprived thereof except in accordance with principles of fundamental justice. Section 11(d) guarantees to those accused of criminal offences the presumption of innocence.] Voluntariness is the basic constituent element of the *mens rea* requirement. The conscious doing of an act (being the *actus reus*) encompasses the intention to do it and therefore constitutes the minimal *mens rea* for general intent offences.

Finally, there is a required connection between the *actus reus* and *mens rea* constituting a crime. This is typically referred to as the principle of contemporaniety. *Actus non facit reum, nisi mens sit rea*: the intent and the act must concur to constitute the crime. That is, the *mens rea* must be directed to the *actus reus* itself, and they must occur, if not simultaneously, at least in tight temporal relation. No act can be criminal without a mental element of fault.

These elements of criminal offences establish a set of basic requirements that criminal law systems must satisfy if they are to conform to principles of fundamental justice. First, criminal law typically requires subjective fault. Exceptions to this rule are just that: exceptional. Moreover, the Crown or prosecution bears the burden of proving every element of the offence, to the criminal law standard of proof beyond a reasonable doubt. This is required by the presumption of innocence. A person accused of a criminal offence has nothing to answer for unless and until the prosecution has proved that he committed the *actus reus*, with the required *mens rea*, duly related to the prohibited outcome. (Duff 2007; Duff 2009; Tadros 2005; Horder 2004; Gardner 2007).

6.3 Responsibility, Liability and Defences

Understanding the elements of a crime is important because it allows us to distinguish four different kinds of answers one might raise to an allegation of criminality: exemptions (youth, insanity, diplomatic immunity), justifications (self-defence, lesser evils), excuses (duress, necessity), and denials that one satisfied all of the elements of the offence. Exemptions and exculpatory defences of justification or excuse have been the subject of considerable philosophical and legal analysis, but they are not relevant to our purposes, because no one thinks voluntary intoxication exempts persons from meeting the demands of the criminal law, nor that it functions as a justification or excuse. If intoxication is relevant to responsibility and liability, it is so because it negates an essential element of the crime alleged.

Often persons answer a criminal charge by raising a *reasonable doubt as to some element of the offence*. Here they are not accepting responsibility for the conduct constituting a crime and raising considerations that block the normal transition from responsibility to liability, as in the case of justifications and excuses. Nor are they denying that they are answerable to the criminal jurisdiction in question or that they are responsible agents fit to answer at all, as in the various kinds of exemptions. Rather, they are denying that they committed the crime at all. That a person cannot be criminally responsible for or liable to punishment on account of conduct not meeting all of the essential elements of the crime charged seems obvious. Suppose a person is charged with a homicide offence, murder or manslaughter. It is a complete answer to the charge that the person one is charged with killing did not die. Bringing about the death of another person is an essential component of the *actus reus* for homicide. It is every bit as much a full answer to deny that one's conduct satisfies the essential *mens rea* or fault elements of the offence charged, though not so intuitively obvious. If an offence requires a particular *mens rea*, that one do something knowingly, or with a specific intention, or being reckless with respect to the risk that one's conduct will bring about a prohibited result, and one does not have the required mental state, one is simply not guilty of the crime. To be guilty of an offence one must satisfy all of its essential elements, and the prosecution must be able to prove that one does satisfy all of those elements, beyond a reasonable doubt. Thus many defences take the form of raising a reasonable doubt as to a required element of the offence charged. Mistake and accident often function this way, defeating either the *mens rea* or *actus reus* elements of the crime.

Automatism is a defence in this same family, in that it functions to defeat an essential element of the crime. Automatism is a defence available to those who "act" without consciousness and voluntary control over their bodily movements. Paradigmatic cases involve persons who bring about a prohibited result while sleepwalking, while in a disassociative state caused by a blow to the head or a severe emotional trauma, or in the throes of a seizure or other condition that undermines their ability to control their bodily movements. If I strike a person, causing him injury, while in any of these states, I will not be held criminally responsible or made liable for that harm. Whether one is in a state of automatism is determined by the degree to which one is in conscious and voluntary control of one's bodily motions and actions. Conceptually, it does not depend upon the cause of one's automatism. Yet the law makes two distinctions within the class of automatistic conduct, based on the cause of the automatism: it distinguishes sane from insane automatism, depending on whether the cause is a disease of the mind as understood in our insanity or mental defect jurisprudence; and within the category of non-insane automatism, it treats differently automatism caused by voluntary intoxication. If automatism is a result of voluntary intoxication, it cannot function to raise a reasonable doubt as to an essential element of the crime charged, for a wide range of crimes. This is problematic, given that automatism seems to defeat both the minimal mental elements of the *actus reus* (voluntary and conscious control), as well as any subjective *mens rea* requirements the offence might have, since there is nothing the person knows, intends, foresees, or adverts to while in a state of automatism. Even if the fault condition is objective negligence, it seems unfair to hold a person responsible for failing to meet the standard of care a reasonable person would meet in circumstances where she is incapable of exercising any care at all. Thus it should raise a reasonable doubt as to both *mens rea* and *actus reus*. As we shall see, in cases of automatism caused by voluntary intoxication, this is not the case, and the automatism defence is denied to intoxicated offenders, even if they would otherwise qualify for it.

6.4 Voluntary or Self-Induced Intoxication

Intoxication, if relevant to questions of criminal responsibility and liability, seems to be so because intoxication can affect a person's mental states, and more especially can diminish a person's capacities that are relevant to responsibility and liability. Indeed, it seems pretty plausible to think that intoxication might be relevant to the mental states of persons at the time they commit an offence, and so it may be used to raise a reasonable doubt as to whether the person had the required *mens rea* for the crime charged. If crimes require subjective *mens rea* – knowledge, intention, malice, planning, deliberation, foresight, awareness, advertent recklessness or wilful blindness – then intoxication should be relevant to assessments of guilt, because it is relevant to an essential element of crimes. An accused person should be able to use the fact of intoxication as an evidential basis for claiming that she lacked the *mens rea* of the offence and so to raise a reasonable doubt as to fault, whatever the fault elements may be. As the New Zealand Court of Appeal put it: "Drunkenness is not a defence of itself. Its true relevance by way of defence, so it seems to us, is that when a jury is deciding whether the accused has the intention or recklessness required by the charge, they must regard all the evidence, including evidence as to the accused's drunken state, drawing such inferences from the evidence as appears proper in the circumstances" (R. v. Kamipeli 1975:616). The success of such arguments will vary depending upon the degree of intoxication and the specific fault requirements of the offence charged. It might be more plausible to assert that a person lacked knowledge of a particular circumstance or foresight of a particular result because she was intoxicated, for example, than to argue that she was not aware of the nature of her act or that she did not act recklessly. But for any crimes requiring subjective fault, whether intent, purpose, knowledge, willful blindness, or advertent recklessness, it seems that intoxication ought to be considered in determining whether the Crown has proved all the elements of the crime beyond a reasonable doubt. (McCord 1990) Intoxication is relevant because it might prevent the formation of the fault element of some crimes. Not surprisingly, then, the intoxication defense began as a common law defense in recognition of the fact that an accused person may be sufficiently intoxicated not to have the subjective *mens rea* for the crime charged.

On the other hand, both policy considerations and general conditions underlying exculpation tend to lend support to a regime in which voluntary intoxication cannot be used to relieve persons of criminal responsibility and punishment. This tension has been played out in law in a number of ways.

The leading modern case is *Director of Public Prosecutions vs. Beard* (1920), a rape and felony murder case heard by the House of Lords. In Beard, the House of Lords developed the distinction between general intent and specific intent offences, and they limited the defense of intoxication to only specific intent crimes. The distinction between the two rests, as the names suggest, upon a difference with respect to the *mens rea* element of the offences. The House of Lords began with the common sense relevance of intoxication to *mens rea*. "That evidence of drunkenness which renders the accused incapable of forming the specific intent essential to constitute the crime should be taken into consideration with the other facts proven in order to determine whether or not he had this intent" (D.P.P. v. Beard 1920: 501–02). This suggests that intoxication should function as the basis of a claim that the accused lacked the required *mens rea* to be guilty of the offence charged, and thus as an evidentiary consideration of relevance to proof of the essential elements of the crime.

But Lord Birkenhead's articulation in Beard of the principles to govern considerations of intoxication in criminal cases has been taken to require something quite different. It has been taken to mark a general distinction between crimes of general and specific intent. Although there is no canonical formulation of the distinction, the *mens rea* for general intent crimes is only a conscious performing of the prohibited act, whereas crimes of specific intent require a further purpose beyond the mere intention to perform the prohibited act, an ulterior purpose, or a fault element greater than recklessness (D.P.P. v. Majewski 1976). Examples of general intent crimes include all forms of assault, manslaughter, mischief, and breaking and entering. Examples of specific intent offences include robbery, breaking and entering with the intent to commit an indictable offence, assault to resist or prevent arrest, murder, theft, aiding and abetting a crime, attempted crimes, and being an accessory after the fact. Several scholars and jurists have challenged the dichotomy between general and specific intent offences as artificial, unprincipled, and indeterminate. (Quigley 1987a, b, c; Colvin 1981; Dickson J. in Leary v. The Queen 1978) While I agree with these critiques of the common law, they are not my purpose here.

The purpose of introducing the general/specific intent distinction was to limit the range of cases in which a "defense of intoxication" could be raised. However specific intent is understood, intoxication may raise a reasonable doubt over whether or not the accused had the specific fault element required. In this sense, intoxication may be a defense available to an accused person charged with a specific intent crime. But intoxication cannot be used to raise a reasonable doubt as to *mens rea* in the case of general intent offences (Leary v. The Queen 1978). Indeed, in many jurisdictions, intoxication can be substituted for the *mens rea* of every general intent crime, so that the prosecution may satisfy its burden of proving fault simply by proving intoxication (D.P.P. v. Majewski 1976; Leary v. The Queen 1978). This substitution rule has been widely debated, and my purpose is not to rehearse that debate or my reasons for thinking the substitution rule is unjust. (Dimock 2009) What matters here is that a person will be held responsible for the crime if it is proved that she committed the *actus reus*, even if she lacked the *mens rea* that would otherwise be required for quilt, if she committed the act while intoxicated. This will be so, moreover, even if the intoxication is extreme enough to raise a reasonable doubt as to the voluntariness of the conduct, even if it is so extreme, that is, as to produce a state of automatism. It is the justification of this practice that I now wish to examine.

6.5 The Fault of Intoxication

The rationale for the substitution rule and its subsequent limiting of the use of intoxication to raise a defense to a criminal charge is defended on a number of different grounds. But all, I suggest, are based upon a particular conception of the intoxicated offender, one which cannot be sustained given how voluntary or self-induced intoxication is understood by the courts. The image is familiar: a person drinks alcohol, consumes narcotics or prescription medication, mixes the two, either with the intent to become impaired, or at least being entirely reckless with respect to whether impairment results. He is blameworthy for his impairment, and so no wrong is done to him if he is held responsible for harms he then does as a result of incapacitating himself.

The willingness to substitute intoxication for the *mens rea* of every general intent offence or to find in intoxication an alternate basis of criminal liability stems from the conviction that individuals who become voluntarily intoxicated are morally blameworthy for doing so. When Canadian courts have addressed the constitutionality of the restrictions on the intoxication defense, many of the Justices have referred to the blameworthiness of becoming voluntarily intoxicated. Thus concerns about whether the restriction violates considerations of fundamental justice, which are centrally concerned with not punishing the morally innocent, are thought to be more easily met, because intoxicated offenders are not morally innocent, just in virtue of their self-induced intoxication. As Lamar C.J. said, intoxicated offenders are not "completely blameless" (R. v. Penno 1990). As he put it: "By voluntarily taking the first drink, an individual can reasonably be held to have assumed the risk that intoxication would make him or her do what he or she otherwise would not normally do with a clear mind."

It would seem, then, that the intoxication rule which allows voluntary intoxication to be substituted for the normal *mens rea* of general intent offences can be justified under a widely accepted principle of responsibility, namely, the "tracing" principle identified by John Martin Fischer and Mark Ravizza. (Fischer and Ravizza 1988) As is well-known, Fischer and Ravizza have argued that it suffices for responsibility that a person exercised guidance control over his action, which control just requires that the person's action issue from their own moderately reasons responsive mechanism. Applied to our case, the position would be that even if the intoxicated offender lacks the capacity to be reasons-responsive after becoming intoxicated, he may still be responsible for his conduct while intoxicated if becoming intoxicated was, at an earlier time, something over which he exercised guidance control. As Fischer and Ravizza put it, "When one acts from a reasons-responsive mechanism at *T1*, and one can be reasonably expected to know that so acting will (or may) lead to acting from an unresponsive mechanism at some later time *T2*, one can be held responsible for so acting at *T2*." (Fischer and Ravizza 1998:50) They describe their view as "a 'tracing' approach: when an agent is morally responsible for an action that issues from a mechanism that is not appropriately reasons-responsive, we must be able to trace back along the history of the action to a point (*suitably related to the action*) where there was indeed an appropriately reasons-responsive mechanism." (Fischer and Ravizza 1988:50–51) The semicompatibilism of Fischer and Ravizza is not only widely adopted among responsibility theorists, but it seems just the kind of theory that the criminal law needs to undergird its practices. So if it has the resources to explain and justify the treatment of intoxicated offenders as responsible for their offences, even when lacking the *mens rea* typically required for them, by tracing back to a choice for which they were responsible (the choice to become intoxicated), then the tracing principle will justify the intuitions about capacities with which we began. The lack of capacity typically exculpates, but not when the incapacity can itself be traced back to a choice for which the incapacitated agent is responsible. Not surprisingly, Fischer and Ravizza use an intoxicated driver as their example to establish the intuitive force of the tracing principle.

Whether the tracing principle can justify holding intoxicated offenders responsible for their offences will depend, however, on whether the choice to become intoxicated is something for which they can be held responsible, and on whether that choice is "suitably related to the [criminal] action". As Fischer and Ravizza note, the tracing principle requires that the person to be held responsible for some act at *T2* must be reasonably expected to know that his conduct at *T1* will or might lead to action on the basis of an unresponsive mechanism at *T2*. He must be able to anticipate, that is, that his earlier choice to consume an intoxicant might lead to acting on unresponsive mechanisms in the future. As they say, "the degree of likelihood employed by the tracing approach would need to be context-relative". (Fischer and Ravizza 1998:50, fn 21) In the context of criminal liability, the degree of likelihood must be above the *de minimus* range if our practices are to satisfy the requirements of fundamental justice. I argue that they do not.

6.6 What Makes Intoxication Voluntary or Self-Induced?

The greatest injustices worked by our current intoxication rules actually stem from the way that voluntary or self-induced intoxication is defined. The problem lays with the responsibility conditions for voluntary intoxication. The image of the intoxicated offender that is relied upon is of a person who imbibes significant qualities of drugs, alcohol or both, over an extended period of time. Even if reaching a state of intoxication or impairment in not intended, any reasonable person engaging in such behaviour must anticipate that impairment might result from his actions. Indeed, it seems simply inconceivable that the person himself did not, at some point in the process of consuming the intoxicants, advert to the risk of impairment that his consumption might have. If this was the only type of person caught by our intoxication rules, they would not likely generate the controversy they have, and they could be justified by the tracing principle. (Although there might still be worries about those whose ingestion of intoxicants is the result of addiction, if addictive desires are not themselves moderately reasons-responsive.) But this is not the only type of person who is deemed to satisfy the conditions for voluntary intoxication.

The conditions on involuntary intoxication are stringent. A person cannot plead involuntary intoxication just because he did not intend to become intoxicated, or if he did not know or even foresee that his conduct would produce intoxication. In order to be involuntary, a reasonable person could not have foreseen intoxication resulting from the person's conduct. If a person ingests or consumes anything which *he knows or ought to know is an intoxicant*, he cannot plead involuntary intoxication (R. v. King 1962). In Canada and elsewhere, there is a rebuttable presumption that impairment from alcohol or drugs is voluntary. Only if there is a reasonable doubt as to a defendant's ability to appreciate and know that he would or might become impaired, an inability for which he is completely without fault, can his subsequent intoxication exonerate. If a person voluntarily consumes alcohol or a drug which he knew or had any reasonable ground for believing might cause him to be impaired, then he cannot use his impairment to escape liability for a crime he then commits, even if he did not intend to become impaired. Among the authorities appealed to in support of this position is Justice O. W. Holmes, who wrote in *The Common Law* that: "As the purpose is to compel men to abstain from dangerous conduct, and not merely to restrain them from evil inclinations, the law requires them at their peril to know the teachings of common experience, just as it requires them to know the law." Applied to intoxication, it has been "taken as a matter of 'common experience' that the consumption of alcohol may produce intoxication and, therefore, 'impairment' . . ., and I think it is also to be similarly taken to be known that the use of narcotics may have the same effect" (R. v. King 1962).

The presumption that persons know that consumption of intoxicants is inherently dangerous and risks impairment is rarely overcome. This is so, even if the resulting intoxication is highly improbable, as long as it is the result of ingesting known intoxicants. Thus even if someone has a completely unpredictable reaction to a small amount of marijuana, for example, or someone else puts drugs into the person's alcoholic drink without his knowledge, his resulting intoxication is not involuntary because it is in part due to his ingesting substances that are known by reasonable people to be intoxicants (R. v. Brenton 1999; R. v. Talock 2003). The lack of fault for the offence due to involuntary intoxication can only exonerate if the intoxication itself was without fault, and fault for intoxication is in practice established merely by the consumption of anything reasonably known to be an intoxicant. Case after case demonstrates that the real test is proof of the voluntary consumption of intoxicants; once voluntary consumption is proved, persons are expected to have common knowledge about the dangers of their consumption, and so recklessness is simply inferred rather than proven. As Clackson J. summed up, "self-induced intoxication ... means the accused voluntarily consumed a substance which he knew or *ought to have known* was an intoxicant and appreciated or should have appreciated that he risked becoming intoxicated" (R. v. Huppie 2008:para. 23; R. v. Chaulk 2007). As another Canadian judge put it, "the law in Canada requires that the Court find that the accused consumed the alcohol. A successful *mens rea* defence would involve evidence that the act of drinking was prompted by threats or mistake and thus not an act of volition. Examples that come to mind of this sort might be: the accused was forced against his will to drink alcohol; or a third party slipped alcohol into the drinks of an unknowing accused; or the alcohol, having been transferred by a third party into an orange juice container, the accused was unaware he was drinking alcohol" (R. v. Thompson 1993:para. 31).

Put positively, if a person knows or ought to know that what he or she is voluntarily consuming is an intoxicant then any resulting state of intoxication is itself deemed to be voluntary. As Dyer J. put it, after reviewing the jurisprudence on voluntary intoxication, "a trial judge in dealing with voluntary consumption of drugs [must] consider whether an accused person knew or had any reasonable grounds for believing that such consumption might cause him to be impaired. In so doing, I do believe the Court should not permit negligence or carelessness on the part of an accused to become a defence. I think persons who take drugs or drink voluntarily are required to act reasonably in taking them and are to be taken to reasonably understand the likely results of taking them in most cases" (R. v. Kataria 2005: para. 102).

In practice, however, the possibility of taking drink or drugs responsibly seems to be ruled out from the start. The courts have ruled, for example, that a person cannot claim to know from experience how long a sleep-aid medication takes to work to escape liability for impaired operation of a motor vehicle, though such arguments would seem to suggest that the accused did not appreciate the risk that he would become impaired while he was in care and control of a vehicle. They have ruled that "It is not necessary for the Crown to show that the appellant knew the degree to which he would be affected. The Crown need only show knowledge that [the intoxicants in question] could affect him and that in fact they did so" (R. v. Jensen 1991:para. 25). Generally, the courts take it as a matter of common knowledge that drugs, whether illicit, prescription or unregulated such as cold medications or sleeping aids, should not be taken with alcohol or at a dosage higher than prescribed or recommended on the packaging, and such knowledge will suffice for proof that any resulting impairment is voluntary.

That voluntary intoxication can result from negligence and yet be the standard of criminal fault in any general intent offence involving crimes against the person has been codified in Canadian criminal law, which establishes gross negligence as a standard of penal fault, and creates an irrebuttable presumption that a person who becomes extremely intoxicated has that fault: he "departs markedly from the standard of reasonable care generally recognized in Canadian society and is thereby criminally at fault" (Criminal Code of Canada, s. 33.1 (2)). Thus if a person commits a general intent offense while voluntarily intoxicated, or a crime against a person even if so severely intoxicated as to be acting involuntarily, he will be deemed to have the *mens rea* necessary for conviction. Negligently becoming intoxicated suffices for criminal fault (R. v. Chaulk 2006).

The case of R. v. Brenton illustrates the problem with this approach. Mr. Brenton shared a marijuana cigarette with his landlady one evening after work. He had prior experience with the drug, though was not a habitual user, and had never had an unusual reaction to it. He smoked the joint hoping to relax so that he could sleep. Instead, he had an extreme and both statistically and subjectively unpredictable reaction to the drug, producing a state of automatism, in which he assaulted his landlady.

He was convicted at trial of the charges, even though the trial judge had a reasonable doubt as to the voluntariness of his conduct or his mental state at the time of the commission of the crimes. On appeal, Mr. Brenton argued that his conviction should be overturned because his intoxication was not voluntary. "The appellant argued, at trial and on appeal, that it cannot be said that he intended to become intoxicated or should have known that he would become intoxicated given the relatively small amount of marijuana he ingested. His purpose for smoking the marijuana was to relax so as to help him sleep. Therefore, it was argued, the result was an unintended and unexpected outcome and thus tantamount to non-voluntary intoxication." Justice Vertes rejected this argument: "I cannot agree with the appellant's submission. Generally speaking, if the ingestion of a drug (or alcohol) is voluntary and the risk of becoming intoxicated is within the contemplation or should be within the contemplation of the individual, then any resulting intoxication is self-induced. Involuntary intoxication is generally confined to cases where the accused did not know he or she was ingesting an intoxicating substance (such as where the accused's drink is spiked) or where the accused becomes intoxicated while taking prescription drugs and their effects are unknown to the accused. This is fairly basic law" (R. v. Benton 1999:paras. 30 and 31). Thus it is voluntary consumption of intoxicants, rather than any subjective appreciation that impairment might result, that is the fault of intoxication, fault that can be substituted for the *mens rea* of any general intent offence. Voluntary intoxication, then, can result from negligence without any subjective awareness of the risk of impairment or subsequent criminality.

That negligence is the fault criterion for voluntary intoxication is extremely important. Many cases involve the combination of alcohol and other drugs, whether banned substances, prescription medications or over-the-counter products. Many drugs in the latter two groups contain warnings against mixing them with alcohol, but the warnings actually suggest that sleepiness might result. While it might be negligent to drive an automobile or operate dangerous equipment in circumstances where one does or ought to anticipate extraordinary tiredness being experienced, it is not at all clear that such a warning suffices to establish that a reasonable person combining a small amount of alcohol with such drugs would or ought to anticipate that he might become violent and actually do or threaten harm to another. The fact pattern in Brenton, involving the consumption of at most half a marijuana joint, which produced a completely unexpected reaction, leading to a loss of voluntary control and violence, raises equal concern. Such an outcome was not subjectively foreseeable, nor, I would argue, even objectively foreseeable. Even a reasonable person would not have anticipated the resulting danger. Nonetheless, the trial judge felt compelled to find the accused guilty, even though entertaining a reasonable doubt as to the voluntariness of Mr. Brenton's conduct. (Criminal Code of Canada s. 33.1 (1)–(3)).

We can now see that the intoxication rules as applied are not actually supported by the tracing principle. The first problem, related to how voluntary intoxication is understood in the law, means that the substitution rule fails to meet the condition of the tracing principle that one can be reasonably expected to know that ingesting an intoxicant will (or may) lead to acting from an unresponsive mechanism at some later time (impairment or loss of capacity). This is so because a person could satisfy the legal requirements for voluntary intoxication without satisfying the requirement that he can reasonably be expected to know that he will later become impaired to the point of being unresponsive, or becoming violent.

There is, moreover, a second way in which our intoxication rules fail to be supported by Fischer and Ravizza's tracing principle. According to their account, we must be able to trace back along the history of the subsequent criminal action to a point (*suitably related to the act of ingesting intoxicants*) where there was an appropriately reasons-responsive mechanism operating. But in fact the acts at *T1* producing intoxication are not "suitably related" to acts of violence that might be committed at *T2*. It is not reasonable to expect that persons engaged in the act of consuming alcohol or drugs can be reasonably expected to know that their conduct at *T1* creates a risk of criminality at *T2*. This is because the risk of criminality from intoxication is in fact so low, objectively speaking, that to say that a person ought to recognize that becoming intoxicated at *T1* constitutes a significant risk of a loss of capacity producing criminality at *T2* is to say that a person ought to believe what is objectively false.

Yet many people seem to think that such a risk is foreseeable from intoxication. Indeed, many judges and academic commentators suggest that becoming voluntarily intoxicated is necessarily reckless. The claim must be a necessity claim if the substitution rule is to be acceptable, because voluntary intoxication creates an irrebuttable presumption of criminal fault for general intent crimes. The problem with this line of argument should now be apparent. The law characterizes voluntary intoxication as intoxication resulting from the consumption of substances the person knew or *ought to have known* were intoxicants, and that he *knew or ought to have known* might cause impairment. Thus the law makes negligence sufficient for voluntariness, rather than the subjective standard of recklessness. But the issues here are too important to settle by semantics, so let's examine whether the ingestion of intoxicants to the point of impairment is necessarily reckless conduct. Only if ingestion of intoxicants really does create a foreseeable risk of criminality will the reasons-responsive mechanisms leading to the decision to consume intoxicants be suitably related to the subsequent criminal conduct (produced as it may be by non-reasons-responsive mechanisms at the time of its occurrence) so as to allow us to trace responsibility from the earlier time to the later. The answer to the question – is the ingestion of intoxicants to the point of impairment necessarily reckless? – is no.

It is surely problematic that a legally innocent action can be a conclusive and irrebuttable basis of criminal fault, indeed, fault for a vast range of crimes, including crimes the commission of which is punishable by life imprisonment. Many judges and legal theorists attempt to meet this concern by claiming that the fault element is the recklessness that necessarily attaches to the act of becoming intoxicated itself. Thus recklessness is the fault element, rather than intoxication per se, and it is satisfied by every voluntarily intoxicated offender. This was the tack taken in Majewski, and it has since been followed by many Canadian judges.

This line of thought has attracted many, in part because it would provide a principled way of distinguishing between general and specific intent crimes, something that has otherwise seemed ad hoc, uncertain and unprincipled. The idea is that specific intent crimes have *mens rea* conditions beyond mere recklessness but general intent crimes require only recklessness. If that was true, and becoming voluntarily intoxicated is necessarily reckless, then the substitution rule would be acceptable. Proof of intoxication would suffice as proof of recklessness and so *mens rea*. But the argument trades on an ambiguity concerning "recklessness." While many general intent offences have recklessness as *mens rea*, recklessness as the fault element of crimes is more constrained than recklessness outside the law. To be guilty of a crime, a person must be reckless *with respect to the criminal act or result* specifically. It is not a crime to be reckless per se. Legal recklessness implies foresight of specific consequences or an awareness of or adverting to risks with respect to a prohibited act or result, and a decision to assume that risk. This presents a dilemma. On one horn, we must suppose that every person who becomes voluntarily intoxicated is reckless with respect to every prohibited act or result that falls within the bounds of general intent offences. This should function as a *reductio ad absurdum* of this way of understanding the argument; we cannot infer such foresight or advertence merely from the fact that a person became voluntarily intoxicated. On the other horn, we must admit that the recklessness evidenced by voluntary intoxication is not of the same kind as reckless in law, and therefore even if intoxicated offenders are reckless in some sense, it is not the sense required for criminal fault.

We should not, however, accept the general claim that becoming intoxicated is necessarily reckless or otherwise morally faulty, even understood in the non-legal sense of recklessness. Recklessness can be inferred from intoxication in some circumstances, but only given additional facts. A person who routinely becomes violent when he drinks alcohol, for example, could reasonably be expected to foresee the danger that he might assault someone if he drinks and so can be considered reckless with respect to that danger. But equally conceivably, a person could take all reasonable steps to avoid harming others while intoxicated.

In an earlier paper, I offered the following counter-example to the claim that voluntary intoxication is necessarily reckless.

> Mary has just achieved some very important personal goal. She has defended her Ph.D., secured a long-sought promotion, or earned tenure. She decides that a party is in order, at which friends, family, and colleagues will celebrate her achievement. But she is a cautious and responsible person, who knows the courts have been doing funny things with respect to host liability specifically and intoxication law in general. Since she also knows that she is likely to imbibe a lot of alcohol at the party, she takes all reasonable precautions. She arranges for the party to be catered by licensed professionals so that there will be no incidents involving food preparation and safety. She ensures that accommodations are made for people who must drive to the party at an inexpensive motel within walking distance from her home and has taxi chits available for local celebrants. Finally, she arranges to have a trusted friend shadow her. Her friend's job is to stay sober and ensure that she does not do anything untoward should she become intoxicated. All is going smoothly on the big night. Her friend is conscientiously performing his duty. Her guests are heartily enjoying themselves, and she raises her glass to every toast made in recognition of her achievement [Miss Manners notwithstanding]. Then, once she is clearly intoxicated, the caterer serves a rare seafood delicacy unknown to many of her guests. Her friend eats a morsel, has an allergic reaction, and dies. At that point, she is agitated and distressed, and intoxicated.

> There seems no reason to accept that she was reckless in becoming intoxicated or that she thereby demonstrated fault sufficient to establish *mens rea* for every general intent offence. Yet according to Canadian law, she has the *mens rea* for all general intent crimes involving violence or bodily interference. (Dimock 2009)

This example still seems to me to stand as a counter-example to the necessity claim, and to provide reason for rejecting the position that proof of voluntary intoxication can ground an irrebuttable presumption of recklessness.

Yet the claim that becoming intoxicated is necessarily reckless persists. It is claimed that it is common knowledge that intoxication is inherently dangerous. Such a claim is especially problematic in a country like Canada, where in most provinces the state itself sells the vast majority of the alcohol available to consumers. In the latest year for which there are statistics (April 1, 2007–March 31, 2008), beer and liquor stores in Canada sold $18.8 billion worth of alcoholic beverages, or 222.9 million litres. Provincial and territorial governments realized a net income of $5.2 billion from the sale of liquor and related products (e.g. liquor licenses). Our governments have not, then, told citizens not to consume alcohol or pharmaceuticals because of the risk of criminality, nor have they made general prior rules against such behavior. To the contrary, members of our society are inundated with advertisements extolling the pleasures of alcohol (including from government-owned liquor retailers) and promoting the ideal of better living through pharmaceuticals. Our governments certainly have not pointed, with a few notable exceptions such as impaired driving, to specific dangers that consuming intoxicants might produce. Instead, our government urges that we "drink responsibly".[2] If the very consumption of alcohol is necessarily criminally reckless, however, then at the very least the government is complicit in that fault, perhaps so much so that it has lost the right to hold citizens to account for it (Tadros 2009).

Chester Mitchell has argued that judicial or legislative treatment of voluntary intoxication as itself criminally negligent or reckless cannot be sustained on the scientific evidence. It is simply not true that the vast majority of people who ingest drugs or drink, even to the point of intoxication, are thereby reckless in doing so. As he says: "For almost all persons, the probability of their drug consumption causing a serious crime is too low to qualify as recklessness. Violent crimes are rarely compared to the common incidence of intoxication or drug-impairment. Furthermore, the relationship between intoxicants and crime is much more problematic, subtle, and indirect than is usually assumed" (Mitchell 1988:78). The claim that becoming intoxicated is itself criminal recklessness simply lacks empirical support.

> For ordinary intoxication, the evidence suggests a probability of resultant harm considerably lower than the level needed for criminal recklessness. The chances of drug users turning to violent or serious crime because of intoxication are at best remote. Most North Americans take alcohol and millions regularly become intoxicated without putting themselves or others at serious risk. Unfortunately, most crime-alcohol studies merely state the proportion of

[2] The Liquor Control Board of Ontario uses "Please drink responsibly" as a regular feature of it community messaging, including advertising on its bags. This suggests that the government thinks it is possible to drink responsibly.

> known criminality involving drug use. This may be as high as 50%. But to judge whether intoxication is reckless we require the opposite statistic, namely the portion of drunken events that involve serious criminal activity. This figure is certainly below 1%. (Mitchell 1988:88–89)

If these facts are correct, as they certainly are in Canada, the eventual criminal act is simply too remote and unforeseeable from the act of becoming intoxicated for intoxication to constitute *mens rea* for it, or for the two acts to be "suitably related" so as to bring them within the scope of the tracing principle. For most people who imbibe intoxicants, it is simply not true that criminal actions fall within the ambit of the act of becoming intoxicated (Gough 1996). The two acts are not "suitably related" such that a person should foresee criminality resulting from the use of intoxicants; not even a reasonable person can foresee connections that are statistically insignificant.

References

Alexander, Larry. 1990. "Reconsidering the Relationship Among Voluntary Acts, Strict Liability, and Negligence in Criminal Law." *Social Philosophy & Policy* 7:84–104.

Colvin, Eric. 1981. "A Theory of the Intoxication Defense." *Canadian Bar Review* 59:750–79.

Criminal Code of Canada, s. 33.1 (2).

Dimock, Susan. 2009. "The Responsibility of Intoxicated Offenders." *Journal of Value Inquiry* 43:339–68.

Dressler, Joshua. 2006. *Understanding Criminal Law*. 4th ed. New York: Lexis.

Duff, R.A. 2007. *Answering for Crime: Responsibility and Liability in the Criminal Law*. Oxford: Hart Publishing.

Duff, R.A. 2009. "Strict Responsibility, Moral and Criminal." *Journal of Value Inquiry* 43: 295–313.

Fischer, John Martin and Mark Ravizza. 1988. *Responsibility and Control: A Theory of Moral Responsibility*. Cambridge: Cambridge University Press.

Gardner, John. 2007. *Offences and Defenses*. Oxford: Oxford University Press.

Gough, Stephen. 1996. "Intoxication and Criminal Liability: The Law Commission's Proposed Reforms." *Law Quarterly Review* 112:335–55.

Horder, Jeremy. 2004. *Excusing Crime*. Oxford: Oxford University Press.

McCord, David. 1990. "The English and American History of Voluntary Intoxication to Negate Mens Rea." *The Journal of Legal History* 11:372–95.

Mitchell, Chester N. 1988. "The Intoxicated Offender — Refuting the Legal and Medical Myths." *International Journal of Law and Psychiatry* 11:77–103.

Quigley, Tim. 1987a. "Specific and General Nonsense?" *Dalhousie Law Journal* 11:75–125.

Quigley, Tim. 1987b. "A Shorn Beard." *Dalhousie Law Review* 12:167–94.

Quigley, Tim. 1987c. "Reform of the Intoxication Defense." *McGill Law Journal* 33:1–48.

Tadros, Victor. 2005. *Criminal Responsibility*. Oxford: Oxford University Press.

Tadros, Victor. 2009. "Poverty and Criminal Responsibility." *Journal of Value Inquiry* 43:391–413.

Cases

D.P.P. v. Beard [1920] 14 Cr. App. R. 159 (HL)

D.P.P. v. Majewski [1976] 2 All E.R. 142 (HL)

Leary v. The Queen [1978] 1 S.C.R. 29

R. v. Brenton [1999] 28 C.R. (5th) 308 at 320 (N.W.T.S.C.)
R. v. Brenton [1999] N.W.T.J. No. 113
R. v. Chaulk [2006] N.S.J. No 407
R. v. Chaulk [2007] N.S.J. No. 301, 2007 N.S.C.A. 84
R. v. Huppie [2008] A.J. No. 989
R. v. Jensen [1991] B.C.J. No. 4060
R. v. Kamipeli [1975] 2 N.Z.L.R. 610 at 616 (C.A.)
R. v. Kataria [2005] B.C.J. No. 2963
R. v. King [1962] 133 C.C.C. 1
R. v. Penno [1990] 2 S.C.R. 865
R. v. Talock [2003] 41 M.V.R. 269 (Sask. C.A.)
R. v. Thompson [1993] O.J. No. 3249

Chapter 7
The Moral Significance of Unintentional Omission: Comparing Will-Centered and Non-will-centered Accounts of Moral Responsibility

Jason Benchimol

Abstract It is reasonable to assume that much wrongdoing for which agents are generally thought blameworthy occurs by way of unintentional omission. In this paper, I explain why certain will-centered accounts of moral responsibility tend to struggle to provide convincing explanations of the theoretical basis for judgments of blameworthiness in cases of unintentional omission. To provide such explanations, these will-centered accounts typically rely upon a "tracing strategy", according to which an agent's blameworthiness for an unintentional omission necessarily presupposes that it is a casual result of some prior blameworthy intentional choice she apparently made. I argue that this sort of appeal to the tracing strategy, upon further inspection, produces distorting implications for the way we ordinarily think about the conditions of legitimate moral criticism in cases of unintentional omission. I conclude by identifying a peculiar assumption that defenders of these will-centered accounts of moral responsibility appear to adopt and that, once rejected, renders the volitionalist's appeal to the tracing strategy unnecessary for purposes of explaining the conditions of blameworthiness for unintentional omission. The upshot of my investigation is rather modest, but it does remain unclear just what advantage, if any, will-centered accounts of moral responsibility enjoy over their rival non-will-centered accounts.

7.1 Introduction

Because so much theorizing about moral responsibility has taken place against a background concern about whether the truth of determinism could be compatible with free will, we should not be surprised that many philosophers have had quite a lot to say about the conditions of moral responsibility for actions and for their consequences. This is presumably because the underlying issue is typically articulated as one that concerns whether the truth of determinism would entail that all of our

J. Benchimol (✉)
Department of Philosophy, University of Washington, Seattle, WA, USA
e-mail: jdbench@uw.edu

N.A Vincent et al. (eds.), *Moral Responsibility*, Library of Ethics and Applied Philosophy 27, DOI 10.1007/978-94-007-1878-4_7,

actions and their consequences are inevitable occurrences given certain antecedent states of affairs that obtained long before our births, and are thus not suitably "free" or "up to us" in the way typically thought necessary to serve as bases for the distinctively moral forms of evaluation involved in praise and blame. Given the prevalence of this particular way of orienting the issue, it is easy to understand why compatibilist and libertarian philosophers have been concerned primarily with explaining how our actions and their consequences can indeed still be "up to us" in the requisite sense to ground legitimate attributions of moral responsibility.

But perhaps this attentiveness to the question of how we can be morally responsible for what we do has inadvertently led to the construction of theories of moral responsibility that are too preoccupied with the conditions of responsible *action*, theories which in turn fail to provide convincing explanations of how agents can be morally responsible for some of the things they *don't* do. Very often, we take certain intuitively morally significant inactions to be legitimate bases for moral criticism of agents. Think of a husband (call him "Mikael") who, after seven years of marriage, completely forgets his own anniversary date. Or, after arranging his schedule to meet a struggling student outside of his normal office hours, a college instructor (call him "Per") subsequently fails to recall the appointment and forgets to show up. Another example: a lifeguard on duty (call her "Abby") falls asleep on the job, during which time an inexperienced swimmer is pulled away from the shore by a strong undertow, and Abby doesn't assist him as she should. Mikael, Per, and Abby are all intuitively blameworthy not, it would seem, on the basis of any particular actions they have performed, but on the basis of certain morally significant inactions. This intuition is supported by noting that judgments that each of these agents has exhibited a morally criticizable measure of ill will or disregard appear to be made appropriate by their inactions. Moreover, it is plausible to suppose that these examples do not constitute rare or anomalous instances of blameworthy inaction. It is, instead, reasonable to assume that much blameworthy wrongdoing occurs by way of this kind of inaction. Any satisfactory general theory of moral responsibility should be able to offer a compelling explanation why judgments of blameworthiness and the kinds of responses associated with them are intuitively appropriate in such cases.

My principal aim in this paper is to explain why certain will-centered approaches to moral responsibility – theories that regard intentional choice or decision as a precondition of legitimate moral criticism – struggle to provide a convincing account of the conditions of blameworthiness for the kind of inaction that is of moral concern in the cases I just introduced. This failure reflects, I think, a lack of attention in the literature on moral responsibility to the moral significance of inaction, and this paper is intended to open avenues for further reflection on this topic. In the next section, I will explain the conception of moral blameworthiness that will guide my inquiry, and I will clarify the precise nature of the kind of inaction that is my present concern. Then, I will briefly discuss how a particular variety of will-centered approaches to moral responsibility have attempted to explain judgments of blameworthiness for this kind of inaction by appealing to a "tracing strategy". I will then subject the way these theories use the tracing strategy to intense critical scrutiny, illuminating different ways I think such use produces distorting implications for the way we ordinarily think about the conditions of legitimate moral criticism in the cases of inaction with which I am concerned. In the final section of the paper, I will expose a peculiar assumption that I think defenders of these will-centered approaches to moral responsibility adopt, and that pinpoints one possible source of their struggle to convincingly explain a substantial set of our intuitive judgments about the conditions of moral blameworthiness. Because non-will-centered theories of moral responsibility can easily reject this assumption, they may be better equipped to provide compelling philosophical explanations of judgments of moral blameworthiness in the cases of inaction that are my chief concern. The upshot of my investigation is rather modest, but it does draw attention to how unclear it is just what advantage, if any, certain will-centered approaches to moral responsibility enjoy over non-will-centered approaches.

7.2 Moral Blameworthiness and Unintentional Omission

My general interest in this paper is in the conditions of moral blameworthiness for certain morally significant inactions. Minimally, moral blameworthiness entails the propriety of a judgment that ill will or disregard has been shown (where proper regard is legitimately expected). In addition, an agent's moral blameworthiness depends crucially upon the propriety of certain distinctly moral kinds of response on behalf of both the offender (e.g., feelings of guilt, remorse, and a desire to apologize and attempt reconciliation) and those offended (e.g., feelings of resentment or indignation, attitudes of disapprobation, and requests for justification and acknowledgement of fault). For convenience, I will sometimes refer to the former kinds of response under the collective heading of "guilt" and the latter kinds of response under the collective heading of "resentment". It is reasonable to suppose that the propriety of a judgment that ill will or disregard has been shown, and the propriety of both guilt and resentment indicates that the conditions of moral blameworthiness are satisfied.

Some philosophers understand "moral blameworthiness" as what T. M. Scanlon has called a "desert-entailing notion".[1] On this view, a correct judgment of moral blameworthiness entails (among other things) that the blameworthy agent deserves to suffer some loss in virtue of what she has done. In a similar vein, others have thought that moral blameworthiness presupposes that it would be morally fair or just to respond to the agent who is blameworthy by applying "informal sanctions" that incorporate distinctly retributive sentiments.[2] My conception of moral

---

[1] Scanlon (1998:274–75).

[2] See Watson (2004). Because some philosophers have assumed that blame carries a characteristic force that requires justification in order for its application to be morally fair, questions about the conditions of moral blameworthiness have sometimes been framed as fundamentally involving the conditions that must be met in order for it to be morally "fair" or "just" for some moral judge to impose sanctions upon a wrongdoer. For an important criticism of the idea that the characteristic force of blame is to be located in these overt sanctioning behaviors, see Hieronymi (2004).

blameworthiness implies neither that an agent who is blameworthy deserves to suffer in virtue of this fact, nor that subjecting her to informal sanctioning behavior is morally fair. By the same token, this conception clearly does not imply the propriety of only what Gary Watson calls "aretaic appraisals".[3] An appraisal of an agent's character or, to use Watson's own term, her "evaluative capacities" as defective or poor in some respect need not involve a specific judgment that ill will or disregard was shown, and unless one has some legitimate stake in the appraisal, need not make guilt or resentment appropriate. So it should be noted that the conception of moral blameworthiness I adopt goes substantially beyond what might be called "negative aretaic appraisal", yet does not go so far as to incorporate any substantive conclusions about the fittingness of overt responses that incorporate retributive sentiments. While any understanding of moral blameworthiness will surely presuppose a corresponding conception of blame, the understanding of moral blameworthiness I have adopted here seems to me to capture features of blame that are most central to that notion as we commonly understand it.

Now I must clarify what I have in mind when I speak of "morally significant inactions". The cases of morally significant inaction in which I am interested are those whereby an agent seems to have violated a legitimate moral expectation not by way of anything she has done, but by way of something she hasn't done. In such cases, it is the fact that the inaction appears to involve the violation of a moral expectation that distinguishes it as "morally significant", thereby raising questions about whether the inaction can be taken as an appropriate basis for moral criticism. Clearly, not every inaction is morally significant in a way that raises such questions. But the example cases I introduced in the previous section are intuitive cases of morally significant inaction, for Mikael, Per, and Abby all appear to have violated legitimate moral expectations in virtue of what they haven't done.[4] I will refer to morally significant inactions involving such violations as "omissions", in order to distinguish them properly from inactions that do not involve such violations and that are thus morally insignificant.[5]

The term "omission", as I have proposed to use it here, is neutral regarding an agent's mental condition vis-à-vis the violation that makes a particular inaction an omission. Therefore, an omission to do s can obtain with or without an agent's awareness that he does not do s. When such awareness is absent, we may call it a case of unintentional omission. Patricia G. Smith has recently offered a compelling analysis of unintentional omission which highlights the fact that all that is necessary and sufficient for an agent's unintentionally omitting to do s is, roughly speaking,

[3] Watson, op. cit.

[4] I think this much can be granted, though I recognize that some will balk at the idea that forgetting an anniversary could involve the violation of a moral expectation. For this reason, I have included the other two example cases which, I take it, rather obviously do involve such violations.

[5] Here I am appealing, somewhat roughly, to Patricia G. Smith's account of omission as it is defended in her papers, Smith (1990), and Smith (2005b). Smith's account is an extension and development of Joel Feinberg's original remarks on the concept of omission. See Feinberg (1984:159–61).

(1) that the agent did not do s, and (2) that, by not doing s, the agent violated a norm of conduct that specifies required behavior for her.[6] Smith explains that:

> there is no positive act and no thought or intention by which to distinguish omission from inaction in the case of unintentional omission. There is only a standard. . . of human conduct, the [violation] of which turns [inaction] into omission by [connecting] it to a particular agent within a specific context. It is this connection that ultimately provides the needed link to agency and responsibility.[7]

While it may be granted that Mikael, Per, and Abby each violate a moral expectation by way of their inactions, this would not by itself entail that each is morally blameworthy, for moral blameworthiness also requires that ill will or disregard was in fact shown.[8] We may, however, assume for the sake of argument that each agent has (somehow) shown a certain degree of ill will or disregard. We can imagine that each would, in virtue of his or her respective unintentional omission, appropriately experience responses characteristic of guilt. Moreover, those who have been neglected, forgotten, or otherwise overlooked would also appropriately experience responses characteristic of resentment. Yet, it is worth noting that nothing in the description of their respective cases thus far suggests the presence of any positive act, thought, or intention either to violate the relevant moral expectations or to show what would readily be recognized by those wronged as ill will or disregard. This leads to a puzzle, I think, because we commonly tend to assume that some such mental act – choice, intention, decision, etc. – is required in order for some state of affairs to be genuinely reflective of ill will or disregard on an agent's behalf. If a positive mental act is necessary in order for it to be true that ill will or disregard was shown, then it is not immediately clear how Mikael, Per, and Abby could be morally blameworthy for their unintentional omissions.

A satisfactory solution to this puzzle will provide a compelling explanation of how an intuitively blameworthy unintentional omission can be reflective of ill will or disregard. Circumstances are plentiful in which agents forget, overlook or otherwise simply fail to act as they should, and we ordinarily take many of these unintentional omissions to constitute grounds for judging that ill will or disregard has been shown. Such circumstances are illustrated by the examples involving Mikael, Per, and Abby. Moreover, unintentional omissions frequently provide occasions both for the omitter to legitimately experience guilt on the one hand, and for those neglected, forgotten, or otherwise overlooked to legitimately experience resentment, on the other. In such cases, our confidence in judgments to the effect that these agents are open to moral criticism for their unintentional omissions depends crucially upon being able to explain how their morally significant inactions can reflect ill will or disregard in the way necessary to underwrite a legitimate attribution of moral blameworthiness.

---

[6] This is admittedly an oversimplification of Smith's account, but for my purposes here, the oversimplification is justifiable.

[7] Smith (2005a).

[8] The violation of a moral expectation entails wrongdoing, but wrongdoing does not by itself entail blameworthiness. This much seems to me to be common ground. For a contrary view, see Norman O. Dahl (1967).

7.3 Volitionalism

In this section, I will briefly explain an approach that certain will-centered accounts of moral responsibility tend to adopt in order to explain how phenomena like unintentional omissions can be reflective of ill will or disregard, despite the fact that no particular mental act involving a choice, decision, or intention appears to be essential to their obtaining. My concern is with volitionalist approaches to moral responsibility, which insist that a condition of moral blameworthiness for some action, omission, or attitude, is that it stem from a conscious mental act called a "volition". Michael J. Zimmerman, a prominent defender of volitionalism, characterizes the notion of a volition as "a decision or choice ... that some event occur, a decision which is accompanied by an intention that it (the decision) be causally efficacious with respect to the event in question."[9] Other notable defenders of volitionalism include Neil Levy and R. Jay Wallace. Levy provides a wonderfully concise articulation of the volitionalist's basic theoretical commitment when he says that "an agent is [morally] responsible for something (an act, omission, attitude, and so on) just in case that agent has – directly or indirectly – chosen that thing".[10] Wallace stresses the fundamental role choice plays in grounding an agent's blameworthiness when he claims that "the primary target of moral assessment ... is the quality of choice expressed in what we do ... Indeed, the degree of our moral fault is determined essentially by the quality of the choices on which we act, regardless of whether we succeed in achieving the ends fixed by these volitional states."[11]

It is reasonable to regard the volitionalist as fundamentally committed to two basic claims about the conditions of moral responsibility and blameworthiness. First, the mental activity involved in intentional choice is the kind of agency that opens one up to moral appraisal in the way required to ground attributions of moral responsibility in its most basic sense.[12] Second, an agent's blameworthiness fundamentally concerns the quality of his will as it is reflected in volitional states (I shall henceforth just use the term "choice" to refer to such states). Choices are what agents are principally morally responsible for. Whether an agent is morally blameworthy, then, depends upon whether the quality of the agent's will reflected in a choice is defective from the moral point of view.[13]

---

[9] Zimmerman (1988).

[10] Levy (2005:2, emphasis in original).

[11] Wallace (1994:128).

[12] Here, I assume that it is uncontroversial that volitionalists must recognize constraints imposed by basic conditions of "moral attributability"; these are conditions that must be satisfied in order for an agent to be morally responsible for some action, omission, attitude, etc. in the first place. Of course, satisfaction of these conditions is not by itself sufficient for moral blameworthiness.

[13] Wallace (op. cit.:132) seems to think that intentionally violating a moral obligation others accept is what constitutes showing ill will or disregard. For Zimmerman, the crucial element of a choice that makes it one for which the agent is culpable, and hence blameworthy, is an occurrent belief that the choice is itself morally wrong. See Zimmerman (op. cit.: 40).

Given this account of the conditions of moral responsibility and blameworthiness, how might a volitionalist explain intuitions that the agents in my example cases are morally blameworthy for their unintentional omissions? Consider Abby's case. The volitionalist picture implies that Abby is morally responsible for unintentionally omitting to assist the swimmer only if her inaction is reflective of some choice she has made, for such a choice is the kind of mental act necessary to make her inaction attributable to her as a basis for further moral appraisal. Likewise, this picture suggests that she is morally blameworthy only if a defective quality of her will (from now on, I will simply take "ill will" or "disregard" to stand for "defective quality of will") is reflected in this choice.[14] So far, the volitionalist picture cannot provide the requisite explanation since, as I have already pointed out, it is clear that no mental act that could possibly be called a choice occurs while Abby dozes and the swimmer struggles for help.

Both Wallace and Zimmerman give a generally clear explanation of how volitionalism should attempt to accommodate cases like Abby's, albeit their explanations differ in certain respects. Their common strategy, however, is to attempt to trace Abby's blameworthiness to some prior episode of choice.[15] The idea is that Abby is blameworthy only if her unintentional omission is either an explicitly foreseen or reasonably foreseeable consequence of some prior choice that reflected ill will or disregard.[16] Because an unintentional omission inherently does not involve any kind of positive mental agency that could possibly be called a choice, and because an agent's blameworthiness is fixed entirely by the quality of her will as it is reflected in her choices, the volitionalist picture implies that the moral significance of Abby's unintentional omission, then, consists entirely in what it reveals about the quality of her will as it was reflected in some prior choice. In other words, Abby's blameworthiness in this case is essentially indirect: the intuition that she is blameworthy on the basis of her unintentional omission must be fully cashed out in a judgment that

---

[14] I take it that the notion of a choice reflecting a particular quality of will is commonly recognized. As I will elaborate in Section 7.5, choices necessarily implicate an agent's evaluations of reasons and other intentional mental states, and the quality of an agent's will seems to be constituted by the quality of just these evaluative mental states.

[15] See Wallace (op. cit.:138–39), and Zimmerman (op. cit.:93). Wallace claims that in cases involving negligence or forgetfulness – e.g., cases like Abby's – "one may have to trace the moral fault to an earlier episode of choice." A concise statement of Zimmerman's alignment with the tracing strategy can be found in his claim that a question of responsibility and blameworthiness "for an omission arises *only* where there is an initial volition of which the omission in question is itself a consequence."

[16] One question that faces the volitionalist, then, concerns just *which* choice it is reasonable to think an agent's moral responsibility and blameworthiness for an unintentional omission are traceable *to*. Volitionalists face a further question of how rigidly to construe the kind of cognitive connection between a choice and a consequence in order for consequence to be a basis for legitimate blame. Wallace (p. 138) seems to understand this cognitive connection as involving the consequence's *reasonable foreseeability* from the agent's perspective at the time of prior choice, while Zimmerman opts for *explicit foresight*. For a fascinating discussion of the problems that the foreseeability constraint poses for the tracing strategy, see Vargas (2005) and a reply by Fischer and Tognazzini (2009).

her unintentional omission is (minimally) a reasonably foreseeable consequence of some prior blameworthy choice.

Of course, it is possible that no prior choice occurred to which Abby's intuitive blameworthiness can suitably be traced. If this is so, then volitionalists face a further question of how to respond. It is of course open to the volitionalist to claim that an intuition that a judgment of blameworthiness is appropriate in Abby's case is flatly unjustifiable if the attempt to trace her blameworthiness to a prior choice fails. In the next section, I will motivate what I take to be a strong case for thinking that this claim ought to be resisted. Indeed, this claim would warrant our acceptance only if no compelling alternative explanation of how an unintentional omission can reflect ill will or disregard is available.

7.4 Problems with the Volitionalist's Use of the Tracing Strategy

In this section, I will attempt to motivate strong skepticism about the volitionalist's capacity to provide a compelling explanation of moral blameworthiness in at least some important cases of intuitively blameworthy unintentional omission by illustrating certain troubling implications that flow from the way volitionalists use the tracing strategy. Some of these concerns are by no means novel, but I will hereby give them novel expression. I will not argue that the notion of tracing is itself philosophically problematic. The following remarks are intended to highlight only what I take to be unsettling about certain implications of the volitionalist picture insofar as it tends to suggest that a very natural conception of the role certain unintentional omissions play in grounding moral criticism is substantially misguided.

Here are the claims I hope to motivate in this section: (1) even when an unintentional omission is not plausibly seen as a result of a prior blameworthy choice, this does not by itself seem to make a judgment of blameworthiness inappropriate and in some cases may even make such a judgment appear more appropriate; (2) the volitionalist's use of the tracing strategy sometimes entails, rather paradoxically, that we should have the least confidence in judgments of blameworthiness in what otherwise appear to be some of the most intuitively obvious cases of blameworthy negligence and forgetfulness involving unintentional omission; (3) the volitionalist's use of the tracing strategy substantially distorts our common sense picture of the kinds of response that blameworthy unintentional omissions intuitively make appropriate; and (4) the volitionalist picture entails that moral criticism of an agent on the basis of unintentional omission alone is always unjustifiable, such that episodes of unintentional omission can never in themselves make a difference to the kind or degree of moral criticism of an agent that is legitimate.

I'll begin by noting one respect in which the volitionalist picture implies a very strong result. It is one thing to say that, for a significant range of cases of intuitively blameworthy unintentional omissions involving neglect, disregard, or forgetfulness, judgments of blameworthiness are justified entirely in virtue of the fact that these unintentional omissions are indicative of a prior blameworthy choice. It is quite another to say that this is so for every unintentional omission that appears blameworthy. Returning to our examples, what exactly must we suppose Mikael previously chose to do? Did he notice the date of the anniversary approaching yet nonetheless choose not to set a reminder? Did Per think, at the moment he agreed to meet with the student, about writing the special appointment down in his day planner but then choose not to do so? Did Abby really notice that she was getting drowsy, and then choose not to go get a cup of coffee? Whatever plausibility each of these stories has, it may be at least as plausible to suppose that no such prior choices in fact occurred. For the distinct possibility remains that at these putative prior moments of choice none of these agents realized that he or she was in a situation in which such choices were available.

This possibility leads to the motivation behind claim (1). One problem for the volitionalist enters when it turns out that an unintentional omission appears to be traceable to just such a failure of awareness rather than to some choice. If such a cognitive failure causally explains an unintentional omission, then a judgment that the agent has exhibited a degree of morally criticizable ill will or disregard is rather obviously not automatically rendered inappropriate. Instead, this prior cognitive failure might only provide additional grounds for judging that ill will or disregard has been shown. This can be so if the prior cognitive failure in question can be seen not merely as a descriptive failure, but as a normative failure that implies the violation of further moral expectations that these agents be attentive to the presence of circumstances in which they may need to take action to avert future wrongdoing.[17] Such episodes of inattentiveness may themselves constitute grounds for judging that ill will or disregard has been shown, and may be what explains a subsequent unintentional omission instead of a choice. Unless the volitionalist is willing, at this point, to very implausibly assert that the mere failure of an initial attempt to trace blameworthiness to a prior choice implies that a judgment of blameworthiness is inappropriate, he will need to engage in still further tracing.

Of course, there is nothing that guarantees that the volitionalist will be successful in this further tracing. Suppose that what explains Abby's falling asleep is not some prior choice she made to avoid taking precautions against dozing, but is instead her failure to be attentive to her situation in a way that would have inclined her to realize that she needs to take action to ensure she can discharge her duties. Now, the volitionalist could attempt to insist that Abby must have made some still prior blameworthy choice that resulted in her subsequent cognitive failure. But it is unclear both what kind of choice this could be, short of a choice to ingest some cognitively disabling substance, and why we should suppose that this is the only way to justify a judgment that she has shown ill will or disregard.

Or suppose that Per's forgetting the special office hours appointment is due to his prior failure to realize that he may need to take steps in order to ensure he remembers. Perhaps the volitionalist will have to claim that Per made some prior

---

[17] For a discussion of the kinds of normative requirements that can make such expectations reasonable, see Goodin (1986).

blameworthy choice that caused this cognitive failure, which in turn caused him to forget the appointment. As I have been trying to stress, it may very well be that no such choices actually took place, or worse, that all we find instead of such choices are still further intuitively blameworthy unintentional omissions to act in a way that would or might prevent a subsequent chain of negligence or forgetfulness. But what is crucial to note is that the mere fact that no such prior choices took place does not, by itself, seem to automatically imply that a judgment of blameworthiness is inappropriate. All this fact seems to imply, to my mind, is that the propriety of this judgment doesn't depend upon anything these agents have done or any of the choices they have made.

This leads to the motivation behind claim (2). There is nothing incoherent in the idea that an unintentional omission for which an agent is intuitively blameworthy might be explainable in terms of prior cognitive failures for which she is also intuitively blameworthy.[18] I have tried to suggest that it is at least as plausible to think that each of my example agent's unintentional omissions resulted from prior blameworthy cognitive failures as it is to think that they resulted from blameworthy choices that more proximally preceded them. The more intuitively blameworthy cognitive failures lie behind the unintentional omission, the more intuitively compelling a judgment of blameworthiness will appear to be, especially if this sequence of cognitive failures leading up to the unintentional omission involves several intuitive showings of ill will or disregard instead of just one. Yet, at the same time, the further this sequence stretches back in the agent's history, the more ad hoc it will be for the volitionalist who genuinely wants to explain the intuition of blameworthiness to insist that what ultimately sets this sequence of deep negligence or forgetfulness in motion is some choice that reflects enough ill will or disregard to which all the agent's intuitive blameworthiness can ultimately be traced.[19]

Now this produces what I think is a very puzzling result. I've suggested that an unintentional omission that stems from several prior blameworthy cognitive failures may in some cases only appear to increase our confidence that moral criticism is appropriate, insofar as this would indicate that the agent has routinely exhibited a deep and pervasive kind of blameworthy negligence or forgetfulness.[20] Yet it is just

[18] Indeed, this kind of case seems analogous to the kind of case that forms the subject matter of Steven Sverdlik's excellent discussion of what he calls "Pure Negligence". He claims that "there do seem to be cases of negligence where there is no deliberate prior abstaining from getting knowledge or a deliberate prior refraining from stopping a loss of knowledge. All that there is, in some cases, is an unwitting violation of a norm, preceded by an indefinitely long period in which it never occurs to the person to consider the relevant risks". See Sverdlik (1993:140–41).

[19] Interestingly, even if such a prior choice can be found, the more distant it is in the agent's history, the harder it will be for this choice to satisfy the foreseeability constraint on the tracing strategy (see note 16). Indeed, for an approach like Zimmerman's that requires explicit conscious foresight of all the consequences of a volition that can be legitimate grounds for moral appraisal of an agent, this constraint may be even less often satisfied.

[20] Indeed, it seems that something like just this kind of explanation applies in cases of persons who, for want of adequate moral reflection, become habitual unintentional wrongdoers who exhibit deep patterns of insensitivity to moral considerations.

this kind of case that forces a difficult choice upon the volitionalist. For he may either (very implausibly) flatly deny that the agent is blameworthy, or else bank on the rather incredible claim that the agent's degree of blameworthiness must be fixed entirely by the quality of her will reflected in some prior choice that supposedly set this chain of deep negligence in motion.[21] Opting for the latter would force the volitionalist to presuppose both that this prior choice reflected monumental ill will or disregard, and that the agent possessed incredible powers of foresight at this prior time of choice in order for any plausible version of the foreseeability constraint on the tracing strategy to be satisfied.[22] Here we see a striking implication of the volitionalist's claim that nothing but a volitional state can reflect an agent's quality of will in the way requisite to ground blameworthiness. For it could turn out that, paradoxically, some of our most intuitively compelling judgments of blameworthiness involving deep negligence or forgetfulness have the least stable theoretical backing on the volitionalist account. Such a result would pull at our intuitions in puzzling ways, for it wouldn't seem acceptable, given certain reasonable assumptions about the very blameworthy quality of will an agent's deep negligence or pervasive forgetfulness would reflect, to stake our confidence in a judgment of blameworthiness in the occurrence of some distant, and supposedly very blameworthy prior choice. But we might also feel at a loss to explain how anything besides a choice could reflect an agent's quality of will, thereby feeling pulled by the thought that our intuition that a judgment of blameworthiness is appropriate indicates that there must have been some prior choice to which all her blameworthiness can be traced.

Now I will attempt to motivate claim (3). This claim states that the volitionalist's use of the tracing strategy produces a substantial distortion of a very natural conception of the content of the kind of responses that blameworthy unintentional omissions seem to make appropriate. This distortion occurs because the volitionalist's use of the tracing strategy directs our attention away from what appears to be the object of principal moral concern in a case of blameworthy unintentional omission, and that consequently seems to be what the agent is open to criticism for. Intuitively, it is Mikael's forgetting the anniversary, Per's forgetting the special appointment, and Abby's failing to assist the swimmer that lead us to judge that each has shown ill will or disregard. This intuition is reinforced by considering the kinds of response that are made uniquely appropriate in virtue of just these episodes of forgetting or neglect. Mikael, Per, and Abby could understandably feel that these episodes by themselves make appropriate such responses as guilt, remorse, and overt

[21] It may seem unfair to suggest that the volitionalist must ground an agent's blameworthiness for a chain of deep negligence or forgetfulness in a single prior choice the agent made. Why couldn't the volitionalist insist that this chain is the result of more than one prior choice? My concern is not with such cases. Rather, my concern is with cases in which a chain of deep negligence or forgetfulness doesn't appear to be owing to *any* prior choices the agent has made. In such cases, I am not claiming that the chain of deep negligence is owing either to one ultimate choice or no choice at all.

[22] See notes 16 and 19 above.

attempts to demonstrate to those whose importance seems to be called into question that the offense, while granting that it was blameworthy, did not stem from any explicit choice to disregard them.[23]

But the volitionalist account suggests that such responses might substantially fail to address the proper object of moral concern in these cases. Instead, these kinds of response, if they were more clear-headed, would directly address not what wasn't chosen, but what was chosen. An adequate attempt at reconciliation on Mikael's behalf might even involve nothing more than expressing his remorse for whatever aspect of his putative prior choice was faulty, for this choice is after all, the volitionalist tells us, the principal object of moral concern in his case. It might actually be misguided for Mikael, Per, or Abby to think that there is any unique way that their respective unintentional omissions make guilt appropriate, or that an adequate attempt at reconciliation should involve acknowledgement that the relevant episode of forgetting or neglect was in and of itself morally problematic. These unintentional omissions need to be acknowledged only inasmuch as recognition of them serves as a path to acknowledgement that a prior choice expressed ill will or disregard, and if the latter acknowledgement occurs without the former, then it seems as though the volitionalist could in principle admit that nothing of moral significance is lost in an attempt at reconciliation. But this seems to be a rather blatant distortion of what we would normally take the principal objects of moral concern in such cases to be, insofar as we tend to think that what needs to be acknowledged when offering an apology or attempting reconciliation is the unintentional omission itself and what it seems to indicate about a wrongdoer's relations to others.

It also seems that appropriate blaming responses on behalf of those who were forgotten or neglected would principally concern the unintentional omission itself and what it seems to reveal about the wrongdoer's relationship to the one who has been forgotten or neglected. Mikael's forgetting would surely seem to make it appropriate for his wife to ask "How on earth could you have forgotten about our special day?!" Similarly, the struggling student might wonder how Per could have been so neglectful, given how much she was depending upon him for his assistance. But the volitionalist picture directs attention away from these episodes of forgetting and neglect, implying that their moral significance in these cases is wholly parasitic on the moral significance of some prior choice these wrongdoers have supposedly made. In all cases, then, the crucial question seems to be one that asks of an unintentional omitter, "How could you possibly have made that choice?!"

Finally, I need to motivate claim (4), which concerns the volitionalist implication that unintentional omissions can never, by themselves, constitute substantive

[23] While this may sound like an attempt at excuse, and so to *affirm* the idea that blameworthiness for the unintentional omission must be traceable from a prior choice, this appearance should be resisted. In such a case, we can imagine that each agent would find it important to point out that the disregard was not explicitly chosen. But this would not entail that each agent would be insinuating that no disregard was *shown*.

bases for moral criticism of an agent. Because an agent's blameworthiness for an unintentional omission is fixed entirely by the ill will or disregard reflected in a prior choice she made, the volitionalist must say that any additional substantive moral criticism of an agent on the basis of an unintentional omission amounts to an acceptance of moral outcome luck. This is because, as we have already seen Wallace claim, the only legitimate targets of moral assessment are qualities of will reflected in choices, and these qualities of will are what they are whether or not any particular unintentional omissions flow from these choices. It follows straightforwardly that, on the volitionalist account, there is never anything intrinsically significant about unintentional omission, from a moral point of view. Unintentional omissions are not grounds for moral criticism of agents over and above any moral criticism that applies to them in virtue of their choices. Assuming that Abby is in fact blameworthy for some choice she made prior to falling asleep, what justification could the volitionalist provide for denying that Abby would be just as blameworthy if the same choice obtained but she never fell asleep? What could possibly be the basis for insisting that Mikael is open to a milder degree of criticism if, after criticizably choosing not to take the necessary steps to ensure he would remember the anniversary, he nonetheless remembers?

At this point, I imagine that many will experience the standard conflicting intuitions typical of consideration of cases of moral outcome luck. Intuitively, it seems that Mikael would be more blameworthy if he both chose not to take precautions to remember his anniversary and forgot, than he would be if he made the same choice but nevertheless remembered. Similarly, a lifeguard who both chooses to brush aside her drowsiness and then falls asleep on the job is seemingly open to a more serious degree of moral criticism than one who chooses similarly, but never falls asleep. Of course, everything depends upon how these cases are described. If falling asleep on the job is an event that reflects additional ill will or disregard over and above whatever ill will or disregard was reflected in Abby's putative prior choice, then she will actually be more blameworthy than she would be if she'd chosen identically, but stayed awake. The challenge here consists in explaining how her dozing could reflect additional ill will or disregard without this being reflected in a choice. If we bring back into focus the volitionalist's claim that only a choice can reflect an agent's quality of will, then such an explanation might be thought to be impossible.

The worries I have tried to motivate in this section are aimed at highlighting some of the distorting implications of the way the volitionalist uses the tracing strategy to explain how certain unintentional omissions can ground legitimate judgments of blameworthiness. By no means have I tried to show, on the basis of the foregoing remarks, that volitionalism essentially fails to specify plausible conditions of blameworthiness. But I do hope that it is now relatively clear that taking volitionalism seriously could require a substantial revision to what I believe is our common sense picture of the way certain unintentional omissions ground judgments of blameworthiness. Next, I will try to cast doubt on the legitimacy of regarding choice as a basic precondition of blameworthiness, in hopes of showing why it is reasonable to think that volitionalism fares no better than rival non-will-centered accounts of moral responsibility, from a theoretical point of view.

7.5 Choosing Between Volitionalism and Non-will-centered Approaches

In this section, my principal aim is to expose a puzzling assumption that the volitionalist appears to adopt and that, if rejected, opens the door for solutions to the worries I motivated in the previous section. In order to accomplish this aim, I must first explain what I think is the most compelling rationale for the volitionalist to use the tracing strategy as he does. I believe that the volitionalist is motivated to use the tracing strategy as he does in order to reconcile his theoretical account of the conditions of blameworthiness with a common and conflicting conviction that ill will or disregard may be directly reflected not only in the choices an agent makes and the actions she performs, but also in some of the choices she doesn't make and some of the actions she doesn't perform. Let me explain why I think this conviction is one that is commonly accepted.

We should begin by noting that nothing in the volitionalist's account of the conditions of blameworthiness precludes his ability to agree that Abby's failure to assist the swimmer is explainable in terms of at least some of her evaluative mental states without its necessarily being a causal consequence of any prior choices she has made. We would quite naturally expect a lifeguard who sincerely believed (however implicitly) that the safety of the swimmers in her care is of utmost moral importance to be motivated by this belief to see to it that she is able to care for them when they need her most. Perhaps the fact that Abby doesn't see to this, then, provides direct evidence of certain evaluative beliefs and attitudes (henceforth, "EM-states") she holds (however implicitly) about the swimmers' safety. If we came to discover that Abby didn't believe their safety was very important, this could plausibly be taken to directly explain her susceptibility toward failing to care for the swimmers as she should.

So, it is at least possible that the fact that Abby does not monitor her situation more attentively indicates that she holds (however implicitly) at least some objectionable EM-states about the importance of the swimmers' safety, which, to my mind, suggests a relatively natural explanation of her inaction in terms of just these objectionable EM-states. It is important to note that the adequacy of this explanation does not depend upon whether any particular underlying EM-states are explanatorily relevant to her unintentional omission; rather, what matters is just that her inaction is capable of being explained in terms of some or other of her EM-states. There are two noteworthy features of this explanation: first, its compatibility with the volitionalist account of the conditions of moral blameworthiness, and second, its illustration of how the fact that an agent does not make certain choices, or does not do certain things, can be directly explainable in terms of certain of her underlying EM-states.

That we often take certain inactions to be directly explainable in terms of some of an agent's underlying EM-states is supported by noting how frequently such explanations are operative in some of our ordinary explanations. If you always fail to think to leave a tip on the table when we dine, I would seemingly have prima facie reason to directly infer that you believe there isn't anything worthwhile or important or useful or desirable about tipping.[24] What is less clear, to my mind at any rate, is why I would have any stronger reason to infer that you explicitly chose to do something that has resulted in your routinely not thinking about whether you should leave a tip.[25] If I keep promising to bring that DVD you asked to borrow, but repeatedly forget to do so, then you could very reasonably take my forgetting as direct evidence of my belief that it isn't terribly important that I make good on my commitment. It isn't obvious why you would have any more compelling reason to think that my repeated forgetting in this circumstance provides direct evidence of any choices I have made.[26] I am not claiming that these particular EM-states are the only ones that can properly explain the relevant inactions. All I mean to point out is that there are at least some circumstances in which we very naturally think that an inaction can be directly explained in terms of certain EM-states themselves, and in which we generally do not think we have any stronger reason to explain such inactions in terms of any choices that an agent has made.

Now, back to Abby's case. Because the volitionalist is antecedently committed to the claim that only choices can reflect ill will and disregard in the way necessary to justify judgments of blameworthiness, he faces considerable pressure to attempt to locate all the relevant mental states that seem to constitute Abby's ill will or disregard and that intuitively explain her unintentional omission in some prior episode of choice. But, even if we assumed that Abby made some such choice, what would make this choice reflective of ill will or disregard is not the fact that it is merely some volitional state called a "choice", but is rather the fact that the evaluative beliefs and attitudes that formed the basis for this choice are morally objectionable. Indeed, to what extent could a choice be said to reflect ill will or disregard if it didn't provide some indication of the precise content and moral quality of the underlying EM-states that constitute its basis? Choices seem to be capable of reflecting ill will or disregard only because they necessarily implicate certain EM-states that, in turn, may be taken by others to be morally objectionable. We have reason to attach moral

[24] Consider a friend who is visiting from a country in which there is no established social practice of tipping. The fact that it does not occur to him to leave a gratuity when paying the check seems to be explainable in virtue of the fact that tipping is not an activity that he sees any reason to regard as important. My frustrated attempts to explain to him how important it is that it *does* occur to him to tip can be seen as my trying to convince him to believe that tipping is important, at least while he is a visitor in my country. What is *objectionable* in this scenario is not some prior choice he has made to ignore the social customs of my culture, but some underlying evaluative belief that directly explains his failure to think to leave a tip.

[25] I am not claiming that your failure to think to leave a tip is *only* explainable in virtue of the presence of these underlying beliefs and attitudes. I am only claiming that such an explanation is possible, and that there may be no reason to think that this kind of failure is explainable only in virtue of some prior choice you have made.

[26] But what about circumstances in which the forgetting is just a kind of "mental hiccup", and doesn't appear to be explainable in virtue of any of the agent's evaluative beliefs and attitudes? I am not saying that these circumstances are impossible. The fact that sometimes an episode of forgetting is explainable in terms of such mental hiccups does not jeopardize my claim that in some cases it might be appropriate to see an episode of forgetting as explainable in terms of an agent's evaluative beliefs and attitudes.

significance to just these underlying EM-states themselves, insofar as they concern our conceptions of ourselves in the world, who and what we value, and what we consider worth doing. Our choices are morally significant, then, just because they necessarily implicate certain of our EM-states. By contrast, it seems strange to say that we have reason to attach moral significance to choices simply because they are moments during which one's mental condition is in some volitional state.

If I am right so far, then we should accept the claim that a choice is reflective of ill will or disregard to the extent that the EM-states that form the basis for this choice are morally objectionable. One way to interpret the motivation behind volitionalism is that the principal target of moral appraisal is not merely a choice insofar as it is a choice, but the moral quality of the EM-states that form the basis for that choice.[27] For it is just these mental states that are capable of being evaluated as acceptable or objectionable from a moral point of view. This seems, to my mind, to be a compelling way to understand what is morally significant about an agent's quality of will, whereby what is centrally at issue in questions of this sort is the moral quality of the particular evaluative beliefs and attitudes that form the basis for the choices an agent makes.

But if we accept that quality of will concerns just the moral quality of these EM-states, then we should wonder why their failure to form the basis for an actual choice entails that they cannot justify a judgment that ill will or disregard has been shown if they are both objectionable and explanatorily relevant to an unintentional omission. At best, the fact that some of an agent's morally objectionable EM-states are reflected in a particular choice provides an explanation of how this particular choice can reflect ill will or disregard. The volitionalist can agree with this; as I have already noted, nothing in his account of the conditions of moral blameworthiness precludes his agreement that certain unintentional omissions are directly explainable in terms of an agent's morally objectionable EM-states. And if, as I have suggested, quality of will concerns just the moral quality of these EM-states, why should we think that these mental states cannot justify a judgment that ill will or disregard has been shown in cases where they are both objectionable and directly explanatorily relevant to her unintentional omission?

One possibility is that the volitionalist thinks that judgments of blameworthiness fundamentally concern an agent's choices because he assumes that an agent's EM-states can reflect ill will or disregard only insofar as they form the basis for some explicit choice she has made.[28] But, before we accept the volitionalist's claim to be

---

[27] Some might object that what is of interest is how the agent deliberates over these evaluative mental states, and how she selects which will be effective in moving her to action and which ones will not. I think this is a very implausible objection, insofar as it seems to present a picture of the agent as something that is capable of standing over and above all her evaluative mental states and distancing herself from them so significantly so as to be constituted purely by her rational will. This is why I do not think it is plausible for a volitionalist to maintain that it is the *fact* that a choice is a choice – a moment of pure self-determination – that is morally significant.

[28] One motivation behind this assumption is that these mental states cannot be identified as "the agent's own" except when they are somehow endorsed or are a basis for the agent's explicit identification with a certain evaluative perspective insofar as she chooses that they be effective in moving

offering the correct account of the conditions of moral blameworthiness, we can reasonably ask for an explicit defense of this assumption. For it is just this assumption that, I think, makes it very difficult for the volitionalist to explain how agents can be open to moral criticism on the basis of unintentional omissions that do not stem from any explicit choices they have made. If this assumption is rejected, then such explanations are much easier to provide, since they will not require one to advocate the kind of indirection and *ad hoc* stipulations associated with the volitionalist's use of the tracing strategy.

Let me provide a brief comment why one might think this assumption worthy of rejection. What seems fundamental for moral blameworthiness, I claim, is just the moral quality of the EM-states that are explanatorily relevant to an agent's conduct, and not the fact (if it is a fact) that these states happened to be implicated in any explicit choice. For whether these states happen to figure into a choice does not seem to change whether their content and moral quality can provide a reasonable basis for objections. Moreover, blaming responses (guilt, resentment, indignation, requests for apology and justification) seem to be responses to further judgments that the particular content and moral quality of an evaluative belief or attitude reflected in one's conduct is objectionable, and not responses to some further perception or belief that an objectionable EM-state is or was ever implicated in a choice. If I am right, then there is no reason to engage in the kind of tracing that the volitionalist endorses in order to explain an agent's blameworthiness for an unintentional omission. For what is important is not whether the unintentional omission can be traced to some prior episode of choice that reflects ill will or disregard, but instead whether the unintentional omission is explainable in terms of certain of an agent's EM-states whose precise content and moral quality would, if implicated in a choice, both entail that the choice reflects ill will or disregard and make various blaming responses appropriate. After all, this seems to be what the volitionalist is ultimately seeking, insofar as he recognizes that moral appraisal concerns the moral quality of just these EM-states. So, armed with this reason, we can reasonably ask the volitionalist to provide an explicit defense of the assumption that these EM-states must form the basis for an explicit choice in order for them to be capable of reflecting ill will or disregard.

P.F. Strawson pointed out that, as parties to interpersonal relationships of many kinds, it matters greatly what our intimates (and even what other strangers) believe to be worthwhile or significant.[29] But it is far from clear that these evaluative beliefs and attitudes matter to us only when they form the basis for a choice. If Mikael (however implicitly) doesn't place the same degree of evaluative significance upon celebrating important relationship milestones as his wife does, his evaluative attitude can, due to its content, be taken by her as a reasonable basis for objections within the context of their relationship, however mild in tone these objections may be. Per's

---

her to action. I will not consider this motivation here since there is much controversy surrounding it, and in any event this motivation is more reasonably seen as a *statement*, rather than as a *defense* of the volitionalist position. For further discussion, see Wallace (2002), Smith (2004), and Hieronymi (2008).

[29] Strawson (1962).

student would seem to have satisfactory grounds for (at least some) resentment if the student came to learn that Per didn't really care about the student's success, and this would be true no matter the particular choices Per has made. We might even feel slightly indignant if we learned that (perhaps only out of boredom and frustration with her job) Abby would rather catch a quick nap than safeguard the swimmers on the beach, and this feeling would be legitimate even if she generally manages to do a fine job staying alert and watching over them.[30] All of this suggests, to my mind at least, that an agent's quality of will is intimately associated with the precise content and moral quality of the EM-states that either potentially or actually form the basis for her actual choices. Here, my aim has been to illustrate how mere knowledge of another's EM-states, particularly those EM-states that concern oneself, can constitute grounds for legitimate (if only mild) objections within the context of an interpersonal relationship, but could also very appropriately give rise to feelings of guilt on behalf of those who recognize that they harbor such objectionable EM-states.[31] This is, I take it, further evidence that an agent's quality of will is a function of the precise content and moral quality of her EM-states, and that it is unclear why these EM-states must figure into any of an agent's explicit choices in order to ground attributions of blameworthiness.

Recent attempts to develop non-will-centered approaches to moral responsibility have elaborated how certain of an agent's EM-states can reflect ill will or disregard even when these states do not form the basis of any choices she has made. The way such explanations proceed is the subject of much attention in the current debate over the conditions of moral responsibility.[32] While I am confident that many of these explanations can be shown to be defensible, my aim in this paper has been, in part, to point out that one way of framing the debate between will-centered approaches to moral responsibility like volitionalism, and its rival non-will-centered approaches is as a debate over whether there is a defensible theoretical rationale for assuming, as the volitionalist does, that all moral blameworthiness for unintentional omission must be traceable to an agent's quality of will as it was reflected in some choice. If this assumption is indefensible, then we will have further reason to think it unclear why we should prefer volitionalism over non-will-centered approaches. Moreover, given the way the volitionalist's use of the tracing strategy tends to distort what may be regarded as a very commonsense picture of the moral significance of unintentional omission, it seems that a non-will-centered approach could more easily explain the important role EM-states play in grounding moral blameworthiness

[30] That indignation is only slightly felt does not indicate, by itself, that the absence of choice substantially mitigates to the point of near excuse. For it may be an implicit assumption that Abby's holding the underlying objectionable evaluative attitude is compatible with her making strong efforts to satisfy her duty. If this is so, then the overall quality of the reactive sentiment we experience will be conditioned by this further assumption, and the concomitant attitudes of approval this further assumption entails.

[31] Indeed, guilt seems appropriate when one realizes, as a result of one's conduct, that one holds an objectionable evaluative attitude or belief one previously hadn't recognized.

[32] See, for example, Arpaly (2003), Sher (2009), Moya (2007), and Smith (2005b).

without incurring the costs of the volitionalist's requirement that all tracing must culminate in a choice.

7.6 Conclusion

My aim in this paper has been to produce strong skepticism about the volitionalist's ability to provide a satisfactory account of the conditions of moral blameworthiness in cases of unintentional omission. I have tried to motivate a compelling case for rejecting the claim that the moral significance of unintentional omission consists entirely in what it indicates about the moral quality of an agent's prior choices and actions. The moral significance of both action and inaction, I suspect, consists in what each indicates about the precise content and moral quality of the underlying evaluative attitudes and beliefs that are explanatorily relevant to an agent's conduct. For this reason, I suspect that theories that have articulated the conditions of responsible agency primarily in actional terms fall short of offering a compelling theoretical explanation of our practices of moral criticism.

Acknowledgments Thanks to Angela M. Smith, Janice Moskalik, and the participants of the University of Delft Conference on Moral Responsibility, Neuroscience, Organization, and Engineering for helpful comments on both written and presented versions of this paper.

References

Arpaly, Nomy. 2003. *Unprincipled Virtue: An Inquiry into Moral Agency*. Oxford: Oxford University Press.
Dahl, Norman O. 1967. "Ought and Blameworthiness." *The Journal of Philosophy* 64:418–28.
Feinberg, Joel. 1984. *Harm to Others*. Oxford: Oxford University Press.
Fischer, John M., and Neal Tognazzini. 2009. "The Truth About Tracing." *Nous* 43:531–56.
Goodin, Robert. 1986. "Responsibilities." *The Philosophical Quarterly* 36:50–56.
Hieronymi, Pamela. 2004. "The Force and Fairness of Moral Blame." *Philosophical Perspectives* 18:115–48.
Hieronymi, Pamela. 2008. "Controlling Attitudes." *Synthese* 161:357–73.
Levy, Neil. 2005. "The Good, the Bad and the Blameworthy." *Journal of Ethics and Social Philosophy* 1:1–16.
Moya, Carlos J. 2007. "Belief and Moral Responsibility." In *Intentionality, Deliberation, and Autonomy: The Action-Theoretic Basis of Practical Philosophy*, edited by C. Lumer and S. Nannini. Burlington, VT: Ashgate pp. 273–287.
Scanlon, Thomas. 1998. *What We Owe to Each Other*. Cambridge, MA: Belknap Press.
Sher, George. 2009. *Who Knew? Responsibility Without Awareness*. Oxford: Oxford University Press.
Smith, Angela M. 2004. "Conflicting Attitudes, Moral Agency, and Conceptions of the Self." *Philosophical Topics* 32:331–52.
Smith, Angela M. 2005a. "Responsibility for Attitudes: Activity and Passivity in Mental Life." *Ethics* 115:236–71.
Smith, Patricia G. 1990. "Contemplating Failure: The Significance of Unconscious Omission." *Philosophical Studies* 59:159–76.
Smith, Patricia G. 2005b. "Feinberg and the Failure to Act." *Legal Theory* 11:237–50.
Strawson, P.F. 1962. "Freedom and Resentment." *Proceedings of the British Academy* 48:1–25.

Sverdlik, Steven. 1993. “Pure Negligence.” *American Philosophical Quarterly* 30:137–49.
Vargas, Manuel. 2005. “The Trouble with Tracing.” *Midwest Studies in Philosophy* 29:269–91.
Wallace, R. Jay. 1994. *Responsibility and the Moral Sentiments*. Cambridge, MA: Harvard University Press.
Wallace, R. Jay. 2002. “Scanlon’s Contractualism.” *Ethics* 112:429–70.
Watson, Gary. 2004. “Two Faces of Responsibility.” In *Agency and Answerability*, edited by Gary Watson, 260–88. Oxford: Oxford University Press.
Zimmerman, Michael J. 1998. *An Essay on Moral Responsibility*. Totowa, NJ: Rowman & Littlefield.

Chapter 8
Desert, Responsibility and Luck Egalitarianism

Diana Abad

Abstract Desert and responsibility are key concepts in political philosophy, most notably in discussions on justice. It is just that people get what they deserve, and what they deserve seems to have something to do with what they are responsible for. This tenet is as close to a fundamental constant as one can get in practical philosophy, so that even some egalitarians, luck egalitarians, make room for exceptions dictated by it: only differences people are not responsible for should be equalized, differences people are responsible for are not unjust, because they are deserved. In this paper I shall contest the second part of this tenet that what people deserve is somehow linked to what they are responsible for. To this end, I shall give a detailed account of the concept of desert in the first half of this paper. In the second half, I shall consider the implications of this for luck egalitarianism, and conclude that while luck egalitarianians can counter some criticisms that are grounded on a wrong understanding of the concept of desert, they cannot rest content in relying on the purely formal notions of responsibility and desert, but need to provide substantial arguments to support their conclusions.

8.1 Desert and Responsibility

Regarding desert, astonishingly many people think that only persons can deserve something, and only in virtue of actions for which those persons are responsible. This is astonishing, to my mind, as in everyday language all sorts of things are said to be deserving in virtue of all sorts of properties. For example, we do say that criminals deserve punishment, and that good pupils deserve to get good marks, but we also say that the most beautiful contestant deserves first prize at the beauty contest, that great paintings deserve to be admired, and that unique landscapes deserve to be preserved.

In this paper I shall examine the conceptual connection between desert and responsibility, and I shall argue that there is none. That is, I shall argue that those who claim that it is a conceptual truth that only persons can deserve something solely for actions for which they are responsible are mistaken. I have absolutely no

D. Abad (✉)
Department of Philosophy, University of Potsdam, Potsdam, Germany
e-mail: diana.abad@uni-potsdam.de

N.A Vincent et al. (eds.), *Moral Responsibility*, Library of Ethics and Applied Philosophy 27, DOI 10.1007/978-94-007-1878-4_8,

idea whether or not the claim that only responsible action can ground desert is true substantially. Personally, I am inclined to doubt it, but that is neither here nor there, as that is not the question I will pursue in this paper. I shall not argue for the truth or falsehood of any given desert judgment. My aim is just to clear up a conceptual confusion.

Since it is the concept of desert I aim to elucidate, and not the concept of responsibility, I shall have a lot to say about the former and rather little about the latter. I will take a lot for granted as far as responsibility is concerned although I realize that things are far from clear in that regard. Most importantly, I will take for granted that we all know what it is to be responsible for an action. Basically, this is already all I have to say about responsibility.

On to desert then.

8.1.1 Desert: The Basics

The first thing to be said about desert is that it is a normative notion, that is, the fact that somebody deserves something implies that she ought to get it, although not unconditionally, but only *pro tanto*.[1] So, the fact that somebody deserves something is always a reason for giving it to her, although not always a conclusive reason. Something more important could count against it. The best team deserve to get the cup, but if the best team do not actually win, they ought not to get it.

The next thing to be said is that desert is a three-place relation, "x deserves y in virtue of z". Let us call x the desert subject, y the desert object, and z the desert base.[2] There are many desert judgments that do not explicitly state a desert base.

Sometimes, we simply say, for example: "The team deserve the cup." This is elliptical, though. One cannot deserve something for no reason at all, but only in virtue of something, the desert base, as Joel Feinberg has shown in his seminal paper "Justice and personal desert", giving the first and most influential analysis of the concept of desert. Moreover, the desert base must be attributable to the desert subject.[3]

Hence, desert judgments like "The team deserve the cup." need to be understood as abbreviated and as always implying a desert base which needs to be attributable to the desert subject, the team in this case. So, we have to supplement the statement with a desert base, for instance like this: "The team deserve the cup because they have played so well.", because having played well is attributable to the team, whereas we cannot supplement the statement like this: "The team deserve the cup because of water's boiling point.", because water's boiling point is not an attribute of the team's.

Here the trouble begins, because it is not quite clear what is "attributable" to a desert subject. Me, I do not mean to say anything more with this than that the desert

[1] Cf. Feinberg (1963:60).

[2] Cf. McLeod (1999:61–2).

[3] Cf. Feinberg (1963:58ff.).

base has to be an attribute of the desert subject's, be it an action or a property. It just has to be theirs, nothing more, nothing less.[4] However, there are others who think that only actions for which the desert subject is responsible are "attributable" to them in the requisite sense.[5] This also means, of course, that only persons can be desert subjects, because other sorts of things cannot perform such actions.

This is the view I shall contest in this part of the paper. I will call it the responsibility view. Before doing so, however, let me explain why this view is so curiously widespread, even though the concept of desert clearly works differently in everyday language.

8.1.2 Feinberg and Rawls

I think the seed for the responsibility view was already laid in Feinberg's analysis of desert. In it, Feinberg is concerned with a particular sort of desert objects: prizes, grades, rewards and punishment, praise and blame, compensations, in short: he is concerned with certain forms of treatment as desert objects only. And the only desert subjects he is concerned with are persons.[6] He exclusively looks at persons who receive these desert objects of prizes, grades, rewards, etc.

Concentrating as he does on persons as desert subjects suggests that only actions for which the desert subjects are responsible can be desert bases, because if only persons can be desert subjects this must be due to something that is peculiar to persons, something like actions for which they are responsible which no other animal or object can lay a claim on.

This is corroborated by the particular set of desert objects Feinberg considers. Only persons deserve these sorts of things, and only in virtue of actions for which they are responsible. It just would be nonsensical to assign punishment, say, to any other sort of desert subject than persons, and it would be unfair to do so on any other basis than an action for which they are responsible.

After having sprung from this seed, the responsibility view throve and prospered further with the publication of Rawls's *A theory of justice* a few years after Feinberg's paper which enormously influenced the subsequent treatment of the concept of desert in philosophical discussion.[7] Rawls as well considers only actions for which persons are responsible as desert bases. As he says in *A theory of justice*:

> The precept which seems intuitively to come closest to rewarding moral desert is that of distribution according to effort, or perhaps better, conscientious effort.[8]

---

[4] Cf. Cupit (1996:92ff.); Feldman (1995:186–7).

[5] Cf. e.g. Sadurski (1985:117); Rachels (1978:157); Rachels (1986:143); Sher (1987:37ff.); Smilansky (1996).

[6] Feinberg (1963:62,55).

[7] Abad (2007:part 1, chap. II).

[8] Rawls (1971:311).

Evidently, a conscientious effort consists in an action for which a person is responsible.

So, it seems as if Feinberg and Rawls subscribe to the responsibility view, and, influential as their theories have been, as if Feinberg and Rawls really are responsible for the responsibility view being so widespread. I think the latter of these claims is true. I do think that Feinberg's and Rawls's analyses of desert are responsible for many people holding the responsibility view.

The former claim, however, is false. Neither Feinberg nor Rawls really held the responsibility view. It is true that they limit their discussion of desert to cases in which persons deserve something in virtue of actions for which they are responsible, but this is due to the fact that they are concerned with examining the particular connections between desert and justice. Still, this restriction does not mean that other things than persons cannot be desert subjects, nor that other things than responsible actions cannot be desert bases. Neither Feinberg nor Rawls excludes the possibility of a painting's deserving admiration. The thing is just that the question whether or not a painting deserves admiration is not a question pertaining to justice.[9]

8.1.3 Against the Responsibility View

Even so, many philosophers hold the responsibility view. So, what is wrong with it?

What is wrong with it is that it puts the cart before the horse. Instead of examining the concept of desert and then deriving from that which individuals may permissibly replace the variables x, y, and z, they try to derive the concept from the individuals which they already know must be the only permissible ones. This is methodologically unsound, and it begs the question whether those individuals really are conceptually the only permissible ones.

Consider, by way of analogy, the predicate "x is a flightless bird", and consider a zoologist, a newbie on the field of ornithology, who is convinced that penguins are the only flightless birds there are. Now one day our zoologist is confronted with an ostrich. There are two ways of reacting open to our newbie-zoologist: first, he can correct his belief and say that penguins evidently are not the only flightless birds there are; or second, he can flatly refuse to recognize an ostrich as a flightless bird and qualify it as something else instead on the grounds that, obviously, it is not a penguin. Clearly, the first way of reacting is the adequate one. Unfortunately, regarding desert, the proponents of the responsibility view take on the equivalent of the second way.

As Wojciech Sadurski, one of the many champions of the responsibility view, puts it representatively:

[9] Cf. Feinberg (1963:55); Pogge (1989:63ff.); Abad (2007:14, 21–9) for a fuller discussion of this point.

> When we are pronouncing judgments of desert, we are inevitably making judgments about persons whom we hold responsible for their actions. It makes no sense to attribute desert... to persons for actions or facts over which they have no control.[10]

This is rather a curious statement about desert judgments. What exactly does Sadurski mean by saying that in talking about desert we "inevitably" talk about persons responsible for their actions, and that talking about other things in connection with desert "makes no sense"? It is obviously not inevitable in the sense that we cannot but, or do not, talk about desert in any other way, because we do so all the time. Let us say, for example, that a man may deserve something good in virtue of his noble birth, as the Ancient Greeks believed. In what sense does it "make no sense" to say this?

Sadurski leaves it at that and does not elaborate what he means. More is the pity, since it needs elaborating, because clearly, that judgment does not "make no sense" such that we could not possibly understand what it means. We do. We might be inclined to disagree, but we understand it alright. There are several other possibilities, though: Sadurski might mean that it is analytically false to say this, or that there is some kind of Strawsonian truth-value gap, or a category mistake, or quite literally, that this sentence is meaningless.

However, as of yet, we have not been offered a concept of desert such that the very meaning of the word excludes such desert judgments or makes them meaningless, or which implies a truth-value gap or a category mistake in such cases. Hence, to say that the desert judgment that a man deserves something good in virtue of his noble birth is analytically false, or meaningless, or that there is a truth-value gap regarding this judgment, or that there is a category mistake, would be to beg the question in a zoologist-reaction-number-2-kind of way as just described.

The desert judgment in question may very well be false, and moreover, it may very well be that only those desert judgments are true that have persons as desert subjects and actions for which they are responsible as desert bases. My point here is purely conceptual. These desert judgments may be false, but not analytically so, and in no sense are they meaningless. If they are false, they are not so because the concept of desert does not allow for these kinds of desert judgments. It does, as I shall go on to show. If they are false indeed, they must be so because of substantial reasons rather than conceptual ones.[11]

The proponents of the responsibility view might mean something else entirely, though. They might say that only desert judgments about persons and the actions they are responsible for are "real" desert judgments, whereas any other desert judgments are merely metaphorical, or derived, just loose talking, or manners of speech. We understand them well enough, but they are not to be taken seriously since they are not to be taken literally. Alternatively, they might want to distinguish different concepts of desert, say, one that pertains to questions of justice and that deals only with persons and responsible actions, as Feinberg and Rawls have it, and other

---

[10] Sadurski (1985:117, cf. fn. 5 above).

[11] Cf. Lamont (1994) for a similar line of argument.

concepts which may be useful in other contexts, all of them "real" concepts of desert and to be taken seriously.

The trouble with this proposal is that it presents us with a fragmented view of desert. On the face of it, the concept of desert works the same way in any of the many varied contexts in which it may be used, it is only the individuals whose names replace the variables that are vastly heterogeneous. So, an analysis of desert as a single, unified concept which covers all cases would be, on grounds of simplicity, superior to an analysis that chopped desert up into different concepts according to context. After all, an analysis of a concept is supposed to take seriously the different ways the concept is actually used and make sense of them. An analysis which resulted in saying that there is no way to make sense of the different uses, that they have nothing in common even though the same word is used, or an analysis that said that most people use a concept in a metaphorical way only, or indeed one that came to the conclusion that people do not know what they are saying really, would be a poor analysis if there was another one available.

So, it is really three problems the responsibility view has: First, it begs the question regarding whether there can be other desert subjects than persons and other desert bases than actions for which those persons are responsible. Secondly, it has to treat other desert judgments as meaningless, where at worst they are false. Thirdly, it fragments the concept of desert.

8.1.4 The Concept of Desert

So, what is the concept of desert?[12] What does it mean to deserve something? To deserve something means that it is appropriate to get it. And what does this in turn mean, that it is appropriate? Propriety, as I will introduce the term, consists of two components: the one is a relation I shall call fittingness, and the second is a certain normative element I shall call requirement.

Fittingness is a pretty straightforward thing. Puzzle pieces, for example, fit each other. But also states of affairs may be said to fit each other. Another way of putting this would be to say that what is fitting is a "response" to what it is fitting to. Returning the ball is a fitting response to having been served in tennis; having been asked what time it is, it is fitting to tell; going for a walk is fitting to the weather's being good; and so on, and so forth. Obviously, unlike particular cases like puzzle pieces, there may be more than one fitting response to given states of affairs. Hence, instead of going for a walk when the weather is good, it may also be fitting to go for a swim, or to hang out your laundry to dry, or to get inside if you are prone to get sunburnt. What is fitting to what really depends on the particular case and its circumstances.[13] To come back to the responsibility view for a second, though: it should be evident that it is not only actions for which persons are responsible that

---

[12] For a full discussion, cf. Abad (2007).

[13] Cf. Bittner (2001:chap. 4). Some of the examples mentioned are his.

can have fitting counterparts. Puzzle pieces and the weather's being good are cases in point.

In the case of desert, the desert object needs to be fitting to the desert base. This is not all there is to it, though, because as I have pointed out at the beginning, desert is a normative notion. So, the second component I have mentioned needs to come in, the normative element of requirement. Desert is a case of not only fittingness, but of propriety, and by that I mean that it is not only a fittingness relation, but one where the fitting counterpart is required.

Clearly, not everything that is fitting is also required, that is, not everything that is fitting is also appropriate. Two puzzle pieces may be put together, but they just as well may not. They do not require being put together as if that were their natural state they belonged in. Just so, the weather's being good does not require that I take a walk. It would just be a good idea, a fitting thing to do. I may as well not. Nothing goes wrong if I do not. By contrast, something does go wrong if what is appropriate does not occur.

Thus, to deserve something means that it is appropriate to get it, and this in turn means that it is fitting and required that the desert subject get the desert object in virtue of the desert base.

However, this still is not all there is to it, because there are cases of propriety which are not cases of desert. That is to say, there are cases where something is fitting and required, but not deserved. Consider for example a major scale. Anyone who has ever played seven notes of any major scale on any musical instrument will know that the eighth note is not only fitting, but required too. That is so because a major scale's seventh note is a leading note that leads on to the eighth note. If the eighth note does not follow the leading note leads to nothing, and that is just not right. Something goes wrong if a major scale's octave is not completed. This is evidenced by the fact that most listeners can hardly bear to hear it so that they add the eighth note either mentally or by singing it. This unbearableness for listeners is explained by the impropriety of the eighth note missing. Hence, it is not only fitting, but appropriate to add the eighth note after having played the first seven of a major scale. Yet, it is not the case that the first seven notes of a major scale deserve that the eighth be added.

To return again to the responsibility view: as requirement is the only difference between fittingness and propriety, and since not only actions for which people are responsible have fitting counterparts, these are also not the only things that require a fitting counterpart, as this last example of the scales shows.

The question now, though, is: as not all cases of propriety are cases of desert, which ones are? Here it would be very easy for the proponents of the responsibility view to jump in and say: only those cases of propriety are also cases of desert where the subject is a person and the base is an action for which she is responsible. To which I respond, as I have already at length in the last section, that this leaves out too many judgments of desert to be taken seriously as a good analysis of the concept.

Instead, I propose that only those cases of propriety are also cases of desert which are based on something fitting or unfitting, or in other words: desert is that propriety that is appropriate in virtue of something "fittingness-affecting". In still other words, desert is something like "second-order fittingness": deserving something means, utlimately, that it is fitting (and required) to get it because one has done or is something (un-)fitting.

I realize of course that at this point at the latest things are getting just a tiny bit intricate, so let me elucidate this by way of some examples. I will use some of those I have mentioned at the beginning:

1. Criminals deserve punishment in virtue of their crimes. This means that punishing criminals is appropriate, and this in turn means that it is fitting and required to punish criminals. What makes it so? Committing crimes, the desert base, is itself something unfitting; let us say breaking and entering is unfitting to the concept and right of property. And this is what makes it fitting and required, that is appropriate, that they be punished. So, punishing criminals is fitting (and required), because their committing crimes is unfitting. Hence, criminals deserve punishment. If committing crimes was not itself fitting or unfitting to anything, if punishing criminals was only fitting (and required), because of their committing crimes period, their punishment would not be deserved but appropriate. The normative force is the same, the punishment is required in just the same sense both times, it is just that in the first case we can say that it is "deserved" whereas in the second it is "appropriate".
2. The most beautiful contestant deserves first prize in the beauty contest. In this case, being the most beautiful is the desert base, so this is what must be fitting to something. Well, the context is a contest and this contest is about beauty, so presumably, being the most beautiful is fitting to the concepts of contest and beauty. If this is so, this is what makes it appropriate that the most beautiful contestant get first prize, and hence she deserves it. Again, if things are not so, that is, if being most beautiful is not fitting to anythings, it is just appropriate period that the most beautiful contestant get first prize.
3. Great paintings deserve to be admired. What makes great paintings great, let us say, is that they exemplify to an extraordinarily high level what art is about. To be honest, I am making this up, I do not know the first thing about art and what makes paintings great. But remember that I am not concerned with the truth or falsity of this desert judgment, but with what it means. So, whoever says that great paintings deserve to be admired says something like this: their greatness is the paintings' desert base; their greatness is fitting to something, let us say to the idea of what art is about; so this is what makes it appropriate to admire them, and therefore they deserve it.
4. Certain landscapes deserve to be preserved. For instance, the UNESCO talks about Natural Heritage Sites like this. The idea is that these landscapes have particular features that are these landscapes' desert bases, and so that these features are fitting to something. Let us say that, whatever those features are, they are unique, and their uniqueness is fitting to Earth's marvelous variety of landscapes. (I am speculating again.) Hence, it is the fittingness of those

unique features that make it appropriate to preserve those landscapes, and so they deserve preservation.[14]

Obviously, not all propriety relations are based on something fitting or unfitting. The example of the major scale was a case in point. Hence, even though it is appropriate to add the eighth note to the first seven, it is not deserved, as playing seven notes of a major scale is not fitting to anything. But if it were, if there was some obscure story in which we could say that, then we would have to say that the seven notes deserve to have the eighth note added.

8.1.5 Conclusion

To wrap it all up: desert is that propriety that is based on something fitting or unfitting. So, propriety is a subset of fittingness; those fittingness relations are also propriety relations in which the fitting counterpart is not only fitting, but also required. In turn, desert is a subset of propriety; those propriety relations are also desert relations which are based on something fitting or unfitting.

This analysis makes clear that actions for which persons are responsible are not the only things there are that have fitting counterparts, or that require the fitting counterparts as appropriate, or in virtue of which one can deserve something. To think so is wrong for the three reasons I have given: it begs the question, it renders too many desert judgments meaningless, and it fragments the concept of desert.

So, the responsibility view of desert is wrong. We have to understand desert as I have explained, and there is nothing in that account that precludes other things than persons to be desert subjects nor other things than actions for which they are responsible to be desert bases.

8.2 Desert and Luck Egalitarianism

Now that the concept of desert and the role responsibility does, or rather, does not, play in relation to it are clear, it can be used to untangle misunderstandings in discussions in political philosophy in which both the concepts of responsibility and of desert figure crucially. One such discussion is the one on luck egalitarianism. It is outside the scope of this paper to engage in a fully fledged analysis of this debate, examine in detail how any given authors use the concepts of desert and responsibility, show how they go wrong on the basis of the foregoing considerations, and set them on the right track. However, I shall give a very rough and exemplary outline of how applying the correct concept of desert can help further the discussion substantially: I shall discuss two critics of luck egalitarianism, Serena Olsaretti and Nicole

[14] It is because of examples of kinds 3 and 4 that Smilansky's defense of the connection between desert and responsibility fails: paintings and landscapes are not ever "positively responsible" for anything, nor can they ever be "negatively responsible", cf. Smilansky (1996:160).

A Vincent, and show, first, how, with the proper account of desert expounded in this paper, luck egalitarianism can counter their criticisms, but also, secondly, that relying on this account of desert is still not enough to vindicate luck egalitarianism.

Luck egalitarianism, to quote Olsaretti, is the position that holds that those inequalities between people are unjust that are traceable to "circumstances that individuals could not reasonably foresee and avoid. By contrast, individuals are justly held responsible for, that is, they are liable to pick up the costs and reap the benefits of, events they could reasonably foresee and avoid".[15] This position is motivated by a powerful intuition Vincent calls the responsibility-tracking intuition, "i.e. the intuition that people should *take* responsibility for those things for which they *were* responsible, and that no one is entitled to expect others to take this responsibility for them".[16] So, the idea is if you make your own free choices and act accordingly, you have to suffer the consequences for better or worse. Hence, if you recklessly drive your motorcycle at high speed without wearing a helmet and have an accident, or freely gamble away all your savings, it is your own fault and you cannot expect your health insurance to pay your hospital bills and social security or anybody else to help you out.[17]

As common and as powerful as the responsibility-tracking intuition is, it is not quite clear what it means. Vincent argues that there are actually two distinct notions of responsibility at play here, one she calls outcome responsibility which involves attributing a particular state of affairs to a particular person, and one she calls liability responsibility which concerns the question "who should now do what" in consequence of that state of affairs being attributable to that person.[18] So, the responsibility-tracking intuition, precisely understood, should really read like this: you have to take liability responsibility for what you are outcome responsible for.[19]

At this point, two questions arise, and though Vincent and Olsaretti both consider both questions they each specially focus on one of them: first, does liability responsibility really follow from outcome responsibility, and secondly, if so, how do we determine what consequences exactly one is liable for given one's outcome responsibility.

8.2.1 How to Determine the Consequences One Is Liable For

To start with the second question, Olsaretti shows that, even assuming that liability responsibility does follow from outcome responsibility it is not as easy to determine what consequences exactly one is liability responsible for given one's outcome

[15] Olsaretti (2009:165–6).

[16] Vincent (2009:41).

[17] These are the examples Olsaretti discusses in her paper.

[18] Vincent (2009:45).

[19] Cf. Vincent (2009:46).

responsibility as luck egalitarians relying on the responsibility-tracking intuition would have it:[20]

> consider Bert's [the reckless motorcyclist's driving at high speed without a helmet and subsequently injured in an accident] case more closely. On reflection, it appears that these consequences are not so self-evident after all. For example, do these consequences include being left to the side of the road? Even if not, is the strength of the obligation on passers-by an obligation to take him to a hospital conditional on the gravity of Bert's condition and/or on the costs, to them, of taking him to a hospital? Should Bert pay for treatment only of those injuries that resulted from the accident itself, or also for medical conditions that resulted from the unforeseeable effect of the accident on certain hitherto unknown predispositions to illnesses? Or even for any medical treatment he will need henceforth? And at what price should the treatment be charged, so that that price may also be deemed "a consequence of his action"? (May a hospital have a policy of charging imprudent motorcyclists more than others?) Are the consequences of Bert's action also that passers-by may appropriate his motorbike from the side of the road? May he lose his job if, once he has recovered from his accident, his limpness makes him a less attractive employee? May he be denied life insurance henceforth?
>
> The list of questions could go on.[21]

So, the responsibility-tracking intuition by itself does not determine what consequences should follow from outcome responsibility. All sorts of consequences issue from a given outcome, and we need to rule out those that are "unduly harsh towards those who end up in dire straits through their own choices"[22] as well as those that "are of the wrong, because irrelevant, sort".[23] Only if we can do this, Olsaretti maintains, are the inequalities that result from people's choices justified on luck egalitarian terms. Hence, in addition to the responsibility-tracking intuition luck egalitarians need what Olsaretti calls a "principle of stakes" which does just that.

The trouble, though, is, according to Olsaretti, that no account of a principle of stakes works, and that, therefore, luck egalitarianism should be rejected.

I am sure Olsaretti is right about most of the candidates for a principle of stakes she considers and that they do not serve to supplement the responsibility-tracking intuition in the requisite way. However, she also considers and rejects desert as a principle of stakes, and here, naturally, I beg to differ from her. Though she clearly sees that there is an advantage to the desert view, namely a "proportionality constraint" which rules out unduly harsh consequences, this is to "deliver too little ... for too high a price",[24] because desert by itself cannot determine what consequences outcome responsibility might justifiably have. Rather, outside considerations are needed, so that this commits us to a view of responsibility as "[uniquely entailing] one's own favoured account of stakes".[25] In the case of desert as a principle

[20] Olsaretti (2009:167, 169).

[21] Olsaretti (2009:172).

[22] Olsaretti (2009:166).

[23] Olsaretti (2009:183).

[24] Olsaretti (2009:185).

[25] Olsaretti (2009:186).

of stakes, this means that, since, "as even defenders of desert have been willing to grant", what someone deserves "is settled by the institutional context in which desert claims are made, rather than by the notion of desert itself".[26] Hence, adopting desert as luck egalitarianism's principle of stakes would mean understanding responsibility as "entailing" institutions that settle desert and, by extension, responsibility, which is said "too high a price", therefore we should not adopt it, and so luck egalitarianism fails.[27]

There are several problems with this line of argument, though. First of all, here is a defender of desert who is not willing to grant that what someone deserves is in every case settled within an institutional context. Sometimes this is the case, but more often than not, it is not. And even the institutional cases of desert are not intelligible without understanding desert preinstitutionally. So, no, desert is not essentially institutional.[28]

Secondly, as I have explained in the foregoing sections, desert involves far more than "proportionality", by which I take Olsaretti to mean what I call "fittingness". While this is a central component, as should be evident by now, it is not all there is to it. Desert is not only fittingness, but required fittingness, that is propriety. Hence, to adopt desert as the principle of stakes for liability responsibility allows us not only to find out which consequences are fitting that a subject bear for her outcome responsibility, but also requires her bearing them. So, the link between outcome responsibility and liability responsibility provided by desert also comes with the requisite normative force. Hence, adopting desert as the principle of stakes does not provide "too little", but just the thing required to serve luck egalitarianism's purposes.

Finally, Olsaretti has a problem with desert as a principle of stakes, because she mistakenly believes that what someone deserves is settled by institutions "rather than by the notion of desert itself", which leads her to conclude that one needs to understand responsibility as entailing institutions. Presumably, if what someone deserved was settled by "the notion of desert itself" the problem would not arise. However, as should be clear from the preceding discussion of desert, "the notion of desert itself" is a formally normative relation that by itself does not determine anything. What desert object a desert subject deserves is in every case, institutional or not, settled by the desert base and nothing else. To say that the subject deserves it is not to settle anything, it is just to say that it is appropriate that she get it. Hence, to demand that what someone deserves to be settled "by the notion of desert itself", because otherwise it cannot serve as a principle of stakes for luck egalitarianism, is unreasonable.

Incidentally, as Vincent shows, the same is true of the notion of responsibility: it "only provides a formal structure within which ... other normative considerations determine how people may be treated, but contrary to what most people seem to

[26] Olsaretti (2009:185).

[27] Cf. Olsaretti (2009:186).

[28] For a full discussion, cf. Abad (2007:16–9).

think responsibility does not generate practical demands of its own".[29] So treating the question of the principle of stakes as "a question of what *responsibility itself* requires",[30] as Olsaretti does, is equally unreasonable.

Thus, that other considerations settle what someone deserves, and by extension what they are liability responsible for, is not to understand responsibility as entailing those other things. This, indeed, would be "too high a price" and absurd too, but since both responsibility and desert are just formal relations that provide normative links between different things, the problem does not arise. No relation conceptually entails the individuals it relates to each other.

These considerations certainly do commit luck egalitarianism to "a particular view about the principle identifying the grounds of responsibility", namely the desert view.[31] I fail to see, though, how this constitutes "too high a price", because this is just what a principle of stakes is supposed to do on Olsaretti's own terms. A problem arises only if we do not keep in mind what sort of responsibility we are talking about here. Obviously, desert cannot ground outcome responsibility. To say that I am only outcome responsible for what I deserve to bring about is bizarre. However, we are not talking about outcome responsibility here, but about liability responsibility. So, in looking for a way to normatively link consequences that are neither unduly harsh nor irrelevant to certain states of affairs someone is outcome responsible for, we are indeed looking for a principle of stakes that identifies the grounds of liability responsibility, and desert can fulfill this need. Far from being too high a price then, this is just what Olsaretti said luck egalitarianism needed.

So, if luck egalitarianism adopts desert as the principle of stakes, then, *contra* Olsaretti, it can rule out consequences that are unduly harsh or irrelevant as consequences someone should be liability responsible for given her outcome responsibility. However, luck egalitarianism still needs to establish that liability responsibility really does follow from outcome responsibility in the first place.

8.2.2 How to Derive Liability Responsibility from Outcome Responsibility

As I have already said, Vincent shows that outcome responsibility and liability responsibility are two different responsibility concepts. Not only do they refer to different objects, but they also are differently orientated in time: while outcome responsibility looks backwards, liability responsibility looks forward. Hence, outcome responsibility refers to a state of affairs one has brought about in the past, whereas liability responsibility refers to consequences one will bear in the future.

Since outcome responsibility and liability responsibility are two quite different concepts of responsibility, Vincent argues that the one does not follow from the other

[29] Vincent (2009:49).

[30] Olsaretti (2009:186).

[31] Olsaretti (2009:185).

"automatically", that is it is not logically entailed, as the responsibility-tracking intuition would have it. Rather, it would need additional normative premises to "bridge the inference gap", for example something like: "those who are outcome responsible for X should take liability responsibility in manner Y". Vincent calls such additional normative premises "reactive norms, since they are norms that govern our reactions to outcome responsible parties".[32] However, luck egalitarians do not offer any reactive norms as bridging premises, but simply assume that liability responsibility automatically follows from outcome responsibility. Since this is wrong, Vincent concludes that the responsibility-tracking intuition must be rejected.[33]

This conclusion is surprising in its abruptness, because, first, we could just have luck egalitarians read Vincent's analysis and surely they would immediately recognize the need to offer reactive norms and do so. Secondly, Vincent herself thinks that there are reactive norms that bridge the inference gap since there are "normative considerations that . . . play a key role in validating the transition from claims about a person's outcome responsibility to conclusions about their liability responsibility".[34] Thirdly, the responsibility-tracking intuition is a very powerful intuition many people share, and not just luck egalitarians. We should be wary of discarding it just like that, but rather see whether there is a way of retaining it without running into the problems Vincent points out.

Regarding the first point that luck egalitarians might just agree with Vincent and belatedly offer reactive norms to supplement their theory, Vincent might reply that this essentially is to give up luck egalitarianism, because, to borrow from Olsaretti, the idea behind luck egalitarianism presumably is to see only those inequalities as justified that can be derived from a liberal concept of freedom of choice and the concept of responsibility which are compatible with luck egalitarianism.[35] Thus, the idea seems to be to start out from concepts as thin as can be so as to get as widespread approval as possible and justify inequalities from there. Suggesting to simply add some reactive norms really amounts to abandoning this underlying idea, because all of a sudden the starting points do not seem to be so thin and universally approvable anymore.

Well, if luck egalitarians really are as inflexible as all that, so much the worse for them, of course. However, I am not convinced that there might not be a more yielding kind of luck egalitarian who would not mind a spot of extra justification for the odd reactive norm or two supplementing the responsibility-tracking intuition. Still, even if there is not, luck egalitarians are not the only people who want to derive liability responsibility from outcome responsibility. In fact, and this is the second point, Vincent herself seems to want to do just that, and she introduces reactive norms to do the very trick.

32 Vincent (2009:47).

33 Vincent (2009:46–8).

34 Vincent (2009:49).

35 Cf. Olsaretti (2009:179).

And to be sure, reactive norms will serve. Vincent correctly argues that we need some additional premises to bridge the inference gap from outcome responsibility to liability responsibility in the responsibility-tracking intuition, and her reactive norms do that. But she also sees that "this now raises the question of where such reactive norms might come from". So, she recognizes the need to justify those norms, because they may allow treating people harshly, and this is where normative considerations of, say, justice, utility, caring, beneficence and so on come in that inform those norms.[36]

However, this will not do. The problem with Vincent's account of reactive norms as bridging premises is that they are arbitrary. Reactive norms would not only provide a link between outcome responsibility and liability responsibility but also spell out the consequences one is liability responsible for. However, as we have seen in the last section, it is important that this be a link such that it connects only the right sort of consequence to outcome responsibility.

Informing reactive norms by normative considerations like utility or caring does not help in this regard. Say we care about our fellow citizens' safety so much that we really want them to wear helmets when riding their motorbikes so as to spare them the ghastly consequences of possible head injuries. Moreover, those head injuries are a real strain on our health insurance system. In order to achieve this we institute a reactive norm that motorcyclists who have an accident while riding without a helmet be ordered to scrape chewing gum from underneath school desks as soon as they recover. This is both caring and not at all too harsh, as almost every motorcyclist is bullied into wearing a helmet by the prospect of this distasteful task resulting in a significant drop in those specific head injuries, and those who are not at least do something useful to pay something back to society. The trouble is that this consequence of gum-scraping is not covered by the responsibility-tracking intuition. What is powerful about the intuition, even though it employs two different responsibility concepts, is that we intuitively see that there is something to the idea that people who are in a situation through their own fault should deal with it themselves, that they should suffer the consequences. However, in the example it is all too natural to ask, "Why gum-scraping?" So, the intuition does not cover any consequences that may arise out of situations people are in through their own fault, but only those that are linked to them in some special way. Linking them through a reactive norm does not work, as there is a reactive norm in place in the example, but we still do not intuitively see that a reckless motorcyclist really should scrape gums. This might be covered by the reactive norm, but it is not covered by the responsibility-tracking intuition.

Therefore, while reactive norms can serve as normative premises bridging the inference gap from outcome responsibility to liability responsibility, they can do so only in an arbitrary way, and thus fail as an explanation of the normative force of the responsibility-tracking intuition.

[36] Vincent (2009:47).

In view of this, Vincent might be tempted to reject the responsibility-tracking intuition altogether: we cannot derive liability responsibility from outcome responsibility automatically, we need reactive norms as additional bridging premises. Reactive norms fail to do the trick, so let us chuck the responsibility-tracking intuition and face it – liability responsibility cannot be derived from outcome responsibility at all.[37] But this would be too easy a dismissal.

Whether or not Vincent believes in the responsibility-tracking intuition, many, if not most, people do. It is such a powerful intuition, and this is the third point mentioned at the outset of this discussion, that we should be loath to go to such lengths as rejecting it if not necessary. And it is not, for we can tell which specific consequences are responses to certain states of affairs they issue from, and which are not. In the first case, the consequences are fitting to what happened before, in the latter, they are not. And the force of the responsibility-tracking intuition, its being so widespread and powerful, indicates that they are not only fitting, but required, hence appropriate. So, as easy as that, we can derive liability responsibility from outcome responsibility: a person should take liability responsibility for a state of affairs she is outcome responsible for, because that is the appropriate thing for her to do.

So, there is a certain link between reckless, helmetless motorcyclists getting into accidents and their paying their hospital bills themselves, namely the latter being a response to the former, while there is no such link – other things being equal – between their getting helmetless into accidents and scraping gum from underneath school desks. Hence, with the help of the notion of a "response" we get what consequences are fitting to what states of affairs. And the responsibility-tracking is evidence for our believing that they ought to be thus linked, that they are not only fitting but appropriate.[38]

We can probably even say that, given the dangers of motorcycling and the fragility of the human body, motorcyclists do something unfitting when they drive without helmets, and therefore, that it is not only appropriate but that they deserve to pay their own hospital bills. Obviously, though, whether or not we can say this, whether the person outcome responsible deserves to take liability reponsibility, depends on the responsibility-tracking example. At the least, however, it is appropriate for her to do so.

Some might worry that this is nothing but an exercise in terminology, that I have invented a new name for the responsibility-tracking intuition, but have not justified it. The last bit of this is true, I have not justified the responsibility-tracking intuition, but that is because that is not my business here. Rather, I have tried to make sense of how exactly to derive liability responsibility from outcome responsibility. In order to do this, I have simply taken for granted that liability responsibility should

---

[37] I do not get this impression from her paper, but in private correspondence Vincent leans that way.

[38] I do not mean to say that this link between outcome responsibility and liability responsibility holds necessarily. As I have argued in the first part of this paper, to say this would need substantial arguments for each situation in which such a link is said to hold. The present discussion, though, is not on this point but on luck egalitarianism, and for the sake of this discussion, I will conveniently assume that we are talking about a situation in which this link does hold.

follow from outcome responsibility. I have done so on evidence of the responsibility-tracking intuition's plausibility and force. The trouble was, as Vincent showed, that the intuition is not enough to derive liability responsibility from outcome responsibility, it needs to be supplemented. Vincent tries to do this with reactive norms, but that will not work. The foregoing considerations show that, rather, the responsibility-tracking intuition needs to be supplemented by the notion of propriety. This is not to give just a new name to the game. It is not to say that persons outcome responsible ought to take liability responsibility because they ought to, it is to say that they ought to because it is appropriate. And that this is not the same is what I have shown in the first part of this paper.

8.2.3 Two Questions or One?

Now it seems as though in the last two sections I have given two rather similar answers to the two quite distinct questions Olsaretti and Vincent focus on, that is on the one hand the question how the transition from outcome responsibility to liability responsibility works, and on the other hand the further question, assuming the transition does work, what consequences one should be liable for given one's outcome responsibility. In answer to both questions I have argued that desert will do the respective trick. So, does it not seem as though I have become confused about what the difference between the two questions is somewhere along the way? Well, no. Rather, the concept of desert is so great that it is capable of doing both tricks at once. Let us see how this works.

Remember that the concept of desert is made up of two components, fittingness and a normative element which makes what is fitting appropriate, that is which requires that the desert subject, characterized by the desert base, get the fitting desert object. The second question, what consequences one should be liable for given one's outcome responsibility, is the question what desert object is a response to a particular desert base a particular desert subject has set. The first question, how liability responsibility follows from outcome responsibility, is the question of the normative force of propriety in this case. I have not specially argued that there is such normative force there in this case, but have simply taken the power of the responsibility-tracking intuition as sufficient evidence for its holding here.

In other words, in the desert relation "x deserves y in virtue of z", the second question concerns the fittingness between y as liability responsibility and z as outcome responsibility of subject x, whereas the first question concerns the transition marked by "deserves".[39]

So, rather than having confused the two questions by employing the concept of desert in the discussion of luck egalitarianism, I have killed two birds with one stone.

---

[39] I have already said in the last section that whether liability responsibility given some outcome responsibility is a case of desert or of propriety is a matter of the particular constitution of the outcome responsibility a.k.a. desert base, and also that nothing hangs normatively on this conceptual distinction.

8.2.4 Luck Egalitarianism

Now, what does all of this mean for luck egalitarianism? Vincent and Olsaretti reject luck egalitarianism, or the responsibility-tracking intuition it rests on the, grounds that luck egalitarians cannot provide answers to the two questions mentioned. I have shown that luck egalitarianism cannot be rejected for that reason, because, if luck egalitarianism is supplemented by the concept of desert as explained, it can provide such answers after all. However, this does not mean that desert is all in the luck egalitarians' court. Luck egalitarians may employ this concept in order to draw the conclusions they want to draw, but that does not mean that desert may not equally well be employed by luck egalitarianism's opponents.

This is so because, as I have now said repeatedly, the *concept* of desert by itself does not determine who deserves what for what, and because, as I have emphasized all along, the concept of desert does not presuppose the concept of responsibility.

So, while it is reasonable to suppose that an unemployed gambler who has lost all his savings in a casino (who is outcome responsible for this) deserves to be barred from welfare aid (ought to take liability responsibility in this manner) it is equally reasonable to suppose that the gambler's situation now being thus that he has no adequate access to food, medicine, and shelter, he deserves to get welfare aid. This being equally reasonable means that in both cases the consequences are equally good responses to the antecedent states of affairs, so that we can say that the gambler both deserves to get welfare aid in virtue of his situation and deserves to be barred from welfare aid in virtue of his outcome responsibility.

Luck egalitarians, therefore, cannot simply point to the gambler's desert in order to draw the conclusion that he ought to be barred from welfare aid, because there are other considerations of desert to be taken into account, and since all of these are equally considerations of desert none of them are more weighty than the others simply on the grounds of their being deserved. So, in this regard the concept of desert will not help the luck egalitarian.

Neither can luck egalitarians point out that it is the gambler's own fault, the gambler is liability responsible and so he should be barred from welfare aid no matter what other desert considerations count against that, because those other desert considerations are not based on responsibility. The answer to that would be: so what? What on Earth is so very special about responsibility that it should break the tie between different considerations of desert, the normative force of which I have already shown does not rest in the slightest on responsibility? We would need additional arguments for that.

Nor can luck egalitarians point to the concept of justice and say that the gambler's deserving to be barred from welfare aid is a matter of justice whereas the gambler's deserving welfare aid is a matter of charity, and justice outweighs charity. Again, this would need some substantial arguments, that justice is only concerned with what people are responsible for, which have as of yet not been given, and that would be a counterintuitively thin notion of justice anyway.[40] After all, it is not

[40] Cf. Vincent (2009:49).

implausible to suppose that giving people what they deserve is always a matter of justice. Moreover, even if the one really was a matter of justice and the other a matter of charity – whoever said that justice was more important?

Well, the luck egalitarian might say, all of this is well and good, and if this was an ideal world in which there was enough for everyone no problem would arise. Alas, our resources are scarce, there is not enough for everyone, not even enough for everyone deserving, so that unfortunately we need to limit distribution in some way. Surely, it is preferable to do so in a just way. And distributing resources according to desert based on outcome responsibility is such a just way after all. So, given the scarcity of resources, such distribution is justified since at least I have granted that it is just.

Certainly, but this would be just to settle the matter by pragmatic considerations. This does not make picking out desert based on outcome responsibility of all desert considerations any more warranted in terms of justice, and it does not settle the matter regarding other possible just ways to distribute scarce resources, that is, this consideration by itself does not show that from among various just ways to distribute scarce resources we should pick the luck egalitarian option.

8.3 Conclusion

So, there is no conceptually necessary link between desert and responsibility. The responsibility view of desert is wrong. Nevertheless, if luck egalitarians avail themselves of the concept of desert, they thereby have an instrument with the help of which they can both explain how to derive liability responsibility from outcome responsibility and what specific consequences one is liability responsible for given one's outcome responsibility. However, it is important for them to note that this is only an instrument with the help of which they can explain these things. The concept of desert is not there to do all their argumentative work for them. They still need to provide substantial arguments to support their conclusions, and so far, these arguments have not been forthcoming.

Acknowledgments This is a revised version of a paper I presented at the conference "Moral responsibility: Neuroscience, organization & engineering" on August 24–27, 2009 in Delft. I thank Rüdiger Bittner, Logi Gunnarsson, Martina Herrmann, Ute Kruse-Ebeling, Nicole Vincent, and the audience at the conference for their help.

References

Abad, Diana. 2007. *Keeping Balance. On Desert and Propriety*. Heusenstamm: Ontos.

Bittner, Rüdiger. 2001. *Doing Things for Reasons*. Oxford: Oxford University Press.

Cupit, Geoffrey. 1996. "Desert and Responsibility." *Canadian Journal of Philosophy* 26:83–99.

Feinberg, Joel. 1963. "Justice and Personal Desert." First published in *Nomos VI: Justice*, edited by Carl J. Friedrich and John W. Chapman, 69–97. New York, NY: Atherton Press. Quoted from *Doing and Deserving. Essays in the Theory of Responsibility*, Joel Feinberg, 55–94. (Princeton, NJ: Princeton University Press, 1970).

Feldman, Fred. 1995. "Desert: Reconsideration of Some Received Wisdom." First published in *Mind* 104: 63–77. Quoted from *Utilitarianism, Hedonism, and Desert. Essays in Moral Philosophy*, Fred Feldman, 177–92. (Cambridge: Cambridge University Press, 1997).
Lamont, Julian. 1994. "The Concept of Desert in Distributive Justice." *The Philosophical Quarterly* 44:45–64.
McLeod, Owen. 1999. "Contemporary Interpretations of Desert. Introduction." In *What Do We Deserve?* edited by Louis P. Pojman and Owen McLeod, 61–9. Oxford: Oxford University Press.
Olsaretti, Serena. 2009. "Responsibility and the Consequences of Choice." *Proceedings of the Aristotelian Society* 109:165–88.
Pogge, Thomas W. 1989. *Realizing Rawls*. Ithaca, NY: Cornell University Press.
Rachels, James. 1978. What People Deserve. In *Justice and Economic Distribution*, edited by John Arthur and William H. Shaw, 167–96. Englewood Cliffs, NJ: Prentice-Hall.
Rachels, James. 1986. *The Elements of Moral Philosophy*. New York, NY: Random House.
Rawls, John. 1971. *A Theory of Justice*. Cambridge: Belknap Press.
Sadurski, Wojciech. 1985. *Giving Desert Its Due: Social Justice and Legal Theory*. Dordrecht: Reidel.
Sher, George. 1987. *Desert*. Princeton, NJ: Princeton University Press.
Smilansky, Saul. 1996. "Responsibility and Desert: Defending the Connection." *Mind* 105:157–63.
Vincent, Nicole A. 2009. "What Do You Mean I Should Take Responsibility for My Own Ill Health?" *Journal of Applied Ethics and Philosophy* 1:39–51.

Chapter 9
Communicative Revisionism

Lene Bomann-Larsen

Abstract Causal determinism may appear more salient when informed by empirical science. Thus even if neuroscience brings nothing substantially new to the debate on free will and human agency, it may enforce a call for revision of moral and legal practices. If our moral agency is a result of causal luck, desert-based moral practices seem unwarranted. A current trend in compatibilism agrees with the Strawsonian approach to moral responsibility in rejecting radical revisionism, but supplies the Strawsonian approach with a contractualist normative foundation. This paper argues that the contractual justification for desert-based moral practices fits well with a communicative theory of punishment. It is argued, however, that while a contractual communicative view on punishment may require some forms of hard treatment, it is unlikely that it will warrant extremely severe treatment. Hence determinism calls for a weak to moderate revision of our punitive practices insofar as these at present impose extreme suffering.

9.1 Introduction

There is some dispute over whether neuroscience brings anything substantially new to the compatibilist/incompatibilist debate on the significance of determinism for moral responsibility, and, as a corollary, whether neuroscience should have any impact on criminal law. Some argue that its impact will be substantial, because hard science has the weight and the prerogative to convince both decision-makers and the general public about what smart philosophers have known for a long time, namely that since there is no free will, and retributive punishment requires freedom of the will, we have to revise our justification for punishment (Vargas 2005; Greene and Cohen 2004), or eliminate punishment altogether (Pereboom 2007). Others maintain that the law makes no assumptions about free will, merely about intent and competence. Intent and competence, to be sure, do not hinge on free will; hence there is no reason why determinism either in its pure philosophical or empirical form should have any revisionary potential with regard to punishment (Morse 2004).

L. Bomann-Larsen (✉)
Department of Philosophy, Classics, History of Art and Ideas, University of Oslo, Oslo, Norway
e-mail: lene.bomann-larsen@hf.uio.no

N.A Vincent et al. (eds.), *Moral Responsibility*, Library of Ethics and Applied Philosophy 27, DOI 10.1007/978-94-007-1878-4_9,

However, even granted that the law makes no assumptions about free will and that the penal institution as such is not threatened by neuroscience, some concerns arise in the wake of scientifically informed determinism that are worthy of consideration. For one, the legitimacy of the penal institution rests partly on its correspondence with a "common sense of justice", and this common sense of justice is arguably informed by folk intuitions about free will (Greene and Cohen 2004). These intuitions may be altered, or deemed illusionary when the truth about human mind and agency revealed by neuroscience hits the public (ibid.). Though we cannot help but act as if our actions are "up to us", in our reflective moments we will realize that up-to-usness is illusory (Smilansky 2000), and hence cannot serve as the basis for penal practices. Second, since punishment by definition involves deliberately imposing suffering on a person, justifying it is a difficult task even in the absence of deterministic challenges. Science enforcing causal determinism does not make the task easier. Even if determining who is "guilty" and who is not in legal terms does not make any explicit references to free will, punishing the guilty appears to make such reference, insofar as its justification at least partly relies on "desert", which seems inextricably connected to free will. This interconnection is described by Galen Strawson as follows:

> What is it to be capable of being truly deserving of praise and blame for one's actions? ... Given that an agent is a moral agent, it is capable of being truly deserving of praise and blame for its choices and actions when and only when it is capable of free choice and free action. (1986:1)

To be deserving of praise and blame, that is, to be morally responsible in "the full sense", is described by Derk Pereboom[1] thus:

> For an agent to be morally responsible for an action is for it to belong to her in such a way that she would deserve blame if she understood that it was morally wrong, and she would deserve credit or praise if she understood that it was morally exemplary. The desert at issue here is basic in the sense that the agent, to be morally responsible, would deserve the blame or credit just because she has performed the action ... and not by virtue of consequentialist considerations. (2007:86)

Desert-entailing responsibility then, is a backward-looking form of responsibility; "Desert is concerned with what the person deserves to get for what she has done" (Smilansky 2000:2). It is thus closely connected to the person; we do not simply judge the action A as bad and point to X as the causal agent of A, but claim that X is bad for doing A, where A belongs to X in some intimate way.

Compatibilists about determinism and moral responsibility may recognize the force of the argument that if our actions are not really "up to us", we cannot be truly deserving of praise and blame, and yet attempt to salvage some concept of desert that does not require ultimate up-to-usness; but which still suffices to warrant our retributive attitudes and the practices that express them. One such (quasi-compatibilist)

[1] Pereboom himself takes it that we cannot have this kind of responsibility under determinism. To him, full moral responsibility requires ultimate control.

attempt consists in giving a contractualist,[2] or interest-based, argument for the legitimacy of our moral practices, which warrants maintaining them largely, if not wholly, unrevised. Considering the kind of creatures we are and what we tend to value – not least our moral agency and the ownership of our own actions – and what we stand to lose, were we to jettison our moral agency, it seems plausible that it is in our interest to leave our moral practices largely intact. Within such a contractualist scheme, the attribution of desert-entailing responsibility is justified with reference to the interest people take in being treated as responsible moral agents whose actions are up to them; that is, in being treated as moral agents for those types of actions for which they are willing to assume responsibility.

However, even if the contractualist argument succeeds in justifying, and hence leaves largely unrevised, our informal moral practices, the notion of desert it engenders may not be sufficiently robust to leave unrevised our *punitive* practices. With a substantive notion of "true desert",[3] which implies that the agent was fully free to choose to do otherwise[4] and still decided to do wrong, it is easier to see hard treatment as something intrinsically *good*. A contractualist notion of desert, on the other hand, requires that the justification of hard treatment must also find its basis in some form of agreement on what is a reasonable mode and scope of punishing those of us who end up as criminals, given the deterministic presumption that our actions are ultimately a matter of luck, in spite of how much we value perceiving of our actions as "up to us". Imagining a veil of ignorance behind which we do not know whether we will be causally lucky or unlucky in terms of moral agency is a useful thought-experiment.[5] My thesis is that under such conditions, we would choose a scheme where punishment is expressed as a form of moral censure, that is, a backward-looking form of punishment connected to "desert", but one in which punishment does not impose severe or extreme suffering (e.g. life-sentences, capital punishment).

This paper argues in support of three claims: (1) the contractualist argument establishes a basis for a publicly instituted censure of wrongdoing, aiming at addressing the offender as a moral agent and offering him an opportunity to repent and reconcile himself with his victim and society; (2) this censure must be expressed in terms of hard treatment; but (3) severe treatment, i.e. imposing extreme suffering, will not be warranted.

---

[2] The "contractualism" I am referring to here is of a Scanlonian kind (Scanlon 2003). It is thus constrained by some normative notions such as fairness and reasonableness. It is not a rationality-based contractualism like Rawls' Original Position, according to which contractors are guided by enlightened self-interest in ignorance of their position in society.

[3] As expounded in the quote from Galen Strawson above.

[4] Not necessarily in terms of the Principle of Alternative Possibilities, but at least in terms of having ultimate control over one's actions by having chosen to be the person who acts in the way one does. Cf. Galen Strawson's Basic Argument (2003).

[5] When I introduce the metaphor of the Veil of Ignorance, this is not intended to be a shift to a Rawlsian situation of choice, but aims merely to illustrate the radical character of the requirement that we should place ourselves at the receiving end of the principles we hold, in order to determine whether they are acceptable.

In Section 9.2, I give a brief outline of a contractualist theory of desert. In Section 9.3 I offer an argument for why contractualist desert is fitted to a communicative theory of punishment (Duff 2001), where the public expression of condemnation (Feinberg 1970) is combined with addressing the offender as a moral agent. In Section 9.4 I sketch the conditions for determining an appropriate mode and scope of punishment. I suggest that under conditions where we are ignorant of how we fare as moral agents, we will choose a form of censure which (1) goes beyond mere symbolic censure and thus involves some form of hard treatment, but which (2) does not impose extreme hardships or irreparable suffering. I also consider, and reject, some objections to both these claims. Section 9.5 concludes the paper.[6]

9.2 Justifying Desert in Contractualist Terms

There is a trend in contemporary compatibilism to provide a Strawsonian conservative approach (P. Strawson 2003) to moral responsibility attribution with a contractualist, or interest-based (Lenman 2006; Bomann-Larsen 2010), normative foundation. The contractualist approach recognizes the force of our reactive attitudes, but also recognizes that there is a problematic inference from the fact that we have and value these attitudes, to allowing these attitudes to justify our moral and punitive practices. By invoking our interest in maintaining our practices, their normative basis is secured because reference to our interests gives the opportunity to fend off accusations of unfairness; it is not unfair to people to treat them as morally responsible agents if it is in their interest to be so treated.

To the contrary, it would be unfair *not* to, because that would amount to an unjustifiable dismissal of the claim of persons to have their legitimate interests taken into account. The alternative to treating a person on the basis of *intrinsic* features of herself or her act (Smilansky 2000:1) is to treat her on account of *extrinsic* features, such as concern for the general good.[7] The wrongdoer will be objectivised, regarded

---

[6] I assume that everything argued in this paper is compatible with even the strongest possible threat from neuroscientifically informed determinism; what may be roughly labeled as the No-Action-Thesis (Morse 2004). Should it turn out to be true that conscious willing is in fact an illusion; i.e. that we merely *feel* like agents (Wegner 2002), we can still want to be treated as the agents we feel like being. Illusionism is fully compatible with a contract-based justification for desert and a communicative theory of punishment; insofar as it is unavoidable to maintain a pragmatically meaningful notion of "intent", and insofar as our agency – illusory or not – *matters* to us. Of course, the argument requires that we are reason-responsive, but even illusionists about conscious willing have to admit that we are reason-responsive at some level, if they are to argue that punishment could work as a deterrent. (Indeed if they are to argue at all without performative contradiction).

[7] It could be objected that the kind of determinism which is presupposed here undermines the distinction between intrinsic and extrinsic features, because if true, all features are in the relevant sense extrinsic. But we do not need to do away with the distinction. Consider for example Neil Levy's argument that even if we do not make conscious decisions, "the mechanisms that make the decisions are ... ours; they have our values, our beliefs, our goals (we have them by them having

as an item to be manipulated or a problem to be managed, or treated in a paternalistic way, as a misbehaving child. And since it is presumably not in our interest to be subjected to rules treating us in this way, the contractualist argument concludes that this form of treatment is wrong.

The contractualist argument provides a justification for treating each other as morally responsible agents in *the full sense*, even on the condition that we are not, in the metaphysical sense, free. Desert-entailing responsibility may be burdensome; as its corollary is blame, resentment and sanctions which are unpleasant to experience, and particularly so when they reflect on the *person*, not simply on the action viewed in agent-neutral terms. Yet, even if it may sometimes be contrary to our interest at a given time t_0 to be treated as full moral agents, it is in general, our lives seen as a whole, in our interest to be treated as such. The reason is that desert-entailing responsibility has another side as well; moral praise and credit. And we cannot have the one without the other; we are rationally committed to hold that we either *are* the kind of beings to whom moral appraisal applies, or we are not. The burdensome upshot of being treated as a moral agent to whom praise and credit applies when one has done something worthy of these responses, is to be subject to resentment, blame and perhaps even punishment when one has done something that is worthy of those responses. But it is a price we are willing to pay, because being treated as moral agents is extremely important to us. As Dennett notes:

> Blame is the price we pay for credit, and we pay it gladly under most circumstances. We pay dearly, accepting punishment and public humiliation for a chance to get back in the game after we have been caught in some transgression. (2003:292)

Moreover, we may even challenge the assumption that we only value negative responses because they are corollaries of positive responses: it is not given that simply because being subjected to blame and resentment is unpleasant, we do not value being subjected to negative moral sanctions when we know that we have done something wrong. In cases where we strongly feel remorse, we may appreciate having our self-reactive attitudes asserted by others, and to be given the opportunity to set things right by sincerely repenting and paying back what we owe.

But how far can the contractualist argument get us in terms of moral responsibility? It can be argued that it does not get us any form of *desert*; it merely suggests a *derivative* notion of moral responsibility (Smart 2003). A hard incompatibilist like Pereboom (2007) accepts that we can attribute responsibility for morally wrongful actions in such a way that we can express moral criticism; that is, in such as way that it makes sense for X to regret that she did A, and opt for improvement in the future (but not in such as way as to assert that X deserves reproach for doing A). Such an approach leaves room for backward-looking apology and forward-looking reform, but not for blame and punitive sanctions. However, as soon as this much is admitted, it seems we already have the raw materials we need to establish a weak

---

them) and when they decide, *we* decide." (Levy 2007:243). Those causal forces that are me, then, are intrinsic features that may be distinguished from causal forces operating outside of me (our outside of my consciousness) and which cannot be attributed to me as a person.

notion of desert. Firstly, it does not make sense to ask X to apologise *sincerely* for a past action without asserting that the action belongs to her in some intimate way. Secondly, it does not make sense to expect moral reform from X with regard to future actions without X herself sincerely taking her past actions to belong to her in some intimate way (Bomann-Larsen 2010).

Respecting a moral agent as such requires some form of correspondence between first-person and third-person responses; that is, between responses to one's own actions versus responses to other people's actions. First-person responses come in (at least) two forms: agent-remorse and agent-regret (Williams 1981). Agent-remorse is the form of self-blame that is the upshot of understanding that one has culpably (intentionally or by a form of culpable negligence or recklessness) done wrong. The appropriate third-person correlate to agent-remorse is blame.[8] Agent-regret, on the other hand, responds to the thought "How much better if it had been otherwise" (ibid.:27), and so does spectator-regret; the spectator, too, will join in and say: "How much better indeed." Were we to reject desert-entailing responsibility, we would be left with only one third-person response; spectator-regret, and ideally with only one form of first-person response; agent-regret. But as long as agents are likely to insist on agent-remorse, the consequence of jettisoning desert-based moral practice is a radical asymmetry between how the agent views her own action as something intrinsically belonging to her, and the third-person response of spectator-regret treating her action as some kind of unfortunate event. As response-types, neither agent-regret nor spectator-regret are specifically directed towards persons (self or other) as *moral* agents; they conflate moral and causal agency and thus conflate intentional actions and mere accidents. Regret-responses therefore do not sufficiently express respect for persons as the moral agents they take an interest in being treated as by others.

The contractualist view gives a justification for leaving unrevised those elements of our moral practices that relate to desert. Let us now turn to how a contractualist justification of desert can inform a theory of punishment, which, arguably, is harder to justify because it involves a stronger imposition of suffering on the agent than does informal moral sanctioning.

9.3 Determinism and Theories of Punishment

Criminal law and the institutionalisation of criminal punishment may be viewed as the public expression of blame. Certain types of moral wrongs are a public concern. I am here relying on Antony Duff's account of crimes as public wrongs (Duff 2007), and in the present context I will only be concerned with punishment for those crimes that are properly speaking also moral wrongs, and which are crimes for that reason; that is, which are condemned *because* they are morally wrongful (as opposed, for instance, to violations of administrative regulations, though it may also be considered morally wrong to violate these because it is wrong to violate legitimate laws

[8] Whether actually expressing blame is appropriate will depend on other factors as well.

(see ibid.:81, 89–93). In short, I am concerned with the type of crimes that can be classified as *mala in se*; wrongful independently of their formal status as crimes.[9] It is mainly for such actions that moral agents may be asked to repent, out of respect for their own moral agency, as well as out of respect for their victims and the moral community as a whole.

If we agree that there is a reason, in contractualist terms, for people to accept desert-entailing moral responsibility, then we have established the *foundations* of a backward-looking theory of punishment that ties the offender to his punishment in terms of desert; in short, the foundations of a retributive theory. That is, we have established the basis for a theory of punishment which addresses past wrongdoing, justified in terms of what we owe to the offender and to the victim of wrongdoing, according to which properly addressing wrongdoing involves treating wrongdoers as *deserving* of censure. This fits well with an expressive or communicative theory of punishment, where, according to Feinberg:

> Punishment is a conventional device for the expression of attitudes of resentment and indignation, and of judgments of disapproval and reprobation, on the part either of the punishing authority or of those "in whose name" the punishment is inflicted. (Feinberg 1970, quoted in Duff 2001:27)

Duff further adds that the communicative theory of punishment

> ...communicate(s) the censure that offenders deserve by portraying punishment as a species of *secular penance*. That account is retributivist: it justifies punishment as the communication of deserved censure (Duff 2001:30).

However, communicative punishment also contains three forward-looking elements in aiming at persuading the offender to *repent*, and hopefully *reform* himself and be *reconciled* with the community (ibid.).

In arguing that a communicative theory of punishment is suited to the contractualist argument for desert, it must be shown why it is better suited than alternative theories. The contractualist argument justifies choosing one scheme in terms of its desirability compared to alternative schemes. Successfully arguing in favour of a communicative theory of punishment therefore partly depends on the lesser desirability of conceivable alternatives.

Traditionally, there are two main contenders to the retributivist justification of punishment solely in terms of what "the guilty deserve to suffer" (Duff 2001)[10]:

---

[9] Though I remain, at present, neutral on the question of how to identify which wrongs are public wrongs, i.e. whether these are to be picked out by a singular principle, such as the harm-principle, or by plural principles, or in terms of communal values (Duff 2001, 2007).

[10] Note that nothing I say in favour of a communicative justification of punishment with reference to desert is intended to set aside the need for protecting society from dangerous offenders. Should the offender be dangerous, he might have to be detained, but the justification for that could be of a different kind – protection of community, not punishment – and should, if so, only be used to the extent necessary for this purpose, and under as humane conditions as possible. For example, we already detain dangerous psychotics, but we do not punish them. The need for protection may come in addition to the retributive element in an expressive or communicative theory, but with a different and not necessarily punitive justification. The question is how much of the material component of

pure consequentialism and abolitionism; whereof, to be precise, the latter is not really a justification for punishment at all, but for its abolition, in whole or part. Abolitionism takes many forms; from the abolition of punishment altogether, to the abolition of particular forms of punishment, e.g. imprisonment as a mode of punishment (Duff 2001:31). Within the free-will debate, the equivalent of (total) abolitionism is often referred to as *eliminativism* about punishment (Pereboom 2007; see also Vargas 2005). Here, it is recommended that the very *concept* of punishment should be eliminated along with the concepts of desert and guilt. In the following I will focus on the strong revisionary claim that punishment as such – as a concept and an institution – ought to be eliminated from our moral practices.

While radically different in crucial respects, both (pure) consequentialist justifications of punishment and various claims to the elimination of punishment have one important feature in common; they see no justification for a backward-looking form of punishment. The perpetrator is not to be treated as deserving of suffering for what she has done in the past, but should be dealt with in a different way and/or for different reasons. Such reasons may be deterrent, protective, and/or corrective/reformatory. While both sets of theories recognise the need for protecting society against harmful actions, they are sceptical towards a backward-looking kind of punishment, simply because it entails no benefit for anyone, apart, perhaps, from the satisfaction of a presumably unjustifiable thirst for revenge. To be sure, both consequentialist and abolitionist theories are proposed independently of the free-will debate, for independent moral reasons, but they are also typically revisionist theories within the determinism/free-will debate, where they seem to acquire an additional edge against retributivism on the basis that if no one is free, everyone is fundamentally innocent on the basis of causal luck, and on this score retributivism cannot satisfy its own basic and absolute prohibition against punishing the innocent. Hence, the issue arising from determinism is not only that retributive punishment does not benefit anyone, but more fundamentally, that such punishment is profoundly unfair. So why bother rescuing retributivism from the threat of determinism? Why not simply bite the bullet and abandon retributivism along with its presuppositions? Why should we not, as Greene and Cohen (2004) suggest, choose – in our reflective moments – a purely forward-looking justification for punishment?

Forward-looking theories offer different answers to the luck problem. Consequentialists are all happy about punishing the innocent (i.e. the unlucky) for the sake of deterrence and protection of the community, that is, to impose suffering on someone for entirely person-extrinsic reasons. Now, it is a familiar argument against consequentialism that punishing the innocent in order to further some social aim amounts to using people as mere means, and granting the truth of determinism reinforces this objection: not only will consequentialist punishment under determinism *open* the door to punishing the innocent (which arguably could be avoided by

imposing suffering can be put into the punishment itself, and how much is left to be justified in terms of protection.

side-constraining consequentialism); it systematically *requires* it, because everyone is by definition innocent.

However, the "use as means" objection begs the question against the consequentialist, who does not believe that there is anything wrong in using people as mere means. The contractualist argument offers a better response, namely that it is hardly justifiable to a person to treat her as a mere means.[11] Hence a purely consequentialist theory of punishment is unlikely to be accepted, given the contractualist argument as a basis for our moral practices.[12] Now, it may be objected that nothing bars contractors behind a veil of ignorance from settling for consequentialist principles which then, by being chosen, are justifiable *ex hypothesi* to those subjected to them. Contractors may well choose principles that treat them as means but give a better prospect of avoiding harm. And admittedly, contractors may conceivably settle for purely consequentialist principles of punishment, but all my argument needs is to show that it is equally or perhaps more plausible that they will not. Although there may be exceptions in some cases, it is not implausible to assume that people in general prefer to be treated as ends, even though this might occasionally harm rather than benefit them, in light of the alternative of giving up their autonomy *tout court* to avoid all kinds of harms.[13]

For those who believe that it is wrong to treat people as mere means, no matter which reason they have for holding the belief, it may seem that the only logical and morally acceptable upshot of determinism is to eliminate the concept of punishment altogether, and replace the punitive institution with an institution that serves the interests of society and individuals in a non-punitive way. Eliminating punishment does not entail that we cannot protect society from dangerous individuals (cf. fn. 9). When necessary, we can justify detaining such individuals in the same way as we justify detaining carriers of highly contagious and dangerous viruses (Pereboom 2007:116). But eliminativists argue that we are not justified in making detainees suffer beyond what is the inevitable consequence of the means of protection. Moreover, detention, or other means for controlling risky behaviour, should be combined with measures for rehabilitation, which can be[14] a way of addressing the person rather than using him as a mere means for some extrinsic end (Pereboom 2007). Yet arguably, something paternalistic seems to be going on once punishment

---

[11] Here both Scanlon and Rawls differ from a classical contractarian like Hobbes. To Hobbes, the value above all values is security, whereas to contemporary contractualists, e.g. justice, freedom and autonomy are rated higher, and thus different justifications are yielded.

[12] Confer Rawls (1999a).

[13] Further, as an anonymous referee has pointed out, an accusation of begging the question could be made against baking into the contract the values that are supposed to be justified by the contract. But it is not question-begging if the assumption about people's reluctance to being treated as means is a psychological rather than a moral one. Contractors choose moral principles on the basis of some commonalities in human psychology. What these commonalities are is of course ultimately an empirical question which cannot be settled here, but again, that it matters to most of us to be treated as somehow "end's in ourselves" is not an implausible assumption.

[14] I say "can be" because arguably, there are forms of rehabilitation that may entail using people as mere means. Cf. Stanley Kubrick's film "A Clockwork Orange".

is replaced with mere rehabilitation, even if rehabilitation is in the best interest of the person. In addition to bereaving persons of the opportunity to truly repent for their past crimes, the reformatory approach conflates classes of offenders who are normally taken to differ in terms of their capacity for exercising moral agency; i.e. it makes no principled distinction between competent adults and the mentally ill, or between adults and children (Bomann-Larsen 2010). In that sense it appears to fall short of paying due respect to persons who take an interest in being treated as competent moral agents, by treating them on a par with non-competent agents. From a contractualist point of view which assumes that most people take an interest in being treated as moral agents, the alternative seems to leave little to be desired.

The contractualist argument states that it is unfair to treat persons contrary to their interest in being treated as morally responsible agents; i.e. to treat them as objects to be manipulated, as children, as anything less than competent adult moral agents. Purely forward-looking theories of punishment fail to take into account the fundamental interests of persons to be treated as if their actions are really up to them. In Antony Duff's words:

> To use censure simply as a useful technique for modifying conduct is to treat the person censured as a not responsible and autonomous subject, but as an object to be manipulated by whatever techniques we can find (Duff 2001:28).

Only some form of backward-looking, that is, retributive, theory seems to sufficiently accommodate the claim of the offender to be treated as a moral agent. What I have referred to as strong (or "positive") retributivism is the view that it is a moral duty to punish the guilty, simply because they are guilty and deserve to be punished. However, it is hard to see how this justification of punishment can be reconciled with the contractualist argument which, after all, takes as given that our moral agency is ultimately a matter of luck. On the strong retributivist account, justice *demands* the punishment of the guilty; hence guilt is a *sufficient* condition for punishment (Duff 2001:19). But this thought is challenged by the rejection of "up to usness" because even though it is in the interest of persons to be treated as moral agents in the desert-sense (say, to be blamed), it does not follow that it is in their interest to be *punished*. Hence, on this scheme guilt is not *sufficient* for punishment as imposed suffering; we need to fulfil an additional condition of *acceptability* of the principles of punishment.

Communicative punishment seems to preserve those elements of retributivism that are desirable to preserve. It retains the idea that punishment is a form of public censure which ties the agent to her past action, but it need not presuppose anything about ultimate "up to usness". It suffices to presuppose the importance to us to be treated as the agents we conceive of ourselves to be, and our acceptance of such treatment in terms of that importance.

9.4 Finding a Reasonable Standard for Determining the Mode and Scope of Punishment as Communication

My first claim was that the contractualist argument for moral responsibility establishes a basis for a publicly instituted censure of wrongdoing, aiming at addressing the offender as a moral agent and offering him an opportunity to repent past actions and reconcile himself with the moral community. Granted that this claim is accepted by the reader as plausible, it is time to turn to the second and third claims, namely that (2) censure must sometimes be expressed in terms of hard treatment, but that (3) severe/extreme treatment is unwarranted.

To the second claim, it can be objected that the contractualist argument merely warrants symbolic punishment, in the form of public moral criticism and demand for public apology, and that this should suffice for reconciling the offender, the victim and the community. This is a rather strong revisionist view, which implies a radical transformation of the expressions of our reactive attitudes to wrongdoing. Still, the view is not implausible. Arguably, what choosers decide on behind a veil of ignorance determines the proper terms of communication. Hence, if the parties agree to a revisionary scheme where repentance is expressed in merely symbolic terms, it can not be objected that symbolic punishment fails to appropriately express condemnation.[15] There are several ways of responding to this objection, however. It is true that whatever the parties behind the veil agree on constitutes the proper terms of communication. But it seems the parties cannot set the terms of appropriate communication at whim. As soon as a backward-looking principle of punishment is accepted, that is, a principle according to which punishment aims to address the perpetrator as a moral agent by communicating society's views on the blameworthiness of her conduct, we are also committed to a proportionality criterion; punitive sanctions must be arrayed according to the degree of blameworthiness or seriousness of the conduct (von Hirsch 1994:125). Proportionality is related to fairness and thus something owed to offenders and victims alike. To punish a minor crime in the same way, or harsher, than a major crime, would be unreasonable and unfair to the offender, but also to the victim of the major crime. Now, the proportionality requirement does not necessarily entail that the treatment must be hard, but as I will argue, there are good proportionality-related reasons for hard treatment. I will return to this shortly.

To the third claim, it can be objected – in an opposite sentiment – that if we take the contractualist argument seriously as establishing full moral responsibility even in a deterministic world, there is no limit at the outset to choosing any degree of punishment that we see fit. Thus either (a) no revision of our penal practices is really needed, and in consequence, causal determinism is bracketed out as irrelevant to theories of punishment; or (b) the contractualist justification for punishment may in fact yield draconian punishment for rather minor offences, if choosers see it fit. I believe this last objection too can be addressed with reference to the proportionality criterion, which is essential to all forms of backward-looking punishment where the sanctions aim to reflect the severity of the wrongdoing. But before returning to the discussion of proportionality, I will elaborate somewhat on the objection (a) that determinism is irrelevant to our theory of punishment and hence that if the contractualist argument succeeds in establishing desert and warranting censure-based punishment, then no revision of our penal practices is needed.

I will argue that in searching for a reasonable standard for determining the acceptable mode and scope of punishment, we must take seriously *both* the fact that our

[15] I owe this point to Kasper Lippert-Rasmussen.

actions are not really up to us *and* the fact that it is in our interest to be treated as if our actions are up to us, in a way that appropriately addresses wrongdoing as something for which the agent is responsible. In other words: (1) we must be able to justify the terms of punishment to those who will (as a matter of causal luck) suffer from it; that is, to potential offenders, and (2) if we are to express censure properly, the censure must communicate society's view on the gravity of the wrong, both in absolute terms and relative to other wrongs; i.e. the punishment must "fit the crime". To let a wrong go by without appropriately addressing it signals that we do not really regard it as wrong (Duff 2001:28). And yet excessive punishment from the point of view of the offender could be rejected by a chooser in the contract situation, who does not know whether he will (as a matter of causal luck) end up as an offender or not. Contractualist communicative punishment thus consists in reaching equilibrium between "too little" and "too much" according to the above-mentioned constraints, and requires that the interests of the perpetrator and the interests of the moral community are balanced.

I have suggested that we employ the metaphor of the veil of ignorance to determine the appropriate measure of communicative contractualist punishment. What is of the essence in this context is that the parties "do not know how they have fared in the natural lottery" (Rawls 1999b:113) – i.e. "that they do not know their own place in the distribution of natural talents and abilities" (Rawls 1999c:178) – including their moral talents and abilities. It is also fundamental that the parties recognise one another as someone who has legitimate claims; that is, as someone to whom justification is owed.

Not knowing how one has fared in the natural lottery implies that one does not know whether one will be lucky or unlucky in terms of the factors that facilitate either moral or criminal behaviour. This reflects the underlying intuition of the fairness objection against retributive punishment in a deterministic world, and of the contract-based response to the objection. The intuition is the same as that driving luck egalitarianism. People are not to be made to carry the burden of (bad) luck, only the burden of their choices.[16] But under determinism, causal luck encompasses

[16] Given this idea, we could arguably be compelled to choose the principles of criminal justice on the same basis as we choose our principles for distributive justice, which entails choosing a scheme for criminal justice which distributes burdens according to the principles that would be most beneficial to those who are the worse off in virtue of bad causal luck. On this interpretation and in the present context, the worse off are those who end up as criminals. However, there is an important difference between criminal justice and distributive justice which does not warrant treating them on the same scale, even if we accept the intuition underlying luck egalitarianism as generally sound. Criminal justice is about *creating* (new) burdens, not distributing already existing burdens. The burdens created by criminal justice do not exist prior to the institutions which create them, and they need not be created at all. So from the idea that when we distribute existing burdens people should only be made to carry the burdens which result from their voluntary choices, nothing follows with regard to how we should distribute the burdens we create; or to whether we should create them at all. The rationale for criminal justice is thus different from the rationale for distributive justice. (I owe this point to Jakob Elster). I hold on to this thought even if it could be argued, as pointed out by an anonymous referee, that criminals do create burdens (directly and indirectly) and therefore, punishing them is a way of redistributing the burdens they have created. I read this

everything, including our choices. The contractual approach responds that it is still in our interest to maintain a distinction between chance and choice which corresponds with the distinction between factors over which we exercise control and factors over which we do not, even if we never exercise *ultimate* control.

Yet, in taking the fact of causal luck seriously, I have to acknowledge that my moral persona is contingent on luck factors and therefore that I should not judge, at the outset, that criminals are some mysterious "others" who deserve to suffer simply for being who they are. We easily grasp the thought that "it could have been me" when witnessing someone being the *victim* of crime. We sympathise with the victim precisely because we can imagine ourselves being in her shoes, and we demand the punishment of the perpetrator as if he had wronged ourselves. It is much harder to imagine oneself as a different moral persona, say, as a murderer, or a rapist. But given that we are not to know whether we will be the lucky or unlucky ones, we are obliged to place ourselves in the perpetrator's shoes as well, and acknowledge, with Scanlon, that "There but for the Grace of God go I" (Scanlon 2000:294). And since one of the things we must take into account when we decide on the severity of punishment is that we might end up as receivers of the punishment, we have reason in the contract situation to not allow extremely severe punishments. Thus our current punitive practices are not unaffected by determinism, and some revision of the mode and scope of punishment is called for.

However, as suggested above, there seems to be something unsatisfactory to merely saying: "I am sorry (for killing your child)" – in particular when the killing has been deliberate. Mere apology does not seem to bring us beyond agent-regret; beyond the: "How much better if it had been otherwise". In order to properly own up to what one has done, then, one must accept the imposition of some form of suffering beyond the mere unpleasantness of public apology. Similarly, society must show how seriously it takes the crime by imposing a fitting amount of suffering. "Censure cannot be expressed adequately in purely verbal or symbolic terms; the hard treatment is necessary to show that the disapprobation is meant seriously" (von Hirsch 1994:121).

To let a wrong go by insufficiently noticed is to silently endorse it, that is, to express that it does not really matter; that it is not important. Take rape as an example. Say we know that the rape is a one-time event. There is no possibility that the offender will ever do it again. Add that no one but the involved parties learns about the rape, so punishing the rapist has no deterrent effects on other potential rapists. In this case there are no forward-looking reasons either for punishing or detaining the rapist. Yet merely to ask the offender to apologise to his victim communicates

---

objection as a version of the "Removal of Unfair Advantage" justification of punishment. While the theory bears with it some interesting challenges, it has been vastly criticised – in my view correctly – for giving a distorted picture of what makes crimes wrongs. "The criminal wrongfulness of rape, for instance, in virtue of which it merits punishment, does not consist in taking an unfair advantage over all those who obey the law" (Duff 2001:23). True, there may be types of crimes where unfair advantage is an appropriate explanation of their wrongness, but these will typically not be the kinds that are *mala in se*, with which I am mainly concerned here. In any event, creating a new burden (punishment) does not nullify the original burden (the crime), it adds another.

a lot: it communicates to the offender that he did not do anything really wrong.[17] It communicates to his victim that she was not really wronged, and, hence, that rape is not really a wrong.

Von Hirsch points out that "if censure conveys blame, its amount should reflect the blameworthiness of the conduct ... the severity of a sanction expresses the stringency of the blame ... Hence punitive sanctions should be arrayed" (ibid.:125). That is, punitive sanctions must be constrained by *ordinal* proportionality. (ibid.:128) Ordinal proportionality compares different crimes in terms of their relative seriousness, and requires that differentiation of punishment should display the relative seriousness of crimes.

Now, symbolic punishments may meet the criterion of ordinal proportionality, that is, there may be different symbolic expressions for different offences. Just like awarded medals which have the same material composition may signify different merits, so too may symbolic punishments signify different types and degrees of wrongdoing.[18] Consider for instance the "Hester Prynne"-sanction; Hester Prynne had an "A" for "adulteress" painted on her forehead. We could imagine a system where criminals were branded, say, "R" for rapist or "M" for murderer. Such branding would amount to differentiated symbolic punishment because the degree of social shaming would reflect the degree of wrongness. However, it seems that for symbolic punishment to work as *punishment*, it would have to be pretty harsh – as in the Hester Prynne-case – in the sense of being truly socially shaming.[19] Otherwise it would fail to communicate the wrongness of the action. Hence even if ordinal proportionality is compatible with symbolic punishment because symbolic punishment may be arrayed, the material content of the punishment (here, in terms of the consequential social stigma and resultant isolation, mistrust and fear which would appear to be its corollaries) seems to be just as harsh, if not even harsher than imprisonment, and *ipso facto* amount to a form of hard treatment.[20]

Let us now turn to the objection to my third claim above that the contractualist argument will not warrant punishment in the form of *severe* or *extreme* suffering. Consider the argument for draconian punishment for drunken driving. Thomas Pogge has argued that a contractualist approach to punishment may in fact yield draconian punishment even for strict liability offences (Halvorsen 2002:fn. 16, 180–81). Drunk driving illustrates this well: Why should we not accept punishment by death for drunken driving, if, say, by executing 10 people we could prevent 1000 deaths caused by drunken drivers?

---

[17] Of course, he will have violated a legal rule, which provides a reason to punish him, but we do not primarily want to communicate that he has violated a regulation; we want to communicate that he has violated his victim. The legal prohibition against rape is after all there because rape is wrong, and it is wrong independent of the law.

[18] I owe this point to an anonymous referee.

[19] If the norms were completely internalized, it could of course be the case that symbolic punishment worked without social shaming. But in one important sense, this would not be punishment at all, but rather some form of self-reproach.

[20] That said, this form of punishment is not ruled out by anything I say here. All I am saying is that hard treatment is a necessary component for punishment to be justified, not that the form of punishment needs to be imprisonment.

Perhaps we would, if the risk of being killed by drunken drivers was severely reduced by the deterrent effect. It is questionable whether it would deter, however; drunken driving is a strict liability crime because the *mens rea* component is absent. People who drive drunk do so because they are drunk and their judgment is impaired, hence it is questionable whether a threat of capital punishment would have a deterrent effect. Of course, it might deter people from drinking, but that is not in itself crime, or it might create an incentive to lock down the car keys, which would be a good thing. But there are other concerns as well. For one, the kind of contractualism I am expounding here is constrained by fairness considerations. Punishing drunken driving *killings* with death leaves a lot of space for moral luck; those who end up as killers are morally unlucky, and it seems unfair to punish someone on the basis of moral luck.[21] Hence, if we accept capital punishment for drunken driving killings, it seems we should also accept if for drunken driving which, accidentally, does not result in someone's death. And even if we do accept capital punishment for killings caused by drunken driving, it is unlikely that we would accept capital punishment for drunken driving which does not result in someone's death. Given global causal luck, the risk of ending up a drunken driver is much greater than the risk of ending up the victim of a drunken driver. After all, most drunken drivers never kill anyone. Knowing this it is not evident that it would be rational to choose the death penalty for drunken driving.

Secondly, I am presupposing that people take an interest in being treated as moral agents – that is the basis for the contractual justification of punishment. This interest can only be served by differentiating between punishments according to degrees of blameworthiness. Drunken driving might result from horrible recklessness, but it is not as bad as murder. Consider capital punishment for drunken driving from the point of view of proportionality. It can of course be argued that since drunk drivers willingly accept the risk of killing others, punishing them by death is not entirely unfitting. And still, drunk driving is not murder, even when it results in unjustified killing. Taking moral agency seriously, we cannot conflate risky behaviour which might cause death – even when in fact it does cause death – with intentionally and deliberately killing another human being. And in terms of ordinal proportionality, the most severe punishments should be spared for the most severe wrongdoings; the ultimate punishment must be spared for the ultimate crime. Hence, if we assign punishment by death for drunken driving, we have exhausted our opportunity to mete out the most severe punishment for the most severe crimes; and arguably, murder is a greater wrong than killing someone by drunken driving.[22]

---

[21] I am assuming that it matters to people to be regarded as agents, even if they are not to take into account what kinds of agents they are, and thus that the principles guiding society should reflect this interest in being treated as agents. This calls for a distinction between mens rea crimes and strict liability crimes, where the latter does not involve any agency control but more, and external, luck.

[22] It could be objected that if the punishment for drunk driving was death, the punishment for murder could be torture + death (I owe this point to Kasper Lippert-Rasmussen). But this seems to violate the proportionality principle as well. i.e. "A head for an eye" seems disproportionate in *cardinal* terms, as discussed below.

However, ordinal proportionality considerations only tell us to array punishments relative to the blameworthiness of different kinds of conduct. It cannot give us an answer to where to set the upper and lower limits for punishment, for instance, what kind of punishment should be given for the most severe crimes. Ordinal proportionality must therefore be paired with *cardinal* proportionality. Cardinal proportionality is non-relative (von Hirsch 1994:129) and sets the limit on justifiable intrusions on the liberty of persons. In addition to the considerations of ordinal proportionality in relation to strict liability offences versus *mens rea* offences above, cardinal proportionality too explains why the former should not be subject to draconian punishments. To live in a society where unintended harm is draconianly punished would be unbearable and intolerably intrusive on people's liberty. Thus, while ordinal proportionality in principle could allow for rather harsh punishments for minor crimes, provided only that the punishments given for graver crimes are even harsher, cardinal proportionality prevents us from harshly punishing lesser wrongs. We could imagine a society which punished throwing gum on the sidewalk with imprisonment.[23] But this seems too intrusive of liberty to be acceptable – not least because humans are fallible, and a society which was not willing to cut people some slack would be extremely difficult to live in.[24] Moreover, we know that in so far as people are allowed to drink, and to own cars, some of us will occasionally get drunk and lose self-control, and jeopardise people's lives by getting behind the wheel. Society accepts this risk, while it could be avoided by banning alcohol or cars. But we take prohibiting either to be overly intrusive and illiberal, and if the prohibition is incompatible with liberal principles then so, it seems, is punishing its accidental consequences by severe means.

Nothing said so far rules out capital punishment for capital crimes, and life-time sentences of imprisonment for major crimes short of murder. Yet I have suggested that the contractualist argument will not allow for extreme punishment. But why is that? Or put differently: where do we set the *maximal* limit on punishment; i.e. the standard in relation to which punitive sanctions are to be arrayed?

Given the contractualist argument, the justifiability of the punishment itself depends on its acceptability to those who are to be punished. What we need to ask, then, is which modes and scopes of punishment it is reasonable to expect those who will suffer the punishment to accept; and we need to ask this in ignorance of whether we will be in the perpetrator's shoes.[25]

---

[23] There are of course many countries that do practice severe punishments for minor crimes; e.g. Singapore, where people suffer imprisonment for littering the streets. I owe this point to an anonymous referee.

[24] I owe this point to Jakob Elster.

[25] It can be objected, as an anonymous referee has, that if contractors who behind the veil do accept a crime-preventing system of hard punishment, it is reasonable to expect them to accept such punishment if they turn out to be offenders. But again, there are certain constraints on the contract: not every conceivable agreement is reasonable. Acceptability is not entailed by agreement – it is entailed by *reasonable* agreement. There are some independent standards determining what the contractors may agree on. Unreasonable agreement may display a failure to take into account the

First, I believe that from that point of view it would not be regarded as acceptable to impose a scheme of punishment that required one to pay with one's life, either in terms of a life-time imprisonment or in terms of capital punishment. Second, even if imprisonment is acceptable as a mode of punishment, extreme conditions in prison such as isolation, brutal treatment and similar hardships are hardly likely to be acceptable. Third, long sentences short of life may be unacceptable. Say a woman becomes a murderer at 20. A sentence of a length that would make it impossible for her to ever have children could be regarded as imposing an unacceptable burden. Basically, while it is plausible that most offenders take an interest in being treated as moral agents and therefore to accept the imposition of some form of suffering as a "vehicle for the expression of condemnation" (von Hirsch 1994:125), it is equally plausible to assume that it is in their interest to be given an opportunity to reconcile themselves with the community. Punitive principles that impose unbearable sacrifices on the part of offenders by closing off all possibility of reconciliation, or by inflicting irreparable harm, may be rejected as unacceptable on the terms that they are not likely to be accepted by those suffering under the principles.

I have argued that in the contract situation we would accept proportionality-constrained backward-looking hard punishment – but not extremely severe punishment – as a means of communicating moral censure. Let us now consider two final objections to this contractualist communicative theory of punishment. First, the hardship of punishment, and hence the message it conveys, is relative; a life-time sentence could arguably be perceived of as a less harsh message to a 90-year old than, say, ten years imprisonment to a 17-year old. Not to mention the message that being sentenced to death conveys to the religious fanatic terrorist aiming to become a martyr. I have argued that the punishment should aim to communicate the degree of blameworthiness of the act, i.e. that the punishment fit the crime. This implies that if two crimes are of identical seriousness, the punishment should be identical too. But it seems identical punishment may communicate different messages to different offenders.[26]

Second, it seems the contract-based argument cannot justify punishing those who for some reason or other do not take an interest in being treated as moral agents at all, either because they lack the capacity to respond to moral reasons, or because they do not want to be members of the moral community.

---

point of view of those subjected to the rules. What I am suggesting is that if the people behind the veil truly take into account that it is ultimately just a matter of luck who ends up as criminals, they might consider that if they were in those unlucky shoes, they would want to be given a second chance. Combined with an interest in being treated as agents in relation to those actions over which they do exercise some control (and not in relation to what merely happens, i.e. outcomes of moral luck), this starting point sustains the distinction between *mens rea* crimes and strict liability offences, while at the same time it should also yield a more forgiving attitude towards the former. Of course, if the contractors are Hobbesian in the sense that their only concern is security, then the picture may look very different, but Hobbesian rationality arguably does not give a plausible account of human psychology.

[26] I owe this point to Kasper Lippert-Rasmussen.

The former objection does not pose a problem that is peculiar to communicative punishment, nor to a contractualist one. Insofar as it poses a problem at all,[27] it does so to *all* theories of punishment, determinism aside. Deterrence-based theories must deal with the problem that a threatened punishment may deter some but fail to deter others, and while there is in principle no reason why deterrence-based theories should not differentiate punishment according to what effectively deters different individuals, doing so would be practically impossible and raise all sorts of epistemic problems. Some 90-year olds may value every day they have left of their lives, some 17-year olds may not care about their lives at all. But the law must strike a uniform compromise on the basis of the presumed efficiency of the threat for all subjects. Similarly, all desert-based theories face the same problem. According to retributivism, the guilty deserve to suffer, but the extent to which the guilty actually *do* suffer will vary widely across different individuals; yet again, the law must be uniform and address all subjects as one.

The latter objection may be warded off in similar way. Any theory of punishment must deal with those who are not to be regarded as full members of the moral community, but who pose a danger to others. While they may be unable to repent, society still needs to protect other citizens from them. "Atypical perpetrators", like psychopaths, pose a problem to any theory of punishment. Only eliminativist theories may avoid this problem, because they do not treat anyone as full moral agents, and reject the very notion of punishment. Hence they need not distinguish between punishable and non-punishable persons. According to this view, we are all in one sense "atypical perpetrators" insofar as we are perpetrators. Yet as suggested in Sect. 9.2, eliminativist theories must carry the justificatory burden of showing why normal, morally competent adults ought to be treated in the same way as those who are usually regarded as incompetent.

Purely consequentialist theories may on their part distinguish between those who are punishable, i.e. able to be deterred by the law, and those who are not (Greene and Cohen 2004). But they, too, need to deal with the latter group, though the former group – the punishable – may include more individuals than it would under a desert-based jurisprudence (i.e. many psychopaths are able to be deterred by the law, but they do not understand the concept of moral wrong and can thus not be *deserving* of punishment). There will then, on any theory of punishment, always be a class of offenders which the theory cannot account for, and which still needs to be dealt with. That is a problem for liberal society, but not one which is peculiar to the theory proposed here. The contractualist communicative theory I have expounded is only idiosyncratic on one score: namely that not only those who fall outside of the moral community for lack of capacity, but also those who choose not to be part of it (because they do not value being treated as moral agents), are unjustifiably punished. That is a bullet the theory should be willing to bite, just as these people must be willing to bite the bullet of being treated as incapable, and be detained should they pose a risk to others, as the upshot of their voluntary alienation.

---

[27] I say "if" because there is still considerable leeway for judges and juries to exercise judgment in individual cases.

9.5 Conclusion

I have argued that even if determinism is true and our actions are not ultimately up to us, we can still justify desert-based moral practices with reference to our interest in being treated as full moral agents. Such a contractual notion of desert gives us the basis for a backward-looking form of punishment as a vehicle for publicly communicating censure of wrongful actions. This contractual communicative theory of punishment is revisionary because it takes seriously the fact that our agency is owed to causal luck, hence the principles of punishment must be justifiable also to those who end up at the receiving end of punishment. It is plausible that parties to a contract, who do not know how they will fare in terms of luck, will accept that some form of hard treatment is required in order to appropriately communicate censure, but that they have reason to reject extreme punishment, that is, punishment which either makes reconciliation with community impossible, or which imposes irreparable damage.

Acknowledgments I want in particular to thank Jakob Elster, Vidar Halvorsen, Kasper Lippert-Rasmussen and an anonymous referee for helpful discussion and useful criticisms during the process of writing this paper. Thanks also to participants at the conference "Moral Responsibility: Neuroscience, Organization & Engineering" at TU Delft, August 24–27 2009, and to Nicole Vincent for opportunity and support.

References

Bomann-Larsen, Lene. 2010. "Revisionism and Desert." *Criminal Law and Philosophy* 4:1–16. doi: 10.1007/s11572-009-9081-x.

Dennett, Daniel. 2003. *Freedom Evolves*. New York, NY: Viking Press.

Duff, R. Antony. 2001. *Punishment, Communication and Community*. New York, NY: Oxford University Press.

Duff, R. Antony. 2007. *Answering for Crime. Responsibility and Liability in the Criminal Law*. Legal Theory Today. Portland, OR: Hart Pub.

Feinberg, Joel. 1970. *Doing and Deserving*. Princeton, NJ: Princeton University Press.

Greene, Joshua, and Jonathan Cohen. 2004. "For the Law, Neuroscience Changes Nothing and Everything." *Philosophical Transactions of the Royal Society of London* 359:1775–785.

Halvorsen, Vidar. 2002. *Ethics, Force and Violence in Policing*. Oslo: Unipub forlag

Lenman, James. 2006. "Compatibilism and Contractualism: The Possibility of Moral Responsibility." *Ethics* 117:7–31.

Levy, Neil. 2007. *Neuroethics. Challenges for the 21st Century*. Cambridge: Cambridge University Press.

Morse, Stephen. 2004. "New Neuroscience, Old Problems." In *Neuroscience and the Law. Brain, Mind and the Scales of Justice*, edited by Brent Garland, 157–98. Washington, DC: Dana Press.

Pereboom, Derk. 2007. "Hard Incompatibilism." In *Four Views on Free Will*, edited by John M. Fischer, Robert Kane, Derk Pereboom, and Manuel Vargas, 85–125. Singapore: Blackwell.

Rawls, John. 1999a. "Two Concepts of Rules." In *John Rawls. Collected Papers*, edited by Samuel Freeman, 20–26. Cambridge, MA: Harvard University Press.

Rawls, John. 1999b. "The Sense of Justice." In *John Rawls. Collected Papers*, edited by Samuel Freeman, 96–116. Cambridge, MA: Harvard University Press.

Rawls, John. 1999c. "The Justification of Civil Disobedience." In *John Rawls. Collected Papers*, edited by Samuel Freeman, 176–89. Cambridge, MA: Harvard University Press.

Scanlon, Thomas M. 2000. *What We Owe to Each Other*. Cambridge, MA: Harvard University Press.

Smart, John J.C. 2003. “Free Will, Praise and Blame.” In *Free Will* (2nd Edition), edited by Gary Watson, 58–71. New York, NY: Oxford University Press.
Smilansky, Saul. 2000. *Free Will and Illusion*. New York, NY: Oxford University Press.
Strawson, Galen. 1986. *Freedom and Belief*. Oxford: Clarendon Press.
Strawson, Galen. 2003. “The Impossibility of Moral Responsibility.” In *Free Will* (2nd Edition), edited by Gary Watson, 212–28. New York, NY: Oxford University Press.
Strawson, Peter. 2003. “Freedom and Resentment.” In *Free Will* (2nd Edition), edited by Gary Watson, 72–93. New York, NY: Oxford University Press.
Vargas, Manuel. 2005. “The Revisionist’s Guide to Responsibility.” *Philosophical Studies* 125:399–429.
von Hirsch, Andrew. 1994. “Censure and Proportionality.” In *A Reader on Punishment,* edited by R. Antony Duff and David Garland, 112–32. New York, NY: Oxford University Press.
Wegner, Daniel M. 2002. *The Illusion of Conscious Will*. Cambridge, MA: MIT Press.
Williams, Bernard. 1981. *Moral Luck*. Cambridge: Cambridge University Press.

Chapter 10
Moral Responsibility and Jointly Determined Consequences

Alexander Brown

Abstract In *Responsibility and Control: A Theory of Moral Responsibility*, John Fischer and Mark Ravizza argue against incompatibilist principles of moral responsibility and offer a compatibilist account of moral responsibility. The book has sparked much discussion and criticism. In this article I point out a significant flaw in Fischer and Ravizza's negative arguments against the incompatibilist Principle of the Transfer of Non-Responsibility. I also criticise their positive argument that moral responsibility for consequences depends on action-responsiveness. In the former case I argue that their putative counterexamples against Transfer NR and Transfer NR* are underdescribed but once fully described depend upon consequence-particulars and not consequence-universals as they claim. In the latter case I argue that their account is unable to cope with quite ordinary cases of jointly determined consequences.

10.1 Introduction

In *Responsibility and Control: A Theory of Moral Responsibility*, John Fischer and Mark Ravizza offer a compatibilist account of moral responsibility which purports to explain both how it is that "inner mechanisms" can lead to acts or omissions for which agents are morally responsible *and* how it is that "outer processes" can lead to consequences for which agents are morally responsible (Fischer and Ravizza 1998).[1] The book has sparked much discussion and criticism, particularly with respect to Fischer and Ravizza's claim that inner mechanisms (that is, mental states leading to acts or omissions) attract moral responsibility just in case they exhibit "guidance control" (see Glannon 1997; Stump 2000; Levy 2002; Ginet 2006; Judisch 2007; McKenna 2008). This account (they claim) is superior to accounts which ground moral responsibility in "second-order volitions" (cf. Frankfurt 1971, 1987). In this article, however, I wish to focus on the outer processes between agents' acts or omissions and the consequences in question. I accept that moral responsibility for consequences must depend on both inner mechanisms and outer

[1] The book brings together and refines material from a series of earlier articles.

A. Brown (✉)
School of Political, Social and International Studies, University of East Anglia, Norwich, UK
e-mail: alexander.c.brown@uea.ac.uk

N.A Vincent et al. (eds.), *Moral Responsibility*, Library of Ethics and Applied Philosophy 27, DOI 10.1007/978-94-007-1878-4_10,

processes, but I wish to bracket off internal mechanisms to focus on external processes.

Having introduced Fischer and Ravizza's negative argument that the inevitability of certain events or consequences does not rule out the possibility of an agent's moral responsibility for those consequences, and their positive argument that moral responsibility for consequences depends on action-responsiveness, I set out to do two main things. First, I attempt to highlight a flaw in Fischer and Ravizza's account of simultaneous overdetermination of consequence-universals. They present some examples in which two actual paths lead to the occurrence of the same consequence, where each path would have been sufficient to make the consequence obtain had the other path not existed. According to Fischer and Ravizza, such "joint" cases undermine "the Principle of the Transfer of Non-Responsibility" (Transfer NR). I shall argue that this is not the case. Since the consequence-universals in the putative counter-examples are underdescribed, the examples in question do not qualify as counter-examples to Transfer NR, but once the relevant consequences are properly fleshed out, they look more like consequence-particulars than consequence-universals.

Second, I investigate cases of jointly determined consequences, where each path is *not* sufficient by itself to bring about the relevant consequence. While examples of simultaneous overdetermination appear in philosophy books, examples of jointly determined consequences are a more familiar part of ordinary moral experience. Take the following description of the execution of a man on death row in Texas:

> The warden told Willingham that it was time. Willingham, refusing to assist the process, lay down; he was carried into a chamber eight feet wide and ten feet long. The walls were painted green, and in the center of the room, where an electric chair used to be, was a sheeted gurney. Several guards strapped Willingham down with leather belts, snapping buckles across his arms and legs and chest. A medical team then inserted intravenous tubes into his arms. Each official had a separate role in the process, so that no one person felt responsible for taking a life. (Grann 2009)

Fischer and Ravizza declare that they intend to establish a wide reflect equilibrium within the domain of phenomena associated with moral responsibility (Fischer and Ravizza 1998:34). If so, then it is important that their account of moral responsibility for consequences can explain our intuitive judgements about examples of jointly determined consequences. I shall argue that as it stands their account is not competent in this regard. If (as they propose) action-responsiveness is a necessary condition for an agent being morally responsible for certain consequences, then an act or omission that only jointly determines a consequence cannot attract moral responsibility given Fischer and Ravizza's definition of action-responsiveness. Yet it seems intuitive to say that such acts or omission can attract moral responsibility for the agents concerned. Therefore, either their definition of action-responsiveness is defective or action-responsiveness is not a necessary condition after all. At the end of this article I put forward my own dedicated accounts of joint moral responsibility for consequences and joint action-responsiveness for consequences which can deal appropriately with these examples.

10.2 Preemptive Overdetermination of Consequences

Typically, a compatibilist approach to moral responsibility will contain both negative and positive arguments: first, it will make the negative argument that it is false to suppose that the thesis of causal determinism is incompatible with attributions of moral responsibility (most notably by identifying counter-examples to incompatibilist principles); second, it will present a positive account of what moral responsibility is grounded in (such as an account of the internal mechanisms in virtue of which agents can be deemed morally responsible for their acts or omissions and an account of the external processes in virtue of which agents can be deemed morally responsible for the consequences of their acts or omissions).[2] I begin with the negative argument before turning to the positive argument.

Fischer and Ravizza reject the incompatibilist principle that a person cannot be held morally responsible for bringing about an event if that event was inevitable, where "inevitable" means that the agent could not have prevented the event from obtaining even if he had acted differently than he did. They do so by evoking Frankfurt-type cases.[3] In their example "Avalanche" we are asked to imagine that Betty is a double agent who has been instructed to explode dynamite at the top of a mountain in order to trigger an avalanche that will destroy an enemy camp in the valley below. However, unbeknownst to Betty, Ralph has been asked by his superiors (who are also Betty's superiors) to place explosives a few feet lower down the mountain than Betty's explosives, and to trigger the avalanche if Betty fails to do so. The superiors are unsure of Betty's commitment to the cause. Fischer and Ravizza argue that even though Ralph's presence is enough to ensure that the avalanche and camp-destruction take place, this does not detract from Betty's moral responsibility. Provided she has guidance control over her own actions, she *is* morally responsible for the consequences (Fischer and Ravizza 1998:155–56). Indeed, they argue that the same could be said even if the story is modified so that if Betty had not placed the charge, then a natural event (erosion) would have triggered the avalanche (157).

The nub of the example is to show that mere inevitability of consequences does not rule out the possibility that an agent could be morally responsible for those consequences. Fischer and Ravizza believe that other Frankfurt-type cases illustrate

---

[2] I do not mean to say that a compatibilist must attempt to do both of these things, only that a complete compatibilist approach would. Nor do I mean to suggest that the business of developing a positive account of moral responsibility is idiosyncratic to compatibilists. For, it is available to an incompatibilist to combine such an account (even the positive account of Fischer and Ravizza) with the requirement that the agent must have genuinely open alternative possibilities (see Ginet 2006:241).

[3] The original Frankfurt case runs as follows. Suppose Black places Jones in a set of circumstances which leave Jones no alternative but to do the thing that Black wants him to do. If Jones begins to look as though he is not going to do as Black desires, then Black will take "effective steps" to ensure that he does, although Jones does not know that Black will intervene. In the end Jones decides to do the thing without Black actually having to step in to make him do it. Although Jones could not have acted otherwise in that sense, we nonetheless tend to think that he is morally responsible for his actions (Frankfurt 1969:835).

the same point (155). Take the example of "Assassin". Imagine that Sam tells his friend Jack of his plan to assassinate the mayor. Jack has his own reasons for wanting to assassinate the mayor and is nervous. He wants to make doubly sure that the mayor is shot and killing. So he hatches a plan to shoot and kill the mayor himself but only if Sam fails to do so for some reason. As it turns out, Sam does shoot and kill the mayor, and Jack (the assassin who ensures that that consequence will obtain no matter what) did not actually play a role in bringing about the shooting and death of the mayor. Since Sam *did* shoot and kill the mayor, it makes sense to say that Sam *is* morally responsible for this consequence, and this holds true in spite of the fact that the mayor being shot and killed was inevitable (given Jack's intentions and abilities).

Fischer and Ravizza refer to what happens in these sorts of cases as *preemptive overdetermination of consequences*, meaning that the ensuring conditions (as in, that Ralph or erosion would have triggered the avalanche and crushed the enemy camp if Betty had not done so, and that Jack would have shot and killed the mayor if Sam had not done so) are preempted by the actual conditions (that Betty did detonate the dynamite and crush the camp, and that Sam did shoot and kill the mayor). These examples demonstrate that, contrary to the incompatibilist principle that the inevitability of consequences rules out the possibility of moral responsibility, it *can be* appropriate to hold agents morally responsible for consequences even in scenarios where those consequences were somehow inevitable.[4]

There is, however, something about these cases that troubles Fischer and Ravizza; and rightly so I think. Let us say that an incompatibilist is someone who holds the following nuanced view about moral responsibility: if an agent is not morally responsible (or no agent is morally responsible) for certain events, and for the fact that those events causally determine other events or consequences, then that agent is not morally responsible (or no agent is morally responsible) for the other events or consequences. This is a view *only about* cases in which events for which an agent is not morally responsible (or no agent is morally responsible) causally determine other events or consequences about which the question of moral responsibility is asked. Yet the examples of Avalanche and Assassin are not cases of this sort. Here the relevent (counterfactual) events for which the agents in question (Betty and Sam) are not morally responsible (or no agent is morally responsible), namely, that Ralph (or erosion) would trigger an avalanche to destroy the camp if Betty does not and that Jack would shoot and Kill the mayor if Sam fails to do so, do *not* causally determine the other events or consequences about which the question of moral responsibility is being asked. The events or consequences in question are *preempted* by the actions of Betty and Sam. As such, the examples of Avalanche and Assassin are strictly speaking beside the point. They do not test the nuanced incompatibilist view. The right way to establish genuine counterexamples to the nuanced incompatibilist view is to present cases in which events for which the agents in question are not morally

[4] For alleged counterexamples in which the preempting agent is not morally responsible after all, see Levy (2002).

responsible (or no agent is morally responsible) *do* bring about consequences for which the agents in question are morally responsible (159–60).

10.3 Simultaneous Overdetermination of Consequences

Fischer and Ravizza take this objection seriously. Nevertheless, they believe that it is possible to construct other cases that are pertinent to the nuanced incompatibilist view. Specifically, they think that cases of *simultaneous overdetermination of consequences* are powerful counterexamples to the nuanced incompatibilist view. Such cases involve two-paths to an event or consequence – one path for which the agent is putatively morally responsible and another path for which the agent is not morally responsible (or no agent is morally responsible).[5] Before introducing these cases, however, I need first to say something about the intended target.

The intended target for cases of simultaneous overdetermination is the Principle of the Transfer of Non-Responsibility (Transfer NR), or two versions thereof:

Transfer NR

(1) If p obtains, and no one is even partly morally responsible for p; and
(2) if p obtains, then q obtains, and no one is even partly morally responsible for the fact that if p obtains, then q obtains; then
(3) q obtains, and no one is even partly morally responsible for q. (152)

and

Transfer NR*

(1) If S is not morally responsible for p; and
(2) S is not morally responsible for the fact if p obtains, then q obtains; then
(3) S is not morally responsible for q. (157)

Fischer and Ravizza claim that respectively Transfer NR and Transfer NR* are susceptible to the following counterexamples.

In "Joint Avalanche" we are asked to imagine that Betty sets off an explosive charge at T1 which triggers an avalanche that crushes an enemy camp at time T3. However, unbeknownst to Betty, whilst she is setting her explosives a nearby glacier is melting, shifting and eroding, and it releases another avalanche that crushes the enemy camp at the exact same time, T3. According to Fischer and Ravizza, Betty

[5] The path for which the agent is putatively responsible must, on Fischer and Ravizza's account, involve guidance control with respect to both inner mechanisms (from mind to act or omission) and outer processes (from act or omission to consequence). Since my interest in this article is with outer processes and not internal mechanisms, I shall not discuss Eleonore Stump's objection that if causal determinism is true and inner mechanisms are constituted by physical matter (i.e. neurons), then the path for which the agent is putatively responsible fails (Stump 2000). For a reply, see Fischer and Ravizza (2000).

is morally responsible for the consequence, *that the enemy camp is crushed at T3*, despite the fact that no one (including Betty) is even partly morally responsible for the fact that if erosion triggers an avalanche, then the enemy camp is crushed at T3. This is presented as a counterexample to Transfer NR, since here we have a case in which there is an event p for which no one is even partly morally responsible that causes another event or consequence q for which an agent *is* morally responsible (i.e. Betty) (162).

In "Joint Assassins" we are to suppose that Sam and Jack simultaneously shoot and kill the mayor. Unlike the case of Assassin, Jack does not wait to see what Sam will do. Rather, he decides to shoot and kill the mayor himself and does so at the exact same moment as Sam (time T2). Although the actions of Sam and Jack are independently sufficient to bring about the consequence, *that the mayor is shot and killed at T2*, in fact both Sam and Jack shoot and kill the mayor. Fischer and Ravizza present Joint Assassins as a counterexample to Transfer NR*. The suggestion is that although Sam is not even partly responsible for the event, *that Jack pulls his own trigger at T1*, nor for the state of affairs, *that if Jack pulls his own trigger at T1, then the mayor is shot and killed at T2*, Sam is morally responsible for the consequence, *that the mayor is shot and killed at T2* (161). (They also show sensitivity to the fact that a change to the timings of Joint Assassins will change the judgement. They imagine a case, "Joint Assassins 2", in which Jack actually fires his gun a few seconds after Sam, and Jack's bullet hits the mayor a few seconds after. In this case they judge that Sam is morally responsible for the consequence, *that the mayor is shot and killed at T2*, whereas Jack is only morally responsible for the consequence, *that the mayor is shot a second time* (118–19). They also imagine a case, "Joint Assassins 3" in which Sam fires first and then Jack second, but because Jack is much closer to the mayor, Jack's bullet hits the mayor first. Here they determine that Jack is morally responsible for the consequence, *that the mayor is shot and killed at T2*, whereas Sam is only morally responsible for the consequence, *that the mayor is shot a second time* (119).)

The alleged power of Joint Avalanche and Joint Assassins lies in the fact that they involve the simultaneous overdetermination of events or consequences. That is to say, they involve "the actual occurrence of two triggering events that both bring about the terminal events simultaneously" (118). This feature makes it possible for there to exist events for which some agent S is not morally responsible (or no agent is morally responsible) that causally determine a consequence for which S *is* morally responsible (or at least one agent *is* morally responsible).[6] This is not possible in cases of preemptive overdetermination because here it is only ever

[6] At first glance, it is not clear why it is important in the case of Assassins that the two agents are acting independently of each other. But perhaps the importance can be underlined as follows. Suppose a married couple are living beyond their means. They rack up large debts they cannot afford to pay off. They each know what the other is doing. Nevertheless, the actions of each agent would have been sufficient to produce debts which they cannot repay. This is a case of simultaneous overdetermination of consequence, but it is not a counterexample of the right sort. That is because it might be argued that the husband is partly responsible for the actions of the wife and vice versa.

the case that one event actually brings about the terminal event or consequence in question.

It is also important to recognise that Fischer and Ravizza's cases of simultaneous overdetermination (along with their cases of preemptive overdetermination) are presented as involving "consequence-universals". A consequence-universal "can be brought about via different causal antecedents" (96). In contrast to this, "a consequence-particular is individuated more finely" (ibid.). In other words, "the actual causal pathway to a consequence particular is an essential feature of it" (ibid.). The more basic distinction here is between what is repeatable or multi-instantiable (universals) and what is non-repeatable or mono-instantiable (particulars). The property black, for example, is a universal because it can be exemplified or instantiated in more than one place at the same time, as when I make the truthful statement that both my shoes and my trousers are black. Moreover, two different properties can be instantiated at the same place and time, as when I make the truthful statement that my shoes are black and shiny. Particulars, by contrast, are non-repeatable. Any particular pair of shoes cannot be in more than one place at the same time. And no two pairs of shoes can occupy exactly the same space at the same time. It is safe to say that if properties like *being black* are simple universals, then consequence-universals are complex universals in the sense that they combine particulars with universal properties. Hence we can say that the consequence-universal, *that the mayor is shot and killed at T2*, is complex because it attributes the universal property of being shot and killed to a particular person, the mayor. Consequence-particulars, by contrast, involve particular properties and lend greater precision to how consequences come about. Sticking with the same example, a consequence-particular might specify who shot and killed the mayor at T2.

Fischer and Ravizza stress that their counterexamples to Transfer NR and Transfer NR* "treat consequences as consequence-universals" (154 n. 5). In the case of Joint Assassins, they propose that Sam and Jack are each morally responsible for the consequence-universal, *that the mayor is shot and killed at T2* (161). The counterexample would not have worked if it had been couched in terms of consequence-particulars. Sam cannot be held morally responsible for the consequence-particular, *that Jack shot and killed the mayor at T2*, just as Jack cannot be held morally responsible for the consequence-particular, *that Sam shot and killed the mayor at T2*. Fischer and Ravizza also distinguish between "descriptive" and "modal" consequence-universals (102). The relevant descriptive consequence-universal in the case of Joint Assassins would be something like, *that the mayor is shot and killed by someone or other at T2*. The relevant modal consequence-universals would be, *if contrary to fact Sam had not shot and killed the mayor at T2, then the mayor would have been shot and killed by Jack alone*, and *if contrary to fact Jack had not shot and killed the mayor at T2, then the mayor would have been shot and killed by Sam alone*. Plainly the counterexample would not have worked if it

This looks likely if each is aware of what the other is doing, each does not attempt to stop the other and each encourages the spending of the other.

had been couched in terms of a modal consequence-universal. This is because Sam, say, cannot be morally responsible for the modal consequence-universal, *if contrary to fact Sam had not shot and killed the mayor at T2, then the mayor would have been shot and killed by Jack alone*.

The upshot is that if cases of simultaneous overdetermination of consequences are to attract moral responsibility in the right way, then it is only because one and the same consequence can be brought about in more than one way, and this is only possible if the relevant consequences are consequence-universals of the right sort. However, it is one thing for Fischer and Ravizza to acknowledge the fact that for their argument about moral responsibility to work they *must* appeal to consequence-universals rather than consequence-particulars; it is quite another to show that consequence-universals rather than consequence-particulars *do* figure in our ordinary attributions of moral responsibility; and yet another thing to demonstrate that the argument *can* work by appealing to consequence-universals rather than consequence-particulars. It is to these further necessary steps in the argument that I now turn.

10.4 Consequence-Universals and Consequence-Particulars

Do consequence-universals figure in ordinary attributions of moral responsibility? Some people might think that in ordinary situations we tend to hold agents morally responsible not for consequence-universals but for instantiations of consequence-universals (i.e. the actual obtaining of consequence-universals) *vis-à-vis* consequence-particulars. Of course, Fischer and Ravizza hold that agents can be morally responsible for both consequence-universals and consequence-particulars (121). In addition to their counterexamples against Transfer NR and Transfer NR* they have another set of arguments to show that agents can be morally responsible for consequence-particulars even in the absence of genuinely open alternative possibilities (98–101).[7] However, the present objection is that their argument that agents can be morally responsible for consequence-universals is misplaced since generally speaking we do not take agents to be morally responsible for consequence-universals just as we do not ordinarily take agents to be morally responsible for Platonic forms.

Even if some people might be tempted to think that consequence-particulars are the only things that matter as far as moral responsibility is concerned, I do not think that this is actually the case. On the contrary, consequence-universals are a feature of ordinary moral discourse and the attribution of moral responsibility. Suppose two brothers are playing football outside of their house. Just as the first brother is about to kick the ball, the second brother shouts out, "There is a spider crawling up your neck!" The first brother is distracted for a moment and accidentally kicks the ball toward the front window, smashing it. Although he kicked the ball into the window,

[7] For an interesting discussion of a possible tension between Fischer and Ravizza's account of guidance control over consequence-particulars and their account of taking responsibility, see Judisch (2007).

he says to the second brother, "It was your fault that the window got smashed because you distracted me." The other replies, "No, you were responsible for the fact that the window got smashed because you took your eye off the ball." Finally, the boys' mother appears on the scene and offers the final word, "Never mind who actually kicked the ball, you were both playing football outside of the house even though I have told you many times not to do so, therefore you are both jointly responsible for smashing the window." Presumably all of these utterances make sense, and they do so because the interlocutors are referring to the consequence-universal, *that the window is smashed by the ball.* (It also seems to me that the attribution of joint responsibility in this case is made plausible by the fact that the boys were engaged in a joint enterprise. I shall have more to say about joint enterprises below.)

Quite apart from the question of whether or not it is appropriate to attribute moral responsibility to agents for consequence-universals, I believe that a more pressing issue is whether or not consequence-universals can work in the way that Fischer and Ravizza intend them to work; whether or not Fischer and Ravizza are able to rely on consequence-universals in the cases of Joint Avalanche and Joint Assassins. I have serious doubts on this score.

Given their description of Joint Avalanche, it is clear that Fischer and Ravizza have in mind two simultaneously occurring events which are both counterfactually sufficient to crush the camp, meaning that if contrary to fact only one of the two avalanches had hit the camp, then it would have been sufficient to crush the camp by itself. Since the two avalanches did hit the camp at the same time and each avalanche would have been sufficient to crush the camp counterfactually, at first glance it seems plausible to say that both avalanches crushed the camp. But this idea is more difficult than it first appears. We are told that two events simultaneously overdetermined the same consequence, but this is metaphorical. It does not tell us *how it is that* the two events actually caused the same consequence at the same moment given the laws of nature in our world – the world for which the theory is intended. Without a proper physical description of the events and consequences in question it is mysterious how two events can simultaneously overdetermine the same consequence.

It deserves mention that avalanches are constituted out of physical things, including volumes of snow, lumps of rock, chunks of ice, tree roots and branches, man-made objects and dust particles. Hence Betty's avalanche B and the natural avalanche A are made up of constituents B/C1, B/C2 to B/Cn and A/C1, A/C2 to A/Cn respectively. The camp is also made up of a number of component parts P1, P2 to Pn and locations L1, L2 to Ln. With this in mind, let us imagine that the camp was being monitored by a network of slow motion cameras. Looking at the camera footage avalanche scientists discover that when the two avalanches hit the camp at time T3, it just so happened that all of the constituents from Betty's avalanche B, as in, B/C1, B/C2 to B/Cn, and only constituents from Betty's avalanche B, crushed all parts of the camp P1, P2 to Pn and occupied all locations L1, L2 to Ln. All of the constituents of the natural avalanche, A/C1, A/C2 to A/Cn, were pushed to the side at the point of impact. The avalanche scientists might account for this surprising set of facts with the hypothesis that Betty's avalanche B had greater velocity than the natural avalanche A. Of course, had the constituents of Betty's avalanche B not crushed the camp and occupied its locations at T3 the constituents of avalanche A would have done so. But this is not what *actually* happened. Given this scientific discovery, the question is whether or not it still makes sense to say that both avalanches crushed the camp. The answer is surely that Betty's avalanche B and not the natural avalanche A crushed the camp. So here we have a case in which at least one person (Betty) *is* morally responsible for an event that causally determined (in part) another event or consequence for which someone (Betty) is morally responsible. So this is not a counterexample to Transfer NR.[8]

At this stage Fischer and Ravizza might insist that I have described a highly unusual turn of events. In most instances of simultaneous crushing of camps (so the counter runs) avalanche scientists expect that the constituents of both avalanches, B/C1, B/C2 to B/Cn and A/C1, A/C2 to A/Cn, will crush different parts of the camp and occupy its different locations. Not only that but snow, ice, rock, trees, objects and dust particles from the two avalanches will merge, meld and combine to form new, mixed constituents, M/C1, M/C2 to M/C3. If this is the case, then we can say that the two avalanches were jointly responsible for crushing the camp. What is more, we can say this even if each avalanche would have been sufficient to crush the camp without the presence of the other avalanche. So once again we do have a counter-example to Transfer NR, namely, a case in which there is an event for which no one is even partly morally responsible (erosion) that causally determined another event or consequence for which at least one person (Betty) *is* morally responsible. However, in order to make this claim Fischer and Ravizza have no choice but to rely on a consequence-particular rather than a consequence-universal. It would not be enough to say that there obtains a consequence-universal, *that the camp is crushed by an avalanche at T3*, which is caused (in part) by an event for which no one is even partly morally responsible. Why? Because that description is quite consistent with the story I told in which constituents from Betty's avalanche B crush all parts of the camp and occupy all locations. In order to rule out this possibility, Fischer and Ravizza must appeal to a consequence-particular, such as, *that a combination of avalanche constituents B/C1, B/C2 to B/C3, A/C1, A/C2 to A/Cn and M/C1, M/C2 to M/C3 crush parts of the camp P1, P2 to Pn at locations L1, L2 to Ln at T3.*

Much the same point applies to Joint Assassins. It is not clear that appealing to the consequence-universal, *that the mayor has been shot and killed at T2*, suffices to show that Sam and Jack are morally responsible. To see why, consider two additional

[8] I do not consider here the fact that there is an ambiguity in the concept of crushing a camp. On one reading, the camp is not crushed until every last part of the camp, P1, P2 to Pn, is crushed. This is "crushed" in the sense of complete obliteration. According to another reading, the camp is crushed only provided that all of the core parts, P*1, P*2 to P*n, are crushed, where the core parts might be the foundation blocks of the main living quarters, the supporting legs of the observation tower, the camp flag, the fence posts, the walls of the ammunition store and the communications dish. This is "crushed" in the sense of rendered useless as a camp but not completely obliterated. I believe that the example could be made to work whichever of the two readings of the concept of crushing a camp is given.

versions of Joint Assassins. In Joint Assassins 4, a forensic pathologist carries out a painstaking autopsy of the mayor's body. The autopsy along with CCTV footage, reveals that both Sam's bullet and Jack's bullet hit the mayor at the exact same moment, but Sam's bullet entered the mayor's heart, while Jack's bullet entered the mayor's stomach. Although either bullet would have been sufficient by itself to cause death, the forensic pathologist determines that it was the bullet entering the heart that caused death. Given this fact, we are inclined to say that Sam killed the mayor, not Jack. This would not count as a counterexample to Transfer NR*, since in this case there is no path for which an agent S is not responsible and that leads to a consequence for which S is responsible. Now consider Joint Assassins 5. Suppose the autopsy reveals that the two bullets entered and exited the mayor's heart at locations L1/L2 and L3/L4 respectively. The forensic pathologist determines that the mayor was killed by virtue of a massive trauma to the heart caused by two bullets entering and exiting the heart at locations L1/L2 and L3/L4 at T2. This implies the actual occurrence of two triggering events which brought about the terminal event simultaneously. And so the counter-example is back in play. However, we can *only* say this because we rely on a consequence-particular, namely, *that the mayor is shot and killed by virtue of a massive trauma to the heart caused by one bullet entering and exiting the heart at locations L1/L2 and a second bullet entering and exiting the heart at locations L3/L4 both at T2*.

The moral of the story is that Fischer and Ravizza's argument against Transfer NR and Transfer NR* does not go through unless the consequences of the putative counterexamples are properly fleshed out, but once the consequences are properly fleshed out we find that they are actually consequence-particulars rather than consequence-universals. Fischer and Ravizza are not unaware of this sort of counter-argument. They refer to it as "the Divide and Conquer strategy" (98). However, they seem to think that the strategy fails in respect of consequence-universals merely because it is possible for agents to exercise guidance control over consequence-universals (101, 106). Yet my objection is not that it is somehow impossible for an agent to exercise guidance control over a consequence-universal. Rather, my objection is that it is difficult to make sense of the claim that two acts can jointly overdetermine the same consequence given our laws of nature without knowing more about the consequences in question. This claim remains mysterious until the contents of the consequences have been fleshed out. But once the contents of the consequences have been fleshed out, they turn out to be consequence-particulars rather than consequence-universals.

Fischer and Ravizza affirm that their counterexamples to Transfer NR and Transfer NR* treat consequences as consequence-universals. If I am correct, then they are mistaken. But so what? Why does it matter if the consequences in question are consequence-particulars as opposed to consequence-universals? Apart from showing that Fischer and Ravizza are mistaken about the nature of their own counterexamples, it matters because telling the stories in terms of consequence-particulars changes our intuitive judgements. If the relevant consequence in the case of Joint Avalanche is the consequence-universal, *that the camp is crushed by an avalanche at T3*, then it opens up the possibility of saying that Betty is fully morally responsible for what happened. But if the relevant consequence turns out to be the consequence-particular, *that the camp is crushed by a combination of avalanche constituents B/C1, B/C2 to B/C3, A/C1, A/C2 to A/Cn and M/C1, M/C2 to M/C3 at T3*, then Betty cannot be fully morally responsible for that consequence, since she is responsible for only some and not all of these avalanche constituents. Likewise, if the relevant consequence in the case of Joint Assassins is the consequence-universal, *that the mayor is shot and killed at T2*, then it seems that both Sam and Jack can be fully morally responsible. However, if the relevant consequence is the consequence-particular, *that the mayor is shot and killed by virtue of a massive trauma to the heart caused by one bullet entering and exiting the heart at locations L1/L2 and a second bullet entering and exiting the heart at locations L3/L4 both at T2*, then neither Sam nor Jack can be fully morally responsible for that consequence. As the case is described above, Sam is not responsible for both bullets, just as Jack is not responsible for both bullets.

Let us now turn from Fischer and Ravizza's negative argument against Transfer NR and Transfer NR* to consider their positive account of what it means for an agent to exercise guidance control over a consequence-universal.

10.5 Jointly Determined Consequences

On Fischer and Ravizza's positive account of moral responsibility, for an agent to be morally responsible for the consequences of his or her acts or omissions it is necessary that the inner mechanism leading to the relevant act or omission is "moderately reasons-responsive" (chap. 3), where the inner mechanism is the "agent's own" (chap. 7) and the agent "takes responsibility" (chap. 8) for it. Furthermore, it is necessary that the act or omission is part of a process of type-P which leads from the act or omission to the consequence in question and is "sensitive to action" or is action-responsive (107). In what follows I wish to concentrate on this notion of action-responsiveness.

According to Fischer and Ravizza, to say that an act or omission is part of a process of type-P that is action-responsive with respect to a consequence C is to say that the process in question involves a person S who moves his body in way B at time T and this is actually sufficient to cause C to obtain at *T+i* given ordinary background conditions, *and* "If S were to move his body in way B* at *T*, all triggering events (apart from B*) which do *not actually* occur between *T* and *T+i* or which *actually* occur and bring about C *simultaneously or subsequently* to *T+i* were *not* to occur, and P-type process were to occur, then C would not occur" (120). So, for example, in the case of Joint Assassins we can say that Sam's act of pulling the trigger is action-responsive with respect to the consequence, *that the mayor is shot and killed at T2*, if and only if Sam's act is part of a process leading from the act to the consequence which is such that Sam's pulling the trigger is actually sufficient for the shooting and killing of the mayor at T2 given ordinary background conditions, and in the absence of other triggering events (i.e. another assassin) Sam's not pulling the trigger does not lead to the shooting and killing of the mayor at T2. Fischer and

Ravizza assume that the bullets are fired under ordinary atmospheric conditions and that such ordinary background conditions are part of the process that actually leads to the consequence (113).

Fischer and Ravizza believe that action-responsiveness is a necessary condition for attributing moral responsibility for consequences. To support this belief, they offer the example of "Missile 3". Imagine that an evil woman, Elizabeth, has launched a missile toward Washington, D.C. However, a second woman, Joan, has another weapon which she can fire at Elizabeth's missile so as to deflect it to a less populous area of the city. Due to her position, the missile's trajectory and the nature of her own weapon, Joan cannot actually prevent the incoming missile from hitting the city. But she can deflect Elizabeth's missile between neighbourhoods, say, from Columbia Heights to Glenmont. Fischer and Ravizza contend that because Joan is involved in a process which is *not* action-responsive with regard to the consequence-universal, *that Washing, D.C. is bombed*, she is not morally responsible for that consequence. This holds even if it *is* the case that Joan is responsible for the consequence-particular, *that Washing, D.C. is bombed at Columbia Heights rather than Glenmont* (95).

However, I shall now try to show that Fischer and Ravizza's account of action-responsiveness cannot capture our intuitions in an important range of cases. To be more specific, I will offer three examples that although do *not* contain a person S who moves his body in a way that is sufficient to cause C to obtain, and as such do not qualify as examples of action-responsiveness according to the proposed definition, do nevertheless seem to involve moral responsibility at an intuitive level.[9] All three examples involve persons whose acts *jointly determine* certain consequences.[10]

The first example, which I call Revolutionaries, involves *cumulative* shooting and killing. Imagine that two revolutionaries, working independently and without knowledge of each other's plans, both set out to kill a government official, each with a single bullet. However, because they are both farmers and not trained soldiers they are not very accurate. Consequently, they each shoot the mayor in parts of his body that other things remaining equal would not cause death. Yet the cumulative effect of both bullets is enough to cause death. In this example I think it makes sense to say that each revolutionary is *jointly* responsible for shooting and killing the government official even if the actions of each assassin, taken in isolation, did not cause death.

[9] I shall not discuss here an example put forward by Glannon (1997) in which an agent is in a situation such that even though her act was not, and could not have been, sufficient to bring about or prevent the occurrence of an undesirable consequence directly, she is nevertheless morally responsible for the consequence through her own negligent interference in the actions of another person who is in a position to determine what happens directly.

[10] I do not intend to consider cases of analytic joint responsibility; that is to say, cases in which it is true by virtue of the meanings of the terms that two agents are responsible for the consequence in question since the consequence must involve joint action. For example, we might say that two people must be jointly responsible for the consequence, *that the boss had an affair with his secretary*, since given the ordinary meaning of "an affair" the consequence must be the result of the joint actions of two agents. This is captured by the popular dictum, "it takes two to tango".

The second example, which I shall call Fundamentalists, involves shooting and killing as a *joint enterprise*. Suppose two religious fundamentalists set out to kill the leader of their country on the grounds that they believe he is standing in the way of the creation of a religious state. Due to the heavy security protecting the leader the fundamentalists have to work together in order to smuggle a rifle into the building opposite the leader's residence. The first fundamentalist smuggles in the frame, barrel and magazine of the rifle, while the second smuggles in the sights and the ammunition. The collaboration does not end there. While the first fundamentalist loads the rifle and holds it steady, the second lines up the crosshairs and pulls the trigger. Here we have a case in which two agents act in conjunction in pursuit of a common goal that they simply could not achieve working alone. Although only one of the fundamentalists pulls the trigger, it seems that they are both *jointly* morally responsible for shooting and killing the leader in the sense that they were both part of a joint enterprise. That they are both jointly morally responsible holds true even though there is *not* one person S whose acts caused the consequence C to obtain.

The third example, call it Firing Squad, involves *probabilistic* shooting and killing. Imagine that an army training facility commandant has set up a firing squad whose task it is to execute a deserter. The firing squad is composed of six marksmen all of whom are good shots. The commandant instructs each of the marksmen to aim at the deserter's head from a close range and to shoot at the same moment. However, unbeknownst to the marksmen, the commandant only loads one of the six rifles with live ammunition; the other five rifles are loaded with blanks. The marksmen select the rifles at random and out of sight of the commandant. They are all wearing hearing protectors. Neither the commandant nor the marksmen know which particular marksman had been given the rifle loaded with live ammunition such that in the end nobody knows who actually shot and killed the deserter. Needless to say, all we know is that for each marksman there is a 16.67 percent probability that he shot and killed the deserter. But this is not the same as saying for each marksman that his actions caused the death of the deserter. This is unlike the case of Assassins in which, according to Fischer and Ravizza's description, there is a 100 percent probability that each assassin shot and killed the mayor. As a way of reflecting what is unknown about the shooting and killing of the deserter in Firing Squad, we might say that the marksmen *jointly* shot and killed the deserter.

On Fischer and Ravizza's positive account of moral responsibility and action-responsiveness, in order to attribute moral responsibility to a person it is necessary that he moves his body in way B at time T and this is actually sufficient to cause C to obtain. In the foregoing examples, each particular person did not move his body in a way that was actually sufficient to cause the relevant consequences to obtain. Not only that, but there are (by stipulation) no other acts or omissions which are sufficient to cause the consequence. That is to say, there are no other genuine trigger events to be screened out assuming that a trigger event is "an event which is such that, if it were to occur, it would *initiate* a causal sequence leading to C" (110–11). Nevertheless, these examples intuitively involve persons who *are* morally responsible for the consequences in question or at least are *jointly* morally responsible for the consequences in question. If I am right in this intuitive judgment, then these examples directly challenge Fischer and Ravizza's account of action-responsiveness or their assertion that action-responsiveness is a necessary condition of moral responsibility.

What is interesting about these examples is that they exist on the margins of what Fischer and Ravizza have in mind when they say that moral responsibility for consequences may only be attributed to persons when their acts or omissions are involved in consequence-obtaining processes that are themselves "sensitive to action". This is another way of saying that the relevant acts or omissions must make a difference to what actually happens. All of my examples involve particular acts that can make a difference to what actually happens but only in the sense that they make a difference to what actually happens (as in, they cause the terminal event to obtain) provided that they are combined with other acts or omissions. To make the same point slightly differently, the acts do not qualify as triggers in the strict sense, since if the act occurs by itself, then it is not enough to initiate the consequence. Nevertheless, each act is crucial to a joint act or a set of acts that is a trigger in that sense.

10.6 Possible Replies

How might Fischer and Ravizza respond? I do not think that they have the option of accepting that action-responsiveness is not a necessary condition for attributing moral responsibility. This would be to significantly change the character of their view of moral responsibility. It would also render their account of inner mechanisms discontinuous with their account of outer processes. But neither, I think, do they have the option of simply ignoring the above examples. Examples of jointly determined consequences do not fall on the penumbra of our ordinary moral experience. On the contrary, such examples are fairly typical of the sorts of questions of moral responsibility that we face every day. Consider the joint responsibility of prison guards for death row executions, the joint responsibility of parents for the bad behaviour of their children, the joint responsibility of a group of thugs for beating up and killing a neighbour who dares to challenge them, the joint responsibility of members of terrorist organisations for planning and carrying out atrocities, the joint responsibility of multiple generations for global warming.

Alternatively, Fischer and Ravizza might try to insist that the foregoing examples are not counterexamples to their account on the grounds that their definition of action-responsiveness *does* apply to these examples after careful reflection. Recall that according to Fischer and Ravizza's definition, an act or omission is part of a process of type-P that is action-responsive with respect to a consequence-universal C if and only if the act or omission is actually sufficient for C to obtain and a different consequence would have obtained if the act or omission had not occurred and all other triggering events that would have been sufficient to cause C are not in play. Much depends on what the relevant process is. If the relevant process for each act has narrow scope, then it involves that act and only that act along with its ordinary background conditions. In which case, when it comes to the foregoing examples the processes in question are not action-responsive with respect to their consequences. Yet if the relevant process for each act has wide scope, then it involves that act along with its ordinary background conditions and possibly other people's acts as well. In which case, the processes in question can be action-responsive in these examples.

However, this raises the difficulty of identifying in advance which is the operative process in any given example: is it the narrow scope process or the wide scope process? After all, someone might attempt to abdicate moral responsibility for the consequences of an act on the grounds that his or her act was part of a process that had narrow scope and was thereby not action-responsive in relation to the consequence, while others will argue (perhaps the victims of the act) that the person should be held morally responsible for the consequences on the grounds that the act was part of a process that had wide scope and was action-responsive.

In fact, Fischer and Ravizza "concede both that process individuation is problematic and that [they] do not have an explicit theory of process individuation" (113). Nevertheless, they insist that "all that is required for our purposes is that there be agreement about some fairly clear cases" (ibid.). But what would that agreement look like? Perhaps the idea is that the operative process will be defined as being whichever process produces an attribution of moral responsibility that most people find intuitive. But then the task of process identification becomes ad hoc. Furthermore, where it is vague whether or not someone is morally responsible, it remains vague what the relevant process is. Fischer and Ravizza seem willing to accept this outcome. "If we are unsure about an agent's moral responsibility for a consequence in precisely those cases in which we are unsure about process individuation, then at least the vagueness of our theory will match the vagueness of the phenomena it purports to analyze" (ibid.). Nevertheless, this outcome may seem disappointing to some people. Ideally (they might say) we want a theory of moral responsibility that has the power to make us sure about examples concerning which we had been previously unsure.

In light of all this, it seems to me that in order to capture our ordinary intuitions about jointly determined consequences we need new accounts of moral responsibility and of action-responsiveness which are especially designed for examples of that sort. As well as accounts of individual moral responsibility for consequences and individual action-responsiveness for consequences we need dedicated accounts of joint moral responsibility for consequences and joint action-responsiveness for consequences. With this in mind, let us say that an individual is jointly morally responsible for a consequence C if and only if he or she is morally responsible for the internal mechanism leading to his or her own act or omission *and* his or her act or omission is jointly action-responsive with respect to C along with the act or omission of at least one other individual who is also morally responsible for the internal mechanism leading to his or her own acts or omissions. An individual's act or omission is jointly action-responsive with respect to a consequence C if and only if it along with the acts or omissions of at least one other individual is part of a process of type P which is sufficient for C to obtain, and a different consequence would have obtained if it along with the other acts or omissions had not occurred and all other triggering events that would have been sufficient to cause C are not in play. Taking into consideration my earlier discussion of consequence-universals and consequence-particulars, I leave it open as to whether C is a universal or particular.

The reader might wonder why I have not mentioned the possibility of an individual being jointly morally responsible for a consequence that has been jointly causally determined by his or her acts or omissions along with a *natural event* as opposed to the acts or omissions of at least one other person or moral agent. My hunch is that it would be linguistically odd to speak of *joint* moral responsibility in such cases, since here moral responsibility would be shared between a person and a natural event. This hunch is supported by the view that reason-responsiveness is a necessary condition for moral responsibility and by the fact that this condition cannot be satisfied by a natural event. So, I propose that in such instances we speak instead of a person being *partly* morally responsible for the given consequence, where this is by virtue of her being morally responsible for the internal mechanism involved *and* her acts or omissions being jointly action-responsive with respect to that consequence along with the natural event. The definition of joint action-responsiveness remains the same in this proposed account of *part* moral responsibility for consequences except that natural events are added to the right hand side of the biconditional.

With these accounts of joint moral responsibility for consequences and joint action-responsiveness for consequences in place, I believe that it is now possible to make intuitive judgements about my three examples. In Revolutionaries, we can say that each of the revolutionaries is jointly morally responsible for the consequence, *that the government official was shot and killed*, because (by stipulation) each revolutionary was morally responsible for his own internal mechanisms *and* both of their actions were jointly action-responsive with respect to that consequence. One might say that their actions each contributed – in a cumulative fashion – to a process that was action-responsive with respect to the consequence. I propose similar judgements for Fundamentalists and Firing Squad. In the example of Fundamentalists, the two sets of actions were jointly action-responsive – by dint of the fundamentalists' joint enterprise – with respect to the consequence, *that the leader was shot and killed*. And in Firing Squad, the acts of each of the marksmen were jointly action-responsive in respect of the consequence, *that the deserter was shot and killed* – by virtue of the fact that together their acts had a 100 percent probability of bringing about that consequence.

Before concluding, I offer the following comment on how Fischer and Ravizza might respond to my accounts. They might argue that there is no need to augment their theory with my new accounts, since they can deal with my three examples of jointly determined consequences in the following way. When an individual agent is part of a joint activity, the question of moral responsibility pertains to the group or corporate entity. We can then apply the existing account of moral responsibility to that corporate entity as the relevant *agent*. Hence, Fischer and Ravizza might say that a corporate entity is morally responsible for a certain consequence just in case its behaviour issues from its own, suitably reasons-responsive internal mechanism *and* its behaviour is part of a process which is action-responsive with respect to that consequence. This account would not be applicable to examples where an individual's acts or omissions jointly determine a consequence along with a natural event. That is because in such situations there is no corporate entity with a suitably reasons-responsive internal mechanism. Yet it could potentially work for my three examples.

Now there certainly are occasions when it is fitting to inquire into the moral responsibility of a corporate entity or group. We often say that nations are morally responsible in this way. But what happens to the moral responsibility of individuals in all of this? Surely we do not want to lose that dimension altogether. At this point Fischer and Ravizza could try to argue that the moral responsibility of the individual flows from the moral responsibility of the group. Provided they can explain how it is that groups have suitably reasons-responsive internal mechanisms, they might argue that an individual is morally responsible for the consequences of a group's behaviour just in case he or she is a voluntary member of the group, he or she played some part in the group's reasons-responsive internal mechanism and the group's behaviour is part of a process that is action-responsive in relation to the consequences. However, none of this means that we are somehow uninterested in the particular part played by individual members in bringing about the relevant consequences. For, we cannot take it as read that every member's behaviour is action-responsive with respect to the consequences. And arguably we might want to draw a moral distinction between someone whose acts or omissions do actually figure in the relevant action-responsive process and someone whose acts or omissions do not. In addition to this, one cannot rely on the existence of group moral responsibility to explain individual moral responsibility in the case of Revolutionaries (and other similar cases) because here the individuals under discussion have no knowledge of each other and are not associates.

Hence the purpose of my schema is to account for joint moral responsibility of individuals by making it explicit that an individual's acts or omissions must be jointly action-responsive in relation to the relevant consequences along with the acts or omissions of other individuals with whom that joint moral responsibility is to be shared. What is more, I have provided a story or set of stories that hopefully explain *how it is possible* for the acts or omissions of individuals to become parts of jointly action-responsive processes along with the acts or omissions of other individuals. These stories involved associates and members of groups as well as non-associates and isolated agents. In my three examples I explained the occurrence of joint action-responsiveness in terms of *accumulation*, *joint enterprise* and *probability*. This means that I can use my schema to account for the possible existence of joint moral responsibility without necessarily having to rely on the existence of corporate entities or groups with their own suitably reasons-responsive internal mechanisms.

In this article I have put to one side the question of internal mechanisms and focused instead on external processes. (There might be a need for an account of joint moral responsibility in respect of joint internal mechanisms in the event that examples come to light which call for such an account.) I have pointed out a flaw in Fischer and Ravizza's negative argument that the inevitability of certain events or consequences does not rule out the possibility of an agent's moral responsibility for those consequences. I have also been critical of their positive argument that moral responsibility for consequences depends on action-responsiveness. In the former case I argued that their putative counterexamples against Transfer NR and Transfer NR* are underdescribed but once fully described depend upon consequence-particulars and not consequence-universals as they claim. In the latter case I argued that their account is unable to cope with quite ordinary cases of jointly determined consequences.

References

Fischer, John, and Ravizza, Mark. 1998. *Responsibility and Control: A Theory of Moral Responsibility*. Cambridge: Cambridge University Press.
Fischer, John, and Ravizza, Mark. 2000. "Replies." *Philosophy and Phenomenological Research* 61:467–80.
Frankfurt, Harry. 1969. "Alternative Possibilities and Moral Responsibility." *Journal of Philosophy* 66:829–39.
Frankfurt, Harry. 1971. "Freedom of the Will and the Concept of a Person." *Journal of Philosophy* 68:5–22.
Frankfurt, Harry. 1987. "Identification and Wholeheartedness." In *Responsibility, Character, and the Emotions: New Essay in Moral Psychology*, edited by Ferdinand Schoeman. Cambridge: Cambridge University Press. pp. 27–45.
Ginet, Carl. 2006. "Working with Fischer and Ravizza's Account of Moral Responsibility." *Journal of Ethics* 10:229–53.
Glannon, Walter. 1997. "Sensitivity and Responsibility for Consequences." *Philosophical Studies* 87:223–33.
Grann, David. 2009. "Trial by Fire: Did Texas Execute an Innocent Man?" In *The New Yorker*, September 7. Available at: www.newyorker.com/reporting/2009/09/07/090907fa_fact_grann, last accessed July 1, 2011.
Judisch, Neal. 2007. "Reasons-Responsive Compatibilism and the Consequences of Belief." *The Journal of Ethics* 11:357–75.
Levy, Neil. 2002. "Excusing Responsibility for the Inevitable." *Philosophical Studies* 111:43–52.
McKenna, Michael. 2008. "Saying Good-Bye to the Direct Argument the Right Way." *Philosophical Review* 117:349–83.
Stump, Eleonore. 2000. "Review: The Direct Argument for Incompatibilism." *Philosophy and Phenomenological Research* 61:459–66.

Chapter 11
Joint Responsibility Without Individual Control: Applying the Explanation Hypothesis

Gunnar Björnsson

Abstract This paper introduces a new family of cases where agents are jointly morally responsible for outcomes over which they have no individual control, a family that resists standard ways of understanding outcome responsibility. First, the agents in these cases do not individually facilitate the outcomes and would not seem individually responsible for them if the other agents were replaced by non-agential causes. This undermines attempts to understand joint responsibility as overlapping individual responsibility; the responsibility in question is *essentially* joint. Second, the agents involved in these cases are not aware of each other's existence and do not form a social group. This undermines attempts to understand joint responsibility in terms of actual or possible joint action or joint intentions, or in terms of other social ties. Instead, it is argued that intuitions about joint responsibility are best understood given the *Explanation Hypothesis*, according to which a group of agents are seen as jointly responsible for outcomes that are suitably explained by their motivational structures, invoked collectively: something bad happened because they didn't care enough; something good happened because their dedication was extraordinary. One important consequence of the proposed account is that responsibility for outcomes of collective action is a deeply normative matter.

11.1 Joint Moral Responsibility Without Individual Control

Sometimes a number of individuals seem *jointly* morally responsible for events over which they, as individuals, had no control. Consider a simplified case:

> *The Lake:* Alice, Bill and Cecil each have a small boat in East Lake outside their town. One day last spring, each painted the boat and, unknown to the others, poured excess solvent into the lake. In the back of their heads, they all knew that this could affect the wildlife, but each of them decided that it would be a hassle to dispose of the solvent in a safe way and hoped that nothing bad would happen. However, as the solvent from all three diffused throughout the lake over the next few days, its concentration became high enough everywhere to prevent micro-organisms in the lake from reproducing during the next few weeks, thus leaving higher organisms without food and effectively wiping out all fish in the lake.

G. Björnsson (✉)
Linköping University, Linköping, Sweden

University of Gothenburg, Gothenburg, Sweden
e-mail: gunnar.bjornsson@liu.se

N.A Vincent et al. (eds.), *Moral Responsibility*, Library of Ethics and Applied Philosophy 27, DOI 10.1007/978-94-007-1878-4_11,

> The concentration of solvent exceeded the threshold for the microorganisms by quite some margin: although the solvent from only one of the three would not have been enough to kill off the fish, the solvent from any two would.

Let us assume that all three agents satisfied conditions of moral accountability. They were not being forced or manipulated to do what they did and they had both the capacity to reason and reflect on the values involved and the relevant sort of control over their own decisions and actions. Then it seems that we can rightly hold them responsible for recklessly pouring solvent into the lake. But to just about everyone that I have confronted with the case, it also seems clear that they are morally responsible *for the death of the fish*, that is, for an outcome of their actions over which they had no control as individuals. Similarly, it seems that voters can be morally responsible for the outcome of a referendum, citizens for toppling a dictatorial regime, consumers for good or bad practices of companies they patronize, and frequent flyers and drivers of SUVs for climate effects, even though, as individuals, they could not have significantly affected those outcomes, practices or effects.

The question of this paper concerns the conditions for such joint responsibility for outcomes of collective actions. In the next section, I explain why a case like *The Lake* provides difficulties for standard ways of understanding collective responsibility. In Section 11.3, I propose a preliminary analysis of joint responsibility based on variations on *The Lake*. To support this analysis, Section 11.4 introduces the *Explanation Hypothesis*, a model of our concept of moral responsibility that was developed to account for various aspects of individual moral responsibility for decisions, actions and outcomes. In Section 11.5, I show how the Explanation Hypothesis subsumes and deepens the analysis of Section 11.3. In Section 11.6, finally, I suggest a way of turning the Explanation Hypothesis' characterization of our *concept* of moral responsibility into an account of moral responsibility as such. One of the important consequences of the proposed account is that responsibility for outcomes of collective action is a deeply normative matter.

Some caveats are in order. First, the concern of this paper is *moral, retrospective responsibility for events*. Space prevents me from saying anything about the tight and interesting connections between this topic and other questions discussed under the heading of "responsibility" – questions concerning legal liability, moral or legal obligations to *ensure* outcomes or to *take* responsibility for outcomes by compensating those harmed, and questions about what characterizes responsible persons, or responsible decision procedures. Second, since the concern is with joint responsibility of *individual* agents, I will not say anything about the claim that collectives can be responsible for an outcome when *none* of their members are. (For recent defences of "autonomous" corporate responsibility, see Arnold 2006; Pettit 2007; Tännsjö 2007; Copp 2007; for criticism see Corlett 2001; Haji 2006; McKenna 2006; Miller 2007.) Third, the primary concern here is with *outcome* responsibility rather than responsibility for decisions. The conditions under which individuals are responsible for their decisions are themselves highly contestable, but I will assume that all individuals in the cases discussed are autonomous, in control of their own decisions and actions, capable of rational deliberation, suffering from no motivational maladies, and, as a result, responsible for their own acts or failures to act. Fourth, since our concern is with difficulties pertaining specifically to the understanding of how individuals are *jointly* responsible for outcomes, I will assume that other difficulties pertaining to outcome responsibility can be overcome, in particular the fact that outcomes often depend on factors outside the agent's control. (For discussion, see Feinberg 1968:681–82; Nagel 1976; Sverdlik 1987:74; May 1992:42–45; Enoch and Marmor 2007). Finally, although it is clear that individuals can be jointly responsible for good outcomes, I will follow most of the literature and focus on responsibility for *bad* outcomes. It should be clear, however, that the discussion generalizes.

11.2 Difficulties

As we shall see, neither the standard notion of individual responsibility for outcomes, nor typical strategies for making sense of collective moral responsibility explain the intuition that the agents in cases like *The Lake* are responsible for the outcomes in question.

On a standard conception, an individual agent is morally responsible for a harm to the extent that some morally faulty aspect of her behaviour played a significant causal role in producing that harm (Feinberg 1968:674; May 1992:15). The difficulty is to see how the reckless acts of the agents in *The Lake* play a significant causal role.

We have already noted that no one agent made any difference to the survival of the fish given the other acts, so significance cannot require such *difference making*. On the other hand, the solvent contributed by each agent was causally involved in bringing about the outcome. But causal *involvement* cannot in itself be what accounts for individual responsibility for the collective outcome. Suppose that there are two solvents. Solvent X works as before, preventing microorganisms from reproducing, but it can do so by means of either of two distinct but equally powerful chemical processes, X1 and X2, depending on whether solvent Y is present. Solvent Y is itself incapable of doing any damage except in extreme concentrations, but will favour process X2 in the presence of solvent X. Suppose further that whereas Bill and Cecil poured solvent X into the lake, Alice contributed solvent Y, thus slightly changing the way the solvents from Bill and Cecil prevented micro-organisms from reproducing. Then it is not clear that she would be morally responsible for the outcome.

Intuitively, it might seem that the relevant causal involvement would have to be one of at least *facilitating* the causal process, or make it more likely to produce the outcome (cf. Petersson 2004). But while that might be true for responsibility for outcomes of individual actions, it is not required in *The Lake*. Suppose that when the concentration of solvent reaches above what would be provided by two polluters, the process by which the microorganisms are prevented from reproducing is both slowed down and made more open to possible disturbances, thus slightly decreasing the objective probability of the outcome. Then it is true of each of the polluters that he or she actually (but unwittingly) lowered the probability that the fish would die and obstructed that process to some degree, given the actual contribution from the other two. Nevertheless, the three polluters would still seem to be jointly responsible for the death of the fish; it still died because of their actions.

Now consider the corresponding case with only one agent involved:

Adam's Lake: Because of rare but naturally occurring processes, a poisonous substance is produced in the mud at the bottom of the lake. The amount would be just enough, by itself, to prevent the microorganisms from reproducing. Over the same period, Adam is painting his boat, recklessly pouring excess solvent into the lake, solvent containing the very same poisonous substance. The overall result is that the lake contains more than enough to kill off the microorganisms. In fact, at this concentration, the processes preventing the reproduction are a little slower than they would have been if Adam had not disposed of his solvent this way. In the end, though, the microorganisms are wiped out.

Though it is clear that Adam is morally responsible for recklessly pouring solvent into the lake, most people seem reluctant to say that he is responsible for the death of the fish. At the very least, it was much clearer that Alice, Bill and Cecil were so responsible in *The Lake*. This strongly suggests that the responsibility attributed to the three is fundamentally collective. *Taken together*, the faulty behaviours of Alice, Bill and Cecil clearly played a significant causal role in wiping out the fish; *individually*, they did not.

The problem posed by *The Lake* for standard accounts of responsibility for outcomes of individual action is equally a problem for attempts, like that of Stephen Sverdlik (1987), to reduce collective or shared outcome responsibility to individual outcome responsibility. But it also poses a problem for other standard attempts to understand forms of collective or shared responsibility, whether reductive or not. Since the most obvious cases in which we hold agents responsible for an outcome *as a group* are cases where they have either worked together towards some goal or failed to do so, such attempts are often cast in terms of actual or possible joint agency or joint intentions (e.g., Held 1970; Rescher 1998; Kutz 2000; Miller 2006; Sadler 2006; Shockley 2007). Less obvious and more controversial are cases where members of a community are responsible for outcomes of acts by other members because members empower and are empowered by each other, and thus "shares in what each member does, and ... should feel responsible for what the other members do" (May 1992:11).

The Lake fits neither of these patterns. Since Alice, Bill and Cecil performed their acts independently and without knowledge of the others, they had no intentions to act together with the others. Nor is it likely that our ascription of joint responsibility relies on the assumption that they could reasonably have formed such intentions. Moreover, we have no reason to think that they form a group the members of which empower each other. For all we know, they might see each other as enemies. Still, they seem jointly morally responsible for the death of the fish.

What is clear from *The* Lake and similar examples is that a number of individuals can be jointly responsible for an outcome if, *together*, they play a significant causal role for that outcome. Structurally, this relation between the actions of the individuals and the outcome is similar to well-known attempts to analyse causes, not as necessary conditions or difference makers, but as non-redundant parts of nomically sufficient conditions for effects (Mackie 1974; cf. Wright 1988). In *The Lake*, the actions of the three agents are pair-wise sufficient for the outcome, each action being a non-redundant part of such a pair. It might thus be tempting to explain the joint responsibility of the three agents in such terms (Braham and van Hees 2010). Unfortunately, any such attempt will run into deep problems with cases of what David Lewis (1986b) calls "causal preemption". Suppose that instead of pouring solvent into *East Lake*, Alice built a contraption that monitored the concentration of solvent in the lake and set it to empty her bucket of solvent into the lake should the level not rise high enough to kill the fish. Since Bill and Cecil contributed enough solvent, Alice's contraption was never triggered. In this case, she clearly would not be responsible for the outcome, even though her action would be a non-redundant part of sufficient conditions for the death of the fish (conditions including her action and the contribution of either Bill or Cecil).[1]

Elsewhere I have defended a way for theories of causation dealing in sufficient conditions to adequately account for cases of causal preemption (Björnsson 2007). But something more would need to be said even with such an account at hand. The fact that Adam poured solvent into the lake was a non-redundant part of a sufficient condition for the death of the fish, together with the fact that some volume of mud at the bottom of the lake emitted the same amount of poisonous substance; yet Adam's responsibility for that outcome is much less obvious than that of Alice, Bill and Cecill in *The Lake*. Apparently it matters whether the actions of other agents are involved; the fundamental problem of joint responsibility is *why*. This is where I hope to make progress.

11.3 A Preliminary Analysis of Responsibility for Outcomes of Collective Action

To understand joint responsibility, the first thing to be clear about is the required relation between the collective and the outcome for which they are responsible. As a first approximation, what is required seems to be that, together, the responsible agents play a significant role in the *explanation* of the outcome: the fish died *because of* Alice, Bill and Cecil. With some qualifications, this is very much in line with the idea that individual outcome responsibility requires that the individual's behaviour played a significant causal role in the outcome. However, talk about *causal* (as opposed to *explanatory*) role suggests that the responsible parties *brought about* or *produced* the outcome rather than merely *let it happen*, and we know that production is not required for outcome responsibility:

> *The Well:* Eric, Fiona and George are spending a Sunday afternoon in the woods, each thinking that he or she is the only person within miles. Suddenly they hear cries for help

[1] Other problems are provided by probabilistic case where there are no causally sufficient conditions for outcomes, and so-called "switching" cases, where necessary parts of sufficient conditions seem to change the way an outcome happens without being causally responsible for it (cf. the case where Alice contributes solvent Y). These are also problems for counterfactual analyses in the tradition of David Lewis (1973); for discussion, see e.g. (Collins et al. 2004; Björnsson 2007).

> coming from an area with especially dense vegetation. Although the cries are disturbing and continues for a long while, each ignores them while thinking that they could be part of a prank, or that whatever might be going on is none of their business. Had they walked in the direction of the cries, however, they would have found a woman, Hannah, who had accidentally fallen into a partially overgrown old well but was hanging onto a ledge a meter or so down, screaming for help and slowly losing her grip. Since no one came to her help, Hannah eventually fell down into the dried up well and died as she hit the rocks at the bottom. The story could have ended differently, however. One person would not have been able to pull her up without help, but had any two of those who heard her cries come to her rescue, they would have been able to save her.

It seems that if they learned the truth of what happened, Eric, Fiona and George could rightly blame themselves for not having investigated the call closer. But it also seems that they are to some extent morally responsible for the fatal *outcome* of the accident (though not, of course, for the accident itself), and they certainly seem responsible for the fact that Hannah wasn't saved. They could have saved her, but they did not. As in *The Lake*, the responsibility involved seems to be essentially collective. In a version of *The Well* – *Esther's Well* – Esther is the only person in place to hear Hannah's cries. Like Eric, she ignores the cries for dubious reasons; like Eric she would have been unable to save Hannah even if she had responded. But whereas Eric, Fiona and George seemed clearly responsible for the fact that Hannah wasn't saved, Esther clearly is not. *Esther's Well* highlights the essentially joint nature of Eric's, Fiona's and George's responsibility in *The Well*, just as *Adam's Lake* did in relation to *The Lake*.

In *The Well*, unlike in *The Lake*, there is a sense in which none of the three were *involved* in the process leading to the final outcome: indeed, it seems that they could all have been absent and nothing in that process would have been different (ignoring minute differences in the gravitational field and the like). Nevertheless, it seems that their inaction *explains why* Hannah wasn't saved. This is the notion of "explaining why" that seems relevant for our ordinary attribution of moral responsibility in these cases.

Thus far I have suggested that *the agents* should play a significant role in the explanation of the outcome. But more needs to be said about the required sort of involvement. As we have already seen from *The Well*, the relevant involvement need not consist of any particular sort of positive *intentional action*: perhaps Eric was sitting on a rock, Fiona climbing a tree, and George running across a meadow instead of helping Hannah. Similarly, no *decisions* on part of members of the group need to be involved in the explanation. Perhaps none of the three even considered the possibility of finding out whether they could help; perhaps they just noted, absent-mindedly, that someone seemed to be in need of help but failed to see any reason to take action. That would not seem to remove their responsibility as long as they could have considered the possibility to help, and would have done so if they had cared more about the needs of others. That no decision is needed can be made even clearer with a case involving negligent ignorance where there is no awareness of risk involved. Suppose that Alice, Bill and Cecil poured the solvent into the lake while being unaware of its lethal potential. They could still be responsible for the outcome if the reason they were unaware was that they lacked concern for the environment or for taking in relevant information, and if that explained why they failed to react to the warning signs on the cans of solvent.

In all these variations, we might say that some morally "faulty" aspect of behaviour explains the outcome, but the behaviour seems faulty only because it is explained by the wrong sensitivity to values, or the wrong motivational structure. If Alice, Bill and Cecil were ignorant of the solvent's lethal potential due to other factors than a lack of appropriate concern, their responsibility for the death of the fish is undermined. Similarly, suppose that George was wearing headphones and did not hear Hannah's cries for help. Or suppose that he heard the cries and started walking towards the well but was trapped by impenetrable vegetation blocking his way and delaying him until it was too late. In neither case would he seem to be responsible for the outcome. The best explanation for that, it seems, is that in these cases, unlike in the original scenario, George's concern or lack of concern fails to explain why he didn't reach the well in time.

Another thing to notice is that the outcome needs to be explained by the motivational structure in a "normal" way. If Dave finds out that Alice, Bill and Cecil lack appropriate concern for the environment and draconically proceeds to poison their lake to teach them a lesson, their lack of concern might be part of the explanation of the death of the fish in the lake, but they are not thereby morally responsible for it. Similarly, if George's lack of concern for others had made him ignore a discussion of feasible paths through the forest, and if as a result he was stuck in the mud and unable to heed Hannah's call, it is not clear that he is thereby morally responsible for not having come to her rescue.

Judging from the variations of *The Lake* and *The Well*, it seems that the two groups of people are responsible for the outcomes because the outcomes are explained (in a "normal" way) by the agents' motivational structures. The fish died because Alice, Bill and Cecil lacked appropriate concern for the environment; Hannah's accident had a fatal outcome because Eric, Fiona and George lacked appropriate concern for their fellow human beings. The same seems to hold for cases of moral responsibility for *good* outcomes. Suppose that each member of a trio discovers and mends a leaking sewer out of concern for the environment and that the reduction of pollution secured by any two of them would have been enough to save the fish in the nearby lake, but not the reduction secured by only one agent. Then it would seem reasonable to say that the fish survived because these three individuals cared about the environment, and they would seem to be correspondingly (jointly) responsible for that outcome.

The question remains, however, whether we can expect this analysis to survive still further variations, and whether it generalizes to other cases of collective responsibility. Moreover, we have yet to explain why the *individuals* are jointly responsible for the outcomes, given this diagnosis. It is one thing to say that the group is responsible, another to say that the members of the group are, and it might be thought that attributions of moral responsibility in cases like these involve some kind of mistake. Perhaps our desire to hold someone responsible prompts us to *confusedly* assign joint responsibility for outcomes on the ground that (a) each individual is responsible for wrongfully risking some bad effect – an adverse environmental effects, say – and (b) what they risked actually took place because of these wrongdoings, taken collectively. The suspicion that there is something amiss with our judgments gains force from a comparison of Alice's responsibility in *The Lake* and Adam's in *Adam's Lake*. In spite of performing identical actions the upshots of which are causally involved in bringing about the death of the fish in the same way, and in spite of the fact that their actions resulted from identical motivational structures, Alice's responsibility was *much* clearer than Adam's. And in spite of acting in the very same way as Esther for the very same reasons and having exactly the same possibility to save Hannah – i.e. none – only Eric seemed responsible for the fact that Hannah wasn't saved. This is bound to strike some readers as arbitrary.[2]

I address these issues in the next three sections. Section 11.4 introduces an independently motivated hypothesis about our concept of individual retrospective moral responsibility, the *Explanation Hypothesis*. In Section 11.5, I explain how it subsumes the analysis of joint responsibility developed in this section. This gives us reason to think that our present analysis will generalize to further cases. Moreover, it suggests that the different attributions of responsibility to Alice and Adam are no more arbitrary than attributions of outcome responsibility in general. Although the Explanation Hypothesis is primarily an empirical hypothesis about our concept of responsibility, supported by its predictive power, it strongly suggests an account of moral responsibility. In Section 11.6, finally, I introduce that account – *Explanatory Responsibility* – and discuss how it makes issues of outcome responsibility deeply normative.

11.4 The Explanation Hypothesis

In two recent papers (Björnsson and Persson 2009, 2011), Karl Persson and I have argued that a wide variety of intuitions about individual responsibility for decisions, actions and outcomes can be explained if we understand our concept of moral responsibility as shaped by our interest in holding people responsible. What follows is a brief and simplified version of that story.

People hold each other responsible for a variety of events in a variety of ways. We blame or express indignation towards people who have brought about or failed to prevent something bad for lack of proper concern, and praise or express moral admiration towards those who have brought about or let happen something good at remarkable costs to themselves. Sometimes our expressions of so-called "reactive" attitudes are as simple as a frown or a smile. At other times we are more elaborate, punishing or demanding explanation or compensation, or distributing rewards and honours. And we direct analogues of all these reactions towards ourselves.

Our interest in holding people responsible is largely an interest in shaping motivational structures – values, preferences, behavioural and emotional habits, etc – in order to promote or prevent certain kinds of actions or events that we like or dislike.

---

[2] See (Zimmerman 1985:116–17) for an argument that seems to assume that differences of this sort cannot make for different degrees of responsibility.

Consciously or unconsciously, we often hold ourselves and each other responsible for various outcomes so that we will behave responsibly and take into account possible outcomes of the sort that we have been held responsible for. This is not to deny that we often hold people responsible for reasons of desert, without an eye to deterring or encouraging agents or third parties. The claim is merely that general reformative interests very much drive and shape our practices of holding people responsible. (For instance, consider the way expressions of indignation are placated when agents express regret and real motivation to avoid repeats, and consider plausible evolutionary rationales for our reactive attitudes.)

In order for our practices of holding people responsible to reliably affect outcomes in this way, they need to be targeted at motivational structures of types that are (a) systematically tied to those outcomes and (b) tend to be amenable to modification when targeted by these practices, and need to be so when (c) instances of the motivational structure type explain the outcome in a salient straightforward way that supports learning.

Undoubtedly, our concept of moral responsibility plays a central role in determining whom to hold responsible for what. In particular, expressions of indignation and requests for explanation are withheld when we conclude that the putative target of these practices was not responsible for the objectionable decision, action or outcome. Since our concept of moral responsibility plays this role, it would not be surprising if it has been shaped by the need to identify proper targets for our practices of holding people responsible, identified by conditions (a) through (c) above.[3]

This provides motivation for what we call the "Explanation Hypothesis", an empirical hypothesis about the conditions under which we take people to be retrospectively morally responsible for some event:

> *The Explanation Hypothesis*: People take P to be morally responsible for E to the extent that they take[4] E to be an outcome of a type O and take P to have a motivational structure S of type M such that GET, RR and ER hold:
>
> > *General Explanatory Tendency (GET)*: Type M motivational structures are part of a reasonably common sort of significant explanation of type O outcomes.
> >
> > *Reactive Response-ability (RR)*: Type M motivational structures tend to respond in the right way to agents being held responsible for realizing or not preventing type O outcomes.

---

[3] In connecting moral responsibility to reactive attitudes and practices of holding responsible, this hypothesis is closely related to a category of accounts starting with Peter Strawson's (1962) paper "Freedom and Resentment". In (Björnsson and Persson 2011) we indicate how our particular way of spelling out this connection avoids some of the standard objections raised against such accounts.

[4] In saying that people "take" GET, RR and ER to hold, I do not mean that they are consciously aware of the considerations defined by these conditions in making their judgments of responsibility under these descriptions, only that judgments are in fact determined by such considerations.

Explanatory Responsibility (ER): S is part of a significant explanation of E of the sort mentioned in GET.

My focus here will be on the two explanatory requirements, GET and, in particular, ER, but a few words are needed to avoid misunderstanding of RR. It is meant to capture the idea that certain types of motivational structures are impervious to blame, praise or other practices of holding people responsible, and that this undermines moral responsibility. RR thus explains why we typically take moral responsibility to be diminished when behaviour is driven by compulsion, phobias, severe personality disorders and extreme stress.

Since RR concerns how motivational structures respond to blame, praise, etc., it is easy to think that the Explanation Hypothesis understands judgments of moral responsibility as forward-looking, concerned with whether holding someone responsible would reform her behaviour. That would be a misunderstanding, however. The fact that someone's motivational structure is of a *type* that tends to respond in the right way does not mean that it is likely to do so in this case. A particular instance of a type that tends to respond appropriately might resist reform: disdain might satisfy RR, but disdain for morality might be self-protecting. Moreover, various extraneous factors might mask the motivational structure's disposition to react in the right way: perhaps the agent is disposed to react adversely to criticism, say, or perhaps she suffered from a stroke immediately after her action and no longer has the cognitive capacity to understand what she is held responsible for. To be directly forward-looking, judgments of moral responsibility would have to be sensitive to such masks, but they clearly are not; they are essentially backward-looking, concerned with what *explained* the outcome in question.

Among motivational states and outcomes that satisfy RR, there are basically two kinds of explanation that also satisfy GET: First, events are often explained by the fact that we want them sufficiently, as our desires guide our goal-directed cognitive mechanisms ("The trial was all due to Dr. Ortega's relentless passion for justice"; "Her tragic death was due to Mr. Inza's obsession with revenge"). Second, the fact that we do not sufficiently want something not to happen often explains why we let it happen ("The new factory was allowed to pollute the river because the CEO didn't care about the environment"; "He missed his daughter's game because he cared more about his work than about her").[5] Consequently, we take people to be responsible for a bad outcome when we think that it happened because they wanted them ("Mr. Inza is to blame for her death") or because they didn't care enough to prevent them ("The pollution is the CEO's fault"), and take people to be responsible

[5] It is an interesting question whether GET-satisfying explanations require awareness on part of the agent that the sort of outcome in question might take place or whether it can be enough that the person would have been aware and acted on the information if the person had possessed a different motivational structure. We are currently investigating this, and preparatory studies suggest that most people come down on the latter side. For some of the philosophical controversy, see (Zimmerman 2008:chap. 4; Sher 2009).

for a good outcome when it happened because they wanted it ("Dr. Ortega deserves all credit for the trial").[6]

According to the Explanation Hypothesis, our everyday concept of an *explanation why something happened* is at the core of our thinking about moral responsibility. One key feature of that concept is that it is highly *selective*. Suppose that a house has just burned down and that we are asked why. In answering, we could list a number of conditions, each of which might be a necessary part of complex sufficient condition for the outcome: there was a thunderstorm, the house was hit by lightning an hour earlier, the house consisted largely of combustible matter, there was oxygen in the air, etc.[7] All of these conditions, and countless more, might be part of a *full* causal story leading up to the fact that the house burned down, but only a small subset will stand out when we want to give a condensed explanation of that fact. When we do, the fact that the house was hit by lightning will likely grab our attention, whereas the fact that the house consisted of combustible matter or that there was oxygen in the air would be taken for granted as part of what we might call the explanatory "background". Typically, the explanatory background consists of conditions that are generally to be expected whereas attention grabbers are conditions that violate such expectations. Generally speaking, we expect houses to be built from some amount of combustible material, and we certainly expect there to be oxygen in the air, but we do not in the same way expect houses to be hit by lightning at some given time.

Our everyday notion of explanation is selective in another way too. The bolt of lightning that hit the house itself had a causal genesis, and there were numerous causal intermediaries between the fact that the house was hit by lightning and the fact that it burned to the ground. These conditions are not likely to be seen as part of the explanans, however. When we provide explanations of an event, we cite a condition that we take to provide a particularly *telling* explanation among those leading up to that event, a condition that satisfies our explanatory interests without immediately raising new and urgent why-questions. If we wonder why the house burned down and are told that the attic insulation caught fire, we will probably wonder *why* the insulation caught fire, and if we are told that there was a separation of positive and negative charges in the neighbouring atmosphere, we are likely to ask how *that* explained that the house burned down. By contrast, if we are told that the house was hit by lightning, we will probably be satisfied: we take a house's being hit by lightning to be both the sort of thing that just happens and the sort of thing that causes houses to burn down.

---

[6] It is possible that GET should be restricted to these two broad kinds of explanation.

[7] In (Björnsson 2007) I argue that our causal reasoning is *primarily* directed towards sufficient rather than necessary conditions and that this is explained by the connection between causal thinking and instrumental reasoning: instrumental reasoning is primarily directed at ensuring certain states of affairs rather than making them possible. The priority of sufficiency over necessity explains why causation is compatible with many varieties of overdetermination and ultimately explains why responsibility is not a matter of difference making. (All this simplifies matters by ignoring probabilistic causation and explanation.)

When condition ER in the Explanation Hypothesis refers to a *significant* explanation, that means an explanation that satisfies our explanatory interests and background assumptions or, differently put, fits our *explanatory frame*. The selective nature of significant explanations makes the Explanation Hypothesis a surprisingly powerful account of judgments of moral responsibility. Obviously, the hypothesis can account for the fact that we take people to be responsible for most intended outcomes of their actions: because of our powerful goal-directed mechanisms, such outcomes are straightforwardly explained with reference to what we want to achieve, and most of our everyday preferences satisfy RR. But relying on the selective nature of significant explanations also provides a unifying account of how a wide variety of otherwise disparate phenomena affect judgments of responsibility. As I have argued elsewhere (Björnsson and Persson 2009, 2011), it explains why we take it that (a) external force, (b) threats and (c) ignorance mitigate moral responsibility to various degrees, as well as why we take it that (d) those who actively participate in the production of an outcome have a higher degree of responsibility for it than those who merely allow others do it, that (e) someone who takes initiative is more responsible than someone who tags along, and that (f) agents are more responsible for known negative than for known positive side-effects that the agent does not care about. It also explains why judgments of responsibility tend to be undermined by considerations suggesting that (g) our decisions are a matter of luck, (h) our actions are, ultimately, the upshots of events over which we have no control, (i) our behaviour can be given reductionistic, mechanistic explanations, or that (j) the felt conflict between determinism and moral responsibility is lessened when people consider concrete cases, and especially cases involving grave moral transgressions.

11.5 The Explanation Hypothesis and Collective Responsibility

The explanatory power of the Explanation Hypothesis, along with its etiological motivation, gives us reason to think that the everyday concept of retrospective moral responsibility has a structure that straightforwardly incorporates our preliminary analysis of joint responsibility in Section 11.3: in cases of joint responsibility, the motivational structures of all participants are seen as parts of a significant explanation of the outcome. This gives us independent reason to expect further cases of joint responsibility to conform to the same analysis, thus providing a first answer to the generalization worry.

More specifically, the Explanation Hypothesis explains both why we take the agents of *The Lake* to be responsible for the death of the fish and why we take them to be *jointly* responsible. We see them as *responsible* for the outcome because the three conditions GET, RR and ER are satisfied for each of them, and we see them as *jointly* responsible because their motivational structures are part of a significant explanans only taken together with the motivational structures of the other two.

Start with the last claim. Compare the following two answers to the question: why did the fish in the lake die?

(1) Alice, Bill and Cecil didn't care about the environmental effects of their actions.
(2) Alice didn't care about the environmental effects of her actions.

Whereas (1) sounds like a perfectly good explanation, (2) is clearly problematic, for two reasons. First it brings attention to the fact that Alice's carelessness made no difference to the outcome because there would have been enough solvent in the lake without it, and although difference making doesn't always undermine explanatory claims it might do so in this case.[8] But (2) is also problematic because it focuses on Alice at the exclusion of Bill and Cecil who played exactly the same role in killing off the fish. Both these defects are absent in (1). That the trio didn't care about the environmental effects of their actions straightforwardly explained why they poured solvent into the lake, and the resulting concentration of solvent explained why the fish died. Of course, not all their actions or all the solvent was needed for that outcome, but there is no privileged subset of these actions that would provide a better explanans. For example, if we explained the death of the fish by mentioning the carelessness of Alice and Bill, we would misleadingly suggest that Cecil had less to do with the outcome than the other two. For that reason, such a restricted explanans would not provide us with an acceptable straightforward explanation.

Now consider the claim that the motivational structure of *each* agent satisfies GET, RR and ER for the outcome in question. First, it satisfies GET because the outcome is explained by a lack of concern to avoid that sort of outcome in the normal way. The most common explanation of this type will be one in which an *individual's* lack of concern explains the outcome, but we frequently explain outcomes in terms of attitudes of members of a group: "The kids next door play loud music because they don't care about the neighbours"; "Sweden rejected the Euro because many Swedes were afraid of losing political independence"; etc. Second, the motivational structures also satisfy RR: we have assumed that the individuals involved satisfy conditions needed for individual responsibility for decisions and action. Finally, we have just seen that the individual agent's motivational structure satisfies ER, as it is alluded to in the joint explanation given by (1).

Contrast this case with *Adam's Lake*. Just like Alice's lack of environmental concern, taken on its own, Adam's lack of concern does not itself strike us as straightforwardly explaining the death of the fish. But whereas Alice's is *part* of a significant explanation that satisfies ER, expressed in (1), it is not clear that Adam's is. For example, the following answer to the question of why the fish died in *Adam's Lake* seems strained:

(3) Adam didn't care about the environment and a poisonous substance was produced at the bottom of the lake.

---

[8] The model of causal judgment developed in (Björnsson 2007) explains the restricted role of difference making or counterfactual dependence in causal judgments and shows why the lack of counterfactual dependence might undermine the claim that Alice's carelessness caused or explained the death of the fish in the lake. This effect would be even stronger in the version of *The Lake* where her contribution actually lowered the probability of the outcome.

Although both conjuncts mention conditions that are part of a complete causal explanation of the death of the fish, their conjunction does not form the most *salient* explanation of the outcome. It would be considerably more natural to appeal to the fact that the lake was poisoned, as the causes of the poisoning are diverse. Moreover, among those causes, the fact that a poisonous substance was produced at the bottom of the lake would likely be seen as more significant than Adam's contribution, since it actually made a difference to the outcome.

Intuitions about *The Well* are explained almost exactly as intuitions about *The Lake*. Eric, Fiona and George are seen as jointly responsible for the fact that Hannah wasn't saved because that fact is naturally explained with reference to *their* lack of concern, but not with reference to, say, Eric's lack of concern in particular. The defect of an explanation singling out one individual is more strongly marked than in *The Lake*. "Why wasn't Hannah saved?" "Because Eric didn't care to see whether he could help!" The answer invites the reply that Eric couldn't have saved Hannah on his own, and does so even more strongly than (1) invited the reply that the fish would have died without Alice's action: at least Alice's action was directly causally involved in blocking the reproduction of the microorganisms whereas Eric's inaction made no definite difference at all.[9] (This explanatory inadequacy is of course even more accentuated in *Esther's Well*, where Esther's lack of care clearly does not explain why Hannah wasn't saved.)

What we have seen, then, is how the Explanation Hypothesis supports the diagnosis of joint responsibility provided in Section 11.3. Given that so many other aspects of our thinking about moral responsibility is well understood given this account, we should expect further variations on the cases discussed here to conform to the same pattern.

For similar reasons, we should hesitate before saying that typical intuitions about cases like *The Lake* result from confusedly attributing joint responsibility based on (i) *individual responsibility for decisions and actions* and (ii) *non-distributive collective responsibility for an outcome*, that is, collective responsibility that does not imply corresponding responsibility for members of the collective. The argument given here suggests that intuitions of joint responsibility rely on the same sort of considerations as do intuitions about individual responsibility. From the point of view of our concept of retrospective moral outcome responsibility, then, the attribution of joint responsibility is in no way arbitrary. Nor is it arbitrary, from an etiological point of view, that we should have a concept that yields this pattern of judgments; a focus on cases with a straightforward explanatory connection between

[9] The Explanation Hypothesis also implies that subtle differences in characterizations of outcomes might yield different verdicts about moral responsibility. It is intuitively clear that Eric, Fiona and George are responsible for the fact that Hannah wasn't saved, but it is less clear that they are responsible for her death. If we ask why she wasn't saved, it is natural to cite, say, the trio's lack of concern, but if we ask why she died, it is considerably more natural to cite the fact that she fell into an old well or didn't watch where she was going than to cite the non-intervention. Different explananda yield different explanatory frames: unlike the fact that she died, the fact that she wasn't saved implies that she was in danger, thus relegating her initial fall into the well to the explanatory background.

suitable motivational structures and outcomes is crucial for the sort of moral reform that much of our everyday practice of holding people responsible is aimed at. One might worry, though, that it is *unfair* that Alice should be held responsible (together with Bill and Cecil) for the death of the fish whereas Adam is not, given that both were equally reckless and contributed solvents that were similarly causally involved in processes leading to the death of the fish. But this is a familiar problem for outcome responsibility in general, not specifically for joint responsibility or for the analysis proposed here. Factors outside the control of an agent are part of what determines the outcome of her behaviour: only one of two equally reckless drivers is responsible for the death of a child, because only one had a child run out into the street in front of him; only one of two equally courageous and skilled lifeguards is responsible for having saved a life, because only one had the opportunity.

Thus far, we have seen how the Explanation Hypothesis handles cases of joint responsibility without individual control. But it also predicts that people might be seen as jointly rather than individually responsible for an outcome even in cases where each individual could have prevented the outcome. Think of a version of *The Well* where any one of Eric, Fiona and George could have saved Hannah using a winch next to the well. We might still be reluctant to say that *Eric* is responsible for the fact that Hannah wasn't saved because it arbitrarily picks out Eric at the exclusion of the other two. The significant explanans is still that *none of the three* cared enough to go see whether help was needed; that corresponds to the most natural assignment of responsibility, namely jointly, to all of them.

Another prediction, borne out by almost every discussion of distributive collective responsibility, is that we will ascribe joint responsibility in many cases where agents act together, with joint intentions, since these tend to be cases where agents' motivational structures are involved in straightforwardly explaining the intended outcome. Similarly, intuitions about corporate responsibility bear out the prediction that we will ascribe moral responsibility for outcomes to corporations (organizations, nations, clubs) insofar as we take them to have structures that both straightforwardly explain their actions or omissions and corresponding outcomes and are open to modification by practices of holding these corporations responsible (see e.g. French 1984; May and Hoffman 1991).

For both cases of joint action and cases of corporate moral responsibility, the Explanation Hypothesis predicts attributions of quite different degrees of responsibility to different members of a collective that are causally involved in producing or failing to prevent some outcome. For example, we might think that a stream has been polluted because a certain company doesn't care about the environment, but we do not thereby think that the janitor at the company headquarters is responsible for the pollution. He might have somehow facilitated the process leading to the pollution, but his motivation is not thereby part of a *significant* explanation in the way that the motivational structures of the CEO or members of the board are likely to be. And the same might be true about a member of the board who voted against the polluting activity, or even about someone who voted for it because she thought that that was the way to minimize the harm by allowing her to minimize the resulting pollution.

11.6 Explanatory Responsibility and the Normativity of Retrospective Outcome Responsibility

As we have seen, the Explanation Hypothesis promises a unified account of our judgments of individual and collective responsibility, an account that sees our ascription of essentially *joint* responsibility in cases like *The Lake* or *The Well* as integral to our thinking about moral responsibility in general. Moreover, although it does not say what the relation of moral responsibility *is*, it strongly suggests an account of that relation. Given the Explanation Hypothesis' account of our concept of moral responsibility, it might seem reasonable to assume that the relation of moral responsibility corresponds to what is identified when the concept is applied without any mistakes, that is, when GET, RR and ER hold.

Things are not quite that simple, however, because the selective nature of our explanatory judgments makes them sensitive to differences in explanatory frames. For example, it seems that when people are encouraged to abstract away from the level of detail that we employ in everyday explanations of actions and to focus on causal factors outside agents' control, they are less inclined to find motivational structures explanatorily significant, and less inclined to ascribe responsibility (Björnsson and Persson 2009, 2011). In the same way, explanatory judgments often depend on *normative* expectations or ideals. Suppose that that a child falls and breaks an arm during some rough and tumble play. A person who thinks that mothers ought to be strongly protective of their children is more likely to explain this fact with reference to the mother's lack of protective concern, and thus more likely to take the mother to be responsible for the accident.[10]

This frame-dependence of our concept of moral responsibility means that if there is a determinate, objective, truth of the matter as to whether people are responsible for certain outcomes, the "significant explanations" referred to in GET and ER needs to be restricted. The most obvious way to do so is to require that they are significant relative to a *correct explanatory frame*: relative to *correct* normative ideals, *correct* background assumptions, and *relevant* explanatory interests and explanatory perspectives. "Objectifying" the Explanation Hypothesis, we would thus get the following characterization of moral responsibility:

> *Explanatory Responsibility:* P is morally responsible for E to the extent that E is an outcome of a type O and P has a motivational structure S of type M such that GET, RR and ER hold relative to a correct explanatory frame.

Obviously, Explanatory Responsibility only implies determinate judgments of responsibility given substantial assumptions about what the correct explanatory frames are. This is not the place to defend some such assumptions,[11] but the fact

---

[10] For empirical data illustrating some effects of normative expectations on explanatory judgments, see e.g. (Alicke 1992; Knobe and Fraser 2008; Hitchcock and Knobe 2009; Sytsma et al. 2010).

[11] In (Björnsson and Persson 2011) we argue that explanatory frames of the sort that motivate most of our everyday judgments of moral responsibility should be preferred to the frames that are induced by sceptical arguments against moral responsibility.

that moral responsibility would depend on the correctness of normative expectations is itself a highly significant consequence.[12] Because of it, fundamental issues in normative ethics are directly relevant to questions of moral responsibility.

As an example, consider how issues of joint responsibility are affected by the disagreement about the existence of reasons to do one's own part in a cooperative scheme even when others are known not to, or to "keep one's own hands clean". Thus far, I have discussed cases where, for all the agents knew, their acts could have made a difference individually to the outcome for which they are responsible. Moreover, this feature might seem essential to the cases. For example, if Alice had poured solvent into the lake knowing for sure that it would make no significant environmental difference or even slowed down ongoing damage, that could clearly undermine her responsibility for the death of the fish as her contribution would no longer be explained with reference to a lack of care. But suppose that there are moral reasons for people to do their part in appropriate cooperative schemes that do not depend on the possibility of actually significantly furthering the ultimate point of these schemes. Then people might be jointly responsible for bad outcomes that they, as individuals, *knew* they could not prevent: if they had *all* been more concerned to do their part, the outcome would have been different.

If there are non-consequentialist reasons of this sort, their strength will also have major impact on what we are responsible for. Given high enough normative expectations that people should avoid working for or purchase the goods of organizations that are responsible for certain bad outcomes, it will seem that great many people without direct causal influence on these outcomes are nevertheless responsible for them, i.e. for such things as the effects of a company's environmental policy, the persecution of members of organized labour in undemocratic countries, or the enactment of severe oppression of civilians on occupied territories. After all, if people had cared more and been more "principled", many such things could have been very different. This in turn raises difficult questions about the relation between normative expectation and psychological realism: since it seems unlikely that people will live up to these expectations under present circumstances, are they really reasonable? If correct, Explanatory Responsibility makes clear just how such questions are central to issues of collective responsibility, by being directly relevant for the identification of significant explanations.

Acknowledgments Earlier versions of this text have been presented and received valuable input at the *International Conference on Moral Responsibility* in Delft, August 2009 at the Centre for Applied Ethics at Linköping University, at the Department of Political Science and the Department of Philosophy, Linguistic and Theory of Science at University of Gothenburg, and at the Department of Philosophy, Lund University. I am also grateful to participants at the CEU 2009 summer school on moral responsibility, and for comments from Ibo van de Poel and an anonymous reviewer for this volume.

[12] For related discussions of how normative aspects affect judgments of responsibility, see (Smiley 1992).

References

Alicke, Mark D. 1992. "Culpable Causation." *Journal of Personality and Social Psychology* 63:368–78.

Arnold, Denis G. 2006. "Corporate Moral Agency." *Midwest Studies in Philosophy* 30: 279–91.

Björnsson, Gunnar. 2007. "How Effects Depend on Their Causes, Why Causal Transitivity Fails, and Why We Care About Causation." *Philosophical Studies* 133:349–90.

Björnsson, Gunnar, and Karl Persson. 2009. "Judgments of Moral Responsibility: A Unified Account." *Society for Philosophy and Psychology*, 35th Annual Meeting 2009 PhilSci archive. http://philsci-archive.pitt.edu/archive/00004633/.

Björnsson, Gunnar, and Karl Persson. 2011. "The Explanatory Component of Moral Responsibility." *Noûs*. 45. Doi: 10.1111/j. 1468-0068.2010.00813.x

Braham, Matthew, and Martin van Hees. 2010. "An Anatomy of Moral Responsibility." http://www.rug.nl/staff/martin.van.hees/Anatomy.pdf

Collins, John, Ned Hall, and L.A. Paul. eds. 2004. *Causation and Counterfactuals*. Cambridge, MA: The MIT Press.

Copp, David. 2007. "The Collective Moral Autonomy Thesis." *Journal of Social Philosophy* 38:369–88.

Corlett, J. Angelo. 2001. "Collective Moral Responsibility." *Journal of Social Philosophy* 32: 573–84.

Enoch, David, and Andrei Marmor. 2007. "The Case Against Moral Luck." *Law and Philosophy* 26:405–36.

Feinberg, Joel. 1968. "Collective Responsibility." *The Journal of Philosophy* 65:674–88.

French, Peter A. 1984. *Collective and Corporate Responsibility*. New York, NY: Columbia University Press.

Haji, Ish. 2006. "On the Ultimate Responsibility of Collectives." *Midwest Studies in Philosophy* 30:292–308.

Held, Virginia. 1970. "Can a Random Collection of Individuals Be Morally Responsible?" *The Journal of Philosophy* 67:471–81.

Hitchcock, Chrisopher, and Joshua Knobe. 2009. "Cause and Norm." *Journal of Philosophy* 106:587–612.

Knobe, Joshua, and Ben Fraser. 2008. "Causal Judgment and Moral Judgment: Two Experiments." In *Moral Psychology*, edited by Walter Sinnott-Armstrong, Vol. 2, 441–47. Cambridge, MA: MIT Press.

Kutz, Christopher. 2000. *Complicity*. New York, NY: Columbia University Press.

Lewis, David. 1973. "Causation." *Journal of Philosophy* 70:556–67. Reprinted in Lewis 1986a, 159–72.

Lewis, David. 1986a. *Philosophical Papers*, Vol. II. New York, NY: Oxford University Press.

Lewis, David. 1986b. "Postscripts to 'Causation'." *Philosophical Papers*, Vol. II, 172–213. New York, NY: Oxford University Press.

Mackie, John. 1974. *The Cement of the Universe*. Gloucestershire: Clarendon Press.

May, Larry. 1992. *Sharing Responsibility*. Chicago, IL: University of Chicago Press.

May, Larry, and Stacey Hoffman. 1991. *Collective Responsibility: Five Decades of Debate in Theoretical and Applied Ethics*. Lanham, MD: Rowman & Littlefield.

McKenna, Michael. 2006. "Collective Responsibility and an Agent Meaning Theory." *Midwest Studies in Philosophy* 30:16–34.

Miller, Seumas. 2006. "Collective Moral Responsibility: An Individualist Account." *Midwest Studies in Philosophy* 30:176–93.

Miller, Seumas. 2007. "Against the Collective Moral Autonomy Thesis." *Journal of Social Philosophy* 38:389–409.

Nagel, Thomas. 1976. "Moral Luck." *Proceedings of the Aristotelian Society, Supplementary Volumes* 50:137–51.

Petersson, Björn. 2004. "The Second Mistake in Moral Mathematics Is Not About the Worth of Mere Participation." *Utilitas* 16:288–315.
Pettit, Philip. 2007. "Responsibility Incorporated." *Ethics* 117:171–201.
Rescher, Nicholas. 1998. "Collective Responsibility." *Journal of Social Philosophy* 29:46–58.
Sadler, Brook Jenkins. 2006. "Shared Intentions and Shared Responsibility." *Midwest Studies in Philosophy* 30:115–44.
Sher, George. 2009. *Who Knew?* New York, NY: Oxford University Press.
Shockley, Kenneth. 2007. "Programming Collective Control." *Journal of Social Philosophy* 38:442–55.
Smiley, Marion. 1992. *Moral Responsibility and the Boundaries of Community: Power and Accountability from a Pragmatic Point of View*. Chicago, IL: University of Chicago Press.
Strawson, Peter F. 1962. "Freedom and Resentment." *Proceedings of the British Academy* 48:1–25.
Sverdlik, Steven. 1987. "Collective Responsibility." *Philosophical Studies* 51:61–76.
Sytsma, Justin, Jonathan Livengood, and David Rose. 2010. "Two Types of Typicality: Rethinking the Role of Statistical Typicality in Ordinary Causal Attributions." [Preprint] URL: http://philsci-archive.pitt.edu/id/eprint/5372 (accessed 2011-07-07).
Tännsjö, Torbjörn. 2007. "The Myth of Innocence: On Collective Responsibility and Collective Punishment." *Philosophical Papers* 36:295–314.
Wright, Richard W. 1988. "Causation, Responsibility, Risk, Probability, Naked Statistics, and Proof: Pruning the Bramble Bush by Clarifying the Concepts." *Iowa Law Review* 73:1001–77.
Zimmerman, Michael. 1985. "Sharing Responsibility." *American Philosophical Quarterly* 22: 115–22.
Zimmerman, Michael J. 2008. *Living with Uncertainty*. Cambridge: Cambridge University Press.

Chapter 12
Climate Change and Collective Responsibility

Steve Vanderheiden

Abstract Can persons be held morally responsible for harmful consequences that result from the acts or omissions of their nation or society, even if they conscientiously avoid contributing toward those consequences *qua* individuals? What if those acts and omissions, together with a great many other similar ones committed against the backdrop of social norms that tolerate and even encourage such harmful behavior, contribute to a global environmental problem that gives rise to valid claims for compensation on the part of those harmed by it, but where discrete instances of harm cannot be attributed to any specific persons as directly causally responsible? Such is the case with global climate change, which results in part from social norms that are permissive of polluting activities and which often frustrate efforts to avoid them, rather than being caused by culpable individual choices alone, in which case individual fault and responsibility could more plausibly be assigned. Furthermore, the harm associated with climate change is caused by aggregated greenhouse pollution from a great many untraceable point sources rather than being the direct result of discrete emissions of heat-trapping gases by particular persons, undermining standard accounts of individual moral responsibility and thus giving rise to claims for assigning responsibility collectively instead. But holding nations and peoples collectively responsible for climate change raises objections from the perspective of individual moral responsibility, at least insofar as some persons may be implicated *qua* members of groups when they are faultless as individuals.

12.1 Introduction

Policy responses to climate change challenge conventional accounts of moral responsibility in various ways, and the normative concept of responsibility serves as the theoretical linchpin of climate justice (Vanderheiden 2011). But what does it mean to be responsible in the context of global climate change? Consider first the purely causal sense of responsibility, in which person P is responsible for outcome X insofar as P's actions bring about, intensify, or increase the probability

S. Vanderheiden (✉)
Department of Political Science, University of Colorado, Boulder, CO, USA

Centre for Applied Philosophy and Public Ethics (CAPPE), Canberra, ACT, Australia
e-mail: vanders@colorado.edu

N.A Vincent et al. (eds.), *Moral Responsibility*, Library of Ethics and Applied Philosophy 27, DOI 10.1007/978-94-007-1878-4_12,

of X occurring, as applied to unmitigated anthropogenic climate change. Through their greenhouse gas (GHG) emissions, all persons contribute toward climate change in some way since all emit carbon dioxide through respiration, but the wide variation among individual emission rates entails equally wide variation in *causal responsibility* for the various harms associated with climate change. Moreover, those harms are not expected to be evenly distributed across persons or peoples, with the least advantaged suffering disproportionately from climatic disturbances.[1] Without yet invoking any normative account of responsibility, this causal analysis reveals that those expected to suffer the most damaging effects of global climate change are among the least responsible for causing it. Such an empirical observation invites obvious normative evaluation, constructing an account of moral responsibility from its causal counterpart. It might be unobjectionable if persons were to suffer climate-related harm in exact proportion to their causal contributions to the problem, measured in terms of their GHG emissions (or, as I've argued, their luxury emissions).[2] If this was the case, greenhouse pollution could be seen as imprudent but not unjust, as persons soiled their own nests but imposed no externality costs upon others. In so doing, they would bear one kind of responsibility for their actions and resulting outcomes (i.e. warranting the harm that they impose upon themselves), but this responsibility would invite only prudential rather than moral critique. But in fact many suffer climate-related harm for which they are minimally causally responsible or not responsible at all (by a fault-based standard), while others causally contribute far more than their share to the problem but escape most of its insidious effects.

It is through such an analysis of causal responsibility for climate change that judgments concerning moral responsibility for its mitigation and adaptation can be made. One might endorse the following principle of responsibility in reference to the causes and consequences of climate change: No person should be made to suffer harm (or bear responsibility) from environmental problems beyond their share in having caused such problems, and those responsible for causing those problems should bear liability for ensuring that this is so, in proportion to that responsibility. To speak of *liability responsibility*[3] is to focus on the assignment of remedial costs necessary for ensuring that all and only those causing climate change bear its

---

[1] According to the Intergovernmental Panel on Climate Change, "the impacts of climate change will fall disproportionately upon developing countries and poor persons within all countries, and thereby exacerbate inequities in health status and access to adequate food, clean water, and other resources." (Intergovernmental Panel on Climate Change 2001).

[2] In contrast to the survival emissions that persons cannot avoid producing in the process of meeting basic needs and for which persons cannot be faulted, luxury emissions are associated with activities that are not necessary for survival and thus form the basis for fault-based liability for climate-related harm. See Vanderheiden (2008:especially chap. 5).

[3] I take this term from Hart (1968), but use it in a slightly different way. Hart argued that the "primary sense" of responsibility concerned charges that, if established, entail "liability to punishment or blame or other adverse treatment", but focus especially on remedial or compensatory orders that issue from assessments of liability. That is, my focus is on how determinations of liability responsibility inform who should pay for resulting harm.

costs, and in proportion to those costs. The assignment of liability costs could be used to fund *mitigation* efforts, which reduce the anthropogenic drivers of climate change by either reducing GHG emissions or sequestering those gases after they are released, or efforts at *adaptation*, which seeks to shield humans from climate-related harm once changes to the climate system are underway. In some cases, liability can be justifiably assigned in the absence of moral fault or even causal responsibility, as when potential rescuers are assigned the liability for saving famine victims by virtue of their capacity and proximity alone. This kind of capacity-based responsibility does not involve assessments of vicarious responsibility, where some are held morally responsible for the actions of others, since it can be assigned even when none are at fault for some potentially bad outcome such as a famine and does not necessarily involve blame or moral disapprobation. Typically, however, capacity-based liability is not employed when fault-based moral responsibility is available, as remedial burdens to avoid or compensate for bad outcomes are thought to accrue to faulty parties first when such parties can be identified, and only fall to capable but faultless parties when they cannot.

My interest here lies in the justification for assigning climate-related remedial liability to some apparently faultless parties when faulty parties can be readily identified, and in failing to assess such liability proportionate to either causal responsibility or fault. Both present problems from the perspective of responsibility theory, since each involves some outcome that is inconsistent with the imperative to hold persons responsible for all and only their personal contributions toward common environmental hazards, and each is complicated by assessments of collective national responsibility for climate change. In the first instance, as Paul Harris has argued, holding entire nations liability responsible for climate change obscures the wide disparity among individual GHG emission rates within both industrialized and developing countries (Harris 2009). In practice, assessments of national responsibility for climate change typically depend on average per capita emissions, making no distinctions between those well above and those well below those averages in finding citizens to be responsible for their national emissions. When entire nations engage in mitigation activities that are financed through tax revenues, such as transportation infrastructure upgrades, tax assessments that finance such activities are typically not indexed to the GHG emissions of taxpayers that are in effect held liable for those mitigation efforts. When nations commit funds toward adaptation projects, they typically also do so through general tax revenues, ignoring distinctions between the relative causal contributions made by various taxpayers. In practice, national liability for climate-related mitigation and adaptation efforts is assigned to persons on the basis of the income categories to which tax rates are indexed but to neither causal responsibility nor fault for climate change. Given that some residents of high-polluting nations take great pains to minimize their personal carbon footprints, often at considerable expense to themselves, this blanket assignment of liability seems initially to be objectionable from the perspective of individual moral responsibility.

One might view the assignment of collective responsibility to entire nations for climate change mitigation and adaptation as a mere administrative convenience, delegating individual liability assessments to national governments, to be made on the basis of individual causation and fault. For example, under the Kyoto Protocol the United States incurred a mitigation burden on the basis of its GHG emissions that would require significant reductions in national emissions as well as costly offsets – had the U.S. ratified the protocol – but this liability assignment merely delegated authority for assessing fault and responsibility to the national government and took no position on how it was to be domestically allocated among persons, groups, and industry sectors. What looks like an assignment of collective responsibility entailing vicarious liability for at least some persons at the international level need not entail any vicarious liability at the national or subnational level. Domestically, liability could be assigned to individual persons in proportion to their contributory fault for climate change, as for example through some form of carbon tax. None would need to be held vicariously liable for climate-related harm toward which they did not personally contribute, so typical objections to collective responsibility would not necessarily follow from international burden-allocation schemes. Viewing the assessment of national responsibility for climate-related harm in this way, however, belies the important sense in which the benefits of historical patterns of greenhouse pollution accrue even to those residents of high-emissions countries that take significant pains to minimize their personal carbon footprints and the manner in which the costs of significant national mitigation and adaptation efforts must be borne by entire societies, even if those costs are equally distributed among all of its members. Part of the collective liability for climate change that is assigned to entire nations can be reduced to individual liability, but part cannot, and this latter aspect of responsibility for climate change makes opting out or absolving oneself of responsibility for climate-related harm impossible, but justifies the blanket assessments of national liability that have been part and parcel of international climate policy development.

Indeed, I shall argue that the assignment of collective liability to nations for climate change mitigation and adaptation is not a mere administrative convenience, nor does it impose morally objectionable forms of vicarious liability upon persons that cannot validly be implicated in their home country's role in causing climate change and related remedial responsibility to minimize the harm that it causes to others. Rather, it rests partly upon a kind of moral responsibility for climate-related harm from which none in industrialized nations can completely extricate themselves and in which many residents of developing countries are also complicit. As Christopher Kutz notes, "the notion of participation rather than causation is at the heart of both complicity and collective action" (Kutz 2000:138), and persons cannot help but participate in the systems of advantage and disadvantage that have been shaped by national GHG emissions patterns and against the backdrop of social norms that structure individual emission patterns. Since climate change is not caused exclusively by the isolated acts of atomistic individuals, but is also a product of collective forces like culture, public policy and social norms, entire societies can validly be viewed as collectively causing significant proportions of their national emissions, for which they must be held collectively responsible. By participating in these forces – and persons cannot help but participate in them even if they also aim to resist and reform those social forces – persons acquire at least a minimal complicity in the harm that results such that assessments of national responsibility for climate change need not be seen as violating principles of individual moral responsibility. Unlike forms of collective responsibility that rest of the causation and fault of only part of the larger collectivity, holding some vicariously liable for harm toward which they are in no way individually responsible, the form of responsibility that best captures the sort of national responsibility on display in climate change is what Joel Feinberg terms *contributory group-fault: collective and distributive*. This model illuminates the important link between individual acts and the broader social context in which they are embedded, and offers a reply to objections lodged from the perspective of individualistic conceptions of responsibility that began this chapter. It holds that all residents of nations held liable for climate change mitigation and adaptation are responsible for climate change in at least some significant sense, and therefore that we must all take steps to mitigate our collective contributions to the problem as well as assist those who are threatened by it.

12.2 Fault, Responsibility, and International Climate Policy

In assessing national liability for climate-related harm, the 1992 United Nations Framework Convention on Climate Change (UNFCCC) declares that mitigation, adaptation, and compensation costs should be allocated among the world's nations according to their "common but differentiated responsibilities" for the problem (United Nations 1992). This judgment follows from the recognition that all nations are to some extent responsible in that persons everywhere emit some of the heat-trapping gases that cause the phenomenon, but considerable variation exists among nations in terms of their per capita emissions, levels of economic development, and past and ongoing proactive efforts to abate those hazardous emissions originating within their borders. As I have argued elsewhere (Vanderheiden 2008), this standard is best understood as invoking fault-based rather than strict liability, where parties are assigned remedial burdens based upon their relative causal contributions to the problem combined with some assessment of moral fault. Indeed, debates over the meaning of the "differentiated responsibilities" language and the burden-allocation formula that it entails have focused upon the manner in which such fault can be defensibly assessed. Strict liability (in which fault plays no role, as parties are held liable only for their causal contributions to harm) would unjustifiably jettison the morally relevant difference between the survival emissions that persons and peoples cannot avoid generating through basic activities associated with biological needs and the luxury emissions that cause the avoidable harm of anthropogenic climate change. According to the analysis that faults parties for their luxury but not survival emissions, none can be faulted for acts that are necessary for survival (as *ought* implies *can*), but assessments of fault may legitimately be applied to those activities that generate harmful emissions above the survival threshold, and agents producing these harmful emissions may defensibly be held liable for redressing the harm that results.[4]

But fault-based liability requires complicated normative judgments that are unnecessary under assessments of strict liability, even when applied to individual persons in relatively simple cases of harm. Judgments of fault require more than determinations of causal responsibility for climate change, which can readily be quantified from existing data on historical greenhouse gas emission patterns. Fault relies on judgments of moral responsibility rather than mere causation, and is most commonly understood in terms that defy its straightforward application to collective entities like nations. Individual persons can be faulted for actions that result in harm to no one and can be faultless despite causing harm to others,[5] with the attribution of fault and assignment of liability turning on mental states that have no parallel in collective entities like nations or cultures. Given the apparent dependence of judgments of fault on cognitive capacities and forms of agency that only individual persons have and exercise, we must ask: Can collective entities like nations be held responsible for harm through fault-based liability at all? Must a remedial global climate regime instead seek out those individuals that are morally responsible for the problem, seeking to assess liability for climate-related harm through billions of separate determinations? If collective responsibility cannot coherently rest on judgments of national fault, the enterprise of assessing national liability for climate-related harm may be an indefensible one.

In allocating climate-related costs to nations rather than persons, nations are assumed to exercise a kind of collective agency that is not fully reducible to individual agency, and some persons are bound to be held responsible for the faulty acts of others. Rather than assigning remedial responsibility to individuals in proportion to their historical emissions (as in an ex post carbon tax), this approach relies upon a kind of collective responsibility where societies are held to be at fault in a way that does not reduce to faulty individual acts or decisions. At least part of my responsibility *qua* American is based not on my past individual emissions, but on the effects of national affluence on my life prospects and global climate, for which I am also responsible, even if I cannot be faulted for these advantages. Another part is based in the harmful social norms in which I have participated and/or not adequately challenged, and which condition the greenhouse-polluting acts that contribute toward high per capita rates of national emissions. I owe some compensation to the victims

[4] Some claim that this sort of backward-looking attribution of responsibility is untenable in cases where individual persons lack non-polluting options or the resources to employ them instead of polluting ones, suggesting that responsibility for climate change be instead assessed in terms of forward-looking obligations to remedy. See, for example, Fahlquist (2009). My concern here is both backward-looking at causal responsibility and moral fault as well as forward-looking toward remedies, using the former to inform the latter. To the extent that better options are not available, as where persons have no mass transit options for commuting to work and so must drive personal automobiles, individual causation is at least partly the product of collective fault in failing to make more sustainable options available.

[5] Perhaps the best account of the disjuncture between assessments of moral responsibility and the consequences of an action can be found in Nagel (1979).

of climate change because of the state policies and social norms that are complicit in causing the problem and undermining potential solutions to it, from which I have benefitted in the past and continue to do so, however reluctantly. Even if I avoid contributing to climate change directly, it might be argued, I can be faulted for my indirect contributions to the problem.

However, this judgment about the sources of my responsibility for compensating those harmed by collective activities in which I participate appears to violate the standard conditions for assessing liability, which requires contributory fault. As Joel Feinberg notes:

> First, it must be true that the responsible individual did the harmful thing in question, or at least that his action or omission made a substantial causal contribution to it. Second, the causally contributory conduct must have been in some way faulty. Finally, if the harmful conduct was truly "his fault", the requisite causal connection must have been directly between the faulty aspect of his conduct and the outcome. It is not sufficient to have caused harm and to have been at fault if the fault was irrelevant to the causing. (Feinberg 1970:222)

From this individualistic conception of causal agency, collective liability in the climate case inevitably but unjustly holds some persons responsible for harm that is in no way their fault. It does this by imposing upon entire nations a liability burden, which not only declares all its citizens to be at fault in producing a global environmental hazard but also would presumably be born by the nation at large through general taxation, rather than mandating that individuals be held liable for their personal contributions to the problem. In reply to this objection, I shall consider how citizenship in a democratic society might affect one's responsibility for this global environmental problem, beyond whatever individual responsibility one might have as greenhouse polluter. My claim is that the justification for holding an entire nation responsible for climate change depends on whether its cause is seen as aggregated individual emissions only, or whether its causes are also (and, in my view, properly) regarded as being a function of citizenship, membership in a culture, and participation in networks of social norms. If the latter, it becomes considerably more difficult (if not impossible) for Americans to extricate themselves from responsibility for the problem, regardless of their individual emissions or personal preferences, and the use of collective responsibility in climate policy becomes less problematic.

12.3 Democracy and Collective Responsibility

To what extent can persons be implicated for the polluting actions of their fellow citizens, even when they themselves conscientiously aim to minimize their individual greenhouse footprints? Does democratic citizenship diffuse responsibility for climate change among an entire populace, even when considerable variation exists among individual pollution patterns? Do citizens assume responsibility for the greenhouse pollution rates of their fellow citizens, when these are conditioned by the social norms and public policies (or lack thereof) for which they are collectively responsible? These questions aim to link democratic citizenship with collective responsibility for those adverse consequences caused by one's fellow citizens, treating citizenship as the source of responsibilities and well as privileges and regarding the relationships of social solidarity that define citizenship as a potential source of liability for the harmful actions of others.

Climate-related harm displays some of the characteristics of a collectively produced hazard for which responsibility cannot be fully ascribed to individual citizens. Although the GHG-emitting actions and choices of individual citizens can be identified as among the causes of a nation's aggregate emissions, so too can public policies, social norms, and public infrastructure be seen as causally responsible for these collectively generated harms. The citizen driving long distances to and from work may be the proximate cause of the emissions that she produces through her automobile's petroleum combustion, but she may rightly claim that the lack of more efficient personal automobiles (itself a product of a lax regulatory state that fails to encourage automobile fuel efficiency combined with social norms that attach status to fuel-inefficient vehicles) is also partly to blame for the greenhouse pollution from her commute, as is the lack of an adequate mass transit option or affordable housing located closer to her place of employment. Such factors play a causal role in structuring her choice, making difficult or impossible more sustainable individual actions, and yet are themselves not obviously caused by identifiable individuals that could be held responsible for them. When democratic societies fail to enact adequate anti-pollution regulations, develop norms of affluent consumption that equate polluting with higher social status, and build cities and towns without a sustainable transit infrastructure or decent housing that is proximate to jobs that make such housing affordable, these failures are the fault of the group itself, even if no individual member can be faulted for them. When whole societies are held responsible for the collected but evidently faultless acts of individual members, as in holding an entire nation of reluctant car commuters responsible for their aggregate greenhouse emissions, it would seem that collective responsibility is being applied where individual responsibility would be un-warranted.

Such cases tempt us to exonerate collectively-produced harm when no group members can be held individually and fully responsible for causing it, but such exoneration would raise its own set of problems for individual responsibility. Writing about national responsibility, David Miller identifies this problem as one of ensuring that persons are held responsible for their own acts and choices, but not those of others, which he takes to comprise the normative core of individual responsibility. Linking responsibility and justice, he articulates the two-sided nature of individual responsibility, describing its imperative as holding that "as far as possible we want people to be able to control what benefits and burdens they receive, but we also want to protect them against the side effects, intended or unintended, of other people's actions" (Miller 2004:245). In cases where groups make collective decisions or engage in collective actions, even where some group members oppose those decisions or abjure those actions, it is sometimes impossible to assign responsibility to discrete individuals. In such cases, the two parts of this justice aim conflict: either we can hold entire groups responsible for consequences that are beyond the control of some members, or we fail to protect others against the harmful effects of group actions. From the perspective of group members, it may seem entirely unjustified to hold reluctant participants in collective actions or omissions responsible for the consequences that result from those actions, particularly when some members actively oppose them, but from the perspective of the victims of group actions it is preferable to hold some group members vicariously responsible than to exonerate entire groups when culpable individual parties cannot be identified. Unless the group is held liable for its collective action, the victims of that action may be forced to bear the costs of harm for which they are not responsible, but this group liability may have to be borne by some faultless individual members if faultless external victims are to be adequately compensated for the harm that they are made to suffer.

In an example analogous to problems of assessing national responsibility for climate-related harm, Miller considers groups displaying "cooperative practices" characteristics such as a polluting firm in which a dissenting minority of its employees opposes that pollution, favoring instead the purchase of some costly anti-pollution controls in order to avoid it. Because a numerical minority, these conscientious employees are overruled by those for whom additional private costs on behalf of avoiding a public nuisance are seen as imprudent. Although opposing the group's final decision by voting against it, can they still be held responsible for the resulting pollution-related harm? Miller argues that they can be held responsible, under some circumstances, if "they are the beneficiaries of a common practice in which participants are treated fairly – they get the income and other benefits that go with the job, and they have a fair chance to influence the firm's decisions – and so they must be prepared to carry their share of the costs, and in this case the costs that stem from the external impact of the practice" (Miller 2004:253). Insofar as members have fair and meaningful opportunities to influence group actions – decisions are not made by a small clique of elites against the will of the majority, for example – the mere fact that some oppose the group's final decision cannot exonerate them from responsibility, so long as they benefit from the cooperative endeavor. As Miller claims of such groups, "participating in the practice and sharing in the benefits may be sufficient to create responsibility" (Miller 2004:253). Thus, he suggests, the more open and democratic the group, the more each member must be held responsible for its decisions, whether or not they personally supported them.

This sort of collective responsibility is essential for ensuring group accountability and preventing individuals from becoming moral free riders, harmlessly dissenting from group decisions when possible in order to create benefits for the entire group at some external costs to others and then invoking this ineffective dissent as a grounds for deflecting responsibility. If available as a means for escaping responsibility for group actions, citizens might seek to avoid the burdens and duties of citizenship *en masse*, transferring their democratic agency to unrepentant polluters (in the climate case) that can provide cover for their ongoing harm on the pretext that they would have preferred to have been legally prohibited from polluting but didn't have anyone palatable to vote for in the last election. If merely registering some opposition to harmful group actions was sufficient to exonerate individual members from fault and liability for them, when those same members could enjoy the private benefits of their reluctant public nuisance nonetheless, then dissent would cease to be sincere or effective and could become a cynical means of obtaining the benefits of membership without accepting its burdens. Dissenters would merely be shirking their responsibility, and might be unfavorably compared to those voting in favor of harmful group actions that at least in principle accept responsibility for the public nuisance from which they derive private benefits. As Miller suggests, refusing the benefits of harmful group actions would be the only way to demonstrate the sincerity of one's opposition to them, and this sort of principled dissent would be the only way of altering this insidious incentive structure.

But forfeiting the benefits of membership in affluent industrialized democratic society is not easily accomplished, and may be altogether impossible. Some benefits are public goods from which none can be excluded, however reluctantly citizens may participate in such consequences of social affluence as democratic governance, political stability, and economic opportunity. By nature, such goods accrue to all, regardless of whether or not citizens voluntarily accept them. Insofar as democratic citizenship constitutes what Miller terms a cooperative practice, is it possible for citizens to escape from this sort of collective responsibility for climate change, short of exercising their exit option from society? Must they go beyond standard avenues of democratic participation before their opposition to some harmful policy can be regarded as adequately sincere, and would such measures release them from responsibility even if ineffective? The illogic of wishing that one's nation or residence had avoided past greenhouse pollution is especially evident. Can one tenably embrace post-materialist environmental values in a pre-industrial society, or regret the economic bases upon which many of one's inherited advantages were forged without undermining the very advantages which make such regret possible? Indeed, a complete opting out of the advantages of residing within nations whose affluence depended on high rates of greenhouse pollution may not be possible at all, but it may be possible to reduce one's personal share of responsibility by acting in ways that tend toward minimizing future bad social conduct or refusing advantages that stem from past bad conduct. The issue concerns the shares of individual responsibility for collective decisions in a democracy, including those to allow ongoing GHG pollution, and to this problem we now turn.

In considering whether fault and liability for social failures to enact sufficient climate policies can be applied to citizens themselves, including those actively encouraging the adoption of such policies, we might consider examples of vicarious fault and liability from other domains of theory. Persons are held vicariously liable for the acts of others when they specifically authorize those acts, as is paradigmatically seen in the principle-agent relationship within military hierarchies. In just war theory, soldiers in the field are obligated to follow orders without question, within reasonable limits, so that while they may be at fault for wartime atrocities, the moral blame and legal liability is typically attributed to commanding officers issuing the orders or failing to control the conduct of those under their command. But can fault and liability similarly transfer in other such principal-agent relationships? Decisions about whether to wage wars are typically made by civilian leaders rather than military commanders, so vicarious liability may likewise be transferred from military commanders to political authorities, and perhaps in turn to those citizens of democratic states in whose name and presumably with whose consent the war is waged. Since democratic governments function as agents that are authorized by principals within the electorate, citizens are in this sense responsible for the actions of their government, even if they personally oppose them, as Miller claims. But are all citizens equally responsible for the harmful actions of their states or governments, by the mere fact of the principal-agent relationship that defines democratic governance? If so, this form of vicarious liability stretches principal-agent causality much further than does just war theory, and arguably by conflating ineffective resistance to power with acquiescence to and support of it.

Michael Walzer, in considering the case for reparations for victims of aggressive wars, notes that such reparations are generally paid for through taxation of all a nation's citizens (a form of liability), not just the active supporters of the war, and over time such that many who had nothing to do with the decision to wage war continue to bear collective responsibility for it (Walzer 1977:297). This does not, he thinks, pose a particularly difficult philosophical problem for moral responsibility so long as they are only held liable and not guilty for the war's atrocities.

Attributions of liability (as in reparations) are not necessarily attributions of legal or moral guilt, he suggests, but are rather judgments based upon the existence of harm, the finding of fault, and the demand of justice to compensate victims for their injuries. Making such responsibility collective rather than individual, even if this implicates a war's opponents along with its supporters, acknowledges the causal role of citizenship in a state's decision to wage an aggressive war. In the context of global climate policy, where the citizens of causally responsible nations may be held liable for mitigation and adaptation burdens even if they exercised no control over national climate policies, Walzer's parsing of liability and guilt may be attractive. Insofar as national responsibility for climate-related harm is translated into individual citizen responsibility for paying shares of those national liability burdens, climate-related liability resembles reparations for unjust war in that both involve culpable collective actions but questionable individual culpability for harmful state actions or omissions, and both hold individual citizens liable for this collective culpability as the only way in which the collective itself can discharge its remedial obligations. Responsibility for climate change in nondemocratic states mirrors Walzer's description of responsibility for unjust wars in those same states, as both incur obligations to compensate victims for the harm that they are made to suffer regardless of citizen control of relevant policies, and both discharge this remedial responsibility through individual assignments of shares of this collective liability. Yet, Walzer's analysis holds persons liable for decisions over which they as citizens of nondemocratic states have no control, seemingly violating the core tenet of moral responsibility, which insists that individuals be at fault if they are to be held liable for some harm.

Of course, citizenship confers far greater responsibility in democratic states than it does in authoritarian ones, and Walzer also considers the case of a state opting to wage war from open and democratic processes, arguing that more widely dispersed decision-making power in democracy connotes similarly dispersed responsibility for bad state decisions, basing culpability on a sliding scale according to the extent to which each citizen wields their various powers of resistance. Who, he asks, should be held responsible for the decision to wage unjust war? Those "who voted for it and who cooperated in planning, initiating, and waging it" must be held most responsible for its atrocity, he argues, including those soldiers who, in their capacities as citizens though not in their capacities as soldiers, shared in the decision to wage the war. Those who voted against the war, he provisionally suggests, cannot be morally faulted for it, although they may later be held liable for harm that results. But what about those citizens who didn't vote? Walzer suggests that they are blameworthy for their "indifference and inaction" in failing to do what they could have done to oppose an unjust policy, "though they are not guilty of aggressive war." Here, though, attributions of fault-based liability would not be inappropriate.

The moral language of guilt and blame is invoked against the apathetic citizen, suggesting that omissions can be faulted alongside actions when either results in some avoidable bad outcome and that fault turns on an individual's capacity to affect group actions. This control condition mirrors that of standard accounts of individual moral responsibility, as citizens are held accountable not only for what they personally do but also for what they fail to do in politics. Even if one was to abstain from personally emitting unsustainable levels of greenhouse gases, one's failure to exercise political responsibility on behalf of sustainable climate policy confers fault and triggers liability for climate-related harm without the need for vicarious responsibility. As Larry May argues, "the degree of individual responsibility of each member of a putative group for the harm should vary based on the role each member could, counterfactually, have played in preventing the inaction" (May 1992:106). Suppose that the anti-war minority could have won the decision had they staged marches and demonstrations rather than merely voting, but they opted not to. Would they then bear responsibility? Walzer thinks so, "though to a lesser degree than those slothful citizens who did not even bother to go to the assembly", since their more active but incomplete resistance is less faulty than the predictably ineffective acquiescence of the nonvoter. Fault among citizens in democratic regimes is thus assigned in proportion to their missed opportunities to wield their various powers of citizenship in defense of justice and against injustice. Given the magnitude of the injustice of aggressive war, the democratic citizen is obligated, he argues, to "do all he can, short of frightening risks, to prevent or stop the war" (Walzer 1977:300–01).

As Walzer suggests, democracy can be regarded as "a way of distributing responsibility", and insofar as citizens have some control over their collective decisions they must also be held responsible for them. Those with more control, whether by virtue of their office or influence in democratic societies or their being in a better position to resist collective decisions outside of standard political processes, may be held assigned greater responsibility for collectively-produced harm than may those with less control, and even if all citizens are to some degree responsible for what they do together. Collective responsibility in wartime and its aftermath therefore sometimes extends even to those citizens that opposed the war at the ballot box or public forum, insofar as they did not do all they could reasonably have done to stop it. Here, citizens are the principals that collectively bear responsibility for the decisions of the state, which acts as their agent. Collective responsibility thus serves a valuable social role in expressing and strengthening the solidarity of groups that share mutual interests or bonds of affection, strengthening norms and encouraging cooperation. But it also raises objections from the principle of responsibility, since the group's fault does not readily reduce to the faults of all individual members held liable for group actions and decisions. The same is true of collectivized responsibility for climate change, as fault that is widely disparate among fellow citizens is obscured by blanket assignments of group liability.

12.4 Social Norms and Collective Fault

Climate change may be caused by individual actions, but significant contributing causes of those actions are state policies and social norms, and in the contemporary United States neither prohibits individual emissions at levels well above those which are globally sustainable. Despite its several democratic deficits, the US government remains answerable to its citizens during periodic elections and through inter-election pressure groups, so the American citizenry must shoulder some share of responsibility for the failure of its government to make adequate domestic climate change mitigation policy, and perhaps also for its continued obstruction of global climate policy efforts, given its widespread passive support for its government's active opposition to global efforts to reduce emissions. But the government's failure to adequately address global climate change is not merely an institutional shortcoming, since social norms are too permissive of pollution to generate genuinely democratic support for taking the necessary policy steps to avoid dangerously high greenhouse gas concentrations from accumulating, much less to achieve those aims in the absence of coercive policies. Part of the problem is a public culture constructed around the personal automobile, large living spaces, high resource consumption, and little regard for the consequences of these upon the world's less fortunate. Democratic decisions ultimately reflect this culture, and the shared values and common identity it fosters create the necessary conditions for attributing collective responsibility as well as generating the preferences for which such attributions are necessary. Prior to those political decisions lies a culture that is inimical to meaningful action to reduce emissions, and that culture can only be the product of society taken as a collectivity, and irreducible to individuals.

The key to linking group fault and liability with individual acts and choices lies within the roles played by social norms and practices and the culture in which they are bound. Describing this role, Howard McGary finds individuals to be culpable for social practices in which they acquiesce, even if they don't personally support or participate in them. A practice, he writes, is "a common accepted course of action that may be over time habitual in nature; a course of action that specifies certain forms of behavior as permissible and others as impermissible with rewards and penalties assigned accordingly" (McGary 1991:79). According to McGary, individual fault is based partially on personal control over group actions, but persons can escape responsibility for group actions without stopping those actions if they are powerless to affect group outcomes and they refuse to accept unjust enrichment from collectively-produced harm. Here, fault-negating acts of "disassociation can involve publicly denouncing a practice, but only if that is all that one can do, and a refusal to accept any enrichment that occurs as a result of the faulty practice" (McGary 1991:83). Given the inescapable benefits that accrue to members of affluent industrial societies that are primarily responsible for causing climate change, one might infer that citizens of such societies might mitigate their personal fault by publicly opposing the harmful polluting practices and those social norms in which they are embedded, along with taking care not to personally contribute to collectively-produced harm by reducing their own greenhouse emissions to sustainable levels, but that they cannot escape fault and liability altogether. Insofar as climate-related harm is at least partially caused by norms and practices, which provide the context in which individuals make choices and societies set policy, none are held vicariously responsible for environmental harm for which they are not at least at some fault.

Similarly, Kutz finds the concept of "collective intention" to be the key to understanding collective responsibility, wherein individual persons can be complicit in harmful outcomes that they cannot cause by themselves. According to his Complicity Principle:

> (Basis) I am accountable for what others do when I intentionally participate in the wrong they do or the harm they cause. (Object) I am accountable for the harm or wrong we do together, independently of the actual difference I make. (Kutz 2000:122)

What matters for holding individuals morally responsible for collective actions and their outcomes is not the control that each member exercises over group actions or the difference that each makes on their own in producing or avoiding the bad outcome, but it is their "intentional participation in a collective endeavor directly links them to the consequences of that endeavor" (Kutz 2000:138). Social norms may structure our interactions with others and condition our priorities, but we cannot be excused from culpability for contributing toward harmful outcomes merely because our actions are not expressly condemned by those norms. Rather, persons reinforce norms by participating in them and by not challenging or resisting them, but norms themselves are a collective rather than an individual product. To the extent that they are implicated in the causal processes that produce harmful acts, people can be held collectively responsible for these norms and thus the behavior they encourage. As Kutz argues, "it is both a reasonable and a necessary expectation upon agents inhabiting a crowded social landscape that they be prepared to deal with the costs imposed upon others by their freely chosen projects" (Kutz 2000:154). To the extent that persons fail to resist or challenge harmful norms, they freely endorse them and thus are complicit in the outcomes that result.

Likewise, May describes this relationship between individual and group, mediated by culture and based in group identity, as a form of metaphysical guilt, which "arises out of each person's shared identity, out of the fact that people share membership in various groups that shape who these people are, and that each person is at least somewhat implicated in what any member of the group does" (May 1991:240). Like McGary, May argues that the "moral taint" of metaphysical guilt "arises from the fact that nothing is done to prevent the harms or at least to indicate that one disapproves of them. Due to these failures, the individual does nothing to disconnect himself or herself from those fellow group members who perpetrate harms" (May 1991:240–41). For May, however, this form of responsibility is existential rather than causal, in that by "condemning or disavowing what one's community has done", one "changes that part of one's self which is based on how one chooses to regard oneself" (May 1991:247). If we define ourselves by our choices, we acquire this taint by our choice not to disassociate from the harm that groups to which we belong cause through actions in which some but not all group members participate. Our identity is bound up in what the group does, May suggests, and we are responsible as individuals to avoid personal associations with harmful group actions even if we do not ourselves commit them.

Although May is concerned with the appropriateness of what Bernard Williams terms "agent regret" rather than legal liability (Williams 1981), his diagnosis of the link between individual failures and group fault is instructive for climate change. Individuals become tainted, according to May, from their solidaristic relationships with others in a culture that encourages or allows harmful action, and their willing participation in harmful social norms, where "cultures are both the product of individual actions and attitude, and also the producers of new actions and attitudes in the world" (May 1991:246). Because individual citizens can be faulted for acquiescing to harmful social norms that provide the context for harmful actions by others, they are not held vicariously liable under a climate policy that assigns mitigation and adaptation burdens to them, since they are responsible for one set of causes (the social norms that condition polluting behavior by others) if not for another (that behavior). What we do conditions what others see as permissible and impermissible, and May's account of the mediating role of culture recognizes this link between individual and collective agency. The permissive culture of industrialized nations like the United States implicates those who fail to sufficiently challenge the norms by which high rates of greenhouse emissions are produced, even if they do not produce those emissions personally. Because persons can be more or less faulty in their participation in this culture, fault and liability can be greater or lesser depending upon the efforts by which persons challenge this culture. Since May argues that collective responsibility cannot vary among group members, he terms this form of group-based taint shared responsibility, implying the presence of individual responsibility alongside that assigned to groups.

Others endorse similar versions of collective responsibility but deny that it must be equally shared by all group members. Feinberg, for example, considers the deeply ingrained racism practiced by whites in the post-bellum American South, where only some group members took part in acts of violence against blacks but where "99 percent of them, having been shaped by the prevailing mores, whole-heartedly approved of them" (Feinberg 1968:686). Although the vast majority actively or passively reinforced a hostile environment for blacks – faulty acts for which they may be held responsible – what about that one percent that disapproved? According to

Feinberg, the extent to which they could be implicated in the group's fault – with the community's passive supporters guilty of abetting those actually undertaking violent attacks – depends upon the pains they took to distance themselves from the acts of the majority; acts that appear to go beyond mere voice and appear closer to exit options. One might plausibly oppose this racism, he suggests, but to do so would "totally alienate" a person from the white Southern community, and such total alienation would be "unlikely to be widely found in a community that leaves its exit doors open". Commenting on the same example, Miller argues that one cannot escape collective responsibility merely by speaking out or voting against such practices, but rather "must take all reasonable steps to prevent the outcome occurring" (Miller 2004:255).

Here, the more demanding standard for extricating oneself from responsibility for harm caused by group actions – separately endorsed by Walzer, Feinberg, Miller, McGary, Kutz, and May – is more plausible, requiring democratic citizens to take all reasonable and prudent steps to avoid individually contributing to a problem, whether through individual emissions or through acquiescence with harmful social norms or solidarity with polluting activities. Merely voting against some candidate or policy is insufficient, since such passive opposition to something that finds support not only from other citizens but also through prevailing social norms amounts to too meager an attempt to avoid personally contributing to the problem. Given their vast historical and ongoing responsibility for climate change, Americans cannot merely vote for a losing candidate or ballot measure, return to their oversized homes, park the SUV in their three-car garages, and reasonably expect to be exonerated from liability for the harm associated with climate change. To do so would not only be to personally contribute toward the harm in question, but is also to fully participate in the harmful culture and reinforce the harmful norms on which the group's culpability rests. Exercising political responsibility requires more than low-cost and ineffective action. One must, as Miller argues, "take all reasonable steps" to prevent climate change from occurring – not only at the ballot box or public forum but also in everyday consumer decisions and the manifold ways in which persons may reinforce or challenge prevailing social norms; which all contribute, albeit in different ways, to the problem. And even then, the impossibility of forgoing all unjust enrichment from residing within an historical greenhouse polluter only allows citizens of industrialized nations to mitigate rather than negate their personal responsibility and thus liability for climate-related harm.

Thus, the sort of collective responsibility involved in anthropogenic climate change most closely resembles what Feinberg terms *contributory group-fault: collective and distributive*, as there is contributory fault on the part of all group members, so no one's fault is vicarious and (nearly) all are somehow at fault, if unequally so (Feinberg 1968:683). Hence, as May suggests, this sort of group liability need not run afoul of individual moral responsibility, as all are at fault for climate change, whether directly or indirectly. Fault need not be distributed equally among group members – more liability may be attributed those who are more causally responsible – but all members are responsible in some way for the harm in question, and so can be held liable for it.

12.5 Conclusion

From such examples, a preliminary picture emerges concerning each person's share of the collective responsibility that attaches to citizenship in those nations most responsible for anthropogenic climate change. Even though national per capita averages obscure a wide range within individual emissions, the aggregate rate of fossil fuel combustion within the United States is plainly too high to avoid collective (if distributive) fault, yet those patterns of behavior that generate such high emissions are supported by social norms in the same way that white racism in the post-bellum South was the product of such norms. As is the case in Feinberg's racism example, some may be more responsible than others for contributing to climate change and so might be assessed greater liability for compensating those harmed by it, but none escape some fault altogether, at least insofar as all benefit from group activities that result in greenhouse pollution, regardless of whether or not they personally support those activities. Unlike Feinberg's drowning example, however, none can be released from responsibility by the acts of others, as national GHG mitigation cannot be accomplished by a single rescuer. Such a conclusion need not dismay those pressing their governments to take action to abate national emissions as well as personally reducing their own carbon footprints, for such collective responsibility is part and parcel of democratic citizenship. Justice requires that, insofar as culpable parties owe compensation to the victims of climate change, it also requires those at greater fault to pay more than those at lesser fault. Nothing in the general claims of collective responsibility diminishes the sense of individual responsibility discussed above. More importantly, nothing in the conception of either individual or collective responsibility absolves democratic citizens of their duty to ensure that their government and society does all that it can to avoid harming others. In this sense, the sort of collective responsibility invoked in global climate policy is wholly consistent with the individualistic conceptions of responsibility upon which it has been premised.

References

Fahlquist, Jessica. 2009. "Moral Responsibility for Environmental Problems – Individual or Institutional?" *Journal of Agricultural and Environmental Ethics* 22(2):109–24.

Feinberg, Joel. 1968. "Collective Responsibility." *The Journal of Philosophy* 65:674–88.

Feinberg, Joel. 1970. *Doing and Deserving*. Princeton, NJ: Princeton University Press.

Harris, Paul. 2009. *World Ethics and Climate Change*. Edinburgh: Edinburgh University Press.

Hart, H.L.A. 1968. *Punishment and Responsibility*. New York, NY: Oxford University Press.

Intergovernmental Panel on Climate Change, Climate Change. 2001. *A Synthesis Report. A Contribution of Working Groups I, II, and III to the Third Assessment Report of the IPCC*, edited by R.T. Watson and the Core Writing Team, 12. Cambridge: Cambridge University Press.

Kutz, Christopher. 2000. *Complicity: Ethics and Law for a Collective Age*. New York, NY: Cambridge University Press.

May, Larry. 1991. "Metaphysical Guilt and Moral Taint." In *Collective Responsibility: Five Decades of Debate in Theoretical and Applied Ethics*, edited by Larry May and Stacey Hoffman, 239–54. Savage, MD: Rowman & Littlefield.

May, Larry. 1992. *Sharing Responsibility*. Chicago, IL: The University of Chicago Press.

McGary, Howard. 1991. "Morality and Collective Liability." In *Collective Responsibility: Five Decades of Debate in Theoretical and Applied Ethics*, edited by Larry May, and Stacey Hoffman, 77–87. Savage, MD: Rowman & Littlefield.
Miller, David. 2004. "Holding Nations Responsible." *Ethics* 114:240–68.
Nagel, Thomas. 1979. "Moral Luck." In *Nagel Mortal Questions*, 24–38. New York, NY: Cambridge University Press.
United Nations. 1992. *United Nations Framework Convention on Climate Change*. http://unfccc.int/essential_background/convention/background/items/2853.php
Vanderheiden, Steve. 2008. *Atmospheric Justice: A Political Theory of Climate Change*. New York, NY: Oxford University Press.
Vanderheiden, Steve. 2011. "Climate Justice as Globalized Responsibility." In *Cosmopolitan Conceptions of Climate Change*, edited by Paul Harris. Cheltenham: Edward Elgar.
Walzer, Michael. 1977. *Just and Unjust Wars*. New York, NY: Basic Books.
Williams, Bernard. 1981. *Moral Luck*. New York, NY: Cambridge University Press.

Chapter 13
Collective Responsibility, Epistemic Action and Climate Change

Seumas Miller

Abstract This article undertakes four tasks: (1) outline a theory of joint action, including multi-layered structures of joint action characteristic of organizational action; (2) utilize this theory to elaborate an account of joint epistemic action – joint action directed to the acquisition of knowledge, e.g. a team of scientists seeking to discover the cause of climate change; (3) outline an account of collective moral responsibility based on the theory of joint action (including the account of joint epistemic action); (4) apply the account of collective moral responsibility to the issue of human-induced, harmful, climate change with a view to illuminating both retrospective responsibility for causing the harm and also prospective responsibility for addressing the problem in terms of mitigation and/or adaptation.

13.1 Introduction

In this paper I set myself four connected tasks and the paper is in four sections corresponding to these tasks. In Section 13.2 I elaborate the notion of Joint Action (JA) in its various aspects, including certain forms of institutional action, e.g. the actions of a government (Miller 2001:chap. 2). This notion of joint action underpins my concept of joint epistemic action developed in Section 13.3 and my notion of collective responsibility outlined in Section 13.4. In Section 13.2 I introduce various technical notions, such as that of a multi-layered structure of JA, which are necessary in order for it to be seen that the forms of institutional action in question are at bottom the joint actions of individual human beings and, therefore, individual human beings can be held morally responsible for them.

I analyse and argue for a particular species of joint action, namely, joint epistemic action (Miller 2008). In the case of the latter, but not necessarily the former, agents have epistemic goals, e.g. scientists seeking to acquire knowledge of climate

S. Miller (✉)
Centre for Applied Philosophy and Public Ethics, Australian National University, Canberra, ACT, Australia

Charles Sturt University, Canberra, NSW, Australia

Department of Philosophy, Delft University of Technology, Delft, The Netherlands
e-mail: seumas.miller@anu.edu.au

N.A Vincent et al. (eds.), *Moral Responsibility*, Library of Ethics and Applied Philosophy 27, DOI 10.1007/978-94-007-1878-4_13,

change. The notion of joint epistemic action is a novel notion and the idea that coming to have beliefs (and therefore coming to have knowledge) could be action has been disputed. Moreover, in the theoretical literature on collective moral responsibility, indeed on moral responsibility more generally, epistemic responsibility, i.e. responsibility (including collective moral responsibility) for epistemic action has not been previously identified, nor theorized as a concept in its own right. While joint epistemic action can be morally significant, it differs from non-epistemic forms of responsibility in important respects, e.g. typically, epistemic failures are in themselves less morally serious than (so to speak) behavioural moral failures and tend to derive their moral significance from the behaviour they enable.

In Section 13.4 I outline a general notion of collective moral responsibility (Miller 2010:chap. 4). This notion includes the notion of collective moral epistemic responsibility. It is important to understand the notion of collective moral epistemic responsibility and how it relates to collective moral responsibility in general, since typically morally significant complex joint actions, including institutional action and the joint actions of large groups, have as a key element morally significant joint epistemic action for which agents can be held morally responsibility. Moreover, joint epistemic action is deeply implicated in climate change debates – the issue I address in Section 13.5 – as the influential stand taken by climate change skeptics makes abundantly clear.

In Section 13.5 I put to work the theoretical machinery developed in Sections 13.2, 13.3, and 13.4 and address the question of the moral responsibility for harmful, climate change caused by human action.

The issue of moral responsibility for human-induced, harmful climate change is an intellectually difficult and controversial one. Common sense might lead us to ascribe some moral responsibility to each of us for the harm caused. However, this has been disputed by theorists. For example Sinnott-Armstrong argues that individual citizens (who, for example, drive gas-guzzling SUVs) are not morally responsible for the harm done by human-induced climate change (Sinnott-Armstrong 2005). Sinnott-Armstrong goes on to hold governments morally responsible. Aside from illustrating the potential discrepancy between common sense and applied philosophical theory, it also raises the issue of the moral responsibility of institutions and institutional actors and the relationship of institutional moral responsibility to that of individual human beings. Specifically, is institutional action reducible to the action of individual human agents? If not, then we could have a situation in which an institution, e.g. a government, was morally responsible for harmful climate change but no individual human being (including individual members of that government) was responsible. Indeed, this is precisely the view of many influential contemporary theorists, including Margaret Gilbert (Gilbert 1992; Miller and Makela 2005) and David Copp (Copp 2007; Miller 2007, 2010). If so, then what is the analysis of institutional action that makes this possible; not, I submit, the analyses provided by atomistic individualist accounts (Narveson 2002).

A central purpose of this paper is to display the continuity between individual and institutional moral responsibility for actions: the continuity between, for example, the moral responsibility for harmful climate change of individual citizens and that of governments. Moreover, as noted above, in the available theoretical discussions of collective moral responsibility, indeed moral responsibility more generally, epistemic responsibility, e.g. of climate scientists, has not been distinguished and differentiated from behavioural responsibility. Accordingly, my broad aim in this paper is to provide a much needed theoretical framework for this highly complex, interconnected set of issues, and to illustrate some of the ways in which this framework can be applied to illuminate the various kinds and levels of moral responsibility in play in the current climate change debates. In so doing I take myself to be demonstrating the explanatory power, fecundity and utility of my novel individualist, joint-action-based account of collective moral responsibility, on the one hand, and to be taking the initial steps toward mapping the nature and strength of some of the key moral responsibilities in play in responding to harmful, human-induced climate change, on the other.

For convenience, I will sometimes refer to joint action that is not joint epistemic action as joint behavioural action – thereby signaling the presence of bodily behaviour – notwithstanding that joint epistemic action and joint behavioural action (in this restricted sense) do not exhaust the types of joint action and also that joint epistemic action typically involves some form of observable behaviour.

13.2 Joint Action

Joint actions are actions involving a number of agents performing interdependent actions in order to realise some common goal (Miller 2001:chap. 2). Examples of joint action are: two people dancing together, a number of tradesmen building a house and a team of researchers conducting an attitudinal survey. Joint action is to be distinguished from individual action on the one hand, and from the "actions" of corporate bodies on the other. Thus an individual walking down the road or shooting at a target are instances of individual action.

The concept of joint action can be construed very narrowly or more broadly. On the most narrow construal we have what I will call, *basic* joint action. Basic joint action involves two co-present agents each of whom performs one basic individual action, and does so simultaneously with the other agent, and in relation to a collective end that is to be realised within the temporal and spatial horizons of the immediate face-to-face experience of the agents. A basic individual action is an action an agent can do at will without recourse to instruments other than his or her own body. An example of a basic individual action is raising one's arm; an example of a basic joint action is two people holding hands.

If we construe joint action more broadly we can identify a myriad of other closely related examples of joint action. Many of these involve intentions and ends directed to outcomes outside the temporal horizon of the immediate experience of the agents, e.g., two people engaging in a two hour long conversation or three people deciding to build a garden wall over the summer break. Others involve intentions and ends directed to outcomes that will exist outside the spatial horizon of the immediate experience of the agents, and involve instruments other than the agent's bodies. Thus two people might jointly fire a rocket into the extremities of the earth's atmosphere.

Still other joint actions involve very large numbers of agents, e.g., a large contingent of soldiers fighting a battle.

13.2.1 Joint Procedures (Conventions)

Basic joint actions can also be distinguished from, what I will call, joint procedures. An agent has a joint procedure to x, if he x-s in a recurring situation, and does so on condition that other agents x. (Procedures are different from repetitions of the same action in a single situation, e.g., rowing or skipping.) Thus Australians have a procedure to drive on the left hand side of the road. Each Australian drives on the left whenever he drives, and he drives on the left on condition the other agents drive on the left. Moreover, joint procedures are followed in order to achieve collective goals, e.g., to avoid car collisions. Joint procedures are in fact conventions (Miller 2001:chap. 3).

It is important to distinguish conventions from social norms. Social norms are regularities in action involving interdependence of action among members of a group, but regularities in action that are governed by a moral purpose or principle (Miller 2001:chap. 4). For example, avoiding telling lies is a social norm. Some regularities in action are both conventions and social norms, e.g., driving on the left hand side of the road. Conventions and social norms are necessary elements of institutional action and it is important for my purposes in this paper that they can be understood in individualist terms.

13.2.2 Joint Institutional Mechanisms

We can also distinguish between joint procedures (in the above sense) and, what I will call, joint mechanisms (Miller 2001:chap. 5; 2010:chap. 1). Examples of joint mechanisms are the device of tossing a coin to resolve a dispute and voting to elect a candidate to office. Joint mechanisms are typically – but not necessarily – constitutive elements of social institutions (Miller 2010) and when they are they are joint institutional mechanisms.

In some cases, that these joint mechanisms are used might be a matter of having a procedure in my earlier sense. Thus, if we decided that (within some specified range of disputes) we would always have recourse to tossing the coin, then we would have adopted a procedure in my earlier sense. Accordingly, I will call such joint mechanisms, joint procedural mechanisms.

Joint mechanisms (and, therefore, joint procedural mechanisms) consist of: (a) a complex of differentiated but interlocking actions (the input to the mechanism); (b) the result of the performance of those actions (the output of the mechanism), and; (c) the mechanism itself. Thus a given agent might vote for a candidate. He will do so only if others also vote. But further to this, there is the action of the candidates, namely, that they present themselves as candidates. That they present themselves as candidates is (in part) constitutive of the input to the voting mechanism. Voters vote *for candidates*. So there is interlocking and differentiated action (the input). Further there is some result (as opposed to consequence) of the joint action; the joint action consisting of the actions of putting oneself forward as a candidate and of the actions of voting. The result is that some candidate, say, Jones is voted in (the output). That there is a result is (in part) constitutive of the mechanism. That to receive the most number of votes is to be voted in, is (in part) constitutive of the voting mechanism. Moreover, that Jones is voted in is not a collective end of all the voters. (Although it is a collective end of those who voted for Jones.) However, that the one who gets the most votes – whoever that happens to be – is voted in, is a collective end of all (or nearly all) of the voters.

Joint mechanisms play a central role in institutional action and as is the case with conventions and social norms, it is important for my purposes in this paper that they can be understood in purely individualist terms and by recourse to my core notion of joint action.

13.2.3 Organisations, Institutions and Multi-Layered Structures of Joint Action

Organizations consist of an (embodied) formal *structure* of interlocking roles (Miller 2001:chap. 5; Miller 2010:chaps. 1 and 2). An organizational role can be defined in terms of the agent (whoever it is) who performs certain tasks, the tasks themselves, procedures (in the above sense) and conventions. Moreover, unlike social groups, organizations are individuated by the kind of activity that they undertake, and also by their characteristic ends. Many organisations are also social institutions. Social institutions are organisations with a moral dimension by virtue of, for example, the authority relations they involve and the fact that their collective ends are also collective goods (Miller 2010:chap. 2). Thus governments have as a collective end the regulation of other institutions (a collective good), universities the end of discovering knowledge (a collective good), and so on.

A further defining feature of organizations is that organizational action typically consists in, what I have elsewhere termed, *a multi-layered structure of joint actions* (Miller 2001:chap. 5; Miller 2010:chaps. 1 and 2). One illustration of the notion of a layered structure of joint actions is an armed force fighting a battle. Suppose at an organizational level a number of joint actions ("actions") are severally necessary[1] and jointly sufficient to achieve some collective end. Thus the "action" of the mortar squad destroying enemy gun emplacements, the "action" of the flight of military planes providing air cover, and the "action" of the infantry platoon taking and holding the ground might be severally necessary and jointly sufficient to achieve

[1] Here there is simplification for the sake of clarity. For what is said here is not strictly correct, at least in the case of many actions performed by members of organizations. Rather, typically some threshold set of actions is necessary to achieve the end; moreover the boundaries of this set are vague.

the collective end of defeating the enemy; as such, these "actions" taken together constitute a joint action.

At the first level there are individual actions directed to three distinct collective ends: the collective ends of (respectively) destroying gun emplacements, providing air cover, and talking and holding ground. So at this level there are three joint actions, namely those of the members of the mortar squad destroying gun emplacements, the members of the flight of planes providing air cover, and the members of the infantry taking and holding ground. However, taken together these three joint actions constitute a single joint action. The collective end of this second level joint action is to defeat the enemy; and from the perspective of this second level joint action, and its collective end, these (first level joint) constitutive actions are (second level) individual actions. I note that typically in organisations not just the nature but the quantum of the individual contributions made to the collective end will differ from one agent to another.

Obviously, given the crucial role of institutions and institutional actions in harmful climate change, it is important for my purposes in this paper that organisations that are institutions can be understood in purely individualist terms and by recourse to my core notion of joint action; hence the significance of the technical notion of a multi-layered structure of joint action.

13.2.4 Collective Ends

Joint actions are interdependent actions directed toward a common goal or end. But what is such an end? This notion of a common goal or, as I shall refer to it, a collective end, is a construction out of the prior notion of an individual end. Roughly speaking, a collective end is an individual end more than one agent has, and which is such that, if it is realised, it is realised by all, or most, of the actions of the agents involved; the individual action of any given agent is only part of the means by which the end is realised. The realisation of the collective end is the bringing into existence of a state of affairs. Each agent has this state of affairs as an individual end. (It is also a state of affairs aimed at under more or less the same description by each agent.) So a collective end is a species of individual end (Miller 2001:chap. 2; Miller 2010:chap. 1).

This completes my general theory of joint action, the individualist theory which underpins my account of collective moral responsibility, including the moral responsibilities of institutions and institutional actors. However, although I have provided a theoretical account of joint action and its various permutations, I have not elaborated an account of a key species of joint action that, as climate change skepticism illustrates, is deeply implicated in harmful climate change, namely, joint epistemic action. In what follows my task is to analyse joint epistemic action in terms of my general theory of joint action, and thereby enable the provision of a theory of collective moral responsibility which accommodates both joint behavioural action and joint epistemic action. I begin with an account of epistemic action in general, since this notion is far from transparent and its existence has largely been ignored (Goldman 1999; Miller 2008).

13.3 Epistemic Action

As noted above, epistemic action is action directed to an epistemic goal, especially knowledge. I take it that the key notion of knowledge in play here is propositional knowledge, i.e. "knowing that", as opposed to, for example, "knowing how". Moreover, I will assume in what follows that knowledge is justified true belief. Naturally, it could be argued – by recourse to Gettier cases, for example – that justified true belief is not sufficient for knowledge. Here I will assume that such counter-examples can be defeated by, for example, an additional condition to the effect that the justification relied on by a true believer does not itself essentially depend on any falsehoods (Lehrer 1987).

Justified true belief is a serviceable definition of knowledge for our purposes here, albeit by no means is it a complete or definitive one. Let us now turn to the notion of epistemic action (Goldman 1999; Miller 2008).

13.3.1 Knowledge, Belief and Action

The justification of a true belief involves reasoning that provides a good and decisive justification for the believer to truly believe the content of the belief in question. Moreover, this reasoning is in large part theoretical, as opposed to practical, reasoning. For it is reasoning that terminates in a belief (or structure of beliefs), as opposed to an action.

So justification is of two sorts: justification in relation to actions, and justification in relation to beliefs.

An important difference is that actions can often be done at will, e.g., I can raise my right arm now, whereas apparently this is not so for belief acquisition, e.g., if I believe that the world is round I cannot simply decide to believe that it is flat. Moreover, this contrast can lead one to opt for a sharp division between questions of morality and questions of knowledge. Morality, it might be held, pertains only to actions (and habits, including virtues and vices) for which one can be held responsible, whereas belief acquisition – and, therefore, knowledge acquisition – not being under one's control can have no intrinsic moral dimension. To be sure, knowledge acquisition involves the application of principles of rationality, e.g. in relation to good and bad evidence for one's beliefs, but such principles do not include, on this view, any specifically moral principles.

However, it is doubtful that moral properties can be ascribed only to the actions, agential conditions or other states for which someone can be held morally responsible (usually the person who performed the action, is possessed of the condition or caused the state in question). Consider someone brought up in a racist society or a paedophile who was himself routinely subject to sexual abuse as a child and developed paedophilia as a consequence. Indeed, lack of autonomy and, therefore, of the ability to act with moral responsibility is itself a moral deficiency, notwithstanding that one might not be responsible for this lack, e.g. if one was raised as a slave or became a drug addict in one's mother's womb. If it be objected that *someone* is morally responsible for these deficiencies of character, even if not the person possessed of them, it can be replied that this is not obviously so in some of these examples, such as the racist society which has never had any exposure to non-racism, or the drug addict whose drug addict mother became pregnant as a result of being raped. But in any case there are examples where it is clearly not the case that anyone is morally responsible, such as that of a person whose violent temper is caused by some neurological defect.

Moreover, the contrast between actions and beliefs should not be overstated.[2] First, even if one cannot freely choose between believing that p and believing that not p, one can certainly in many instances freely choose to have neither the belief that p nor the belief that not p; one can do so by refraining from inquiring or otherwise investigating whether or not it is the case that p. And, of course, in such cases typically one can freely choose to investigate whether or not that p, in which case one is in effect choosing to come to have either the belief that p or the belief that not p, depending on the outcome of the investigation. In short, one can often freely choose between an absence of belief and the presence of belief with respect to some matter. For many beliefs are, and can only be, acquired after a process of investigation, e.g. the belief that Sutcliffe is the Yorkshire Ripper (or that he is not) could not have been acquired if detectives had not decided to investigate the murders of Yorkshire prostitutes. That is, without this act of will – to conduct an investigation – the detectives would simply not have had a belief as to the identity of the Yorkshire Ripper; they would have remained in a state of ignorance.

So much for choosing whether or not to have a belief with respect to some matter; but are there cases in which one can freely choose between having the belief that p and having the belief that not p? As long as the notion of freely choosing is understood broadly, then it seems that there are many such cases.

Beliefs are often the terminal point of an act of judgement, and evidence-based acts of judgement are typically freely performed. Consider, for example, an examinee who comes to believe on the basis of a series of calculations that the answer to a complex mathematical problem is zero. The examinee is not absolutely certain that the answer is zero; after all she well knows that she could have made a mistake. However, after checking she is very confident that her judgement is correct. As it turns out the examinee has given the right answer based on valid mathematical reasoning. Surely the inference based judgement that terminated in her belief that the answer was zero was freely performed; certainly she is held responsible for providing this answer and marked, awarded prizes and so on, accordingly. Here I am not simply claiming that she freely chose to try to answer the mathematical problem, although this is also true. Rather I am claiming that although her act of judgement was "compelled by logic", it was, nevertheless, freely performed. Indeed, in these

---

[2] I accept the arguments of Montmarquet (Montmarquet 1993: chap. 1) to the conclusion that one can be directly responsible for some of one's beliefs, i.e. that one's responsibility for some of one's beliefs is not dependent on one's responsibility for some action that led to those beliefs. In short, doxastic responsibility does not reduce to responsibility for actions. However, if I (and Montmarquet) turn out to be wrong in this regard, the basic arguments in this chapter could be recast in terms of a notion of doxastic responsibility as a form of responsibility for actions.

types of case there is no tension between the "compulsion" of logic and the exercise of freedom.

Now consider a second example. The belief that Sutcliffe was the Yorkshire Ripper was formed as a result of the detectives' judgement that on the basis of the evidence gathered he was the Yorkshire Ripper. Naturally, their judgement was not freely made in the sense that the detectives could have made any old judgement that they felt like making, including a judgement that was completely inconsistent with the evidence. But freely performed judgements are not to be identified with capricious or irrational judgements.

In this respect judgements are akin to actions in general; an action that is "compelled" by reason does not thereby cease to be a freely chosen action. Suppose that A desires to go home immediately after work to relax and have dinner, and also that A has promised A's spouse that A will do so; in addition, suppose that A has no other competing desires or obligations, and also that the only available means for A to get home is for A to take the bus. Needless to say, A takes the bus home. For A has good and decisive reasons to take the bus home, and A has no reasons to perform any competing action. So A's taking the bus home is "compelled" by reason; but it is no less a freely performed action for being so. It remains true, of course, that A could have chosen to do otherwise than take the bus home, albeit this might have been somewhat psychologically difficult for A, given A is a rational being.

Now suppose a police officer uses a tazer gun on an armed offender in self defence, and could not have done otherwise if he was to preserve his own life. Here the police officer has acted freely, notwithstanding that "he had no other choice" rationally speaking; that is, his action was fully rationally justified and the alternative (to allow himself to be killed) was without rational justification (assuming tazer guns are a form of non-lethal force). Indeed, it may well be that given the threat to his own life, he would have found it psychologically difficult not to use the tazer gun; nevertheless, his action was freely performed.

So the sharp contrast drawn between belief formation and actions with respect to being freely chosen does not hold up. Moreover, our examples have revealed a further analogy. In both the case of the rational use of the tazer gun and the evidence-based judgement of Sutcliffe's guilt there is a further dimension, namely, a moral dimension. In both cases the "actions" have moral significance. In one case, a life is at stake, in the other case life imprisonment (at least) is at stake. Accordingly, it is doubtful that the epistemic sphere (pertaining to knowledge) exists entirely independently of morality, notwithstanding that knowledge acquisition can be, and often is, without moral significance.

One can be held morally responsible for failing to pursue knowledge or for arriving at false beliefs on the basis of sloppy evidence gathering. Naturally, the knowledge in question must have moral significance. In criminal investigations, for example, the knowledge (or false belief) in question almost always has moral significance, at least potentially, since crimes are typically immoral acts. In scientific work on climate change, at least in contemporary settings, the knowledge acquired has moral significance by virtue of the potential for massive harm that climate change brings with it.

And there is a further point to be made here. Truth is teleological: assertions, judgements, beliefs and so on aim at the truth and are deficient in so far as they fail and are false. So qua maker of judgements, former of beliefs, assertor and so on, one ought to aim at the truth and do so for its own sake. To this extent truth-aiming is an epistemic norm that is intrinsic to the kinds of epistemic acts in question. However, some kinds of knowledge are worth having for their own sake by virtue of being an inherent human good, as opposed to being merely instrumentally valuable or of trivial interest. More specifically, such knowledge is inherently valuable by virtue of being a constitutive element of human understanding. This is an additional property of some epistemic states; it is not a necessary feature of all epistemic states. Accordingly, the norms governing human understanding are not simply the purely epistemic norms governing the narrower practice of knowledge acquisition per se. Moreover, in the light of human understanding being a human good, the norms governing human understanding are moral, or quasi-moral, norms.

13.3.2 Joint Epistemic Action

Thus far we have discussed joint action and epistemic action in general terms. It is now time to bring these two notions together and focus on the resultant notion of joint epistemic action. Joint epistemic action is joint action that has a collective epistemic end, e.g. the acquisition of knowledge.

Naturally, many truth-aiming attitudes or actions, such as beliefs, inferences, perceptual judgements, assertions to one-self, and so on are individual, not joint, actions or attitudes. Moreover, I am not an advocate of irreducibly collective beliefs (Gilbert 1992:chap. 5) or of collective subjects that engage in some form of irreducibly, non-individualist reasoning or communication (Pettit 2001:chap. 5; Miller and Makela 2005). However, much knowledge acquisition is performed by individuals acting jointly to realize a collective epistemic end, e.g. a team of linguistic experts who work together to discover the meaning of some lost manuscript.

Many speech actions, including acts of assertion are joint epistemic acts (Miller 2008). Assertion typically involves a speaker (assertor) and a hearer (audience) and the practice of assertion involves, I suggest, three connected features. Firstly, assertions have a communicative purpose or end; they are acts performed in order to transmit beliefs, true beliefs, and often knowledge (justified true beliefs). Secondly, they are acts at least constrained by considerations of truthfulness. It is central to the practice of assertion that participants (in general) aim at the truth, or at least try to avoid falsity. Thirdly, speakers purport to be, or represent themselves as, or make out that they are, aiming at the truth. Indeed, they make out not only that they are aiming at the truth, but also that they have succeeded in "hitting" the truth.

Assertions are joint actions and, more specifically, joint epistemic actions. Assertion is a joint epistemic action involving a speaker and hearer each having as their end that the hearer gain knowledge and that each has this end is a matter of mutual knowledge, i.e. the end in question is a collective end.

Naturally, speakers can assert insincerely in which case they do not have the collective end of knowledge acquisition by the hearer; hence the definition of assertion involves the weaker condition mentioned above, namely, that speakers purport to be aiming at the truth.

Assertions and like speech acts are governed by epistemic norms. Thus it is held that the speaker epistemically ought to tell the truth and that the hearer epistemically ought to trust the speaker; if these norms are infringed then the collective end is likely not to be realized. Moreover, this collective end itself has a normative character in the context of the speech act; the acquisition of knowledge by the hearer ought to be the aim and result of an assertion. Indeed, I suggest that this normative condition with respect to the collective end of assertions is in part definitional of this type of speech act and explains, in particular, how it is that speakers purport to be aiming at the truth (Miller 2008).

These epistemic norms are often also social norms in my above-mentioned sense, i.e. they are mutually believed by a community (at least one community) to have moral content. Hence there is the community-wide (and surely correct) belief that a speaker morally ought not to mislead a hearer by pretending to comply with the epistemic norm to tell the truth but not do so; in most (all?) linguistic communities lying is (correctly) mutually believed to be morally wrong.

More generally, epistemic action, including the acquisition of knowledge, involves procedures, e.g. verification procedures such as observation, interviewing suspects. Many of these procedures are epistemic norms.

These procedures include joint procedures (i.e. conventions, as described above). Thus each uses the procedure, given others do and they realize a collective end, namely, that we come to have knowledge. For example, testimony is a joint procedure in this sense.

These joint procedures include joint institutional mechanisms (as described above). For example, the replication of experiments by scientists is a joint institutional mechanism in this sense. The collective end here is that the initial experimental outcome is verified or remains unverified (and is possibly disconfirmed); the result is that (say) the initial experimental outcome is verified (as opposed to remaining unverified or being disconfirmed).

As is the case with joint action more generally, some joint epistemic action has no moral significance, e.g. two people jointly solving a crossword puzzle. However some joint epistemic action has profound moral significance, e.g. designing the atom bomb, discovering the cure for cancer. Moreover, some epistemic joint procedures and joint procedural mechanisms have moral significance, e.g. clinical trials for drugs.

Notwithstanding these similarities with respect to moral significance between joint epistemic action and joint action more generally there are important differences. I do not have the space to elaborate these differences here. However, I note that, typically, epistemic actions – including joint epistemic actions – are in themselves less morally significant than behavioural actions. Specifically, epistemic failures are in themselves less morally serious than behavioural failures. This is in part because epistemic actions (and omissions) tend to derive their moral significance from the behaviour they enable or (more indirectly) from the consequences of the behaviour that they enable. Thus the discovery of the properties of various combinations of chemicals and, specifically, how to make gunpowder (joint epistemic activity) enabled military forces to more effectively destroy buildings in which civilians were housed and to commit other atrocities of war (joint behavioural activity). But this epistemic activity did not cause these morally reprehensible outcomes and those who discovered the chemical properties and processes in question are not responsible for war crimes; rather these civilian deaths were intentionally caused by the military personnel in question and they should be the ones brought before the relevant war crimes tribunal. On the other hand, joint epistemic action in which the epistemic end is qua collective end aimed at as a means to achieve evil, as in the case of scientists engaged in designing and building weapons of mass destruction is a different matter; in such cases joint epistemic action might attract a high degree of (collective) moral responsibility for the final outcome.

As we saw was the case with joint behavioural action, there are some multi-layered structures of joint epistemic action, including joint epistemic actions undertaken by the members of organizations. Consider a major crime squad undertaking a criminal investigation.

At the first level there is joint epistemic action. Here are three instances of this. (1) The victim communicates the crime (assault) and a description of the offender to a police officer; note that the speech act of assertion is a joint epistemic action, as is the process of asking and answering questions. (2) Two detectives interview a suspect to determine his motive and opportunity; this is a joint epistemic action. (3) The forensic team analyses the physical evidence, e.g. DNA; this is a joint epistemic action.

At the second level there is a joint epistemic action constituted by the three first level joint actions but with an additional collective end, namely, that of solving the crime. The crime squad solves the crime; this is a joint epistemic action. Moreover, the crime squad solving the crime is a multi-layered structure of joint epistemic action comprised, as it is, of the three first level joint epistemic actions directed to the second level collective end of solving the crime.

13.4 Collective Moral Responsibility

Let me now outline my account of collective moral responsibility (Miller 2006). I note that this account is underpinned by my analyses of joint action (including joint epistemic action), and by the various technical notions derived from basic joint action (e.g. joint mechanisms, multi-layered structures of joint action) that are required for the understanding of institutional action. I further note the above-mentioned desideratum that my account of collective moral responsibility display the continuity between collective moral responsibility for joint behavioural action and collective moral responsibility for joint epistemic action, notwithstanding the differences between them (in particular, the typically greater stringency of moral obligations with respect to joint behavioural action by comparison with moral obligations with respect to joint epistemic action).

We need first to distinguish some different senses of responsibility (Miller 2001:chap. 8; Miller 2010:chap. 4). Sometimes to say that someone is responsible for an action is to say that the person had a reason, or reasons, to perform some action, then formed an intention to perform that action (or not to perform it), and finally acted (or refrained from acting) on that intention, and did so on the basis of that reason(s). Note that an important category of reasons for actions are ends, goals or purposes; an agent's reason for performing an action is often that the action realises a goal the agent has. As we have seen, such goals could include epistemic goals in which case the action is an epistemic action. I will dub this sense of being responsible for an action "natural responsibility", i.e. intentionally performing an action and doing so for a reason.

On other occasions what is meant by the term, "being responsible for an action", is that the person in question occupies a certain institutional role, and that the occupant of that role is the person who has the institutionally determined duty to decide what is to be done in relation to certain matters. For example, the computer maintenance person in an office has the responsibility to fix the computers in the office, irrespective of whether or not he does so, or even contemplates doing so. Since fixing a computer will typically involve an epistemic task of finding out the cause of the problem, the computer maintenance person has an institutional responsibility to perform certain epistemic tasks.

A third sense of "being responsible" for an action, is a species of our second sense. If the matters in respect of which the occupant of an institutional role has an institutionally determined duty to decide what is to be done, include ordering other agents to perform, or not to perform, certain actions, then the occupant of the role is responsible for those actions performed by those other agents. We say of such a person that he is responsible for the actions of other persons in virtue of being the person in authority over them. Thus a schoolteacher might be held to be responsible for some of the epistemic failures of her students, e.g. their failure to learn the letters of the alphabet.

The fourth sense of responsibility is, of course, moral responsibility. Roughly speaking, an agent is held to be morally responsible for an action – including an epistemic action – if the agent was responsible for that action in one of our first three senses of "responsible", and that action is morally significant.

Here the notion of a morally significant action is an imprecise term of art designed to cast the net widely rather than a precise definitional term. An action is obviously morally significant if it morally ought to be performed or morally ought not to be performed. Thus the action could be intrinsically morally wrong, as in the case of a human rights violation. Or the action might be the means to a morally good or bad end, or the outcome that it actually had might be morally good or morally bad. However, an action might be morally significant even though it is neither the case that it morally ought to be performed nor the case that it morally ought not to be performed. It might be morally permissible, for example, or it might be one option in a moral dilemma in which there is nothing to choose, morally speaking, between the available options.

As with behavioural actions, epistemic actions can be morally significant in a number of ways. As we saw above, they can be morally significant by virtue of the ends that they serve or the outcome that they produce, e.g. discovering the cure for cancer and thereby saving lives. Moreover, knowledge and false belief can have moral significance independently of their consequences. Some knowledge (and the corresponding false beliefs) is morally significant simply in virtue of being by definition (so to speak) moral knowledge, e.g. knowledge that the guilty ought not to be punished. Again, some knowledge and corresponding false beliefs have an implicit moral content and, as such, are morally significant. For example, the false moral belief (based on an error in the identification procedure) among police and the community that a suspect is a paedophile.

Some knowledge is such that certain persons have a moral right to it; accordingly, the epistemic acts that realize these rights have moral significance. For example, perhaps citizens have a right to know about climate change. Again, there are rights that others not know certain things, e.g. some privacy rights.

We can now make the following quasi-definitional claim concerning moral responsibility:

1. If an agent is responsible for an action – including an epistemic action – in the first, second or third senses of being responsible, and the action is morally significant, then – other things being equal – the agent is morally responsible for that action, and – other things being equal – can reasonably attract moral praise or blame and (possibly) punishment or reward for the action.

Here the term "action" also refers to omissions and to the intended outcomes of actions. Further, the first "other things being equal" clause is intended to be cashed in terms of the capacity for moral agency; for example, a psychopath might not have the capacity to make moral judgements and thus ought not to be held morally responsible for his actions. The second "other things being equal" clause is to be cashed in terms of justificatory or exculpatory conditions, such as that the agent was not coerced, could not reasonably have foreseen the consequences of his or her action, and so on. It is also important to note that – consistent with this quasi-definition – agents can be held morally responsible for the morally significant foreseeable outcomes of their actions and omissions, notwithstanding that such outcomes were not intended or otherwise aimed at.

Having distinguished four senses of responsibility, including moral responsibility, let me now turn directly to collective responsibility.

As is the case with individual responsibility, we can distinguish four senses of collective responsibility. In the first instance I will do so in relation to joint actions.

Agents who perform a joint action – including a joint epistemic action – are responsible for that action in the first sense of collective responsibility. Accordingly, to say that they are collectively responsible for the action is just to say that they performed the joint action. That is, they each had a collective end, each intentionally performed their contributory action, and each did so because each mutually believed the other would perform his contributory action, and that therefore the collective end would be realised.

Here it is important to note that each agent is individually (naturally) responsible for performing his contributory action, and responsible by virtue of the fact that he intentionally performed this action, and the action was not intentionally performed by anyone else. Of course the other agents (or agent) believe that he is performing, or is going to perform, the contributory action in question. But mere possession of such a belief is not sufficient for the ascription of responsibility to the *believer* for performing the individual action in question. So what are the agents *collectively* (naturally) responsible for? The agents are *collectively* (naturally) responsible for the realisation of the (collective) end which results from their contributory actions. Consider a team of three detectives trying to solve a burglary; one is conducting an interview of the suspect, one an interview of the witness, and the third is checking fingerprints found at the crime scene. Each is individually (naturally) responsible for completing his task (assuming the tasks are completed, i.e. the fingerprints are found to match those of the suspect, the witness identifies the suspect as the burglar and the suspect confesses). Moreover, the three detectives are collectively (naturally) responsible for bringing it about that the crime is solved.

Again, if the occupants of an institutional role (or roles) have an institutionally determined obligation to perform some joint action – including a joint epistemic action – then those individuals are collectively responsible for its performance, in our second sense of collectively responsibility. This is the case in our detective scenario. Here there is a joint institutional obligation to realise the collective end of the joint epistemic action in question, namely, to solve the crime. In addition, there is a set of derived individual institutional obligations; each of the participating detectives has an individual institutional obligation to perform his or her contributory action. (The derivation of these individual institutional obligations relies on the fact that if each performs his or her contributory action then it is probable that the collective end will be realised.)

There is a third sense of collective responsibility which might be thought to correspond to the third sense of individual responsibility. The third sense of individual responsibility concerns those in authority and is a species of institutional responsibility. Suppose the members of the cabinet of country A (consisting of the prime minister and her cabinet ministers) collectively decide to exercise their institutionally determined right to abandon the country's carbon tax in the light of its unpopularity in the electorate. The cabinet is collectively (institutionally) responsible for this policy change.

There are a number of things to emphasise here. First, the notion of responsibility in question here is, at least in the first instance, institutional – as opposed to moral – responsibility.

Second, the "decisions" of committees, as opposed to the individual decisions of the members of committees, need to be analysed in terms of the notion of a joint institutional mechanism introduced above. So the "decision" of the cabinet can be analysed as follows. At one level each member of the cabinet voted for or against the carbon tax policy; and let us assume some voted in the affirmative, and others in the negative. But at another level each member of the cabinet agreed to abide by the outcome of the vote; each voted having as a collective end that the outcome with a majority of the votes in its favour would be pursued. Accordingly, the members of the cabinet were jointly institutionally responsible for the policy change, i.e. the cabinet was collectively institutionally responsible for the change.

A corresponding example in relation to joint epistemic action would be a decision on the part of an investigations management committee in a police organisation not to investigate a case of reported fraud on the grounds that in the context of limited investigative resources due to government cutbacks, the reported fraud in question was less serious and less likely to be solved than other competing pending fraud cases.

Third, in so far as an organisation, such as a government comprised of the prime minister, the cabinet ministers and the members of the supporting government bureaucracy, makes and implements a policy then, by virtue of the earlier introduced notion of a multi-layered structure of joint action, the participating organisational actors (i.e. the relevant individual human beings who occupy those organisational positions) can, at least in principle, be held collectively institutionally responsible for that policy being in place. Naturally, there are differential degrees of responsibility attaching to different members of an institution, e.g. some lower echelon institutional actors may have diminished institutional responsibility by virtue of their subordinate role. (There is a further complication here in the case of the traditional Westminster system of government. For under that system there is a convention whereby the cabinet minister is taken to be institutionally responsible for certain failings of the members of his or her bureaucracy. However, this does not affect the general point that all the members of an organisation could be held collectively institutionally responsible for realising some collective end of that organisation on the basis of having contributed to it qua occupant of their organisational role.)

What of the fourth sense of collective responsibility, collective *moral* responsibility? Collective moral responsibility is a species of joint responsibility on the view that I am advocating. Accordingly, each agent is individually morally responsible, but conditionally on the others being individually morally responsible: there is interdependence in respect of moral responsibility. This account of collective moral responsibility arises naturally out of the account of joint actions. It also parallels the account given of individual moral responsibility.

Thus we can make our second quasi-definitional claim about moral responsibility:

2. If agents are collectively responsible for the realisation of a joint action – including a joint epistemic action – in the first, second or third senses of collective responsibility, and if the joint action is morally significant then – other things being equal – the agents are collectively morally responsible for that joint action, and – other things being equal – can reasonably attract moral praise or blame, and (possibly) punishment or reward for performing it.

As is the case with the above corresponding claim in respect of individual responsibility, the term "joint action" refers to joint omissions and also to outcomes that are the collective end of prior joint actions (as in the case of multilayered structures of joint action). Moreover, the first "other things being equal" clause is intended to be cashed in terms of capacity for moral agency, and the second in terms of justificatory or exculpatory conditions. Finally – and consistent with this quasi-definition – agents can be held collectively morally responsible for the morally significant foreseeable outcomes of their joint actions and omissions, notwithstanding that such outcomes were not collective ends of the agents in question.

In accordance with this second definitional claim, collective moral responsibility for epistemic states can legitimately be ascribed to a set of agents if those epistemic states are morally significant and are the collective ends. Moreover, as in effect just mentioned, agents can be held collectively morally responsible for the morally significant foreseeable outcomes of their joint epistemic actions.

Suppose, for example, that a team of scientists working for the military discover how to make the atomic bomb; the scientists are collectively morally responsible for this morally significant knowledge and potentially (to some degree) morally responsible for the intended or foreseeable use to which it is put by the military. However, as noted above, the matter of the degree, if any, of collective moral responsibility for the indirect morally significant outcomes of joint epistemic action is far from clear cut.

Thus far we have elaborated, and displayed the relationships between, various theoretical notions, notably those of joint action, joint epistemic action, joint institutional mechanisms, multilayered structures of joint action, institutional action and collective moral responsibility. Importantly, my notion of collective moral responsibility crucially depends on the prior defined notions of joint action and joint epistemic action; moreover, the notion of institutional action – applicable when it is the collective responsibility of institutions and institutional actors that is in question – crucially depends on the notions of a joint institutional mechanism and of a multilayered structure of joint action. It is now time to apply this theoretical machinery to the question of collective moral responsibility for harmful, climate change caused by human action.

13.5 Climate Change

Evidently the emission into the atmosphere of excessive quantities of GHG or green house gases (importantly carbon, and to a lesser extent methane) produced by human activities (notably the burning of fossil fuels) are causing changes in global climactic conditions (especially global warming), which are in turn likely to have catastrophic consequences for human and other life forms on the planet, if the rate of emissions is not slowed and ultimately stabilised at an acceptable level. The changes in question include the melting of the ice-caps and consequent rising sea levels, variations in seasonal rainfall patterns which impact negatively on food production, and increased levels of natural disasters such as hurricanes, tsunamis and the like. While there is dispute about the direct empirical evidence for global warming and what, if anything, ought to be done by way of response, there is general agreement in relation to the high and increasing levels of human-induced carbon emissions, in particular, and the reality of the "greenhouse effect" (Gardiner 2004; Vanderheiden 2008).[3] Moreover, it is indisputable that thus far (i.e. since the Industrial Revolution in the late 18th century) it is the developed economies that have contributed the lion's share of human-induced carbon emissions, albeit developing economies, notably China and India, are now major contributors.

In what follows I abstract away from the details, ignore extreme forms of climate skepticism and simply assume that the human race is likely to suffer catastrophe at some point in the future unless it addresses the problem of human-induced climate change and does so quite soon.[4]

Let us first address the issue of collective responsibility with respect to a relatively discrete, self-contained, type of environmental problem, namely, the required response to immediately pending disasters such as tsunamis and focus, in particular, on the collective responsibility for joint epistemic action in such cases. I then turn to the generic, multi-level, underlying and long term problem of collective moral responsibility for harmful climate change caused by humans. In doing so I differentiate the various kinds of collective behavioural and epistemic responsibilities in play and display the relationships between them.

Consider the 2004 Indian Ocean tsunami that devastated areas of Indonesia, Thailand and Sri Lanka. The relevant officials in these countries mutually know that tsunamis can bring death and destruction on a large scale. Accordingly, there is a need (among other things) for early warning systems to enable people to avert disaster, at least to the extent of preventing or minimising loss of life. So there is a collective (behavioural) end which is also a collective (moral) good (Miller 2010:chap. 2), namely, that members of the relevant community (or communities) avert disaster. However, there is in addition a collective epistemic end the realization of which is necessary to achieve the prior collective behavioral end, namely, that there be mutual knowledge of any impending tsunami. Given that the collective epistemic end is a necessary means to achieving a collective moral good, then the collective epistemic end has moral significance and so, by the lights of our above-described account of collective responsibility, there is (other things being equal) a collective moral responsibility to realize this epistemic end.

As we have seen, in the tsunami scenario joint action is required to realize a collective epistemic end, namely, mutual knowledge of any impending tsunami. However, the required "joint action" is actually a multi-layered structure of joint epistemic action (in our above-described sense) with constitutive joint epistemic

3 The "greenhouse effect" works roughly as follows. GHG simultaneously admit short wave solar radiation while blocking some of the long wave radiation emanating from the earth's surface thereby ensuring that the temperature at the earth's surface is greater than it otherwise would be.

4 Weaker epistemic assumptions are, of course, consistent with accepting the need to act to avoid catastrophe, e.g. that catastrophe has a 50 percent chance of taking place if we do not act or even that we are not sure of the probability in question.

actions e.g. the design of the early warning system. Note that such large scale, multi-layered structures of joint actions are typically constituted by both joint behavioural actions, e.g. constructing detectors of seismic activity, and joint epistemic actions, e.g. communications with respect to any impending tsunami.

Designing, building and deploying an early warning system for tsunamis in the Indian Ocean is a multi-layered structure of joint action which is also an institution (Miller 2010:chap. 2) in which roles are established, tasks allocated and so on, in order to realize the overarching collective epistemic end. Accordingly, there is no barrier to holding the individuals in question collectively (i.e. jointly) morally responsible for the existence of such a system or, alternatively, for its non-existence (a joint omission). Moreover, in the light of the moral significance of averting disaster and saving lives, the institutional responsibilities of the role occupants to perform joint epistemic tasks such as monitoring undersea volcanic activity that are the necessary means to avert such disasters, are collective moral responsibilities and quite stringent ones (albeit they fall short of being morally responsible for the deaths themselves).

Let us now turn to the generic global issue of collective moral responsibility for harmful, climate change caused by human action.[5]

The Intergovernmental Panel on Climate Change's (IPCC) 1990 Report drew the world's attention to harmful climate change consequent upon (in particular) humanly produced carbon emissions. Accordingly, since 1990 each one of millions of the earth's human inhabitants, especially in the developed world, have not only made a minute causal contribution to current massive environmental damage and consequent large-scale harm to humans, e.g. climate change causing rising sea levels and flooding of Pacific Island villages, they have done so knowingly (in some sense, but see below). Can we conclude from this that the millions in question are collectively morally responsible for the harm already done and the future harm already in train? Naturally, we here rely on the above-described theoretical account of collective moral responsibility, since the meaning in ordinary language of the term, "collective moral responsibility", is more or less indeterminate and (as noted above) if one turns to the theorists one finds an array of competing theoretical accounts with diverse practical implications.

To assist in the identification of the nature, and determination of the strength, of the moral responsibility in play in the climate change scenario, let us contrast that scenario with the following stabbing scenario. Assume that in the stabbing scenario there are just five men who each intentionally stab a sixth man, Smith, having as an end (a collective end) that Smith die as a consequence of his wounds, and having no good reason to kill Smith. Assume further that Smith does in fact die from these stabbings, albeit the stab wounds inflicted by any one of the agents was neither necessary nor sufficient for Smith's death. Clearly, each of the five is fully

[5] I will not concern myself in what follows with the common resource or "sink" issue; roughly, the issue of the injustice arising from the fact that the citizens of developed economies have exhausted the limited capacity of the earth to absorb carbon emissions and, thereby, denied others from their "fair share" of that common resource (Gardiner 2004).

morally responsible for deliberately and unjustifiably killing Smith and, if the facts of the case emerged, each would be found guilty of murder by a competent court of law. I note that the stabbing scenario straightforwardly exemplifies collective moral responsibility as presented in my above account, i.e. there is a morally significant collective end which is aimed at by each and to which each makes an individual intentional causal contribution.

One important difference between the climate change and the stabbing case as described thus far is that in the stabbing case, but not in the climate change case, each had as an end that the harm be done; in the climate change scenario there are foreseen untoward consequences but they are not intended or otherwise aimed at. Let us then adjust the stabbing case so that each stabs Smith in the knowledge that he would die but without having this as an end. I note that each of the men remains morally responsible for killing Smith; a court of law would find them guilty, if not of murder, then of a somewhat lesser, but still very serious, offence such as culpable homicide; moreover, by the lights of our theory there is no collective moral responsibility – because no joint action as such – however, there is aggregate individual moral responsibility (a notion sometimes confused with collective moral responsibility). At any rate, the two scenarios are now apparently relevantly similar, the only difference being the number of participants (millions versus a handful) and the magnitude of the causal contribution that each makes (minute versus substantial). Naturally, these differences are morally important, however I am trying to identify additional moral considerations.

Let us further elaborate the climate change scenario. Each of us unavoidably produces carbon emissions and, therefore, necessarily makes some contribution to the total quantum of carbon emissions produced by human activity; each of us has to do so in order to survive. By contrast, each of the five men does not need to stab or otherwise interfere with Smith in order to survive. Nevertheless, if each of us had reduced our carbon emissions to the level required for us to survive (or even somewhat above that level), i.e. if each of us had foregone luxury emissions, then the harm consequent upon our 1990–2010 emissions would in turn have been reduced to a morally acceptable level.

Assume that the large scale harm caused by this total quantum of luxury emissions was foreseeable. Thus each individual (or most of them) was aware of the likelihood of the harm consequent upon this quantum of luxury emissions. Assume further that each individual, considered on his or her own, could have avoided the production of his or her contributing luxury emissions, e.g. by selling his or her car and any of his appliances which use a large amount of electricity generated by burning coal, installing a solar energy heater in his roof, becoming a vegetarian, and quitting his or her job at a petrol station in favour of going on welfare. Accordingly, each is not only fully, individually, naturally responsible for the minute luxury emissions he or she individually produced, each is also fully, individually, *morally* responsible for those emissions since they have moral significance; they are a causal contribution to the large-scale harm. Is it morally wrong to do something which is in itself morally innocuous, but which you know will make a tiny causal contribution to a massive harm? (Naturally, there are morally relevant differences in the size of contributions made by individuals and, crucially, differences between the average (and aggregate) contributions of the members of developed nation-states and those of undeveloped and developing nation-states (Pickering, Vanderheiden and Miller 2010).) Surely it is, at least in some cases. If so, then it is presumably a minor wrongdoing. At any rate, I am going to assume that in the climate change scenario each of the millions is fully morally responsible for a minor wrongdoing (in the sense of knowingly, albeit unintentionally, contributing causally to harming others). Similarly, each of the five men in the stabbing scenario is fully, naturally and morally responsible for his knife stabs – it being a further question whether each is fully morally responsible for Smith's death.

As we have seen, the millions considered in aggregate are *causally* responsible for the large-scale harm done by the carbon emissions. (And being causally responsible for harming others is typically a morally relevant consideration, including in relation to climate change, albeit it does not constitute moral responsibility in the sense elaborated above since it does not necessarily involve knowledge that the harm will be caused (Shue 1992).) Similarly the five men are in aggregate causally responsible for the death of Smith.

However, each of the five men is in addition fully morally responsible for (let us say) culpable homicide. By contrast, it would be absurd to claim that each of us is fully morally responsible for the large scale harm caused by the totality of 1990–2010 luxury carbon emissions, e.g. Jones is not fully morally responsible for the loss of habitats and lives consequent upon the climate change in question. Rather each of the millions has at most a radically diminished moral responsibility for the large-scale harm resulting from the 1990–2010 emissions.

Doubtless, the reason for the absurdity of the claim of full individual moral responsibility for the massive harm lies in part in the large numbers involved in the climate change scenario and the fact that each makes a tiny causal contribution to harming (for the most part) future persons. Moreover, in the climate change scenario the action performed by each (his or her carbon emissions) are not harmful per se, but rather in aggregate have harmful effects that are in the distant future, at the end of a long and complex causal chain, and (most of) the persons in harm's way are notional in the sense that they do not yet exist. In such contexts of causal responsibility, moral responsibility is diffuse (and is a species of aggregate individual moral responsibility, as opposed to collective moral responsibility per se). Moreover, the idea of moral responsibility is likely to be somewhat inchoate in the minds of the agents in question, and likely also (relatedly) to lack a strong psychological underpinning.

In these respects, aggregate individual moral responsibility for harmful climate change is different from the aggregate moral responsibility of the five men for the wrongful killing of Smith.

So far so good, but I suggest that we have still not identified all the important moral differences between the two scenarios. What moral consideration is there, in addition to those just mentioned, by virtue of which each of the five men is fully morally responsible for Smith's death, but each of us is not fully morally responsible for the harm consequent on 1990–2010 luxury carbon emissions? I suggest that a key difference is that practically speaking – as opposed to as a matter of logic – the five men could have acted otherwise and, if they had, Smith would still be alive, but the millions could not have acted so as to avert the harm done by the 1990–2010 emissions (future emissions and the consequent harm are another matter – see below). Let me defend this claim.

The two main positive responses to human-induced, harmful, climate change are mitigation and adaptation measures. Mitigation measures are aimed at reducing carbon emissions and consist of interventions in the causal chain at the point at which human activities cause environmental damage (e.g. by emitting excessive quantities of carbon). Adaptation measures are interventions in the causal chain at the point at which environmental damage, e.g. rising sea levels resulting from global warming, causes harm to humans, e.g. flooding of coastal villages. Thus relocating to higher ground is adaptation. Presumably in the long term mitigation must take priority, since in the long term ever-increasing carbon emissions will make the planet uninhabitable. At any rate, I take it that it is the reshaping of existing institutions, and the development of new technologies, in the service of mitigation and/or adaptation that is the principal means by which to avert the harm to present and future humans caused by environmentally damaging emissions and, specifically, a necessary means if 1990–2010 luxury emissions were to have been reduced to the level at which the consequent harm would in turn not rise above a morally acceptable level.[6]

Accordingly, only if each (or most or a very large percentage) of the millions of the earth's human inhabitants could have, jointly with the others (or most of the others), during the period 1990–2010, formed a collective end to avert the harm consequent upon luxury emissions, and devised and deployed the institutional and technological means to realize this end, e.g. mutual knowledge of required emission reduction targets, "clean" energy organisations, compliance mechanisms, then is it the case that all (or most) of the millions are collectively morally responsible for the harm caused by 1990–2010 luxury emissions. Note the dependence of the realization of a collective behavioural end on joint epistemic action (the collective end of which is mutual knowledge of emission reduction targets).

However, I suggest that between 1990 and 2010 each (or most) of the (relevant) millions could not reasonably be expected to have, jointly with the others, formed the requisite collective end, and designed and implemented the technological and institutional means to realize it. For one thing, and notwithstanding the 1990 IPCC Report, it is not the case that there was sufficiently widespread and adequate mutual knowledge – that is, each not only knows but also knows that most others know etc. – of harmful, humanly produced, luxury carbon emissions among members of

[6] I realize that the latter claim, in particular, is disputable. However, given that those in the developed world were responsible for the lion's share of carbon emissions during this period, and given the dependence of most citizens on current institutions and technologies, it is surely plausible that reshaping institutions and developing new technologies would have been necessary. For example, return to a more primitive economic and technological system is not for modern citizens a feasible option.

the relevant populations; nor was there such mutual knowledge of the necessary institutional and technological means to reduce these emissions.

For another thing, even if the members of these populations had the necessary mutual knowledge they were not in a position themselves to implement such fundamental institutional and technological change. Here it is important to understand that while it might be feasible for each individual member of a large group to do x, it might not be feasible for all or most of the members of the group to do x; to suppose otherwise is to commit a version of the fallacy of composition. Thus while it might be possible for any singe member of a community to go on welfare, it is not possible for everyone to do so; since with everyone out of work eventually there would be no welfare funds to be dispersed. Again, while it might be feasible for one or a minority of people to immediately and simultaneously switch to alternative energy sources, it is not feasible for everyone to do so immediately and simultaneously, since an entire national – indeed, international – system of energy infrastructure based on fossil fuels cannot be replaced overnight but will take decades of well-planned and coordinated institutional redesign and technological development. I conclude that the millions are not collectively morally responsible for the harm in question, and each is certainly not fully morally responsible for that harm (including for the initial reasons given above).

It might be argued in response to this that the members of the relevant governments are collectively morally responsible for the harm in question since (within the 1990–2010 time frame) they could have acted in accordance with the collective end to avert the harm, and devised and implemented the required mitigation and adaptation measures by causing the necessary redesigning and reshaping of relevant institutions. Notwithstanding the collective action problems faced by national governments (e.g. if one nation-state substantially cuts carbon emissions and the others don't then the first will be significantly economically disadvantaged), and the pressure to maintain the status quo applied by powerful corporations (e.g. oil companies) and community interest groups (e.g. mining communities), arguably the members of these governments are collectively morally responsible for failing to put in place policies to avert or substantially ameliorate the harm done (or about to be done) by 1990–2010 luxury carbon emissions. However, the members of the governments in questions are not morally responsible for the harm itself; a few thousand politicians did not produce a quantum of luxury carbon emissions sufficient to cause the massive harm in question.

Thus far we have discussed collective moral responsibility for the harm caused by 1990–2010 luxury carbon emissions; that is we have been concerned with retrospective collective moral responsibility. It is now time to look at things prospectively and to consider the collective moral responsibility to act to avert future harms.

I take it that the potential future harms in question are catastrophic if the increasing level of global luxury carbon emissions is not slowed and then stabilized in the coming decades. Moreover, I take it that for this to occur there needs to be joint action commencing in the very near future on the part of (at least) the USA, the major European nations, Japan and the major emerging economies, especially China and India. Further, it is clear that the joint action in question will not only need to realize the collective end (or ends) in question, it will entail an allocation of burdens, especially in respect of emission reduction targets, and the burdens should reflect the quantum of past emissions, the capacity to bear the burdens and so on (Pickering, Vanderheiden and Miller 2010). However, I will not address these issues of allocation and distributive (including intergenerational) justice here (Gardiner 2004; Vanderheiden 2008).

As we have seen, there are an array of collective epistemic moral responsibilities in relation to luxury carbon emissions that derive from the collective moral behavioral responsibility to avert the catastrophic future harms consequent upon such emissions.

As we have also seen, these collective, epistemic, moral responsibilities pertain to the means to realise a collective end, namely, averting future large-scale harms, and the means in question include a wide variety of institutional rearrangements and of new technologies.

Moreover, these multiple, collective, epistemic, moral responsibilities attach to the members of a variety of different groups. Crucially, we do not need to go beyond the ascription of moral responsibility to individual human beings. I will focus attention on three of these groups, namely, members of governments, climate scientists and citizens.

In the light of the catastrophic nature of the potential harm in question and the need for knowledge of climate change, climate scientists have an epistemic, moral responsibility to acquire the required knowledge, and members of government (and of the media) have an epistemic, moral responsibility to disseminate this knowledge to their citizens. These responsibilities are also institutional responsibilities; for example, an important acknowledged institutional responsibility of governments is to protect the lives and habitats of their citizens and, therefore, to provide to the citizenry such information as is necessary to achieve this.

However, in the light of our account of collective moral responsibility, we can now understand these responsibilities as collective moral responsibilities and not simply as aggregates of individual responsibilities or as corporate responsibilities that attach to the institutions or groups in question per se. For in the case of the climate scientists, the intellectual work in question is a joint enterprise that ultimately yields mutual knowledge of climate change, as it already to some extent has e.g. with respect to the greenhouse effect (notwithstanding, that at any point in time there will be scientific disputes). In the case of the governments, the collective responsibility in question is an institutional responsibility now to be understood as the joint moral responsibility of the members of each of these governments. Naturally, the nature and strength of these moral responsibilities is relative to the magnitude of the potential harm in question and the period of time available to avert it. But it is also a function of the extent to which these moral responsibilities have been, so to speak, institutionalized, e.g. by the creation of institutions and associated institutional roles, such as a department of climate change headed up by a minister for climate change. As our theory makes clear, collective moral responsibility and institutional responsibility interact, and give direction to, and mutually reinforce, one another.

On the plausible assumption that the reality of human-induced, harmful, luxury carbon emissions is no longer seriously disputed by the world's governments, or that if it is by some, it morally ought not to be, then an important collective moral responsibility of national governments is to see to it that emission reduction policies are designed (joint epistemic action) and implemented (joint behavioral action).[7] This is in effect a collective moral responsibility with respect to the reshaping and/or establishment of institutional arrangements (notably economic ones), i.e. with respect to multi-layered structures of joint action comprised of both joint epistemic and joint behavioral tasks.

The collective moral responsibilities of governments operate at two levels, namely, inter-governmental joint action (where the various separate governments cooperate on carbon emissions policies, e.g. emissions targets agreed (hopefully) at international gatherings such as Kyoto and Copenhagen), and intra-governmental joint action (where the members of a single government cooperate on carbon emissions, e.g. via a national carbon tax).

The collective moral (epistemic and behavioural) responsibility of governments at the intra-governmental or national level reduces to the collective moral (epistemic and behavioural) responsibility of the relevant individual members of the government in question qua member of that government. This is an instance of the collective moral responsibility that can attach to the morally significant decisions of a joint institutional mechanism (as described above).[8]

I also note that the collective moral (epistemic and behavioural) responsibility of governments at the *inter-governmental* level reduces to the collective moral (epistemic and behavioural) responsibility of the relevant individual members of each of the governments in question (in each case qua member of his or her own government). This is an instance of the collective moral responsibility that can attach to the morally significant decisions of a multi-layered structure of joint action and, indeed, a multi-layered structure of joint action that comprises a multi-layered structure of joint institutional mechanisms, one at the international level and a number of others at the national level.

---

[7] Designing a public policy (on my account) is in essence a process of finding out a complex – and hitherto unknown – means to achieve a prior, given collective end e.g. the end of reducing carbon emissions. Moreover, a policy is simply a linguistic structure of propositions describing the means to achieve that end – as such it is essentially an epistemic structure – and if the alleged means are not actually means then it has failed epistemically. (And if the policy maker is not aiming at actually finding a means but simply (say) pretending to find one then this is deception.) Accordingly, many policies are not implemented and remain only as documents in the filing cabinets of bureaucrats. So I am distinguishing between a policy and its implementation. Implementation is principally a behavioural matter. I reiterate that joint epistemic action typically involves joint behavioural action and vice-versa.

[8] And in so far as the notion of a government includes the bureaucracy which implements its policies, this is an instance of the collective moral responsibility that can attach to a multilayered structure of joint action.

Finally, let me turn briefly to the moral responsibilities of citizens, especially citizens of democracies given their greater capacity to influence the policies of their governments. Twenty years after the 1990 ICCP Report and in the wake of numerous, widespread and ongoing mass media reports on climate change and governmental climate change policies, there is mutual knowledge of the climate change issue and of the claims on the part of credible authorities that catastrophe awaits if it is not addressed. Accordingly, there is at the very least an aggregate of individual moral responsibilities on the part of citizens of each of the democracies to inform him or herself (epistemic action) in relation to carbon emissions, government carbon emissions policies and the like. Is there also a collective moral responsibility to vote for a political party (behavioral action via a joint institutional mechanism) that has rational and fair policies to address adequately the problem of human-induced, harmful carbon emission? Presumably, the answer to this is in the affirmative, given the reality and magnitude of the problem and given that the prior aggregate of individual epistemic responsibilities of citizens to inform themselves with respect to carbon emissions etc. have been adequately discharged (or even if they have not, they morally ought to have been).

There are further collective moral responsibilities of citizens that now follow, including to comply with (behavioral action) rational and fair policies on mitigation and adaptation measures in order to realize the morally significant collective ends of these measures, and also to establish conventions and social norms with respect to carbon emission reduction, e.g. to use forms of public transport that reduce per capita carbon emissions. The latter involving as it does attitudinal changes, notably in mutual knowledge, is in large part an exercise in implicit joint epistemic action (Miller 2001:chap. 2).

References

Copp, David. 2007. "The Collective Moral Autonomy Thesis." *Journal of Social Philosophy* 38(3):369–88.

Gardiner, Stephen. 2004. "Ethics and Global Climate Change." *Ethics* 114(3):555–600.

Gilbert, Margaret. 1992. *Social Facts*. Princeton, NJ: Princeton University Press.

Goldman, Alvin. 1999. *Knowledge in a Social World*. Oxford: Clarendon Press.

Lehrer, Keith. 1987. *Knowledge*. Oxford: Oxford University Press.

Miller, Seumas. 2001. *Social Action: A Teleological Account*. New York, NY: Cambridge University Press.

Miller, Seumas. 2006. "Collective Responsibility: An Individualist Account." *Midwest Studies in Philosophy* 30(1):176–93.

Miller, Seumas. 2007. "Against the Moral Autonomy Thesis." *Journal of Social Philosophy* 38(3):389–409.

Miller, Seumas. 2008. "Collective Responsibility and Information and Communication Technology." In *Moral Philosophy and Information Technology* edited by J. van den Hoven and J. Weckert. New York, NY: Cambridge University Press. pp. 226–250.

Miller, Seumas. 2010. *The Moral Foundations of Social Institutions: A Philosophical Study*. New York, NY: Cambridge University Press.

Miller, Seumas, and Pekka Makela. 2005. "The Collectivist Approach to Collective Moral Responsibility." *Metaphilosophy* 36(5):634–51.

Montmarquet, James. 1993. *Epistemic Virtue and Doxastic Responsibility*. Lanham, MD: Rowman and Littlefield.
Narveson, Jan. 2002. “Collective Responsibility.” *Journal of Ethics* 6(2):179–98.
Pettit, Philip. 2001. *A Theory of Freedom*. London: Polity.
Pickering, Jonathan, Steve Vanderheiden, and Seumas Miller. 2010. “Ethical Issues in the United Nations Climate Negotiations: A Preliminary Analysis of Parties’ Positions.” Accessed April 1, 2010. www.cappe.edu.au.
Shue, Henry. 1992. “The Unavoidability of Justice.” In *The International Politics of the Environment* edited by A. Hurrell and B. Kingsbury. Oxford: Oxford University Press. pp. 373–397.
Sinnott-Armstrong, Walter. 2005. “Its Not My Fault: Global Warming and Individual Moral Obligations.” In *Perspectives on Climate Change* edited by W. Sinnott-Armstrong and R. Howarth. Amsterdam: Elsevier. pp. 285–299.
Vanderheiden, Steve. 2008. *Atmospheric Justice*. Oxford: Oxford University Press.

Index

N.A Vincent et al. (eds.), *Moral Responsibility*, Library of Ethics and Applied Philosophy 27, DOI 10.1007/978-94-007-1878-4,

MIX
Papier aus verantwortungsvollen Quellen
Paper from responsible sources
FSC® C105338

If you have any concerns about our products,
you can contact us on
ProductSafety@springernature.com

In case Publisher is established outside the EU,
the EU authorized representative is:
Springer Nature Customer Service Center GmbH
Europaplatz 3, 69115 Heidelberg, Germany

Printed by Libri Plureos GmbH
in Hamburg, Germany

Natural Language Processing for Software Engineering

Scrivener Publishing
100 Cummings Center, Suite 541J
Beverly, MA 01915-6106

Publishers at Scrivener
Martin Scrivener (martin@scrivenerpublishing.com)
Phillip Carmical (pcarmical@scrivenerpublishing.com)

Natural Language Processing for Software Engineering

Edited by

Rajesh Kumar Chakrawarti

Ranjana Sikarwar

Sanjaya Kumar Sarangi

Samson Arun Raj Albert Raj

Shweta Gupta

Krishnan Sakthidasan Sankaran

and

Romil Rawat

Scrivener Publishing

WILEY

This edition first published 2025 by John Wiley & Sons, Inc., 111 River Street, Hoboken, NJ 07030, USA and Scrivener Publishing LLC, 100 Cummings Center, Suite 541J, Beverly, MA 01915, USA

For more information about Scrivener publications please visit www.scrivenerpublishing.com.

Wiley Global Headquarters
111 River Street, Hoboken, NJ 07030, USA

For details of our global editorial offices, customer services, and more information about Wiley products visit us at www.wiley.com.

Library of Congress Cataloging-in-Publication Data

ISBN 9781394272433

Front cover images supplied by Adobe Firefly
Cover design by Russell Richardson

Set in size of 11pt and Minion Pro by Manila Typesetting Company, Makati, Philippines

Printed in the USA

10 9 8 7 6 5 4 3 2 1

Contents

Preface

The book's goal is to discuss the most current trends in applying natural language processing (NLP) approaches. It makes the case that these areas will continue to develop and merit contributions.

The book focusses on software development that is based on visual modelling, is object-orientated, and is one of the most significant development paradigms today. To reduce issues throughout the documentation process, there are still a few considerations to make. To assist developers in their documentation tasks, a few aids have been developed. To aid with the documentation process, a variety of related tools (such as assistants) may be made using natural language processing (NLP). The book is focused on software development and operation using data mining, informatics, big data analytics, artificial intelligence (AI), machine learning (ML), digital image processing, the Internet of Things (IoT), cloud computing, computer vision, cyber security, Industry 4.0, and health informatics domains.

1

Machine Learning and Artificial Intelligence for Detecting Cyber Security Threats in IoT Environmment

Ravindra Bhardwaj[1]*, Sreenivasulu Gogula[2], Bidisha Bhabani[3], K. Kanagalakshmi[4], Aparajita Mukherjee[5] and D. Vetrithangam[6]

[1]*Deparment of Physics and Computer Science, Dayalbagh Educational Institute (Deemed to be University), Agra, Uttar Pradesh, India*
[2]*Department of CSE (Data Science), Vardhaman College of Engineering, Shamshabad, Hyderabad, India*
[3]*Department of Computer Science and Engineering, University of Engineering and Management (UEM), New Town, West Bengal, India*
[4]*Department of Computer Applications, SRM Institute of Science and Technology (Deemed to be University), Trichy, India*
[5]*Department of Computer Science and Engineering, Institute of Engineering and Management, University of Engineering and Management (UEM), New Town, Kolkata, West Bengal, India*
[6]*Department of Computer Science & Engineering University, Institute of Engineering, Chandigarh University, Mohali, Punjab, India*

Abstract
The Internet of Things (IoT) refers to the increasing connectivity of many human-made entities, such as healthcare systems, smart homes, and smart grids, through the internet. Currently, a vast amount of material and expertise has been widely spread. These networks give rise to several security threats and privacy concerns. Intrusions refer to malevolent and unlawful actions that cause harm to the network. IoT networks are susceptible to a diverse range of security issues due to their widespread presence. Cyber attacks on the IoT architecture can lead to the loss of information or data, as well as the sluggishness of IoT devices. For the past twenty years, an Intrusion Detection System has been utilized to ensure the security of

**Corresponding author*: ravindrabhardwaj2@gmail.com

Rajesh Kumar Chakrawarti, Ranjana Sikarwar, Sanjaya Kumar Sarangi, Samson Arun Raj Albert Raj, Shweta Gupta, Krishnan Sakthidasan Sankaran and Romil Rawat (eds.) Natural Language Processing for Software Engineering, (1–14) © 2025 Scrivener Publishing LLC

data and networks. Conventional intrusion detection technologies are ineffective in detecting security breaches in the Internet of Things (IoT) because of the distinct standards and protocol stacks used in its network. Regularly analyzing the vast amount of data created by IoT is a tough task due to its endless nature. An intrusion detection system (IDS) is employed to safeguard a system or network against unauthorized access by actively monitoring and identifying any potentially malicious or suspicious activities. Machine learning technologies provide robust and efficient approaches for mitigating these distinct hazards. The establishment of a robust machine learning system is the key to acquiring networks that are free from any form of threats.

Keywords: Machine learning, Internet of Things, security, privacy, attacks, vulnerability, intrusions

1.1 Introduction

The use of connected devices made ordinary chores easier and more efficient. They also provide a lot of information that is of great use. Connected automobiles, for example, may be able to take use of services that provide driver assistance. Medical devices give detailed patient records. The unfortunate reality is that a digital assault is possible on any device that is capable of establishing a connection to the internet. In worst case, many of these devices are missing even the most basic safety safeguards. According to the authors of the report, almost all of the data flow associated with the internet of things (98%) is not secured. This information may be obtained by anybody with little effort. To repeat, devices that are connected to the Internet of Things provide fraudsters with an easy target. Not only might their information be stolen, but perhaps other sensitive data as well. Using one of these devices is a frequent strategy used by hackers to gain access to a company's internal network. The sheer number of these devices and the settings they control may be enough to pique the interest of a cyber-attacker [1] as given in Figure 1.1: Increasing Number of DDOS Attacks [Source: Cisco Annual Internet Report 2018-2023] and in Figure 1.2: Threats to Internet of Things.

In a smart environment, any number of items, including databases of user credentials, electronic sensors, CCTV installations, access controls, personal electronic devices, recorded biometrics, and so on, might be the target of an attack. It is essential to protect the confidentiality, integrity, availability, authentication, and authorization features of the IoT architecture from a security point of view [2]. DDoS attacks are becoming more common, and Cisco's Annual Internet Report (2018-2023) White Paper forecasts that the total number of DDoS attacks would more than double

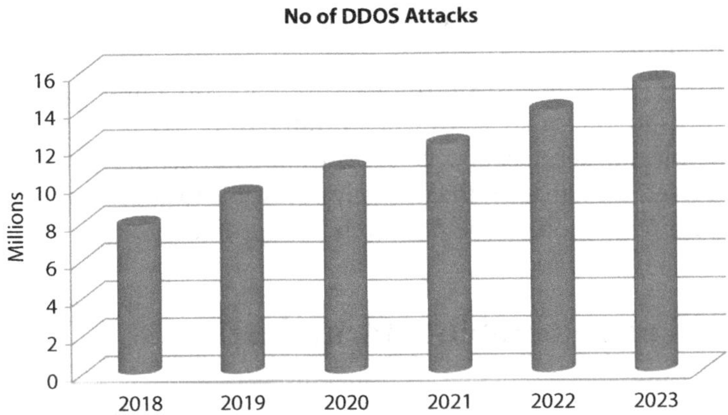

Figure 1.1 Increasing number of DDOS attacks [Source: Cisco Annual Internet Report 2018-2023].

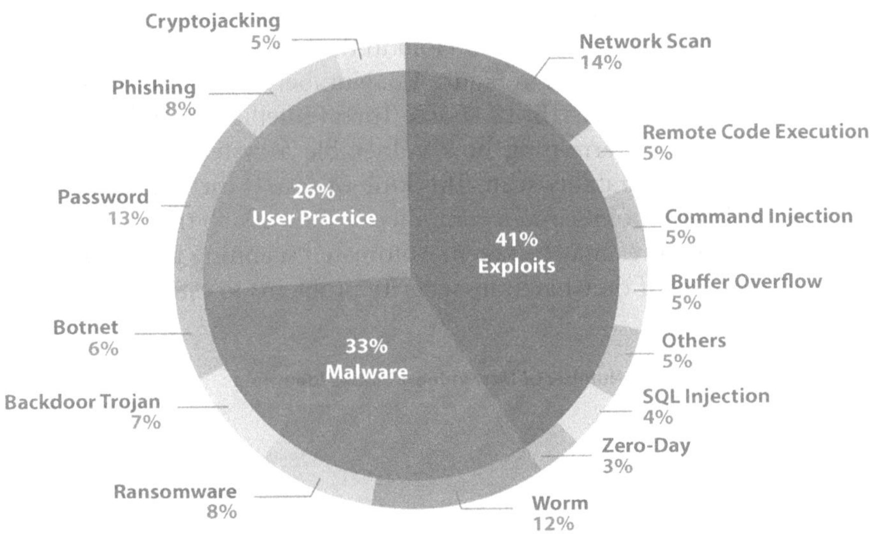

Figure 1.2 Threats to Internet of Things.

from the 7.9 million that were seen in 2018 to anywhere over 15 million by 2023 as shown in Figure 1.1.

According to the survey, 57% of IoT devices that are connected via this insecure traffic are susceptible to medium- to high-severity attacks, making them an easy target for cybercriminals [3]. In addition, the survey found that 41% of attacks target IoT vulnerabilities by scanning them against publicly available databases of known security flaws. The analysis is shown in Figure 1.2.

According to the Internet of Things Threat Report published by Palo Alto Networks in March 2020, 98% of all traffic from IoT devices is unencrypted, giving attackers a chance to eavesdrop. This network contains sensitive and private information that is easily accessible to attackers, who may then sell the information on the dark web for a profit.

1.2 Need of Vulnerability Identification

Vulnerabilities in IoT network are increasing every year. As shown in Figure 1.3, IoT environment is experiencing, a large number of new vulnerabilities every year. All the Internet of Things applications—smart city, smart farming, smart healthcare, smart transportation, and smart traffic—are experiencing new vulnerabilities and increasing number of attacks every year. Also, vulnerabilities and attacks are increasing every year. Number of vulnerabilities has increased threefold in the last decade and twofold in last five years as represented in Figure 1.3: Number of New Vulnerabilities Identified in IOT [Source- IBM X-Force Threat Intelligence Index 2022].

The process of determining how vulnerable a system is to attack is referred to as a vulnerability scan. This kind of scan is carried out to identify potential entry points into a computer or network so that appropriate preventative measures may be taken. Automated scanning methods check applications to see if they have any security problems to establish whether

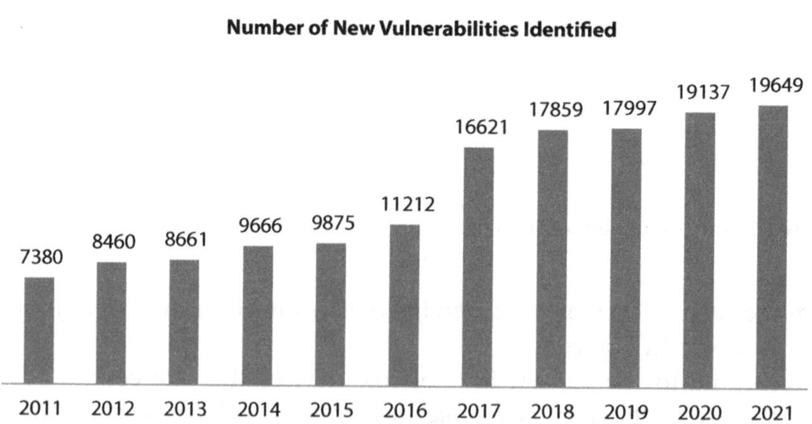

Figure 1.3 Number of new vulnerabilities identified in IoT [Source- IBM X-Force Threat Intelligence Index 2022].

or not there are vulnerabilities in an organization's internal network. Users are spared the time and effort required to carry out hundreds or even thousands of manual tests for each kind of vulnerability since vulnerability scanners automate the process of searching for security issues in a system.

To maintain the integrity of the system's protections, it is essential to assign vulnerabilities a severity ranking before putting into action any remedial procedures. Common Vulnerability Scoring System (CVSS) is a tool that administrators may use to prioritize security problems according to the severity level associated with each fault. The CVSS score of vulnerability is a standard metric that is not developed for unique network architecture. Despite the fact that the frequency and impact of vulnerabilities affect the security risk level of a specific network, the CVSS score of vulnerability is a standard metric. In addition to the severity score, a number of other factors also affect the level of security risk that is posed by the organization's underlying infrastructure. These factors include the age and frequency of vulnerabilities already present in the system, as well as the impact that exploiting vulnerability has on the system. For this reason, it is advised that, when doing risk level calculations, these components, together with the CVSS severity score, be used. This will allow for effective network security risk management.

1.3 Vulnerabilities in IoT Web Applications

The authors of [4] provide a code inspection-based strategy. To identify a number of mistakes hidden inside the process, this method makes use of code inspection. It is said that the offered approach may be used to locate each and every vulnerability in the NVD. Using this classifier might assist in more accurately identifying potential security flaws.

In addition, a web crawler was developed by Guojun and his colleagues [5]. This web spider collects papers that are connected to one another. The TF-IDF is essential to the methodology. Medeiros *et al.* [6] were the ones who first proposed the approach for evaluating the quality of the code. The concepts that underlie data mining are built on this methodology, which acts as the basis for those concepts. New techniques for identifying web server vulnerabilities were developed by [7].

Authors [8] have developed an innovative method for locating vulnerabilities in web applications. In addition to this, static analysis and data mining directly from the source code are used. Researchers [9] came to the conclusion that XML injection is a critical issue that exists in all web applications.

The vast majority of recently published web apps continue to be plagued by XML injection difficulties.

According to research by [10], a large percentage of such norms rely on online application security. Security measures designed to prevent code injection attacks on web applications were the primary focus of these studies. But even if the notion of acceptance is clearly defined and extensively concealed in almost all international standard regulations, the number of assaults is rising because of flaws in the infusion of code. This is the opinion of the developers. To reduce safety gauges, it is crucial to inform engineers and clients about the relevance of these metrics and to urge them to fulfil the standards with meticulous care. The time we waste waiting for this type of instruction and support is just not acceptable.

Authors [11] spoke about the significant factors that are engaged in the life cycle of product innovation. In addition, a number of software engineers have introduced security mechanization tools and processes that can be used at any stage of the software development life cycle (SDLC) to enhance the stability and quality of even the most fundamental digital systems. In addition to this, they requested that all organizations working to improve networks place a higher priority on planning, education, risk assessment, threat modelling, audits of architecture configuration, secure coding, and assessments of data that has been sent and received after it has been processed.

Wang and Reiter [12] developed a method for mitigating denial of service attacks by making use of a website's diagrammatic structure to counter flooding assaults. When visiting the destination website, a valid customer has the opportunity to quickly get a reward URL by clicking on a referral link provided by a reputable source. The proposed paradigm has no requirements in terms of infrastructure, and it does not call for any changes to be made to the code that users use when they access websites. The WRAPS framework, in addition to the intentions that its creator had for it, was provided. Nearly all of the smart assaults on websites recycled old strategies and methods from earlier attacks. There is a wide number of guises under which one may launch an assault against a strategy or an approach. They may also be seen in circumstances that are not related to the web. Attacks on a website's business logic may be harmful to the website itself, but attackers can also utilize websites as a go-between to accomplish their goals.

The SQLProb [13] will remove the user input and check to see whether it complies with the syntactic requirements of the query. This is accomplished by applying the formula that was inherited and then improving it. The SQLProb is a comprehensive discovery approach that does not need any modifications to be made to either the application or the database. This allows it to avoid the complexity of polluting, learning, and instrumenting code. In addition, neither education nor metadata are required in order to go on with the material's approval procedure.

Authors presented a complete stream-based WS-security handling architecture in their paper [14]. This design improves the level of preparedness in the administration processing and raises the level of resistance to different kinds of DoS assaults. When leaking is used as a strategy, their engine is able to handle standard WS-Security application scenarios.

The author [15] has examined the vast majority of the conventional criteria that are used to judge Web service quality. The majority of the measures, including performance, consistency, adaptability, limit, strength, exception handling, correctness, uprightness, openness, accessibility, interoperability, and security, all fall below the average level.

Hoquea *et al.* [16] took into consideration the activities that may be taken as well as the probable results or degrees of harm. Following that, the designer divides the assaults into a number of distinct categories. They consistently offered a scientific classification of attack equipment to assist in the organization of security specialists. This was done to help in the prevention of potential threats. They delivered a detailed and well-organized examination of existing tools and frameworks that may aid attackers as well as system defenders. Their focus was on tools and frameworks that are available now. The writers have included a description of both the benefits and drawbacks of the tools and frameworks in the event that you are interested in learning more about them.

Binbin Qu *et al.* [17] provided an explanation of the method that lies behind a model design. The construction of a pollutant dependency diagram for the program requires many steps, one of which is a static examination of the program's source code. They employ a limited state automaton to adhere to the attack model while communicating the pollutant string estimate and verifying the robustness of the program's protections for user input. All of this takes place while maintaining the integrity of the attack model. They utilized the framework model for computerized recognition based on the examination of the spoils and placed it into operation.

1.4 Intrusion Detection System

An incursion refers to any malevolent or dubious activity that jeopardizes the security of a computer or network. Intruders may originate from either internal or external sources. Internal intruders conceal themselves within the targeted network and acquire elevated privileges to deliberately harm the network infrastructure. External intruders surreptitiously extract data from the target network while remaining concealed outside of it. Internal attacks are initiated by nodes that are either malevolent or compromised, whereas external assaults are initiated by entities that are external to the system. An intrusion detection system (IDS) refers to any hardware or software that can identify and alert to potentially malicious activity on a network or computer system. Moreover, it may also be employed to detect any dubious activities or breaches within the system. Typically, when a network or system behaves abnormally, it suggests the occurrence of anything violent, harmful, or illegal. Although the majority of intrusion detection systems (IDS) mostly depend on identifying and reporting anomalies, there are a handful that excel in detecting intrusions that are overlooked by conventional firewalls. In terms of safeguarding the system from harm, intrusion detection systems (IDS) function similarly to firewalls by preventing unauthorized individuals from gaining access.

There are a total of three categories of intrusion detection systems based on the source of data, four groups based on the technique of analysis, and an additional three groups in total.

The Host-Based Intrusion Detection System (HIDS) software is placed on a computer to monitor, evaluate, and gather data on the traffic and suspicious activities of that specific system. In addition, it analyses not just the traffic activity, but also the system calls, file system changes, inter-process communication, and program running on the computer (Zarpelío *et al.*, 2017). HIDS utilizes data collected from the operating system and application software to detect suspicious activities. When a host-based intrusion detection system (HIDS) is deployed, it is capable of detecting intrusions solely on the host where it is installed. Installation of HIDS eliminates the need for extra software to identify threats on the system. Intruder detection systems are designed to detect and identify instances of unauthorized access or attacks from within a protected area. The installation cost is substantial due to the requirement of individual Host-based Intrusion Detection Systems (HIDS) for each device as given in Figure 1.4: Host-based IDS.

The Network-Based Intrusion Detection System (NIDS) safeguards network nodes by capturing and scrutinizing all network packets for malicious activities. Figure 1.5 displays the structure of the NIDS. The sensor is strategically positioned in a vulnerable region inside the

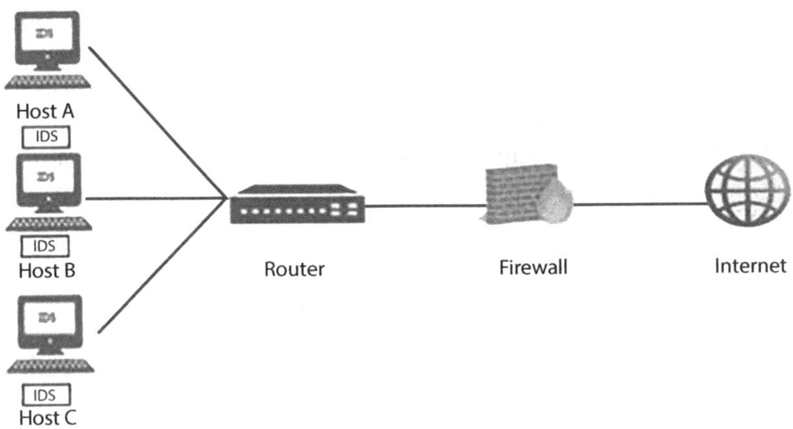

Figure 1.4 Host-based IDS.

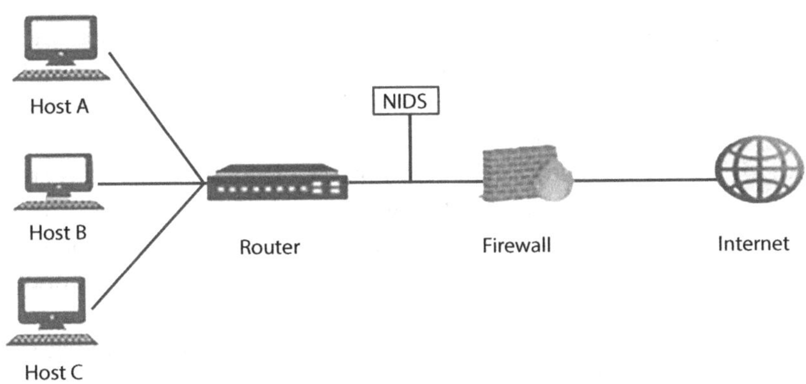

Figure 1.5 Network-based intrusion detection system.

network, bridging the server and the network. The NIDS monitors both incoming and outgoing communications. If the system identifies any network risks, it will need to respond rigorously in order to safeguard itself. One possible course of action is to prohibit network access from the specified IP address, while another alternative is to inform the responsible party through warning notifications. Determining if the NIDS has noticed their potential intrusions might provide a challenge for a thief. Monitoring extensive networks is under the purview of only a limited number of intrusion detection systems. To mitigate potential security risks, it is imperative to implement scanners, sniffers, and network intrusion detection tools. These measures are necessary to safeguard against various malicious activities such as IP spoofing, DOS assaults, DNS name corruption, man-in-the-middle attacks, and arp cache poisoning. These vulnerabilities arise due to the inherent weaknesses in TCP/IP protocols represented in Figure 1.5 Network-Based Intrusion Detection System.

Hybrid Intrusion Detection Systems (HIDS) integrate the functionalities of several intrusion detection systems to identify and expose intrusions. A hybrid intrusion detection system integrates data from both the network and the host agent or system to create a full overview of the network system. The hybrid technique is the most effective strategy for intrusion detection. Prelude is an example of a hybrid intrusion detection system.

1.5 Machine Learning in Intrusion Detection System

Soft computing makes it possible to build intelligent machines that are able to solve challenging issues that arise in the real world but are beyond the purview of standard mathematical modelling. These kinds of problems cannot be adequately modelled using traditional methods. It has a high tolerance for approximate information, ambiguity, imprecision, and merely a partial view of the environment [18], which enables it to emulate the way individuals form their opinions and make decisions. In this section, we will have a brief discussion on the many different techniques to soft computing that may be used in the process of detecting intrusions.

The genetic algorithm (GA) is a search engine that has been in use since it was conceived in Holland. This search engine is both strong and adaptable. There it first emerged in its current shape for the first time. Because of advances in technology, it is now possible to recreate the natural process of evolution that takes place in uncontrolled environments. The GA may be seen in this way as an example of a global search process that depends on randomness. The concept of "survival of the fittest" is applied by the algorithm to the challenge of developing ever more accurate approximations of a solution to the issue.

The most experienced people in the sector are recruited to teach the next generation, which ultimately results in the development of novel solutions to the issue. If this approach is used, the newly recruited staff members could be better able to address the current challenge [19]. The fitness function enables us to get insight into how well people fared on the aspects of the exam that were the most challenging [20].

PSO was first developed in 1995 by [21], who drew their inspiration from the way fish and birds congregate in groups known respectively as flocks and schools. In an effort to discover a solution, a "population" of particles is moved over the damaged region at specified speeds and rotated clockwise and anticlockwise. By employing the stochastic calibration approach and taking into consideration the best preceding and best adjacent locations of the particles, the velocities of the particles may be changed appropriately. A random number generator is what's needed to get this done.

A kind of logic known as fuzzy logic is one that employs the practice of approximation. The paradigms for optimization and classification used in machine learning are both underpinned by evolutionary computing, which is based on genetic and natural selection-based evolutionary processes. The origin of these evolutionary processes may be traced back to evolution. The majority of the time, genetic algorithms are used [22] in applications that are based on the actual world of business.

In contrast to the conventional naive Bayesian classifier, the HNB may take on a variety of forms depending on the circumstances. Finding the attribute's hidden parent needs the inclusion of a further layer in the HNB model, which necessitates the addition of this layer. The structures of the HNB components may be inferred with the help of Naive Bayes. Each characteristic has a hidden past that was fostered to bring together the many energy that it symbolizes. For the purpose of providing an overview of the covert parents, we may make use of the mean of weighted one-dependency estimators [23, 24].

The support vector machine, sometimes known as an SVM [25, 26] for short, is a technique to classification that is grounded on statistical learning theory (SLT) [27–29]. Another kind of system that is comparable is known as a hyper-plane classifier. In support vector machines (SVM), a good hyper-plane is one that successfully separates the classes while keeping the amount of interclass overlap to a bare minimum.

Deep neural networks, more often referred to as DBNs, are generative graph models that are used in machine learning. These networks are built on latent variables, which are also referred to as hidden units. These networks simply link the levels themselves, and not the units that are included inside those levels.

We may look at the model that was built by researchers and published in [24] as an illustration of one method that can be used to determine attributes for an intrusion detection system.

1.6 Conclusion

The issue of safety is of utmost importance in the context of IoT and other types of pervasive connectivity. There is a growing probability that attacks would focus on companies and organizations that utilize IoT. Traditional cybersecurity systems face multiple obstacles when attempting to detect zero-day threats. The invader exploits the privileges offered by the IoT architecture to acquire valuable data. There are few security risks that are widely recognized, and even fewer that involve slow and unnoticed attacks. An effective strategy to tackle these unexpected challenges is to construct intrusion detection systems using machine learning techniques. Cyberattacks on the Internet of Things architecture may result in data loss or information loss, as well as IoT device sluggishness. To guarantee the security of data and networks, intrusion detection systems have been in use for the last 20 years. Because the Internet of Things (IoT) uses unique standards and protocol stacks, traditional intrusion detection methods are not successful in identifying security breaches in its network. Because the amount of data generated by IoT is infinite, it is difficult to regularly analyze it. A system or network is protected from unauthorized access by an intrusion detection system (IDS), which actively monitors and detects any potentially harmful or suspicious activity. Machine learning technologies offer reliable and effective methods for reducing these specific risks.

References

1. Raghuvanshi, A., Singh, U.K. *et al.*, Intrusion Detection Using Machine Learning for Risk Mitigation in IoT-Enabled Smart Irrigation in Smart Farming. *J. Food Qual.*, 2022, 1, 1–8, 2022.
2. Abhishek, R., Singh, U.K., Phasinam, K., Kassanuk, T., Internet of Things-Security Vulnerabilities and Countermeasures. *ECS Trans.*, 107, 1, 15043–15053, 2022.
3. Raghuvanshi, A., Singh, U.K., Joshi, C., A Review of Various Security and Privacy Innovations for IoT Applications in Healthcare. *Adv. Healthcare Syst.*, 1, 43–58, 2022, doi: 10.1002/9781119769293.ch4.
4. Zhang, Q. and Wang, X., SQL injections through back-end of RFID system, in: *2009 International Symposium on Computer Network and Multimedia Technology. CNMT 2009*, pp. 1–4, IEEE, 2009.
5. Li, Z. *et al.*, VulPecker: an automated vulnerability detection system based on code similarity analysis. *ACM, Proc. of the 32 Annual Conference on Computer Security Applications*, p. 201213, 2016.

6. Guojun, Z. *et al.*, Design and application of intelligent dynamic crawler for web data mining, in: *Automation (YAC), 2017 32nd Youth Academic Annual Conference of Chinese Association*, pp. 1098–1105, IEEE, 2017.
7. Medeiros, I., Neves, N., Correia, M., Detecting and removing web application vulnerabilities with static analysis and data mining. *IEEE Trans. Reliab.*, 1, 54–69, IEEE, 2016.
8. Masood, A. and Java, J., Static Analysis for Web Service Security – Tools & Techniques for a Secure Development Life Cycle. *International Symposium on Technologies for Homeland Security*, pp. 1–6, 2015.
9. Medeiros, I. and Neves, N., Detecting and Removing Web Application Vulnerabilities with Static Analysis and Data Mining. *IEEE Trans. Reliab.*, 1, 1–16, 2015.
10. Salas, M.I., de Geus, P.L., Martins, E., Security Testing Methodology for Evaluation of Web Services Robustness - Case: XMLInjection. *IEEE World Congress on Services*, pp. 303–310, 2015.
11. Madan, S., Security Standards Perspective to Fortify Web Database Applications from Code Injection Attacks. *International Conference on Intelligent Systems, Modelling and Simulation*, pp. 226–233, 2010.
12. Teodoro, N. and Serrao, C., Web application security: Improving critical web - based applications quality through in - depth security analysis, in: *International Conference on Information Society (i- Society)*, pp. 457–462, 2011.
13. Wang, X. and Reiter, M.K., Using Web-Referral Architectures to Mitigate Denial-of-Service Threats. *J. IEEE Trans. Dependable Secure Comput.*, 7, 2, 203–216, 2010.
14. Liu, A., Yuan, Y., Wijesekera, D., Stavrou, A., SQLProb: a proxy-based architecture towards preventing SQL injection attacks, in: *Proceedings ACM Symposium on Applied Computing (SAC'09)*, pp. 2054–2061, 2009.
15. Gruschka, N., Jensen, M., Lo Iacono, L., Luttenberger, Server-side Streaming Processing of WS-Security. *IEEE Trans. Serv. Comput.*, 4, 4, 272–285, 2011.
16. Ladan, M.I., Web Services Metrics: A Survey and A Classification. *J. Commun. Comput.*, 9, 7, 824–829, 2012.
17. Hoque, N., Bhuyan, M.H., Baishya, R.C., Bhattacharyya, D.K., Kalita, Network Attacks: Taxonomy, tools and systems. *J. Comput. Netw. Appl.*, 1, 13–26, 4 October 2013, doi: doi.org/10.1016/j.jnca.2013.08.001.
18. Kulshestha, G., Agarwal, A., Mittal, A., Sahoo, A., Hybrid Cuckoo Search Algorithm for Simultaneous Feature and Classifier Selection. *IEEE International Conference on Cognitive Computing and Information Processing (CCIP)*, pp. 1–6, 2015.
19. Visumathi, J. and Shunmuganathan, K.L., A computational intelligence for evaluation of intrusion detection system. *Indian J. Sci. Technol.*, 4, 1, 28–34, Jan 2011.
20. Wang, B., Yao, X., Jiang, Y., Sun, C., Shabaz, M., Design of a Real-Time Monitoring System for Smoke and Dust in Thermal Power Plants Based

on Improved Genetic Algorithm. *J. Healthc. Eng*, 2021, D. Singh (Ed.), pp. 1–10, Hindawi Limited, UAE, 2021, https://doi.org/10.1155/2021/7212567.
21. Mohanasundaram, S., Ramirez-Asis, E., Quispe-Talla, A., Bhatt, M.W., Shabaz, M., Experimental replacement of hops by mango in beer: production and comparison of total phenolics, flavonoids, minerals, carbohydrates, proteins and toxic substances, *Int. J. Syst. Assur. Eng. Manage.*, Springer Science and Business Media LLC, UAE, 2021, https://doi.org/10.1007/s13198-021-01308-3.
22. Almahirah, M.S., S, V.N., Jahan, M., Sharma, S., Kumar, S., Role of Market Microstructure in Maintaining Economic Development. *Empirical Econ. Lett.*, 20, 2, 01–14, 2021.
23. Chaudhary, A., Tiwari, V.N., Kumar, A., Analysis of Fuzzy Logic Based Intrusion Detection Systems in Mobile Ad Hoc Networks. *Int. J. Inf. Technol.*, 6, 1, 183–198, June 2014.
24. Rathore, N. and Rajavat, A., Smart Farming Based on IOT-Edge Computing: Applying Machine Learning Models For Disease And Irrigation Water Requirement Prediction In Potato Crop Using Containerized Microservices, in: *Precision Agriculture for Sustainability*, pp. 399–424, Apple Academic Press, UAE, 2024.
25. Patsariya, M. and Rajavat, A., A Progressive Design of MANET Security Protocol for Reliable and Secure Communication. *Int. J. Intell. Syst. Appl. Eng.*, *12*, 9s, 190–204, 2024.
26. Rathi, M. and Rajavat, A., Investigations and Design of Privacy-Preserving Data Mining Technique for Secure Data Publishing. *Int. J. Intell. Syst. Appl. Eng.*, *11*, 9s, 351–367, 2023.
27. Dubey, P. and Rajavat, A., Effective K-means clustering algorithm for efficient data mining, in: *2023 2nd International Conference on Vision Towards Emerging Trends in Communication and Networking Technologies (ViTECoN)*, pp. 1–6, IEEE, 2023, May.
28. Nahar, S., Pithawa, D., Bhardwaj, V., Rawat, R., Rawat, A., Pachlasiya, K., Quantum Technology for Military Applications. *Quantum Comput. Cybersecur.*, 1, 313–334, 2023.
29. Pithawa, D., Nahar, S., Bhardwaj, V., Rawat, R., Dronawat, R., Rawat, A., Quantum Computing Technological Design Along with Its Dark Side. *Quantum Comput. Cybersecur.*, 1, 295–312, 2023.

2

Frequent Pattern Mining Using Artificial Intelligence and Machine Learning

R. Deepika[1*], Sreenivasulu Gogula[2], K. Kanagalakshmi[3], Anshu Mehta[4], S. J. Vivekanandan[5] and D. Vetrithangam[6]

[1]*Department of AI&DS, B V Raju Institute of Technology, Narsapur, Telangana, India*
[2]*Department of CSE (Data Science), Vardhaman College of Engineering, Shamshabad, Hyderabad, India*
[3]*Department of Computer Applications, SRM Institute of Science and Technology (Deemed to be University), Trichy, India*
[4]*Department of Computer Science and Engineering, Chandigarh University, Mohali, Punjab, India*
[5]*Department of Computer Science and Engineering, Dhanalakshmi College of Engineering, Dr V P R Nagar, Manimangalam, Tambaram, Chennai, India*
[6]*Department of Computer Science & Engineering, University Institute of Engineering, Chandigarh University, Mohali, Punjab, India*

Abstract

Frequent pattern mining is a very active topic in the field of data mining. Numerous researchers have considered it since its beginning. The dimensions of all areas expand exponentially with the advancement and accumulation of data. The ability to effectively and easily assess and extract time-sensitive information from large datasets is essential for making informed decisions and uncovering new knowledge. Data mining is the use of sophisticated analytics on large databases to discover previously unidentified links, patterns, and trends. Efficient and adaptable handling of large-scale data is crucial for retrieving information and making informed decisions. Data mining is the systematic analysis of vast quantities of data to uncover previously undiscovered correlations, patterns, and trends. Since the inception of the World Wide Web, there has been a rapid and significant increase in the quantity of data that is stored and can be accessed electronically. Data mining, which refers to the process of extracting new insights from data, has

**Corresponding author*: deepika.r@bvrit.ac.in

Rajesh Kumar Chakrawarti, Ranjana Sikarwar, Sanjaya Kumar Sarangi, Samson Arun Raj Albert Raj, Shweta Gupta, Krishnan Sakthidasan Sankaran and Romil Rawat (eds.) Natural Language Processing for Software Engineering, (15–28) © 2025 Scrivener Publishing LLC

become a crucial tool for both business and academic sectors. With the introduction of the Internet, there has been a rapid increase in the quantity of data stored and available online. Consequently, the methods for extracting valuable information from this extensive collection of data have become crucially significant in several domains, such as business and academics. Frequent Item Set Mining is a very popular technique for getting significant insights from datasets.

Keywords: Frequent pattern mining, decision tree, KNN, accuracy, machine learning

2.1 Introduction

Data mining is the systematic exploration of extensive databases to discover noteworthy and previously unidentified patterns [1]. The step described by Fayyad *et al.* for Knowledge Discovery in Databases (KDD) is included in this approach. Data cleaning, integration, selection, transformation, mining, pattern assessment, and knowledge representation are all integral components of the continuing process known as Knowledge Discovery in Databases (KDD). Data mining may be used to several types of data. The approaches and procedures may vary when used to different sorts of data. The patterns extracted from data might vary in terms of their nature and the specific sort of data mining task. Data mining jobs may be broadly classified into two categories: descriptive and predictive. Predictive data mining utilizes existing data to generate predictions, whereas descriptive data mining aims to explain the overall characteristics of the provided data.

Bayes' hypothesis and relapse inquiry were employed in the 1700s to distinguish designs from noise (1800s). Increases in PC innovation have led to a broader variety and higher capacity for information. Hands-on information examination has expanded as the quantity and complexity of informative indexes have grown. There have been a variety of software engineering breakthroughs that have led to this progress, such as the discoveries of neural systems, bunching, hereditary computations (1950s), decision trees (1960s), and support vector machines (1980s) [2].

In a decision tree, each node represents an evaluation of some attribute's value, and each branch represents the evaluation's outcome. The tree's leaves represent classes or distributions of classes. It's a cinch to convert from decision trees to characterization rules. Decision trees can cope with a lot of information. When it comes to storing data, they use a tree structure that is intuitive and simple to learn. Using a decision tree is a straightforward process that requires just a few easy steps to understand and put together. Decision tree enlistment computations have been used in a wide range of fields, including medical, manufacturing, budgeting, cosmology, and subatomic research [3].

Both AI and data mining heavily rely on tree-based learning approaches. It's no secret that these strategies have been in use for a long time. There is nothing over the top about them, and that's exactly what makes them so endearing. When making decision trees, a top-down strategy is often used to identify a univariate split that boosts some local basis (for example, gain percentage) until the leaf segments of the tree are sufficiently pure. Pessimistic Error Pruning uses heuristics that may be measured, while Reduced Error Pruning uses a single set of pruning to determine this utility.

It is a very costly strategy to employ the Naive Bayes classifiers as leaf hubs in all of the first-level child hubs (evaluated by cross-approval), yet this is the only way NB Tree can deliver them in a decision tree. At each node, students analyze additional characteristics as straight, quadratic, or calculated attribute elements, and these elements are then sent down the tree in the same manner that they were processed before. However, despite the fact that root-to-leaf probability dispersions are referred to as disseminations, leaf hubs remain the primary classifiers [4].

This study introduces a recursive Bayesian classifier. One hundred percent accuracy in decision tree enlistment has previously been achieved by a variety of methods, and many of them have been successful. As a result, these new approaches were time-consuming and difficult to learn, and this was the major issue. Recursively dividing the data into places where there is a suspicion of constraining freedom is the most significant aspect. Planning from perceptions of the item to choices based on those perceptions is how judgements about the objective value of anything are made [5].

Determining whether a system is well on its way to attaining its objective is the most prominent usage of decision trees in tasks research. Restrictive probabilities may be calculated using decision trees. A decision tree (also known as a tree outline) is a decision aid that employs a tree-like diagram or model to describe alternatives and their probable outcomes, such as chance event effects, asset expenditures and utility. The decision tree induction approach has been used effectively in master frameworks to gather information. It is possible to use decision trees to enrol people from a variety of data sources [6].

2.2 Data Mining Functions

Information mining is an assortment of procedures for proficient computerized disclosure of beforehand obscure, substantial, novel, helpful, and reasonable examples in enormous databases. The examples must be significant with the goal that they might be utilized in an endeavor's dynamic procedure [7]. Information mining procedures can be gathered as follows as given in Figure 2.1: Data Mining Methods:

- Classification-It is necessary to classify the supplied information event into one of the objective classes that have already been identified or defined. One of the models may be whether a customer is a trustworthy client or a defaulter in Visa's interchange information base, based on his distinct segment and previous purchase characteristics [8].
- Estimation-Like order, the motivation behind an estimation model is to decide an incentive for an obscure yield trait. In any case, in contrast to grouping, the yield quality for an estimation issue is numeric as opposed to clear cut.
- Prediction-It isn't anything but difficult to separate forecast from grouping or estimation.

The primary distinction lies in the fact that the predictive model extrapolates results into the foreseeable future rather than providing directives

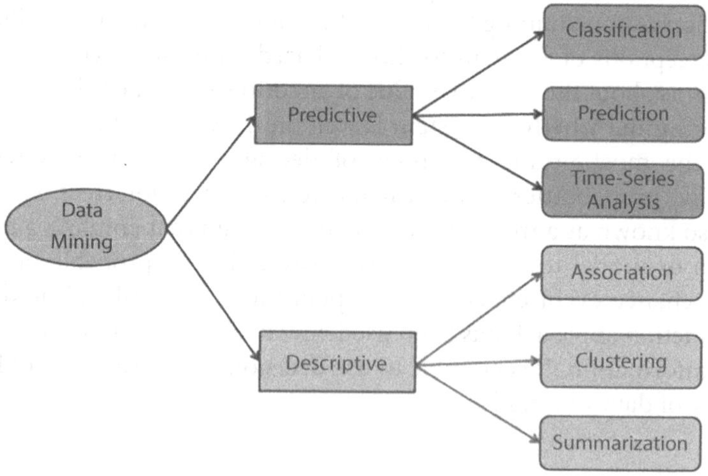

Figure 2.1 Data mining methods.

for actions in the here and now. The discontinuous or quantitative nature of the output characteristic can be chosen. One illustration of what a model might entail is making a forecast regarding the value of the Dow Jones Industrial Average at the end of the following week, and explains the history of a decision tree as well as its possible applications in more detail.

- Association rule mining-Here interesting hidden rules called affiliation rules in a huge value-based information base is mined out. For example, the standard {milk, margarine >biscuit} gives the data that at whatever point milk and spread are bought together scone is additionally bought, with the end goal that these things can be set together for deals to build the general deals of every one of the things [9].
- Clustering-Clustering is an uncommon kind of grouping where the objective classes are obscure. For example, given 100 clients they must be characterized depending on certain comparability measures and it isn't biased [10].

The fundamental application zones of information mining are in Business investigation, Bioinformatics, Web information examination, text investigation, sociology issues, biometric information examination and numerous different spaces where there is extension for shrouded data recovery. A portion of the difficulties before the information mining analysts are the treatment of unpredictable and voluminous information, conveyed information mining, overseeing high dimensional information, and model enhancement issues [11].

In the coming areas, the different stages happening in an ordinary information mining issue are clarified. The different information mining models that are usually applied to different issue spaces are additionally examined in detail in the coming areas.

2.3 Related Work

Information readiness or pre-preparing is a significant advance where the information is made reasonable for handling. This includes cleaning information, information changes, choosing subsets of records, and so on. During the process of setting up one's understanding, there are two stages: determination and change. Methods of deliberation for the collection of information can be applied to the process of data extraction. To accomplish this work, one will first need to perform a search within the database to retrieve the desired characteristics. The process of converting unstructured, unprocessed data into a shape that can be processed effectively by an information management or storage system is referred to as "data transformation." Another name for this process is "data articulation."; e.g., symbolic information types are changed over into numerical structure or straight-out structure [12].

Models such as decision trees, neural systems, and so on are built using the above-mentioned information. To uncover hidden patterns in data, information mining is a method of applying various tactics to data. Finding several models (or capabilities) that describe and identify information classes or concepts is the task of orderly management. An extensive amount of preliminary data was analyzed to derive the inferred model (i.e., information protests whose class mark is known). Different structures may be used to communicate with the inferred model, such as IF-THEN rules, decision trees, scientific formulas, or neural networks.

Grouping techniques like the decision tree are well-known. Tree-like structure with each hub represents a choice on one of the following values: the tree's branches represent the decisions made, while its leaves represent the many classes. A decision tree is both predictive and expressive. Using a decision tree, one can see how the information that were gathered connects.

A decision tree is a useful instrument for planning in the fields of data mining and artificial intelligence. It allows one to shift from more subjective evaluations of an object to more objective evaluations of the object's value. These tree models are known by a few different names, including the layout tree for the purpose of analyzing a particular outcome and the regression tree for the purpose of analyzing repetition, to name just two examples. (ceaseless result). The branches and greenery of the trees are meant to represent the relationships that exist between the various components that come together to form the various organizations. Data is used in an approach to artificial intelligence known as decision tree learning, which results in the generation of a decision tree.

The purpose of the computation is to become familiar with the judgment capacity that is stored in the information and then use it to organize new sources of data given a large number of models (preparing information) represented by some organization of characteristics. The objective of the computation is to become familiar with the judgment capacity that is stored in the information. (for example, sex, position, foundation). One can determine the discriminative strength of each characteristic that can most effectively separate the dataset by applying either the idea of data addition or the Gini list. Both of these methods are described in the following sentence. While common programs such as CART and IBM's intelligent digger make use of the Gini list concept, well-known decision tree algorithms such as ID3, C4.5, C5, and so on depend on data development to determine the next best property [13].

The algorithm determines the characteristics of the first dataset, which are the p-value for the number of positive models and the n-value for the number of negative models. After that, the sample is divided along the chosen characteristic (by making use of v-decisions), and the information gain is computed. This process is replicated for each individual piece of real estate until the location that provides the most significant increase in data gain is selected to serve as the primary nerve center. There are surprisingly few distinctions between ID3, C4.5, and C5 and other similar formats, despite the fact that they all use data gain principles. The techniques that are used to generate and present decision trees are broken down and analyzed in this section.

Continuous and discontinuous feature management is possible with C4.5. To deal with irreversible characteristics, C4.5 first establishes a limit; and then, it separates the list into those whose attribute respect is higher than the limit, and those whose attribute respect is not exactly or exactly equal to the limit. When assembling data with missing quality attributes, it is beneficial to have C4.5's missing attribute support because it enables designate qualities to be distinguished as "?" for missing. The lacking property approximations are not used in either the addition or the entropy calculations. The notion of clipping is utilized by C4.5. After the tree has been constructed, the algorithm will iteratively traverse it to prune away insignificant branches and replace them with leaf nodes where appropriate. C5.0 is a substantial enhancement over C4.5 in terms of both the speed at which it operates and the effectiveness with which it uses memory. Additionally, it makes use of forward-thinking ideas such as bolstering, which are broken down into their component parts in later portions of the theory.

Calculations based on the data gain theory will be more charitable to characteristics that have a greater number of qualities as the number of target groups increases, whereas calculations based on the Gini list will be less generous in this regard. Therefore, contemporary researchers are making an effort to improve decision tree exhibits by utilizing techniques such as pre-pruning (the removal of unnecessary tree nodes during tree assembly) and post-pruning (the removal of tree nodes after tree construction), and others as well.

Computations involving decision trees can be performed with CS4 in a variety of ways, including Bagging, Boosting, and Random Backwoods. Within the framework of the cross-approval set, a hub is only eliminated if the subsequent reduced tree produces results that are comparable to the initial one. Because the presentation is based approximatively on an approval set, this technique of tree pruning has the drawback that the actual tree can only make use of a smaller amount of information. However, over time, C4.5 will generate a certain amount of error based on the act of preparing the information itself. This error will be calculated using the upper limit of a confidence stretch, which is generally 25%, and will be applied to the re-replacement error. The estimated within one standard deviation of the anticipated error of the wheel. The additional cutting function known as sub tree rising in C4.5 provides a number of different options, including reduced mistake clipping as one of them. In the event that a sub tree is elevated, a lower hub might take the position of a higher hub, and vice versa; this would cause a reorganization of the tests.

A point-by-point outline on how C4.5 conducts its post-pruning is given in [14]. Different calculations for decision tree acceptance incorporate ID3 (antecedent of C4.5), C5.0 (replacement of C4.5), CART (grouping and relapse trees) [8], LMDT (Linear Machine Decision Trees) [15], OC1 (slanted classifier, etc. as given in Figure 2.2: A Sample decision tree-Partial view.

A decision tree is depicted in Figure 2.2 from a perspective that only shows portion of the tree. It gives a number of options to choose from, including the fact that one can keep playing if the outlook is good and the humidity is about typical.

It is common for a decision tree to be overfit when it is constructed using data from the training set. This indicates that the tree does an excellent

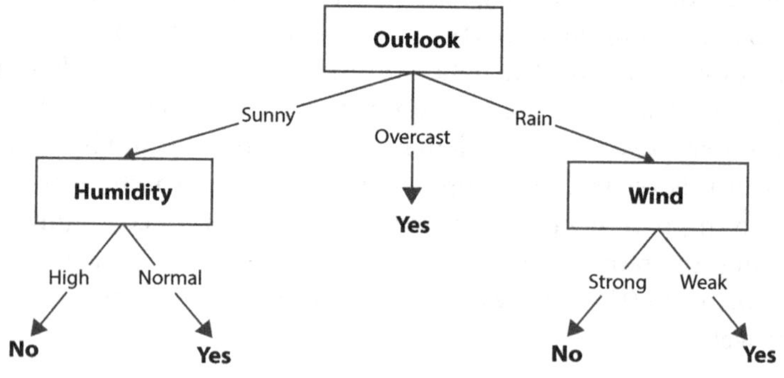

Figure 2.2 A sample decision tree—partial view.

job of training, as its name suggests. If the display contains content that isn't immediately apparent, the quality of the display as a whole will suffer. Therefore, it is possible to "shave off" hubs and sections of a decision tree, essentially substituting an entire sub tree with a leaf hub, if it comes to be established that the average error rate in the sub tree is greater than that in a single leaf. This is because "shaving off" refers to the process of removing a hub or section of a decision tree. The procedure of categorization is made easier as a result.

The process of performing trimming on a complicated decision tree aims to make it more controllable while also progressively expanding its scope. During a procedure known as "post trimming," some of the tree's branches are pruned away after it has reached its complete maturity, and younger trees are estimated with the help of test data. At this point, the ultimate tree will be chosen to be the one that is the least complicated and contains no mistakes.

Pre-pruning is another technique, which involves stopping the development of the tree at an earlier stage than normal. If a tree's overall soundness proportion is lower than a certain essential number, then the tree does not have a center. Choosing the appropriate accent, on the other hand, can be a difficult task. The C4.5 decision tree framework developed by Quinlan is a good example. The overwhelming majority of research involving decision trees focus on techniques to improve the presentation, such as clipping. In this article, we detail how we exploited data for insights into communities that have received inadequate research attention. Calculations based on decision trees are used in this situation to establish both graduation projections and the fundamental variables that contribute to graduation.

Included is a diagram illustrating the relationships between information extraction, the sharing of databases, and other topics such as artificial intelligence, measurements, and the visualization of data. It determines which of a large number of potential factors affecting a result are the most important, and then makes suggestions for strategies that can be used to organize demonstrations or forecast outcomes. It also describes in detail how the information that can be stored in a clustering framework's disorder network, which keeps track of both actual and intended configurations that can be used to evaluate the performance of a model.

In the context of a standard business task, information is presented in the shape of a table of tests, also known as instances. Each instance has a unique collection of distinguishing characteristics, also known as traits, as well as a designation that indicates the division to which it belongs. It describes an innovative method for evaluating characteristics by making use of genomic calculations as the primary tool.

The process of information extraction makes it possible to obtain data that has already been muddled and has the potential to be helpful. It is a form of instruction that makes use of computer algorithms to carry out an exhaustive search for recurring patterns in data. The extraction of useful knowledge from large amounts of data is one implementation of AI. Acquisition by association, or clustering, is an assumption of concept acquisition. The purpose of concept learning is to enable students to acquire an understanding of the significance of a general category after being presented with numerous instances, both positive and negative, of the category in question. Therefore, it draws a Boolean-valued competence conclusion based on the training occurrences. Unlike other methods of concept acquisition, arrangement learning can be expanded beyond the confines of a single educational setting. Finding models that are able to classify occurrences into the various preparatory instances that correspond to them is ultimately the objective of the learning process [16].

2.4 Machine Learning for Frequent Pattern Mining

To improve its effectiveness, the PSO algorithm will take use of the fact that many different kinds of animals, including fish and birds, exhibit behavior similar to that of a swarm. Within the parameters of the search, each particle has a position and velocity and these are completely unique in themselves, and they are free to move in any way that they see fit. The velocity and mobility of the particle are still constrained as a direct consequence of this, and the particle is directed to the location of any previously successful particles [17]. In addition to this, the particle is directed to the location of any other particles that have successfully completed their tasks in the past without causing any mishaps. It is now possible, as a result of the application of a predetermined set of rules to the technique in question, to characterize both the rate of motion and the location of each particle at every particular instant in time.

Identification 3 (ID3) is a method that use a decision tree to categorize instances in an iterative manner according to the values and features of those instances. It is generated from the most complex to the simplest using a collection of instances and the required features in that order. These groups were then further subdivided. When the set included inside a certain subtree is equal to the set of instances that belongs to a comparable category, the set in question is designated as a leaf node within the given subtree. Information theoretical criteria are taken into consideration whenever a characteristic is being chosen for testing purposes. The reduction in entropy will result in an increase in the information gain at each node [18].

Decision trees are often used in machine learning models for the purpose of data classification because of their speed and accuracy. When using this method, tree trimming may be accomplished in a number of different ways, making it a very adaptable practice. The result of the trimming is one that can be comprehended with ease. A number of academicians are of the opinion that taking down trees might be utilized as a means of overfitting. The C4.5 technique [20–22] includes an iterative classification that is used to further improve the categorization of the data until only pure leaf nodes are left, at which point the process comes to a conclusion. This iterative classification can be found in the method's outline. By using this strategy, it is possible to get the most out of the training data, while also eliminating the demand for rules [23, 24] that only signal a specific behavior in the data [19]. This is because it is practical to get the most out of the training data.

In recent years, the use of the technique known as the support vector machine (SVM) has seen significant growth in this sector. A helpful strategy for data categorization [25–27] is the use of a linear or non-linear separation surface in the input space. This may be done either linearly or non-linearly. The support vector machine (SVM) seeks to construct a model that reliably predicts the goal values of new data by using just the characteristics of the test data. The data collected during the training phase are used to construct the model. The support vector machine (SVM) provides a dependable approach for pattern categorization that maintains a high level of accuracy while simultaneously lowering the danger of overfitting. When there are just two types of classes present in the data, SVM may be used. Using SVM, data is categorized by locating the hyperplane that most effectively separates all of the data points into distinct categories. The hyperplane of a support vector machine (SVM) that has the greatest difference in margin between two classes of data is considered to be the optimal hyperplane for an SVM. When the slab is at its widest point parallel to the hyperplane, there are no data points located inside the boundary of the slab itself. Because of their close closeness to the hyperplane that separates the slab, the points along the slab's border are regarded to be support vectors. In fuzzy SVM, a membership value is assigned to each sample determined by its correlations with the values of other samples. There are many different ways in which each input sample contributes to the process that ultimately results in a choice being made. A radial basis function kernel has also been found to improve the performance of a support vector machine (SVM) [20].

2.5 Conclusion

Data mining is the act of applying complicated analytics to enormous datasets to discover hidden links, patterns, and trends. This has been done to uncover previously unknown information. The handling of huge amounts of data must be both efficient and adaptable to facilitate the retrieval of information and the making of well-informed decisions. It finds trends, correlations, or patterns in massive datasets that were not previously there. This is the objective of the process known as data mining. Since the inception of the World Wide Web, there has been a quick and large growth in the quantity of data that has been preserved and is available electronically. The capability of mining data for patterns and linkages that have not been identified before has become a vital resource in a variety of disciplines, including academia and business. As a result of the proliferation of the Internet, the quantity of data that can be kept and accessed online has increased at an exponential rate. As a consequence of this, methods for extracting insights from this mountain of data have become an essential component in a variety of disciplines, including educational institutions and commercial enterprises. It is standard practice to utilize a technique known as frequent item set mining to extract meaningful information from databases.

References

1. Haoxiang, W. and Smys, S., Big Data Analysis and Perturbation using Data Mining Algorithm. *J. Soft Comput. Paradigm (JSCP)*, 3, 01, 19–28, 2021.
2. Sivakami, M. and Prabhu, P., Classification of Algorithms Supported Factual Knowledge Recovery from Cardiac Data Set. *Int. J. Curr. Res. Rev.*, 13, 6, 161–166, 2021. ISSN: 2231-2196 (Print) ISSN: 0975-5241 (Online).
3. Bora, A., Gowri, NV., Naved, M., Pandey, P.S., An Utilization Of Robot For Irrigation Using Artificial Intelligence. *Int. J. Future Gener. Commun. Netw.*, 14, 1, 23–38, 2021.
4. Raghuvanshi, A., Singh, U., Sajja, G., Pallathadka, H., Asenso, E., Kamal, M. *et al.*, Intrusion Detection Using Machine Learning for Risk Mitigation in IoT-Enabled Smart Irrigation in Smart Farming. *J. Food Qual.*, 1, 2022, 1–8, 2022, doi: 10.1155/2022/3955514.
5. Jasti, V. *et al.*, Computational Technique Based on Machine Learning and Image Processing for Medical Image Analysis of Breast Cancer Diagnosis. *Secur. Commun. Netw.*, 2022, 1–7, 2022, Available: 10.1155/2022/1918379.
6. Hemamalini, V., Rajarajeswari, S., Nachiyappan, S., Sambath, M., Devi, T., Singh, B., Raghuvanshi, A., Food Quality Inspection and Grading Using

Efficient Image Segmentation and Machine Learning-Based System. *J. Food Qual.*, 2022, 1–6, 2022, doi: 10.1155/2022/5262294.
7. Raghuvanshi, A., Singh, U., Joshi, C., A Review of Various Security and Privacy Innovations for IoT Applications in Healthcare. *Adv. Healthcare Syst.*, 1, 43–58, 2022, Available: 10.1002/9781119769293.ch4.
8. Agrawal, R., Imielinski, T., Swami, A., Mining Association Rules between Sets of Items in Large Databases. *ACM Sigmoid Rec.*, 22, 2, 207–216, 1993, https://doi.org/10.1145/170036.170072.
9. Agrawal, R. and Srikant, R., Fast Algorithms for Mining Association Rules. *Proceedings of the 20th VLDB Conference Santiago*, Chile, pp. 487–499, 1994.
10. Al-bana, M.R. and Farhan, M.S., An Efficient Spark-Based Hybrid Frequent Itemset Mining. *Data (MDPI)*, 7, 11, 1–22, 2022, https://doi.org/https://doi.org/10.3390/data7010011.
11. Al-Maolegi, M. and Arkok, B., An Improved Apriori Algorithm For Association Rules. *Int. J. Nat. Lang. Comput.*, 3, 1, 21–29, 2014, https://doi.org/10.5121/ijnlc.2014.3103.
12. Magdy, M., Ghaleb, F.F.M., Mohamed, D.A.E.A., Zakaria, W., CC-IFIM: an efficient approach for incremental frequent itemset mining based on closed candidates. *J. Supercomput.*, 79, 7, 7877–7899, 2022, https://doi.org/10.1007/s11227-022-04976-5.
13. Ming-Syan, C., Jiawei, H., Philip, S.Y., Data Mining: An Overview from a Database Perspective. *IEEE Trans. Knowl. Data Eng.*, 8, 6, 866–883, 1996, https://doi.org/10.1109/69.553155.
14. Park, J.S., Chen, M.S., Yu, P.S., An Effective Hash-Based Algorithm for Mining Association Rules. *ACM Sigmoid Rec.*, 24, 2, 175–186, 1995, https://doi.org/10.1145/568271.223813.
15. Sandhu, P.S., Dhaliwal, D.S., Panda, S.N., Bisht, A., An improvement in apriori algorithm using profit and quantity. *2nd International Conference on Computer and Network Technology, ICCNT 2010*, pp. 3–7, 2010, https://doi.org/10.1109/ICCNT.2010.46.
16. Shuwen, L. and Jiyi, X., An Improved Apriori Algorithm Based on Matrix. *12th International Conference on Measuring Technology and Mechatronics Automation (ICMTMA)*, pp. 488–491, 2020, https://doi.org/10.1109/ICMTMA50254.2020.00111.
17. Singh, H. and Dhir, R., A New Efficient Matrix Based Frequent Itemset Mining Algorithm with Tags. *Int. J. Future Comput. Commun.*, 2016, 355–358, 2013, https://doi.org/10.7763/ijfcc.2013.v2.184.
18. Sun, L.N., An improved apriori algorithm based on support weight matrix for data mining in transaction database. *J. Ambient Intell. Hum. Comput.*, 11, 2, 495–501, 2020, https://doi.org/10.1007/s12652-019-01222-4.
19. Mishra, A.K., Tyagi, A.K., Dananjayan, S., Rajavat, A., Rawat, H., Rawat, A., Revolutionizing Government Operations: The Impact of Artificial Intelligence in Public Administration, in: *Conversational Artificial Intelligence*, pp. 607–634, 2024.

20. Vivekanandan, S.J., Ammu, S.P., Sripriyadharshini, R., Preetha, T.R., Computation Of High Utility Itemsets By Using Range Of Utility Technique. *J. Univ. Shanghai Sci. Technol.*, 23, 4, 94–101, 2021.
21. Rathore, N. and Rajavat, A., Smart Farming Based on IOT-Edge Computing: Applying Machine Learning Models For Disease And Irrigation Water Requirement Prediction In Potato Crop Using Containerized Microservices, in: *Precision Agriculture for Sustainability*, pp. 399–424, Apple Academic Press, USA, 2024.
22. Patsariya, M. and Rajavat, A., A Progressive Design of MANET Security Protocol for Reliable and Secure Communication. *Int. J. Intell. Syst. Appl. Eng.*, *12*, 9s, 190–204, 2024.
23. Rathi, M. and Rajavat, A., Investigations and Design of Privacy-Preserving Data Mining Technique for Secure Data Publishing. *Int. J. Intell. Syst. Appl. Eng.*, *11*, 9s, 351–367, 2023.
24. Dubey, P. and Rajavat, A., Effective K-means clustering algorithm for efficient data mining. *2023 2nd International Conference on Vision Towards Emerging Trends in Communication and Networking Technologies (ViTECoN)*, IEEE, pp. 1–6, 2023, May.
25. Pithawa, D., Nahar, S., Bhardwaj, V., Rawat, R., Dronawat, R., Rawat, A., Quantum Computing Technological Design Along with Its Dark Side. *Quantum Comput. Cybersecur.*, 1, 295–312, 2023.
26. Shrivastava, M., Patil, R., Bhardwaj, V., Rawat, R., Telang, S., Rawat, A., Quantum Computing and Security Aspects of Attention-Based Visual Question Answering with Long Short-Term Memory. *Quantum Comput. Cybersecur.*, 1, 395–412, 2023.
27. Rawat, R., Chakrawarti, R.K., Raj, A.S.A., Mani, G., Chidambarathanu, K., Bhardwaj, R., Association rule learning for threat analysis using traffic analysis and packet filtering approach. *Int. J. Inf. Technol.*, *15*, 6, 3245–3255, 2023.

3

Classification and Detection of Prostate Cancer Using Machine Learning Techniques

D. Vetrithangam[1]*, Pramod Kumar[2], Shaik Munawar[3], Rituparna Biswas[4], Deependra Pandey[5] and Amar Choudhary[6]

[1]*Department of Computer Science & Engineering University Institute of Engineering, Chandigarh University, Mohali, Punjab, India*
[2]*Computer Science and Engineering Ganga Institute of Technology and Management, Jhajjar, Haryana, India*
[3]*Department of CSE Kakatiya Institute of Technology and Science Warangal, Hanamkonda, Telangana, India*
[4]*Department of Basic Science and Humanities, IEM Newtown, UEM, Kolkata, India*
[5]*Department of ECE, Amity School of Engineering & Technology (ASET), Amity University, Lucknow, Uttar Pradesh, India*
[6]*Department of ECE, Alliance College of Engineering & Design (ACED), Alliance University, Bengaluru, Karnataka, India*

Abstract
Carcinoma is a significant contributor to the death rates of individuals. Reducing the amount of time it takes to diagnose a patient is very necessary to improve their prognosis. Diagnostic imaging and other traditional methods are used by highly trained medical professionals to identify any telltale indicators that may be present in the bodies of their patients. In spite of the abundance of medical imaging data, manual diagnosis may still be subjective and time-consuming due to the fact that people's perceptions differ so much from one another. One of the primary reasons for the variability is the collecting of data from medical imaging. A proper diagnosis may be more difficult to get as a result of this. When performing activities such as machine learning and the processing of complex pictures, it is important to make use of the most advanced computational power available.

**Corresponding author*: vetrigold@gmail.com

Rajesh Kumar Chakrawarti, Ranjana Sikarwar, Sanjaya Kumar Sarangi, Samson Arun Raj Albert Raj, Shweta Gupta, Krishnan Sakthidasan Sankaran and Romil Rawat (eds.) Natural Language Processing for Software Engineering, (29–42) © 2025 Scrivener Publishing LLC

Ever since the 1980s, there has been a persistent effort to develop a computer-aided diagnostic system that has the potential to help in the early diagnosis of a wide variety of malignancies. According to the most recent estimates, around one-seventh of men will be diagnosed with prostate cancer at some point in their life. This illness claims the lives of so many men every year, and it is unbearable that the number of men who are diagnosed with prostate cancer continues to climb. It is a tragedy that this number continues to rise. A powerful diagnostic system that is capable of managing high-resolution, multi-dimensional MRI images is an absolute need, in addition to computer-aided design (CAD) software. In the present moment, I am focusing my attention on a project that will make it easier for us to achieve our shared goals. Scientists are now studying methods to improve the speed, accuracy, and precision of computer-aided design (CAD) technology since it has been shown to be valuable. CAD technology has been demonstrated to be effective, as shown by the evidence. The development of techniques for the diagnosis and classification of prostate cancer via the use of MRI image processing and machine learning is the fundamental objective of this study as well.

***Keywords*:** Prostate cancer, prediction, machine learning, feature extraction, image segmentation, accuracy

3.1 Introduction

The prostate, a relatively small organ that plays a crucial role in the male reproductive system, is an essential component of sexual reproduction. It is very important for the fluid that is generated by the prostate gland, which is referred to as semen, to assist in the passage of sperm through the male reproductive system. The most important thing is to make sure that it is situated between the bladder and the tube that is responsible for releasing pee from the body, which is the upper urethra. In spite of the fact that melanoma is more prevalent in males, prostate cancer (PC) is the main cause of death among men due to cancer. This is a significant reason for worry for the public health of the whole world. The unregulated expansion of cells inside the gland itself is the primary factor that leads to the development of prostate cancer [1]. There is a possibility that the pace of development of cancer in the peritoneal cavity will differ from patient to patient. The prostate is the only organ that can sustain the development of slow-growing tumors. It is believed that around 85 percent of all cases of pancreatic cancer are slow-progressing variations of the disease. It is very necessary to keep oneself in a state of heightened awareness to properly navigate these circumstances [2]. The second kind of pancreatic cancer has the potential to spread to other parts of the body, in contrast to the first type, which is less aggressive. It is only via the use of reliable monitoring methods [5] that it is possible to differentiate between these two types of development. Physical inspections performed on a regular basis may, in many instances, discover personal computers at an early enough level. It is essential to ascertain the precise anatomical location of the prostate gland to begin the process of formulating a treatment plan once the prostate gland has been identified. Only via the implementation of screening procedures that are dependable and efficient is it possible to obtain a high chance of survival. The utilization of magnetic resonance imaging (MRI), transrectal ultrasonography (TSUS), and prostate specific antigen (PSA) tests are often used in the process of screening for prostate cancer [3]. The provision of standard parameters for magnetic resonance imaging (MRI) was the major objective of the modifications that were made to the initial guidelines for prostate MRI. Both of these things were done in addition to concentrating on the categorization of clinical relevance. In accordance with the first directive, this is not something that should be done. With each new issue, the objective is to provide a higher standard of excellence for photography and journalism. There have been a number of studies conducted in recent times that have focused on the outcomes of notions that are founded on these principles. There are a few restrictions that need to be carefully addressed when diagnosing extremely tiny lesions that have incurred severe damage. However, it is feasible to categorize a PC lesion as clinically significant by utilizing one of these approaches. The findings of this research have significant implications for the staging of cancer since they demonstrate that the use of a PI-RADS technique may make it simpler to detect cancer that has spread beyond the prostate. This has occurred as a result of the infection spreading beyond the prostate, which is the reason for this [4]. The data that are maintained in biological databases, which are accessible to scientists, are a veritable treasure trove [15]. It is becoming more difficult to get actionable insights due to the ever-increasing volumes of data. The term “machine learning” refers to the process by which computers may enhance their intelligence and performance by watching and replicating human activities, comparing their findings to those of other datasets, and generating new information from start. The growth of this kind of learning was brought about by the widespread use of data mining, which is an essential component of knowledge mining. One of the most important aspects of machine learning is the ability to recognize patterns and quickly derive inferences from a wide variety of datasets. The evaluation of ligand libraries may be carried out automatically via the use of machine learning methods [6, 7].

3.2 Literature Survey

Rampun *et al.* [8] utilized a median filter and an anisotropic diffusion filter to achieve their results. Due to the similarity between noise and edge gradients in photographs with a low signal-to-noise ratio, removing noise can be a challenging task. Consequently, removing background noise from pictures becomes a challenging task. While it is possible to detect noise gradients using a thresholding approach, their limits are not as apparent as one might anticipate. Samarasinghe and colleagues [9] employed a three-dimensional sliding Gaussian filter in their study. A plethora of innovative and thorough alternatives to this scanning process have been proposed. These options might assist in addressing issues such as noise distribution in MPMRI images. Shrinkage methods can exploit the sparsity provided by wavelet decomposition to improve MPMRI images. Orthogonal transformations are utilized in the wavelet transform for practical purposes in the real world. This metamorphosis is occurring right in front of you. The unwanted noise signal might still be present when the Rician distribution is used in the wavelet transform. To account for the scattering of noise in the data, modifications were made to the wavelet and scaling parameters. Lopes *et al.* [10] employed a methodology that integrates detection and estimating techniques to remove noise from T2W pictures. The computation starts with the wavelet coefficients that contain noise and then proceeds with the wavelet coefficient that is free from noise, achieved using a posteriori maximum estimate. By resizing the pictures, it was guaranteed that the PZ region would have a standard deviation of zero after the normalization process. Subsequently, the instructional and evaluative uses of the normalized multi-parametric MRI images were examined. By employing defined dynamic ranges for the intensities of the MPMRI sequences, the authors were able to ensure stability in the segmentation process. We successfully achieved our goal by employing this approach. The MPMRI images seem distorted due to the presence of background noise and the bias field of the endorectal coil [11]. The presence of a bias field in MRI images may account for the observed variations in signal intensity. Consequently, there is a substantial disparity in the luminosity of similar tissues across different areas of the picture. As the computer-aided design process progresses, it becomes more and more demanding. Training images are essential as segmentation and classification are fundamentally educational processes. Image-based training is crucial. To develop a dependable automated diagnosis, it is crucial to gather photographs of individuals from the same group with similar signal intensities. Whether or not the patients have cancer is inconsequential. Variations in outcomes can occur across patients, despite the use of the same tools, protocols, and circumstances. Viswanath *et al.* [12] employed the piecewise linear normalization approach to standardize the T2W pictures. This enabled us to ensure that the outcomes would be uniform while also eliminating individual variances among patients. The aim of this approach was to get a homogeneous visual aspect in the photographs. One component of the investigation included identifying and replicating the original foreground by employing methods for piecewise linear normalization. Most medical image analysis algorithms heavily depend on atlases for the process of segmentation. Firstly, it excels in low-definition and pixel-resolution situations. Tian *et al.* [13] obtained the required results from their study of prostate MRI data by integrating the graph cut segmentation approach with the concept of superpixels. Utilizing copy-and-paste segmentation has the benefit of diminishing the requirements for memory and processing resources. Human interaction is necessary during setup as the process is only partially automated. Martin *et al.* [14] propose a method for reconstructing the prostate from MRI data using a segmentation technique that involves deformable models and atlases. The utilization of a malleable model enabled the atlas-based method to precisely align the shape of the prostate cancer with its surrounding boundaries. A likelihood-based strategy may be used to accurately detect the exact position of the prostate. The work conducted by Vincent and his colleagues [15] provides a comprehensive description of an automated method for segmenting the prostate in MRI data. The underlying idea was based on the concept of "active appearance". The optimization process employs a multi-start technique to enhance performance and ensure accurate alignment of the model with the test photographs. This is our approach to ensure that we meet all the requirements. The researchers utilized an atlas-based matching method to generate the autonomous partitioning of the prostate, as described by Klein *et al.* [16]. To do this, the target image was compared to an extensive collection of annotated atlas photographs. The investigation encompassed all aspects. Their registration procedure was lenient, and they employed manual segmentation and classification methodologies [28, 29]. By merging the corresponding pictures throughout the segmentation step, it becomes possible to achieve MR prostate image segmentation after the registration stage is completed. One potential strategy for prostate segmentation is to use deformable models that incorporate both internal and exterior energy sources. The internal energy of the prostate causes it to become flatter, while external energy helps to make it longer. The approach proposed by

Chandra *et al.* [17] for independently and effectively segmenting prostate pictures obtained by scanning does not require the use of an endorectal coil. This approach was devised with the aim of segregating the photos [30–32]. During the training phase of the initialization strategy, this case-specific deformable system generates a distinct triangulated surface and image feature system for each individual patient. Picture feature systems can alter the original appearance of an image by employing the technique of template matching. Another developing trend in automated prostate segmentation systems is the use of approaches that combine several atlases with deformable models. Yin and colleagues [18] employed a very dependable and fully automated technique for prostate segmentation in their experiment. The prostate mean shape system is improved by employing the graph-search approach. Upon employing a standardized gradient field to perform cross-correlation on the prostate, the procedure is concluded. The material presented here is expected to enhance our comprehension of the historical background and development of the prostate. Deformable models are beneficial in situations when noise or abnormalities in the data result in undesired borders of the prostate. By employing a graph-cutting methodology, one may obtain a thorough and unproblematic result without encountering any difficulties arising from excessive segmentation. The graph cut technique was initially employed for prostate segmentation, as stated in the work conducted by Mahapatra and colleagues [19]. The acquired semantic data is employed for this objective. Precise determination of the volume and location of the prostate can be achieved by employing a super-voxel segmentation method that relies on random forests. The use of images and environmental data to educate random forest classifiers facilitated the further enhancement of prostate volume. Utilizing a Markov random field for graph cuts in prostate segmentation has the potential to enhance their performance. Puech *et al.* [20] created a set of rules based on data obtained from hospital IT systems to forecast the outcomes of tests. The fundamental components of supervised learning for data organization are similarity metrics and k-nearest neighbor (k-NN) algorithms. K-means clustering is an unsupervised method for classifying datasets that involves dividing the data into k distinct groups through an iterative process. The variable "k" is used to express the number of iterations in this situation. The number of adjacent centroids defines the unique designation assigned to each point in the feature space. Once we have confirmed that the centroid coordinates of each cluster are the same, we next proceed to update the means and generate a new mean for each cluster. Once all possible modifications to the centroids have been taken into consideration, the process of assigning and adjusting them will ultimately lead to an accurate outcome. K is a renowned and often utilized notation for denoting the number of cluster classes. Linear discriminant analysis (LDA) is the most successful approach for separating the two groups, making it the preferred choice. As a result, disputes across different categories increase, but differences within the same category decrease. The Naive Bayes classifier is widely regarded as the most superior option by a significant number of individuals. Using the idea of independent feature dimensions, this classification method might be referred to as "probabilistic classification." By utilizing this strategy, it is possible to attain the highest achievable posterior probability for picture categorization. An frequently used method for classification is adaptive boosting, also known as AdaBoost. The AdaBoost ensemble learning algorithm has not been publicly released until [21]. The objective of this strategy is to create a robust classifier by merging many ineffective learners. AdaBoost (AdB) generally outperforms random forest (RF) when comparing the outcomes. This specific classifier has a preference for learning procedures that are not efficient, such as decision stumps, classification trees, and regression trees. Lopes and his colleagues employed an AdaBoost classifier to carry out the classification strategy for their inquiry. Class labeling, a type of sparse kernel-based classification, largely relies on Gaussian processes. This method is commonly known as the "kernel approach" since it utilizes the whole training dataset to generate new labels. Sparse kernel classification algorithms have the ability to accurately assign a label to an unknown picture by using only a tiny portion of the annotated examples in the training dataset [22]. A support vector machine (SVM), which is a sparse kernel approach, is used to identify the optimal linear hyperplane for separating data into two label classes and maximizing the margin of error. To accomplish this, classes were partitioned based on the most efficient linear hyperplane. Support vector machines excel as classifiers in real-world scenarios due to their robustness and ability to generalize.

3.3 Machine Learning for Prostate Cancer Classification and Detection

Here we will go over the machine learning methods that are employed in MR scans to identify prostate cancer. Image preprocessing makes use of the histogram equalization approach. You can see things more clearly now. For effective picture segmentation, the fuzzy C-means method is employed. Interactions at the Grey Level among the many possible approaches to feature extraction, matrix is one to consider. There are three classification approaches that get the most attention: K-nearest neighbors, Random Forest and Adaboost. Digital X-rays, MRI, CT, and PET images are just a few examples of the many imaging modalities that could benefit from histogram equalization, a basic methodology in image processing. When one uses this technique, the pictures get clearer and more detailed. It is critical to obtain high-quality photos to correctly diagnose the illness and use these images for diagnosis. If any noises were previously muted in the image, they may be brought to light during the histogram equalization step, which follows processing. This technique is commonly employed in medical imaging analysis, as stated in [23]. This method produces an imperfectly distributed histogram of grey levels by employing grey operations. To do this, the image's grey mapping is determined. Clustering is a method that may be used to find hidden correlations in photos by merging similar patterns into larger groups. Clustering is the process of organizing items into groups based on the shared qualities between them. The FCM technique generates membership values, which are utilized for data item classification. Next, the data are partitioned after optimizing the object function using the least squares technique [24]. Feature extraction is a method in image processing that might reduce the amount of data that has to be kept. To do this, we take a set of feature subsets and eliminate any dimensions that aren't relevant or needed. To restore the texture's characteristics without compromising the pixel-to-pixel correspondence, GLCM is the method of choice. One way to achieve this aim is to find the values of the co-occurrence of grey levels. When building the general linear model (GLM), one can choose a direction of ş = 0, 45, 90, or 135 degrees and a length d from 1 to 5. Generating the GLM is subsequently accomplished using the conditional probability density functions p(I|j, d, ş). To achieve this objective, the GLCM algorithm is employed. The physical distance between two samples, measured as the inter-sample distance (d), is one such example. It is also possible to find the likelihood that these samples are physically connected (i,j | d,ş) using a function that is another example. [25] Among the many noteworthy characteristics of the GLCM are its energy, homogeneity, correlation, and contrast.

One of the many areas where KNN excels is in classification issues; this is because it is a supervised approach. Remember that this method consistently yields the same results with each given set of training data. Using the value in the population that is most comparable to any of the samples, one may give a class to any or all of the samples. If one wants to know how close two pixel coordinates are to each other, he/she may use the following equation to find their Euclidean distance. All of these considerations lead to the same conclusion: grouping the pixels together from the start would have been better. Using the K-nearest neighbors (KNN) algorithm, one may find the neighborhood where the distance between any two neighbours is the lowest. Within the algorithm, this neighborhood is represented by the letter K. The number of nearby residences should be your first consideration. It is usual practice to have an even number of courses when there are just two. Specifically, at that stage of the process, the neighborhood nearest to the subject is calculated using the value K = 1. A consequence of this sort would be the most basic and uncomplicated kind [26].

The phrase "random forest" was created because the model may generate forests that appear to be random. Rarely will you hear RF called "random forest." Using this method, you can build a set of decision trees, and then you can teach each tree independently. All of the possible answers to the questions and many of the available selection possibilities are contained in the present "forest of trees," which was generated using this approach. This is why more precise estimates were produced by include their input into the computations [27].

For classifiers that aren't performing up to pace when it comes to data classification, an approach called "AdaBoost" can be employed to boost their performance. To begin, we will assign relative importance to each observation using the AdaBoost method. The subsequent iterations will place a greater emphasis on the correctly identified observations and a lesser emphasis on the erroneously classified ones. The results will prove this by showing that a clear trend exists. When it comes to increasing the effectiveness of the classifier, all that is necessary is the usage of weights, which reflect the class membership of an observation. As a consequence of this, mistakes in classification will reduce. With the "boosting" approach, which entails providing children with a series of tailored fits, it is likely that pupils who are experiencing problems in school could benefit from the treatment. The successive models [28] in the series add increased weight to the data that were previously rejected during the first phase of the series.

3.4 Conclusion

One of the leading causes of mortality among those aged 65 and older is cancer. There is a significant correlation between the date of a patient's diagnosis and the likelihood that they will survive. In addition to doing standard diagnostics, the trained eyes that evaluate medical pictures for indicators of cancer also perform this examination. These professionals are on the lookout for symptoms that might show that cancer is developing inside the body. Due to the vast quantity of medical imaging data and the wide range of inter-observer variability, manual diagnosis is a time-consuming process that is also susceptible to subjectivity. It is possible that the diversity might be linked to the substantial amount of data that is contained in medical imaging. It is more challenging to arrive at an accurate diagnosis as a result of this consideration. Image processing and machine learning operations that are very complex need the most advanced computer hardware available. Over the course of many decades, researchers have been working on a computer-aided diagnostic system with the intention of assisting medical professionals in the early identification of cancer. A diagnosis of prostate cancer is something that about one out of every seven men will get at some time in their lives. There has been an increase in the number of men who have been diagnosed with prostate cancer, and there has also been an increase in the number of deaths that have been caused by the illness. For the purpose of collecting high-fidelity and multi-faceted magnetic resonance imaging (MRI) images, it is necessary to have a diagnostic system that is suitable in conjunction with computer-aided design (CAD) capabilities. One of the projects that the researcher is now working on is designed to assist us in achieving our goals. Researchers are now concentrating their efforts on enhancing the speed, accuracy, and precision of the computer-aided design (CAD) technologies that are already available. With the use of machine learning, this study presents a model that is capable of accurately evaluating photographs, recognizing distinctive characteristics, and acquiring new abilities.

References

1. Vilanova, J.C., Catalá, V., Algaba, F., Laucirica, O. (Eds.), *Atlas of Multiparametric Prostate MRI: With PI-RADS Approach and Anatomic-MRI-Pathological Correlation*, Springer, USA, 2017.
2. Cameron, A., Khalvati, F., Haider, M.A., Wong, A., MAPS: a quantitative radiomics approach for prostate cancer detection. *IEEE Trans. Biomed. Eng.*, 63, 6, 1145–1156, 2016.
3. Jasti, V., Zamani, A., Arumugam, K., Naved, M., Pallathadka, H., Sammy, F. *et al.*, Computational Technique Based on Machine Learning and Image Processing for Medical Image Analysis of Breast Cancer Diagnosis. *Secur. Commun. Netw.*, 2022, 1–7, 2022, doi: 10.1155/2022/1918379.
4. Giannini, V., Vignati, A., Mirasole, S., Mazzetti, S., Russo, F., Stasi, M., Regge D.2016. MR-T2-weighted signal intensity: a new imaging biomarker of prostate cancer aggressiveness. *Comput. Methods Biomech. Biomed. Eng.: Imaging Vis.*, 4, 3–4, 130–134, 2022.

5. Chaudhury, S., Krishna, A.N., Gupta, S., Sankaran, K.S., Khan, S., Sau, K., Raghuvanshi, A., Sammy, F., Effective Image Processing and Segmentation-Based Machine Learning Techniques for Diagnosis of Breast Cancer. *Comput. Math. Methods Med.*, 2022, 6 pages, 2022, https://doi.org/10.1155/2022/6841334.
6. Weinreb, J.C., Barentsz, J.O., Choyke, P.L., Cornud, F., Haider, M.A., Macura, K.J., Margolis, D., Schnall, M.D., Shtern, F., Tempany, C.M., Thoeny, H.C., Verma, S., PI-RADS Prostate Imaging– Reporting and Data System: 2015, Version 2. *Eur. Urol.*, 69, 1, 16–40, 2016.
7. Abu Sarwar Zamani, L., Anand, K.P.R., Prabhu, P., Buttar, A.M., Pallathadka, H., Raghuvanshi, A., Dugbakie, B.N., Performance of Machine Learning and Image Processing in Plant Leaf Disease Detection. *J. Food Qual.*, 2022, 7 pages, 2022, Article ID 1598796, https://doi.org/10.1155/2022/1598796.
8. Rampun, A., Zheng, L., Malcolm, P., Tiddeman, B., Zwiggelaar, R., Computer aided detection of prostate cancer in t2-weighted mri within the peripheral zone. *Phys. Med. Biol.*, 61, 13, 4796–4825, 2016.
9. Samarasinghe, G., Sowmya, A., Moses, D.A., Semi-quantitative analysis of prostate perfusion mri by clustering of pre and post contrast enhancement phases, in: *Biomedical Imaging (ISBI), 2016 IEEE 13th International Symposium*, pp. 943–947, IEEE, 2016.
10. Lopes, R., Ayache, A., Makni, N., Puech, P., Villers, A., Betrouni, N., Prostate cancer characterization on MR images using fractal features. *Med. Phys.*, 38, 1, 83–95, Jan 2011.
11. Styner, M., Brechbuhler, C., Szckely, G., Gerig, G., Parametric estimate of intensity inhomogeneities applied to MRI. Medical Imaging. *IEEE Trans.*, 19, 3, 153–165, 2000, ISSN 0278-0062.
12. Viswanath, S.E., Bloch, N.B., Chappelow, J.C., Toth, R., Rofsky, N.M., Genega, E.M., Lenkinski, R.E., Madabhushi, A., Central gland and peripheral zone prostate tumors have signi_cantly di_erent quantitative imaging signatures on 3 Tesla endorectal, *in vivo* T2-weighted MR imagery. *J. Magn. Reson. Imaging*, 36, 1, 213–224, Jul 2012.
13. Tian, Z., Liu, L., Zhang, Z., Fei, B., Superpixel-based segmentation for 3D prostate MR images. *IEEE Trans. Med. Imaging*, 35, 3, 791–801, 2016.
14. Martin, S., Troccaz, J., Daanen, V., Automated segmentation of the prostate in 3D MR images using a probabilistic atlas and a spatially constrained deformable model. *Med. Phys.*, 37, 4, 1579–1590, 2010.
15. Vincent, G., Guillard, G., Bowes, M., Fully automatic segmentation of the prostate using active appearance models, in: *Proceedings of the 15th International Conference on Medical Image Computing and Computer-Assisted Intervention (MICCAI) Grand Challenge: Prostate MR Image Segmentation 2012*, p. 7. Nice, France, 1–5 October 2012.
16. Klein, S., Van Der Heide, U.A., Lips, I.M., Van Vulpen, M., Staring, M., JP, P., Automatic segmentation of the prostate in 3D MR images by atlas matching using localized mutual information. *Med. Phys.*, 35, 4, 1407–1417, 2008.

17. Chandra, S.S., Dowling, J.A., Shen, K.-K. *et al.*, Patient specific prostate segmentation in 3-Dmagnetic resonance images. *IEEE Trans. Med. Imaging*, 31, 10, 1955–1964, 2012.
18. Yin, Y., Fotin, S.V., Periaswamy, S., Kunz, J., Haldankar, H., Muradyan, N., Cornud, F., Turkbey, B., Choyke, P., Fully automated prostate segmentation in 3D MR based on normalized gradient fields cross-correlation initialization and LOGISMOS refinement, in: *Medical Imaging 2012: Image Processing*, vol. 8314, p. 831406, International Society for Optics and Photonics, USA, 2012.
19. Mahapatra, D. and Buhmann, J.M., Prostate MRI segmentation using learned semantic knowledge and graph cuts. *IEEE Trans. Biomed. Eng.*, 61, 3, 756–764, 2014.
20. Puech, P., Betrouni, N., Makni, N., Dewalle, A.S., Villers, A., Lemaitre, L., Computer-assisted diagnosis of prostate cancer using DCE-MRI data: design, implementation and preliminary results. *Int. J. Comput. Assist. Radiol. Surg.*, 4, 1, 1–10, Jan 2009.
21. Freund, Y. and Schapire, R., A decision-theoretic generalization of on-line learning and an application to boosting. *J. Comput. Syst. Sci.*, 55119–139, 1, 68–78, 1997.
22. Bishop, C.M., *Pattern recognition and machine learning*, Springer-Verlag New York, Inc., Secaucus, NJ, USA, 2006.
23. Kalhor, M., Kajouei, A., Hamidi, F., Asem, M.M., Assessment of Histogram-Based Medical Image Contrast Enhancement Techniques; An Implementation. *2019 IEEE 9th Annual Computing and Communication Workshop and Conference (CCWC)*, pp. 0997–1003, 2019, doi: 10.1109/CCWC.2019.8666468.
24. Vela-Rincón, V.V., Mújica-Vargas, D., Mejía Lavalle, M., Magadán Salazar, A., Spatial αα-Trimmed Fuzzy C-Means Algorithm to Image Segmentation, in: *Pattern Recognition. MCPR 2020. Lecture Notes in Computer Science*, vol. 12088, K. Figueroa Mora, J. Anzurez Marín, J. Cerda, J. Carrasco-Ochoa, J. Martínez-Trinidad, J. Olvera-López (Eds.), Springer, Cham, USA, 2020, https://doi.org/10.1007/978-3-030-49076-8_12.
25. Benco, M., Kamencay, P., Radilova, M., Hudec, R., Sinko, M., The Comparison of Color Texture Features Extraction based on 1D GLCM with Deep Learning Methods. *2020 International Conference on Systems, Signals and Image Processing (IWSSIP)*, pp. 285–289, 2020, doi: 10.1109/IWSSIP48289.2020.9145263.
26. Uddin, S., Haque, I., Lu, H. *et al.*, Comparative performance analysis of K-nearest neighbour (KNN) algorithm and its different variants for disease prediction. *Sci. Rep.*, 12, 6256, 2022, https://doi.org/10.1038/s41598-022-10358-x.
27. Jackins, V., Vimal, S., Kaliappan, M. *et al.*, AI-based smart prediction of clinical disease using random forest classifier and Naive Bayes. *J. Supercomput.*, 77, 5198–5219, 2021. https://doi.org/10.1007/s11227-020-03481-x.

28. Mahesh, T.R., Dhilip Kumar, V., Vinoth Kumar, V., Asghar, J., Geman, O., Arulkumaran, G., Arun, N., AdaBoost Ensemble Methods Using K-Fold Cross Validation for Survivability with the Early Detection of Heart Disease. *Comput. Intell. Neurosci.*, 2022, 11 pages, 2022, Article ID 9005278 https://doi.org/10.1155/2022/9005278.
29. Rathi, M. and Rajavat, A., Investigations and Design of Privacy-Preserving Data Mining Technique for Secure Data Publishing. *Int. J. Intell. Syst. Appl. Eng.*, *11*, 9s, 351–367, 2023.
30. Dubey, P. and Rajavat, A., Effective K-means clustering algorithm for efficient data mining, in: *2023 2nd International Conference on Vision Towards Emerging Trends in Communication and Networking Technologies (ViTECoN)*, IEEE, pp. 1–6, 2023, May.
31. Chauhan, D., Singh, C., Rawat, R., Chouhan, M., Conversational AI Applications in Ed-Tech Industry: An Analysis of Its Impact and Potential in Education. *Conversational Artif. Intell.*, 1, 411–433, 2024.
32. Chauhan, D., Singh, C., Rawat, R., Dhawan, M., Evaluating the Performance of Conversational AI Tools: A Comparative Analysis. *Conversational Artif. Intell.*, 1, 385–409, 2024.

4

NLP-Based Spellchecker and Grammar Checker for Indic Languages

Brijesh Kumar Y. Panchal[1,2]* and Apurva Shah[3]

[1]*Computer Science and Engineering Department, Faculty of Technology and Engineering, The Maharaja Sayajirao University of Baroda, Vadodara, Gujarat, India*
[2]*Computer Engineering Department, Sardar Vallabhbhai Patel Institute of Technology (SVIT)-Vasad, Gujarat Technological University (GTU), Anand, Gujarat, India*
[3]*Computer Science and Engineering Department, Faculty of Technology and Engineering, The Maharaja Sayajirao University of Baroda, Vadodara, Gujarat, India*

Abstract
Natural language processing (NLP) is a field that combines linguistics with computation. It falls under the umbrella of artificial intelligence (AI) and has prompted the development of a related topic known as computing linguistics. This field focuses on natural language processing in computing systems. A number of sentences, which are linguistic units consisting of one or more words connected based on a predetermined set of rules known as grammar, comprise a natural language. Grammar checking refers to the process of verifying the syntactic correctness of phrases and is a widely used technique in the field of language engineering. Spellchecker is an application that examines potential instances of incorrect spelling within a given text. It identifies and occasionally recommends keywords spelled incorrectly in a given text. The rate of mistake detection and error correction increases as the size of the spellchecker's lexicon increases. The goal of this study is to look at the techniques and procedures used by spellcheckers and grammar checkers for Indian languages, with the ultimate goal of producing comprehensive literature. Thus, one can create a more accurate system. This study

**Corresponding author*: panchalbrijesh02@gmail.com

Rajesh Kumar Chakrawarti, Ranjana Sikarwar, Sanjaya Kumar Sarangi, Samson Arun Raj Albert Raj, Shweta Gupta, Krishnan Sakthidasan Sankaran and Romil Rawat (eds.) Natural Language Processing for Software Engineering, (43–70) © 2025 Scrivener Publishing LLC

concludes by examining the many characteristics present in current spellcheckers and grammar checkers targeting Indian language.

Keywords: Spellchecker, grammar checker, Indic languages, natural language processing (NLP), rules-based, machine learning, artificial intelligence (AI)

4.1 Introduction

Individuals often make grammatical as well as spelling errors when composing articles. This issue mostly affects those who are not good at the rules of language writing, leading to a significant investment in work and time in identifying and correcting spelling and grammatical errors. Therefore, individuals need a software application that facilitates automated grammatical and spelling checking while writing. Spellcheckers and grammar checkers are significant aspects of the study of natural language processing (NLP), and it is considered a well-established problem in NLP. The primary focus of this task is to rectify a range of faults in the text, including but not limited to spelling, punctuation, grammatical, and word-choice errors. This chapter introduces NLP-based spellchecker and grammar checker techniques in 1st part; the 2nd part describes a grammar checker scenario; and the 3rd part discusses the study of grammar checkers in the context of Indic languages.

4.2 NLP-Based Techniques of Spellcheckers and Grammar Checkers

4.2.1 Syntax-Based

Under this method, the provided text is parsed fully. Upon parsing, each phrase is given a parse tree depending on the grammar of the base language. If full parsing fails, the text is regarded as being wrong. Hence, the parser should be as thorough as possible in order to lower the number of false alarms. The key benefit of this strategy is that regardless of the kind of mistake, the grammar checker will recognize all wrong sentences if the grammar supplied is full, that is, if it covers all conceivable syntactic rules of the language. Unfortunately, it is impossible to clearly enumerate all of a natural language's syntactic rules owing to ambiguities in natural languages. Therefore, even for phrases that are accurate, the parser may yield more than one parse tree. This method only allows for the detection of false sentences. Nevertheless, additional rules that parse poorly constructed sentences are needed to inform the user of the issue; this method is referred to as constraint relaxation. A statement is considered wrong and a rule description and recommendation may be offered if it can only be parsed using this additional rule.

4.2.2 Statistics-Based

In this technique, a list of part-of-speech (POS) tags is provided using an annotated corpus. Certain sequences from these created sequences will be highly frequent, while others are likely to not appear at all. Sequences that often occur will be accepted as accurate in other texts, but rare sequences will result in mistakes. The existence of a sizable volume of POS-annotated data is a crucial prerequisite for using this technique. Also, the grammatical characteristics necessary for determining an agreement in the underlying language must be reflected in the employed POS tags.

4.2.3 Rule-Based

In this manner, a text that has at least been POS-tagged is compared against a set of predetermined rules in the form of mistake patterns. If one of such patterns is identified, the text is incorrect. Words, their POS tags, or even chunk tags may be used directly as the foundation for patterns. This scheme is similar to the statistics-based plan, except that all the rules are created by hand. Contrary to syntax-based systems, rule-based systems will never be finished. Even if there are many mistake rules present, it is almost impossible to anticipate every grammatical inconsistency; therefore, there will always be some errors that it misses. It is nevertheless preferable to have some problems go undiscovered than to have an insufficient parser generate unwanted false alarms. This method differs from others in that each rule may be individually enabled or disabled, and the system can provide detailed error messages along with beneficial comments, including explanations of grammatical rules. Using this strategy, the system may be expanded gradually by beginning with only one rule and adding more rules one at a time.

4.2.4 Deep Learning-Based

Artificial neural networks, which are machine learning (ML) algorithms, specialize in deep learning. Deep learning methods have recently been reported to be extensively used and to have achieved effective outcomes. One of the key factors in the achievement of deep learning methods is the freedom they provide when selecting the architecture. In ML research for natural language processing, deep learning approaches were at the forefront. Deep learning, a relatively new topic, goes beyond symbols to represent words as vectors. The semantic meaning of words is encoded in vectors. Deep learning learns vectors for words. One may quantify the distance between the vectors for two words rather than merely assuming that they are equal or unequal, as with symbols, and this measure of distance can provide a potent mechanism for generalization. Deep learning may discover, for instance, that the meaning of the phrase "I feel concerned" is more similar to that of "I feel nervous" than to "I feel tired." A grammar checker built on top of deep learning is called DeepGrammar. It uses deep learning to build a model of language, which it then applies in three phases to check text for errors: (1) Calculate the probability that the text was intentionally written. (2) Try to create wording that is more plausible and similar to the original material. (3) Show the user the text as a potential correction if such material is discovered.

4.2.5 Machine Learning-Based

Machine learning (ML) and NLP are key components in the course of transforming an artificial agent into an artificial "intelligent" agent. An artificially intelligent system can now process more information from its environment and reply to it in a manner that is easy for users to understand because of advancements in natural language processing. Natural language must pass through many stages of processing before a computer can understand it. This method consists of many steps, including morphological analysis, syntactic analysis, semantic analysis, discourse analysis, and pragmatic analysis. People often apply these analytical activities sequentially. In some ways, ML significantly improves almost all of these NLP procedures.

4.2.6 Reinforcement Learning-Based

Machine learning includes reinforcement learning, making it a subset of artificial intelligence. It enables software agents and machines to autonomously decide the best course of action within a certain situation to optimize performance. The reinforcement signal, sometimes referred to as easy reward criticism, is necessary for the agent to learn its behavior. As a subfield of ML and an extension of artificial intelligence, reinforcement learning makes it possible for machines and software agents to automatically decide what behavior is most appropriate in a given situation optimize performance. The reinforcement signal, which is straightforward reward feedback, is needed for the agent to learn its behavior.

4.3 Grammar Checker Related Work

In 2002, this study [1] discussed that the two-pass parsing method is essentially established to cut down on repetition in the grammar rules created for sentence analysis' phrase structure. The sentence is first parsed using some basic phrase structure grammar (PSG) rules. Failure results in the application of the movement restrictions and a reparative punishment. The approach examines declarative sentences for grammatical and structural errors. Implementing two-pass parsing is a novel and distinctive way to address challenging parsing issues. It enables you to maintain a simpler computational grammar while yet covering the widest possible variety of phrases. Without truly delving into the specifics of transformation grammar, it offers you a taste of how transformations work. When a declarative Urdu phrase is entered, the developed system will check it for grammar faults, and if any are discovered, it suggests fixes. The system's implementation validates the two-pass parsing strategy and the suggested learning algorithm.

In 2002, the researchers [2] presented the computational model that will be used to create a grammar checker for Urdu. The model employs the two-pass parsing technique to analyze sentences. The two-pass parsing method is primarily used to cut down the redundancy of the grammar rules for phrase structures that were developed for the analysis of sentences. At first, some base PSG rules are used to analyze the sentence. If the sentence cannot be parsed, movement rules are applied and then rewritten. The model is used to check for grammar and structural errors within declarative sentences. Two-pass parsing is a unique and innovative method for solving complex parsing challenges. It helps you make computational grammar simpler while covering a full range of sentences. Furthermore, it lets you experience a number of transformations and functions without getting into the transformational grammar's specifics. Finally, researchers have implemented the model. The system implemented can take an explicit Urdu sentence as an input and then check its grammar. If any errors are detected, it provides optional corrections to the incorrect sentence. This system is implemented to prove the two-pass parsing method and the algorithm proposed for the computational model.

In 2007, this study [3] developed the Nepali Grammar Checker, which is undergoing testing and development. It is described in this chapter along with its architectural and system design. This grammar checker was developed using a modular methodology and is made up of several components. The overall integrated system then uses these components as a pipeline. It is designed to look for grammatical problems in Nepali, including nominal and verbal agreements, parts of speech inflections, phrase and clause structures, and many types of language structures. The study and production of the first two modules—the tokenizer and the morphological analyzer—of the modules suggested in the architecture and system design of the Nepali Grammar Checker have been partly finished. The two modules have prototypes that are being tested including their complex management capabilities. As new information from their search effort becomes available in the future, the suggested architecture and system design of the Nepali Grammar Checker may vary.

In 2008, this article [4] described the grammar-checking system that was urbanized to detect grammatical mistakes within Punjabi texts. The system employs the full-form lexicon to analyze the morphology and uses rules-based techniques for POS tagging and phrase chunking. The scheme takes an innovative move toward an agreement to ensure that at the level of clause and phrase, the grammatical information provided through POS tags in the form of feature–value pairs is analyzed. The scheme can notice and advise corrections for various grammatical mistakes that result from the absence of an agreement or the arrangement of words in different phrases and phrases, etc. To our knowledge, this grammar-checking system is the first system to be reported in Indian languages. This chapter outlined the specifications for designing and operating the grammar-checking system for Punjabi. This system can detect numerous grammatical mistakes found in official Punjabi documents. As far as the researchers know, this is the first system of its kind applicable to Punjabi and different Indian dialects. The researchers hope this study will help close the gap in Punjabi and other languages in NLP. In addition, this research will inspire future researchers to continue creating advanced tools supporting Punjabi. This system aims to detect different grammatical errors in legal texts written in Punjabi. Identifying grammatical errors primarily focuses on ensuring that false alarms are kept to a minimum. The system gives enough details for each detected error so the user can understand what the error is and why it is being identified. The system also offers suggestions if it is possible to correct the errors.

This chapter outlined an innovative method of performing grammar checks with the help of clause and phrase information paired with grammatical information (POS data) in the form of feature value. This method can be used for languages with advanced resources, such as a full-parser pattern, and the pattern-matching methods cannot recognize other agreements. The online version of this grammar checking is accessible for free with three additional resources for the Punjabi language: the morphological analyzer, the tagger for POS, and the word chunker. The morphological analyzer is available as a free download for non-commercial usage.

In 2009, this study [5] focused on Punjabi language POS and grammar checker, an associate of the Modern Indo-Aryan family of languages, and is the subject of this study's POS tagging research. It was suggested to utilize a tagset for applications like grammar checking. This fine-grained tagset is completely based on the grammatical groups concerned in several types of concord in ordinary Punjabi sentences. The inflectional morphology of Punjabi words provide the basis for many of the morpho-syntactic traits used in this tagset. Because there is not a tagset for Punjabi or other Indian languages, this one was created with an emphasis on the agreement aspects of these languages. The grammar elements needed for agreement testing in Punjabi documents are not entirely covered by the tagsets for other languages. Also discussed is a rule-based tagger that was created using this tagset. This will be the first POS tagger for Punjabi to be released. For the languages that share grammatical traits with Punjabi, more especially the languages of the Modern Indo-Aryan family, the tagset given in this chapter is suggested for grammar testing and other purposes of a comparable kind.

In 2012 [6], researchers presented a unique method of "Hindi" grammar checker in their paper. The system used a complete dictionary for morphology analysis as well as rules-based systems. In this method, the researchers suggested a system that uses rules that is compared to the input Hindi sentence at a minimum and tagged. This method is similar to the approach based on statistics. However, all rules are designed by the researchers themselves. This rule-based Hindi Grammar Checker system was implemented productively for basic Hindi sentences only. The marks are quite positive. The benefit of this method is that the time it takes for grammar checks and analysis of the entire sentence is much less than other schemes. The reason for the higher performance is the fact that it will only look at patterns that are the same in terms of the words that are present in an input sentence, and does not take into account all patterns that are stored in the database. The researchers said that the system performance is further enhanced by adding more rules to the database manually.

In 2014, this paper's researcher [7] planned a spellchecker and grammar checker system designed to detect spelling errors and correct errors in text or a text using the hybrid approach. Grammar checker is an application that helps to determine grammar errors within the written text. Making a spellchecker or grammar checker program for Indian languages like Punjabi creates new problems that cannot be found in English, making the design of spellcheckers and grammar checkers a challenge. The biggest hurdles to overcome are that there is no fundamental layout for the Punjabi keyboard and no standard format approved for Punjabi spelling. There are numerous different grammatical features of Punjabi which makes it distinct when compared to other languages. Punjabi is the 12th most popular spoken language. The most important requirement for creating any spell-checker is to have a dictionary of various words from the language that can function as a lexicon. This paper sought to create an application that is a hybrid mix of grammar checking for Punjabi only. The system first checks for spelling errors and later for grammar errors within the content. If a text input is sent to the system, it goes through grammar and spell checkers before moving on to a grammar checker. A scalable, comparable algorithm was proposed that is a hybrid of grammar checker and spellchecker for Punjabi, which reduces time and costs. The purpose of the paper was to suggest an approach that is a mix of grammar checker and spellchecker for the Punjabi language. The projected system initially checks spelling errors, and after correcting spelling mistakes, it examines grammatical mistakes. The output is a document that is spelling error-free and grammar error-free. The correctness of the system is 83.5%. As per the researcher of this paper, this system can be improved to handle more complex sentences in the future. The system's accuracy was also improved. Other researchers could utilize this system for other languages, too.

In 2015, this study [8] provided a grammatical model analysis of Assamese sentences, which grew from general computational, linguistic, and psycholinguistic study. Linguists and NLP practitioners rely on parsing to decipher the syntactic and semantic details of a language's grammar. Free world order, ambiguity, and inefficiency are only some of the issues that make natural language text difficult to parse. For the Assamese language, the researcher suggested a model using the top-down parsing technique and a context-free grammar (CFG) with a restricted vocabulary. In this research, the researcher described a top-down predictive parsing method for analyzing basic Assamese phrases. Our suggested grammar for Assamese sentences only takes into account six different sorts of elements of speech. Future studies have to take into account as many possible sentence patterns in Assamese as well as other aspects of the language.

In 2015, the researcher [9] worked on developing Tamil morphological generators and analyzers. Making a comprehensive and effective operating system is quite different from making a morphological generator or analyzer for demonstration purposes. Making a system that provides 60% to 65% coverage is not too difficult. It is challenging to raise the efficiency over 65% and to a realistic level of 95% to 97%. Instead of being broad and detailed, the majority of the current descriptions concentrated on a vertical feature that is limited. The coverage that was attained included the descriptions of the previous work, which is often never more than 50%. The assessment technique revealed that the effectiveness of the morphological analyzer created by the current team for Tamil is really impressive. The creation of a morphological analyzer, which includes the analysis of verbal complex, has several natural language applications, including lemmatization, text production, machine translation, and parsing. Additionally, it aids document retrieval and word processing applications like spell checking and text input as well as voice applications like text-to-speech (TTS) synthesis and speech recognition. Assigning POS tags to the verbal complex is made easier by locating the categorical details of the verbal forms.

In 2016, this research paper [10] presented methods that can be utilized to enhance the current Punjabi Grammar Checker. In this study, two key actions, *i.e.*, the morphological analyzer and POS tagger, were enhanced to improve the efficiency of the current Punjabi Grammar Checker. After enhancing these two functions, development of significant magnitude in the current Punjabi Grammar Checker was noticed. In this study, a cross approach was adopted to ensure POS tag disambiguation in Punjabi. The researcher employed an amalgamation of rule-based and statistically-based methods in this method. The hybrid system was implemented with two distinct phases. The first output from the morph was provided as input to the rule-based POS tagger. In the case of a rule-based POS tagger, it was implemented in an exacting order. Every rule is paired with an initial condition known as an entry condition. If the first condition is satisfied, the rule will be relevant, and the researcher will follow the next rule. A common rule is changing tag A to B subject to the previous tag being C. This rule checks the first condition when the preceding tag is C. Then, relate this rule to modify tags from B to A or be relevant to the next rule. The first conditions for the applicability of rules usually depend on words, tags, and other morphological characteristics. For instance, the rules could be to change tag A to tag B with the first requirement being the preceding word contains the word "W." In this stage, the majority of the confusion can be resolved by the handwritten rule. In the next phase, the production of rule-based taggers for POS was used as input to the hidden Markov model (HMM) statistical tagger for POS. In this stage, all ambiguities that still need to be solved by the rule-based system are clarified. In the statistical method, a bi-gram hidden Markov model was employed. The annotated text of about 20,000 words was used to train and estimate the HMM parameter. An annotated corpus is built using a rule-based tagger. The method of maximum likelihood was employed to determine the parameter. The researcher used the Viterbi algorithm to create this method.

In 2016, research [11] techniques for enhancing the current Punjabi Grammar Checker were offered in this study work. To improve the presentation of the current Punjabi Grammar Checker, two primary activities—the morphological analyzer and the POS tagger—were upgraded in this study. Development and creation in the current Punjabi Grammar Checker were seen after upgrading these two tasks. First, the morphological analyzer and POS tagger, two upgraded modules, were examined separately. The grammar checker was then evaluated once the upgraded modules were swapped out for the standard ones. The morphological analyzer was much improved, as indicated in paper. The percentage of words that the morphological analyzer failed to identify decreased by 5–6%. The study also demonstrated an 8–9% development in the disambiguation. Despite an additional 0.5% to improper disambiguation, this may had been overlooked since disambiguation was much improved. Again, according to other study, the morphological analyzer and the POS tagger both contributed to a 27% and 20% decrease in false alarms, respectively.

In 2017, this paper's [12] author designed a grammar-checking system that works for the Hindi language. All of the elements needed for developing a grammar checker were designed from scratch. Certain mechanisms such as morph, POS tagger, and error detection systems were created using a statistical approach, and grammar correction systems were created using a rule-based approach. This system was tested against four types of mistakes. In an unnatural test of sequence-to-sequence strategies for sentence correcting, the researcher discovered that models based on characters tend to be more efficient than models based on words and models that encode sub-word information through convolutions, and modelling the results as a sequence of diffs increases the efficiency over conventional techniques. The most effective sequence-to-sequence model improves over our strongest phrase-based machine translation models, which has access to similar information in the range of six M2 (0.5 the GLEU) points. In addition, in the CoNLL-2014 standard setup's data-driven environment, the researcher showed that the modelling diffs can yield comparable or higher M2 scores when using simplified models or significantly smaller data sets than prior sequence-to-sequence methods. Our research shows that, on an extensive, professionally-annotated data set, a sequence-to-sequence model based on the character can result in significant efficiency advantages over a current smart machine text (SMT) system that includes task-specific features such as ceteris paribus. Additionally, when you consider the crowd-sourced environment of CoNLL data, where there are only a few sentences that have been professionally annotated in training, modelling diffs provide the possibility of making adjustments that increase the effectiveness of the sequence-to-sequence model for the job.

In 2018, in this paper's [13] review of rule-based Gujarati grammar the researchers said that NLP is the abbreviation. It has become a hot topic for study. The study of NLP and its applications reveals how a computer can comprehend natural language speech and text and modify it to perform amusing and practical tasks. Natural language processing (NLP) uses the word "language" to refer to natural languages like Gujarati, Hindi, and English. The main goal of this work is to evaluate the tech that is already in use and to determine the best way to use some of its NLP applications to construct Gujarati grammar. Our major emphasis is on the rule-based function since Gujarati has its own set of specific rules for mixing the consonants, vowels, and modifiers, much like every other language written in Indian script. The development of Gujarati grammar using current technology and appropriate NLP ideas, similar to other languages, is the primary emphasis of this study. The Gujarati language's grammar really requires a lot of labor to execute. The consistency of the Gujarati language and its grammar is the biggest practical issue. Here, the researcher attempted to at least provide a clear path for some of the NLP's language-based rules. Any researcher may in the future utilize a rule-based morphological strategy for classifying Gujarati and expand on this work by implementing grammar rules that may be utilized for other studies in the field of NLP.

In 2019, researchers of this paper [14] tested this system and it showed general accuracy of 0.83, recall of 0.91, and F-measure of 0.87. The grammar-checking software reviewed input sentences. If the sentence was not grammatically correct, then the program provided a suggestion for correcting the sentence if the developed system can check each sentence one at a time. The sentence was then ended with a sentence ending. The system developed was primarily created for sentences with a simple structure in the Hindi language, however, certain compound sentences can be processed to identify and correct mistakes. If the sentence was valid, it was displayed correct. In this research, the author suggested a hybrid method to create a grammar checker tool for identifying and correcting grammatical errors in the Hindi language. This can be described as the fundamental design for the Hindi Grammar Checker. The proposed system can detect and correct grammar mistakes caused by a lack of agreement between nouns and verbs in terms of numbers and gender. The system is designed to work only for short sentences in the Hindi language. The system also checks for issues relating to the lack of agreement between verb and noun or adjective and noun. Therefore, the researcher could further extend the research work to more complex sentences, *i.e.*, complex sentences and compound sentences in Hindi. Further, algorithms for detecting and correcting other kinds of errors, such as an error in the style, an error caused by postposition, and the use of words that are not necessary, could also be used.

In 2020, this paper's [15] researcher said that modern society's reliance on language as its primary means of communication is rooted in its long and storied past. The quality of a language depends in large part on its grammar. Researchers were schooled our whole lives to understand and communicate with one another via a body of information researchers have amassed, learned in accordance with rules, and a limited relevance. Furthermore, the ability to transfer this level of understanding into a computer, where it can interpret and categorize contextual evidence into the correct syntactical form, thereby validating that the information was in the correct form, is incredibly important right now due to the complexity of the task involved. This study discussed the problem and argued that the Dravidian language Kannada might benefit from the development of a tool to check its grammar. Among the first explanations would be the fact that the language's complexity presents a challenge, and therefore using a rule-based approach is a simpler way to go and makes it feasible to adequately identify recognized problems. A language expert is needed to construct hundreds of parallel standards that are hard to maintain. In this work, researchers proposed a model that makes use of a deep learning technique to train an LSTM (long short-term memory) neural network using a large dataset, with the help of Word2Vec, TensorFlow, and the Keras packages to retain information contextually. The suggested approach is efficient at detecting grammatical errors. In this study, researchers provided a deep-learning model for the Kannada language that uses the Word2Vec technique for granular embedding and was then trained in a neural network with an LSTM layer, which keeps the word's etymology in mind while learning its meaning. One shortcoming was the lack of a sizable annotated corpus for the Kannada language. The process of stemming and lemmatizing the data would further improve the paper by allowing for more uniform word interpretation. Additional work is needed to test the system on a much larger dataset in order to fine-tune the model and to make it easily available for future research.

In 2020, this study [16] worked toward constructing a flexible and comprehensive Arabic auditor that can deal with vowelized texts. An automatic grammar checking system may enhance the excellence of the text, lower the expenses of proofreading, and contribute to grammar instruction. The "Arabic Grammar Detector" was termed (AGD). Based on an addiction grammar and decision tree classifier model, AGD was effectively built. Its goal was to identify the proper syntactic dependencies of a phrase by extracting patterns of grammatical rules from a projective addiction network. The present implementation included practically all standard Arabic grammar rules for both vowelized and non-vowelized texts. Utilizing the Tashkeela corpus, AGD was assessed. More than 94% of grammatical problems were caught and fixes were also suggested. An Arabic grammar auditor is a complicated system that needs the assistance of experts in the area as well as substantial linguistic study and resources. This study presented an in-depth grammar auditor that uses a novel methodology. It seeks to identify grammatical mistakes in Arabic texts that include vowels and those that do not, as well as suggest how to fix them. This technique is based on the projective dependency graph's grammar, whose rules are taken from the hierarchy of grammatical rules that authors have created. In essence, the dependencies are synthesized in order to identify the most precise pattern of grammatical rules based on the properties of the sentence words and to determine the correct end-mark based on the output of the decision tree classifier model. Researchers have seen encouraging outcomes with this strategy. The AGD now gives more accurate findings than human auditing. An example of an AGD demonstration is provided in the appendix. The AGD system performance will be improved by posting it online for public usage and making use of user comments. The no projective dependency graph is included as a third element to improve the AGD's handling of Arabic odd permutation instances.

In 2021, researchers [17] worked on a rule-based Bengali Grammar Checker. A rapidly expanding area of artificial intelligence technology is computational linguistics, sometimes known as NLP. However, there has not been much progress made in this area of Bengali language. Spell checking, TTS, and optical character recognition (OCR) for Bengali have all been worked on. Researchers developed a method to verify the grammar of Bengali text since there has not been much effort done on Bengali grammar checking. Researchers drafted a few grammar rules that take into account the basic interdependencies of the various components of speech in order to examine the grammar of Bengali phrases. Researchers used pretrained parts of speech (POS) taggers to break phrases into words before running our grammar software on them. This essay explained the use of POS tagging and grammatical rule checking to spot grammatical mistakes and misplaced words in Bengali phrases. By defining the sentence's parts of speech and then checking the sentence's structure against a set of rules, this approach identified structural grammatical faults in Bengali sentences. An accurate Bengali Grammar Checker is currently being implemented via a number of initiatives. An online platform for rule-based Bengali grammatical verification was the goal of this project. Even so, there are a number of tools available to deal with the processing aspect of NLP for Bengali grammar. No single platform verifies every rule to identify mistakes in Bengali phrases' grammar. This study tackled this problem and developed a platform that uses rules to verify Bengali sentence construction. The contribution of this study consists of categorizing words into seven parts of speech tags and entity rules for verifying nouns, adjectives, and verb phrases produced in accordance with Bengali grammar rules and programmed into the system to discover incorrect terms. In the future, a better POS tagger might be added to the system, greatly increasing its efficiency. The statistical approach might also be used to develop a recommendation system.

In 2021, this study [18] covered the continuing development of a deep neural network-based grammatical mistake detector for the Tamil language. This suggested grammar checker detected crucial subject-predicate agreement issues. In this instance, our focus is particularly on the agreement error between verbal predicates and nominal subjects. Additionally, researchers produced the first Tamil grammatical mistake annotated corpus ever. In order to capture syntactic information, the authors also used multilingual pre-trained language models. The researchers discovered that IndicBERT performed better on our tasks. With the use of our grammar-error annotated data, researchers improved the IndicBERT pre-trained model before implementing this grammar checker as a multi-class classification on top of it. The F1 score produced by this baseline model is 84.0. Researchers are now working to make this suggested approach better by using a dependency parser. Using a cutting-edge methodology, researchers have created a baseline purpose for Tamil grammatical mistake detection. The program described here looks for grammatical mistakes in sentences where the denominative subject and verbal predicate agree on the person number and gender. To capture the Tamil structures, researchers employed a multilingual pre-trained model. It was then adjusted using the grammatical error annotated data researchers produced. The authors discovered that compared to other pre-trained models, the IndicBERT model provides greater accuracy. For an unknown test set, our baseline model displays an F1 Score of 84.0%. To train the grammar checker, the researcher will produce additional annotated data using ThamizhiMorph, a morphological analyzer. To capture syntactic information like subject and predicate, the present model depends on a pre-trained model. A syntactic parser may be used to achieve this, and the syntactically parsed data may improve the score. As a result, as a further step, the researcher will test the suggested system by including syntactic information such as subject and predicate information into our datasets using a Tamil dependency parser named ThamizhiUDp.

In 2022, this paper [19] outlined the architecture and layout of the Nepali Grammar Checker, which is currently under study and improvement. The process is modular that has a grammar checker consisting of self-governing units. The units function as a pipeline to the in general system. Its grammar checker aims to check grammar errors, such as verbal and nominal agreement, parts of speech inflections, clause and phrase structure, and the different types of sentence structures for Nepali. The modules suggested in the system and architectural plan of Nepali Grammar Checker work on the investigate and the growth of the initial two modules, namely the tokenizer and the morphological analyzer, were completed. A prototype of both modules is also available and is being tested with additional features for difficulty handling. As previously talk about, the planned architecture and system concept for this system Nepali Grammar Checker is subject to modifications as the results of their research are made public in the future.

In 2023, this paper's researchers [20] introduced Vyakranly as a Hindi Translation and Grammatical Error Detection Toolkit specifically designed for the Indian language Hindi. The primary aims of Vyakranly include the identification and rectification of spelling errors in Hindi text, the detection and repair of grammar errors in Hindi sentences, as well as the translation of English to Hindi and Hindi to English texts. Notable aspects of our research include the identification of Hindi spelling, as well as the detection of corrections and grammatical errors. Finding historical literature in Hindi is difficult because it lacks digital information and has a more intricate morphology than English.

In 2024, researchers [21] gave a solution under consideration that integrates an improved orthography corrector algorithm with a DeepSpeech2 model architecture that utilizes bilingual encoder symbol derived from transformers and gated recurrent units. The method used in this study enhanced existing decoding algorithms, such as greedy or prefix beam search. It utilized post-processing methods particularly tailored for alterations in the Gujarati language. To train the model, we collected high-quality Gujarati speech data from several speakers, both male and female, using crowd-sourcing. This ensured that we applied the most optimum parameter values. Overall, there was an important 17.20% decrease in word error rate (WER). Furthermore, this research examined a range of analytical methodologies aimed at detecting mistakes that arise from diacritics, consonants, independent components, homophones, and half-conjugates. The enhancement of the Automated speech recognition (ASR) system's general efficacy was attained by the acquisition of a more profound understanding of the Gujarati language and the subsequent use of these strategies.

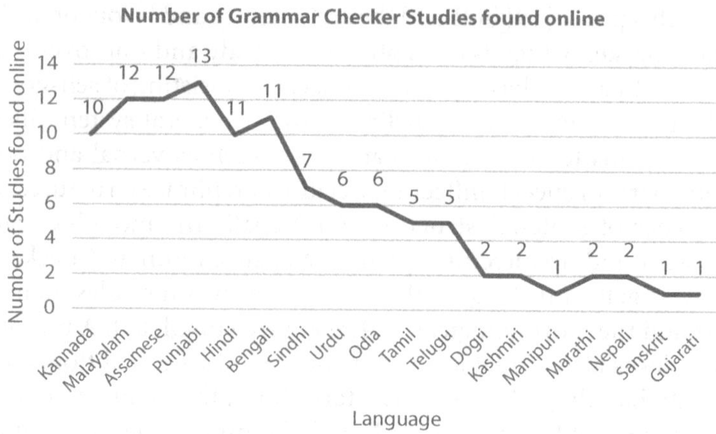

Figure 4.1 Indic language grammar checker research studies found online as of March 2024.

The graphical representation of the number of grammar checker studies found online up to March 2024 is shown in Figure 4.1. More than 109 research papers are available, all on purely Indian language grammar checkers. The highest number of research was found in South Indian languages compared to other Indian languages.

4.4 Spellchecker Related Work

In 2002, researchers [22] presented the Assamese Spellchecker are being considered. At first, the checker resorted to a dictionary lookup. If the dictionary did not have an entry for the term, a suggestion generator provided some replacements. After generating ideas using three different methods and ranking them, the final results were shown to the user. Spellchecker results were shown to be adequate in studies of manuscripts including over 5000 words, including juktaksharas. The Resource Centre for Indian Language Technology Solutions at the Indian Institute of Technology Guwahati is also looking into ways to include its Assamese to English online dictionary into the spellchecker software. Users may choose any of the two languages, type a word, and get the translation in the other. The spellchecker is being modified to work with the dictionary; currently, it exists as a Computer-generated imagery (CGI) software on the web server and its integration with the dictionary is under progress. Databases are made up of dictionaries, which include information on the term, including its definition, grammatical classification, pronunciation, pronunciation, antonyms, and synonyms. The performance of spell checking might be improved with the addition of an additional data set including the Soundex code of all Assamese words. Assamese bigram sequences have been gathered, and the list may be updated in the future. The code to identify spelling errors through a bigram search has also been built.

In 2012, the researchers [23] described the total design and implementation of a Kashmir Spellchecker and presented them this research paper. There were no things undertaken for the Kashmiri language, despite the fact that all main word processors present spell checking for English and in many European languages, with many Indian languages like Hindi, Urdu, Sanskrit, Tamil, and Kannada. The spellchecker for Kashmir that was developed is a standalone application that is not a component of any text editor. Researchers only corrected non-real word errors in this system. About 80% of errors are caught by the framework, and it offers 85% of the right suggestions. Future research will focus on the identification and correction of real word errors. This system can be used for other languages as well, but researchers should incorporate it as an add-on for Open Office and must first create a lexicon for those other language families.

In 2013 [31], this paper's researchers [24] discussed language authorities or consortiums that standardize word spellings, which are then made accessible in dictionaries or lexicons. For example, the word "produkt" is not included in the English dictionary. Therefore, in Urdu, "produkt" is a non-word but "produkt" is a properly spelt word. In today's digital world, text is often represented electronically. English is one of several languages with a variety of applications and additional tools. On the other hand, the creation of applications for less resource-intensive languages like Urdu is still in its infancy. When people compose material digitally on computers, spelling is crucial. The fact that terabytes of text are contributed in the form of corpora or other types of material that need to be spell checked and that doing so manually is very difficult is not taken into account. Numerous spell-checking methods were investigated and assessed in this paper. Spell checking may be done using each one of them independently or in combination. Reverse edit distance approach, a version of the edit distance technique, was used to recommend appropriate words for non-words in spellcheckers for many languages. For an Urdu word of length "n," candidates are selected by doing 86n+41 comparisons. Although the Urdu language has a rich literary history in South Asia, it lacks resources for computer-based projects. The spelling mistake detection and repair functionality in various electronic applications is the main emphasis of this study. The focus of this effort is on assembling a variety of spell-checking and error-correction methods that may be used to fix Urdu spelling mistakes. The difficulty of the reverse edit distance method is calculated to be 86n + 41. The method must be created for Urdu even if it has already been done for languages like English.

In 2015, the researchers [25] described Hindi Spellchecker. The three basic functions of this technology are error detection, error repair via providing recommendations, and error substitution. Approximately 83.2% of spelling mistakes are caught by the algorithm, which also offers 77.9% of the right word recommendations. The HINSPELL-Hindi spell checking system, which is not a feature of any word processor, is presented in this article. Only non-word mistakes are dealt with by this approach. Future studies will focus on actual grammatical faults. The system reports a detection rate of 83.2% and a correction rate of 77.9%. There is room for development in the deployment of SMT with lower reaction time as the correctness of the system grows but the system's answer time also increases after using SMTTechnique. HINSPELL may be adjusted for usage with various languages by changing the dictionary and keyboard.

In 2015, the researchers [9] described Tamil as a difficult inflectional language, which makes developing a morphological analyzer for it difficult for computer linguists. Tamil morphological generators and analyzers are being developed. Making a comprehensive and effective operating system is quite different from making a morphological generator or analyzer for demonstration purposes. Making a system that provides 60 to 65% coverage is not too difficult. It is challenging to raise efficiency over 65% and to a realistic level of 95% to 97%. Instead of being broad and detailed, the majority of the current descriptions concentrate on a vertical feature that is limited. The coverage that is attained by including the descriptions of the previous work is often never more than 50%. The assessment technique reveals that the effectiveness of the morphological analyzer created by the current team for Tamil is really impressive. The creation of a morphological analyzer, which includes the analysis of verbal complex, has several natural language applications, including lemmatization, text production, machine translation, and parsing. Additionally, it aids with document retrieval and word processing applications like spell checking and text input as well as voice applications like TTS synthesis and speech recognition. Assigning POS tags to the verbal complex is made easier by locating the categorical details of the verbal forms.

In 2016, the researchers [26] described a comprehensive plan and growth of a spellchecker for Kashmir and presented this as the research paper's main goal. There have not been anything undertaken for the Kashmiri language, despite the fact that all main word processors offer spell checking for English and in many European languages, along with many Indian languages like Hindi, Urdu, Sanskrit, Tamil, and Kannada. The spellchecker for Kashmir that was developed is a small program that is not a component of any word processor. Researchers have only corrected non-real word errors in this system. About 80% of errors are caught by the system, and it offers 85% of the right recommendations. Future research will focus on the identification and alteration of real word fault. This system can be used for other languages as well, but researchers will have enforce it as an add-on for Open Office and will need to start creating a lexicon to use it.

In 2016, the researchers for this study [27] claimed that a spellchecker is a tool to evaluate words in a text, check their spelling, and, if a spelling error is found, provide recommendations for replacement terms. Numerous studies on spellcheckers for Indian and European languages are available. However, there are not many for Tamil, maybe due to the language's inherent difficulty and great inflectional complexity. This research suggests an efficient method for identifying and fixing errors in Tamil spell checking. A new hybrid method is put into practice by combining n-gram and stemming techniques with a tree-based algorithm. The results of our testing demonstrate that our system can accurately identify spelling errors and provide the majority of workable options for repairing misspelled words with at least 91% accuracy. The performance of mistake detection and correction modules for the Tamil language was compared in this study. In this regard, several test word sets were used to evaluate and apply the tree-based method, n-gram, minimal edit distance, stemming, and lemmatization techniques. The results show that the tree-based algorithm is a much better method for error identification than the other two approaches and that the n-gram methodology, which uses stemmed words, provides the greatest proposal for fixing misspelled words. The results of our testing show that our system can accurately identify spelling errors and provide the best advice for correcting misspelled words with at least 91% accuracy. The n-gram technique is unable to suggest a repair for misspelled words since the accuracy decrease is associated with terms that are not included in the created corpus.

In 2016, this paper's researchers [28] described a program called "Spell Checker" which deals with spelling mistakes and spelling variations (SV). All misspelled words are noted and given the opportunity to be corrected. The content is examined for spelling mistakes and suggestions for repair are given when using this software as an edit. Telugu is an agglutinating language with a highly intricate morphology and a voluminous system of morphophonemic. Telugu has both internal and exterior sandhi, which is something that is noticeable. Telugu has a lot of vocalic and consonantal sandhi, both of which have been extensively examined. It is a very difficult process to determine the precise sandhi kind and separate it suitably. An assortment of linguistic modifications at word borders are known as external sandhi. These modifications resemble phonological processes like deletion, insertion, and substation. In Telugu, external sandhi is often mirrored orthographically. In these situations, external sandhi results in the development of forms that are morphologically impossible to analyze, creating a challenge for all types of NLP applications. In this essay, researchers go into great depth on the Telugu external sandhi procedures and the Spell Checker computer software.

In 2018, the suggested study [29, 37] was the first of its type and an innovative endeavor that concentrated on utilizing deep learning to construct a spellchecker for Malayalam. Two procedures made up the spellchecker: mistake detection and repair. An LSTM-based neural network is used in the error detection part and is trained to recognize misspelled words and the exact location where the mistake happened. The F1 score is used to calculate the error detection accuracy. By choosing the most likely term from the list of candidate words, errors may be corrected. One of the difficulties in doing this task is the lack of clear data. This paper used a simple neural network model. The use of sophisticated neural network topologies for experimentation was hampered by limited computing resources. Despite these restrictions, the suggested approach outperformed the conventional unicode splitting techniques. The outcomes may be significantly enhanced with access to massive clean corpora. Advanced neural network models [38, 39] still need improvement, and it is time to compare their performance to that of the current spell checking techniques. This investigation demonstrates that the word splitting used in the suggested strategy outperformed unicode splitting. Deep learning [40] was used to construct a spellchecker that is capable of both mistake detection and repair. The character level spellchecker for Malayalam is hopeful and merits more investigation.

In 2019, the researchers of this paper [30] prepared the primary objective of this paper which is to provide the best possible alternative spellings for Bengali terms and to identify instances where they have been misused. Any technique that utilizes the Bengali language may take advantage of the platform designed to verify spelling since it is a universal component that can be included into any system. Because of its intricate nature and grammatical constraints, developing an effective spellchecker for Bengali is usually a significant undertaking. The rule is frequently broken in Bengali, which is termed exceptional. In light of this, researchers offer an algorithm that is a clever hybrid of many well-known methods, such as edit distance and Soundex matching. Researchers can predict which incorrect Bengali words are most likely to be suggested after combining existed algorithms and running them through the decoding Bangla familiar to the algorithms.

In 2020, according to the paper's reviewer [31], the functionality of word processors, search engines, and social media platforms is heavily reliant on their grammar and spell checks. Spellcheckers are language-analysis programs that scan a text for spelling errors. If there are any accidental typos in the content, the user is alerted. Researchers are in need of a thorough investigation of the field of spell-checking, including aspects such as power, limitations, handled errors, performance, and evaluation standards. Spellcheckers for some languages are available in literature, and although they all have distinct designs, they all have similar features. This study applies the principles of a methodical literature re-examination of the domain of spell-checking. The methods of the methodical literature re-examination are used on 130 selected articles that were published in prestigious journals, conferences, and workshops related to the subject of spell checking more languages, and a wider variety of creations. During these stages, research questions are developed, research papers are chosen, inclusion and exclusion criteria are used, and pertinent data is extracted from the selected research articles. The major sub-areas of the literature on spell checking are categorized by language. Afterwards, each sub-area is covered in depth based on the method used. To get the outcome of this study, a number of articles are evaluated according to predetermined standards. This article explains how spellcheckers may be created using techniques from different domains, such as morphology, POS, chunking, stemming, and hash tables. It also describes the main problems that researchers ran across and the direction that spell-checking research will go in the future. A basic linguistic tool of NLP, spellcheckers are used in email clients, social media, search engines, information extraction, proofreading, and information retrieval, among other uses. In order to clearly distinguish between them, the spellcheckers of any language are evaluated based on the scripts, approach used, available tools, corpus size, performance, and error handled. The comparative research indicated above also helps choose the spellchecker that fits the language category in question the best in terms of accuracy and ease of use. Of all the spellcheckers available, the Assamese language's categorization and confusion-set-based spellchecker is the finest. Nonetheless, there are two notable spellcheckers available for distinct scripts in the Punjabi language group, and they are both rather effective. Additionally, the n-gram-based spell checking performs very well in the Tamil language category, while the Medical (MED)-based spellchecker carry out best in the Urdu language area. Existing spellcheckers for Telugu are based on depth algorithms and statistical techniques. The spellchecker based on deep learning performs better in this language area. The n-gram and MED based spellchecker for Malayalam produce the same results as other spellcheckers available today. Moreover, there is a single spellchecker for other languages like Sindhi, Odia, and Kashmiri, and it works really well. This article also describes the use of rule-based, statistical, and deep learning technologies in the spell-checking industry. The rule-based techniques do check for spelling by using heuristics based on chunking, stemming, morphology, and POS. The statistical methods use word counts, word frequencies, and word characteristics for spell checking. While statistical and rule-based techniques are quite effective in identifying non-word errors, their applicability to real-world errors is restricted. Spellcheckers based on deep learning are necessary to manage such errors. These techniques work rather well in preventing real-world errors. Although research on magical deep learning methods is still in its early stages, the encouraging results thus far suggest that similar techniques might be useful in the future for other languages to enhance spell-checking performance. This article also describes the challenges faced by the researchers, such as the complexity of time and space, the inability to distinguish words in certain scripts that are context-sensitive, and having to understand context-sensitive spelling.

In 2020, the researchers [32] described that the lives of a sizable portion of computer users are made possible by the unseen but essential role played by spellcheckers. The majority of text-manipulating software, including office packages with anything from basic note-taking tools to fully functional word processors and search engines, are included with it. Text is tokenized by spellcheckers to check for grammatical and spelling mistakes. Although they function for the majority of European languages, existing spellcheckers do not take into consideration the linguistic characteristics of Indian languages like Tamil. There is an additional complication to how Tamil text should be treated for tools like spell checking due to problems with Tamil's unicode encoding representation. Three alternative spellcheckers—bloom-filter, symspell, and LSTM-based—are implemented and tested for Tamil. For lookup recommendations and validation, Symspell is quite quick. Although not precise enough for daily usage, LSTM implementation is an intriguing area of research that has not yet been fully explored. Despite the fact that it is difficult to develop a fully automated spellchecker, it is worthwhile to try to make one since spelling and grammar checking is essentially an Artificial general intelligence (AGI) issue. The current spellcheckers operate in various situations using a variety of different criteria. Grammarly and other such programs are excellent for English. Due to its current infrastructure, it has daily access to a vast quantity of data that it can use to learn from and enhance its algorithms. Researchers look forward to creating such a platform for Tamil with the help of the collective effort from the Tamil speaking community, even if our endeavor is just an initial step in that regard.

In 2021, the researchers of this paper [33] prepared and introduced a Gujarati spellchecker tool 'Jodani,' which is a mechanism on root words and employs string similarity metrics to recognize incorrectly spelled words before attempting to auto-correct the word or suggest syntactically appropriate terms. Jodani determines the proper spelling of a Gujarati word and returns a list of recommendations for the wrong word. The spelling accuracy and list of suggestions are created using the Levenshtein edit distance, and procedures for handling inflected words and sorting the suggestions are devised. The accuracy of 91.56% demonstrates the effectiveness of Jodani's method, which outperforms the existing Gujarati spellchecker. Further improvements can be made by overcoming the assumption that the initial character of the entered word is valid. Machine learning approaches, such as the neural network, can also be used to enhance the order of suggestions.

In 2022, this paper's researchers [34] discussed that a spellchecker is a piece of software that indicates words in a text that could be misspelled. Regardless of the language, a spellchecker is a necessary function of any word processor. The spellchecker looks for misspelled words in the written text and offers the finest correction options. In this study, a hybrid design and implementation method was used for the first time to create a Dogri spellchecker. The main parts of this system are error detection, suggestion-based error correction, and manual or automated error replacement following the suggested technique. The system discovered 80.79% of misspelled words and accurately proposed 74.72% of incorrect words.

In 2023, this paper's researchers [35] found an analysis of the construction of a model aimed at identifying incorrect Assamese words inside digital information. When deciding the spelling of a word, the proposed model considered the contextual information inside the sentence. The comment underscores the fact that many Assamese words possess several interpretations and may not align with the intended context of a given remark while being written accurately as per the dictionary. The chosen methodology utilized two distinct ML methodologies, namely LSTM and bidirectional long short-term memory (BiLSTM). The findings indicated that the suggested move towards significantly improving the identification of spelling errors in the Assamese language, surpassing the presentation of other studies. The BiLSTM model achieved the highest accuracy of 89.52% in the suggested strategy.

In 2024, This research [36] aimed to remedy the lack of a reference point for the job by creating a comprehensive parallel corpus consisting of 7.7

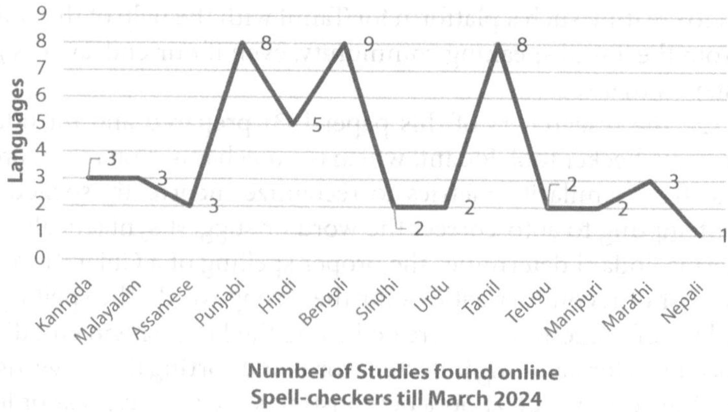

Figure 4.2 Indic language Spellchecker research studies found online as of March 2024.

million source-target pairs. Additionally, we investigated the unexplored capabilities of transformers. In addition to the corpus, we presented a novel approach called Panini, which utilizes transfer learning to achieve well-organized, monolingual, transformer-based correction of Bangla grammatical errors. This method has gained recognition as the leading approach for this task, outperforming both BanglaT5 and T5-Small by 18.81% and 23.8% in terms of accuracy scores, and 11.5 and 15.6 in terms of SacreBLEU scores, respectively. The technique's empirical results provide evidence supporting its superiority over other techniques in capturing complex language rules and patterns. Furthermore, we compared the effectiveness of our suggested approach to the Bangla paraphrase task. This comparison demonstrates its higher performance, surpassing the previous cutting-edge technique in this work. The BanglaGEC corpus and Panini, as well as the baselines for BGEC and the Bangla paraphrase task, are openly available resources.

A graphical depiction of the number of spellchecker studies available online as of March 2024 can be seen in Figure 4.2. There are more than 50 research publications available that focus just on spellchecking in the Indian language. Bengali and Punjabi languages have the most study findings when compared to other Indian languages.

4.5 Conclusion

Overall, this study describes the current scenario of an NLP-based spell and grammar checker system for Indian languages. A total of six types of spell and grammar checker development techniques are explained very briefly. Afterwards, researchers focus on in-depth spell and grammar checker studies with a critical explanation of each paper. Through that critical discussion, one can find the research gap in the current system. If one can work on Indian languages based on NLP research, this system may help them elaborate on their research in the right way. The main issue of Indic languages NLP research is the limited resources of each language, mainly datasets. One can find his or her own way to the next NLP research path through this study in the context of Indian languages only.

References

1. Kabir, H., Nayyer, S., Zaman, J., Hussain, S., Two pass parsing implementation for an Urdu grammar checker, in: *Proceedings of IEEE international multi topic conference*, pp. 1–8, 2002.
2. Kabir, H., Two-pass parsing implementation for an Urdu Grammar Checker. *International Multi Topic Conference, 2002. Abstracts. INMIC 2002*, pp. 51–51, 2002, doi: 10.1109/INMIC.2002.1310158.
3. Bal, B.K., Shrestha, P., Pustakalaya, M.P., Dhoka, N.P., Architectural and system design of the Nepali grammar checker, in: *PAN localization working paper*, 2007.
4. Gill, M. and Gurpreet, L,., A Grammar Checking System for Punjabi. *IEEE – International Conference*, 1, 149–152, 2008.
5. Gill, M.S., Lehal, G.S., Joshi, S.S., Part-of-speech tagging for grammar checking of Punjabi. *Linguist. J.*, 8, 6–22, 2009.
6. Bopche, L. and Dhopavakar, G., Rule Based Grammar Checking System for Hindi. *J. Inf. Syst. Commun.*, 3, 1, 45–47, 2012, ISSN: 0976-8742 & E-issn: 0976-8750.
7. Kaur, J. and Kamal, G,., Hybrid Approach for Spell Checker and Grammar Checker for Punjabi. *Int. J. Comput. Sci. Software Eng.*, 4, 6, 62–67, June 2014.
8. Sarma, H., Das, D., Kashyap, K., Grammatical Error Detection Model for Assamese Sentences. *Int. J. Adv. Res. Comput. Commun. Eng.*, 4, 11, 529–531, 2015.
9. Sankaravelayuthan, R., Spell and grammar checker for Tamil', 1, Wiley, 2015, 10.13140/RG.2.1.3700.6803.
10. Sharma, and Lehal, G.S., Improving existing Punjabi Grammar Checker. *2016 International Conference on Computational Techniques in Information and Communication Technologies (ICCTICT)*, pp. 445–449, 2016, doi: 10.1109/ICCTICT.2016.7514622.
11. Sharma, S.K. and Lehal, G.S., Improving existing Punjabi Grammar Checker. *2016 International Conference on Computational Techniques in Information*

and Communication Technologies (ICCTICT), New Delhi, India, pp. 445–449, 2016, doi: 10.1109/ICCTICT.2016.7514622.
12. Schmaltz, A., Alexander, Y.K., Rush Stuart, M., Shieber, M., Adapting Sequence Models for Sentence Correction. *Proceedings of the 2017 Conference on Empirical Methods in Natural Language Processing*, Copenhagen, Denmark, pp. 2807–2813, Association for Computational Linguistics, Harvard University, September 7–11, 2017.
13. Patel, N. and Patel, D., Research review of Rule Based Gujarati Grammar Implementation with the Concepts of Natural Language Processing (NLP), 1, Wiley, 2018, 10.6084/m9.jetir.JETIRA006276.
14. Mittal, M., Sharma, S.K., Sethi, A., Detection and Correction of Grammatical Errors in Hindi Language, Using Hybrid Approach. *Int. J. Comput. Sci. Eng.*, 7, 5, 421–426, May 2019, E-issn: 2347-2693.
15. Hulipalled, B. C, V. R. and Simha, J.B., Kannada Grammar Checker Using LSTM Neural Network. *2020 International Conference on Smart Technologies in Computing, Electrical and Electronics (ICSTCEE)*, Bengaluru, India, pp. 332–337, 2020, doi: 10.1109/ICSTCEE49637.2020.9277479.
16. Alothman, A. and Alsalman, A.M., An Arabic Grammar Auditor Based on Dependency Grammar. *Adv. Hum. Comput. Interact.*, 2020, 10 pages, 2020, Article ID 8856843 https://doi.org/10.1155/2020/8856843.
17. Fahim Faisal, A.N.M., Rahman, M.A., Farah, T., A Rule-Based Bengali Grammar Checker. *2021 Fifth World Conference on Smart Trends in Systems Security and Sustainability (WorldS4)*, London, United Kingdom, pp. 113–117, 2021, doi: 10.1109/WorldS451998.2021.9514031.
18. Murugesapillai, D., Ravinthirarasa, A., Dias, G., Sarveswaran, K., Neural-based Tamil Grammar Error Detection, in: *Proceedings of the First Workshop on Parsing and its Applications for Indian Languages*, NIT Silchar, India, NLP Association of India (NLPAI), pp. 27–32, 2021.
19. Bal, B.K., Shrestha, P., Madan, P., Pustakalaya, Patandhoka, Nepal, Architectural and System Design of the Nepali Grammar Checker, 1, Wiley, 2022.
20. S., R., S., V., T., S., K., R., Gadhikar, L., Vyakranly : Hindi Grammar & Spelling Errors Detection and Correction System. *2023 5th Biennial International Conference on Nascent Technologies in Engineering (ICNTE)*, Navi Mumbai, India, pp. 1–6, 2023, doi: 10.1109/ICNTE56631.2023.10146610.
21. Bhagat, B. and Dua, M., Improved spell corrector algorithm and deepspeech2 model for enhancing end-to-end Gujarati language ASR performance, e-Prime. *Adv. Electr. Eng. Electron. Energy*, 7, 100441, 2024, ISSN 2772-6711, https://doi.org/10.1016/j.prime.2024.100441.
22. Das, M., Borgohain, S., Gogoi, J., Nair, S.B., Design and implementation of a spell checker for Assamese, in: *Language Engineering Conference, 2002. Proceedings*, IEEE, pp. 156–162, 2002.
23. Lawaye, A.A. and Purkayastha, B.S., Kashmiri spell checker and suggestion system. *Communications*, 21, 2, 123, 2012.

24. Iqbal, S., Anwar, W., Bajwa, U., II, Rehman, Z., Urdu spell checking: Reverse edit distance approach, in: *Proceedings of the 4th workshop on south and southeast asian natural language processing*, pp. 58–65, 2013.
25. Mishra, A. K., Tyagi, A. K., Dananjayan, S., Rajavat, A., Rawat, H., Rawat, A., Revolutionizing Government Operations: The Impact of Artificial Intelligence in Public Administration, in: *Conversational Artificial Intelligence*, pp. 607–634, 2024.
26. Lawaye, A. and Purkayastha, Design and Implementation of Spell Checker for Kashmiri. *Int. J. Sci. Res.*, 5, 199–200, 2016.
27. Sakuntharaj, R. and Mahesan, S., A novel hybrid approach to detect and correct spelling in Tamil text. *2016 IEEE International Conference on Information and Automation for Sustainability (ICIAfS)*, Galle, Sri Lanka, pp. 1–6, 2016, doi: 10.1109/ICIAFS.2016.7946522.
28. Uma Maheshwar Rao, G. and Amba, P., *Kulkarni, Christopher Mala & Parameshwari K., 2012*, Telugu Spell-Checker. Vaagartha, Editors- Shivarama Padikkal Tariq Khan, p. 57, 2022.
29. Sooraj, S., Manjusha, K., Kumar, M., Soman, K.P., Deep learning based spell checker for Malayalam language. *J. Intell. Fuzzy Syst.*, 34, 1427–1434, 2018, 10.3233/JIFS-169438.
30. Saha, S., Tabassum, F., Saha, K., Akter, M., Bangla spell checker and suggestion generator PhD diss, United International University, USA, 2019.
31. Singh, S. and Singh, S., Systematic review of spell-checkers for highly inflectional languages. *Artif. Intell. Rev.*, 53, 4051–4092, 2020, https://doi.org/10.1007/s10462-019-09787-4.
32. Murugan, S., Bakthavatchalam, T.A., Sankarasubbu, M., *SymSpell and LSTM based Spell-Checkers for Tamil*, Wiley - USA, 2020.
33. Patel, H., Patel, B., Lad, K., Jodani: A spell checking and suggesting tool for Gujarati language. *2021 11th International Conference on Cloud Computing, Data Science & Engineering (Confluence)*, pp. 94–99, 2021, doi: 10.1109/Confluence51648.2021.9377072.
34. Jamwal, S.S. and Gupta, P., A Novel Hybrid Approach for the Designing and Implementation of Dogri Spell Checker, in: *Data, Engineering and Applications. Lecture Notes in Electrical Engineering*, vol. 907, S.L. Peng, J. Agrawal, R.K. Shukla, D.N. Le (Eds.), Springer, Singapore, 2022, https://doi.org/10.1007/978-981-19-4687-5_53.
35. Phukan, R., Neog, M., Baruah, N., A Deep Learning Based Approach For Spelling Error Detection In The Assamese Language. *2023 14th International Conference on Computing Communication and Networking Technologies (ICCCNT)*, Delhi, India, 2023, doi: 10.1109/ICCCNT56998.2023.10306972.
36. Hossain, N., Bijoy, M.H., Islam, S. *et al.*, Panini: a transformer-based grammatical error correction method for Bangla. *Neural Comput. Applic.*, 36, 3463–3477, 2024, https://doi.org/10.1007/s00521-023-09211-7.

37. Rathi, M. and Rajavat, A., Investigations and Design of Privacy-Preserving Data Mining Technique for Secure Data Publishing. *Int. J. Intell. Syst. Appl. Eng.*, *11*, 9s, 351–367, 2023.
38. Dubey, P. and Rajavat, A., Effective K-means clustering algorithm for efficient data mining, in: *2023 2nd International Conference on Vision Towards Emerging Trends in Communication and Networking Technologies (ViTECoN)*, IEEE, pp. 1–6, 2023, May.
39. Shrivastava, M., Patil, R., Bhardwaj, V., Rawat, R., Telang, S., Rawat, A., Quantum Computing and Security Aspects of Attention-Based Visual Question Answering with Long Short-Term Memory. *Quantum Comput. Cybersecur.*, 1, 395–412, 2023.
40. Rawat, R., Chakrawarti, R.K., Raj, A.S.A., Mani, G., Chidambarathanu, K., Bhardwaj, R., Association rule learning for threat analysis using traffic analysis and packet filtering approach. *Int. J. Inf. Technol.*, *15*, 6, 3245–3255, 2023.

5

Identification of Gujarati Ghazal Chanda with Cross-Platform Application

Brijeshkumar Y. Panchal

Computer Engineering Department, Sardar Vallabhbhai Patel Institute of Technology (SVIT)-Vasad, Gujarat Technological University (GTU), Anand, Gujarat, India

Abstract

Ghazal is a well-known poetry form of Indian literature. The Ghazal genre is centuries old, dating back to seventh-century Arabic poetry. In the 12th century, the Ghazal moved throughout South Asia. A Ghazal is a lyrical representation of both the anguish of loss or estrangement and the pleasure of love in the midst of that pain. As with many other languages, Guajarati Ghazal has numerous types of Gujarati Ghazal "Chanda". In this chapter, the researcher attempted to identify Gujarati Ghazal "Chanda" in the form of percentage using an android application and website platform. This researcher used the concept of Unicode, by inputting the string and converting it into characters. Then, their Unicode is generated and pushed into the stack. The output is compared with the fixed Unicode defined for the Gujarati character; if they matched, then the input in the new string will be in the form of 1's and 2's, which are then compared within the HashMap, and if they matched, it will give the output for the same simple Unicode. In the current scenario with few research gaps, the system has 72% accuracy for the identification of Gujarati Ghazal Chanda. The Gujarati language history, Ghazal history, and how to attempt a Ghazal are the contents of this chapter.

***Keywords*:** Identification of chanda, Gujarati, Ghazal, chanda, cross-platform, identification chanda, poetry

---

Email: panchalbrijesh02@gmail.com

Rajesh Kumar Chakrawarti, Ranjana Sikarwar, Sanjaya Kumar Sarangi, Samson Arun Raj Albert Raj, Shweta Gupta, Krishnan Sakthidasan Sankaran and Romil Rawat (eds.) Natural Language Processing for Software Engineering, (71–94) © 2025 Scrivener Publishing LLC

Abbreviations

Ghazal	ગ઼ઝલ
Chand	છંદ
Matlaa	મત્લા
Radif	રદિફ
Qaafiyaa	કવ્વાલી
Maqtaa	મક્તા
Beher	બહેર
Misra	મશિરાઆ
Śēra	શેર

5.1 Introduction

5.1.1 The Gujarati Language

Gujarati is classified as an element of the southwestern part of the New Indo-Aryan language family, which is a subdivision of the Indo-Iranian stem of the Indo-European language relatives [1]. Gujarati is the official language of the Gujarat state and is widely spoken in various regions of South Asia, including Maharashtra, Rajasthan, Sind, lower Punjab, Madhya Pradesh, and Karnataka [2]. The Parsi, Hindu, Muslim, and Jain communities in the Persian Gulf, East and South Africa, Britain, North America, and Australia also speak Gujarati. Gujarati is the sixth most prevalent language in India in terms of resident speakers, with 55.5 million individuals speaking it, accounting for around 4.5% of the overall Indian population as of 2011. As of 2007, the number of native speakers ranked it as the 26th most commonly used tongue on a global scale. Subjects of study include history and literature [3]. Old Gujarati, Middle Gujarati, and Modern Gujarati are three distinct periods in the history of the Gujarati language. Old Gujarati refers to the period from the 12th to the 15th centuries; Middle Gujarati refers to the period from the 15th to the 18th centuries; and Modern Gujarati refers to the period from the 18th century onward [4].

The origins of this may be traced back to a specific literary form in Old Western Rajasthani, even though there is evidence of Jain Prakrit discourse and studies by Middle Indian grammarians of Nagara Apabhramsa, a literary Apabhramsa of Gujarat. The Bharates-varabahubaliräsa, composed in 1185, is the oldest known Gujarati literary work from the 12th century [5]. There are collections of prose and poetry that were composed starting in the 13th century. These collections consist of the regular poem Vasantaviläsa and the 14th-century commentary called the Sadavaśyakabalabodhavrtti. Narasimha Mehta's (c. 1414–1488) devotional songs ushered in a new period in poetry and earned a prominent position in its literary history. *Mumbai Samăcar*, a Gujarati daily founded in 1822, is among the most ancient newspapers in Asia. The Bombay Parsis engages in recreation a pioneering role in the growth of Gujarati and Urdu theater [6] as shown in Figure 5.1, which illustrates the vowels of the Gujarati language [7].

Dialects of Gujarati, spoken along the Baroda-Ahmedabad Corridor, is considered as the standard or prestigious dialect [7]. The question is whether the list of Nagari Brhma's carries the same meaning. The position of recurrent platform ("RP") is subject to debate. Additional variations of the Gujarati language are Surati, Carotari, Käthiwārī, and Pātānī, which correspond to the southern, central, Saurashtra, and northern regions of Gujarat, respectively [8]. Pakistani Gujarati is likely a subdialect of the Păţăni language, and the practice of code flipping is declining as the younger population transitions to Urdu and regional languages [9]. Speakers of the Muslim faith, both in that location and in other places, clearly use a significant number of words from the Perso-Arabic language, which is their second-greatest source of vocabulary after Sanskrit. This is particularly evident in discussions related to religion and culture. Parsi Gujarat, a kind of language used by the Zoroastrians of the Indian subcontinent, is easily understood. Swahili loanwords have been incorporated into the East African Gujarat language. Kacchi (Kachchi) is a language that is in the semantic middle ground between Gujarati and Sindhi, and it is also affected by Marwārī [10] as shown in Figures 5.2 and 5.3, which illustrate the consonants and conjunct consonants of the Gujarati language, respectively [7].

Figure 5.1 Vowels of the Gujarati language [7].

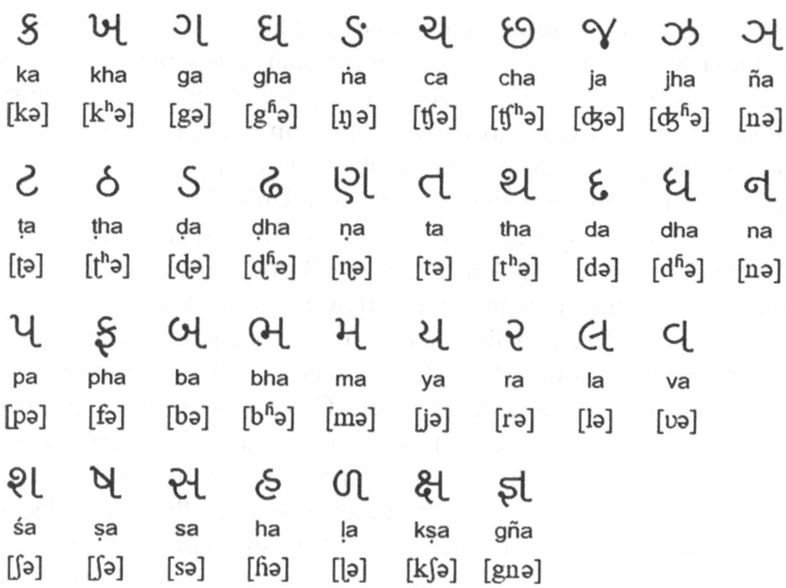

Figure 5.2 Consonants of the Gujarati language [7].

Figure 5.3 Conjunct consonants of the Gujarati language [7].

Gujart Grammar's phonetics are distinct due to the presence of muttered vowels that have evolved from the last /h/ sound, as well as two open vowels, /e/ and /5/. There is no difference in the length of the /i/ and /u/ vowels. Nouns, adjectives, and pronouns may be variable or invariable. There are three genders, counting the neuter, and two numbers. Direct and oblique forms undergo inflection, with the latter using post-positions

૦	૧	૨	૩	૪	૫	૬	૭	૮	૯
મીંડું	એકડો	બગડો	ત્રગડો	ચોગડો	પાંચડો	છગડો	સાતડો	આઠડો	નવડો
mīṃḍuṃ	ekaḍo	bagaḍo	tragaḍo	cogaḍo	pāṃcaḍo	chagaḍo	sātaḍo	āṭhaḍo	navaḍo
0	1	2	3	4	5	6	7	8	9

Figure 5.4 Numerals of the Gujarati language [7].

'મહાબલી' લખવાનો વિચાર સાત-આઠ વર્ષ પહેલાં આવ્યો હતો. મહાકવિ તુલસીદાસના (૧૫૩૨-૧૬૨૩) બે પ્રસંગોથી આકર્ષિત થયો હતો. એમને ૧૬મી સદીમાં વિચારોનું લોકતંત્રિકરણ કરવાનું જે જોખમ ઉઠાવ્યું હતું, તે આજે પણ સરાહનીય છે. તુલસીદાસ દ્વારા 'રામચરિતમાનસ' (૧૫૭૪-૧૫૭૬) લખાયા પહેલાં રામકથા પર વર્ણ વિશેષનો એકાધિકાર હતો. રામકથા બધાં માટે સુલભ ન હતી. સાધારણ લોકો રામકથાના આદર્શો અને એના સંદેશા જાણવા માટે કથાવાચક બ્રાહ્મણો પર આશ્રિત હતા. તુલસીદાસે આ એકાધિકારને તોડી નાખ્યો હતો. મધ્યકાળમાં કોઈ ધાર્મિક એકાધિકારને તોડવો કઈ સરળ કામ નહોતું. એમને જે લગન અને નિર્ભરક્તાથી જોખમ ભર્યું કામ કર્યું હતું એ પ્રશંસાને પાત્ર છે.

Figure 5.5 Sample text in Gujarati.

and clitics [11]. Verbal forms exhibit distinctions in terms of time, modality, and aspect. Verbal nouns and adjectives with auxiliaries create a wide range of obligation and desiderative forms. The vocabulary is abundant in passive, causative, and double causative verbs (Cardona, 1965). Vector or compound verbs, which are often found in New Indo-Aryan languages, are used in limited situations with precise meanings [12] as shown in Figures 5.4 and 5.5, which present the numerals of the Gujarati language and sample text in Gujarati, respectively [7].

5.2 Ghazal

Ghazal is considered the core part of the people of Gujrat. Upon analysis, researchers of the current market noticed that no applications have been developed especially to find Chanda of Gujarati Ghazal. While discussing with various literature experts, this researcher came to know that this is a good initiative to start because new learners who will choose this field. This researcher had a chance to contribute to our native language [13].

Here, this researcher used the concept of the Unicode for the identification of Ghazal Chanda. What is Unicode? Unicode is a standard for computers created to reliably and individually encode characters found in all written languages worldwide. The Unicode standard uses hexadecimal to represent characters. For instance, the Latin letter A is defined by the number 0x0041. Thus, this researcher used this concept, by inputting the string and converting it into characters. Then, their Unicode is generated and pushed into the stack. The output is then compared with the fixed Unicode defined for the Gujarati character, and if they matched, then the input the new string will be in the form of 1's and 2's, which are then compared within the HashMap, and if they matched, it will give the output for the same Unicode. The second thing this researcher did for this project involves the accuracy calculator: inputting the string follows the same process of the Unicode method, and if it matches, it will give the accuracy percentage as output [14].

Furthermore, this researcher used a number of modules for performing the same operation to match the string with the HashMap table. This researcher also used the stack for inputting the data; if any Matra comes out after popping, it will give an output of 2 depending on its strength; otherwise, it will give an output of 1 for the single character as well as for the Matra with a lower strength, which helps us find the Chanda of the string.

Orthograph, a work from 1592 (Mistry, 1996), confirms that a script based on a version of Devanagari has been used to write Gujarat and Kacchi since the 16th century. When printing was introduced in the 1830s, a cursive style took the place of the traditional Sanskrit script that was previously employed in both prose and poetry. There are a total of 45 symbols used to indicate independent and conjunctive forms [14]. These symbols include 8 vowels, 34 consonants, anusvära, visarga, and a velar nasal grapheme. Gujarati, a language written from left to right, is notable for its lack of head strikes and its use of different phonemic alterations. Similar to other characters inherited from Brahmi, it is clear that a post-consonantal /a/ is implied in a consonant that does not include diacritics. The numbers originating from Devanagari were adopted, although the forms of the digits 3, 5, 6, and 9 were changed.

One can create a Ghazal in Gujarati by following these simple guidelines [15]:

1. Select a subject or topic for the Ghazal. This might be anything that inspires you, whether it is spirituality, nature, or love.
2. Put your Ghazal together with a sequence of topically as well as emotionally related couplets, or "sher." Every couplet

needs to be able to stand on its own and express a whole idea.

3. Continue the Ghazal using the same rhyming pattern. The most typical pattern in Gujarati ghazals is AA, BA, CA, and so on, with the rhyme scheme being the same in both lines of each couplet.
4. In every couplet, use the radif, a word or phrase that repeats at the end of the second line. The Ghazal is more cohesive and has a feeling of flow because of its refrain.
5. Through the couplets, convey your feelings, ideas, and visuals while eloquently and poetically expressing the core of the selected topic.
6. The Ghazal's meter and rhythm should be observed since they enhance its melody and impact.

These instructions will help you write a stunning and moving Gujarati Ghazal.

5.3 History and Grammar of Ghazal

The Ghazal form has been around for centuries, going all the way back to seventh century Arabic poetry. The popularity of Ghazal increased over South Asia in the eleventh century. A Ghazal is a poetic look of the grief of loss or alienation, as well as the joy of love in the midst of such misery. Now, focus on Chanda; what is Chanda? It is the study of poetic meters and verse from numerous Gujarati Ghazalkar; learners may understand the structure of Ghazal and its five rules, namely, "Matlaa", "Radif", "Qaafiyaa", "Maqtaa", and "Beher" [16]. The basic unit of ghazal is Śēra. A ghazal is made up of three or more stocks. The shares of a ghazal are connected by the same rhyme, the same type of kafia, and the same verse. Two rows of a share are called two Misra. The first syllable of the ghazal is called Matla, both of which have to maintain the Radif-Kafia scheme in Misra. The Radif-Kafia scheme established in Matla then has to be carried out throughout the ghazal. Matla can be more than one. Shares other than Matla do not have a Radif in the first Misra. In the second Misra, the plan of Radif-Kafia has to be maintained [17, 18] as given in Table 5.1. Understanding Matra with a poetic line is shown in Table 5.2.

In Ghazal, researchers can identify Ghazal Chanda in a word-to-word and a character-to-character basis. Note that if one character has 1 matra, it means it is લ; if there are 2 matras, it means it is ગા.

Table 5.1 Understanding Matra.

1 = લ
2 = ગા

Table 5.2 Understanding Matra with a poetic line.

એ	ક	ધા	રી	ફૂ	લ	ની	કે	વી	અ	દા	છે
ગા	લ	ગા	ગા	ગા	લ	ગા	ગા	ગા	લ	ગા	ગા
2	1	2	2	2	1	2	2	2	1	2	2

Take an example of Ghazal with a few Chandas:

(1) એકધારી ફૂલની કેવી અદા છે.-
ગાલગાગા / ગાલગાગા / ગાલગાગા-
2122/2122/2122 - ખફીફ છંદ.

(2) ઝરુખે ખીલી છે ઉદાસી –
લગાગા / લગાગા / લગાગા – 1
122 / 122 / 122 - મુતકારબિ છંદ

(3) સાથ ચાલી દુઃખી સૌને કરવા હતા-
ગાલગા / ગાલગા / ગાલગા / ગાલગા-
212 / 212 / 212 / 212 મુતદારકિ છંદ.

5.4 Literature Review

The study on part-of-speech tagging for Gujarati using conditional random fields was suggested by Chirag Patel and Karthik Gali in 2008. A machine learning approach for Gujarati part-of-speech tagging has been presented by the author. The machine learning portion is finished. A cross-platform (CRF) model is a useful tool to use. This is taken into consideration when selecting the attributes that CRF receives. Considering the linguistic component of Gujarati, Gujarati now has a lower position than other languages in terms of resource scarcity. There are only around 600 manually marked records. There are 26 tags in the tagset. Tags is the national language of India tagset (IL). The algorithm has a high success rate. Gujarati texts have a 92% accuracy rate. A total of 10,000 words make up the training corpus. The corpus for the test consists of 5,000 words. Researchers have trained a CRF on

Gujarati, which provides an insight into the language. With a 92% accuracy rate, researchers have learned from their experiments. It was discovered that if language-specific rules could be formed into CRF features, the accuracy would improve and can be attained at extremely high levels. The CRF is a group of people who work together to learn from both labeled (600 sentences) and untagged (600 sentences) data. In addition, there are untagged data, which total 5,000 sentences. We can deduct from the errors that the training was ineffective. As the amount of data grows, the number of terms that are unknown decreases will be found in the corpus of the exam, which will Increase the precision. We might also make use of a machine, lexicons, morphs, and other usable resources whenever they are constructed, etc. [19].

In 2013, Miral Patel and Prem Balani proposed a study on Clustering Algorithm for the Gujarati language. They assert that natural language processing is still a work in progress. Natural language processing entails assessing the language's structure and then accurately tagging each word with its grammar basis. Researchers have a set of 50,000 tagged words and are attempting to cluster those Gujarati words using a provided technique; they have also defined their own processing algorithm. There are numerous clustering algorithms available, for example, single linkage, complete linkage, and average linkage. The number of clusters that will be produced is unknown; therefore, it all depends on the data set provided. Clustering is a step in the stemming process. Stemming is the process of extracting the root from its term. "Cats", for example, is equal to cat+s, which means cat is a noun and is not plural. After clustering the tagging words, the results were quite evident, although clustering may be done with multiple languages and tag sets. The conclusion is that clustering with tagged words gives more than 98% accuracy, and clustering on tagged words is an intermediate step on the way to stemming [20].

In 2017, Utkarsh Kapadia and Apurva Desai proposed work on Rule-Based Gujarati Morphological Analyzer. In this chapter, the author also proposes a Rule-Based Gujarati Morphological Analyzer. Gujarati, like other Indo-Aryan languages such as Hindi and Marathi, has a large morphological vocabulary. Many NLP applications, such as machine translation, grammar inference, and information retrieval, require morphological analysis. Researchers have provided a morphological analyzer based on a rule-based approach in this research. We created a Gujarati morphological analyzer based on hand-coded inflectional and derivational rules derived from word and affix regularities. For sentence tagging, the same method was employed in the point-of-sale (POS) tagger. In addition, we have included a full account of the morphological phenomena found in

Gujarati. A lexical dictionary of root words is constructed. Manually generated rules are created in collaboration with linguists. The analyzer program accepts a Gujarati sentence and outputs its grammar class, gender, number, tense, and personal information, as well as its root words. Both inflectional and derivational morphemes are supported by the tool. Using material from essays and short stories, we were able to achieve an accuracy of 87.48%. Aside from its high accuracy, rule-based systems have some drawbacks. For starters, creating an exhaustive rule-based system for any natural language is tough. Second, if a suffix does not match any of the rules, the system may not produce any results. It is difficult to develop rules independent of language because they are so reliant on it [21].

The Gujarati Language: Research Issues, Resources, and Proposed Method on Word Sense Disambiguation is a paper that Tarjni Vyas and Amit Ganatra proposed in 2019. In this publication, the researchers spoke about the Gujarati language, word sense disambiguation (WSD), and Gujarati Wordnet. Because of this, it has been discovered that the deep learning strategy performs better in Gujarati WSD. However, one of its drawbacks is that it requires a large number of information sources, without which preparation is almost impossible. On the other hand, it employs information sources to choose word meanings in a particular context. Because of this, deep learning techniques seem to be more suitable for handling word meaning disambiguation, yet the procedure can never be simple since real languages are ambiguous. The contextual similarity between an example and an unknown paragraph is compared using this model. Use a growing number of training examples and choose the optimal features that include most of the vocabulary for effective generalization. Compared to Hindi, Gujarati has a more advanced use of colloquial terminology, which also differs by area. The Gujarati alphabet may contain words with multiple spellings since it is a more complex alphabet than the English alphabet. It is also likely that some data were saved with misspelled words since the writer of the data did not speak Gujarati. While solutions are suggested here, they are only the beginning; most strategies have not yet been investigated in Gujarati [22].

In 2019, Lata Gohil and Dharmendra Patel suggested a project on sentiment analysis of film reviews in the Gujarati language using machine learning. This text discusses the authors' description of how language is handled in a typical manner. It controls the presentation of data to determine the source's intention for the material. The cause might be attributed to either gratitude (positive) or academic investigation (negative). This work presents a connection between the results achieved by implementing the calculation arrangement using different classifiers, such as K-nearest-neighbor (KNN) and multinomial naive Bayes (MNB). The collected data have been carefully evaluated by considering the extreme film datasets and their correlation with the available evidence. This study examines the impact of the word level count vectorizer and term frequency-inverse document frequency (TF-IDF) on the sentiment analysis of films. The investigators found that the MNB classifier produces more precise outcomes when utilizing the TF-IDF vectorizer compared to the count vectorizer. Additionally, the KNN classifier yields similar accuracy results for both the TF-IDF and the count vectorizer. The researchers in this study compiled a film review dataset in the Gujarati language. They then applied two distinct machine learning-based classification techniques to this data-set, using count and TF-IDF vectorizer components. The objective was to evaluate the sentiment of movie evaluations in the Gujarati language. The findings of the sentiment study indicate that the TFIDF vectorizer features provide superior outcomes in comparison to the count vectorizer features. After evaluating the performance parameters of accuracy, recall, precision, and F-score, we found that the MNB model provided more accurate predictions when using TF-IDF data compared to count vectorizer data [23].

In 2020, Saif Ali Alsaidi, Ahmed T. Sadiq, and Hasanen S. Abdullah presented a study on the classification of English poetry utilizing text mining and rough set theory. The contributors discussed text classification, a technique of classifying articles into predetermined groups based on their textual content. This work aims to address the issue of categorizing poems in English into specific categories using text-mining techniques and machine-learning algorithms. In the suggested model, the authors used text preprocessing on the document file to decrease the number of features and minimize dimension. The preprocessing step transforms the textual poem into features and eliminates irrelevant features using text mining techniques such as tokenization, stop word removal, and stemming. To further reduce the feature vector, two feature selection methods were employed. The categorization task was then performed using rough set theory as the machine learning algorithm. The authors achieved a successful classification rate of 88% with the proposed model. Categorizing English poems is challenging without performing preprocessing steps to reduce the number of features. One way to achieve this is by removing stop words, which eliminates unimportant features. However, even after this step, there may still be a large number of features. To further reduce the features, stemming can be applied to bring many words back to the same root word. Finally, a filter for feature selection can be used to select the most significant characteristics [24].

In 2021, Bhavin Mehta and Bhargav Rajyagor proposed work on Gujarati poetry classification based on emotions using deep learning. They attempted to express emotions through Gujarati poetry by utilizing a range of characteristics found in Gujarati poems. Gujarati poems provide a unique perspective on sentiment capturing in this study. "Kavan" is a collection of Gujarati poems based on the Indian concept expressed in "Navarasa". More than 300 poems were grouped into nine feelings indicated in "Navarasa" in the anthology. The result accuracy of the emotion classification task from the Gujarati poetry corpus was determined to be up to 87.62%. The authors discovered that there was limited research study for the classification of Gujarati poetry on the basis of the notion of "Navarasa" after conducting a literature review. The emotions expressed in the poem have a close link to the poem; poets have written poems that are full of emotions. The authors of this study experimented with the Indian idea of "Navarasa" to establish an automatic system for classification of poetries based on emotions present in the poem. The authors have compiled a collection of poems known as the "Kavan" Gujarati poetry corpus. They found that their system functioned admirably for emotion identification and categorization from Gujarati poetry based on the results obtained [25].

In this research work, we presented a proposed model for word segmentation or "sandhi" in Gujarati language using a purely engineering-based approach. A slight effort is made to create a link between the concept of Gujarati Grammar and the reality of its execution. As a result, not every South Asian language is familiar with the grammar notion Sandhi. However, Gujarati, Tamil, Sanskrit, Devnagri, and Hindi all have a significant role in this concept. The term "language" in NLP refers to natural languages such as Gujarati, Hindi, and English, which humans use to communicate on a daily basis. The majority of NLP research has focused on English and other European languages. In the last few years, NLP research on Indian languages such as Gujarati has begun. This paper's main focus is on demonstrating the road map for implementing the Gujarati grammatical term "sandhi ()." Sandhi is a word segmentation technique that is found in most South Asian languages, including Devnagri, Sanskrit, Hindi, and Gujarati, as well as Chinese and Thai. "Sandhi causes phonetic alteration at the word boundaries of a written chunk (small section), and the sounds at the conclusion of the word combine to form a single chunk of the character sequence." The rule-based application of "sandhi" is the focus of our attention. Gujarati language (grammar) has its unique set of rules for mixing consonants, vowels, and modifiers, just like every other Indian scripting language. We have come up with a set of guidelines for putting "sandhi ()" into practice. There are numerous sandhi rules, each denoting a distinct set of phonetic alterations described in Gujarati grammatical tradition. The Sandhi does not modify the meaning or grammatical structure of the words in question. Sandhi is a voluntary procedure that is solely dependent on the writer's awareness. They presented a method for Gujarati sandhi splitting based on raw text words. Though the approach is only described for Gujarati, it might be used for any language if some stated rules are followed [26].

In 2022, Parita Shah, Priya Swaminarayan, and Maitri Patel stated in their work, "A Sentiment Analysis of Gujarati Text using Gujarati Senti word Net", that sentiment analysis is a critical component of decision-making. This region sees a lot of research for the English language. In comparison to English, there is very little development in this subject for Indian languages. Gujarati is a nearly undiscovered language for this assignment. People prefer to use their local language on the Internet; therefore, more data in the form of movie reviews, product evaluations, and social media posts, among others, are available in regional languages, necessitating the need to mine these data in order to comprehend their opinions. Several tools and resources have been produced for the English language, but just a handful have been established for Indian languages. Gujarati is a language with limited resources for this task. The goal of this study is to create a sentiment lexical resource for Gujarati that can be used to analyze sentiment in Gujarati literature. Gujarati SentiWordNet is based on Hindi SentiWordNet and IndoWordNet's synonym relations of words. We make a twofold contribution: the Gujarati SentiWordNet is being created, while the Gujarati corpus is being generated in order to assess the lexical resource that has been created. The usefulness of the generated resource is demonstrated by the evaluation result. By utilizing synonym relations, this method is used to construct G-SWN using Hindi SentiWordNet and IndoWordNet. The resulting resource can be used to analyze Gujarati text for sentiment. The proposed method can be used to build sentiment lexical resources for any of the IWN languages. The Gujarati tweets corpus was created to test the lexical resource that was generated. Two annotators annotated the corpus for positive and negative polarity classes. Cohen's kappa, a statistical measure of inter-annotator agreement, was 0.55 for this corpus. The resulting annotated corpus contains 863 tweets, 442 of which are positive and 421 are negative. The accuracy of G-SWN utilizing this gold standard corpora was 52.72% for unigram presence and 52.95% for simple scoring classifiers. Results demonstrate the moderate performance of G-SWN. G-SWN provides the baseline for further studies. Future work can become comprehensive by the creation and use of antonym family members. By incorporating WSD, higher accuracy can be achieved [27] as given in Algorithm 5.1: Ghazal Chand Identifier.

Proposed Algorithm:

Algorithm 5.1: Ghazal Chand Identifier

Input: Ghazal Line
Output: Chand of Given Line for Ghazal
Initialize: an array array[] with words of ghazal , token string

1. array[]=split[poem]; // delimiter = ' '(space)
2. for(word:array)
3. for (characterpoint : word)
4. stack.Push(character point)
5. while(stack!=empty)
6. if(size==1) then tokenstring+='1' and pop()
7. Else
8. Top = stack.pop()
9. Below = stack.pop()
10. If('top'+'below' = la)then tokenstring+='1'
11. Else tokenstring+='2'
12. Initialize Map<Integer, String> lagastring , fill with pre-defined tokens
13. For (Map.Entry<Integer,String> var : lagastring.entrySet())
14. Comparator percentage (tokenstring,var)

This is an algorithm of Ghazal Chand Identifier; it helps us to identify the Chand of ghazal. Initialize the map of Chand that is meant to match a line inputted for Ghazal Chand. Split the line with space as delimiter. Iterate over each word and then fill it in stack. Get the top two values and compare them to its combination. If it is a single letter, then add "1" to the token string. If the combination of code points corresponds to the letter ला, then add "1" to the token; if the combination of code points corresponds to the letter गा, then add "2" to the token . Similarly, generate the token and pass it to a percentage calculator parser function whose parameters are the values of the already initialized Chand tokens. Obtain the matching percentage from this function as shown in Figure 5.6.

5.5 Proposed System

There are five phases in the approach we use to create ghazal apps. Before working on the first line of any ghazal, you may want to read the first step (i/p લીમડાને આવી ગયો તાવ જીરે). The second phase is a transitional stage where the ghazal lines are combined into a single string without any white space in between. (short after trimming: લીમડાનેઆવીગયોતાવજીરે). In the previous step, the matras of the string produce tokens of numbers 1 for લ and 2 for ગા (Generation of token: 212222122122). In the following stage, the converted string of tokens 1 and 2 is compared to the system's predefined Chands. If the dataset matches, the Chand is created as an output as presented in Figures 5.7 to 5.13, respectively.

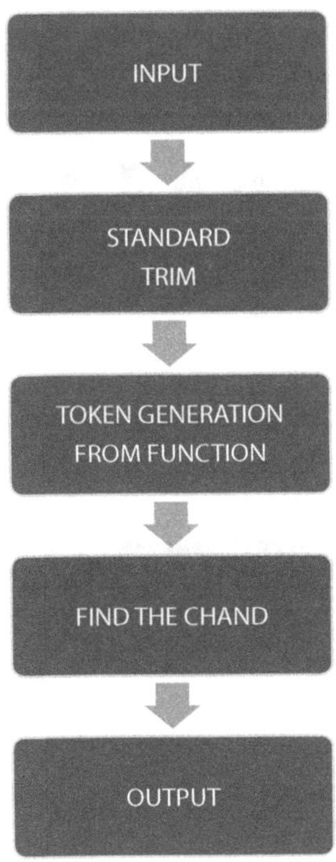

Figure 5.6 Proposed system.

Figure 5.7 Splash screen.

Figure 5.8 Login screen.

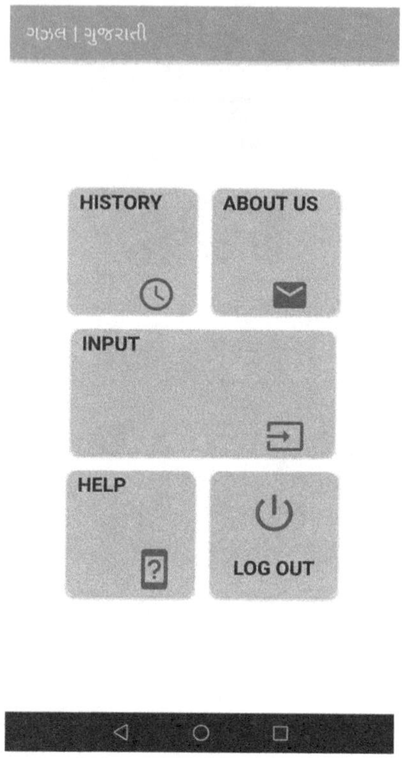

Figure 5.9 Home screen.

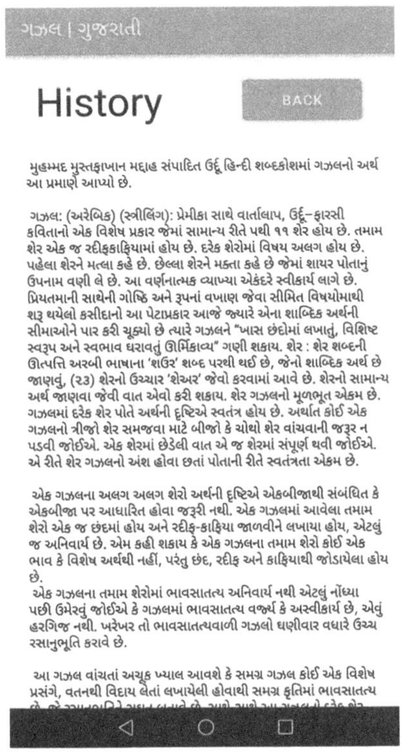

Figure 5.10 History screen.

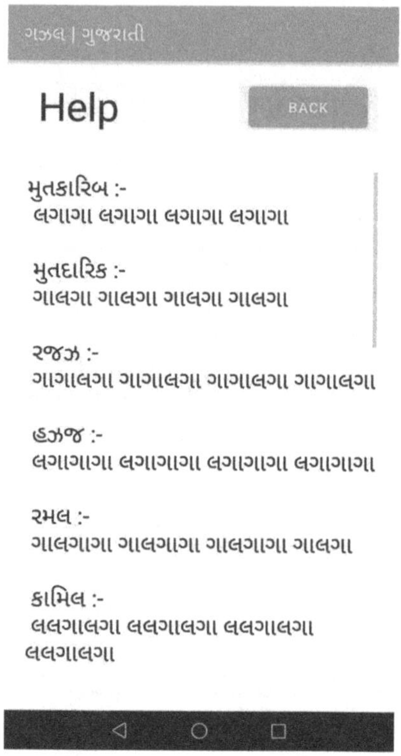

Figure 5.11 Help screen. Type of chanda.

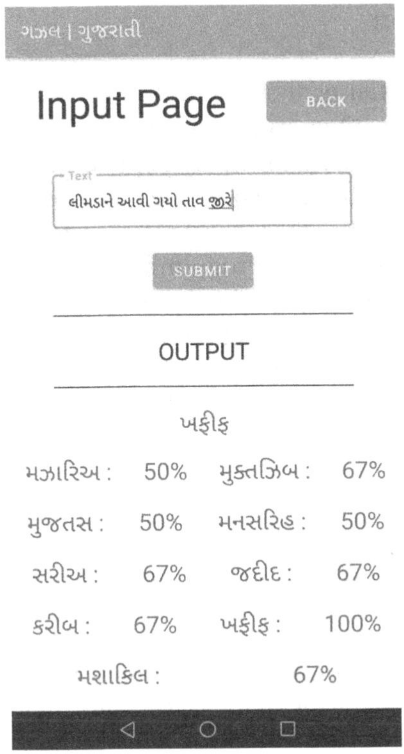

Figure 5.12 Ouput for Khafif Ghazal.

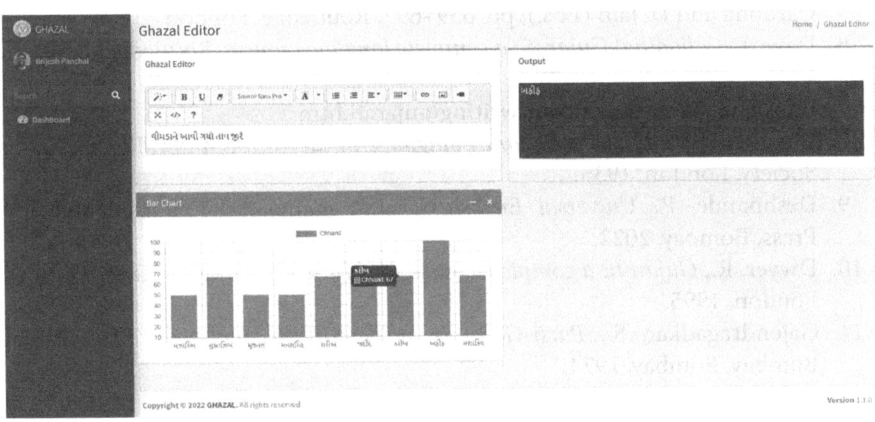

Figure 5.13 Website output for Khafif Ghazal.

5.6 Conclusion

This system is an initial or first attempt in the field of the Gujarati NLP research community. One can identify the Gujarati Ghazal Chanda through this system. Among the many popular genres of poems in Indian literature is the Ghazal. In this paper, researchers of this chapter developed a cross-platform to identify the Ghazal meter. A total of 19 meters are used in this system. Simple Python programming has been used in this proposed system. With the help of this system, budding writers of Gujarati may improve their poetry writing. Gujarati language history, grammar, and steps of the Gujarati Ghazal writing process are described in this chapter. Overall, this chapter's content may be quite beneficial to Gujarati language lovers.

References

1. Acharya, S., *Kacchi sabdávali [Kutchi vocabulary)*, Gujarat Vidyapith, Ahmedabad, 1966.
2. Acharya, S., *Halari dialect*, Gujarat Vidyapith, Ahmedabad, 1985.
3. Bhandari, A., *Gujarati vakyaracanã [Gujarati syntax)*, University Grantha Nirmāṇa Board, Ahmedabad, 1990.
   Bhayani, H., *Gujarati bhāṣhanum aitihäsika vyakarana [A historical grammar of Gujarati)*, Gujarat sahitya akādami, Gandhinagar, 1988.
4. Cardona, G., *A Gujarati reference grammar*, University of Pennsylvania Press, Philadelphia, 1965.
5. Cardona, G. and Suthar, B., Gujarati, in: *The Indo-Aryan languages*, G. Cardona and D. Jain (Eds.), pp. 659–697, Routledge, London, 2003.
6. Dave, J., *Colloquial Gujarati: a complete language course*, Routledge, London, 1995.
7. https://www.omniglot.com/writing/gujarati.htm
8. Dave, T., *A study of the Gujarati language in the 16th century*, Royal Asiatic Society, London, 1935.
9. Deshpande, P., *Universal English-Gujarati dictionary*, Oxford University Press, Bombay, 2022.
10. Dwyer, R., *Gujarati: a complete course for beginners*, Hodder Headline PLC, London, 1995.
11. Gajendragadkar, S., *Parsi-Gujarati: a descriptive analysis*, University of Bombay, Bombay, 1974.
12. Joshi, U., Raval, A., Shukal, Y. (Eds.), Gujarati sahityano itihasa, in: *History of Gujarati literature*, vol. 4, Gujarātī sahitya parisad, Ahmedabad, 1973-1981.

13. Vishal, History of Ghazal, in: *Something about Everything*, 31 May 2016, Web.
14. Mishra, A. K., Tyagi, A. K., Dananjayan, S., Rajavat, A., Rawat, H., Rawat, A., Revolutionizing government operations: The impact of artificial intelligence in public administration. in: *Conversational Artificial Intelligence*, pp. 607–634, 2024.
15. Snyder, B.H. and Margery, Poetry: What Is the History and Definition of a Ghazal?, in: *Thought Co*, 22 Apr. 2016, Web.6.
16. Doty, G., A Short History of the Ghazal, in: *A Short History of the Ghazal*, 2007, Web.
17. Nahar, S., Pithawa, D., Bhardwaj, V., Rawat, R., Rawat, A., Pachlasiya, K., Quantum technology for military applications. in: *Quantum Computing in Cybersecurity*, pp. 313–334, 2023.
18. Sikarwar, R., Shakya, H. K., Kumar, A., Rawat, A., Advanced security solutions for conversational AI. in: *Conversational Artificial Intelligence*, pp. 287–301, 2024.
19. Patel, C. and Gali, K., Part-Of-Speech Tagging for Gujarati Using Conditional Random Fields. *Proceedings of the IJCNLP-08 Workshop on NLP for Less Privileged Languages*, January 2008, pp. 117–122.
20. Patel, M. and Balani, P., Clustering Algorithm for Gujarati Language. *Int. J. Sci. Res. Dev.*, 1, 3, 2321–0613, 2013, ISSN (online).
21. Pithawa, D., Nahar, S., Bhardwaj, V., Rawat, R., Dronawat, R., Rawat, A. Quantum computing technological design along with its dark side. in: *Quantum Computing in Cybersecurity*, pp. 295–312, 2023.
22. Vyas, T. and Ganatra, A., Gujarati Language: Research Issues, Resources and Proposed Method on Word Sense Disambiguation. *Int. J. Recent Technol. Eng. (IJRTE)*, 8, 2S11, September 2019, ISSN: 2277-3878.
23. Namdev, A., Patni, D., Dhaliwal, B. K., Parihar, S., Telang, S., Rawat, A., Potential threats and ethical risks of quantum computing. in: *Quantum Computing in Cybersecurity*, pp. 335-352, 2023.
24. Alsaidi, S.A., Sadiq, A.T., Abdullah, H.S., English poems categorization using text mining and rough set theory. *Bull. Electr. Eng. Inf.*, 9, 4, 1701–1710, August 2020, DOI: 10.11591/eei.v9i4.1898, ISSN: 2302-9285
25. Mehta, B. and Rajyagor, B., Gujarati Poetry Plassification based on Emotions using Deep Learning. *Int. J. Eng. Appl. Sci. Technol.*, 6, 1, 358–362, 2021, ISSN No. 2455-2143.
26. Noonia, A., Beg, R., Patidar, A., Bawaskar, B., Sharma, S., Rawat, H., Chatbot vs Intelligent Virtual Assistance (IVA). in: *Conversational Artificial Intelligence*, pp. 655-673, 2024.
27. Shah, P., Swaminarayan, P., Patel, M., Sentiment analysis on film review in Gujarati language using machine learning. *Int. J. Electr. Comput. Eng. (IJECE)*, 12, 1, 1030–1039, February 2022, DOI: 10.11591/ijece.v12i1. PP-1030-1039, ISSN: 2088-8708.

6

Cancer Classification and Detection Using Machine Learning Techniques

Syed Jahangir Badashah[1]*, Afaque Alam[2], Malik Jawarneh[3], Tejashree Tejpal Moharekar[4], Venkatesan Hariram[5], Galiveeti Poornima[6] and Ashish Jain[7]

[1]Department-ECE, Sreenidhi Institute of Science and Technology, Yamnampet, Hyderabad, Telangana, India
[2]Department of Computer Science and Engineering, Bakhtiyarpur College of Engineering, Patna, Bihar, India
[3]Oman College of Management and Technology, Muscat, Oman, INTI International University, Subang, Malaysia
[4]Yashwantrao Chavan School of Rural Development, Shivaji University, Kolhapur, Maharashtra, India
[5]Department of Practice of Medicine, Vinayaka Mission's Homoeopathic Medical College and Hospital, A Constituent College of Vinayaka Mission's Research Foundation Deemed to be University, Salem, Tamil Nadu, India
[6]Presidency University, Bangalore, India
[7]Department of Computer Applications, The Bhopal School of Social Sciences, Bhopal, India

Abstract

A doctor may use pictures from an MRI, CT, or X-ray to find bone cancer. The manual process is laborious and time-consuming, requiring specific understanding. Therefore, developing a system that can automatically discern between healthy and cancerous bones is crucial. Cancer-damaged bones feel different than neighboring healthy bones. Nevertheless, a few of the sample's images have morphological characteristics associated with both healthy and malignant bone. It becomes difficult to categorize them as a result. This article presents Machine learning and image processing based statistical pattern recognition framework for classification and detection of bone cancer. MRI and CT scan images are used as input data set

Corresponding author: syd_jahangir@yahoo.co.in

Rajesh Kumar Chakrawarti, Ranjana Sikarwar, Sanjaya Kumar Sarangi, Samson Arun Raj Albert Raj, Shweta Gupta, Krishnan Sakthidasan Sankaran and Romil Rawat (eds.) Natural Language Processing for Software Engineering, (95–112) © 2025 Scrivener Publishing LLC

in this framework. Images quality is improved using the Gaussian Elimination. In the end, classification is performed using the CNN and LSTM. Models are trained and tested with sufficient data.

Keywords: Cancer, classification, detection, gaussian elimination, machine learning, accuracy, CNN, LSTM

6.1 Introduction

Early detection is vital in all types of cancer, but particularly in breast cancer, due to its chronic nature and the usual delay in diagnosis. Given the current situation, it is imperative to take immediate action on the problem of predictive detection. The considerable global research undertaken on cancer detection encompasses several aspects, allowing for speculation on the potential results of a predictive technique. To reduce the negative impact of cancer on health, it is crucial to tackle issues related to accurately evaluating the risk for those with a high susceptibility and facilitating cancer prognosis for patients. Predictive cancer detection models not only identify individuals with a high risk of developing cancer, but they also provide current knowledge on how to assess the probability of cancer. Consequently, it simplifies the process of arranging and carrying out clinical cancer trials, so facilitating the advancement and evaluation of risk-benefit indices. This, in turn, enables an evaluation of the financial burden and effect of cancer. However, the previously indicated models may be used to evaluate the effectiveness and delivery of the medicines [1]. A malignant tumor, also known as a malignant neoplasm, is an aberrant proliferation of cells that has the ability to metastasize to other parts of the body, resulting in the disease known as cancer. Conversely, not all tumors are cancerous, hence benign tumors do not metastasize. Several symptoms that are often seen in various cancers include: a palpable mass, abnormal or excessive hemorrhaging, a chronic cough, significant unintentional weight loss (>10%), irregular bowel movements, and so forth. Over one hundred different types of cancer may affect a person. Cancer is characterized by uncontrolled cell proliferation, which occurs when the normal regulation of cell growth and production is disrupted [2]. According to the statistics, tobacco is accountable for around 22% of all cancer-related deaths. Alcohol use, sedentary lifestyle, obesity, and bad dietary habits together account for 10% of all deaths. Infections, ionizing radiation, and environmental pollutants are among the least common of these dangers. Although these factors may play a part in cellular gene modifications, it is conceivable that the formation of cancer necessitates considerably more substantial changes in DNA. Approximately 5-10% of cancer occurrences are attributed to genetic defects that are passed down through generations. While cancer signs may be apparent, other diagnostic procedures, such as a biopsy or medical imaging, may be necessary to definitively establish the diagnosis. Unfortunately, even being diagnosed and undergoing several rounds of treatment, there is still a silent risk of the malignant form reappearing, which requires precise identification and prompt prediction. The prediction models developed using machine learning theory will be essential after all these factors have been considered. The field of cancer prediction has widely used machine learning techniques. The potential applications of predictive analytics in the healthcare business are many. Due to the crucial significance of identifying cancer at an early stage and accurately forecasting its progression, the utilization of real-world data on cancer patients has immense potential for the advancement of more efficient prediction techniques. However, to create accurate prediction models, it is essential to include appropriate and relevant features [3].

Cancer is becoming more prevalent and lethal, with a rising number of cases and fatalities worldwide. Conversely, there is a perception that the increasing amount of data might provide new opportunities for tackling this issue and creating a predictive solution based on data analysis. There seems to be a significant association between verified cases and medical records, which, with further investigation, may uncover factors that assist in predicting cancer. Therefore, it is essential to use methodologies that rely on data analysis and machine learning techniques [4].

6.2 Machine Learning Techniques

Prior to embarking on an in-depth exploration of machine learning methods and their practical implementation in particular situations, it is crucial to fully comprehend the meaning and importance of machine learning. Machine learning is a specific area of research within the science of artificial intelligence. It involves the use of probabilistic, statistical, and optimization techniques to learn from past examples. The earlier training provides advantages for the classification of new data, pattern identification, and trend prediction. Data analysis and interpretation are performed using machine learning methodologies, similar to those used in statistics. On the other hand, machine learning methods that rely on statistics use unconventional optimization strategies that utilize model data or patterns, along with absolute conditionality (IF, THEN, ELSE), conditional probabilities (the probability of X given Y), and Boolean logic (AND, OR, NOT). All of the aforementioned strategies closely resemble the way humans really assess and categorize objects [5].

Machine learning has always relied on established methods of probability and statistics for detection. Machine learning, in contrast, is far more powerful and practical since it enables the generation of suggestions or conclusions that traditional methods cannot achieve. Statistical approach often includes the use of multivariate regression and correlation analysis. Effective conventional techniques depend on the assumption of variables' independence and linear organization for the interpretation of data. Traditional statistical approaches often prove inadequate when variables exhibit conditional dependence and their interactions are nonlinear. Machine learning excels in the field of cancer diagnosis. The majority of genetic structures exhibit nonlinearity, with their parameters being time-dependent. There are many simple physical formations that have a linear shape and whose characteristics are essentially unrelated to each other. There is no guarantee that cancer diagnoses with machine learning will provide satisfactory outcomes. A comprehensive understanding of the issue and the constraints of the available data are essential for the success of any method. Furthermore, a key factor in the effectiveness of the approach is a thorough understanding of the assumptions and limitations of the algorithms. A machine learning experiment may be deemed successful by meticulous planning, appropriate use of learners, and verification of outcomes. The traditional saying suggests that if low-quality data are inputted, the output will also be of low quality. Likewise, if the quantity of variables surpasses the anticipated instances, an unnecessary succession of learners will be created. The selection of input data does not impact the amount of execution for these sets of learning algorithms [6]. The "curse of dimensionality" refers to the difficulty of handling a large number of variables within a limited number of situations. This "curse" also impacts several statistical procedures and machine learning techniques. To resolve this problem, one may either decrease the number of variables (features) or increase the number of training samples. A section-to-feature ratio higher than 5:1 is often expected. The breadth and variety of the training set are crucial. It is crucial that the training examples include a diverse array of data types that the learner is expected to come across. Overtraining or overfitting happens when there is a scarcity of examples and little diversity in the training data. When confronted with fresh information, an excessively trained learner may have difficulty in understanding or categorizing it. Traditional statistics have been shown to be sometimes more effective and accurate than machine learning. This suggests that the user's original hypothesis about the data's interdependence and lack of linearity was inaccurate. This does not imply a deficiency in machine learning; instead, it depends on making the correct choice. Uniform treatment is not universally observed in all machine learning approaches [7].

Diverse tactics provide disparate outcomes on various challenges. For instance, although some machine learning algorithms effectively evaluate the size of genetic domains, others perform quite poorly. Furthermore, certain methodologies may not be appropriate for the current situation owing to underlying assumptions or data prerequisites. Identifying the optimal strategy for a certain problem is a challenging task. Therefore, it is recommended to use several machine learning techniques to conduct experiments on each provided training dataset. There is a common misunderstanding about machine learning that stems from the fact that its ability to recognize patterns and trends often results in unexpected findings. Nevertheless, by meticulous analysis of the data, a human specialist may identify various trends and patterns. Machine learning simplifies the process of sickness detection by providing a less complicated method for identifying patterns and creating classification systems [8–12].

The desired result is the foundation for classifying these algorithms. Supervised learning approaches depend on a "prescient provider," often a teacher, who supplies a labeled set of training data or examples. The tagged samples assist the program in acquiring knowledge on how to optimize the input data for efficient production planning. An instance of this may be a categorized training dataset that has a series of indistinct images depicting the numeral 8. Under the supervision of an instructor, an apprentice may practice the skill of taking notes on all the images labeled as "8." The goal is to provide an accurate and undistorted representation of the method's outcomes. The classroom is the most prevalent setting for pupils to acquire knowledge. Unsupervised learning involves a set of examples that lack labels. Whether a novice is able to see the prototype or discern the categories mostly depends on their own observation skills. Graduate students are the individuals who are most prone to demonstrating this particular type of learning. Unsupervised learning algorithms include methods such as K-means clustering, hierarchical clustering, and self-organizing feature maps (SOMs). These techniques produce clusters from unprocessed, unlabeled, or unclassified raw data. In the future, these clusters might potentially be used to begin classifiers or provide categorization suggestions [13–16].

The SOM approach demonstrates a distinct design of an artificial neural network. The technique relies on altered weights that correlate to input vectors, using a training set that includes a grid of artificial neurons. Initially, the SOM approach is intended to serve as a substitute for the functional characteristics of the genetic brain. The procedure starts with a collection of artificial neurons, each of which has a substantial function in the ultimate outcome. In a winner-take-all process, which is a competitive network, they function as a component where a vector of inputs is designated as the leading candidate and the weights are modified to closely resemble the input vector. This method is dependent on this particular facet of competitive learning. Each one is surrounded by a cluster of nodules. When a node emerges victorious in a conflict, the weights of its neighboring nodes are also altered, but not to the same extent. A lesser displacement in weight happens when the neighbor is geographically far from the winner. A vast quantity of cycles is thus used in doing this operation repeatedly for each input vector. The outcome of the competition might significantly differ based on the inputs provided. The end result is a neural network that can effectively connect certain clusters or prototypes in the input dataset to its output nodes. It is crucial to bear in mind that all machine learning algorithms, both before and after a cancer diagnosis, depend on supervised learning. Moreover, conditional prospects or conditional judgments often serve as the foundation for the categorization and organization procedures of these supervised learning systems.

The use of Support Vector Machines (SVMs) for cancer diagnosis is a modern machine learning technique. Support vector machines (SVMs) are well recognized in the field of machine learning, but they have not yet gained much recognition in the fields of pre-diagnosis and cancer diagnostics. For instance, in the context of breast cancer, SVMs may be used indirectly to distinguish between people with favorable and unfavorable prognoses by comparing the number of axillary metastases to the tumor mass. Two separate clusters have been found. The objective of the support vector machine (SVM) machine learning system is to identify the linear equation that optimally optimizes the distance between the two groups. If a single cluster were to include additional variables like as volume, metastases, and estrogen receptor satisfaction, the rows of division would be transformed into planes. If more variables were provided, a hyperplane would be used to explain the division. Subsequently, the support vectors, which delineate the boundaries between the two classes, reinforce the position of this hyperplane. In the SVM method, the data is first divided into two groups using the maximum range to produce a hyperplane. Given this circumstance, it implies that the region between the hyperplane and the closest examples (the boundary) is maximized. Support vector machines (SVMs) use non-linear kernels to accomplish nonlinear classifications. Using a non-linear kernel may help convert data from a linear characteristic space to a non-linear element space numerically. Applying diverse kernels to various data sets automatically enhances the presentation of an SVM classification. SVMs, similar to ANNs, may be used for diagnosing many difficulties including prototype recognition and classification, medical diagnosis, verbal and content identification, protein utility calculation, and deviating from manual handwriting inspection [17–19].

6.3 Review of Machine Learning for Cancer Detection

The collaboration between techniques for identifying new information and ways for safely processing current data is essential. Implementing this will enhance the usability of a cancer prediction algorithm, perhaps facilitating timely identification and effective management. The number 20 is represented by the numeral [20]. Various renowned global research institutions generate and distribute publicly available cancer datasets that are considered benchmarks in the area. The UCI repository and the SEER database are widely used in several studies, making them the preferred choices among researchers. Reference [21] used the Wisconsin breast cancer dataset to construct and assess many prediction models. To assess the effectiveness of different data mining methods, the authors in [22] used the SEER dataset. An effective method for using machine learning theory is to formally express the problem of cancer prediction as a binary classification algorithm. This method is effective for the majority of cancer types. To diagnose an event or assess its severity, the mathematical model will analyze the connections and patterns among the necessary information and predict the classification of the current stage. Support Vector Machines (SVMs) are categorization algorithms that have been used in recent breast cancer research [23, 24]. The utilization of an SVM-based classifier model enables accurate classification of cancer-related data, regardless of whether it is in numerical or visual format. This powerful technique [43–46], based on the theory of optimal separating hyperplanes, facilitates early detection of cancer and prediction of survival outcomes for patients in advanced stages. The research on breast cancer presented in reference [25] demonstrated that Support Vector Machines (SVMs) were the best suitable method. In a study conducted by [26], an SVM model trained on clinical data achieved a remarkable accuracy of 95.5% in predicting breast cancer. The clinical prognosis of new patients was accurately predicted by using the medical history of patients with cancer who had similar characteristics. This approach had the highest accuracy rate of 66.7% when evaluated with a linear kernel support vector machine [27]. A crucial prognostic indicator for the long-term survival of patients with gastric cancer was used to train a support vector machine using 5-fold cross-validation [28]. The classifier has an average sensitivity of 88.5% and an average specificity of 78.5%. Support vector machines have been used in recent studies to develop classification techniques. According to reference [29], support vector machines (SVMs) are the optimal choice for using breast cancer data in the field of predictive analytics. The Wisconsin breast cancer database, consisting of 699 tuples, was analyzed using predictive analytics. One of the four approaches outlined in [30], the support vector machine (SVM), was used for this analysis. In [31], it was shown that a support vector machine (SVM) was the most efficient method for selecting features in many breast cancer datasets. The authors of [32] achieved greater prediction accuracies in identifying cancer gene markers by using a supervised transductive SVM technique. DTs, or decision trees, are characterized by their ability to quickly acquire and carry out prediction tasks. These predictors are based on information entropy. Reports indicate that the use of DT resulted in a 93% accuracy rate for predicting outcomes in the SEER database [22]. To differentiate between normal and malignant stomach tissues, the researchers used the Classification and Regression Tree (CART) approach to classify their Raman infrared spectra [33]. The predictive sensitivity for these input parameters was determined to be 88.9% on the validation dataset, while the specificity was reported to be 92.9%. The most effective model for forecasting the five-year survival rates of lung cancer patients, using a combined database from Michigan and Harvard, was found to be a Decision Tree (DT) based on the C5.0 algorithm, as stated in reference [34]. Cancer prediction research heavily relies on the use of decision tree (DT) based classifiers. The breast cancer datasets in [31] were examined using decision trees (DTs) and classification and regression trees (CARTs), both with and without feature selection. To predict susceptibility to breast cancer using the standard Wisconsin dataset, a Decision Tree (DT) was used as one of the six classification algorithms indicated in reference [35]. A cross validated technique using a Decision Tree (DT) based on the J48 algorithm obtained an accuracy of 97% in diagnosing non-small cell lung cancer and its two primary subtypes [36]. Artificial Neural Networks (ANNs) are becoming more prevalent in cancer prediction [37]. One of the five unique prediction methods employed in [21] was a multilayer neural network. An artificial neural network (ANN) was trained utilizing several characteristics, including age and mammography findings, to achieve a high accuracy rate of 96.5% in predicting breast cancer susceptibility [38]. Using a testing data set consisting of 40 women in the control group and 40 women in the cancer group, a feed-forward artificial neural network (ANN) obtained prediction metrics of 82.5% specificity and sensitivity [39]. The purpose was to find bio-proteins that function as multiple indications for the identification of breast cancer. The use of Artificial Neural Networks (ANNs) in predicting cancer recurrence was extensively explained in reference [40]. The estimation and forecasting of survival for patients with non-small lung cancer was conducted using Artificial Neural Networks (ANNs) [41]. To forecast risk variables for the prognosis of gastric cancer patients, a back propagation artificial neural network (ANN) achieved an average classification rate of 84.16%. This was accomplished by using several pathological and laboratory feature [42]. K-Nearest Neighbors (KNN) is a fundamental approach of classification. This lazy-learning strategy is used to develop a classification rule, which relies on the occurrences in the training data. Its user-friendly interface makes it very popular among academics worldwide. Aloraini used the K-Nearest Neighbors (KNN) algorithm in their prediction methodology, as documented in reference [21] of the UCI Machine Learning (ML) repository. Instance-based classifiers, such as K-Nearest Neighbors, are often used while constructing cancer prediction models. Based on a study conducted in [29], which used the UCI machine learning library to predict breast cancer recurrence, it was shown that a KNN classifier was the most efficient method overall. One of the techniques used in the study cited in [35] also uses KNN.

6.4 Methods

This section presents a convolutional neural network based framework for cancer image classification and detection. MRI images are first preprocessed using Gaussian Filter to remove noises. Then images are classified by CNN and LSTM deep learning techniques as shown in Figure 6.1: A Framework for Cancer Image Classification and Detection.

To get the desired result, the picture must first be filtered and then enhanced. The results of segmentation performed on photographs obtained with a mobile phone may be affected by a broad variety of factors due to the nature of the photographs themselves. Resizing a picture, lowering the amount of noise in it, and improving it are all examples of processes that are included in pre-processing. It's possible for a digital picture to include a broad array of sounds. Because of this, there is a possibility of picture noise, which renders conventional thresholding ineffective. It is necessary to reduce the amount of noise in the photos. Image noise is the accidental change in a photograph's brightness or coloring that occurs across the image. A picture may include several kinds of noise, including Gaussian noise, noise with salt and pepper patterns, noise with shot patterns, and

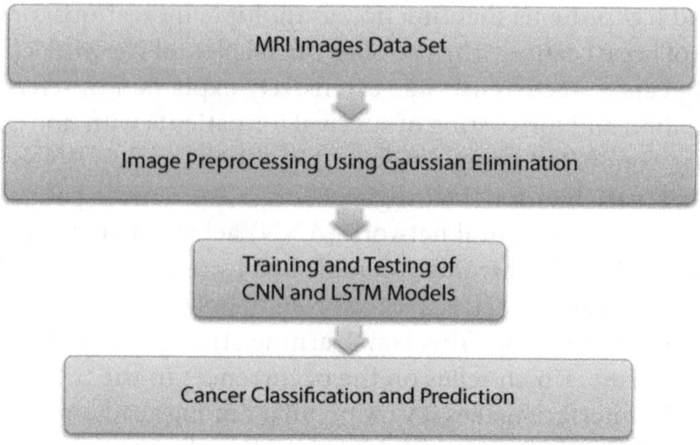

Figure 6.1 A framework for cancer image classification and detection.

quantization noise. There is a possibility that filters such as the median and the Wiener can eliminate these blips in the data. A number of different morphological techniques may be used to reduce the overall loudness of an audio source. The median and Gaussian filters each have their own unique effect on how bright individual pixels are made to seem. To achieve the aim of reducing the amount of background noise, GF was used. In the process of Gaussian filtering, the significance of the intensity of any particular pixel is replaced by a weighted average of the intensities of the pixels that are next to it [18].

Because it is an RNN network with gates such as I/P, forget, and O/P in addition to an additional memory cell, the LSTM (Long Short-Term Memory) [25] algorithm is a well-liked option. The need for gradient descent may be avoided by using LSTM networks because of their capacity to remember information for a protracted period of time. This enables the networks to better recognize patterns and sequences. The data is kept current by using input and output gates in between the time steps. When using Equation 6.2, the information that will be stored in the memory cell is determined by the input gate I. The Forget Gate (f) erases all prior memories by reorganizing the cell's present state in accordance with Equation 6.1. This renders all previous information superfluous. The output gate (y), which is the last phase, is responsible for controlling the data that is sent on to the succeeding stage. As a result of the fact that all three gates are connected to the memory cell, it is possible to monitor the timing of the output. LSTM is shown in Figure 6.2: LSTM network.

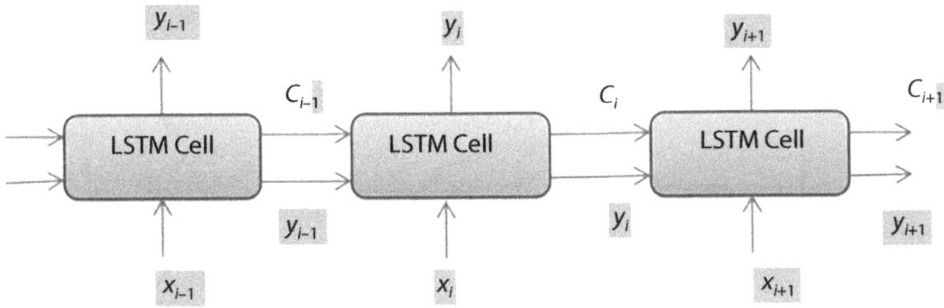

Figure 6.2 LSTM network.

$$f_t = \sigma(w_f.[y_{t-1}, x_t] + b) \tag{6.1}$$

$$i_t = \sigma(w_i.[y_{t-1}, x_t] + b) \tag{6.2}$$

The LSTM network is outlined in Figure 6.4. At each time step, an input i.e. the embedding x_i is fed into the network and the output y_i is determined based on the current embedding x_i, previous output y_{i-1} and the past cell state c_{i-1}. Cell state is capable of adding or removing the information.

There are several hidden layers in a CNN, and two of those levels are the convolution and pooling layers [26]. Image processing is one of its strong suits, and it has the ability to discover dependencies. The features are extracted from the information that is fed into the system using the convolution layer. Convolutional operations are carried out on the embedding matrix using this process. The embedding matrix is where the word embedding vectors that were generated by the word embedding approaches may be found stored. Following the convolution layer in a CNN is a layer called the pooling layer, which is responsible for performing operations such as dimensionality reduction and feature selection through pooling. It is conceivable to carry out a process that involves maximum pooling, a procedure that involves minimum pooling, or an operation that involves average pooling.

After the features have been acquired, they are utilized as input into a neural network that has already had all of its connections fully constructed. The activation functions are responsible for producing the output. The convolutional neural network is seen here in Figure 6.3: Convolution Neural Network. This study made use of two convolution layers together with average pooling to achieve its results.

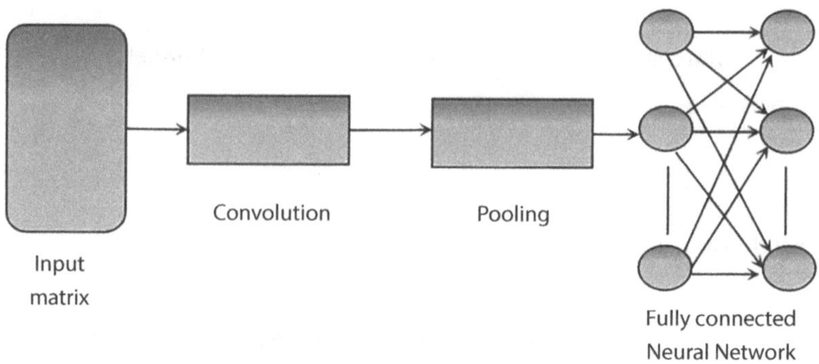

Figure 6.3 Convolution neural network.

6.5 Result Analysis

For experimental work, a total of 200 images were selected at random. 160 images were used for training of model, 20 images were used for validation and remaining 20 images were used for the testing of the model. Images were preprocessed to remove noise using Gaussian filter. Classification

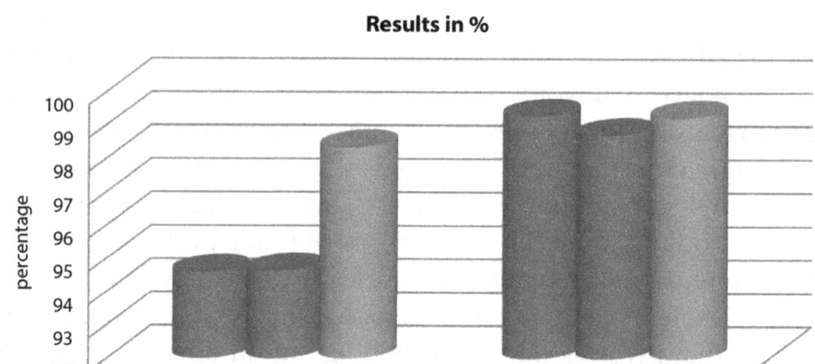

	LSTM	CNN
Accuracy	94.56	99.24
Sensitivity	94.6	98.67
Specificity	98.3	99.2

Figure 6.4 Result comparison of classifiers.

was performed using CNN and LSTM deep learning techniques. Results are shown below in Figure 6.4: Result Comparison of Classifiers.

Sensitivity:

$$\text{Sensitivity} = \frac{\text{TP}}{(\text{TP} + \text{FN})}$$

Where TP stands for True Positive and FN stands for False Negative

Specificity:

$$\text{Specificity} = \frac{\text{TN}}{(\text{TN} + \text{FP})}$$

Where TN stands for True Negative and FP stands for False Positive

Accuracy

$$\text{Accuracy} = \frac{\text{TN} + \text{TP}}{(\text{TN} + \text{TP} + \text{FN} + \text{FP})}$$

6.6 Conclusion

Early detection is essential in cases of breast cancer, primarily because late diagnosis is prevalent. The matter of anticipatory detection is currently of utmost significance. The existing literature has not provided enough evidence to apply the prediction technique universally in response to these issues. To effectively manage cancer-related illness and death, it is crucial to have precise cancer risk assessment for persons at high risk and to define the prognosis for cancer patients. Predictive cancer models have enabled recent advancements in risk assessment and the identification of high-risk patients. Developing such predictive models facilitates the process of strategizing and designing clinical cancer studies, as well as constructing benefit-risk indices. These models can assist in estimating the cost, impact, and effectiveness of cancer treatments and management.

References

1. Yershova, K., Yuan, J.-M., Wang, R., Valentin, L., Watson, C., Gao, Y.-T., Hecht, S.S., Stepanov, I., Tobaccospecific n-nitrosamines and polycyclic aromatic hydrocarbons in cigarettes smoked by the participants of the shanghai cohort study. *Int. J. Cancer*, 139, 6, 1261–1269, 2016.
2. Louie, A.V., Haasbeek, C.J., Mokhles, S., Predicting overall survival after stereotactic ablative radiation therapy in early stage lung cancer: Development and external validation of the amsterdam prognostic model. *Int. J. Radiat. Oncol. Biol. Phys.*, 93, 1, 82–90, 2015.
3. Euhus, D.M., Smith, K.C., Robinson, L., Stucky, A., Olopade, O., II, Cummings, S., Garber, J.E., Chittenden, A., Mills, G.B., Rieger, P., Esserman, L., Crawford, B., Hughes, K.S., Roche, C.A., Ganz, P.A., Seldon, J., Fabian, C.J., Klemp, J., Tomlinson, G., Pretest prediction of BRCA1 or BRCA2 mutation by risk counselors and the computer model brcaproj. *Natl. Cancer Inst.*, 94, 844–851, 2002.
4. Tyrer, J., Duffy, S.W., Cuzick, J., A breast cancer prediction model incorporating familial and personal risk factors. *Statist. Med.*, 23, 1111–1130, 2004.
5. Bianchi, F., Bracci, R., Rosati, S., Galizia, E., Belvederesi, L., Loretelli, C., Giorgetti, G., Giorgi, F., Cellerino, R., CRCAPRO: A statistical model to evaluate the risk of mmr mutations, *J. Clin. Oncol.* in:, *2005 ASCO Annual Meeting Proceedings*, June 2005, vol. 23, p. 9693.
6. Colditz, G.A., Rosner, B.A., Speizer, F.E., Risk factors for breast cancer according to family history of breast cancer. *J. Natl. Cancer Inst.*, 88, 6, 365–371, 1996.
7. Spasic', I., Livsey, J., Keanec, J.A., Nenadic', G., Text mining of cancer-related information: Review of current status and future directions. *Int. J. Med. Inf.*, 83, 9, 605–623, June 2014.
8. Brown, W.R. and Ahnen, D.J., The international health care burden of cancers of the gastrointestinal tract and liver. *Cancer Res. Front.*, 1, 1, 1–9, February 2015.
9. Mishra, A. K., Tyagi, A. K., Dananjayan, S., Rajavat, A., Rawat, H., Rawat, A., Revolutionizing Government Operations: The Impact of Artificial Intelligence in Public Administration. in: *Conversational Artificial Intelligence*, pp. 607–634, 2024
10. Bellazzi, R. and Zupan, B., Predictive data mining in clinical medicine: Current issues and guidelines. *Int. J. Med. Inf.*, 77, 2, 81–97, February 2008.
11. Ramachandran, P., Girija, N., Bhuvaneswari, T., Early detection and prevention of cancer using data mining techniques. *Int. J. Comput. Appl.*, 97, 13, 48–53, July 2014.
12. Matsuno, R.K., Costantino, J.P., Ziegler, R.G., Anderson, G.L., Li, H., Pee, D., Gail, M.H., Projecting individualized absolute invasive breast cancer risk in asian and pacific islander american women. *J. Natl. Cancer Inst.*, 103, 12, 951–961, June 2011.

13. Chlebowski, R.T., Chen, Z., Anderson, G.L., Rohan, T., Aragaki, A., Lane, D., Dolan, N.C., Paskett, E.D., McTiernan, A., Hubbell, F.A., Adams-Campbell, L.L., Prentice, R., Ethnicity and breast cancer: Factors influencing differences in incidence and outcome. *J. Natl. Cancer Inst.*, 97, 6, 439–448, March 2005.
14. Spitz, M.R., Hong, W.K., Amos, C., II, Wu, X., Schabath, M.B., Dong, Q., Shete, S., Etzel, C.J., A risk model for prediction of lung cancer. *J. Natl. Cancer Inst.*, 99, 9, 715–726, March 2007.
15. Spitz, M.R., Etzel, C.J., Dong, Q., Amos, C., II, Wei, Q., Wu, X., Hong, W.K., An expanded risk prediction model for lung cancer. *Cancer Prev. Res.*, 1, 4, 250–254, 2008.
16. Hoggart, C. *et al.*, A risk model for lung cancer incidence. *Cancer Prev. Res.*, 5, 6, 834–846, 2012.
17. Nahar, S., Pithawa, D., Bhardwaj, V., Rawat, R., Rawat, A., Pachlasiya, K., Quantum technology for military applications. in: *Quantum Computing in Cybersecurity*, pp. 313–334, 2023.
18. Suthar, H., Rawat, H., Gayathri, M., Chidambarathanu, K., Techno-Nationalism and Techno-Globalization: A Perspective from the National Security Act. in: *Quantum Computing in Cybersecurity*, 137–164, 2023.
19. Amir, E., Evaluation of breast cancer risk assessment packages in the family history evaluation and screening programme. *J. Med. Genet.*, 40, 11, 807–814, 2003.
20. Rawat, R., and Rajavat, A., Perceptual Operating Systems for the Trade Associations of Cyber Criminals to Scrutinize Hazardous Content. *IJCWT*, 14, 1, 1–19, 2024.
21. Sikarwar, R., Shakya, H. K., Kumar, A., Rawat, A., Advanced Security Solutions for Conversational AI. in: *Conversational Artificial Intelligence*, 287–301, 2024.
22. Delen, D., Walker, G., Kadam, A., Predicting breast cancer survivability: a comparison of three data mining methods. *Artif. Intell. Med.*, 02, 34, 113–127, 2005.
23. Chauhan, D., Singh, C., Rawat, R., Dhawan, M., Evaluating the Performance of Conversational AI Tools: A Comparative Analysis. in: *Conversational Artificial Intelligence*, 385–409, 2024.
24. Tseng, C.-J., Lu, C.-J., Chang, C.-C., Chen, G.-D., Application of machine learning to predict the recurrence-proneness for cervical cancer. *Neural Comput. Appl.*, 24, 13116, 2014.
25. Kim, W., Kim, K.S., Lee, J.E., Noh, D.Y., Kim, S.-W., Jung, Y.S., Development of novel breast cancer recurrence prediction model using support vector machine. *J. Breast Cancer*, 2, 15, 230–238, 2012.
26. Eshlaghy, A.T., Poorebrahimi, A., Ebrahimi, M., Razavi, A.R., Ahmad, L.G., Using three machine learning techniques for predicting breast cancer recurrence. *J. Health Med. Inform.*, 4, 124, 2013.
27. Chan, L.W.C., Machine learning of patient similarity: A case study on predicting survival in cancer patient after locoregional chemotherapy, in: *IEEE*

International Conference on Bioinformatics and Biomedicine Workshops (BIBMW), 2010.
28. Pithawa, D., Nahar, S., Bhardwaj, V., Rawat, R., Dronawat, R., Rawat, A., Quantum Computing Technological Design Along with Its Dark Side. in: *Quantum Computing in Cybersecurity*, 295–312, 2023.
29. Rawat, R., Telang, S., William, P., Kaur, U., CU, O. K. (Eds.). *Dark Web Pattern Recognition and Crime Analysis Using Machine Intelligence*. IGI Global, 2022.
30. Rathi, M. and Gupta, C., An approach to predict breast cancer and drug suggestion using machine learning techniques. *ACEEE Int. J. Inf. Technol.*, 1, 4, 23–31, 2014.
31. Lavanya, D. and Usha Rani, K., Ensemble decision tree classifier for breast cancer data. *Int. J. Inf. Technol. Convergence Serv.*, 1, 2, 17–24, 2012.
32. Maulik, U., Mukhopadhyay, A., Chakraborty, D., Geneexpression based cancer subtypes prediction through feature selection and transductive svm. *IEEE Trans. Biomed. Eng.*, 60, 4, 1111–1117, 2013.
33. Namdev, A., Patni, D., Dhaliwal, B. K., Parihar, S., Telang, S., Rawat, A., Potential Threats and Ethical Risks of Quantum Computing. in: *Quantum Computing in Cybersecurity*, 335–352, 2023.
34. Mihalache, L., Suresh, S., Yaosuo, X., Manjrekar, M., Modeling of a small distribution grid with intermittent energy resources using MATLAB/SIMULINK, in: *Proc. 2011 IEEE Power and Energy Society General Meeting*, pp. 1–8, 2011.
35. Ravi kumar, G., Ramachandra, G.A., Nagaman, K., An efficient prediction of breast cancer data using data mining techniques. *Int. J. Innov. Eng. Technol.*, 2, 4, 139–144, August 2013.
36. Venkat, D.M., Rasheed, M.A., Ali, M., Classification of lung cancer subtypes by data mining technique, in: *IEEE International Conference on Control, Instrumentation, Energy and Communication (CIEC)*, 2014.
37. Shrivastava, M., Patil, R., Bhardwaj, V., Rawat, R., Telang, S., Rawat, A., Quantum Computing and Security Aspects of Attention-Based Visual Question Answering with Long Short-Term Memory. in: *Quantum Computing in Cybersecurity*, 395–412, 2023.
38. Noonia, A., Beg, R., Patidar, A., Bawaskar, B., Sharma, S., Rawat, H., Chatbot vs Intelligent Virtual Assistance (IVA). in: *Conversational Artificial Intelligence*, 655–673, 2024.
39. Zhang, F. and Chen, J.Y., A neural network approach to multibiomarker panel development based on LC/MS/MS proteomics profiles: A case study in breast cancer, in: *22nd IEEE International Symposium on Computer-Based Medical Systems*, vol. *2009*, 2009.
40. Ritthipravat, P., Artificial neural networks in cancer recurrence prediction, in: *IEEE Computer Engineering and Technology 2009. ICCET09*, vol. 02, 2009.

41. Lee, L.G., Lee, C.Y., Park, I.K., Kim, D.J., Park, S.Y., Kim, K.D., Chung, K.Y., Number of metastatic lymph nodes in resected non-small cell lung cancer predicts patient survival. *Pubmed/ NCBI*, 01, 85, 211–215, January 2008.
42. Rawat, R., Chakrawarti, R.K., Sarangi, S.K., Choudhary, R., Gadwal, A.S., Bhardwaj, V., eds. *Robotic Process Automation*. John Wiley & Sons, 2023.
43. Shrivastava, M., Patil, R., Bhardwaj, V., Rawat, R., Telang, S., Rawat, A., Quantum Computing and Security Aspects of Attention-Based Visual Question Answering with Long Short-Term Memory, in: *Quantum Computing in Cybersecurity*, pp. 395–412, 2023.
44. Rawat, R., Chakrawarti, R.K., Raj, A.S.A., Mani, G., Chidambarathanu, K., Bhardwaj, R., Association rule learning for threat analysis using traffic analysis and packet filtering approach. *Int. J. Inf. Technol.*, *15*, 6, 3245–3255, 2023.
45. Rathi, M. and Rajavat, A., Investigations and Design of Privacy-Preserving Data Mining Technique for Secure Data Publishing. *Int. J. Intell. Syst. Appl. Eng.*, *11*, 9s, 351–367, 2023.
46. Dubey, P. and Rajavat, A., Effective K-means clustering algorithm for efficient data mining, in: *2023 2nd International Conference on Vision Towards Emerging Trends in Communication and Networking Technologies (ViTECoN)*, IEEE, pp. 1–6, 2023, May.

7

Text Mining Techniques and Natural Language Processing

Tzu-Chia Chen

Department of Artificial Intelligence, Tamkang University, New Taipei City, Taiwan

Abstract
Text mining is an important branch of data mining that is used to analyze the text data. Text data is any type of data like structured data, unstructured data, and semi-structured data. All types of data are collected from different sources such as multimedia applications, mobile apps, digital systems, etc. These data are beneficial to get a good insight, meaningful results. We use data mining techniques like Support Vector Machine (SVM), Random Forest (RF), Multilayer Perception (MLP), Naive Bayes (NB), etc. to analyze the hidden relationship between data. We use three kinds of data types in text mining.

Keywords: Text mining, machine learning, natural language processing, SVM, random forest

7.1 Introduction

Text thematic organizing is an essential human activity in the modern digital era. The demand for strong algorithms capable of interpreting and extracting valuable insights from massive amounts of digital data has grown in tandem with the proliferation of high-tech devices and software. For this aim, data mining has shown to be an effective approach. To find useful patterns and correlations in massive datasets, data mining sometimes involves looking at the data from several angles and then summarizing it [1]. Data can take the form of any processable fact, picture, table, number, or text.

Email: tzuchiachen1688@gmail.com

Rajesh Kumar Chakrawarti, Ranjana Sikarwar, Sanjaya Kumar Sarangi, Samson Arun Raj Albert Raj, Shweta Gupta, Krishnan Sakthidasan Sankaran and Romil Rawat (eds.) Natural Language Processing for Software Engineering, (113–126) © 2025 Scrivener Publishing LLC

By systematically searching for and analyzing intriguing patterns in large amounts of unstructured material, text miners hope to unearth previously unknown and potentially valuable information [2]. Figure 7.1 shows the process of text mining, which is also known as intelligent text analysis or knowledge finding in text.

The raw dataset that is acquired is frequently inconsistent and ambiguous, as seen in Figure 7.1. This is the reason why the preprocessing stage is so important for applications that include text mining. The phases that are often included in the process of preparing unstructured data for text mining are visualized in Figure 7.2. The natural language processing techniques that are included in these methods include stemming, the removal of stop words, and part of speech tagging (POS), which assigns tags to each word, such as nouns, adjectives, and so on.

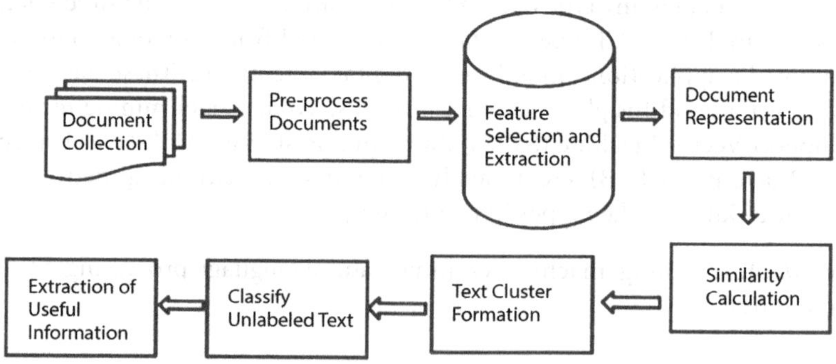

Figure 7.1 Steps in text mining.

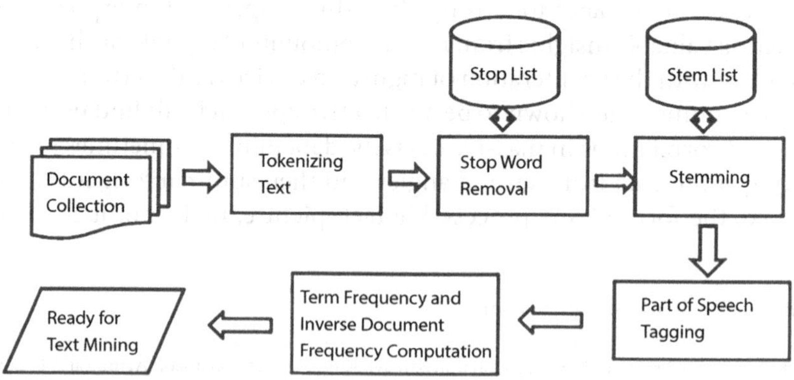

Figure 7.2 Stages of preprocessing text.

The vector space model, often known as the VSM, is the basis for the majority of text retrieval algorithms. This model represents data by considering texts to be a collection of words. To generate a feature vector of words for each text, the VSM makes use of either the term frequency or the term weight [3]. The objective of the feature selection process is to pick a subset of the characteristics of the original document that are capable of functioning effectively as a representation. To develop new features that are more pertinent to the problem at hand, the process of feature extraction entails changing the information that is being entered. To quantify the degree to which two documents are similar to one another, it is usual practice to utilize pair-wise similarity measures like as the Cosine and Jaccard similarity measures [4]. These measures are based on feature vectors. This is accomplished by employing similarity values that are bound by a threshold to build groups of connected documents. In the following step, further unlabeled material can be categorized using a variety of different methods as shown in Figure 7.2: Stages of Preprocessing Text.

7.2 Text Classification and Text Clustering

The goal of text clustering, an unsupervised method, is to arrange text documents into clusters based on their similarities and differences [5]. Image processing, pattern recognition, machine learning, and market segmentation are just a few of the many areas where clustering is now being studied. Clustering of text texts is the main emphasis of this thesis. When dealing with extremely huge datasets that contain several features of diverse sorts, text mining compounds the difficulties of clustering. As a result, applicable clustering methods face novel computational challenges. In response to these needs, a number of algorithms have surfaced and found use in practical data mining applications [6].

Most clustering techniques rely on two things: the availability of a similarity measure that may identify documents to be grouped together and a certain number of clusters. It is not always possible to predict in advance how many clusters will emerge. Documents are represented based on phrase or pair wise context, and the similarity link between the sentences may be found using tree representation similarity, according to a critical review of contemporary document clustering techniques [7]. But as the amount of data grows, the computational complexity and time required by this method skyrocket. Even when two words appear in a document at the same frequency, one of them may be more important to the meaning of the sentences than the other. This is a big problem with most text mining approaches since they use term frequency to determine a term's value in the document [8].

Data mining and machine learning communities devote a great deal of time and energy to studying classification. In classification, as opposed to clustering, the challenge is to assign labels to freshly encountered testing data; in contrast, clustering makes use of an existing set of pre-classified training data. To learn the descriptions of classes and to classify fresh data, the training data is utilized. Researchers from several fields have spent decades studying the classification problem. Text, multimedia, social networks, and even biological data are just a few of the many issue areas that might benefit from categorization. Additionally, the issue might arise in other contexts, including those with imprecise or flowing data. The data domain and issue scenario significantly impact the underlying algorithms, making classification a relatively broad topic. The test cases that cannot be observed are divided into categories according to the class label in the classification issue. Although clustering is often used to group instances, there is a significant distinction between the two issues. When it comes to clustering, the segmentation is accomplished by looking for similarities between the feature variables, without knowing how the groups are structured beforehand. Segmentation for classification purposes is based on a training dataset that stores information about the grouping structure as a target variable. Therefore, although clustering and data segmentation are both founded on ideas of similarity, in practice, it is possible to make substantial departures from similarity-based segmentation. Thus, supervised learning is used to describe the classification problem, whereas unsupervised learning is used to describe clustering. Some of the most common approaches to classification include decision tree induction, fuzzy logic, genetic algorithms, case-based reasoning, k-nearest neighbor classifier, and Bayesian networks.

7.3 Related Work

The movie review dataset is very useful for individuals to think about and make decisions about a wide variety of real-world challenges. A lot of people get other people's opinions before they make a final choice. Knowledge may be extracted from a wide range of study areas, including sentiment analysis, opinion mining, and text classifications. Reviewing films is one use case for sentiment analysis. Analyzing people's emotions isn't as simple as the term suggests. The categorization [18] of the movie review data from the dataset requires a number of preprocessing processes. The leading relevant research in sentiment analysis and text mining has been presented by researchers. The writers have gone over the sentimental content and the major effects of word of mouth on internet stores and customers. To determine the degree of reliance between different polarity ranges of terms, they used a coefficient of correlation (CC) and a natural language processing (NLP) method for positive/negative bag of words (BOW) [9]. Various viewpoints published in Roman-Urdu and English have been culled from a blog, and the authors have addressed text categorization in a WEKA setting. In terms of accuracy, Naïve Bayes (NB) surpasses Decision Tree (DT) and K-Nearest Neighbors (KNN), two of the three classification approaches they have used. The authors have covered topics such as deep learning-based sentiment analysis of Twitter databases. To analyze Twitter data, they used a Convolution Neural Network (CNN), which is great for extracting data from bigger texts and, by extension, for sentiment analysis. When compared to SVM and NB approaches, the proposed CNN method performs better. Studies on regional languages, such as Kannada (the official language of Karnataka), have focused on sentiment analysis. Using both ML and semantic methods, they analyzed sentiment and classified texts from Kannada online articles into an English-language dataset; ML methods outperformed semantic learning methods on average with the Kannada dataset. The authors have suggested an approach to user nature identification that relies on SoftMax based attitude detection. By considering the user's attitude, the accuracy and reliability of emotion prediction may be significantly enhanced. Utilizing tweets collected from the microblogging platform Twitter, the proposed algorithm is assessed [10]. With the use of sentiment analysis, the authors were able to improve their findings while analyzing text-based data from Chinese microblogs. The authors propose a novel approach to sentiment analysis for text categorization using text-based hidden Markov models (Text Mms). By including text semantic similarity, the authors' suggested tenor factorization approach enhances the factor's primary purpose of discovering comparable users, revealing the data's underlying characteristics, and forecasting users' preferences. Customers' reviews have been worked on by the authors. To do sentiment analysis, we randomly selected reviews [11]. Subject models and other popular CSTM text analysis techniques are shown to be ineffective when dealing with brief texts, according to the authors. We found that our CSTM beat the state-of-the-art short text topic conventional model in experiments conducted on real-world datasets. Wang, To examine the polarity of sentiment for brief texts, the authors have presented Senti-related, a unique cross-domain sentiment classification technique based on SRI. When working with unlabeled data from the target domain,

Senti-related uses SRI to extend feature vectors. An issue that has sparked global discussion on social media, the Syrian refugee crisis has impacted millions of individuals and has prompted researchers to probe popular sentiment and opinion on the matter. They looked at pertinent tweets in both Turkish and English to see how people felt about the subject on Twitter. Additionally, they have examined the contrasting tone of the recovered tweets. To discover feature-opinion pairs and disclose the orientation of extracted opinions, the authors have presented two distinct approaches to building rule-based systems. The authors have proposed other classifiers for text data classification. Twenty newsgroups and IMDb have contributed to their data set [12]. Several methods, including KNN, RF, and NB, have been used by the writers to examine the movie evaluations. Opinion mining systems that express user's favorable or negative opinion at different levels have been the subject of research. We can extract feelings from the web and anticipate online client preferences using the same approach for predicting views. This might be useful for marketing research. Due to the importance of views, which we seek out anytime we must make a choice, a lot of recent study has focused on how our feelings and opinions are processed. Using a logistic regression classification model and an artificial bee colony algorithm, the authors have developed a new approach to spam detection. They have tested it on three separate datasets and shown that it can effectively handle high-dimensional data. Using text semantic analysis, the authors have proposed and implemented a system to better identify and categorize spam. Moreover, they have implemented spam detection in their respective domains using automatically collected semantic characteristics. Experts have deliberated how to identify and categorize ham data and e-mails that include both text and images. Three algorithms were used for spam e-mail classification: KNN, NB, and the reverse DB-SCAN method. The accuracy, precision, sensitivity, and specificity of these classifiers were found to be good when tested both before and after data preprocessing. Various evaluations pertaining to email spam filters have been proposed by the writers. A wealth of data on spam filters is included in this article [13]. To classify words for spam email filtering, researchers have proposed a feature selection-based semantic ontology. The spam email filter was built using Information Gain, Latent Dirichlet Allocation, a generative statistical model, and a semantic-based FST. Spam detection and detection-cum-analysis of hacked accounts are two interrelated issues that the authors have primarily addressed. up this publication, they have also filled up several gaps in the research that will be necessary for future studies. To identify spam, the authors have created a model that uses the Sender Policy Framework (SPF) protocol to examine the IP addresses of A and MX records. Using N-gram text data and an IDF feature selection approach, the authors have developed a new spam filter methodology. They have also provided an algorithm to balance distributions and a model for a regularized Deep Multilayer Perceptron Neural Network with rectified linear units called DBB-RDNNReL. Better text categorization accuracy was also attained when they evaluated spam filter performance with various ML techniques. The authors have researched the shortcomings of signature-based systems and spam blacklisting systems, and they have presented an ID3 algorithm for spam filtering based on the decision tree approach. According to [14], the suggested method outperformed competing algorithms in terms of accuracy. In the WEKA setting, the authors have implemented the Random Forest ML technique. Their spam email filter is quite effective and has very few features. To examine the efficacy of classifiers for spam and ham document categorization, the authors have used supervised ML algorithms such as NB, Perceptron, and C4.5. Naïve Bayes classifier, which outperforms other algorithms in terms of accuracy, has been proposed by them. The authors have classified spam emails using the SVM light program, which uses four kernel functions. Additionally, they have analyzed the dataset and computed several utility functions, such as TF, IDF, and TF-IDF. When applied to the email, the proposed SVM classifier improved the accuracy of the spam classification. When compared against more traditional methods of spam filtering, such as black lists and white lists, the authors' proposed Logistic Model Tree Induction approach in a WEKA environment outperformed the competition. When it comes to spam filtering, the authors have suggested using the Negative Selection Algorithm (NSA) to discover anomalies. For the Enron1 spam e-mail dataset, the suggested technique achieved an accuracy of 93.14 percent. To assess database performance, the writers have used distributed memory, distributed bag of words, cosine similarity, and auto encoder techniques. Due to the extensive representation of features, space complexity is a significant downside. Distributed memory and the distributed bag of words method have produced huge dictionaries for their respective word vectors, but the ever-increasing quantity of their vocabulary poses a dilemma when it comes to fixing the spam e-mail issue [15]. To lessen the spatial and temporal complexity, the authors propose using the Word Net ontology in conjunction with semantic based approaches and similarity metrics to reduce the number of textual characteristics that are extracted. By combining the FST with Principal Component Analysis (PCA) and Correlation Feature Selection (CFS), the authors were able to improve computing speed while simultaneously reducing spatial complexity. They have created a program called Concept Drift Analyzer that uses a k-fold cross-validation approach to accurately recognize ham and spam emails. When it comes to adversarial risk categorization, the authors have looked at the NB algorithm and the ACRA framework. An extension of anti-spam filtering, the authors have proposed the multi-objective optimization problem. This study used three new evolutionary multi-objective algorithms: SMS-EMOA, CH-EMOA, and MOEA/D, which are based on decomposition. For e-mail categorization with a low confidence level, our method outperforms another spam filter and optimizes the performance of heterogeneous ensemble classifiers. To train the classifier with high-quality data, the authors have suggested a novel method for producing phishing e-mail examples. Additionally, they have introduced quantitative assessment techniques, strengthened the generalizability of classifier control quantity sequence pairs, and built six resource generators and a communication connection selector. To overcome the uncertainty that arose from polysemy in spam e-mail detection, the authors propose using NB classification in conjunction with a conceptual and semantic similarity method. For permanent spam email categorization, the authors have presented a new model termed ELCADP. They evaluated the suggested model's performance with existing approaches for spam e-mail document categorization and found that it outperformed the competition. To categorize phishing emails, the authors have presented a new Remove Replacement Feature Selection Technique (RRFST) in addition to two decision tree methods [16]. The authors have put forward the ALO-Boosting technique for spam email classification. This approach makes use of ALO to choose the best feature subset, which is then fed into a boosting algorithm to improve classification accuracy. Irrelevant communications were a major factor in digital investigations, according to the authors. When it comes to digital investigations into spam emails, this letter gives a lot of useful information. The authors gathered information regarding spam e-mails and hint about hackers using five such cases. With the use of an e-mail spam corpus, the authors presented a text analytics approach that effectively detects threads and spam e-mails. To categorize spam, it used the text keyword matching approach with the corpus. This helped to avoid the inbox from being inundated with useless emails. To detect spam emails, the authors combined a logistic regression classification model with an artificial bee colony technique. To test their model's efficacy, they compared it to the existing model and utilized three separate datasets that were accessible to the public. Two studies have been conducted by the authors to detect SMS spam. The first trial assessed the suggested approach's performance, whereas the second employed a Bayesian network classifier testing method in conjunction with a cost-sensitive strategy [17].

7.4 Methodology

This section contains machine learning and feature selection-based methodology for text mining. This method consists of a text data set as input. First of all, features are selected using particle swarm optimization algorithm. Then machine learning algorithms are tested with testing data. The accuracy of algorithms is measured to correctly classify records. Finally, prediction of records is performed. The proposed methodology is shown below in Figure 7.3.

To improve its effectiveness, the PSO algorithm will take use of the fact that many different kinds of animals, including fish and birds, exhibit behavior similar to that of a swarm. Within the parameters of the search, each particle has a position and velocity that are completely unique to itself, and they are free to move in any way that they see fit. The velocity and mobility of the particle are still constrained as a direct consequence of

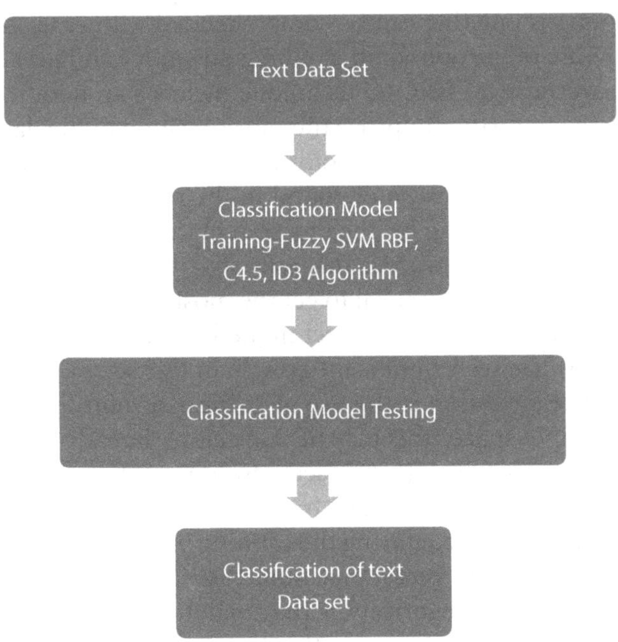

Figure 7.3 Machine learning based framework for text mining.

this, and the particle is directed to the location of any previously successful particles. In addition to this, the particle is directed to the location of any other particles that have successfully completed their tasks in the past without causing any mishaps. It is now possible, as a result of the application of a predetermined set of rules to the technique in question, to characterize both the rate of motion and the location of each particle at every particular instant in time.

Identification 3 (ID3) is a method that use a decision tree to categorize instances in an iterative manner according to the values and features of those instances. It is generated from the most complex to the simplest using a collection of instances and the required features in that order. These groups were then further subdivided. When the set included inside a certain subtree is equal to the set of instances that belong to a comparable category, the set in question is designated as a leaf node within the given subtree. Information theoretical criteria are taken into consideration whenever a characteristic is being chosen for testing purposes. The reduction in entropy will result in an increase in the information gain at each node.

Decision trees [19, 20] are often used in machine learning models for the purpose of data classification [21–23] because of their speed and accuracy. When using this method, tree trimming may be accomplished in a number of different ways, making it a very adaptable practice. The result of the trimming is one that can be comprehended with ease. A number of academicians are of the opinion that taking down trees might be utilized as a means of overfitting. The C4.5 technique includes an iterative classification that is used to further improve the categorization of the data until only pure leaf nodes are left, at which point the process comes to a conclusion. This iterative classification can be found in the method's outline. By using this strategy, it is possible to get the most out of the training data, while also eliminating the demand for rules that only signal a specific behavior in the data. This is because it is practical to get the most out of the training data.

In recent years, the use of the technique known as the support vector machine (SVM) has seen significant growth in this sector. A helpful strategy for data categorization is the use of a linear or non-linear separation surface in the input space. This may be done either linearly or non-linearly. The support vector machine (SVM) seeks to construct a model that reliably predicts the goal values of new data by using just the characteristics of the test data. The data collected during the training phase are used to construct the model. The support vector machine (SVM) provides a dependable approach for pattern categorization that maintains a high level of accuracy while simultaneously lowering the danger of overfitting. When there are just two types of classes present in the data, SVM may be used. Using

SVM, data is categorized by locating the hyperplane that most effectively separates all of the data points into distinct categories. The hyperplane of a support vector machine (SVM) that has the greatest difference in margin between two classes of data is considered to be the optimal hyperplane for an SVM. When the slab is at its widest point parallel to the hyperplane, there are no data points located inside the boundary of the slab itself. Because of their close closeness to the hyperplane that separates the slab, the points along the slab's border are regarded to be support vectors. In fuzzy SVM, a membership value is assigned to each sample determined by its correlations with the values of other samples. There are many different ways in which each input sample contributes to the process that ultimately results in a choice being made. A radial basis function kernel has also been found to improve the performance of a support vector machine (SVM).

7.5 Conclusion

Text data is a treasure trove of information, but deciphering massive amounts of it requires a lot of work in terms of content organization, retrieval, and linking. The process of automatically extracting valuable information from massive amounts of unstructured text, such as blog posts, correspondence, internal reports (e.g., medical records), financial reports, research papers, account statements, and a plethora of web documents, among many others. Text mining is an emerging multidisciplinary discipline that brings together fields such as computational linguistics, statistics, data mining, machine learning, and information retrieval. Many businesses see text mining as a lucrative strategy because the vast majority of data is stored in text format (more than 80%). This chapter contains machine learning and feature selection-based methodology for text mining. This method consists of a text data set as input. First of all, features are selected using particle swarm optimization algorithm. Then machine learning algorithms are tested with testing data. The accuracy of algorithms is measured to correctly classify records. Finally, prediction of records is performed.

References

1. Mishra, A. K., Tyagi, A. K., Dananjayan, S., Rajavat, A., Rawat, H., Rawat, A., Revolutionizing Government Operations: The Impact of Artificial Intelligence in Public Administration. in: *Conversational Artificial Intelligence*, pp. 607–634, 2024.

2. Radovanovic, M. and Ivanovic, M., Text Mining: Approaches and Applications. *Novi Sad J. Math.*, 38, 3, 227–234, 2008.
3. Wang, X., Tang, J., Liu, H., Document clustering via matrix representation, in: *Proceedings of 11th IEEE International Conference on Data Mining*, pp. 804–813, 2011.
4. Schaeffer, E.S., Survey on Graph Clustering. Elsevier *Comput. Sci. Rev.*, 1, 1, 27–64, 2007.
5. Li, C.H., Yang, J.C., Park, S.C., Text categorization algorithms using semantic approaches, corpus-based thesaurus and WordNet. *Expert Syst. Appl.*, Elsevier, 39, 765–772, 2012.
6. Zhang, W., Yoshida, T., Tang, X., Wanga, Q., Text clustering using frequent itemsets. *Knowl.-Based Syst.*, Elsevier, 23, 379–388, 2010.
7. Lam, W. and Hwuang, R., An active learning framework for semi-supervised Document Clustering with language modeling. *Data Knowl. Eng.*, 68, 49–67, 2009.
8. Pithawa, D., Nahar, S., Bhardwaj, V., Rawat, R., Dronawat, R., Rawat, A., Quantum Computing Technological Design Along with Its Dark Side. in: *Quantum Computing in Cybersecurity*, pp. 295–312, 2023.
9. Luo, Y., Xu, B., Cai, H., Bu, F., A Hybrid User Profile Model for Personalized Rec ommender System with Linked Open Data. *Enterprise Systems Conference (ES)*, Shanghai, pp. 243–248, 2014, doi: 10.1109/ES.2014.16.
10. Nahar, S., Pithawa, D., Bhardwaj, V., Rawat, R., Rawat, A., Pachlasiya, K., Quantum technology for military applications. in: *Quantum Computing in Cybersecurity*, pp. 313–334, 2023.
11. Shrivastava, M., Patil, R., Bhardwaj, V., Rawat, R., Telang, S., Rawat, A., Quantum Computing and Security Aspects of Attention-Based Visual Question Answering with Long Short-Term Memory. in: *Quantum Computing in Cybersecurity*, pp. 395–412, 2023.
12. Cremonesi, P., Koren, Y., Turrin, R., Performance of recommender algo rithms on top-n recommendation tasks, in: *Proc. of the fourth ACM conference on Recommender Systems*, ACM, New York, USA, pp. 39–46, 2010.
13. Bansal, N. and Koudas, N., Blogscope: A system for online analysis of high volume text streams, in: *Proceedings of the 33rd international conference on very large databases*, VLDB, pp. 1410–1413, 2007.
14. Fei Jiang, F.M., Pei, J., Chee Fu, A.W., Ix-cubes: iceberg cubes for data warehousing and olap on xml data, in: *CIKM '07: Proceedings of the sixteenth ACM conference on Information and knowledge management*, ACM, New York, NY, USA, pp. 905–908, 2007.
15. Chakravarthy, V.T., Gupta, H., Roy, P., Mohania, M., Efficiently linking text docu ments with relevant structured information, in: *VLDB '06: Proceedings of the 32nd International conference on very large data bases*, VLDB Endowment, pp. 667–678, 2006.

16. Lin, C.X., Ding, B., Han, J., Zhu, F., Zhao, B., Text Cube: Computing IR Measures for Multidimensional Text Database Analysis. *Eighth IEEE International Conference on Data Mining*, 2008.
17. Namdev, A., Patni, D., Dhaliwal, B. K., Parihar, S., Telang, S., Rawat, A., Potential Threats and Ethical Risks of Quantum Computing. in: *Quantum Computing in Cybersecurity*, pp. 335–352, 2023.
18. Shrivastava, M., Patil, R., Bhardwaj, V., Rawat, R., Telang, S., Rawat, A., Quantum Computing and Security Aspects of Attention-Based Visual Question Answering with Long Short-Term Memory, in: *Quantum Computing in Cybersecurity*, pp. 395–412, 2023.
19. Rawat, R., Chakrawarti, R.K., Raj, A.S.A., Mani, G., Chidambarathanu, K., Bhardwaj, R., Association rule learning for threat analysis using traffic analysis and packet filtering approach. *Int. J. Inf. Technol.*, *15*, 6, 3245–3255, 2023.
20. Sikarwar, R., Shakya, H. K., Kumar, A., Rawat, A., Advanced Security Solutions for Conversational AI. in: *Conversational Artificial Intelligence*, 287–301, 2024.
21. Patsariya, M. and Rajavat, A., A Progressive Design of MANET Security Protocol for Reliable and Secure Communication. *Int. J. Intell. Syst. Appl. Eng.*, *12*, 9s, 190–204, 2024.
22. Chauhan, D., Singh, C., Rawat, R., Chouhan, M., Conversational AI Applications in Ed-Tech Industry: An Analysis of Its Impact and Potential in Education, in: *Conversational Artificial Intelligence*, pp. 411–433, 2024.
23. Chauhan, D., Singh, C., Rawat, R., Dhawan, M., Evaluating the Performance of Conversational AI Tools: A Comparative Analysis, in: *Conversational Artificial Intelligence*, pp. 385–409, 2024.

8

An Investigation of Techniques to Encounter Security Issues Related to Mobile Applications

Devabalan Pounraj[1*], Pankaj Goel[2], Meenakshi[3], Domenic T. Sanchez[4], Parashuram Shankar Vadar[5], Rafael D. Sanchez[6] and Malik Jawarneh[7,8]

[1]Department of Computer Science and Engineering, Bonam Venkata Chalamayya Engineering College (Autonomous), Dr. B. R. Ambedkar Konaseema District, Andhrapradesh, India

[2]Applied Science And Humanities, G. L. Bajaj Institute of Technology and Mangement, Gr. Noida, India

[3]Apeejay Stya University, Sohna, Haryana, India

[4]Cebu Technological University-NEC, City of Naga, Cebu, Philippines

[5]Yashwantrao Chavan School of Rural Development, Shivaji University, Kolhapur, Maharashtra, India

[6]Cebu Institute of Technology-University, Cebu, Philippines

[7]Oman College of Management and Technology, Muscat, Oman

[8]INTI International University, Subang, Malaysia

Abstract

Since its introduction, malware has been used to attack mobile devices. Fraudulent mobile applications and inserted harmful apps are the two main forms of standalone mobile malware assaults. A thorough grasp of the permissions stated in apps and API calls is essential if one wants to successfully defend against mobile malware's cyber risks. Permission requests and API calls are used in this study to create an effective categorization model. There are many APIs that Android applications utilize, thus to make it easier to detect malicious apps, the authors have come up with three alternative categorizing strategies: ambiguous, hazardous, and disruptive. Mobile malware often asks for harmful permissions to access sensitive data, as shown by the findings, which show that malicious apps use a different set of API calls than benign ones.

**Corresponding author*: devabalanme@gmail.com

Rajesh Kumar Chakrawarti, Ranjana Sikarwar, Sanjaya Kumar Sarangi, Samson Arun Raj Albert Raj, Shweta Gupta, Krishnan Sakthidasan Sankaran and Romil Rawat (eds.) Natural Language Processing for Software Engineering, (127–142) © 2025 Scrivener Publishing LLC

This article presents a comprehensive literature review of various methods to deal with Android malware and related security concerns. This article contains an analytical investigation of various methods used for tackling malwares in Android operating system. This study found that the machine learning algorithms like Support Vector Machine and Convolution Neural Network are most accurate in classification and prediction of malwares in Android operating system.

Keywords: Security, privacy, android, malware, counter measures, machine learning techniques, blockchain

8.1 Introduction

The Android malware detection challenge has been intensively explored by the academic security research community. On fixed datasets, machine learning approaches that have been developed in the past often have high detection rates. According to a few, the forecast times are also rather rapid. However, the criteria for malware detection go well beyond these figures of merit; therefore most of them are not adequate for real-world implementation [1]. Schematic representation is shown below in Figure 8.1.

As a result of the proliferation of Android apps and smartphones, the Internet of Things is rapidly becoming a reality. There has been a

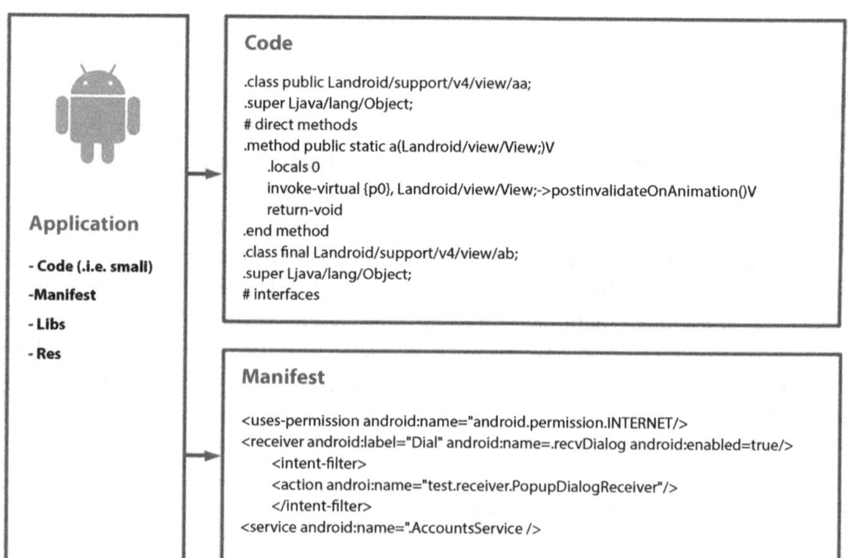

Figure 8.1 Schematic representation of android app.

considerable increase in the number of malicious software threats that are aimed at smartphones that run Android. In addition, owing to the widespread use of the Android operating system in Internet of Things devices, it is difficult to protect against attacks of this sort that are launched by malicious software. It is likely that the combination of machine learning methods and blockchain technology might improve the capabilities of Android Internet of Things devices to identify malware. Clustering, classification, and the blockchain are all components of the sequential process that was used in the introduction of the new technique. Clustering and classification techniques are used by machine learning to successfully capture malware data on the blockchain [2].

Malware [14] is always growing, both in terms of its diversity and its level of complexity, which makes it more difficult for detection technologies to keep up. The makers of malicious software use a broad variety of intricate methods whenever they wish to generate a new edition of the infection. To circumvent detection mechanisms and preserve the original functionality of the malicious code, these tactics include deleting, changing, or adding API calls that aren't really necessary [3].

Developers of malicious software [4] often focus their attention on the most widely used platforms in their efforts to infect the greatest number of devices feasible. The reason for this is that Android has been the subject of attacks on a consistently regular basis. The majority of efforts to battle malware on Android are focused on detection, with the objective of preventing infected devices from ever being infected in the very first place. For the purpose of automatically classifying malware samples and taking the appropriate measures to reduce the effect of those samples, this is a vital component.

It is possible to spread a significant number of malware samples on Android since they are variations of strains that are already known. Because of this, the security of an Android platform is dependent on a robust classifier that is able to manage large sample numbers. Automating variation detection and categorization is critical for detecting fraudulent activity and obtaining representative characteristics, particularly when dealing with larger datasets. Scalability plays a significant role in automating these processes, which is necessary for discovering fraudulent conduct. A deep neural network is made up of several layers, each of which has the capacity to learn and adjust its unique parameters to improve its classification accuracy. The computability of computers has been significantly improved by recent advancements in parallel computing and processing power [5, 6].

8.2 Literature Review

Malware identification is one of the several tedious and difficult parts of network security [1]. The proliferation of mobile devices and network approaches has greatly exacerbated the problem of malware, such as code obfuscation and zero-day attacks, on computer systems and networks. Methods for detecting malware that use machine learning (ML) have been suggested by several. The fast expansion of malware variants and assaults by adversarial examples (AEs) mean that research into malware detection is still continuing. Data visualization and adversarial training on detectors based on machine learning constitute our novel approach to the present constraint in malware detection. The ability to distinguish between various malware types will be greatly enhanced by this. With an average accuracy of 96.25% across all malwares evaluated, and a maximum accuracy of 97.33% according to experimental findings utilizing the MS BIG malware database and the Ember database, the suggested technique is able to thwart zero-day assaults. Malware assaults on the IT sector, particularly on AI and the Internet of Things, have increased noticeably. As the first general ML-based visualization tool for malware and variant detection, this work suggests Visual-AT, a universal binary format. To discover and evaluate variations of the same infection and previously undetected malware, another AT approach is used. This method makes use of visual data that has been altered by two ML algorithms. The experimental findings show that the proposed technique is more accurate and resilient than state-of-the-art ML-based malware detectors. Finally, the Visual-AT can accurately identify malware with a rate of up to 97.33% and an average detection rate of 96.56%. By reducing false positive rates by 81.17% and improving detection accuracy by 28.14%, Visual-AT outperforms both earlier and more modern machine learning-based visual identification methods.

It would be fascinating to see how the Visual-AT is used in novel situations, such as hierarchical labeling, given that the AEs are trained for every classification task using a horizontal label set (e.g. Animal-Dog-Poodle). Audio and voice processing are only two of the many possible applications of Visual-AT, which may make imposition and identification easier. Making the Visual-AT approach more relevant to other sorts of malware assaults, such the protection against the specialized attack termed Distributed Denial of Service (DDoS) [20–23], is another tough topic that requires study. Finally, there are a lot of ways the Visual-AT approach may boost machine learning [24–26] and computer security.

In this study, the authors address some of the most important issues that need to be considered before implementing Android malware detection systems in production environments [2]. A prospective approach must be contrasted with a constant stream of dynamic facts. A more accurate and realistic picture of detection performance may be obtained by simulating the continual flow of unknown file items into the classification process using streams of evolving data.

The authors created and used an ensemble method to detect Android malware automatically, taking into consideration the given real-world constraints. Because of its speed and reliability, Support Vector Machines use as inputs Atomic Naive Bayes classifiers that are built on several APK feature categories. Our example research successfully identified distinct forms of malware using different atomic classifiers, according to the authors. A model trained on 120,000 samples of a massive data stream has never previously had its results made publicly accessible.

The sensing, healthcare, and remote monitoring industries are just a few of the many that are benefiting from the Internet of Things (IoT) and its revolutionary changes to the environment [3]. Sending out a broadcast of all the malware data recorded in the blockchain's history makes it easy to spot any new infection. Producing weights for each set of characteristics, constructing an optimization parametric study, and continuously removing features with low weights that are redundant are all required steps in implementing the clustering strategy. The naive Bayes classifier is used to obtain the many properties of Android malware. The naive Bayes classifier use decision trees to glean additional crucial features for classification and regression, making it a very accurate and durable classifier. Our final strategy makes use of the permission blockchain to store real data acquired from extracted attributes in blocks of a distributed malware database, which speeds up and improves the accuracy of run-time malware detection.

Malware that targets Android phones has also proliferated in tandem with the exponential growth of Android smartphones [4]. One possible aspect is that third-party programs made for Android may run on any Android device, regardless of the OS. A key differentiator of Android is its inter-process communication capability, which enables components to be reused between processes. This is a great approach for the Android framework to access a lot of third-party services. Commonly, this kind of communication is managed by binding messaging objects called intents during runtime. Permissions and other well-studied characteristics may not be able to capture viral intentions as precisely as intents, which provide semantically rich information. This decision will be the worst one to make in the long run. You may maximize its potential by combining it with other well-known features. Out of a total of 7,406 applications, 1846 were found to be clean and 5,5600 to be contaminated. Among Android permissions, 83% could be identified and 91% of Android Intents could be identified. Using both features together raises the detection probability to 95.5%.

To deduce malicious activity, this study suggests novel algorithms that use associative principles and are based on recurrent subsequence alignment. The proposed technique [5] considers the chronology and probability of transitioning between two API invocations in the call sequence to detect groups of malwares that have similar dangerous behavior. It is not required that these subsets be sequential. Because they may be used in dynamic analysis scenarios, the following malware classification method is resistant to obfuscation and evasion strategies based on API call perturbation. The results show that it beats two well-known methods for malware detection: one that uses Markov chains and another that makes use of API call sequence matching techniques. In this experimental assessment, the suggested strategy outperformed its rivals in terms of categorization performance.

In this paper, the authors showcase the CANDYMAN approach to Android malware detection, which combines dynamic analysis with Markov chains. Using Markov chains and dynamic analysis approaches, it is possible to extract useful information from malware samples in the form of an ordered series of states. With this information, we may design features that can be used to classify things. By using Deep Learning algorithms and unbalanced learning approaches, among other machine learning techniques, the authors train a library of malware samples from various families. After that, they assess the proposed method. The Drebin dataset originally had 179 malware families; however, 4,442 samples were selected from 24 distinct families due to a lack of appropriate and relevant samples. The validity and relevance of these samples were further assessed. The experimental results in this dataset demonstrated an exceptionally high rate of accuracy, measuring 81.8% [6].

There are a lot of Android applications that track trends, customer preferences, and industry news [7]. The open-source nature of Android makes it possible for unlicensed app shops, and the platform's lack of app screening makes it inevitable that harmful software will infect Android-based smartphones and tablets. In response, specialists have devised a strategy that safeguards Android users against harmful applications by constructing a model that use ensemble Rotation Forest (RF). They utilized a dataset of 2,130 samples to test the plan's efficacy. An accuracy rate of 88.56% and a sensitivity of 88.10% we both attainable with the proposed approach.

The suggested method's accuracy was tested using a widely-used support vector machine (SVM) model. Its accuracy was found to be 3.33% higher than that of the SVM model. The outcomes of the tests demonstrated that this approach shows great promise for detecting malware on Android devices.

Users of the Android operating system have been somewhat worried about data security since its debut. Whether or not an app's special features can withstand viral attacks is highly dependent on those features. If Android malware detection is an issue, a Siamese network might be a solution. Feature grouping is an alternative to traditional methods for choosing the most appropriate API requests and permissions. We provide a Feature Centralized Siamese Convolutional Neural Network (FCSCNN) to speed up the identification process. A database's mean centers for benign and malicious data are first retrieved using the FCSCNN. We can find out what category an application belongs in by comparing its distance from the two centers. Findings from the "VirusShare" dataset show that the suggested method, FCSCNN, can detect viruses in less than 0.1 second with an accuracy of 98.07 percent [8]. An F-measure of 94.3% was achieved when the suggested strategy was used to a real-world dataset of 27,891 Android applications [9].

A technique for identifying Android malware using features collected from instruction call graphs is proposed in this work [10] based on previous research. When presented with a balanced dataset, deep neural networks make greater use of their exploration capabilities to distinguish between safe and hazardous execution routes. There isn't a publicly accessible model for Android malware detection available right now. A synthetic data set is used in this study. To find the best values for statistical indicators, we use a grid search strategy that takes into account both network parameters and hyper-parameters. We put the proposed technique through its paces using a dataset consisting of 24,650 negative samples and 25,000 positive ones. When comparing baseline classifiers with metrics for deep network architecture statistics, runtime is one of the metrics employed. A table displays the outcomes. A total of 91.42 percent accuracy, with an extra 91.11 percent F-measured, is achieved by the malware detection service that is supplied, according to the research.

Being able to detect malware is crucial for smart device security [11]. Despite its inability to identify zero-day assaults or polymorphic infections, signature-based approaches continue to be widely used. A hybrid approach is recommended for Android malware detection. This post will provide a strategy for analyzing Android apps that integrates heuristic and signature-based approaches. In this context, "reverse engineering" refers to disassembling an Android app to get its manifest and binary files.

The authors extracted manifest and binary files, as well as identified Android malware, using state-of-the-art machine learning methods. Using a battery of tests, they put a suite of classifiers through their paces to get there. When it comes to recognizing binary files, SVM is the way to go, but when it comes to identifying manifest.xml files, KNN is where it's at. The methodology demonstrated promising outcomes in malware identification when tested on benchmark datasets.

The authors of this paper [12] provide a new method for detecting malware that makes use of convolution recurrent neural networks and opcode sequences. Executable files are statistically defined as a collection of machine codes. Malware detection using opcode sequences is a theoretical possibility. A malware detection system that uses deep learning using these sequences as input and a method for extracting opcode sequences have been described in detail. The next stage involves a front-end convolutional auto encoder operating at the opcode level and a back-end dynamic neural network classifier. The experimental results showed that the suggested model had a 95% TPR, a receiver operating characteristic-area under the curve of 0, and a detection accuracy of 96%. Opcode sequences were the gold standard for malware detection back then, with a 97% success rate and an 82% false positive rate. The suggested model's accuracy was 96%, which was somewhat lower than the current method, but its TPR was 95%, which was much higher. The suggested approach is more effective at detecting harmful software because of this.

Customers are at risk from zero-day malware [13] samples because no safeguards are in place to prevent freshly found, unexpected activity. To deal with zero-day malware, prior information is essential for malware detection. The experts agree that it's bad when a once-dangerous feature becomes its real form. This implies that when confronted with new dangers, tightly linked feature-engineering that uses previous domain expertise may not work. In lieu of human specialists, this study employs a deep learning neural network that is completely ignorant of any possibly harmful characteristics. Examples of these traits include app permissions and the usage of hidden Android APIs. Three significant advantages are associated with our method. A malware detector for Android has been created using AI and machine learning. It can identify, rank, and categorize threats without the need for malware domain knowledge. The authors used Drebin and AMD benchmarks to assess our model's functionality in zero-day scenarios. Compared to state-of-the-art approaches, the proposed model achieved detection rates as high as 81% and 91%, respectively, a 57% improvement. With F1 scores of 0.9928 on the Drebin dataset and 0.9963 on the AMD benchmark dataset, respectively, overall detection performance was improved by an average of 77% when compared to current best practices. The findings were further contextualized by this.

An open vulnerability exists in the Android operating system because malicious programs (also termed malware) often find methods to circumvent the security mechanisms, and consumers are unaware of malware before downloading an app. Many techniques based on machine learning have been developed to identify malware in data collected via static analysis in an effort to address this issue. The authors summarized previous research on the topic and test the efficacy of supervised machine learning methods using the Drebin dataset's static analysis data. With the use of six well-known classification approaches, each with its own unique set of characteristics, they want to identify Android malware and features. With a small set of features, the proposed model was able to obtain good classification accuracy.

A meteoric rise in malware assaults has accompanied the widespread use of cellphones. When viruses use covert strategies, signature-based approaches struggle to detect them [15]. This study introduces the PIndroid framework, a tool for detecting malicious Android applications. When it comes to anti-malware solutions, PIndroid is the only one that uses Ensemble approaches in combination with permissions and intents. The suggested solution had the highest reported success rate of 99.8 percent across 1,745 real-world applications. The suggested method seems to be successful in detecting harmful applications, according to the empirical data.

Hackers have often targeted Android due to its widespread use and ease of access. Hackers are constantly developing new methods of attack and finding new security flaws in Android as Google rolls out new versions of the operating system. The security and resource restrictions of Android provide unique obstacles for malware attack detection and investigation. The authors of this work suggest several novel behavioral methods for classifying and detecting Android malware [16]. Decompiling the Android malware dataset allows one to construct an encoded list of potentially malicious API classes and functions. Following the generation of several sequence alignments for various malware types utilizing the encoded patterns, the profile hidden Markov model is used. An unknown program's potential danger may be assessed using a log probability score. Outperforming state-of-the-art approaches to Android malware detection, this framework achieves a remarkable 94.5% detection accuracy.

There has been a lot of buzz lately around Android malware detection [17]. Models for mobile virus detection are often constructed using machine learning approaches. Both static and dynamic application information may be gathered by these models. Hopefully, a far broader range of static and dynamic properties will be retrievable. Malware data is famously hard to collect owing to its intrinsic variety and its high dimensionality. It is possible to identify zero-day malware with the use of unsupervised malware detection technologies. In this scenario, an unsupervised feature reduction approach might be used to lower the data's dimensionality. This paper proposes a feature learning approach called Subspace based Restricted Boltzmann Machines (SRBM) to potentially reduce the dimensionality of virus detection data. Initially, the initial data set is searched for several subspaces. In addition, every subspace is given its own unique RBM. By combining the results of the hidden layers of the trained RBMs, a lower-dimensional data representation is produced. The features learnt by SRBM outperform those by other feature reduction methods when performance is assessed using clustering evaluation metrics. Datasets from OmniDroid, CIC2019, and CIC2020 show that NMI, ACC, and Fscore are effective.

Four malware detection methods—k-medoid-based next-neighbors (KMNN), all nearest neighbors (ANN), weighted all nearest neighbors (WANN), and first-closest (FNN)—use Hamming distance to identify sample similarity [18]. This approach has the potential to stop the spread of malware via an alarm system. There is a wealth of information here on detection techniques and the algorithms that go along with them. To verify their usefulness, a thorough evaluation of suggested similarity-based detection methods is carried out. Our analysis makes use of three datasets, including Drebin and malware as well as Contagio and Genome, which include both high-quality and low-quality Android applications. Classifier's efficacy was shown by comparing its results with those of the FalDroid methods, the PDME (program dissimilarity measure based on entropy), and a handful of other state-of-the-art algorithms. Several factors, such as API, purpose, and authorization, were examined on these three datasets. The data shows that the suggested algorithms are state-of-the-art with an accuracy rate of over 90% and, under some circumstances (such as when taking API features into account), over 99.99 percent.

The Android operating system has caused a tsunami wave of change in the mobile and portable device industries. This free and open-source mobile platform runs on virtual computers and can support a diverse ecosystem with millions of devices. There has been a meteoric rise in the amount of malware aimed at Android devices; at present, 99 percent of all malware detected on smartphones is Android-specific. There are other methods for evaluating and detecting malicious Android apps that have been published in academic journals. Because Android malware has evolved and proliferated so rapidly in recent years, it has become more difficult to identify new types of Android malware. Our 'End to End Deep Learning Architectures that detect and attribute Android malware using opcodes retrieved from application bytes' [19] are specialized learning models that have been designed to handle this challenge. By using neural networks with bidirectional long short-term memory (BiLSTMs), which outperform the current state-of-the-art, it is possible to identify static behavior in Android malware. Recurrent neural networks, Long Short-Term Memory networks, and their Bidirectional variant are the neural networks used in our study. For static malware analysis, our study also makes use of conventional neural architectures like Diabolo networks (autoencoders), deep convnets, and generative graphical models like deep belief networks. There is now a better bytecode dataset thanks to the inclusion of three publicly available and autonomously updated bytecode datasets. Results showed an F1-score of 0.996 and an accuracy of 0.999 on a dataset of over 1.8 million Android applications.

To keep up with the rapid growth of the IoT, cyber-physical systems (CPS) that use IoT principles to provide a range of services have become a focus for malware research and detection. Malware detection and analysis have already achieved great strides with the use of cutting-edge machine learning techniques like deep learning. But there are some problems with this method as well. The authors claim that certain methods aren't as reliable as they should be due to the presence of noise and outliers in the available malware datasets. The conclusion is that malware categorization might need some work. To get around this issue, it could be conceivable to combine correntropy with deep learning models. Below, we outline our technique [20] for malware detection and analysis, which involves reconstructing the loss function of a popular deep learning model called the Convolutional Neural Network (CNN). This allows us to find outlier behaviors. For challenging datasets with a high noise level, the mixed correntropy is a useful similarity metric to use. Results from testing the suggested method on both a popular benchmark dataset and a real-world malware dataset demonstrate its efficacy in learning.

8.3 Results and Discussions

Malware detection is one of the most difficult parts of network security. Anti-malware detection approaches that are based on machine learning (ML) have been suggested. The suggested strategy is able to avoid the zero-day attack and achieve up to 97.73 percent accuracy.

There has been an increase in the amount of malware targeting Android phones. Intents, which are late runtime binding messaging objects, are often responsible for this communication. An overall number of 7406 applications were examined, of which 1846 were found to be clean and 5560 contaminated. A total of 91% of Android Intents were identified, while an equal amount of 83% of Android permissions were identified. It can be identified 95.5% of the time when both traits are utilized in conjunction with one another.

To evaluate the suggested approach, machine learning techniques such as imbalanced learning methods and Deep Learning algorithms are utilized to train a dataset of malware samples from a range of families. According to the Drebin dataset, 179 separate malware families were represented, resulting in 4,442 samples divided among 24 distinct malware families, which were then chosen for relevance and validity owing to a scarcity of relevant and valid samples. The experimental findings reveal an accuracy rate of 81.8 percent for this dataset, which is an extremely high rate for this dataset [6].

The FCSCNN starts by determining the benign and malicious mean centers in the database. The distance between an application and the two centers is measured to determine which class to give it. The "VirusShare" dataset has been used to demonstrate that the proposed strategy FCSCNN is 98.07 percent accurate and takes less than 0.1 second to identify infections [8].

Our proposed approach for detecting mobile malware was shown to be successful using a real-world dataset of 27,891 Android apps, with an F-measure of 94.3%. Our approach to malware forensics and mobile app analysis, we feel, will be very valuable [9].

8.4 Conclusion

Malware has been used to target mobile devices since they were first introduced. The two most common types of independent mobile malware attacks are fraudulent mobile applications and malicious apps that are embedded within legitimate mobile applications. If one wishes to effectively protect against mobile malware's cyber threats, one must have a comprehensive understanding of the permissions provided in applications and API requests. Using permission requests and API calls, this research aims to develop an efficient classification model. Because there are several APIs that Android applications make use of, the authors have devised three additional categorization methodologies to make it simpler to identify malicious applications: confusing, dangerous, and disruptive, among others. According to the research, mobile malware often requests detrimental rights to access sensitive data, as shown by the fact that malicious applications make use of a distinct set of API calls than benign apps. An in-depth examination of the literature on several ways for dealing with Android malware and associated security problems is presented in this article. This article is a comprehensive look at how other people have dealt with Android malware and other security issues. This article is about different ways to deal with malware in the Android operating system. This study found that machine learning algorithms like the Support Vector Machine and the Convolution Neural Network are the best at classifying and predicting malware in the Android OS.

References

1. Liu, X., Lin, Y., Li, H., Zhang, J., A novel method for malware detection on ML-based visualization technique. *Comput. Secur.*, 89, 101682, 2020, Available: 10.1016/j.cose.2019.101682 [Accessed 6 January 2022].
2. Palumbo, P., Sayfullina, L., Komashinskiy, D., Eirola, E., Karhunen, J., A pragmatic android malware detection procedure. *Comput. Secur.*, 70, 689–701, 2017, Available: 10.1016/j.cose.2017.07.013 [Accessed 6 January 2022].
3. Kumar, R., Zhang, X., Wang, W., Khan, R., Kumar, J., Sharif, A., A Multimodal Malware Detection Technique for Android IoT Devices Using Various Features. *IEEE Access*, 7, 64411–64430, 2019, Available: 10.1109/access.2019.2916886.
4. Feizollah, A., Anuar, N., Salleh, R., Suarez-Tangil, G., Furnell, S., AndroDialysis: Analysis of Android Intent Effectiveness in Malware Detection. *Comput. Secur.*, 65, 121–134, 2017, Available: 10.1016/j.cose.2016.11.007 [Accessed 6 January 2022].
5. D'Angelo, G., Ficco, M., Palmieri, F., Association rule-based malware classification using common subsequences of API calls. *Appl. Soft Comput.*, 105, 107234, 2021, Available: 10.1016/j.asoc.2021.107234 [Accessed 6 January 2022].
6. Martín, A., Rodríguez-Fernández, V., Camacho, D., CANDYMAN: Classifying Android malware families by modelling dynamic traces with Markov chains. *Eng. Appl. Artif. Intell.*, 74, 121–133, 2018, Available: 10.1016/j.engappai.2018.06.006 [Accessed 6 January 2022].
7. Zhu, H., You, Z., Zhu, Z., Shi, W., Chen, X., Cheng, L., DroidDet: Effective and robust detection of android malware using static analysis along with rotation forest model. *Neurocomputing*, 272, 638–646, 2018, Available: 10.1016/j.neucom.2017.07.030 [Accessed 6 January 2022].

8. Kong, K., Zhang, Z., Yang, Z., Zhang, Z., FCSCNN: Feature centralized Siamese CNN-based android malware identification. *Comput. Secur.*, 112, 102514, 2022, Available: 10.1016/j.cose.2021.102514 [Accessed 6 January 2022].
9. Alazab, M., Alazab, M., Shalaginov, A., Mesleh, A., Awajan, A., Intelligent mobile malware detection using permission requests and API calls. *Future Gener. Comput. Syst.*, 107, 509–521, 2020, Available: 10.1016/j.future.2020.02.002 [Accessed 6 January 2022].
10. Pektaş, A. and Acarman, T., Learning to detect Android malware via opcode sequences. *Neurocomputing*, 396, 599–608, 2020, Available: 10.1016/j.neucom.2018.09.102 [Accessed 6 January 2022].
11. Rehman, Z. *et al.*, Machine learning-assisted signature and heuristic-based detection of malwares in Android devices. *Comput. Electr. Eng.*, 69, 828–841, 2018, Available: 10.1016/j.compeleceng.2017.11.028 [Accessed 6 January 2022].
12. Jeon, S. and Moon, J., Malware-Detection Method with a Convolutional Recurrent Neural Network Using Opcode Sequences. *Inf. Sci.*, 535, 1–15, 2020, Available: 10.1016/j.ins.2020.05.026 [Accessed 6 January 2022].
13. Millar, S., McLaughlin, N., Martinez del Rincon, J., Miller, P., Multi-view deep learning for zero-day Android malware detection. *J. Inf. Secur. Appl.*, 58, 102718, 2021, Available: 10.1016/j.jisa.2020.102718 [Accessed 6 January 2022].
14. Syrris, V. and Geneiatakis, D., On machine learning effectiveness for malware detection in Android OS using static analysis data. *J. Inf. Secur. Appl.*, 59, 102794, 2021, Available: 10.1016/j.jisa.2021.102794 [Accessed 6 January 2022].
15. Idrees, F., Rajarajan, M., Conti, M., Chen, T., Rahulamathavan, Y., PIndroid: A novel Android malware detection system using ensemble learning methods. *Comput. Secur.*, 68, 36–46, 2017, Available: 10.1016/j.cose.2017.03.011 [Accessed 6 January 2022].
16. Sasidharan, S. and Thomas, C., ProDroid — An Android malware detection framework based on profile hidden Markov model. *Pervasive Mob. Comput.*, 72, 101336, 2021, Available: 10.1016/j.pmcj.2021.101336 [Accessed 6 January 2022].
17. Liu, Z., Wang, R., Japkowicz, N., Tang, D., Zhang, W., Zhao, J., Research on unsupervised feature learning for Android malware detection based on Restricted Boltzmann Machines. *Future Gener. Comput. Syst.*, 120, 91–108, 2021, Available: 10.1016/j.future.2021.02.015 [Accessed 6 January 2022].
18. Taheri, R., Ghahramani, M., Javidan, R., Shojafar, M., Pooranian, Z., Conti, M., Similarity-based Android malware detection using Hamming distance of static binary features. *Future Gener. Comput. Syst.*, 105, 230–247, 2020, Available: 10.1016/j.future.2019.11.034 [Accessed 6 January 2022].
19. Amin, M., Tanveer, T., Tehseen, M., Khan, M., Khan, F., Anwar, S., Static malware detection and attribution in android byte-code through an end-to-end

deep system. *Future Gener. Comput. Syst.*, 102, 112–126, 2020, Available: 10.1016/j.future.2019.07.070 [Accessed 6 January 2022].
20. Luo, X., Li, J., Wang, W., Gao, Y., Zhao, W., Towards improving detection performance for malware with a correntropy-based deep learning method. *Digit. Commun. Netw.*, 7, 4, 570–579, 2021, Available: 10.1016/j.dcan.2021.02.003 [Accessed 6 January 2022].
21. Nahar, S., Pithawa, D., Bhardwaj, V., Rawat, R., Rawat, A., Pachlasiya, K., Quantum Technology for Military Applications, in: *Quantum Computing in Cybersecurity*, pp. 313–334, 2023.
22. Pithawa, D., Nahar, S., Bhardwaj, V., Rawat, R., Dronawat, R., Rawat, A., Quantum Computing Technological Design Along with Its Dark Side, in: *Quantum Computing in Cybersecurity*, pp. 295–312, 2023.
23. Shrivastava, M., Patil, R., Bhardwaj, V., Rawat, R., Telang, S., Rawat, A., Quantum Computing and Security Aspects of Attention-Based Visual Question Answering with Long Short-Term Memory, in: *Quantum Computing in Cybersecurity*, pp. 395–412, 2023.
24. Rawat, R., Chakrawarti, R.K., Sarangi, S.K., Patel, J., Bhardwaj, V., Rawat, A. and Rawat, H. eds. *Quantum Computing in Cybersecurity*. John Wiley & Sons, 2023. https://onlinelibrary.wiley.com/doi/book/10.1002/9781394167401
25. Patsariya, M. and Rajavat, A., A Progressive Design of MANET Security Protocol for Reliable and Secure Communication. *Int. J. Intell. Syst. Appl. Eng.*, *12*, 9s, 190–204, 2024.
26. Rathi, M. and Rajavat, A., Investigations and Design of Privacy-Preserving Data Mining Technique for Secure Data Publishing. *Int. J. Intell. Syst. Appl. Eng.*, *11*, 9s, 351–367, 2023.

9

Machine Learning for Sentiment Analysis Using Social Media Scrapped Data

Galiveeti Poornima[1*], Meenakshi[2], Malik Jawarneh[3,4], A. Shobana[5], K.P. Yuvaraj[6], Urmila R. Pol[7] and Tejashree Tejpal Moharekar[8]

[1]Presidency University, Bangalore, India
[2]Apeejay Stya University Sohna Haryana, Haryana, India
[3]Oman College of Management and Technology, Muscat, Oman
[4]INTI International University, Subang, Malaysia
[5]Department of Computer Applications, Sri Krishna Arts and Science College, Coimbatore, India
[6]Department of Mechanical Engineering, Sri Krishna College of Engineering and Technology, Coimbatore, India
[7]Department of Computer Science, Shivaji University, Kolhapur, India
[8]Yashwantrao Chavan School of Rural Development, Shivaji University, Kolhapur, Maharashtra, India

Abstract
Social media encompasses a wide range of internet apps that enable users to share, find, and engage with material created by other users. The number of persons utilizing social media increases by up to 3.80 million on a daily basis. By the start of 2020, the number of internet users is projected to reach 1 billion. Social media is a significant catalyst for acquiring and disseminating information in several domains such as entertainment, commerce, science, politics, and crisis management. It enables users to publish and share a diverse range of media formats, including text, videos, pictures, and audio. By conducting data analysis on social media, a person can access a wide range of information, including trends, concerns, and key individuals. Sentiment Analysis (SA) aims to ascertain the emotional response of individuals towards a specific service, business, or product. Sentiment analysis utilizes a diverse range of approaches, strategies, and tools to identify and extract subjective information, such as views and attitudes, from a given language.

**Corresponding author*: varaprabha.lita@gmail.com

Rajesh Kumar Chakrawarti, Ranjana Sikarwar, Sanjaya Kumar Sarangi, Samson Arun Raj Albert Raj, Shweta Gupta, Krishnan Sakthidasan Sankaran and Romil Rawat (eds.) Natural Language Processing for Software Engineering, (143–154) © 2025 Scrivener Publishing LLC

Traditionally, SA has sought to assess any information that is accessible to the public on the Internet. When utilized in conjunction with theme analysis, sentiment analysis has the capability to accurately detect both positive and negative emotions. Deep Learning Techniques (DLTs) are valuable in Sentiment Analysis (SA) because they have the ability to teach both supervised and unsupervised categories. DLTs comprise several network types such as feature presentation, phrase modeling, text creation, word representation estimation, vector representation, and sentence classification.

Keywords: Sentiment analysis, deep learning social media scrapped data, twitter data, accuracy, CNN, SVM, AdaBoost

9.1 Introduction

The most vivid representation of a person's deeds is found in their opinions. Subjective feelings such as viewpoint, sentiment, attitude, and so on had a significant impact on the actions of humans. The decisions and convictions that we make are influenced by the way in which other people view and feel about the world. When it comes to making decisions, we frequently consult with one another to get their perspectives on the matter. Considering that the opinion of the general public regarding their goods and services is always significant to them, this is something that can be beneficial to both individuals and a big number of organizations [1].

Even the typical consumer will examine reviews published by individuals who have already purchased a product before making a final choice about whether or not to purchase it. Customers' reviews and star ratings are shown next to each product on online marketplaces such as Amazon.com. These reviews are helpful in providing the buyer with recommendations of things to purchase. The utilization of social media platforms, such as Facebook, Twitter, and blogs, among others, for the purpose of conveying desires, accusations, and feelings regarding any service, product, or topic has witnessed a significant increase among users of a significant number of different countries. It is possible for a person to convey his/her opinion in connection to many different things, including an event, a person, a product, or even an organization. Components and features are examples of possible parts that make up an entity. A phone, for example, is an example of a thing. There are several components that make up the mobile device known as a "phone," including the battery, the screen, and so on. The quality of the camera and the voice are two examples of the traits that it possesses. Either by directly addressing any entity or by drawing parallels between them, individuals have the ability to communicate their thoughts in a number of different ways. Take into consideration the following example to better demonstrate the distinction between the two as follows: "battery life of Nokia is more than iPhone." In the first scenario, the speaker is expressing his/her viewpoint regarding the "battery life" feature of a Nokia phone. In the second scenario, he/she are comparing the two companies, Nokia and iPhone, and the battery life features that each of them possesses [2].

Despite the fact that surveys, interviews, and other antiquated techniques of acquiring and assessing opinionated data are still utilized, sentiment analysis by hand is an unattainable undertaking due to the vast volume of opinionated data and the absence of structure in this data. Methods that are capable of automatically extracting sentiment from unstructured opinionated data are required as a result of this. To sort through this mountain of subjective data, we are employing a wide range of Natural Language Processing (NLP) activities. Particularly, sentiment analysis is gaining popularity due to its objective of polarity classification. This objective can be accomplished through binary or multiclass classification, and it generates outcomes such as positive or negative, neutral or thumbs up or thumbs down. The application of sentiment analysis (SA) to the study of public opinion and sentiment exposes the influence on individuals as well as the impact on the community as a whole during the course of the research. Opinions are the primary foci of sentiment analysis [3].

As a result of the flood of biased data, sentiment analysis has developed into a significant area of research in recent years. Simply put, it is extremely important for the advancement of artificial intelligence. In particular, the meteoric expansion of recommendation websites, blogs, and social networking platforms such as Twitter and Facebook has attracted the interest of a great number of organizations in the field of sentiment analysis. When it comes to finding new customers and successfully selling their products, businesses and corporations rely on this kind of subjective information [4]. A wide range of user-generated content (UGC) that may be found on the internet, including blog posts, reviews, comments, and other forms of online material, can be subjected to automated sentiment analysis. To put it another way, it analyzes a piece of text to determine how people are feeling and then assigns a label to that feeling, such as positive, negative, neutral, furious, sad, etc. To summarize, Sentiment Analysis, which is sometimes referred to as Opinion Mining, is a method that is utilized in the field of machine learning (ML) that employs text analysis, computational linguistics, and natural language processing to classify the feelings that individuals have regarding any certain matter [5].

9.2 Twitter Sentiment Analysis

Analysis of sentiment has been the primary focus of studies for a considerable amount of time. Students in academic institutions have shown an interest in sentiment analysis as a method for determining the viewpoints of the general public on a number of different subjects. It has become an indispensable instrument, whether it be for a single individual or for a major organization that is making a decision based on opinionated data that is available to the public. A rising number of companies, including the government, are incorporating sentiment analysis into their marketing strategies and are offering financial assistance for projects that are relevant to this field. The various types of sentiment research that may be performed on social media can also lead to wonderful business opportunities. Systems that provide recommendations and models that are based on customer relationships stand to gain a great deal from its deployment. For the purpose of illustrating the argument, it is helpful for recommendation systems to determine which features customers appreciate and for them to eliminate features that elicit negative feedback. Despite the fact that there has been a consistent interest in sentiment analysis for a considerable amount of time, the field has only recently witnessed a significant increase in the amount of study [6].

Since its inception in the 1950s, sentiment analysis has been used for the goal of extracting opinions from written texts. On the other hand, the explosion of web 2.0 itself is directly responsible for the extensive use of sentiment analysis to opinionated data found online. When compared to the extensive histories of linguistics and Natural Language Processing (NLP), the amount of study conducted on opinions and sentiments before to the year 2000 was rather unrepresentative. Prior to the widespread recognition of sentiment analysis, the majority of the older publications focused their attention on examining a wide range of themes, including affects, metaphors, points of view, and a variety of other subjects. Prior to the introduction of the World Wide Web (WWW), there may have been a scarcity of data that was available digitally and contained expressions of opinion. People have turned to the time-honored method of word-of-mouth (WOM) to learn about people's ideas and feelings regarding any given topic or situation. This is due to the fact that the internet has not advanced technologically [7].

Word-of-mouth marketing, often known as WOM, was defined by S. Tokes and Lomax as "interpersonal communication regarding product or services regardless of whether the receiver regards communicator as impartial." Before the World Wide Web became widely known, organizations would traditionally rely on polls, surveys, and interviews to gather information about people's opinions. The subject of study known as sentiment analysis has always been one that is both fascinating and dynamic. However, with the advent of web 2.0, individuals have never before had access to a platform that is unparalleled in its ability to express their insightful opinions on a broad variety of topics. Numerous factors are contributing to the rising interest that researchers are displaying in the field of sentiment analysis. It is possible that one of the contributing factors is the fact that sentiment analysis offers a substantial number of potential applications across a wide range of industries, such as healthcare, politics, social events, finance, and many others. By making good use of the vast volumes of sentiment-bearing opinionated data that are available to the public, organizations and government enterprises have the potential to significantly benefit from accessing this information. Another, more obvious reason is that this is the case. It has been observed that the rise of social media technology has coincided with the emergence of sentiment analysis as a subject of study [8].

When it comes to the dissemination of information and the expression of opinions, Twitter stands out as the social media platform with the most users. Through the use of this casual platform, individuals from all over the world are able to send and receive messages. It is because of this that a lot of natural disasters have been brought to the notice of the general population. It all began in 2006 as a platform for sending and receiving text messages (SMS), but since then, it has expanded significantly beyond its intended purpose. This is largely due to the efforts of social media influencers and well-known celebrities who use it to engage with their individual audiences, whether for personal or business purposes. According to research (https://learn.g2.com/Twitter-statistics), there are more than 321 million individuals who use Twitter on a daily basis, and they transmit an average of 500 million tweets with their accounts. This day and age, Twitter remains one of the most popular microblogging services due to the fact that millions of users submit millions of tweets every single day. There is an opportunity for brand expansion on Twitter due to the fact that businesses are able to communicate with and gain a better understanding of their customers through the platform's opinionated data. The fact that more than 80 percent of the material is not organized is a further insult. "Tweet" is the term used to describe a message that is posted by an individual on the microblogging service Twitter. Given that, the maximum number of characters that can be included in a tweet is 160. As a consequence of this, tweets are written in a manner that is less formal [9, 10].

There is a significant amount of interest in the study of Twitter sentiment analysis at the present time. This information can be utilized by both the government and corporations to evaluate the effectiveness of their systems in the midst of the flooding of subjective data that is freely available on the internet [18–21]. Twitter is considered to be one of the most popular microblogging websites, where users frequently communicate their thoughts, opinions, and attitudes regarding a wide range of topics and events. Twitter is the most popular social networking platform [22–24], and it is used by not only the regular person but also politicians and celebrities. The elections for the Lok Sabha, the decision regarding the Ram Mandir, the decision regarding the shutdown, and the decision regarding demonetization are just a few instances of the events that cause Twitter to become flooded with tweets that are related to the current topic. It is enlightening to observe how individuals are feeling about a variety of subjects and current events based on the tweets that they have released [11].

In spite of the fact that there is a plethora of opinionated content available on Twitter in the form of tweets, manually gathering the vast amount of data, extracting relevant information, and then synthesizing the opinions that have been gathered into a meaningful manner is a big job. What this demonstrates is the importance of using software that analyzes sentiment. Despite the fact that opinionated data in the form of tweets is relatively unstructured, group thoughts from a variety of persons are more illuminating than individual perspectives. In addition, the vast majority of the digital data that can be accessed online is unstructured, meaning that it is not organized in any specific way (https://learn.g2.com/structured-vs-unstructured-data). The distillation and extraction of relevant information from data that carries sentiment [25] is required to improve the quality of decisions that are made for society as a whole. Sentiment analysis on Twitter can be of use in this regard.

According to [12], the basic objective of Twitter sentiment analysis is to extract the feelings that are associated with a text, which in this case is tweets.

Analysis of Twitter sentiment has been the subject of a great number of previous research, which have utilized a wide range of features and approaches (including lexicon-based, machine learning, and hybrid ways of thinking). The work that researchers have done on Twitter sentiment analysis has achieved considerable results, according to their reports.

To further extract the essential information from opinionated data, a number of methods for sentiment analysis [13] have been developed. The vast majority of research projects that have been conducted on Twitter sentiment analysis have utilized supervised machine learning approaches.

These techniques entail training classifiers with data that has been labeled. Despite this, there is a dearth of research that compares a large number of various state-of-the-art classifiers that make use of different characteristics. Through a comparison of the performance of a number of state-of-the-art classifiers in respect to features, the major objective of this thesis is to offer a solution to the problem that has been presented. The objective is to determine which classifiers offer the greatest degree of success when applied to particular sets of characteristics. [14–19] Several classifiers will be evaluated on several domains, including a public benchmark dataset and a real-time Twitter dataset (in which real-time tweets are obtained from Twitter). These datasets will be used to test the algorithms.

9.3 Sentiment Analysis Using Machine Learning Techniques

The methods that were used may be seen in Figure 9.1.

This section consists of three classification techniques: Support Vector Machine, AdaBoost, and Convolutional Neural Network.

Support Vector Machine (SVM) is an excellent choice to study if you are seeking for an algorithm that may assist you in recognizing pedestrians. A common method for displaying images that are produced by computer vision algorithms is to use a non-linear matrix that is composed of square

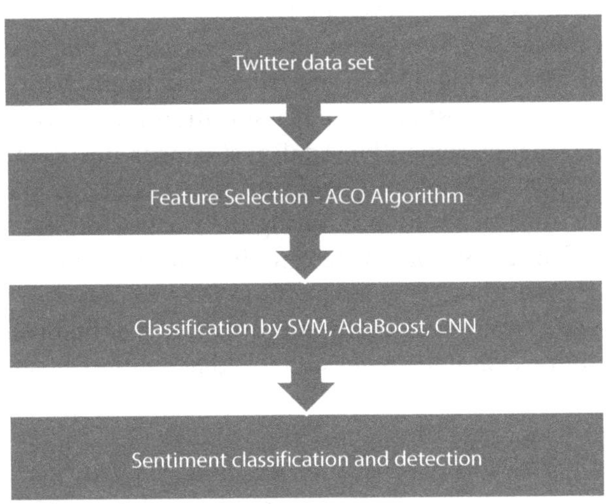

Figure 9.1 ACO-CNN deep learning model for sentiment classification and detection.

pixels. For an object to be accurately classified, it is required to first extract the distinctive qualities of the item from an image. It is possible to extract features from photos by employing approaches that have been tried and tested for a long time at feature extraction. For the purpose of determining whether or not an image displays pedestrians, a number of binary classifiers, such as support vector machines (SVMs), are utilized. To accomplish this, the support vector machine (SVM) constructs a hyperplane that connects the non-linear data points of the images. After that, it classifies each point into one of two binary categories. By increasing the distance between the data point and the hyperplane, it is possible to get a higher level of classification accuracy. One example of its application is the procedure of employing a support vector machine (SVM) to identify favorable characteristics in photographs [18].

AdaBoost is the name given to the innovative gradient-boosting approach that was first developed by researchers at the University of Michigan for the purpose of binary classification. After the initial tree decision tree has been constructed, its performance on the training data is utilized to assess the usefulness of the tree. This evaluation will establish whether or not the tree decision tree is useful in your decision-making process. Through the utilization of a number of distinct classification techniques, this approach results in the generation of a single strategy that encompasses everything. The initial model is constructed by beginning with the data required for training. Other models are built to correct any errors that may have been present in the initial model. If they are able to accurately predict the data contained in the training set, then the models are considered to have been developed; otherwise, they continue to be created until the maximum number of models possible is reached. Ultimately, the process of integrating all of the earlier classification models resulted in the creation of the most effective classification model. As a result of its ability to detect pedestrians, the AdaBoost sensor has garnered a lot of attention from professionals. To begin the process of computing the feature values, we must begin by translating the images into what are known as rectangular frames. Simply by designating the series of windows in any order, pedestrians and other people who use the road can be easily differentiated from one another. The same steps are taken as before, but this time the windows in the example image are picked in a different order than they were in the previous instance. With the exception of that, there has been no alteration. The procedure of categorizing windows can be repeated until a cascade of categorization criteria is constructed [19]. Any windows that are not rejected by any of the models are regarded to be pedestrian windows. There is no limit to the number of times you can perform this operation.

When confronted with this circumstance, the first model disregards windows that are obviously not belonging to pedestrians, the second model disregards windows that are less obviously not belonging to pedestrians, and so on.

On the other hand, when applied to big datasets, machine learning techniques have very little practical application. There are a number of reasons for this, including underfitting, sophisticated models, and inadequate optimization of resources. The effectiveness of the procedures is immediately blamed on these impediments, which are directly accountable for the reduction. By applying deep learning networks to big datasets, individuals may be able to acquire new knowledge, improve their ability to predict outcomes, and take action based on those predictions. The implementation of "deep learning" has made it possible for computer models to acquire the capability of learning from both textual and visual data. In response to the boom in the amount of data that is available, a number of distinct deep learning architectures have come into being. The effectiveness of these designs has been demonstrated to be superior when compared to other conventional machine learning techniques.

In the realm of deep neural networks, a convolutional neural network is among the most popular and extensively utilized designs. The area of computer vision makes use of this type of network (CNN). Layers that comprise a convolutional neural network (CNN) include the convolutional layer, pooling layer, activation layer, and connected convolutional layer. A deep convolutional neural network (CNN) is characterized by an extensive network of interconnected convolutional layers (Figure 9.1). Information traveling through the convolutional layer is primarily filtered by it. In the convolutional layer, there is a filter that is applied to a small subset of the input picture's pixels, say 3 x 3.

An operation known as "dot" is applied to the pixel values by the filter, and the effect of this operation is controlled by a weight that has been calculated in advance. Because of this, the size of the picture's data point matrices is decreased once the convolutional layer has been applied to the image. Through the process of back propagation with the matrices that are transmitted to the activation layer, the matrices of the activation layer train the network and provide the network with nonlinearity. The size of the filter matrix and the number of sample layers are both reduced by the process of pooling, which involves merging samples. The sort of layer known as a max layer selects only one property from each category rather than all of them. The output of the max layers is utilized by the linked layer to come up with a collection of candidate label probabilities. To obtain these probabilities, the connected layer is utilized. It is important to take into account the most likely consequence while selecting a label.

9.4 Conclusion

The objective of behavior analysis, also known as sentiment analysis (SA), is to determine the emotional reaction of individuals to a particular service, business, or product. When it comes to identifying and extracting subjective information, such as views and attitudes, from a given language, sentiment analysis makes use of a wide variety of methodologies, strategies, and technologies. Throughout its history, SA has made it a priority to evaluate any and all information that is available to the general public on the internet. At the same time as it is utilized in combination with topic analysis, sentiment analysis has the capacity to accurately detect both positive and negative feelings. The capacity of Deep Learning Techniques to teach both supervised and unsupervised categories makes them an invaluable tool for Sentiment Analysis, which allows for the analysis of sentiment. DLTs are comprised of a number of different types of networks, including feature presentation, phrase modeling, text creation, word representation estimation, vector representation, and sentence classification. This chapter presents a deep learning-based technique to perform sentiment analysis on Twitter scrapped data.

References

1. Bollen, J., Mao, H., Zeng, X., Twitter mood predicts the stock market. *J. Comput. Sci.*, 2, 3, 1–8, 2011.
2. Karabulut, Y., Can Facebook predict stock market activity?, SSRN eLibrary, pp. 1–58, 2013, http://ssrn.com/abstract=2017099 or http://dx.doi.org/10.2139/ssrn.2017099. Accessed 2 Feb 2014.
3. Liu, B., Sentiment Analysis and Subjectivity, in: *Handbook of Natural Language Processing*, Marcel Dekker, Inc., New York, NY, USA, 2009.
4. Richmond, J.A., Spies in ancient Greece. *Greece Rome (Second Series)*, 45, 01, 1–18, 1998.
5. Rawat, R., Kaur, U., Khan, S.P., Sikarwar, R., Sankaran, K., *Using Computational Intelligence for the Dark Web and Illicit Behavior Detection*. IGI Global. 1, 2022, https://doi.org/10.4018/978-1-6684-6444-1.
6. Kharde, V.A. and Sonawane, S.S., Sentiment Analysis of Twitter Data: A Survey of Techniques. *Int. J. Comput. Appl.*, 139, 975–8887, 2016, doi: 10.5120/ijca2016908625.

7. Khairnar, J. and Kinikar, M., Machine learning algorithms for opinion mining and sentiment classification. *Int. J. Sci. Res. Publ.*, 3, 6, 1–6, 2013.
8. Zhang, T., An Introduction to Support Vector Machines and Other Kernel-based Learning Methods. A review, Association for the Advancement of Artificial Intelligence (www.aaai.org), 2001.
9. Vateekul, P. and Koomsubha, T., A Study of Sentiment Analysis Using Deep Learning Techniques on Thai Twitter Data, 2016.
10. Pang, B. and Lee, L., Opinion Mining and Sentiment Analysis. *Found. Trends Inf. Retr.*, 2, 1–2, 1–135, 2008.
11. Chauhan, D., Singh, C., Rawat, R., Dhawan, M., Evaluating the Performance of Conversational AI Tools: A Comparative Analysis. *Conversational Artificial Intelligence*, pp. 385–409, 2024.
12. Castellanos, M., Dayal, M., Hsu, M., Ghosh, R., Dekhil, M., U LCI: A Social Channel Analysis Platform for Live Customer Intelligence, in: *Proceedings of the 2011 international Conference on Management of Data*, 2011.
13. Zhang, W., Yoshida, T., Tang, X., Ho, T.B., Improving effectiveness of mutual information for substantival multiword expression extraction. *Expert Syst. Appl.*, 36, 10919–10930, 2009, doi: 10.1016/j.eswa.2009.02.026.
14. Liu, B., Sentiment Analysis and Opinion Mining. *Synth. Lect. Hum. Lang. Technol.*, 5, 1–167, 2012, doi: 10.2200/S00416ED1V01Y201204HLT016.
15. Yu, Y., Lin, H., Meng, J., Zhao, Z., Visual and Textual Sentiment Analysis of a Microblog Using Deep Convolutional Neural Networks. *Algorithms*, 9, 41, 2016, doi: 10.3390/a9020041.
16. Hagenau, M., Liebmann, M., Neumann, D., Automated news reading: Stock price prediction based on financial news using context-capturing features. *Decis. Support Syst.*, 55, 685–697, 2013, doi: 10.1016/j.dss.2013.02.006.
17. Kim Boes, A.I., Buhalis, D., Wilkinson, P.F., An Empirical Study on the Relationship between Twitter Sentiment and Influence in the Tourism Domain. *Ann. Tour. Res.*, 28, 1070–1072, 2012, doi: 10.1016/S0160-7383(01)00012-3.
18. Pak, A. and Paroubek, P., Twitter as a Corpus for Sentiment Analysis and Opinion Mining. *Proc. Seventh Conf. Int. Lang. Resour. Eval.*, pp. 1320–1326, 2010, doi: 10.1371/journal.pone.0026624.
19. Rawat, R., Chakrawarti, R.K., Sarangi, S.K., Choudhary, R., Gadwal, A.S., and Bhardwaj, V., eds. *Robotic Process Automation*. John Wiley & Sons, 2023.
20. Patsariya, M. and Rajavat, A., A Progressive Design of MANET Security Protocol for Reliable and Secure Communication. *Int. J. Intell. Syst. Appl. Eng.*, *12*, 9s, 190–204, 2024.
21. Rathi, M. and Rajavat, A., Investigations and Design of Privacy-Preserving Data Mining Technique for Secure Data Publishing. *Int. J. Intell. Syst. Appl. Eng.*, *11*, 9s, 351–367, 2023.
22. Dubey, P. and Rajavat, A., Effective K-means clustering algorithm for efficient data mining, in: *2023 2nd International Conference on Vision Towards*

Emerging Trends in Communication and Networking Technologies (ViTECoN), pp. 1–6, IEEE, 2023, May.

23. Nahar, S., Pithawa, D., Bhardwaj, V., Rawat, R., Rawat, A., Pachlasiya, K., Quantum Technology for Military Applications, in: *Quantum Computing in Cybersecurity*, pp. 313–334, 2023.
24. Pithawa, D., Nahar, S., Bhardwaj, V., Rawat, R., Dronawat, R., Rawat, A., Quantum Computing Technological Design Along with Its Dark Side, in: *Quantum Computing in Cybersecurity*, pp. 295–312, 2023.
25. Rawat, R., Telang, S., William, P., Kaur, U., C.U., O., *Dark Web Pattern Recognition and Crime Analysis Using Machine Intelligence*. IGI Global, 2, 2022, https://doi.org/10.4018/978-1-6684-3942-5.

10

Opinion Mining Using Classification Techniques on Electronic Media Data

Meenakshi

Apeejay Stya University Sohna, Haryana, India

Abstract
Both businesses and consumers have changed their viewpoint in reaction to the movement of the Web from being a producer of information to being a receiver of information. Consequently, an increasing number of individuals are opting to make judgments using online platforms. Companies highly value these evaluations as they provide impartial depictions of the customer's genuine sentiments. Although possessing such information ensures substantial advantages, it also presents notable challenges.

One significant factor behind this phenomenon is the widespread availability of social media applications. Prior to the advent of technology, individuals relied on personal networks of family and friends to obtain information for informed purchasing choices.

However, in the present day, the internet has taken control, and individuals rely on online assessments to inform their purchasing decisions. Moreover, rather than engaging in face-to-face interactions, numerous individuals seek for these types of evaluations on the internet. A plausible rationale for this predicament is the surge in the prevalence of social media. Internet users now have the ability to access a vast amount of information that may be advantageous to both companies and their customers. Although this data is undeniably beneficial, the overwhelming number of views required for just one product has resulted in choice fatigue. To mitigate choice fatigue for individuals and facilitate effective decision-making for enterprises, the root-cause analysis approach offers a comprehensive and accurate understanding of products. Aspect extraction, often referred to as opinion target extraction, and sentiment identification, also called opinion mining,

Email: mt6458@gmail.com

Rajesh Kumar Chakrawarti, Ranjana Sikarwar, Sanjaya Kumar Sarangi, Samson Arun Raj Albert Raj, Shweta Gupta, Krishnan Sakthidasan Sankaran and Romil Rawat (eds.) Natural Language Processing for Software Engineering, (155–168) © 2025 Scrivener Publishing LLC

are two components of root-cause analysis. Sentiment analysis is to ascertain the reviewer's overall position about a certain product. Consequently, both customers and companies may more effectively evaluate the advantages and disadvantages of their products. Both organizations and consumers can gain advantages by enhancing the root-cause analysis method proposed in this thesis. Support Vector Machines (SVM), Random Forest, Multilayer perception and CNN algorithms are efficient in opinion mining task.

***Keywords*:** Opinion mining, machine learning, electronic media analysis, natural language processing

10.1 Introduction

Electronic media analysis refers to the process of examining and comprehending media content that is transmitted through electronic platforms, such as the internet, radio, and social media. Electronic media analysis aims to decode the information transmitted through various channels and understand its effects on society and individuals. There are other approaches to examining electronic media, including:

Content analysis: This involves thoroughly analyzing the language, graphics, and themes of a program or website, which are the components of media messaging. Through the examination of media information, content analysts are able to identify patterns, such as the occurrence rate of a specific sort of message or the way in which a given issue is presented.

Discourse analysis: To accomplish this, we need to analyze the terminology and speech used by the media to identify the extent to which it affects our perspective of the world. Through the process of discourse analysis, the assumptions and values that are included within media messages may be retrieved from them.

Audience analysis: Studying the cognitive and emotional responses of different demographic groups to media messages is a crucial aspect of this discipline. Different groups of people have different reactions and understandings of media messages, and these understandings affect their attitudes and actions. Conducting audience analysis can assist in identifying these distinctions.

Social media analysis: As part of this procedure, data from social media platforms are examined to provide further insights as to how users communicate and share information on these websites. By utilizing social media analytics, we are able to discern patterns in the data shared on these platforms and analyze the manner in which individuals engage with it.

Natural language processing (NLP) is a subfield of artificial intelligence that focuses on comprehending how humans and computers communicate with one another. It has the potential to be a useful instrument for analyzing information that is presented in the form of text, audio, and video. The scope of this concept encompasses a broad variety of techniques that enable robots to comprehend and generate material that may be utilized by humans. Natural language processing and programming languages are two quite different things. There is a huge distinction between the two. On the other hand, the collection of mathematical operations that they have made available is not static. A computer program that instructs a machine on what to perform is what creates the definition of a computational task. There are currently no compilers or interpreters available for natural languages such as Hindi, English, German, and French. This is a very unfortunate situation. When it comes to language processing, the process often involves converting human-spoken utterances into numerical data, which computers may subsequently use for analysis and interpretation. In addition to this, its objective is to produce natural language writing that is semantically consistent and intelligible. Natural language generation (NLG) and natural language understanding (NLU) are both acronyms that stand for "natural language generation" and "natural language understanding," respectively. A sufficient amount of emphasis cannot be placed on the intricacy of human language. While this is going on, natural language processing (NLP) is emerging as a solution to the growing demand for computer programs that are able to comprehend human pronunciation [1].

Natural language processing techniques that were used in the past depended on linguistics-based strategies, such as part-of-speech (POS) tagging, which drew a solution from the most fundamental semantic and syntactic aspects of a language. An increasing number of people are using NLP into their day-to-day lives. For example, when a user begins typing a search phrase into a search engine, an application can attempt to estimate the following words that the user will type. Smartphones, tablets, laptops, and even ships that already have software loaded on them attempt to recognize human spoken orders and attempt to carry them out. Numerous well-known services, such as chatbots, social media monitoring, language translation, voice assistants, and spam filters, are dependent on the natural language reading capabilities of computers. Natural language processing (NLP) has witnessed the introduction of a broad variety of unique solutions in recent years, which are employed by a wide spectrum of customers. These solutions have been developed by different companies. Among these users are those who construct websites, do research, create conversational artificial intelligence applications, and a great many more [2].

10.2 Opinion Mining

The fast rise of Web 2.0 has led to a significant amount of content being shared on electronic media platforms such as reviews, comments, tweets, blogs, and more. Businesses can gain valuable insights by examining this sort of data. The analysis of electronic media material was previously ignored. In the present day, several firms heavily depend on content analysis to ascertain the public's perception of their brand. However, commercial organizations now face a significant hurdle in accurately gauging public sentiment from internet sources. In this context, there is a need for a completely self-governing system that can gather, assess, and categorize user sentiment among a vast amount of digital media data. Sentiment analysis (SA) is the field of computer science that focuses on analyzing public opinion, attitude, and judgement using subjective input such as text, audio, video, and more. Opinion Mining is an area of social learning.

Social learning refers to the acquisition of knowledge and skills via active engagement and collaboration with others. It involves the exchange of information and knowledge among individuals or groups, usually facilitated by digital platforms. Classrooms, online communities, social media groups, and professional networks are all instances of informal and formal settings where social learning may occur. Students engage in social learning through verbal communication, collaborative effort, and mutual knowledge acquisition. By engaging in their studies, students have the opportunity to enhance their communication, critical thinking, and problem-solving skills, as well as develop a deeper understanding of the subject matter [3].

Furthermore, individuals can gain advantages in both their personal and professional spheres by developing and nurturing social interactions and networks through social learning. Emotions play a vital role in driving behavior, highlighting the importance of social learning in sentiment analysis. The firm use social learning to analyze and monitor the content trends associated with the product. Consumer satisfaction significantly influences repurchase behavior and word-of-mouth recommendations. Individuals have the ability to exercise their voting rights to either support or oppose a leader depending on their sentiments towards his beliefs and personality. Authorities possess the power to implement necessary actions to prevent potentially violent demonstrations or marches if public opinion towards these activities suggests a high probability of violence.

Opinion mining utilizes machine learning, data analysis, and natural language processing techniques to derive quantitative sentiment assessments from unstructured text. There are several approaches available for doing this task. Practically, one may manually do the task by conducting online searches for authentic blog posts, thoroughly reading them, and thereafter assessing the sentiment or polarity of the comments area. However, an algorithm can accomplish the task with more efficiency and precision. Data-driven sentiment analysis systems undergo a process of iterative evolution as machine learning algorithms are used to perform sentiment scoring. Sufficient training samples, in the form of annotated texts tagged with sentiment, are essential for training sentiment analysis algorithms. Experts extract and annotate these samples of training data [4].

10.3 Related Work

Recent deep learning efforts have generated state-of-the-art models that have sparked interest in sentiment analysis. The main difficulty in past sentiment analysis research is understanding the semantic relationships between target properties of sentences in their respective contexts. The reason for this is the significant correlation between the contextual factors of the input phrases and the extent to which they match the desired attribute. Therefore, it is advisable to include both contextual and targeted training connections. Authors developed a model that is reliant on the target. The model employs two Long Short-Term Memory (LSTM) units, positioned on both the right and left sides, to get representations that are contingent upon the target. Furthermore, it implicitly extracts the semantic connection between the goal feature of the text and the contextual factors in the ASA task. This approach can augment traditional word embeddings by including target aspect word representations. An Attention Mechanism is employed to capture the relationship between the aspect and its context [5].

The authors developed a flexible deep learning system using Apache Spark for analyzing massive amounts of data on smartphones. The findings indicate that DL with spark has superior efficiency in comparison to other spark models.

The authors offered two more strategies that may be used to extract relevant attitudes from the surrounding contexts of targets. Additionally, they applied spectral clustering (SC) to the industry-standard dataset following the training of the model using a typical backpropagation technique. Compared to the baseline models, this one had superior performance in properly forecasting emotion. Several research have demonstrated that deep learning algorithms have the ability to automatically collect important input from the ASC. Nevertheless, most of these approaches evaluate the target data directly [6].

The authors introduced two LSTM algorithms that focus on extracting target and aspect information using attention. Therefore, the attention mechanism in the SC paradigm enhances the ASC task by assigning greater significance to the most crucial components of a sentence. The experimental results indicated that both techniques offer a superior understanding of the connections between context and sentiment, in comparison to the baseline models. In their study, the authors showed that utilizing a RAM with attention mechanism may efficiently gather pertinent information from different words in a phrase. They also proposed a technique to measure the significance of each word and its context by employing a multiple attention mechanism [7].

The authors introduced a unique approach to predict sentiment polarity. This strategy depends on understanding the temporal connections between different aspects. The authors created a novel target-based methodology to tackle this issue. This model depicts the relationship between each word and its corresponding context word inside the aspect. This model employs a Convolutional Neural Network (CNN) to address the limitations of the traditional attention mechanism in identifying specific features. The TSC target information was included into word representations by deep transformation. Consequently, the model consistently outperforms several advanced models in terms of accuracy and acquires a deeper understanding of abstract contextual information [8].

The authors emphasized the significance of independently and collaboratively obtaining background and target information. The interactive attention network model is able to comprehend the interactions between target and contextual information by isolating them. This model had impressive performance on the SemEval 2014 datasets, showcasing its ability to acquire significant features for context-based and target-based Aspect Sentiment Analysis (ASA). The attention mechanism in the model enables it to identify the target features that hold the most significance by analyzing their semantic orientation [9].

To preserve the associations between aspect words and their surrounding context, a model based on attention-based encoders was developed. In their study, the authors employed a positional attention mechanism with a penalized feature to improve the performance of the ASA task inside a single sentence. The objective was to enhance the disparity of attention weights closer to the aspect [10].

The ASC problem was addressed by analyzing Chinese review sentences using Knowledge-Enhanced Neural Networks, as described. The objective was to ascertain subjective and situation-dependent components. The sentiment knowledge graph was utilized to ascertain the sentiment polarity of every aspect-pair. The model demonstrated superior performance compared to conventional models when evaluated on the Chinese automobile review dataset, resulting in more thorough sentiment analysis outputs [11].

The authors constructed a deep memory network for sentiment classification by employing a location encoding and content attention strategy. Most SA studies uncover explicit attitudes, whether they are voiced explicitly or indirectly. Explicit emotions have gained considerable attention and made great progress in both the corporate and academic domains. The absence of vocabulary to articulate certain emotions indicates that unspoken sentiments continue to be a problem [12].

To address the issues related to implicit sentiment analysis (SA), the authors suggested employing Bi-LSTM with multi-polarity orthogonal attention. The Bi-LSTM model is more effective than the usual attention mechanism in identifying important aspects with sentiment information in implicit sentiment analysis. Aspect-embedding has been extensively employed for aspect group categorization in ASA activities. However, the depiction of the relationship between aspect-terms and aspect-categories is insufficient [13].

The authors suggested a position-based hierarchical technique to extract important information from phrase segments. The results obtained from trials done on four standard datasets demonstrated that the proposed strategy surpassed other strategies in terms of improving ASC performance. The authors developed a novel approach that incorporates LSTM into the hidden representations to enable both coarse and fine-attention techniques. Rather than depending on location data, most deep learning approaches emphasize the importance of attention when representing each component. ASC's performance may be enhanced by leveraging the multi-level knowledge from SSC and incorporating the position information from several stages. To tackle the problem of long-range dependencies, the authors introduced a novel attention-based model that captures the semantic connections among the identified features in a phrase. The IMDB and Yelp 2018 datasets were extensively studied to enhance the performance of sentiment classification by acquiring conceptual semantic understanding of documents [14–18].

10.4 Opinion Mining Techniques

The progression of digital services in the domain of electronic media has been extraordinary. Microblogging encompasses personal perspectives, firsthand encounters, and recommendations, making it the most effective medium for sharing daily events. This multimedia material includes textual information, photographs, and hyperlinks to external websites. Social marketing, political campaigns, academics, and journalists heavily depend on electronic media to distribute their perspectives on current events and commercial products. The internet greatly streamlines our everyday life by enabling the efficient completion of complex tasks. Online ratings and reviews have become essential in consumers' decision-making process when buying things. Customer feedback is a vital component of product development. Electronic media, the latest digital platform, allows people to share the most current local, national, and global news. An effective method for understanding people's viewpoints on various matters is by utilizing sentiment analysis (SA), which relies on online customer reviews. The information produced by electronic media users effectively conveys customers' thoughts, emotions, and demands on infrastructure, products, and services.

10.4.1 Naïve Bayes

The Naive Bayes approach is a probabilistic classification technique that applies the Bayes theorem. This method of data classification assumes that characteristics are independent of one other, meaning that the presence of one characteristic does not restrict the presence of another feature. The phrase "naive" accurately characterizes it. Despite this oversimplification, Naive Bayes often produces good outcomes in practical situations, especially in the context of text classification problems. This technique utilizes the probabilities of the attributes in the data point to ascertain the probability of the data point belonging to a specific class. Firstly, we calculate the prior probability of each class by dividing the training data by the total number of observations in that class. Next, when presented with a class, we calculate the conditional probability of each characteristic. The chance of a data point belonging to a specific class is obtained by multiplying the prior and conditional probabilities of all its attributes. However, when the independence requirement is adequately robust, Naive Bayes may be used to other classification problems. These approaches provide benefits because of their computational efficiency and ability to achieve excellent performance with less training data.

10.4.2 Support Vector Machine

Support Vector Machine (SVM) is a supervised technique commonly employed for regression and classification tasks. The procedure ascertains the optimal hyperplane for segregating the data points into their respective classes. The support vectors are the closest data points to each class, and the hyperplane is chosen to optimize the margin. Support vector machines (SVM) are commonly utilized in the classification of pictures, texts, and bioinformatics. In high-dimensional data, when the number of attributes exceeds the number of data points, the data become even more valuable. SVM is well-known for its ability to handle non-linearly separable data. It accomplishes this by utilizing kernel methods to convert the input into a feature space with higher dimensions. The goal of support vector machines (SVM) is to find the hyperplane that maximizes the margin while minimizing classification error. SVM does this by solving a constrained optimization problem, which involves finding the Lagrange multipliers that satisfy the Karush-Kuhn-Tucker (KKT) conditions. By resolving this optimization problem, we derive the optimal hyperplane for separating the data points into their respective classes, along with the decision function that utilizes this hyperplane to classify newly additional data points. The determination of the decision boundary for the support vector machine is contingent upon the specific issue and model being used.

10.4.3 Decision Tree

Two instances in which decision trees are utilized are classification and regression. To provide this method its functionality, the feature space is partitioned in a recursive manner. The feature and threshold that effectively split the data into the target classes are selected by the algorithm at each phase of the process. This process is repeated for each and every subset until a certain endpoint is reached, such as a maximum depth for the tree or a minimum number of samples for each node. It is possible to make a prediction about a new class after the creation of the decision tree by tracing the path that the tree takes from its root to its leaf node. Most of the training examples that are able to reach that leaf node are successful in achieving the class. They are a well-liked machine learning method due to their ability to handle a combination of continuous and categorical data, as well as their ease of use and interpretability. The unfortunate reality is that they are not always the most effective, and there is a potential that they will be overfit. There is a possibility that they will not perform as well when dealing with noisy data or a decision boundary that is intricate.

10.4.4 Multiple Linear Regression

Multiple linear regression (MLR) is a statistical approach used to predict a continuous dependent variable YY based on one or more independent variables $YX1$, $XX2$,..., $XXnn$. Due to its inability to directly predict categorical variables, it is rarely used as a classifier. Typical implementations encompass logistic regression, decision trees, support vector machines, neural networks, and random forests, all of which are employed to address classification problems. These approaches are more effective at predicting categorical outcomes. Converting the category variable into a numerical one allows for the utilization of multiple linear regression as a classifier. The multiple linear regression model can utilize modified categorical data as an independent variable. However, it is important to note that this system has some imperfections. It may exhibit worse performance compared to other categorization methods or encounter difficulties when dealing with data that have a high number of categories. Therefore, it is rarely employed as the main answer for a classification problem.

10.4.5 Multilayer Perceptron

In the field of machine learning, the multilayer perceptron (MLP) is a well-known feedforward artificial neural network that is utilized for supervised learning tasks such as classification and regression. The input layer, the hidden layer (or layers), and the output layer are the three components that make up the architecture of a multi-layer perceptron (MLP). It is at the input layer that the model obtains the attributes that it uses as input. Every single node in the input layer is responsible for representing a single input feature. The processing takes place in the hidden layers, which are composed of a collection of nodes that apply non-linear modifications to the data that are being received. The nodes that make up a hidden layer collect data from all of the layers that are below them, assign a weight to the inputs, apply an activation function that is not linear to the sum, and then ultimately transfer the output to the nodes that are below it. A possible output value is represented by each node in the output layer, which is where the model's final output is formed once it has been processed. Before training a multi-layer perceptron (MLP), it is necessary to adjust the weights of the connections that exist between the nodes of the network. This is done with the intention of reducing the disparity between the actual outputs and the predicted outputs. In most cases, the optimization technique known as stochastic gradient descent is utilized for this purpose. The authors are able to maintain the accuracy of the weights by repeatedly updating the weights at each layer of the network, beginning with the output and working their way backwards. Backpropagation is the phrase that accurately describes this process.

10.4.6 Convolutional Neural Network

Convolutional Neural Networks (CNNs) are utilized in various text categorization applications (Severyn & Moschitti, n.d.). Examples of text analysis tasks include subject categorization, sentiment analysis, and spam detection. A word embedding matrix is a widely used format for input data in text classification. In this matrix, each row corresponds to a word vector, while each column corresponds to a vocabulary word. Word embeddings are fed into a 1D convolutional layer, which applies filters to the input sequence, enabling the usage of CNNs for text classification. Typically, the filters have different widths, allowing the network to detect patterns with different levels of detail. Following the processing of the output by the convolutional layer, it is then passed on to a max-pooling layer. This layer selects the highest value from each feature map and utilizes it to reduce the dimensionality of the feature maps. The ultimate outcome, often a probability distribution over the possible categories, is produced by transmitting the resulting feature vector across a fully linked layer. To train the network, the weights are adjusted so that the expected output and the actual labels have minimal discrepancy. Popular techniques for this problem involve the use of gradient descent and backpropagation. Multiple benchmarks have demonstrated that Convolutional Neural Networks (CNNs) attain the highest level of performance, which is promising for solving text classification challenges. The performance of the model relies significantly on the quality and amount of the training data, the selection of hyperparameters, and the model architecture, similar to other machine learning models.

10.4.7 Long Short-Term Memory

The Long Short-Term Memory (LSTM) [19, 20] Network is an architecture of neural networks specifically designed to process sequential input, such as text or voice. Long Short-Term Memory (LSTM) networks [21–23], a kind of Recurrent Neural Network (RNN), have the ability to selectively retain or ignore information from previous time steps. Due to their ability to capture long-term relationships and interactions between inputs, activities that include sequential data are very successful in achieving their goals. An LSTM cell is a unit that has the ability to retain information over an extended period of time by utilizing a sequence of memory cells. The gates on these memory cells enable fine control over the incoming and exiting data streams. The input gate decides the data that should be incorporated into the memory cell at the current time step, while the forget gate determines the data that should be eliminated from the memory cell at the previous time step. Currently, the output gate specifies which specific information from the memory cell should be used to generate the output.

10.5 Conclusion

The complexities inherent in human speech provide significant challenges in identifying and extracting pertinent segments from customer assessments. The strategies given in this chapter are essential for efficiently extracting elements from reviews. The objective of sentiment analysis is to ascertain the overall viewpoint of the reviewer on the product under consideration. Consequently, both firms and customers may have the ability to evaluate the advantages and disadvantages of their products more accurately. By enhancing the proposed method of analyzing the fundamental causes of a problem, both organizations and customers may enjoy the advantages. Regarding opinion mining, algorithms such as CNN, Multilayer Perceptron, Random Forest, and Support Vector Machines (SVM) have strong performance. Enhancing the model with additional guidelines to effectively process sarcasm will be a forthcoming improvement. Data patterns with even minimal occurrences can be detected by employing supplementary criteria. This requires an extremely strong model that is capable of accurately capturing even the smallest variations. The authors will explore the possibility of integrating this model into their design or modifying their architecture to incorporate these guidelines at a later time. Further elimination of outdated data can enhance forecast accuracy, even when reinforcements are employed to capture shifts in trends. The ranking issues offer a comprehensive understanding of the significance of each aspect, with the most crucial ones being the study of time requirements and money considerations. To enhance corporate decision-making, it is advisable to prioritize issues that may be promptly resolved or need low expenditure.

References

1. Patil, A. and Thakare, S., Analyzing public sentiment variations on and Facebook. *Int. J. Adv. Res. Comput. Sci. Technol.*, 5, 2, 30–3, April–June. 2017.
2. Sharma, A., Sharma, A., Singh, R.K., Upadhayay, M.D., Hybrid classifier for sentiment analysis using effective pipelining. *Int. Res. J. Eng. Technol.*, 4, 8, 2276–81, August 2017.
3. Mishra, A. K., Tyagi, A. K., Dananjayan, S., Rajavat, A., Rawat, H., Rawat, A., Revolutionizing Government Operations: The Impact of Artificial Intelligence in Public Administration. in: *Conversational Artificial Intelligence*, pp. 607–634, 2024.

4. Zhang, K., Yu Cheng, Y., Agrawal, A., Palsetia, D., Lee, K., Choudhary, A., SES: sentiment elicitation system for social media data. *Icdmsentire*, pp. 129–36, 2011.
5. Tupsoundarya, A. and Dandannavar, P.S., Sentiment expression via emoticons on socialmedia. *Int. J. Res. Appl. Sci. Eng. Technol.*, 6, 6, 2404–8, June 2018.
6. Sharif, W., Samsudin, N.A., Deris, M.M., Naseem, R., Mushtaq, M.F., Effect of negation in sentiment analysis. *Int. J. Comput. Linguist. Res.*, 8, 47–56, June 2017.
7. Nahar, S., Pithawa, D., Bhardwaj, V., Rawat, R., Rawat, A., Pachlasiya, K., Quantum technology for military applications. in: *Quantum Computing in Cybersecurity*, pp. 313–334, 2023.
8. Perdana, R.S. and Pinandito, A., Combining likes-retweet analysis and naive Bayes classifier within twitter for sentiment analysis. *J. Telecommun. Electron. Comput. Eng.*, 10, 1–8, 41–6, April 2018.
9. UmaMaheswari, S. and Dhenakaran, S.S., Sentiment analysis on social media big data with multiple tweet words. *Int. J. Innov. Technol. Explor. Eng.*, 8, 10, 2514–8, August 2019.
10. Sharma, A. and Dey, S., Artificial neural network based approach for sentiment analysis of opinionated text. *ACM Transaction*, pp. 37–42, 2012.
11. Turney, P., Thumbs up or thumbs down? Semantic orientation applied to unsupervised classification of reviews. *Proc. Assoc. Comput. Ling. (ACL)*, pp. 417–24, 2002.
12. Pang, B. and Lee, L., Opinion mining and sentiment analysis. *Found. Trends Inf. Retr.*, 2, 1–2, 1–135, 2008.
13. Tan, S., Li, Y., Sun, H., Guan, Z., Yan, X., Bu, J., Chen, C., He, X., Interpreting the public sentiment variations on twitter. *IEEE Trans. Knowl. Data Eng.*, 26, 5, 1158–70, May 2014.
14. Filho, P.B., Avanço, L., Pardo, T., Nunes, M.D.G.V., NILC–USP: an improved hybrid system for sentiment analysis in Twitter messages, in: *Proceedings of the 8th International Workshop on Semantic Evaluation (SemEval2014)*, 2014.
15. Gonçalves, P., Araújo, M., Benevenuto, F., Cha, M., Comparing and combining sentiment analysis methods, 2014.
16. Iqbal, M., Karim, A., Kamiran, F., Bias-aware lexiconbased sentiment analysis, in: *ACM Symposium on Applied Computing*, pp. 845–50, 2015.
17. Vidya, N.A., Fanany, M., II, Budi, I., Twitter sentiment to analyze net brand reputation of mobile phone providers. *Procedia Comput. Sci.*, 72, 519–26, 2015.
18. Sikarwar, R., Shakya, H. K., Kumar, A., Rawat, A., Advanced Security Solutions for Conversational AI. in: *Conversational Artificial Intelligence*, pp. 287–301, 2024.
19. Patsariya, M. and Rajavat, A., A Progressive Design of MANET Security Protocol for Reliable and Secure Communication. *Int. J. Intell. Syst. Appl. Eng.*, 12, 9s, 190–204, 2024.

20. Rathi, M. and Rajavat, A., Investigations and Design of Privacy-Preserving Data Mining Technique for Secure Data Publishing. *Int. J. Intell. Syst. Appl. Eng.*, 11, 9s, 351–367, 2023.
21. Dubey, P. and Rajavat, A., Effective K-means clustering algorithm for efficient data mining, in: *2023 2nd International Conference on Vision Towards Emerging Trends in Communication and Networking Technologies (ViTECoN)*, 2023, May, IEEE, pp. 1–6.
22. Chauhan, D., Singh, C., Rawat, R., Chouhan, M., Conversational AI Applications in Ed-Tech Industry: An Analysis of Its Impact and Potential in Education, in: *Conversational Artificial Intelligence*, pp. 411–433, 2024.
23. Chauhan, D., Singh, C., Rawat, R., Dhawan, M., Evaluating the Performance of Conversational AI Tools: A Comparative Analysis, in: *Conversational Artificial Intelligence*, pp. 385–409, 2024.

11

Spam Content Filtering in Online Social Networks

Meenakshi

Apeejay Stya University Sohna, Haryana, India

Abstract
In the contemporary period, individuals engage in both professional and personal contacts mostly through electronic modes of communication. Over the past decade, the popularity and influence of email and social media platforms such as LinkedIn, Facebook, and Twitter have experienced a significant and rapid increase. Online social networking platforms and email are exploited by spammers to distribute their messages, taking advantage of their popularity. The spam filtering system must possess sufficient robustness to effectively detect and prevent unwanted communications, hence halting spammers' activities promptly. When attempting to recognize spam communications, the majority of individuals rely on either text-based or collaborative methods. To improve the accuracy of spam detection in emails and social networks, it is necessary to employ strategies that reduce the occurrence of false positives and false negatives. Support vector machines are the most effective method for categorizing and detecting spam emails.

***Keywords*:** Spam e-mail filtering, machine learning, support vector machine, accuracy, online social networks

11.1 Introduction

Electronic communication has become an essential component of contemporary existence. There are two fundamental categories of electronic communication: formal emails and personal online social networks (OSNs). The biggest issue that internet users are currently facing is the widespread

Email: mt6458@gmail.com

Rajesh Kumar Chakrawarti, Ranjana Sikarwar, Sanjaya Kumar Sarangi, Samson Arun Raj Albert Raj, Shweta Gupta, Krishnan Sakthidasan Sankaran and Romil Rawat (eds.) Natural Language Processing for Software Engineering, (169–182) © 2025 Scrivener Publishing LLC

occurrence of spam messages. Spam refers to unsolicited commercial communications delivered over electronic messaging systems with the intention of marketing, spreading hazardous content, engaging in phishing, or just annoying customers. Spam may easily become viral because individuals tend to trust and spread information that others have already shared. Spam is an unproductive and often costly use of time for consumers. Internet consumers encounter the challenging issue of spam, but there are several methods to safeguard themselves from it [1].

11.1.1 E-Mail Spam

In the present era, the vast majority of individuals opt to interact using electronic mail. An urgent issue is the development of a method to effectively exclude undesirable emails from the email system. A spam filter must possess the qualities of being user-friendly and adaptable to be considered necessary. The exact and accurate filter only produces lower rates of false positives and false negatives. False positives arise when a filter evaluates a message and erroneously categorizes it as spam. The erroneous forecast made by the filter results in unsolicited emails being classified as false negatives. An effective spam filter should have a low percentage of false positives and a high rate of accuracy. Due to the potential danger caused by spam emails, categorizing them as "ham emails" in users' inboxes raises the likelihood of unwittingly causing damage to their systems [2].

Another concern is to the elevated frequency of false positives. Although ham email may not be harmful, it nevertheless gets filtered into the spam folder. As a result, the user can overlook important emails due to her failure to remember to check her spam folder. For a classifier, maintaining a low percentage of false positives and false negatives is of utmost importance. A negative connection exists between the rates of true positives and true negatives, and the rates of false positives and false negatives. Consequently, as the rates of false positive and false negative decrease, the accuracy rate increases proportionally with the number of correct classifications. Spam filter attacks may be classified into two primary categories: poison attacks and impersonation attacks. David and his colleagues (2018a) discussed instances of poison attempts in an email conversation. Poisoning is a technique used to decrease the chances of spam detection by including many non-spam terms into spam emails. The spam e-mail perpetrator employs impersonation assaults by hacking into the accounts or computers of unsuspecting users. There are two main approaches to spam filtering: content-based and identity-based. The content-based filter analyzes and ranks emails based on patterns and phrases that are commonly associated with spam. Identity-based spam filtering utilizes a comparison of the sender's email address with a blacklist and a whitelist to accurately detect spam.

Both the whitelist and the blacklist include email addresses of persons whose communications should not be subjected to filtering by the spam filter [3].

11.2 E-Mail Spam Identification Methods

Various techniques can be employed to avoid spam emails, including the utilization of intricate mathematical algorithms to ascertain if an email was solicited or unsolicited. These materials exhibit a significant level of spatial and temporal intricacy. To overcome these issues, there are other alternatives available that do not require any technological expertise. Below is an incomplete compilation of a few of them:

11.2.1 Content-Based Spam Identification Method

Through the utilization of a static spam term corpus, the content-based e-mail spam detection system achieves its goal. With the purpose of categorizing the emails into spam and ham folders based on the frequency with which particular spam keywords appear in the emails respectively. Spammers are able to circumvent content-based spam detection technologies by changing and filtering their emails before sending them to the people they plan to send them to. There is a pattern that spammers may follow while they are spreading spam [4].

As part of their analysis of spam emails, researchers provided a comprehensive breakdown of the methods that spammers employ. The rule-based filtering technique is included in the content-based spam detection strategies. For the purposes of training and email classification, rules are utilized. When it comes to the identification and filtering of spam e-mails, users are required to manually build pattern matching rules, which can be a process that can be time-consuming. Since the activity of spam emails changes over time, it is necessary to have a rule that changes to recognize spam emails. As an illustration of a rule-based algorithm, the RIPPER rule learning algorithm is a good example.

One of the strategies that falls under the area of content-based methods is the identification of spam messages using statistical methods. For the purpose of modeling the data, approaches from the field of machine learning are utilized. Several algorithms have been developed for the purpose of classifying texts; however, for these approaches to be effective, the classifier must first be trained by a human. Among the various types of content-based searching, there is a subgroup that makes use of search engines. Individuals that engage in spamming send emails that contain connections to other websites. The link will lead you to a website that is sponsored by advertisements. It is the responsibility of the search engine to automatically review the content of the websites that are linked in the emails.

11.2.2 Identity-Based Spam Identification Method

The identification of the senders is crucial for the detection of spam emails. This identification mechanism utilizes a list-based method, which incorporates whitelists and blacklists. Users using electronic mail have the ability to create a whitelist and blacklist. Users have the ability to add email addresses to a whitelist or blacklist. Messages originating from email addresses listed in the whitelist are authorized to be delivered to the intended recipients' primary email folders, but messages originating from email addresses listed in the blacklist are automatically directed to the spam folder. In a distributed adaptive blacklist situation, the server is tasked with the responsibility of managing the adaptive blacklist. Upon receiving an email, the e-mail transfer agent triggers the activation of the filter. Examining the email's header may be used to determine whether mails are spam, serving as a method for categorizing spam based on identity. This approach verifies if emails lack a sender ID in the "From" field and if the "To" field has an excessive number of recipient IDs.

11.3 Online Social Network Spam

Email is not the only medium in which spammers and spam messages may be found; social media platforms are also plagued by them. The growth of online social networks (OSNs) such as Facebook, LinkedIn, Twitter, and others is accelerating at an unparalleled rate. It is possible that the unanticipated growth of online social networks (OSNs) might be attributable to two factors: the large number of users and the greater connectedness to the general public. Ignoring the bad features of social networks is not going to get you very far, despite the fact that there are clearly some beneficial advancements in the domain of social networks currently. The most aggravating experience for people who use social media is having to cope with an excessive amount of spam. The amount of inaccurate or unpleasant information that is moving throughout the networks will lead to the emergence of a number of issues that will affect society. Screening out undesired texts may be accomplished in a variety of different ways. The number of spam messages that are transmitted through social media platforms has not greatly diminished, despite the fact that this has been stated [5].

Different types of social spam are available. Common among them are of following types:

- **Bulk Message Spam**
Disseminating several identical copies of material to numerous social network users all at once. Bulk texting may also be used to send ads, false messages, or harmful links to social networks.

- **Malicious Link Spam**
To deceive users, harm their devices, or generate revenue for spammers, malicious links are posted on social networks. Users' comments or postings are a perfect medium for the harmful links to spread.

- **Fake Review Spam**
Users write false reviews to benefit financially from the product service suppliers that reply to them. Its secondary objective is to lessen the product's appeal.

- **Click-bait Spam**
Simply said, clickbait is an enticing headline that, when clicked, takes the reader to a website that offers irrelevant or boring information. In this way, clickbait boosts their financial gain by increasing the amount of page views. Like jacking is a sort of clickbaiting when people post status updates on social media without any prior knowledge or intention.

11.4 Related Work

Spam is a term that refers to unwanted or unwelcome messages that are sent over communication channels such as instant messaging, microblogging sites, and electronic mail. When it comes to email spam filters, users and email service providers (ESPs) alike have a lot of things to complain about. It is necessary for filters to be both resistant to attacks and extremely accurate for them to efficiently identify spam.

The addition of more spam filters ought to result in a reduction in the number of false positives and false negatives. A false positive is the term used to describe the situation in which legitimate emails are mistakenly selected as spam. It is referred to as a false negative when emails that are considered spam are not identified as spam. In spite of the vast number of spam classifiers that are currently available, it is still possible for some spam filter attacks to occur. These attacks include the poison attack and the impersonation attack. A number of popular words are used into poison assaults to reduce the likelihood that spam e-mails would be recognized as spam. Spammers engage in impersonation assaults, in which they give the impression that they are genuine users by utilizing stolen credentials or by compromising their computers in some other way. With this in mind, the objective is to recognize spam and develop a technique of spam filtering that can efficiently differentiate between legitimate emails and those that are not wanted [6].

The email system was improved by adding data from social networks to better boost the effectiveness of spam screening. It was found in a number of studies that when it came to filtering spam, individuals' trust, hobbies, and the degree of closeness in their relationships on social networks were also taken into consideration. However, due to the fact that spam emails are totally generated from social networks, these factors are not sufficient to identify and classify their content. For the purpose of classifying the emails, there were no criteria that were specifically based on the email itself that were calculated. An active learning-based spam message categorization was proposed by the authors as a means of significantly reducing the amount of time required for classification while still preserving accuracy. The technique that they adopted did not take into consideration the categorization of emails that contain photographs.

The utilization of a fuzzy-based technique was the concept behind the classification of spam emails. After conducting an analysis of the structural patterns of the spam messages, the authors decided to implement a fuzzy-based method to reduce the noise point problem. The authors indicated that the selection of features for spam filtering in emails is based on category ratio and word frequency, and that this decision is made independently of the sample size obtained from each class.

One of the potential solutions that the authors have suggested is to use information gathered from social networks to identify spam in emails that were received. The spam filtering strategies that it utilized included both identity-based and content-based methods, in addition to social network approaches. For the purpose of scanning and grading emails that fall under the content-based category, typical spam keywords and patterns are utilized. In the content-based category, impersonation attacks, in which hostile actors appear to be genuine users by compromising their computers or forging their IDs, are extremely frequent. These assaults are considered to be particularly common. One of the most important aspects of identity-based filtering is the whitelist and blacklist of email addresses that are managed by the user. Due to the fact that they rely only on sender email addresses, they are more susceptible to poison assaults. A form of attack that involves cramming spam emails with actual phrases in an effort to make them less likely to be detected as spam is called a spear phishing attack. Email systems rely on a subset of social network indicators, such as proximity, interest, and trust, to differentiate between genuine and spam communications. This allows them to discern between the two types of messages. Bayesian spam filters were utilized to significantly improve accuracy, provide protection against attacks, and ensure effective spam detection. In addition, trust and interest criteria were not taken into account while calculating email networks [7].

Methods of machine learning were utilized by the authors to identify individuals that engage in spamming on Twitter. A significant portion of the information that was utilized for the empirical research consisted of millions of tweets. It was determined that a neighborhood-based detection method would be the most effective way to identify spammers using Twitter. The collection of data on profile-based feature evasion and the validation of evasion tactics were utilized to detect spammers on Twitter.

We were able to detect spam accounts on Twitter by looking at criteria such as the number of followers and tweets that a user had. A thorough investigation was conducted on the 24 detecting factors as well as the many evasion tactics that are utilized by spammers on Twitter. However, the difficulty is that the datasets that were gathered from Twitter and categorized as harmless only contained people who had never posted malicious URLs. This is the case even though some of the accounts that were included in the datasets might possibly be hazardous [8].

Researchers have devised a technique that may be used to identify spammers on social media platforms. For the purpose of identifying spammers, a method that is based on supervised machine learning was proposed. The contents of the message and the actions taken by the user were related with a number of essential features, and the authors used some of these qualities. For the purpose of identifying spammers, feature selection strategies were utilized in conjunction with Support Vector Machine (SVM) classification algorithms. This allowed for the determination of which qualities were the most important and the amount of weight that should be assigned to each feature. In addition, statistical analysis and human selection were utilized in the process of automatic feature extraction.

The method obtained a high level of performance when it took into consideration the true positive rate of spammers as well as the rate of non-spammers. The technique was proposed by scientists as a means of tracking down potentially hazardous emails [9].

This method, which placed a focus on persistent threats, was superior than other existing tactics because of its recipient-oriented aspect. Preprocessing of the emails with data that was particular to the firm was performed before a random forest classifier was used to categorize the emails that corresponded to the company. Following that, certain properties were retrieved from the mixture. This is very harmful. E-mail is delivered in small batches to individuals or small groups with the intention of deceiving them into believing that it is harmless and that it is suited to their particular need. The threat actors are identified by the network protector based on the significance and quality of their actions. Standard computer network attacks often target web servers and other network-based listening services as their primary targets. However, targeted attacks frequently employ the strategy of social engineering through the use of email. Regrettably, the majority of communities continue to allow email to reach their social networks, which poses a significant threat to their security [10].

The researchers made a presentation on attentive learning for the classification of emails. Email categorization has lately been a topic of discussion because of the large number of emails that are sent and received on a daily basis. Through the utilization of an attentive learning technique, automatic e-mail categorization is able to imitate the natural and ever-changing behaviors of users. Researchers investigated a number of different email classification methods; their findings were based on the activities of users. This email categorization was made feasible by expressing the structure and content of each incoming message as a subset of the feature space, which is referred to as a feature set. Subsequently, a selection of the traits was selected for additional examination. To restate, the feature sets were utilized to choose set classifiers or processes that would be responsible for determining the correctness of the features that been selected. This selection results in high-accuracy judgments on the classification of e-mails into safe and spam categories, and its behavior is so tight-fisted that it is efficient in terms of the amount of time it takes to complete the task.

It has been recommended that adaptable learning frameworks should be utilized in conjunction with adaptive approaches. Sequential input is received by the learning system that is contained inside the framework. After the forecast has been made, the next step is to incorporate new data into the model that is already in place. The Adaptive Bayesian Classifier with Dynamic Features (ABC-DYNF) provides a control and adaptation mechanism that allows it to quickly react to changes in features as well as drifting that is either actual or contextual. Additionally, the ABC-DYNF investigated the effectiveness of email classification performed with a Bayesian Filter (BF), in addition to analyzing the performance of various pre-processing, control, and adaptive algorithms. Email foldering poses a big difficulty because of the behavior that it exhibits, which is always changing. There is also the possibility of adding, removing, or creating a large number of directories throughout the course of time. It is necessary to pick particular qualities to engage in data streaming for textual data. In the realm of email classifiers, adaptive approaches are a game-changer that could not be ignored [11].

A number of scholars raised objections to the digital investigation.

Within the scope of the digital investigation, the examination of hundreds of thousands of artifacts was carried out. Using email is the sole method that allows for the creation of a substantial volume of data and information. E-mail forensics has been used to a wide variety of instances, and all of these investigations have been based on genuine cases that have been investigated. Not only may criminals use spam email to contact potential victims, but they can also utilize it as a tool to develop their scams. As a result of the fact that no forensic tools are capable of reliably identifying suspicious spam e-mails, digital investigators will need to equip themselves with strong knowledge and patience to discover how the essential data are being transmitted through content analysis. The mission of those working in the field of email spam detection is to reduce the number of false positives and false negatives as much as possible, rather than to attempt to extract useful information from spam emails. Spam sent via email provides criminals with a viable channel through which they may communicate their thoughts and views. Furthermore, spam filtering has been utilized as a tool in the investigation of homicides and other types of criminal activity, despite the fact that the information that is retrieved from garbage emails may not be of any use for digital investigations.

11.5 Challenges in the Spam Message Identification

Unfortunately, content-based spam filtering is more vulnerable to poison attacks, which is the main problem with spam message filtering. This approach involves adding several real terms to spam emails to make them less likely to be identified as spam. The impersonation assault is a problem for the identity-based spam filtering. Common users' identities are used in this assault by hacking their computers or faking their IDs. We need spam filters that can withstand attacks and produce fewer false positives and false negatives. Legitimate emails that are incorrectly flagged as spam are known as false positives, whereas undetected spam emails are known as false negatives. While previous research has taken into account trust, interest, and closeness as social network metrics, it has done so only using OSN data and the premise that a lower hop count indicates a closer relationship. The degree of intimacy between two users is, however, heavily influenced by the nature of their connection. So, for active email filtering, it's important to think about the relationship strength as well. If a person wants to build a decent spam classifier, he/she needs to take into account characteristics from both social networks and the email network while assessing spam emails. The most common formats for spam e-mails include both plain text and pictures. Therefore, a spam classifier is considered effective if it takes that possibility into account as well. The Open Source Network (OSN) already has several spam detection and filtering mechanisms available, however such systems need the user to actively enable a spam filter. Unfortunately, users usually won't go to the trouble of manually setting each rule, thus the system might not operate in real time and might only work for one social network. For efficient spam message categorization, picking the right features is just as crucial as picking the right classifiers.

11.6 Spam Classification with SVM Filter

Within the realm of support vector classification, LIBSVM is an integrated piece of software that is utilized. There is a sophisticated classification method known as support vector machines (SVM), which begins with the separation of the available data into training data and testing data. A supervised learning model known as the support vector machine (SVM) [11, 12] is utilized for classification in addition to regression analysis. On the basis of the training examples, support vector machine (SVM) training models construct a model that assigns the test data that does not have a class label to a category that has been predetermined. There is a known class label included in every training data set, as well as various properties or features of the variables that are being observed. The LIBSM application programming interfaces (APIs) [13–15] are utilized to generate a model that is derived from the training data. This model is then utilized to forecast the values of the test data by providing just the test data properties.

For the purpose of spam filtering [16, 17], the tokens or keywords that are included in the emails, as well as the frequency with which these tokens appear in both the spam and the ham emails, are taken into consideration. A value of one is assigned to ham, whereas a value of zero is assigned to spam e-mails. Both the data used for training and those used for testing are scaled to a certain range. The process of scaling ensures that no token will be able to dominate any other token. In the event that the data is not scaled, some keywords may have a larger frequency, which increases the likelihood that they would dominate the words that appear less often. Furthermore, the existence of the least dominating terms is not taken into consideration at all. Following the scaling of the data used for testing and training, the train APIs are utilized to generate the models. The prediction API is utilized to construct predictions for the testing data, and the accuracy of these forecasts is also computed. These predictions are based on the models that were generated and the scaled test data. The support vector machine (SVM) is able to discover a solution to the optimization equation and the parameters that are necessary for performing this optimization after being provided with a training set of label pairs. During the process of generating the models by utilizing the training APIs, equations are discovered.

In high-dimensional space, the support vector machine (SVM) locates a linear separation hyperplane that has the maximum margin. The support vector machine (SVM) is capable of doing non-linear classifications by utilizing kernel techniques in addition to linear classification. Mapping the data into a space with greater dimensions is the method that is used to do non-linear classification. There are four distinct kernels that may be utilized, and they are the linear, sigmoid, polynomial, and radial basis functions. The Radial Basis is utilized by LIBSVM.

11.7 Conclusion

Despite the existence of many real-time spam message filtering algorithms, users still encounter the issue of receiving spam messages in their email and on online social networks (OSN). Spam messages not only have the potential to irritate customers, but they may also lead to significant consequences such as financial losses and a deterioration of trust among users. Hence, both users and service providers want a dependable system that can rapidly identify and eliminate spam messages. If you want to categorize and identify spam emails, support vector machines are the most reliable option. To enhance the categorization of emails in future research, one will have to collect information on the preferences of users, in addition to the existing attributes, and take into consideration the dynamic and evolving nature of these preferences. Regarding the filtering of undesired messages in online social networks (OSN), future goals involve utilizing supplementary datasets, considering new factors, and evaluating the system's effectiveness using various support vector machine (SVM) kernels. One further possibility under consideration is the development of a browser extension that has the capability to analyze incoming data and effectively eliminate spam messages in the online social network (OSN). This extension would utilize social context variables from each social network to achieve its filtering functionality. This extension would have the capability to function on many networks for the purpose of spam filtering, rather than being limited to just one network.

References

1. Cranor, L.F. and LaMacchia, B.A., Spam! *Commun. ACM*, 41, 8, 74–83, 1998.
2. Jain, G. and Sharma, M., Social Media: A Review, in: *Information Systems Design and Intelligent Applications*, pp. 387–395, Springer, India, 2016.
3. Nelson, M., *Spam Control: Problems and Opportunities*, pp. 23–82, Ferris Research, India, USA, 2003.
4. Cormack, G.V., Hidalgo, J.M.G., Sánz, E.P., Feature engineering for mobile (SMS) spam filtering, in: *Proceedings of the 30th annual international ACM SIGIR conference on Research and development in information retrieval*, US, pp. 871–872, 2007.
5. Davidson, T., Warmsley, D., Macy, M., Weber, I., Automated hate speech detection and the problem of offensive language. *Proceedings of the International AAAI Conference on Web and Social Media (ICWSM)*, pp. 512–515, 2017.
6. Dadvar, M. and Trieschnigg, D., Towards context-aware filtering of hate speech content on Twitter. *Proceedings of the International Conference on Weblogs and Social Media (ICWSM)*, pp. 573–576, 2013.
7. Waseem, Z. and Hovy, D., Hateful symbols or hateful people? Predictive features for hate speech detection on Twitter. *Proceedings of the NAACL Student Research Workshop*, pp. 88–93, 2016.
8. Ribeiro, M.H., Araújo, M., Gonçalves, P., Benevenuto, F., SentiBench—a benchmark comparison of state-of-the-practice sentiment analysis methods. *EPJ Data Sci.*, 7, 1, 45, 2018.
9. Zubiaga, A. and Ji, H., Tweet, but verify: epistemic study of information verification on Twitter. *Proceedings of the International Conference on Weblogs and Social Media (ICWSM)*, pp. 641–650, 2014.
10. Mathew, B.K., Bhattacharyya, P., Ghosh, S., Overview of multimedia data processing and analytics in social media: Extraction, summarization, and content filtering. *Multimed. Tools Appl.*, 78, 2, 1573–1611, 2019.
11. Rathore, N. and Rajavat, A., Smart Farming Based on IOT-Edge Computing: Applying Machine Learning Models For Disease And Irrigation Water Requirement Prediction In Potato Crop Using Containerized Microservices, in: *Precision Agriculture for Sustainability*, pp. 399–424, Apple Academic Press, USA, 2024.

12. Patsariya, M. and Rajavat, A., A Progressive Design of MANET Security Protocol for Reliable and Secure Communication. *Int. J. Intell. Syst. Appl. Eng.*, *12*, 9s, 190–204, 2024.
13. Rathi, M. and Rajavat, A., Investigations and Design of Privacy-Preserving Data Mining Technique for Secure Data Publishing. *Int. J. Intell. Syst. Appl. Eng.*, *11*, 9s, 351–367, 2023.
14. Dubey, P. and Rajavat, A., Effective K-means clustering algorithm for efficient data mining, in: *2023 2nd International Conference on Vision Towards Emerging Trends in Communication and Networking Technologies (ViTECoN)*, pp. 1–6, IEEE, 2023, May.
15. Chauhan, D., Singh, C., Rawat, R., Chouhan, M., Conversational AI Applications in Ed-Tech Industry: An Analysis of Its Impact and Potential in Education, in: *Conversational Artificial Intelligence*, pp. 411–433, 2024.
16. Chauhan, D., Singh, C., Rawat, R., Dhawan, M., Evaluating the Performance of Conversational AI Tools: A Comparative Analysis, in: *Conversational Artificial Intelligence*, pp. 385–409, 2024.
17. Park, M. and Fink, E., Examining the effectiveness of social media content moderation: Evidence from Reddit. *Proceedings of the ACM Conference on Computer-Supported Cooperative Work and Social Computing (CSCW)*, pp. 442–453, 2019.t

12

An Investigation of Various Techniques to Improve Cyber Security

Shoaib Mohammad[1]*, Ramendra Pratap Singh[1], Rajiv Kumar[1], Kshitij Kumar Rai[1], Arti Sharma[1] and Saloni Rathore[2]

[1]School of Law, IMS Unison University, Dehradun, India
[2]Invertis University, Bareilly, India

Abstract

Cyber security threats, characterized by a series of assault stages, persistently aim to accomplish a pre-established goal. Due to the intricate nature of these attacks, the intruder is capable of bypassing the target's security defenses and gaining access to a majority of its systems. When accessing data kept in the cloud, there is a genuine risk of experiencing data breaches, compromised credentials, Denial of Service (DoS) assaults, hacked interfaces and Application Programming Interfaces (APIs), permanent data loss, and other significant cybersecurity concerns. Due to the constant innovation of cybercriminals, who continuously develop more advanced methods to avoid detection, it is challenging to both identify and prevent these malicious activities. As digital technology advances, gigabytes and terabytes of data are now generated every second. Businesses in a variety of industries are finding that using the internet to manage their resources and transactions is useful. Given the value of data and the need to safeguard its security and privacy, securing big data remains a major challenge for all solutions. Due to the exponential expansion of network data, intrusion detection is becoming increasingly important, and manual analysis would be either impossible or take the same amount of time as analyzing it. As a result, there is an urgent need for an automated system capable of extracting relevant information from enormous amounts of hitherto untapped data when it comes to network intrusion detection. Data mining can perform a variety of tasks, such as clustering, prediction, classification, and the extraction of association rules between data pieces. This paper discusses machine learning techniques for designing intrusion detection systems for big data networks. In this

**Corresponding author*: shoaib.mohammad@iuu.ac

Rajesh Kumar Chakrawarti, Ranjana Sikarwar, Sanjaya Kumar Sarangi, Samson Arun Raj Albert Raj, Shweta Gupta, Krishnan Sakthidasan Sankaran and Romil Rawat (eds.) Natural Language Processing for Software Engineering, (183–192) © 2025 Scrivener Publishing LLC

approach, the NSL KDD data set is used as input. First, the CFS-correlation feature selection approach is used to pick only relevant features from the NSL KDD data set. The NSL KDD data collection contains 41 features. The number of characteristics was reduced to 16 after applying the CFS algorithm. The 16 attributes are then used by machine learning techniques to classify and predict malware data in the NSL KDD data set.

Keywords: Cyber security, attacks, privacy, vulnerability, machine learning, intrusion detection

12.1 Introduction

The Internet is a global network of linked computers that offers companies and people unprecedented opportunities for communication and cooperation. This phenomenon has prompted people to modify their lifestyle, as seen by the increasing prevalence of online education and e-commerce, which are gradually replacing traditional schools and physical retail stores. The vast and highly intelligent World Wide Web (WWW), with its immense volume of data, has had a significant impact on the overall worldwide security situation over a long period of time. Despite the disclosure of many data breaches by leading security firms, users' accounts are still being consistently compromised. Technological advancement is a crucial factor in all of these recent events. This provides an opportunity for criminals to experiment with novel methods of cybercrime, such as exploiting computer systems and networks [1].

Cybersecurity threats [14], including several phases of attack, persistently aim to accomplish a pre-established goal. Due to the intricate nature of these attacks, the intruder is capable of bypassing the target's security defenses and gaining access to the majority of its systems. Accessing data held in the cloud today poses a genuine risk of data breaches, compromised credentials, Denial of Service (DoS) assaults, hacked interfaces and Application Programming Interfaces (APIs), irreversible data loss, and other significant cybersecurity concerns. Due to the constant enhancement of attackers' sophisticated plans and methods to evade detection, it is challenging to detect and prevent these activities. Due to the fact that these assaults mostly target corporate data and other sensitive information, stopping them poses a significant challenge. Attacks use advanced strategies and often include extensive groups of synchronized personnel using technological infrastructure with extensive Command and Control (C&C) networks of computers. High device densities in wireless networks, caused by the rapid rise of the Internet of Things and vehicle networks, lead to data traffic overflow and pose significant security risks. Assailants consider a range of obstacles and possibilities [2].

Cybercrime encompasses a series of deliberate attacks that are carried out in a systematic manner with the objective of achieving a certain purpose. Assailants meticulously adhere to this sequential procedure to successfully execute their attacks. A Defense architecture that is driven by intelligence and incorporates the cyber kill chain provides a series of steps for the identification and prevention of cyber attacks. The typical cyber death chains include seven distinct stages: reconnaissance, weaponization, delivery, exploitation, installation, command and control, and operations on target [3]. During the reconnaissance phase, attackers do research to identify a suitable target who would enable them to accomplish their objectives. Before proceeding to the next step, referred to as "delivery," the weaponization phase will merge the exploit and malware into a payload. For instance, during the third stage of a cyber attack, hackers could use an email deception to transmit malicious software to the target. The term "Zero-Day" refers to the specific code used in the fourth stage of an attack, enabling adversaries to exploit a vulnerability and gain unauthorized access to the victim's machine [4]. Subsequently, in step five, the attackers construct a durable backdoor or insert malicious code into the target website to ensure continuous access for an extended period. In the sixth step, a command network is established, enabling the attacker to exert remote control over the victim using a command and control (C&C) server. This is facilitated by a malevolent application. Ultimately, the intruders successfully achieve the mission's goal by targeting the victims. The intruder has the potential to engage in clandestine surveillance, pilfer credentials, manipulate or interrupt data, sabotage computer hardware, collect and extract information, as well as covertly modify or extract data. Disrupting just one link in the cyber death chain may bring the onslaught to a total stop. Interrupting the chain early will minimize the amount of damage caused [5].

12.2 Various Attacks [6–9]

Phishing is the biggest cyber danger right now. The neologism "phishing" is a play on the word "fishing" that arose from the idea of utilizing bait to lure in victims. One of the most common ways that hackers target networks and individuals is via phishing attacks, which have claimed the lives of a large number of users. It seems to be coming from a trusted source, but it's really a fake link. It is a sting operation set up by an enemy to steal people's private information. It is a malicious link that, if clicked, will take the user to other malicious websites created by the hacker. Spear phishing assaults occur when the phishing website is primarily designed to target a specific person or business. Cybercriminals prey on people's trusting nature to breach security measures; unfortunately, the majority of internet users nowadays fall prey to such tricks whenever they visit a URL. As a kind of social engineering often used to acquire user data, phishing is among the most subtle yet potent assaults. The perpetrators of phishing attacks may quickly concoct and send out phony emails that include harmful code or links. By installing malicious malware on the victim's PC, the attackers were able to steal sensitive information and send it back to themselves via a backdoor when the user clicked on the misleading URL. In this way, the attacker's server will get the victim's request instead of the legitimate ones. Phishing is the primary vector through which most assaults have gained access to systems. Unless they incur massive losses, victims will remain oblivious to phishing attempts. These phishing links have been the primary vector for most users' falls prey. Phishing emails were formerly a common way for cybercriminals to steal personal information.

In a cryptojacking attack, the hacker takes control of a victim's computer, mobile phone, tablet, or other connected home device and uses it to mine cryptocurrency. To implant crypto mining code on the victim's system, malicious onscreen characters use a malicious connection or infect websites or online ads with JavaScript code. One study by Adguard found that in-program cryptojacking was evolving at a pace of 31%. Cryptojacking is gaining popularity because it allows thieves to make a lot of money with very little effort. The majority of one million registration devices were compromised in February 2018 by the Sominru crypto mining botnet. The admins had mined 8,900 Monero, which is worth about 3.6 million dollars, according to Proofpoint, a cybersecurity company. Two Chinese programmers were accused by the US government a year ago of stealing data from 45 US tech companies, government agencies, and more than 100,000 US Navy personnel. According to the indictment, the defendants compromised systems that remotely managed the information technology infrastructure of governments and businesses worldwide. Businesses that store data for other companies on their servers or remotely manage their clients' IT infrastructure are particularly vulnerable to these types of assaults. Hackers may also target consumers by infiltrating these companies' systems. Looking at the development of sophisticated technologies, most companies will choose cloud solutions to host their IT infrastructure. Companies should go with large cloud providers like Google and Amazon since they are much more secure than smaller companies who are becoming more wary of these kinds of assaults. Since it provides transparency and security via encryption, blockchain is being used in many applications. Among the most promising applications of Blockchain technology, smart contracts stand out. Projects like this use blockchain technology to conduct code, and if certain conditions are satisfied, the result is an advanced resource transfer. Smart contracts will be crucial for all of these applications, from completing financial trades to approved innovation security. Experts promise that clever contracts still contain faults, despite the fact that they have possible used cases. Hackers exploited a flaw in Parity, a multi-signature digital wallet, in 2017 and stole $32 million in advance. Due to the inherent simplicity of the blockchain, the primary concern with protecting the privacy of the savvy contract data is its accessibility. The aggressors have acknowledged this vulnerability formally. In 2019, businesses that employ smart contracts will face a huge challenge.

This year, cybercriminals will target mobile phones more than ever before. There was a 54% increase in new mobile malware variants in 2017, according to the Symantec Internet Security Threat Report. The methods and tools used by cybercriminals to monitor iOS and Android devices are constantly evolving. Talos, a security and intelligence company, discovered a hacker group targeting a small number of iPhones in India at the Mobile Device Management (MDM) conference a year ago. It came out that the hackers sneaked into the devices using social engineering attempts and physical access to steal data. Avoiding downloading files from unknown sites and tapping on connections are the best ways to protect yourself against adaptable malware. Also, keep your mobile operating systems up-to-date; this will make them more resistant to digital threats.

"Associations know the advantages of AI innovation to guard their framework, but they are likewise mindful that assailants have interesting capacities to misuse their framework with that same technology," said Rodney Joffe, senior VP of Neustar, in a published statement. To identify digital threats, several cybersecurity resistance businesses have started to use AI models. Despite this, hackers are able to get through these defenses and launch more sophisticated assaults.

Using generative antagonistic systems, in which two neutral systems compete to uncover the AI computations used by the other, is one way to do this. The developers may easily create a model to circumvent the computation if they happen to stumble into it. Programmers may also get into data sets used to train AI models, which poses a threat in and of itself. They may inject malicious code or change markings so threats are marked as safe instead of questionable.

The goal of cyber espionage is to gain an advantage over a targeted corporation or government agency by means of coordinated, sensitive data or protected technology. For Merriam-Webster, "undercover work" is "the act of spying or utilizing spies to acquire data about the plans and exercises particularly of an outside government or a contending organization." Take it online, and the secret operatives are hordes of evil programmers from all over the globe who employ cyberwarfare to further their own political, economic, or military agendas. From government frameworks to financial frameworks or utilities assets, these hand-picked and highly renowned hackers can shut them down with ease. They have impacted the outcome of worldwide events, impacted political contests, and contributed to the success or failure of enterprises. To sneak into systems or frameworks and remain undiscovered for a long period, many of these attackers use advanced persistent threats (APTs). International espionage is not a new phenomenon; it dates back to the early Middle Ages.

The world of clandestine agents has progressed with the times, and we are now facing a more formidable challenge with digital monitoring. This novel kind of planned and organized risk use digital warfare techniques to gain economic, military, or political benefits. Cybercriminals with exceptional skill are recruited with the goal of disrupting or destroying government or military infrastructure, or to gain unauthorized access to financial systems. From altering the outcome of significant political choices to causing a stir at global events, they are quite capable of creating a situation of total chaos on a global scale. The frustrating part about digital surveillance is that the perpetrator usually follows the standard procedure to ensure that their footprints remain undetectable for a considerable amount of time. As this immoral practice has been gradually adopted, the danger has now spread to other sectors as well. The Verizon 2018 Data Breach Investigations Report states that the major initiatives dealing with the problem of digital covert operations are education, assembly, and open organization. To get access to sensitive material belonging to a government agency or a military foundation, cyber surveillance involves the use of intermediate servers and an unauthorized system or framework. Attacks on traded-off information, which often includes sensitive financial, political, or military data, are a well-known example of this notorious behavior. Onscreen characters allied with governments or nation states seeking to get an advantage are the most common risk entertainers in the world of digital monitoring. Recently, FireEye, a cybersecurity company located in California, exposed the goals of APT39, an Iranian cyber intelligence collecting. The gathering's primary focus continues to be the Middle Eastern media transmission companies. It turned out that the group's covert operations were motivated by a genuine fear for Iran.

When one nation utilizes digital weapons like viruses and hackers to impair another's critical computer systems, they are engaging in cyberwarfare. The goal of these assaults is to cause harm, death, or devastation. In future conflicts, hackers will use computer code to assault enemy infrastructure, fighting side by side with regular soldiers utilizing weaponry like firearms and missiles. A shadowy realm populated by spies, hackers, and top-secret digital weapon projects, cyberwarfare is a perilous and ever-present aspect of global wars. But at this moment, there is a genuine danger that things may swiftly spiral out of control due to the absence of clear regulations controlling online combat and the increasing cyberwarfare weapons race. When one country's computers or data networks are targeted by another, either intentionally or unintentionally, by means such as virus attacks or denial-of-service attacks, this is known as cyberwarfare. Decision-makers in the military and civilian sectors may find advice on how to protect their nation's technological infrastructure against the destructive effects of cyberwarfare in RAND studies.

The term "cyber terrorism" refers to coordinated, coordinated, and targeted electronic assaults against a particular target over the Internet or other networks, emanating from a variety of fear mongering sources with a variety of motivations. Typically, those who oppress people's minds online see their goals as integral components of a nation's fundamental structures or as commercial endeavors.

12.3 Methods

This section presents the design of an intrusion detection system for massive data networks using machine learning methodologies. This framework utilizes the NSL KDD data set as its input. Initially, the NSL KDD data set undergoes processing using the CFS-correlation feature selection technique to only extract the most relevant features. The NSL KDD dataset consists of 41 characteristics. The CFS algorithm was used to restrict the number of features to 16. Machine learning algorithms are then used to classify and predict malware data in the NSL KDD dataset based on these sixteen attributes.

CFS, an integral component of feature selection evaluations, determines the value of an attribute based on its distinct capacity and the extent to which it overlaps with other features. We choose attribute subsets based on their high correlation with the class and low correlation with each other [10].

This approach is ideal for solving classification and regression problems. Support Vector Machines (SVM) identify a hyperplane, which is a line in the case of two-dimensional data, that separates the training data into different classes. This knowledge is then used to categorize new data points. The discovery of the hyperplane, which maximizes the distance between classes, enhances the potential for generalizing hidden data. The Support Vector Machine (SVM) algorithm is known for its superior classification performance, since it provides the highest accuracy on the training set. Data overflow [15–18] is not the result of it.

LS Support vector machines [19–21], such as SVM (Least Square), make no assumptions about the data. There are two primary classifications of support vector machines: linear and non-linear. The representation of training data is often done in a linear manner using a line, sometimes referred to as a hyperplane [11].

The theorem itself is a fundamental principle of Bayesian classification. By using a large dataset, Naive Bayesian Classification techniques provide fundamental foundations that are comparable to decision tree and neural network classification. Naive Bayes classification may be used to represent a subset of dependent attributes. This procedure is used to ascertain the posterior probability P(x|c) for each class. In this study, the outcome is forecasted based on the class with the highest probability. Naive Bayes use a similar methodology to predict various probabilities based on different characteristics [12]. If the weight of each instance in the dataset is determined by the previous results of the base classifier for each of these instances, then the AdaBoost Decision tree [13] uses a dataset that is weighted based on these outcomes. If the instance is misclassified, the weight of subsequent models will be increased, whereas it will remain constant if it is properly classified. The final conclusion is obtained using a weighted vote of the basic classification, where the weight of the model is determined by the misjudgment rate.

12.4 Conclusion

Intrusion detection is becoming increasingly crucial as network data continues to grow at an exponential rate, and manual analysis would either be impossible or take the same amount of time as manually analyzing the data would take. Because of this, when it comes to network intrusion detection, there is an urgent need for an automated system that is capable of extracting important information from large amounts of data that has hitherto been untouched. Data mining can be used to perform a wide range of tasks, including clustering, prediction, classification, and the extraction of association rules between data pieces, among other things. The purpose of this study is to examine machine learning techniques for constructing intrusion detection systems for massively parallel networks to prevent cyber attacks.

References

1. Tang, M., Alazab, M., Luo, Y., Big data for cybersecurity: vulnerability disclosure trends and dependencies. *IEEE Trans. Big Data*, 5, 3, 317–329, 2019.
2. Raghuvanshi, A., Singh, U., Sajja, G., Pallathadka, H., Asenso, E., Kamal, M. *et al.*, Intrusion Detection Using Machine Learning for Risk Mitigation in IoT-Enabled Smart Irrigation in Smart Farming. *J. Food Qual.*, 2022, 1–8, 2022, doi: 10.1155/2022/3955514.
3. Vasan, D., Alazab, M., Venkatraman, S., Akram, J., Qin, Z., MTHAEL: cross-architecture IoT malware detection based on neural network advanced ensemble learning. *IEEE Trans. Comput.*, 69, 11, 1654–1667, 2020.
4. Almoman, O., A Feature Selection Model for Network Intrusion Detection System Based on PSO, GWO, FFA and GA Algorithms. *Symmetry*, 2, 1046, 2020, doi: 10.3390/sym12061046.
5. Raghuvanshi, A., Singh, U., Joshi, C., A Review of Various Security and Privacy Innovations for IoT Applications in Healthcare, in: *Advanced Healthcare Systems*, pp. 43–58, 2022, doi: 10.1002/9781119769293.ch4.
6. Davis, J.J. and Clark, A.J., Data preprocessing for anomaly based network intrusion detection: A review. *Comput. Secur.*, 30, 6–7, 353–375, 2011.
7. Reddy, G.T. *et al.*, Analysis of dimensionality reduction techniques on big data. *IEEE Access*, 8, 54776–54788, 2020.
8. Zhang, Y. and Zhao, Z., Fetal state assessment based on cardiotocography parameters using PCA and AdaBoost, in: *2017 10th International Congress on Image and Signal Processing, BioMedical Engineering and Informatics (CISP-BMEI)*, pp. 1–6, 2017.
9. Abdi, H. and Williams, L.J., Principal component analysis. *Wiley Interdiscip. Rev. Comput. Stat.*, 2, 4, 433–459, 2010.
10. Aggarwal, M., Performance analysis of different feature selection methods in intrusion detection. *Int. J. Sci. Technol. Res.*, 2, 6, 225–231, 2013.
11. Kabir, M.E. and Hu, J., A statistical framework for intrusion detection system. *2014 11th International Conference on Fuzzy Systems and Knowledge Discovery (FSKD)*, pp. 941–946, 2014, doi: 10.1109/FSKD.2014.6980966.
12. Shen, Z., Zhang, Y., Chen, W., A Bayesian Classification Intrusion Detection Method Based on the Fusion of PCA and LDA. *Secur. Commun. Netw.*, 2019, 1–11, 2019, Available: 10.1155/2019/6346708.

13. Shahraki, A., Abbasi, M., Haugen, Ø., Boosting algorithms for network intrusion detection: A comparative evaluation of Real AdaBoost, Gentle AdaBoost and Modest AdaBoost. *Eng. Appl. Artif. Intell.*, 94, 103770, 2020, doi: 10.1016/j.engappai.2020.103770.
14. Revathi, S. and Malathi, D.A., A Detailed Analysis on NSL-KDD Dataset Using Various Machine Learning Techniques for Intrusion Detection. *Int. J. Eng. Res. Technol. (IJERT)*, 2, 12, 1848–1853, December 2013.
15. Chirgaiya, S. and Rajavat, A., Tiny object detection model based on competitive multi-layer neural network (TOD-CMLNN). *Intell. Syst. Appl.*, 18, September 2022, 200217, 2023.
16. Rathi, M. and Rajavat, A., *Analysing Cryptographic and Random Data Sanitization Techniques in Privacy Preserving Data Mining*, vol. 83, Allied Publishers, New Delhi, India, 2023.
17. Rathore, N. and Rajavat, A., Scalable edge computing environment based on the containerized microservices and minikube. *Int. J. Softw. Sci. Comput. Intell. (IJSSCI)*, *14*, 1, 1–14, 2022.
18. Dhar, S., Dhar, U., Rajavat, A., Factors and Attributes of Team Players: A Study of Engineering Students in India, in: *International Simulation and Gaming Association Conference*, pp. 53–60, Springer International Publishing, Cham, 2021, September.
19. Pithawa, D., Nahar, S., Bhardwaj, V., Rawat, R., Dronawat, R., Rawat, A., Quantum Computing Technological Design Along with Its Dark Side, in: *Quantum Computing in Cybersecurity*, pp. 295–312, 2023.
20. Shrivastava, M., Patil, R., Bhardwaj, V., Rawat, R., Telang, S., Rawat, A., Quantum Computing and Security Aspects of Attention-Based Visual Question Answering with Long Short-Term Memory, in: *Quantum Computing in Cybersecurity*, pp. 395–412, 2023.
21. Rawat, R., Chakrawarti, R.K., Raj, A.S.A., Mani, G., Chidambarathanu, K., Bhardwaj, R., Association rule learning for threat analysis using traffic analysis and packet filtering approach. *Int. J. Inf. Technol.*, *15*, 6, 3245–3255, 2023.

13

Brain Tumor Classification and Detection Using Machine Learning by Analyzing MRI Images

Chandrima Sinha Roy[1]*, K. Parvathavarthini[2], M. Gomathi[3], Mrunal Pravinkumar Fatangare[4], D. Kishore[5] and Anilkumar Suthar[6]

[1]*Department of Computer Science and Engineering, JIS College of Engineering, Kalyani, West Bengal, India*
[2]*Department of Computer Science and Engineering, Vels Institute of Science, Technology and Advanced Studies, Chennai, India*
[3]*S. A. Engineering College, Tamil Nadu, India*
[4]*Computer Science and Engineering, Department of Polytechnic and Skill Development DVK MIT World Peace University, Kothrud, Pune, India*
[5]*Department of ECE, Aditya College of Engineering & Technology, Surampalem, India*
[6]*New LJ Institute of Engineering and Technology, Ahmedabad, Gujarat, India*

Abstract
In recent years, there has been a rise in the death rate as a consequence of the proliferation of encephaloma tumors among individuals of all ages. The identification of physical tumors is a challenging endeavor that requires a significant amount of time and effort on the part of medical professionals. This is due to the complex nature of the tumors and the presence of unwanted noise in the MR imaging data. Since this is the case, the diagnosis and location of tumors at an early stage are of the highest significance. The use of medical imaging in conjunction with segmentation and relegation techniques has the potential to deliver an accurate and speedy diagnosis. This is accomplished by monitoring and forecasting the progression of cancer at its various stages. In this article, we provide a method that is based on machine learning and is used to segment and categorize magnetic resonance imaging (MRI) pictures for the purpose of detecting brain cancers. To segment pictures, extract features, and categorize them, this system makes use of the

**Corresponding author*: mail2chandrima@gmail.com

Rajesh Kumar Chakrawarti, Ranjana Sikarwar, Sanjaya Kumar Sarangi, Samson Arun Raj Albert Raj, Shweta Gupta, Krishnan Sakthidasan Sankaran and Romil Rawat (eds.) Natural Language Processing for Software Engineering, (193–206) © 2025 Scrivener Publishing LLC

Naive Bayes method, the Support Vector Machine technique, and the K Nearest Neighbor algorithm.

Keywords: Brain tumor, classification, machine learning, accuracy, precision, recall

13.1 Introduction

The fatality rate has dramatically increased as a result of the growth in the number of encephaloma tumors that have been seen across all age groups over the course of the last several years. The two primary classifications of tumors that form in the brain in an uncontrollable manner are known as benign and malignant disorders. The term "malignant" is used to describe tumors that have an irregular structure that results in the proliferation of cancerous cells from the tumor. Benign tumors are characterized by the presence of normal structures and cells that do not contribute to the development of cancer. When attempting to detect tumors based on physical criteria, medical practitioners face a challenging and time-consuming task. This is due to the fact that tumors are complex and MR imaging data includes signals that are not intended. In light of this, it is of the utmost importance to promptly diagnose and localize the precise position of the tumor. By integrating medical imaging with segmentation and classification algorithms, it is possible to get an accurate early diagnosis. This may be accomplished by monitoring and predicting cancer-prone regions at various levels. [1] Tags are used to safeguard the material of the user.

The procedure of segmenting MRI images, which is both laborious and time-consuming, is required to identify the tissues that are present in brain tumors. With the assistance of segmentation, the structures in medical pictures that are often misinterpreted may be accurately discovered and diagnosed. In the event where the radiologist manually assessed the tumor by utilizing an excessive number of pictures, it is possible that an inaccurate diagnosis was made. It is necessary to have an automated system in place to guarantee that the processing and interpretation of medical images are free of errors caused by humans. the third one Digital image processing encompasses a wide range of fields, including geology, photography, microscopy, astronomy, computer vision, and medical imaging, among others. The process of doing research in the domains of medicine and science comprises a multitude of intricate phases. Medical imaging is a vital initial step that must be taken before artificial intelligence (AI) [25–27] may begin to segment medical photos and assist in computer-aided diagnosis (CAD) [25, 26, 28]. They streamline the process of treatment planning and execution, which brings about an improvement in the efficiency of human-machine interaction during surgical operations. In order to create diagnostic tools that are very helpful in the area of medicine [29, 30], this method comprises the creation of imaging equipment as well as the execution of a therapeutic strategy. An extensive range of medical technologies were used to generate the images of the human body that are shown here. Computer tomography (CT) and magnetic resonance imaging (MRI) are two of the most important instruments that we have at our disposal for non-invasive imaging of the human body. "[4]" is the text that was entered by the user; "[5]" is the text that represents the user.

The buildup of abnormal tissues [2, 3, 11, 14, 19] inside the brain is the most prevalent mechanism that leads to the development of brain tumors. However, these abnormal tissues disrupt the normal processes of tissue synthesis, growth, and death, which causes them to proliferate and increase in an uncontrollable manner. Several different types of medical imaging techniques, such as computed tomography (CT) and magnetic resonance imaging (MRI), have the potential to detect brain cancer instances. Diagnostic imaging techniques, such as computed tomography (CT) and magnetic resonance imaging (MRI), are commonly used by medical professionals in the process of searching for brain malignancies. By providing radiologists and physicians with three-dimensional (3D) images of the brain, magnetic resonance imaging (MRI) and computed tomography (CT) scans may be used to detect brain cancer. Through computerized analysis, specialists may be able to save time and provide more accurate conclusions. This kind of analysis may swiftly detect aspects of a brain tumor and give a comprehensive three-dimensional image. Through the use of automated or semi-automatic tumor segmentation, professionals have the opportunity to liberate their time from the responsibilities of patient treatment planning and follow-up management as shown in Figure 13.1: Steps Involved in MRI Image Processing. The text that they are using is "[6]".

Several obstacles impede the prompt processing of whole MRI images. Examples of these challenges include the presence of bias fields, noise interference, and the inclusion of non-brain tissues. To address this particular problem, we offer a wide array of pre-processing alternatives at our disposal. After processing, photographs need to go through the time-consuming pre-processing phase, which involves removing any non-essential features. Prior to commencing this procedure, it is important to complete the pre-processing phase [4]. Image grayscale conversion, noise reduction, and reconstruction are sequential stages in the pre-processing

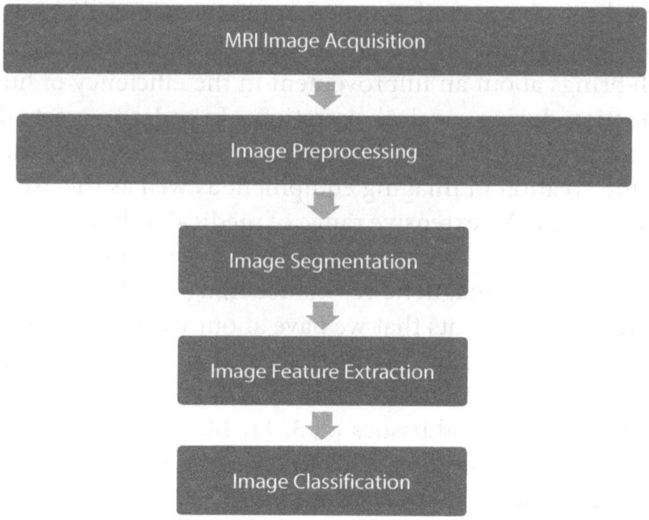

Figure 13.1 Steps involved in MRI image processing.

pipeline. Grayscale image conversion is a commonly used pre-processing method [1]. Various filtering methods are used to eliminate further noise after grayscale processing of the image. To get satisfactory outcomes while obtaining photographs from the database, it is essential to eliminate any background noise. The current approaches being used for noise reduction have notable disadvantages.

Segmentation refers to the process of dividing something into distinct segments or parts. Large images were generated during the process of scanning; medical professionals should possess the ability to visually identify these images manually within a suitable timeframe. It plays a crucial role in clinical diagnostics and is used in computer-assisted surgery and pre-operative planning.

This approach is called feature extraction, and it involves assigning a feature vector to each character simultaneously, which is essentially a representation of the character. Ultimately, the goal is to achieve two challenging objectives: improving the identification rate with the fewest components possible and generating a consistent feature set for several occurrences of the same sign. The current feature extraction approaches failed to prioritize the features for examination in later diagnostics.

Classification: Each piece of data inside a batch is organized into a certain category from a set of predetermined options. Typically, this approach is used to categorize brain images as either normal or malignant. The main objective of classification is to accurately predict the target class for each occurrence in the dataset. The algorithm accomplishes this task by categorizing brain pictures as either containing tumors or being devoid of malignancy. Considering the lack of emphasis on this stage in present approaches, our suggested endeavor would largely concentrate on precisely recognizing MRI images.

13.2 Literature Survey

It is feasible to get information from photographs of the brain by using techniques that are associated with image processing. A number of medical disorders have been successfully diagnosed and treated with the use of magnetic resonance imaging (MRI), which has shown to be effective. Pre-processing a picture consists of the following processes, which are as follows: There are several techniques that may be used to improve the quality of cranium scans, reduce noise, and get rid of artifacts. This image should make it easier to identify the malignancies that are present. To enhance magnetic resonance imaging (MRI) brain imaging of astrocytomas, Suryavamsi *et al.* [7] proposed three techniques: "Histogram Equalization," "Contrast Limited Adaptive Histogram Equalization," and "Brightness Preserving Dynamic Fuzzy Histogram Equalization." The PSNR, RMSE, and MSE metrics are examples of performance measures that have been used to verify these methodologies and quantify the results they provide.

Noise removal from magnetic resonance imaging (MRI) data is the first and most crucial stage in the process of acquiring the target signal. Earlier phases in the pre-processing phase included the use of nuisance regression and independent component analysis. Bianca De Blasi and her colleagues [8] devised a number of different LD cleaning processes to exclude non-BO LD signals from healthy patients as well as those who were suffering from temporal lobe epilepsy. In comparison to data that was only preprocessed in the 0.01-0.1 Hz area, all of the preprocessing pipelines that were investigated improved the temporal features, such as the total signal-to-noise ratio (StNR) and power spectrum density, in the frequency range that corresponds to the resting state. Before beginning the ICA procedure, the authors went through the whole pre-processing pipeline to get the DMN. These pipelines and groups fared better than others when it came to characterizing the posterior cingulate cortex. This was the case when compared to other pipelines and groups.

Pre-processing techniques that have been proposed by Poornachandra and Naveena [9] have the potential to enhance the categorization of glioma tumors, like tumors that are seen in the brain. State-of-the-art deep learning has recently been used in the field of medical imaging. With enhanced segmentation findings, researchers are able to get a better knowledge of brain tumors, which ultimately results in more accurate disease identification and novel therapy choices for patients.

The use of magnetic resonance imaging (MRI) for the diagnosis and staging of cervical cancer has been the subject of intense discussion. The consistency of the picture makes the process of image segmentation much more difficult than it would otherwise be. To enhance the Region Scalable Fitting approach for image segmentation, Setiawan Widyarto and colleagues [10] included pre-processing procedures prior to using a region-based active contour model. In regional areas, the models that were utilized included data on intensity as one of its components. Within the context of the preprocessing step, the 2D-sigmoid function was used to perform processing on the tumor border. The addition of a 2D-sigmoid function during the pre-processing stages resulted in an increase in the contrast of the brain MRI image.

Important characteristics must be extracted by algorithms used for tumor segmentation, a total of eleven. The accuracy of brain tumor segmentation was increased by Jui *et al.* by the use of an enhanced feature extraction component. This component takes into consideration the association between the compression that is induced by the growth of the tumor and the structural deformation experienced inside the brain. MRI volumetric data from the lateral ventricle (LaV) is modified via the use of three-dimensional nonrigid registration and deformation modeling. To validate and make use of LaV deformation feature data for brain tumor segmentation, we will use conventional classification algorithms. Real and virtual patient photographs were used by the author to carry out a comprehensive quantitative and qualitative analysis of the component that was considered for implementation. All indications point to a good outcome for the probe.

Instead of using tissue segmentation or nonlinear registration, Jun Zhang and colleagues depend on landmarks in their suggestion for the extraction of longitudinal structural magnetic resonance images for the purpose of Alzheimer's disease identification. It is necessary for you to locate the distinctive landmarks in the training images before you will be able to recognize them in the testing photographs in a quick and efficient manner. The need for nonlinear registration and tissue segmentation will be avoided by using an approach that identifies landmarks in a short amount of time. With these points of reference in hand, we gather longitudinal data that is relevant to the environment, together with advanced statistical aspects, to evaluate the brain's spatial absorption. In terms of efficiency and performance, the experimental findings demonstrate that our suggested technique outperforms the method that is considered to be the state-of-the-art. This is the case when the method is evaluated on the Alzheimer's Disease Neuroimaging Initiative database, particularly for mental cognitive impairment and Alzheimer's disease. It was determined that the categorizing work was finished with a rate of 88.30 percent [12].

BLADeS is an all-encompassing and completely automated breast computer-aided diagnosis (CAD) system that was created by Gabriele Piantadosi and her colleagues [13]. This system was designed to assist in the identification of breast cancer and lesions. There are a number of modules that Michael Osadebey and his colleagues proposed for a hierarchical design. Some of these modules include breast segmentation, motion artifact reduction, lesion localization, and malignancy-based categorization. For the purpose of providing a fair comparison, the researchers used a cross-validation sample consisting of 42 patients who had histological lesions that were confirmed. The results of the experiments demonstrate that BLADeS was capable of diagnosing breast lesions using T1-weighted DCE-MRI in a totally automated manner, without any involvement from a human being at any stage of the processing chain (processing chain). Tags were used to safeguard the material of the user.

Hsin-Yi Tsai and colleagues [15] presented a novel method that makes use of the Gray-Level Co-Occurrence Matrix (GLCM) to accelerate the process of graphics processing unit (GPU)-based feature extraction. In contrast to its sequential version, which is developed and optimized on a single computer by using MATLAB and C, this technique is deployed on several GPU devices for the purpose of optimizing performance. The suggested technique outperforms the serial version when it is evaluated on GeForce GTX 1080s, with speedups occurring between 25 and 105 times for single-precision MR brain shots and between 15 and 85 times for double-precision MR brain images. For the purpose of testing, the actual percentage of improvement is determined by the size of the ROIs that are employed.

An automatic segmentation approach that is based on Convolutional Neural Networks (CNNs) was reported by Sérgio Pereira *et al.* [16]. More precisely, the system was based on small kernels that were 3 x 3. Not only does reducing the weights of the network provide assistance in preventing overfitting, but it also makes it possible to create patterns that are more detailed. This pre-processing step is not used by CNN-based segmentation algorithms very often; nevertheless, when paired with data augmentation, it yields good results for the segmentation of brain tumors shown in magnetic resonance imaging (MRI) pictures.

The enhanced picture quality that is provided by ultrahigh field (7 T) magnetic resonance imaging (MRI) was used in a semi-automatic segmentation approach that was described by Jinyoung Kim and colleagues [17]. For the purpose of this method, several other structural MRI modalities were used to offer supplemental edge data. The integration of susceptibility-weighted, T2-weighted, and diffusion magnetic resonance imaging (MRI) results in the production of a one-of-a-kind edge indicator function. Each of these modalities was customized to meet the requirements that were special to it. When it comes to geometric active surfaces, having a grasp of the form and structure of the subcortical structures enables more efficient development. To physically separate neighboring buildings from one another, an iterative approach was used. In case that the structures did not overlap, a penalty was given to the division at their borders. There are fifty distinct regions of the brain that are engaged, as stated by Antonios Makropoulos *et al.* [18], beginning with the early preterm period and continuing until the age that is comparable to full term. This study makes use of a unique segmentation approach to investigate the intensity distribution across the whole brain. This is done while taking into consideration the anatomical hierarchy and the physical restrictions. This technique is distinct from the conventional procedures that are based on atlases because, in contrast to manual reference segmentations, it increases the resolution of label overlaps. The findings of the experiments demonstrate that the suggested method is extremely dependable throughout a broad spectrum of gestational ages, ranging from 24 weeks to term-equivalent.

13.3 Methods

Image enhancement and refinement are essential for enhancing its quality. Mobile phone images include several elements that have the ability to affect the segmentation results. The pre-processing of an image involves three stages: scaling, noise reduction, and enhancement. The digital picture may include a multitude of sounds. Basic thresholding is troublesome since it might lead to picture noise generated by ineffective capture. Therefore, it is essential to minimize image noise. Image noise refers to a random alteration in the colors or intensities of a picture. Photographic noise may manifest in several forms, such as periodic noise, film grain, quantization noise, shot noise, salt and pepper noise, and Gaussian noise. To reduce these disruptions, one may use filters such as the Median and Wiener filters. Morphological techniques provide a range of approaches to accomplish noise reduction. Gaussian filtering has the effect of reducing the noise in pictures, but median filtering has the potential to alter the luminosity of individual pixels. Here, the researchers used the GF to eliminate extraneous noise. Instead of using the importance of intensity at each individual pixel, Gaussian filtering used a weighted average of intensities derived from neighboring pixels.

The number 18 was included. Filtering improves the interpretability of pictures for humans and aids in the development of increasingly advanced image processing systems. By manipulating the histogram of the input image to a fixed value, we can guarantee that the distribution of intensities stays unchanged. This technique reliably enhances the overall difference between light and dark areas in photos, which is especially valuable when the image's relevant information is closely related to contrast. By using this technique, it is possible to achieve a uniform distribution of intensities in the histogram. In areas characterized by low contrast, this distinction is significant. Histogram equalization achieves image enhancement by evenly distributing the most common intensities across the picture.

Following the use of dynamic fuzzy histogram equalization to enhance the image, it is then partitioned into many sections and segmented to generate the accurate Region of Interest (ROI). Essential features are then retrieved from these parts. Picture segmentation is the process of identifying and categorizing separate sections within an image. Data may be segmented either based on geographical regions or based on boundaries between different areas. Regions with anatomical or functional characteristics may be categorized based on intensity patterns surrounded by a group of adjacent pixels [20].

This study employs region-based segmentation, a technique that partitions the area of interest (ROI) into subgroups based on distinct patterns or textures. K-means clustering utilizes the local mean as a cluster prototype to partition different interpretations into k groups. To identify clusters within the data, this approach aggregates all the groups represented by the variable k. The algorithm determines the nearest data point by calculating the squared Euclidean distances. The approach categorizes all data points into one of k categories based on the provided characteristics [21].

The K-NN classifier has been used in several research investigations. Pattern recognition employs a multitude of methods to classify items. K-NN utilizes the nearest training samples to classify objects. K-NN acquires knowledge from occurrences. Calculation is deferred until categorization is finished when a locally approximated function is used. KNN is most suitable as a classification approach when there is little knowledge about the historical distribution of the data. KNN is a widely used technique for categorizing patterns. Various observers have found that KNN computing is very effective when used to diverse sorts of data [22].

SVM, developed by Vatnik, has piqued the curiosity of scholars worldwide. The data is first divided into two groups using a support vector machine classifier. Once the classifier has been trained using the training data, a test model is created. At times, multiclass categorization tasks occur. This task will need a substantial number of binary classifiers. Based on several research, SVM demonstrates superior performance compared to other existing classification approaches. Support vector machines are capable of doing image categorization. According to the study, SVMs achieve much greater accuracy compared to other traditional classifiers [23].

13.4 Result Analysis

The researchers have assessed "Dataset-160 and Data-255" from the Harvard clinical college of "architecture" [24]. They assessed "Dataset-160," which includes "Normal-20," "Abnormal-140," and "Dataset-255", which includes 35 normal and 220 abnormal "T2-weighted" MR256x256 axial aircraft encephalon images, over the course of the investigation. Eleven different syndromes were represented by the "Dataset-255" Irregular Encephalon Magnetic Resonance metaphors, which connect to the "Dataset-160" by connecting the seven different syndromes. Among the seven disorders included in "Dataset-160" are Huntington's syndrome, Alzheimer's infection, Alzheimer's illness, and examples of agnosia, glioma, meningioma, Pick's infection, and sarcoma. "Dataset-255" contains images of four new syndromes: chronic subdural hematoma, herpes encephalitis, and a handful of other types of sclerosis. "Dataset-255" as shown in Figure 13.2: Result Comparison of Classifiers.

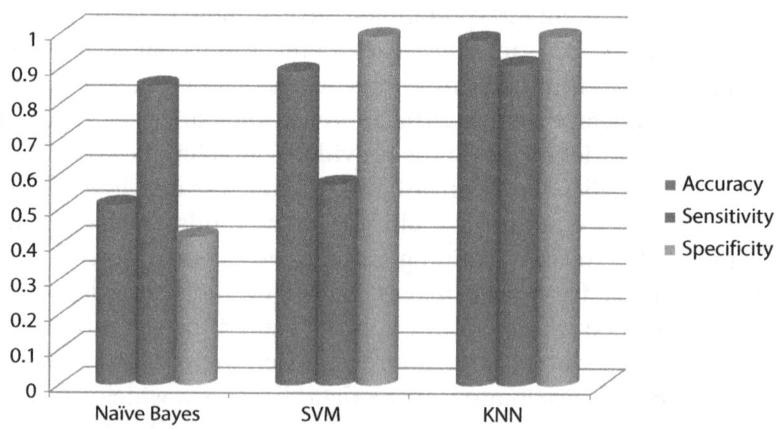

Figure 13.2 Result comparison of classifiers.

13.5 Conclusion

Across all age groups, the death rate has risen due to an increase in encephaloma tumors. Physical tumor identification is difficult and time-consuming for clinicians due to tumor complexity and the involution of noise in MR imaging data. Therefore, it is crucial to diagnose and localize the tumor early on. By combining medical images with segmentation and relegation methods, early diagnosis of malignant tumors at multiple stages becomes possible. To detect brain tumors, our method segments and categorizes MRI images using machine learning. Feature extraction, classification, segmentation, and support vector machine (SVM) and k-nearest neighbor (KNN) techniques are all part of this system. It is doing well, if KNN's accuracy is to be believed. When it comes to specificity, SVM and KNN are neck and neck. Compared to other algorithms, KNN performs better in terms of sensitivity.

References

1. Mohan, G. and Subashin, M., MRI based medical image analysis: Survey on brain tumor grade classification. *Biomed. Signal Process. Control*, 39, 139–161, 2018.
2. Işın, A., Direkoğlu, C., Şah, M., Review of MRI-based brain tumor image segmentation using deep learning methods. *Procedia Comput. Sci.*, 102, 317–324, 2016.
3. Menze, B.J., Jakab, A., Bauer, S., Kalpathy-Cramer, J., Farahani, K., Kirby, J., Burren, Y., Porz, N., Slotboom, J., Wiest, R. *et al.*, The multimodal brain tumor image segmentation benchmark (BRATS). *IEEE Trans. Med. Imaging*, 34, 1993–2024, 2015.
4. Litjens, G., Kooi, T., Bejnordi, B.E., Arindra, A., Setio, A., Ciompi, F., Ghafoorian, M., van der Laak, J.A.W.M., van Ginneken, B., Sánchez, C.I., A survey on deep learning in medical image analysis. *Med. Image Anal.*, 42, 60–88, 2017.
5. Cheng, J., Huang, W., Cao, S., Yang, R., Yang, W., Yun, Z., Wang, Z., Feng, Q., Enhanced performance of brain tumor classification via tumor region augmentation and partition. *PLoS One*, 10, e0140381, 2015.
6. Sachdeva, J., Kumar, V., Gupta, I., Khandelwal, N., Ahuja, C.K., A package-SFERCB-Segmentation, features extraction, reduction and classification analysis by both SVM and ANN for brain tumors. *Appl. Soft Comput.*, 47, 151–167, 2016.
7. Suryavamsi, R.V., Sai Thejaswin Reddy, L., Saladi, S., Karuna, Y., Comparative Analysis of Various Enhancement Methods for Astrocytoma MRI Images.

International Conference on Communication and Signal Processing (ICCSP), pp. 0812–0816, 2018.

8. De Blasi, B., Galazzo, I.B., Pasetto, L., Storti, S.F., Koepp, M., Barnes, A., Menczaz, G., Pipeline Comparison for the PreProcessing of Resting-State Data in Epilepsy. *26th European Signal Processing Conference (EUSIPCO)*, pp. 1137–1141, 2018.
9. Poornachandra, S. and Naveena, C., Pre-processing of MR Images for Efficient Quantitative Image Analysis Using Deep Learning Techniques. *International Conference on Recent Advances in Electronics and Communication Technology (ICRAECT)*, pp. 191–195, 2017.
10. Widyarto, S., Kassim, S.R.B., Sari, W.K., 2Dsigmoid enhancement prior to segment MRI Glioma tumor: Pre image-processing. *4th International Conference on Electrical Engineering, Computer Science and Informatics (EECSI)*, pp. 1–5, 2017.
11. Jui, S.-L., Zhang, S., Xiong, W., Yu, F., Fu, M., Wang, D., Hassanien, A.E., Xiao, K., Brain MRI Tumor Segmentation with 3D Intracranial Structure Deformation Features. *IEEE Intell. Syst.*, 31, 2, 66–76, 2016.
12. Zhang, J., Liu, M., An, L., Gao, Y., Shen, D., Alzheimer's Disease Diagnosis Using Landmark-Based Features From Longitudinal Structural MR Images. *IEEE J. Biomed. Health. Inf.*, 21, 6, 1607–1616, 2017.
13. Piantadosi, G., Marrone, S., Fusco, R., Sansone, M., Sansone, C., Comprehensive computer-aided diagnosis for breast T1-weighted DCE-MRI through quantitative dynamical features and spatio-temporal local binary patterns. *IET Comput. Vision*, 12, 7, 1007–1017, 2018.
14. Osadebey, M., Pedersen, M., Arnold, D., Wendel-Mitoraj, K., No-reference quality measure in brain MRI images using binary operations, texture and set analysis. *IET Image Proc.*, 11, 9, 2017.
15. Tsai, H.-Y., Zhang, H., Hung, C.-L., Min, G., GPU-Accelerated Features Extraction From Magnetic Resonance Images. *IEEE Access*, 5, 22634–22646, 2017.
16. Pereira, S., Pinto, A., Alves, V., Silva, C.A., Brain Tumor Segmentation Using Convolutional Neural Networks in MRI Images. *IEEE Trans. Med. Imaging*, 35, 5, 1240–1251, 2016.
17. Kim, J., Lenglet, C., Duchin, Y., Sapiro, G., Harel, N., Semiautomatic Segmentation of Brain Subcortical Structures From High-Field MRI. *IEEE J. Biomed. Health. Inf.*, 18, 5, 1678–1695, 2014.
18. Makropoulos, A., Gousias, I.S., Ledig, C., Aljabar, P., Serag, A., Hajnal, J.V., David Edwards, A., Counsell, S.J., Rueckert, D., Automatic Whole Brain MRI Segmentation of the Developing Neonatal Brain. *IEEE Trans. Med. Imaging*, 33, 9, 1818–1831, 2014.
19. Iqbal, Z., Khan, M., Sharif, M., Shah, J., ur Rehman, M., Javed, K., An automated detection and classification of citrus plant diseases using image processing techniques: A review. *Comput. Electron. Agric.*, *153*, 12–32, 2018, doi: 10.1016/j.compag.2018.07.032.

20. Zhao, W. and Wang, J., A new method of the forest dynamic inspection color image sharpening process. *2010 3Rd International Conference On Advanced Computer Theory And Engineering(ICACTE)*, 2010, doi: 10.1109/icacte.2010.5579715.
21. Reza, M., Na, I., Baek, S., Lee, K., Rice yield estimation based on K-means clustering with graph-cut segmentation using low-altitude UAV images. *Biosyst. Eng.*, *177*, 109–121, 2019, doi: 10.1016/j.biosystemseng.2018.09.014.
22. Deng, Z., Zhu, X., Cheng, D., Zong, M., Zhang, S., Efficient k NN classification algorithm for big data. *Neurocomputing*, *195*, 143–148, 2016, doi: 10.1016/j.neucom.2015.08.112.
23. Suryawati, E., Pardede, H., Zilvan, V., Ramdan, A., Krisnandi, D., Heryana, A. *et al.*, Unsupervised feature learning-based encoder and adversarial networks. *J. Big Data*, *8*, 1, 2021, doi: 10.1186/s40537-021-00508-9.
24. http://med.harvard.edu/AANLIB/
25. Nahar, S., Pithawa, D., Bhardwaj, V., Rawat, R., Rawat, A., Pachlasiya, K., Quantum Technology for Military Applications, in: *Quantum Computing in Cybersecurity*, pp. 313–334, 2023.
26. Pithawa, D., Nahar, S., Bhardwaj, V., Rawat, R., Dronawat, R., Rawat, A., Quantum Computing Technological Design Along with Its Dark Side, in: *Quantum Computing in Cybersecurity*, pp. 295–312, 2023.
27. Chauhan, D., Singh, C., Rawat, R., Chouhan, M., Conversational AI Applications in Ed-Tech Industry: An Analysis of Its Impact and Potential in Education, in: *Conversational Artificial Intelligence*, pp. 411–433, 2024.
28. Chauhan, D., Singh, C., Rawat, R., Dhawan, M., Evaluating the Performance of Conversational AI Tools: A Comparative Analysis, in: *Conversational Artificial Intelligence*, pp. 385–409, 2024.
29. Shrivastava, M., Patil, R., Bhardwaj, V., Rawat, R., Telang, S., Rawat, A., Quantum Computing and Security Aspects of Attention-Based Visual Question Answering with Long Short-Term Memory, in: *Quantum Computing in Cybersecurity*, pp. 395–412, 2023.
30. Rawat, R., Chakrawarti, R.K., Raj, A.S.A., Mani, G., Chidambarathanu, K., Bhardwaj, R., Association rule learning for threat analysis using traffic analysis and packet filtering approach. *Int. J. Inf. Technol.*, 15, 6, 3245–3255, 2023.

14

Optimized Machine Learning Techniques for Software Fault Prediction

Chetan Shelke[1]*, Ashwini Mandale (Jadhav)[2], Shaik Anjimoon[3], Asha V.[4], Ginni Nijhawan[5] and Joshuva Arockia Dhanraj[6]

[1]Alliance College of Engineering and Design, Alliance University, Bangalore, India
[2]Computer Science and Engineering, Rajarambapu Institute of Technology, Rajaramnagar, Shivaji University, Kolhapur, Maharashtra, India
[3]Institute of Aeronautical Engineering, Dundigal, Hyderabad, India
[4]Department of Computer Applications, New Horizon College of Engineering, Bangalore, India
[5]Lovely Professional University, Phagwara, India
[6]Department of Computer Science and Engineering (AI&ML), School of Engineering, Dayananda Sagar University, Devarakaggalahalli, Harohalli, Kanakapura Road, Ramanagara District, Bengaluru, Karnataka, India

Abstract

Software fault prediction serves to improve testing efficiency and software quality by enabling the early discovery of software problems. This is accomplished via improved program quality. In most cases, the procedure of categorizing is used for the purpose of error detection. During the classification process, coding features and other characteristics are used to produce predictions about the potential occurrence of mistakes. Due to the fact that software defect detection is heavily influenced by poor categorization judgments, it is necessary to have an improved decision-making model to anticipate trends by making use of the attributes retrieved from datasets. Through the use of a collection of software failure datasets, these researchers evaluate the performance of the offered techniques in comparison to that of a wide variety of machine learning classifiers. Accuracy, balance, area under the curve, false alarm rate, detection rate, or recall rate were some of the performance criteria that were used in the evaluation of the recommended approaches.

**Corresponding author*: Chetan.shelke@alliance.edu.in

Rajesh Kumar Chakrawarti, Ranjana Sikarwar, Sanjaya Kumar Sarangi, Samson Arun Raj Albert Raj, Shweta Gupta, Krishnan Sakthidasan Sankaran and Romil Rawat (eds.) Natural Language Processing for Software Engineering, (207–220) © 2025 Scrivener Publishing LLC

***Keywords*:** Scientific programming, machine learning, software fault prediction, software quality improvement

14.1 Introduction

Software faults are errors that prevent the software from functioning correctly and are referred to by that same term. Consequently, the fundamental purpose of the team should be to develop software that is free of mistakes whenever possible. Ineffective software that is both poorly written and poorly performed is a definite method to waste resources (including time, money, and energy). Even if there is no such thing as a perfect system, it is essential that there are as few errors as possible and that their negative effects are minimized. This will allow the system to be utilized more frequently and with a greater degree of assurance. When it comes to software modules, outputs that are wrong could be the result of poor-quality software as well as incorrect programming logic. It is possible that this will result in the client becoming dissatisfied, which will in turn push up the cost of maintenance. A decrease in customer satisfaction may drive the client to urge that the developer solve the issue, or the client may opt to withdraw from the contract entirely. Both of these outcomes are possible. In the end, poor quality and the failure of the project are both potential outcomes that can result from defects. When it comes to software development, metrics not only make it possible to evaluate the effectiveness and quality of a project, but also make it easier to strategically distribute available resources [1].

As a result of the fact that it is not always possible to discover and correct faults while the development process is in progress, it is essential to keep an eye out for them and correct them as soon as you or your teammates see them. It is possible for errors to occur at any stage of the software development process because it is an iterative process. Therefore, to produce a maintenance strategy, it is essential to discover problems in software modules in a methodical manner prior to the deployment of the project. Software development is a process that has the potential to produce a variety of different types of errors. It is possible that it is foolish to believe that these vulnerabilities are introduced into the system at the beginning of the cycle and that they can be addressed as the cycle progresses. Every single stage of the process is open to the chance of making a mistake. The term "software defects" refers to irregularities that occur throughout the process of developing software and result in the software not conforming to the standards that were anticipated [2].

For project managers, the goal of accurately predicting software development cycle (SDLC) errors in a timely way is an ideal goal, but it is also a very tough goal to achieve [3]. In this day and age, it is quite challenging to produce software that is not only dependable but also free of faults, particularly during the development period. During the process of development, there are a number of problems that get increasingly intricate and ambiguous. It is an extremely challenging endeavor to either avoid or deal with all of these problems. It is impossible to guarantee that there will be no errors in the process, regardless of how much preparation or documentation is done. The product's quality suffers as a result of these defects, and customers are dissatisfied with the purchase. Classification and prediction are two independent concerns that can be utilized to express software fault prediction: classification and prediction. The first method can be utilized to assign defect labels to data classes, while the second method can be utilized to create predictions regarding trends on a continuous scale. The distinction between the two kinds of predictions is that one approach makes use of discrete, unordered labels or categorical variables, while the other approach makes use of functions that have continuous values. Through the utilization of this kind of analysis, software defects may be comprehended and treated in a more effective manner [4].

Software defect prediction is a learning issue that involves predicting the chance of software modules having flaws based on previous data. This approach is known as software defect prediction. To derive the defect prediction models, the log files of older versions are analyzed to extract the qualities that correspond to the code. Only by making use of predictions is it possible to arrive at an exact count of the number of defects that are present in the tested module as well as the locations of those defects. Sadly, this requirement has not been satisfied because of the inconsistencies that have been recorded in the defect recording procedure as well as the very complicated nature of the prediction process [5].

Most of the time, SDP models are able to determine whether or not a specific collection of test data contains any errors. Metrics for software can be utilized to ascertain the degree to which the software is prone to defects. In software development process (SDP) models, the state of the software bug is used as the dependent variable. These models make use of independent variables that are acquired and evaluated throughout the software development lifecycle. In the context of software, metrics refer to measurements that are taken of either the software itself or the specifications of the software. Utilizing this is helpful when attempting to quantify the quality of the curriculum. "Continuously applying techniques based on measurement in the process of developing software and its products and in providing meaningful and timely Management Information (MI) along with the methods to improve its products and processes" is the resultant definition of metrics for software development [6].

In numerous occasions, software quality prediction models are constructed using software metrics and defect data from a software project that has already been developed and deployed. This makes it possible to evaluate the development module's fault proneness, which is a significant benefit. A non-defect forecast implies that the current module is of good quality, which provides the opportunity for the resources to be pooled for some other activity. On the other hand, a defect prediction that results in the requirement to shift resources to address the issue is the reverse of what is intended. Our ultimate objective is to find a balance between quality and dependability while making the most of the resources we have currently available to us. As a result of the fact that the model is dependent on the information that is contained in the underlying software measures, selecting the appropriate collection of software measures is an essential component of the process of building a model for computing software quality prediction. Due to the fact that software companies are subject to a penalty when customers report software defects, it is beneficial to have knowledge of the expected number of errors that must be present in a software product at a particular stage of development. To determine when it is appropriate to release a software product, it is necessary to have the ability to forecast the number of issues that will arise at any given stage [7].

Machine learning techniques that are now in use include classification and clustering, which are two of the most prevalent methods. Having characteristics or data of a good quality is absolutely necessary for the operation of data models. If the data is faulty or contains information that is not relevant to the problem at hand, then the accuracy of the model's predictions will be undermined. As a consequence of this, it is of the utmost importance to prepare the data in such a way that it can be less redundant and free of noise. The procedure of selecting features is quite important. Classification is a well-liked method for predicting software defects. It employs a model that is constructed using metrics data of software that has been used in the past to classify the codes of software attributes according to whether or not they are defective. On account of the fact that the classifier is typically the weakest link due to the limited number of features that are used for prediction, it plays an extremely important role in the accurate detection of defects [8].

14.2 Literature Survey

It was recommended that a three-way decision structure be used for the purpose of anticipating software flaws. This decision-making framework takes into consideration costs, and it does so by using the well-known two-stage categorization paradigm as its base. A system that utilizes attribute selection for defect prediction was developed by the authors. This system is built on five different classifiers: Random Forest, Random Tree, LWL, IBk, and KStar. In this study, we evaluated two separate classification learners using six alternative feature selection procedures. Additionally, we assessed approaches that coupled feature selection with data sampling, as well as cases in which feature selection was used on its own. It has been shown via the results of the experiments that the SelectRUSBoost technique greatly increases classification performance when compared to other strategies that have been used in the past. When comparing the performance, the ROC values and accuracy are taken into consideration. According to the findings, the framework was able to successfully cut down on the number of characteristics that were used for each dataset by an average of six times. In addition, it was discovered that LWL performed better than the other four classifiers when it was put through a test with a 10CV or a 10 Cross-Validation and a split percentage of 66%. A validation accuracy grade that is exceedingly low suggests that the model is unable to function properly when dealing with complex data [9].

A Twin Support Vector Machine (TSVM) was used by the writers to make a prediction about the mistakes that would be present in a software product that has been updated. This prototype was far more effective than the ones that came before it. Additionally, when compared to all of the SDP approaches that were offered, the TSVM with a Gaussian kernel function has shown the highest level of efficiency. To maintain a high level of quality in the program, the author was also able to anticipate the shortcomings of the new technique. During the testing phase, the strategy that was advised was already more cost-effective. On the other hand, it was shown that the model of huge data displays very low levels of scalability [10].

The authors proposed the use of a multilayer neural network as a means of significantly enhancing the capacity of learning algorithms to forecast software issues. This article presents a unique technique that blends evolutionary algorithms and the concepts of support vector machines (SVM). With the help of this innovative method, the classification margin was increased to its maximum, and overfitting was avoided. Using three different datasets from NASA, eleven different machine learning prototypes and statistical methodologies were put through their paces to establish how effective the aforementioned procedure was. It was concluded that the process described above offered a higher level of trust and authenticity when compared to the other prototypes. In spite of this, it was found that neural networks greatly increased the degrees of complexity that the models had [11].

For the purpose of determining FCRelevance, the authors used Chi-Square, Relief, and Information Gain. They also quantified FFCorrelation by using Symmetric Uncertainty. To analyze the rate of redundancy and, as a last step, to evaluate the effectiveness of defect predictors, empirical tests were carried out. As a basis for putting the proposed framework into action, real-world projects were used such as NASA and Eclipse. This endeavor resulted in a final product that proved the effectiveness of the framework that was provided and gave advice for achieving feature selection that is cost-effective. On the other hand, the model could not provide satisfactory results when the levels of uncertainty measure were low or equivalent [12].

TSCS is a two-stage cost-sensitive learning technique that combines cost data before, during, and after the feature selection and classification processes. The authors suggested this approach for the SDP. Following that, the feature selection process resulted in the development of three cutting-edge algorithms that were very sensitive to cost. By including cost information into the traditional feature selection methods, it was feasible to generate the Cost-Sensitive Variance Score (CSVS), the Cost-Sensitive Laplacian Score (CSLS), and the Cost-Sensitive Constraint Score (CSCS). These scores could be calculated. There is an increase in the computational complexity when more than one model is used. An additional review of the approaches that have been presented is carried out with the use of seven real data sets that have been generated from NASA investigations. According to the results of the experiments, TSCS performed much better than other cost-sensitive methods when it came to forecasting software problems. During the feature selection process, it was found out that the recommended ways performed better than the other standard methods. This was done to further assure that the utilization of cost information would be effective [13].

A concept for active learning has been developed as a result of research into automating the models that academics have developed to improve their ability to predict which releases would include flaws. When compared to its equivalent learning technique, the results demonstrated that active learning integration with uncertainty sampling performed much better. When it came to discovering and integrating the relevant information in the datasets that were supplied, the scientists discovered that multidimensional scaling with random forest similarity was more successful than feature selection. Improvements were made to the method as a result of three successive versions of Eclipse's flawed module prediction [14].

It was stated that a mechanism existed for forecasting software problems by making use of certain metrics. The authors gave feature selection strategies a great deal of attention and proposed a novel strategy that took a hybrid approach to the problem. The findings indicated that the strategy that was recommended improved the accuracy of categorization. A study was conducted to investigate the influence that feature selection techniques, metrics sets, and dataset size had on the prediction of software defects. One of the drawbacks of this technology is that it allows for the use of several models, which leads to very high levels of computational complexity. The research that was done on the subject demonstrated that support vector machines (SVM) and other soft computing methods provide superior classification accuracy when compared to other classifiers. On the other hand, the performance of SVM is NP-Hard and is reliant on the parameter selection of the kernel module. Despite the fact that grid-based methods and meta heuristic approaches, such as Genetic Algorithm (GA), were successfully used, the solutions that were obtained were not ideal. Additionally, GA had a slow convergence rate [15].

The authors presented a strategy that comprised methods for data sampling that were aimed at addressing class imbalance, as well as a method for feature selection that was focused on picking significant characteristics. To examine software engineering, especially the use of classification models for the purpose of software quality prediction, this investigation was carried out. Whenever data sampling and feature selection are combined, there are a number of considerations that need to be taken into account. This case study makes use of nine different software measurement datasets that were taken from the repository of the PROMISE project. The empirical findings revealed that feature selection making use of sampled data worked better than feature selection making use of original data, and that models for defect prediction functioned equally regardless of the data that was used for training. Although the selection of features is significant, it is not sufficient to determine the accuracy of predictions; the prediction model is of more significance on this front [16].

14.3 Methods

Machine learning procedure for software fault prediction is shown below in Figure 14.1.

It is a usual practice to combine the firefly approach with the ant colony optimization (ACO) algorithm when feature selection operations need to be carried out. This is because the firefly technique is so effective. When it comes to intrusion-related data, the firefly approach is responsible for selecting sub-bands, while the ACO strategy is in charge of managing classification and feature continuity analysis. With the help of the ACO approach, both of the objectives are achieved. One example of such a comparison is the approach that algorithm developers use, which is analogous to the way in which ants construct and upgrade their nest spaces [17].

The support vector machine (SVM) is the most appropriate classifier among others many others since it can be utilized in a wide variety of contexts, including medical diagnosis and identification, pattern recognition, text classification, organism identification, and Chinese character classification, among others and many more. Through the construction of an N-dimensional hyperplane, support vector machines (SVMs) divide the data into two distinct groups: those with the most favorable outcomes are located on one side of the hyperplane, while those with less favorable outcomes are located on the other side. By maximizing the margins between

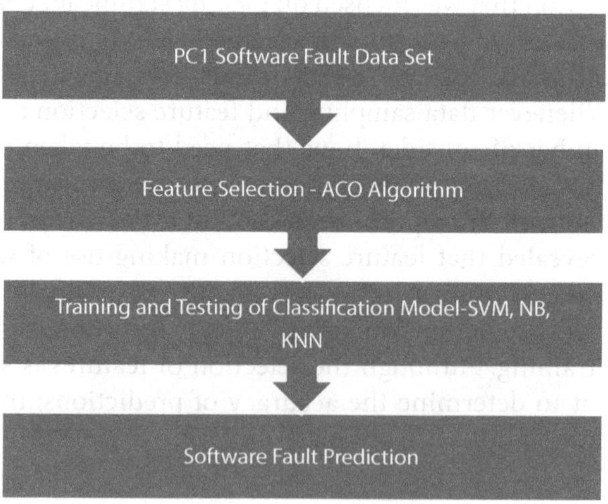

Figure 14.1 Machine learning for software fault prediction.

support vectors and managing non-linear regions, support vector machines (SVM) map data into a space that is not uniform. The hyperplane then executes separation as a result of this mapping [18].

KNN [19] is the most straightforward and effective method for data categorization that everyone can utilize. It is also the most straightforward. In addition to being easy to use and delivering results that are highly competitive, it also has the capability of implicitly computing decision boundaries. Considering that this approach is dependent on having a selection of instances to pick from, there is a possibility that disputes over which characteristics are relevant and which are not would result in findings that are less accurate. To establish whether or not a dataset is n-dimensional, the authors first sum up all of the samples that are included inside the dataset, and then we examine the vector that is produced to determine whether or not it is n-dimensional.

Bayesian classifiers are a kind of statistical classifier [22–24] that makes predictions about the appropriate classes to which data points should belong by assessing the likelihood of class membership. Bayesian classifiers are used in the application of statistics. In a manner that is analogous, the Naive Bayes [25–27] classification approach is significantly dependent on optimum rules; this theorem serves as the basis for the method. There are a number of clear benefits associated with doing so, including the fact that it is easy to put into action and brings about outcomes that can be relied upon. In this study, the authors want to investigate and compare the classification methods used by a number of different convolutional neural network classifiers, as well as the decision tree classifier and the naive Bayes classifier classification system. Under the assumption that the prior probabilities P(c), P(x), and P(x | c) are known, the Bayes theorem may be used to determine the posterior probability P (c | x). Due to the fact that it is predicated on the premise that the effect of a given predictor value (x) on a certain class (c) stays constant across all potential values, the Naive Bayes classifier continues to carry out its typical operations. The concept of "conditional independence" immediately comes to mind when attempting to provide an explanation for this set of circumstances. Among the essential actions involved in the production of a frequency table are the determination of the posterior probability and the classification of characteristics according to the frequency with which they occur. After that, the Naive Bayesian equation is used to get the posterior probability for each of these classes. Those students who belong to the category for whom this prognosis has the greatest likelihood of being right will be the ones to profit the most from its achievement [20]. The Figure 14.2 shows about the Result comparison.

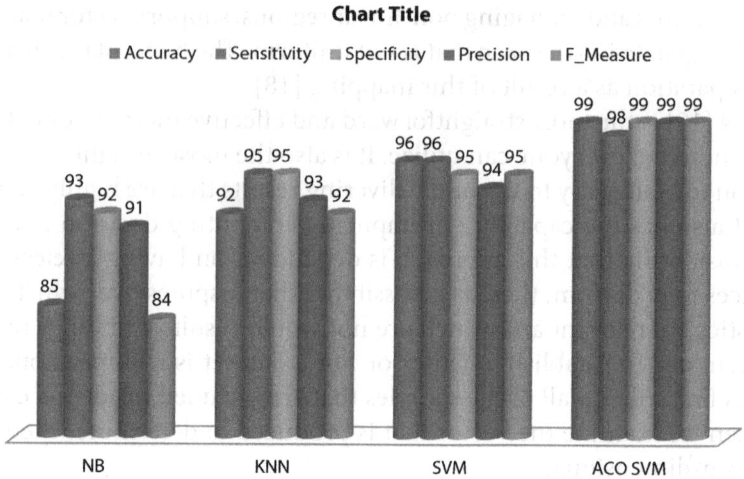

Figure 14.2 Result comparison.

14.4 Result Analysis

The PC1 data collection is used in the scientific research that is being carried out [21]. There are data errors that belong to a specific NASA program that are included in this collection of data. This particular dataset comprises 1,192 records. The data set from PC1 is used as the input for this design. Ant colony optimization is a strategy that selects the characteristics that are most significant. During the training process, the support vector machine is trained using the features that have been chosen in advance. For the purposes of SVM training and testing, the PC1 dataset is used. The performance of the ACO SVM is examined in conjunction with the SVM, Naive Bayes, and KNN classifiers in order to establish its effectiveness.

14.5 Conclusion

In the course of the study, a number of different aspects were investigated, including issues pertaining to the quality of the data, metrics for performance evaluation, metrics for software, and failure prediction. The findings of this study shed light on a range of methodological challenges that were related with software fault prediction jobs. The usage of feature extraction for data with a high dimensionality and classification for data with a data class imbalance associated to software quality issues has been widespread. Both of these techniques have been used extensively. There are a few different metrics that are used to examine the outcomes to determine how accurate the predictions are. The study also revealed difficulties that researchers may examine further to enhance the software defect prediction approach. This was emphasized in order to improve the system.

References

1. Mishra, A., Shatnawi, R., Catal, C., Akbulut, A., Techniques for Calculating Software Product Metrics Threshold Values: A Systematic Mapping Study. *Appl. Sci.*, 11, 11377, 2021.
2. Özakıncı, R. and Tarhan, A., Early software defect prediction: A systematic map and review. *J. Syst. Software*, 144, 216–239, 2018.
3. Son, L.H., Pritam, N., Khari, M., Kumar, R., Phuong, P.T.M., Thong, P.H., Empirical Study of Software Defect Prediction: A Systematic Mapping. *Symmetry*, 11, 212, 2019.
4. Bhavana, K., Nekkanti, V., Jayapandian, N., Internet of things enabled device fault prediction system using machine learning, in: *International Conference on Inventive Computation Technologies*, pp. 920–927, Springer, Cham, Switzerland, 2019.
5. Ramakrishnan, R. and Kaur, A., An empirical comparison of predictive models for web page performance. *Inf. Software Technol.*, 123, 106307, 2020.
6. Padhy, N., Satapathy, S.C., Mohanty, J., Panigrahi, R., Software reusability metrics prediction by using evolutionary algorithms: The interactive mobile learning application RozGaar. *Int. J. Knowledge-Based Intell. Eng. Syst.*, 22, 261–276, 2018.
7. Wang, P., Jin, C., Jin, S.W., Software defect prediction scheme based on feature selection. *International Symposium on Information Science and Engineering (ISISE)*, IEEE, pp. 477–480, 2012, DOI: 10.1109/ISISE.2012.114.
8. Reena, P. and Rajan, B., A Novel Feature Subset Selection Algorithm for Software Defect Prediction. *Int. J. Comput. Appl.*, 100, 17, 39–43, 2014.
9. Jing, X.Y., Ying, S., Zhang, Z.W., Wu, S.S., Liu, J., Dictionary learning based software defect prediction. *Proceedings of the 36th International Conference on Software Engineering*, ACM, pp. 414–423, 2014, DOI:10.1145 / 2568225.2568320.
10. Xu, Z., Xuan, J., Liu, J., Cui, X., MICHAC: Defect Prediction via Feature Selection based on Maximal Information Coefficient with Hierarchical Agglomerative Clustering. *IEEE 23rd International Conference on Software Analysis, Evolution, and Reengineering (SANER)*, vol. 1, IEEE, pp. 370–381, 2016.

11. Xia, Y., Yan, G., Jiang, X., Yang, Y., A new metrics selection method for software defect prediction. *International Conference on Progress in Informatics and Computing (PIC)*, IEEE, pp. 433–436, 2014, DOI:10.1109/PIC. 2014 .6972372.
12. Mandal, P. and Ami, A.S., Selecting best attributes for software defect prediction. *IEEE International WIE Conference on Electrical and Computer Engineering (WIECON-ECE)*, IEEE, pp. 110–113, 2015, DOI: 10.1109/ wiecon-ece.2015.7444011.
13. Dejaeger, K., Verbraken, T., Baesens, B., Toward comprehensible software fault prediction models using bayesian network classifiers. *IEEE Trans. Software Eng.*, 39, 2, 237–257, 2013.
14. Bishnu, P.S. and Bhattacherjee, V., Software fault prediction using quad tree-based k-means clustering algorithm. *IEEE Trans. Knowl. Data Eng.*, 24, 6, 1146–1150, 2012.
15. Gondra, I., Applying machine learning to software fault-proneness prediction. *J. Syst. Software*, 81, 2, 186–195, 2008.
16. Catal, C., Software fault prediction: A literature review and current trends. *Expert Syst. Appl.*, 38, 4, 4626–4636, 2011.
17. Malik, V., Mittal, R., Singh, J., Rattan, V., Mittal, A., Feature Selection Optimization using ACO to Improve the Classification Performance of Web Log Data. *2021 8th International Conference on Signal Processing and Integrated Networks (SPIN)*, pp. 671–675, 2021, doi: 10.1109/ SPIN52536.2021.9566126.
18. Shafaghat, M. and Dezvareh, R., Support vector machine for classification and regression of coastal sediment transport. *Arabian J. Geosci.*, 14, 2009, 2021, https://doi.org/10.1007/s12517-021-08360-0.
19. Goyal, S., Handling Class-Imbalance with KNN (Neighbourhood) Under-Sampling for Software Defect Prediction. *Artif. Intell. Rev.*, 55, 3, 2023–2064, 2021, Available: 10.1007/s10462-021-10044-w.
20. Rahim, A., Hayat, Z., Abbas, M., Rahim, A., Rahim, M.A., Software Defect Prediction with Naïve Bayes Classifier. *2021 International Bhurban Conference on Applied Sciences and Technologies (IBCAST)*, pp. 293–297, 2021, doi: 10.1109/IBCAST51254.2021.9393250.
21. https://www.openml.org/search?type=data&sort=runs&id=1068&status=active
22. Pithawa, D., Nahar, S., Bhardwaj, V., Rawat, R., Dronawat, R., Rawat, A., Quantum Computing Technological Design Along with Its Dark Side, in: *Quantum Computing in Cybersecurity*, pp. 295–312, 2023.
23. Shrivastava, M., Patil, R., Bhardwaj, V., Rawat, R., Telang, S., Rawat, A., Quantum Computing and Security Aspects of Attention-Based Visual Question Answering with Long Short-Term Memory, in: *Quantum Computing in Cybersecurity*, pp. 395–412, 2023.
24. Rawat, R., Chakrawarti, R.K., Raj, A.S.A., Mani, G., Chidambarathanu, K., Bhardwaj, R., Association rule learning for threat analysis using traffic

analysis and packet filtering approach. *Int. J. Inf. Technol.*, *15*, 6, 3245–3255, 2023.

25. Rathi, M. and Rajavat, A., High Dimensional Data Processing in Privacy Preserving Data Mining, in: *2020 IEEE 9th International Conference on Communication Systems and Network Technologies (CSNT)*, 2020, April, IEEE, pp. 212–217.
26. Patsariya, M. and Rajavat, A., Network Path Capability Identification and Performance analysis of Mobile Ad hoc Network, in: *2020 IEEE 9th International Conference on Communication Systems and Network Technologies (CSNT)*, 2020, April, IEEE, pp. 82–87.
27. Dhar, S., Dhar, U., Rajavat, A., Factors and Attributes of Team Players: A Study of Engineering Students in India, in: *International Simulation and Gaming Association Conference*, pp. 53–60, Springer International Publishing, Cham, 2021, September.

15

Pancreatic Cancer Detection Using Machine Learning and Image Processing

Shashidhar Sonnad[1]*, Rejwan Bin Sulaiman[2], Amer Kareem[3], S. Shalini[4], D. Kishore[5] and Jayasankar Narayanan[6]

[1]*Electronics and Communication Engineering, Sharnbasva University, Kalaburagi, Karnataka, India*
[2]*Department of Computer and Information Sciences, Northumbria University, Newcastle, UK*
[3]*Department of Computing, University of Wales Trinity Saint David, Swansea, UK*
[4]*Department of Mathematics, J.N.N Institute of Engineering, Ushaa Garden, Kannigaipair, Chennai, India*
[5]*Department of ECE, Aditya College of Engineering & Technology, Surampalem, India*
[6]*Department of Pharmacology, SRM College of Pharmacy, SRM Institute of Science and Technology Kattankulathur, Chengalpattu District, Tamil Nadu, India*

Abstract
The absence of uniformity in data sources poses challenges for clinical diagnosis. The healthcare industry developments have led to enhanced diagnostic benefits. Medical professionals are optimistic that radiologists will enhance their ability to analyze images and provide accurate diagnoses through the utilization of computer-aided diagnosis technologies. Humans have always been susceptible to many potentially lethal illnesses. Pancreatic adenocarcinoma (PDAC) is a particularly prevalent and lethal illness among those aged 45 and older. PDAC is generally ranked as the fourth most common type of malignancy. CT, MRI, PET scans, and ultrasounds are the often used diagnostic methods for diagnosing disorders. To predict individuals' risk levels and detect symptoms of pancreatic disease for timely surgical preparation, this enables the creation of a reliable diagnostic system for pancreatic cancer using diverse clinical data, such as Structured EHRs, images of jaundiced eyes, and pancreatic CT scans. Extracting patterns from multi-modal

**Corresponding author*: shashidharsonnad1@gmail.com
Jayasankar Narayanan: ORCID: https://orcid.org/0000-0002-6149-2761

Rajesh Kumar Chakrawarti, Ranjana Sikarwar, Sanjaya Kumar Sarangi, Samson Arun Raj Albert Raj, Shweta Gupta, Krishnan Sakthidasan Sankaran and Romil Rawat (eds.) Natural Language Processing for Software Engineering, (221–232) © 2025 Scrivener Publishing LLC

healthcare data is a challenging task due to the pancreas's complex form, volume, and its position in the abdomen. Additionally, there are difficulties in identifying the pancreas, dealing with noisy data, and managing many risk factors associated with the disease. Extracting important disease patterns is currently extremely tough due to the existing state of affairs. Detecting tumors in pancreatic CT images and jaundice eye photographs is a difficult task with the existing segmentation methods. This study aims to extract meaningful disease patterns from clinical data to diagnose pancreatic ailment, taking into account the variety of medical data sources and the lack of a common framework.

***Keywords*:** Pancreatic cancer, machine learning, classification, detection, PSO SVM, accuracy

15.1 Introduction

Pancreatic cancer is one of the leading causes of death from cancer all over the world. In patients who are above the age of 50 and have just been diagnosed with diabetes, there is an increased likelihood that they will develop pancreatic adenocarcinoma (PDAC). About eighty-five percent of the cases were caused by adenocarcinoma of the pancreas, and jaundice is a condition that happens before this cancer develops. The development of pancreatic cancer is a consequence of a wide range of diseases that lead to the malfunctioning of the pancreas. A significant number of these diseases are brought on by structural, social, and environmental changes that occur over the course of time. There are a variety of disorders that can affect the pancreas, including acute pancreatitis, chronic pancreatitis, exocrine pancreatic insufficiency, diabetes, cystic fibrosis, and hereditary pancreatitis. On the other hand, the most significant risk factors for pancreatic cancer are the use of tobacco products, diabetes, exposure to chemicals, heredity, bad eating habits, and excessive intake of alcohol. Pancreatic adenocarcinoma is the fourth most common type of cancer that results in death as a result of cancer. Electronic health records (EHRs) contain information about medical imaging (including CT, MRI, and PET scans, among others) as well as multimodal health clinical data (relating to pancreatic cancer) [1].

A technique known as machine learning is utilized in the process of developing algorithms for disease diagnosis and identification of severity. Following the confirmation of the presence of pancreatic cancer by a patient's scleral bilirubin level, a computed tomography (CT) scan is performed. The stage of the cancer as well as its severity can be determined by CT scans. Medical CT scans in grayscale and color are the inputs for the system that is used for diagnosing pancreatic cancer. Following the extraction of the original data, biomarkers or regions of interest are identified. Considering the pancreatic form and its placement below the stomach, the process of separating the cancer from the normal tissue is a challenging one [2]. The study of computed tomography (CT) scans makes it possible to differentiate between cancerous and non-cancerous tissues, as well as to stage cancer to plan therapies and procedures. How well a diagnostic system is able to recognize patterns of sickness based on patient records can be evaluated using performance metrics such as sensitivity and specificity. In most cases, the metrics of sensitivity, specificity, and false positive rate (FPR) are considered to be adequate for assessing a computer-aided pancreatic cancer diagnostic system. Using multi-modal clinical data, such as structured electronic health records, pictures of jaundiced eyes, and pancreatic computed tomography scans, this study presents strategies for improving the system's performance in terms of sensitivity, specificity, F-score, and error rate in the diagnosis of pancreatic cancer. These strategies are presented in this study [3].

There are two types of health information that are included in clinical data: organized and unstructured health information, as well as medical images. Some of the most common imaging modalities that are used for the diagnosis of pancreatic cancer include scleral recognition, positron emission tomography (PET) scans, ultrasound, computed tomography (CT), magnetic resonance imaging (MRI), and computed tomography (CT). Computed tomography (CT) scans are a type of imaging that involve the use of a focused beam of X-rays that rotates around the body of the patient in a circular motion. It is possible to create cross-sectional views, also known as slices, of the human anatomy through the use of computer processing of the images of the internal organs of the body that were obtained during the scan. Tomographic images, as opposed to traditional X-rays, are given their name due to the fact that these slices produce information that is specific to the images. CT scans of the pancreas are noninvasive methods that can be used to assess a patient's likelihood of developing cancer. These scans involve the collection or stacking of several images of the organ to produce a three-dimensional image that can detect abnormalities such as tumors [4]. One image showing pancreatic cancer is shown in Figure 15.1.

Images of pancreatic cancer obtained using CT and MRI are free of noise caused by patient movement, miscalibration of the detector, and other forms of interference. The noise removal function is essential to the process of image processing since it is necessary for the analysis of the picture. The reduction of noise and the preservation of data can be accomplished by a number of different ways, including linear and non-linear denoising techniques. In addition to protecting the data contained within the image,

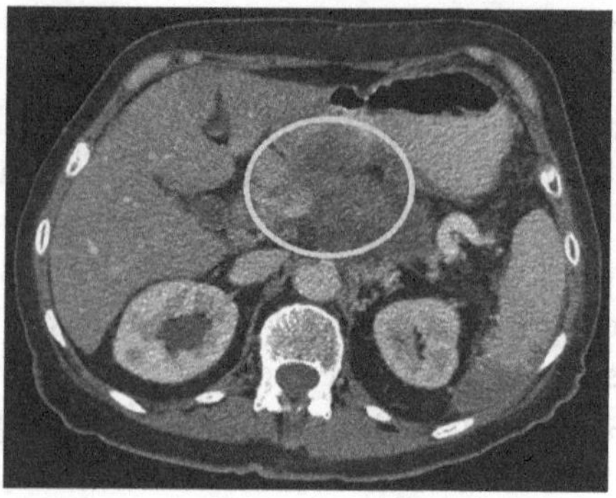

Figure 15.1 Pancreatic cancer tissue in CT scan image.

non-linear filters also give the edges more prominence [5]. Depending on the kind of noise that is present in the image, the proper filter is applied to remove the noise from the image. One can observe the progression of pancreatic tumors by looking at Figure 15.2.

The utilization of ensemble-based classifiers results in a significant improvement in the accuracy of pancreatic cancer classification systems. Learning strategies that are either supervised or unsupervised can be utilized to complete the task of classifying pancreatic segments simultaneously. Supervised learning is used to accomplish the classification of the regions of tumors. The system is intended to acquire knowledge based on the class that is defined for the image. It organizes the test data in accordance

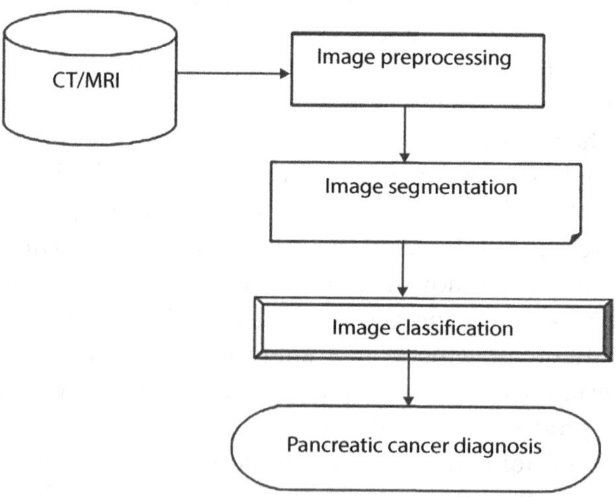

Figure 15.2 Pancreatic cancer detection process.

with the classification that was learned from the structure. During the categorization process, the region of the pancreas that contains the cancer is identified using picture analysis [6].

15.2 Literature Survey

There are two categories of pancreatic tumors: benign and malignant. These categories were determined by utilizing three models that were established [7]: LDA and KNN. Identifying patients who have malignant pancreatic tumors was the motivation for the development of the novel approach, which was developed with the intention of establishing the patient's existence. PLS is utilized in the process of removing Raman spectra data from pancreatic tumors.

Behrouz Alizadeh Savareh and colleagues [8] created a reliable diagnosis model for pancreatic cancer by utilizing miRNA biomarkers. This model was developed utilizing machine learning techniques. Using feature selection methods, the findings assign a score to the miRNAs, and they supply the index with miRNAs that have been chosen for their clinical value as biomarkers for the identification of pancreatic cancer. This demonstrated that the miRNAs with the highest degree of discrimination for the identification of pancreatic cancer have been obtained.

The research conducted by Abu Z. M. Dayem Ullah and colleagues [9] was one of the studies that investigated the link between pancreatic cancer and clinical factors throughout the course of time. It was not possible to conduct an accurate risk assessment for pancreatic cancer in connection to the emergence of co-morbidities and activities that are performed on a daily basis. The judgements may notify risk-stratification methods and improved investigation to persons who are at a higher risk. This is in addition to the fact that they provide systematic recognition of the target population for prospective cohort-based early detection research innovation.

Sk Md Mosaddek Hossain and colleagues [10] laid up the foundation for finding significant regulatory genes and important gene modules by using data from PDAC microarrays. Important regulators were able to examine the patterns and characteristics of gene activity connected to the progression of cancer as a result of this. In addition, the functionalities of the GAN should be rebuilt based on the expected top genes. The difference of partial correlation technique was utilized to accomplish the goal of identifying GAN based on gene function characteristics. Additionally, the recognition of the dynamical GENIE3 (dynGENIE3) technique was made possible by the use of gene regulatory inference.

An investigation was conducted by V. Jackins and colleagues [11] into the application of a Naive Bayes model in a number of disorders, including cancer, with the purpose of determining whether or not a patient was concerned about their illness. An investigation was carried out to analyze and contrast the disease data that were utilized in the model. In addition to demonstrating the efficiency of the classification algorithms, the outcomes of the simulations also highlight the intricacy of the datasets that were utilized.

A bagging of multiple Gaussian mixture approach was developed by Yaoyao Li and colleagues [12] to differentiate between samples that were normal and those that were related to tumors. For the purpose of slicing genomic sequences, it employs a coverage ratio as a rudimentary criterion. Following that, a Gaussian mixture approach was developed to determine the meaning of hazy copy number states. The bagging models were able to detect copy number gains and losses with a great deal greater precision as a result of improvements made to their sensitivity and specificity.

An AdaBoost ensemble method was developed by Sourabh Shastri and colleagues [13] as a part of their research on disease detection in classification. Both imputes and filters were employed by the erythemato-squamous diseases (ESD) team to ensure that the dataset remained in a balanced perspective. To complete the building, both the GB ensemble approach and a method that did not need it were utilized. A shared meta-classifier was utilized by the classes that were part of the GB ensemble technique to generate a variety of static base-classifier combinations possible. Stephen P. Pereira and colleagues [14] presented a review that was developed on the topic of early diagnosis of pancreatic cancer. They investigate the idea of making use of social media. Additionally, his work investigates the application of artificial intelligence in medical imaging and how it is connected to the goals of early discovery. Individualized pre-diagnostic tools for the discovery and validation of biological and epidemiological indicators can be obtained through the construction of new cohorts that are tailored to specific needs.

The identification of pancreatic tumors was spearheaded by Santosh Reddy P and Chandrasekar M when they were working from the ensemble technique [15]. Through the implementation of the intended strategy, the classifiers' capacity to identify pancreatic cancer is improved. The limited visual scheme of mammals serves as the foundation for the development of intelligent artificial picture detection classification. The study that was done by Md. Manjurul Ahsan and his colleagues [16] became the foundation for illness analysis performed by machines. In the beginning, the data about WOS were collected through the use of bibliometric research that was based on published works. There are a number of different domains that are encompassed by the most recent MLBDD algorithms. Some of these domains include kinds of diseases, data categories, applications, and estimating parameters.

15.3 Methodology

Despite the fact that the SVM technique is most frequently utilized for the purpose of achieving classification objectives, it is also capable of addressing challenges associated with regression. By locating a hyperplane, the data can be divided into a number of different groups. The algorithm attempts to maximize the distance between the class data points to locate the hyperplane that is going to be the most effective. This property of maximizing distance is referred to as margin maximization [17]. There are two types of support vector machine algorithms: the linear kind and the non-linear kind. The linear kind is the more common approach. A linear support vector machine classifies the training data by employing a hyperplane as the classification mechanism. In contrast, a non-linear support vector machine (SVM) is built by first substituting each dot product with a non-linear kernel function and then applying the kernel trick to maximum-margin hyper-planes. This process is repeated until the SVM [21–25] is complete. SVM performs exceptionally well in classification challenges that are nonlinear and complex. Furthermore, it provides a reliable form of extrapolation to the data that are uncertain. The current investigation makes use of support vector machines (SVMs) that are fitted with kernels referred to as "linear," "sigmoid," and "radial basis function (RBF)"[25–27] to enhance the categorization of histopathological images and to determine whether or not the characteristics that are retrieved are linearly discriminable or non-linear.

It is a graphical tool that employs branching methodology to represent all of the alternative choice outcomes that are depending on particular variables. This tool is known as a decision tree. Each node within a decision tree represents a feature; each branch represents a decision rule, and ultimately, each leaf node represents an outcome, also known as a target variable. The root node is the first node in a decision tree [24, 25, 28, 29]. It is possible to improve communication and make judgments in the face of uncertainty with the assistance of this method, which provides a visual depiction of a chosen condition. Another method which assists data scientists in arriving at sound findings is by providing them with the capability to perform computations in both the forward and backward directions.

In addition, decision trees are flexible enough to accommodate errors and data that are missing with relative simplicity. It is most appropriate for the method to use instances that are provided in the form of attribute-value pairs. In the context of decision trees, a classification tree or a regression tree are both valid options. A number of different industries, such as banking, finance, remote sensing, and healthcare, stand to gain from the implementation of the algorithm [18].

The Random Forest algorithm works by generating a forest of decision trees by using a randomly selected sample of data [19]. The bagging method is the most used training approach for the Random Forest algorithm. Using a random sample, the model is trained in an iterative manner, and the best prediction is derived by aggregating the results of all of the decision trees. The accuracy of our technique is not affected by outliers, and it continues to function normally even when there is no data available. One of its most notable strengths is that it can process numerical, category, and binary attributes without retaining any of their significance. In addition to this, it provides us with a great concept of which characteristics are going to be the most significant for classification. The banking industry, the automobile industry, the healthcare industry, speech recognition, and the picture and text classification industries have all recently implemented this technique.

15.4 Result Analysis

Patients who were diagnosed with a variety of pancreatic tumors were included in the 500 CT scans of the abdomens that were included in the Medical Segmentation Decathlon (MSD) dataset [20]. When the model was put through its paces, it was tested with 100 photographs, while it was trained using 400 pictures as shown in Figure 15.3: Result Comparison of Machine Learning for Pancreatic cancer Detection.

15.5 Conclusion

Clinical diagnosis is difficult due to the lack of data source standardization. Improvements in the healthcare business have resulted in better diagnostic outcomes. According to clinical professionals, radiologists will be able to evaluate images and make diagnoses more accurately using computer-aided diagnosis technologies. There have always been several infectious diseases that kill humans. Pancreatic adenocarcinoma (PDAC) is a deadly disease

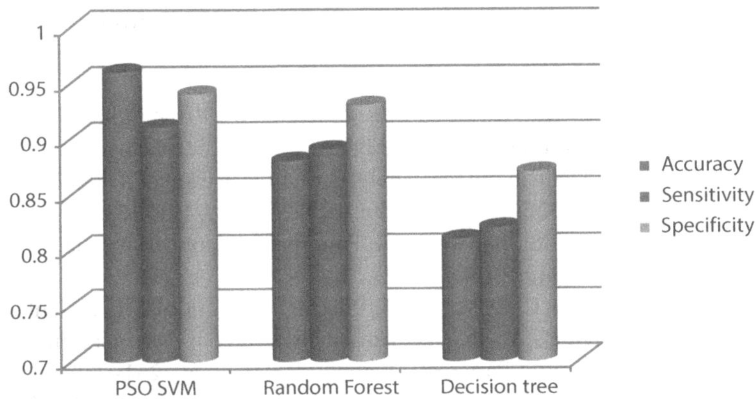

Figure 15.3 Result comparison of machine learning for pancreatic cancer detection.

that primarily affects adults over the age of 45. PDAC is the world's fourth most common cancer. Common diagnostic techniques include computed tomography (CT), magnetic resonance imaging (MRI), positron emission tomography (PET) scans, and ultrasounds. An effective pancreatic cancer diagnostic system that uses multi-modal clinical data, such as structured EHRs, jaundiced eye images, and pancreatic CTs, can be constructed to forecast individuals' risk levels and detect pancreatic disease symptoms for rapid surgery planning. Pattern extraction from multi-modal healthcare data is difficult due to noise, the pancreas' shape and size, its placement in the abdomen, and a variety of other disease-related risk factors. The existing condition makes it extremely difficult to derive useful sickness patterns. The current segmentation approaches make it difficult to detect cancer in images of jaundice in the eyes or pancreatic CT scans. The goal of this research is to identify applicable disease patterns in clinical data to overcome the lack of a universal paradigm for diagnosing pancreatic ailment using multimodal clinical data and a variety of medical data sources.

References

1. Suman, G., Patra, A., Korfiatis, P. *et al.*, Quality gaps in public pancreas imaging datasets: Implications & challenges for AI applications. *Pancreatology*, 21, 5, 1001–1008, 2021.
2. Chen, P.T., Chang, D., Yen, H. *et al.*, Radiomic features at CT can distinguish pancreatic cancer from noncancerous pancreas. *Radiol. Imaging Cancer*, 3, 4, e210010, 2021.

3. Suman, G., Panda, A., Korfiatis, P., Goenka, A.H., Convolutional neural network for the detection of pancreatic cancer on CT scans. *Lancet Digit. Health*, 2, 9, e453, 2020.
4. Jasti, V., Zamani, A., Arumugam, K., Naved, M., Pallathadka, H., Sammy, F. *et al.*, Computational Technique Based on Machine Learning and Image Processing for Medical Image Analysis of Breast Cancer Diagnosis. *Secur. Commun. Netw.*, 2022, 1–7, 2022, doi: 10.1155/2022/1918379.
5. Ryan, D.P., Hong, T.S., Bardeesy, N., Pancreatic adenocarcinoma. *N. Engl. J. Med.*, 371, 1039–1049, 2014.
6. Kenner, B., Chari, S.T., Kelsen, D., Klimstra, D.S., Pandol, S.J., Rosenthal, M., Rustgi, A.K., Taylor, J.A., Yala, A., Abul-Husn, N. *et al.*, Artificial Intelligence and Early Detection of Pancreatic Cancer. *Pancreas*, 50, 251–279, 2021.
7. Yan, Z., Ma, C., Mo, J., Han, W., Lv, X., Chen, C., Chen, C., Nie, X., Rapid identification of benign and malignant pancreatic tumors using serum Raman spectroscopy combined with classification algorithms. *Optik*, 208, 1–10, 2020.
8. Savareh, B.A., Aghdaie, H.A., Behmanesh, A., Azadeh, B., Sadeghi, A., Zali, M., Shams, R., A machine learning approach identified a diagnostic model for pancreatic cancer through using circulating microRNA signatures. *Pancreatology*, 20, 6, 1195–1204, 2020.
9. Dayem Ullah, A.Z.M., Stasinos, K., Chelala, C., Kocher, H.M., Temporality of clinical factors associated with pancreatic cancer: a case-control study using linked electronic health records. *BMC Cancer*, 21, 1–13, 2021.
10. Hossain, S.M.M., Halsana, A.A., Khatun, L., Ray, S., Mukhopadhyay, A., Discovering key transcriptomic regulators in pancreatic ductal adenocarcinoma using Dirichlet process Gaussian mixture model. *Sci. Rep.*, 11, 1–15, 2021.
11. Jackins, V., Vimal, S., Kaliappan, M., Lee, M.Y., AI based smart prediction of clinical disease using random forest classifer and Naive Bayes. *J. Supercomput.*, 77, 5198–5219, 2021.
12. Li, Y., Zhang, J., Yuan, X., BagGMM: Calling copy number variation by bagging multiple Gaussian mixture models from tumor and matched normal next-generation sequencing data. *Digit. Signal Process.*, 88, 90–100, 2019.
13. Shastri, S., Kour, P., Kumar, S., Singh, K., Mansotra, V., GBoost: A novel Grading-AdaBoost ensemble approach for automatic identification of erythemato-squamous disease. *Int. J. Inf. Technol.*, 13, 959–971, 2021.
14. Pereira, S.P., Oldfield, L., Ney, A., Hart, P.A., Keane, M.G., Pandol, S.J., Li, D., Greenhalf, W., Jeon, C.Y., Koay, E.J., Almario, C.V., Halloran, C., Lennon, A.M., Costello, E., Early detection of pancreatic cancer. *Lancet Gastroenterol. Hepatol.*, 5, 7, 698–710, 2020.

15. Santosh Reddy, P. and Chandrasekar, M., PAD: A Pancreatic Cancer Detection based on Extracted Medical Data through Ensemble Methods in Machine Learning. *Int. J. Adv. Comput. Sci. Appl.*, 13, 2, 1–8, 2022.
16. Ahsan, M.M., Luna, S.A., Siddique, Z., Machine-Learning-Based Disease Diagnosis: A Comprehensive Review. *Healthcare*, 10, 3, 1–18, 2022.
17. Joloudari, J., Saadatfar, H., Dehzangi, A., Shamshirband, S., Computer-aided decision-making for predicting liver disease using PSO-based optimized SVM with feature selection. *Inf. Med. Unlocked*, *17*, 100255, 2019, doi: 10.1016/j.imu.2019.100255.
18. Lu, Y., Ye, T., Zheng, J., Decision Tree Algorithm in Machine Learning. *2022 IEEE International Conference on Advances in Electrical Engineering and Computer Applications (AEECA)*, Dalian, China, pp. 1014–1017, 2022, doi: 10.1109/AEECA55500.2022.9918857.
19. Rajathi, V., Azeem A, S.A., S.S.P., Earlier Detection of Diabetes Using Random Forest Algorithm. *2022 1st International Conference on Computational Science and Technology (ICCST)*, Chennai, India, pp. 173–178, 2022, doi: 10.1109/ICCST55948.2022.10040471.
20. http://medicaldecathlon.com/
21. Rathi, M. and Rajavat, A., High Dimensional Data Processing in Privacy Preserving Data Mining, in: *2020 IEEE 9th International Conference on Communication Systems and Network Technologies (CSNT)*, pp. 212–217, IEEE, 2020, April.
22. Patsariya, M. and Rajavat, A., Network Path Capability Identification and Performance analysis of Mobile Ad hoc Network, in: *2020 IEEE 9th International Conference on Communication Systems and Network Technologies (CSNT)*, pp. 82–87, IEEE, 2020, April.
23. Dhar, S., Dhar, U., Rajavat, A., Factors and Attributes of Team Players: A Study of Engineering Students in India, in: *International Simulation and Gaming Association Conference*, pp. 53–60, Springer International Publishing, Cham, 2021, September.
24. Nahar, S., Pithawa, D., Bhardwaj, V., Rawat, R., Rawat, A., Pachlasiya, K., Quantum Technology for Military Applications, in: *Quantum Computing in Cybersecurity*, pp. 313–334, 2023.
25. Pithawa, D., Nahar, S., Bhardwaj, V., Rawat, R., Dronawat, R., Rawat, A., Quantum Computing Technological Design Along with Its Dark Side, in: *Quantum Computing in Cybersecurity*, pp. 295–312, 2023.
26. Chauhan, D., Singh, C., Rawat, R., Chouhan, M., Conversational AI Applications in Ed-Tech Industry: An Analysis of Its Impact and Potential in Education, in: *Conversational Artificial Intelligence*, pp. 411–433, 2024.
27. Chauhan, D., Singh, C., Rawat, R., Dhawan, M., Evaluating the Performance of Conversational AI Tools: A Comparative Analysis, in: *Conversational Artificial Intelligence*, pp. 385–409, 2024.

28. Shrivastava, M., Patil, R., Bhardwaj, V., Rawat, R., Telang, S., Rawat, A., Quantum Computing and Security Aspects of Attention-Based Visual Question Answering with Long Short-Term Memory, in: *Quantum Computing in Cybersecurity*, pp. 395–412, 2023.
29. Rawat, R., Chakrawarti, R.K., Raj, A.S.A., Mani, G., Chidambarathanu, K., Bhardwaj, R., Association rule learning for threat analysis using traffic analysis and packet filtering approach. *Int. J. Inf. Technol.*, *15*, 6, 3245–3255, 2023.

16

An Investigation of Various Text Mining Techniques

Rajashree Gadhave[1]*, Anita Chaudhari[2], B. Ramesh[3], Vijilius Helena Raj[4], H. Pal Thethi[5] and A. Ravitheja[6]

[1]*Computer Engineering, Pillai HOC College of Engineering and Technology, University of Mumbai, Mumbai, Maharashtra, India*
[2]*Mumbai University, Mumbai, India*
[3]*Institute of Aeronautical Engineering, Dundigal, Hyderabad, India*
[4]*Department of Applied Sciences, New Horizon College of Engineering, Bangalore, India*
[5]*Lovely Professional University, Phagwara, India*
[6]*Department of Civil Engineering, SVR Engineering College, Nandyala, Andhra Pradesh, India*

Abstract

Text summaries are generated from huge quantities of unstructured text, such as customer evaluations, internet log entries, and social media postings, and are an important feature of text mining systems. These synopses emphasize the key data representing the whole text or judgment. There are two major approaches to completing a summary task: extractive and abstractive. The extractive approach identifies the meat of the document, which contains all of the information, and extracts it to make the summary. In comparison to the other method, the abstractive methodology is more difficult since it creates summaries based on the document's keywords and semantics. The visually appealing summary job is challenging due to redundancy, a large text volume, unpredictability, and the semantics of natural language. Because of the task's complexity and breadth of applicability, researchers from the academia and business have been working hard on it. This study focuses on two major areas of text mining: feature-based text summarization and text similarity detection, both of which use machine learning-based methods.

**Corresponding author*: rgadhave@mes.ac.in

Rajesh Kumar Chakrawarti, Ranjana Sikarwar, Sanjaya Kumar Sarangi, Samson Arun Raj Albert Raj, Shweta Gupta, Krishnan Sakthidasan Sankaran and Romil Rawat (eds.) Natural Language Processing for Software Engineering, (233–244) © 2025 Scrivener Publishing LLC

Keywords: Text mining, clustering, classification, text summarization, text detection, machine learning

16.1 Introduction

There are a number of essential characteristics that should be considered when evaluating customer evaluations for the purpose of using them in decision-making for various commercial reasons. Most of the time, these evaluations appear to be disorganized and do not provide any hints about anything. For the purpose of achieving corporate goals, it is necessary to provide a concise summary of the most important aspects of these components. A great number of machine learning algorithms have previously rated and summarized the many elements available. The use of consumer preferences as a means of evaluating review components is given top priority in this study with the intention of assisting stakeholders in making more informed business decisions. When seen from the point of view of the customer, this reduces the difficulty of improving aspect ranking [1].

Methods of optimal and parallel large-scale analysis, in addition to machine learning, have been researched for their potential application in the process of summarization. This not only makes the summaries of a high quality, but also makes it possible to analyze extraordinarily large amounts of input from customers. Both machine learning and parallel approaches may be utilized to improve the performance of text summarization solutions. The current state of research in text mining is centered on issues concerning the representation of text, categorization of text, clustering of text, summarization of text, and modeling of hidden patterns [2].

The process of text mining involves the examination of vast quantities of unstructured material to obtain valuable insights. In the context of artificial intelligence, text mining and natural language processing may be viewed as techniques that assist in the extraction of meaningful information from excessive volumes of text. It is possible that this may be exploited for extra analysis, which would be advantageous for the operations of the establishment. There are a few different names for text mining, including data mining and analytics that apply to text. In our day and age, the internet has emerged as a significant source of data, and with it are enormous quantities of material that are not organized in any particular way. The great bulk of this unstructured data is derived from reviews that were posted by millions of different consumers. When these evaluations are subjected to quantitative analysis, companies may be able to arrive at more accurate conclusions. The identification of features and the summary of content that are useful are the two most fundamental reasons for the extensive usage of text mining and its applications. These are accomplishments that can be done using the procedures of feature extraction and text summarizing. By incorporating textual comments into these tasks, they are able to gain a deeper understanding of the operational challenges that are faced by potential customers. It is vital to increase the performance of automatic text summarization systems to deal with the large volumes of data that are created by the internet in the modern day [3].

Aspect ranking algorithms that have been developed lately take advantage of aggregation that is founded on domain ontology. Utilizing domain knowledge on its own will not be sufficient to make the system totally useable. It requires a higher level of precision in aspect ranking in accordance with the preferences of consumers and the knowledge of the area. The purpose of document or collection of input and text document summary is to generate a version of the original document or documents that are more condensed in length. At the moment, the bulk of approaches revolve around the concept of extracting certain words that contain descriptive information from a text. This summary is anything that is made up of a collection of these sentences. When it comes to extracting the semantic information of texts and applying it to build summaries, there are approaches that are more advanced than others [4].

The purpose of feature-based extractive summarizing algorithms is to search through customer reviews for terms that are relevant to the compilation of a summary that can be helpful. Nevertheless, in actuality, the vast majority of online assessments involve the use of tagging to uncover information on the domain in terms of emotion. Machine learning approaches, such as the parallel k-means clustering algorithm, have been utilized extensively by researchers to expedite the process of grouping and summarizing large datasets. This has been done to speed up the process. To solve the challenge of summarizing, Ferrari developed a method that made use of map-reduce, clustering, topic modeling, and semantic similarity. Both clustering and topic modeling are utilized by the system to summarize the texts.

Within the framework of the hybrid method, semantic data, knowledge models, and dictionaries are all included. Systems that are too intricate, such as this one, have repeatedly been unsuccessful. The amount of research that has been done on feature extraction and ranking algorithms that integrate domain knowledge with semantic information is insufficient. Better outcomes would be achieved with the use of this sort of system. The fact that it would be pointless to examine each and every one of these characteristics, the assignment that requires summarizing requires that they be ranked. It's possible that we may go over a number of things that don't provide anything of value to the experience of the customer [5].

A parallel process is utilized in the most recent development of systems for the construction of feature-based summaries. The concept of map-reduce is utilized in each and every one of these approaches to the processing and analysis of enormous volumes of data. Redundancy is yet another significant issue that arises with these systems. This thesis has a primary emphasis on aspect rating and summarization as its primary foci. The performance of existing aspect ranking systems, which have been created using graph-based and semantic techniques, could be improved by leveraging customer preferences as a basis for improvement. Although approaches that are based on semantic information have demonstrated some degree of promise, the effectiveness of these methods is contingent on the data that are contained within the content. The result of this is the development of a new ranking algorithm that takes into consideration the preferences of authors as well as domain knowledge that is generated from ontologies.

When it comes to the challenge of summarization, conventional approaches such as k-means clustering, optimization, and parallel processing lack the necessary effectiveness. At the core of these systems are issues that arise with regard to redundancy and scalability challenges. Because of this, three distinct methods of aspect summary have been proposed, which are as follows: In the first contribution, an implementation of a k-means method that combines optimization principles with distributed clustering is accomplished. A "bag of words" and real-valued vectors are examples of text representation models that are utilized in the second addition, which also makes use of the PSO approach. PSO's diversity enhancement and multi-objective functions are utilized in the development of this technique. An investigation on in-node optimization with combiner is included in the final plan. Through the utilization of map-reduce optimization, it is possible to scale even the largest datasets.

16.2 Related Work

In today's world, the availability of a wide range of text document sources has been made possible by computational automation. In the process of creating tools for text mining, one of the primary objectives is to organize the content of the text and identify patterns from among it. The process of text mining is comparable to that of data mining; however, text mining may handle data sets that are formless or semi-structured, whereas data mining methods are often utilized for the management of structured material [6].

Text mining is a subprocess of data mining that is widely used for the aim of extracting significant patterns and insights from huge volumes of unstructured textual data. It is also known as knowledge discovery. A wide range of methodologies from a variety of fields are applied in this text mining process. These methodologies include machine learning, visualization, statistics, knowledge management, natural language processing, information retrieval, case-based reasoning, database technology, and text analysis. Text mining has emerged as a fast- increasing field in the field of computer science [7]. This is due to the emergence of big data and artificial intelligence.

Text mining is a savior for computers that are attempting to validate unstructured computer data. This technique makes use of a wide variety of algorithms to transform free-form text into patterns that may be put into implementation. Text mining serves three primary functions: text summarization, text categorization, and text clustering. Each of these functions is important. An introduction to text mining, several approaches for text mining, and applications for text mining are all discussed in this study [8].

The practice of text mining is a branch of data mining. Data mining is the process of attempting to learn more by examining data. The technique of collecting relevant information from enormous volumes of text is referred to as text mining on the internet. In light of this, text mining is a process that includes extracting patterns from unstructured text [9]. This is analogous to the way that structured data is exploited in data mining.

Pattern discovery techniques provide the foundation for the majority of the methods that are used to find patterns. This strategy includes a number of different components, including data retrieval, topic extraction, clustering, and summarization [10]. For the purpose of information, extraction, an algorithm is aware of the key phrases and connections included inside a text. For the goal of accomplishing such, the pattern matching method is utilized. A comparison of the text that was entered by the user with the text sequences that were pre-defined is required to implement a pattern matching strategy. This approach is more effective for investigating huge text collections than other approaches. There is no simple method that can be utilized to transform the data that was retrieved into a format that is structured. In light of this, post-processing is an essential step [11]. The process of summarization is crucial to text mining. To put it in another way, summarizing is the process of delivering a concise overview of a lengthy document while maintaining the message or goal that is the primary focus of the text. It provides the user with assistance in judging the usefulness of the material. The process of compression is tied to summarization [12], despite the fact that it is not in a form that can be read by humans. Clustering does not make use of preexisting class labels; rather, it clusters items that are comparable together into groups according to the degree to which they are similar to something else. Few of the numerous categories that text clustering algorithms fall into include partitioning algorithms, agglomerative clustering algorithms, and fundamental parametric modeling-based techniques [13]. These are only few of the text clustering algorithms.

NLP stands for "natural language processing," which refers to the process of transforming human speech into a format that can be read by electronic devices. The basic objective of natural language processing [14] is to construct a computer system that is capable of analyzing, comprehending, and producing natural language processing. Among the various disciplines that make use of it, some examples include the translation of human languages, the creation of fictional worlds, and the development of robotic systems [15].

A KNN-based machine learning strategy was proposed by V. Bijalwan *et al.* [15] in 2014. This approach was proposed for the purpose of text and document mining. Data retrieval, also known as information retrieval (IR), is the process of looking for information in a variety of formats, including relational databases, documents, text, multimedia files, and the Internet. Internet search, automatic summarization, document clustering and classification, information filtering, image object extraction, online searching, and digital library searches are only some of the numerous applications of IR. Additional applications include the extraction of image objects. To categorize a particular query, the KNN (K-nearest neighbor) technique takes into account not just the document that is geographically closest to it, but also the categories of the k documents that are geographically closest to it. This is the fundamental premise that underpins the KNN approach. When this is taken into consideration, the Vector approach may be considered a subset of the KNN technique, where k is equal to 1. A vector-based, distance-weighted matching technique is utilized in this study, which is comparable to Yang's work in that it evaluates the degree of document similarity. Pictured below is a diagram that illustrates a schematic representation of the process of retrieving and indexing records. The KNN algorithm displayed the highest level of accuracy when compared to the Naive Bayes and Term-Graph algorithms. The temporal complexity of KNN is a significant drawback, despite the fact that it exceeds all of its competitors in terms of accuracy.

A hybrid feature selection technique for text classification that is based on an enhanced genetic algorithm was proposed by Abdullah Saeed Ghareb *et al.* [16] in the year 2016. This approach makes use of a hybrid search methodology that combines the advantages of filter feature selection techniques with an improved generalized algorithm (EGA) in a wrapper operation. This allows the method to concurrently improve classification performance while also addressing the large dimensionality of the feature space. To begin, we will discuss the EGA concept, which is founded on the operators for mutation and crossover. The crossover operation is carried out by splitting chromosomes (feature subsets) with session and document frequencies of chromosome entries (features). This is in contrast to the process of mutation, which is conducted by assessing the classifier execution of the original parents and the significance of features. Therefore, rather than depending on chance and random selection, the processes of mutation and crossover are carried out in accordance with the data that are pertinent. A concept for software that builds mind maps by utilizing a text mining method was proposed by Robert Kudeliu *et al.* [17] in the year 2011. The use of a mind map, which is based around a particular word or idea, allows for the visual representation of an assortment of things, including words, thoughts, projects, and other items. Mind maps may be applied for a variety of purposes, including but not limited to the following: research, organizing, problem solving, decision making, and writing. Additionally, they can be utilized for idea development, picturing, and classification. A graphic picture of a typical mind map is shown to us in reference number 119. The online page was downloaded in great detail to ensure that all of the essential information was there, which made this web data source appropriate.

The Rough Set Based Approach is one of the methods that Libiao Zhang *et al.* [18] proposed for the categorization of text. As a source of information on the internet, the gathering of textual materials has become increasingly important and significant. Text categorization is an important technology which plays a significant role in the management and organization of information. The fact that text categorization has become increasingly significant and relevant, researchers from all walks of life have developed an interest in the subject. In the beginning of this study, a variety of different feature selection approaches, algorithms for implementation, and applications of text categorization are presented. To enhance the performance of text categorization, there is a requirement for the development of additional novel strategies and methodologies. The reason for this is that the information that is retrieved by the data-mining algorithms that are currently being used for text classification has a sufficient amount of noise to provoke ambiguity in the process. The information extraction process and the practice of knowing both contribute to the creation of this ambiguity. Increasing the efficiency of the information extraction process and making effective use of the knowledge that has been gathered has been an essential step, but it has also been a considerable challenge. Utilizing a Rough Set decision-making process is advocated for the purpose of achieving more accurate document categorization in situations when standard text classification procedures are unsuccessful.

An approach that is based on fuzzy logic [18] was proposed for the purpose of text mining [19] and document clustering. The purpose of this article is to illustrate the application of fuzzy logic to text mining to cluster various documents. There is a possibility that the truth in fuzzy logic, which is a model of mathematical reasoning, might be biased. It can take on values between zero and one, which can be either completely true or completely false. Instead of relying on exact logic, it relies on approximations to make its decisions. It is the termination criteria that is utilized to decide when the iteration of the FCM algorithm comes to an end. The value of E can range anywhere from 0 to 1, and it is used to make this determination. To a lesser extent than E, the values of the fuzzy c-partition matrix have seen the most significant alteration.

The Huffman Encoding technique formed the foundation for the text clustering approach that was developed by Maria Muntean and colleagues [20] in the year 2014. An innovative strategy to enhance the accuracy of text data clustering is presented by the authors. Before expressing these attributes as numbers in the cluster assessment stage, our system encodes the textual contents of a dataset using the Huffman encoding technique. This is done before the cluster assessment step. We have achieved a significantly greater level of clustering accuracy when compared to the outcomes of more traditional methods. In the event that the dataset just contains string characteristics that require clustering, then this method will be effective. An in-depth explanation of the Huffman encoding algorithm.

16.3 Classification Techniques for Text Mining

16.3.1 Machine Learning Based Text Classification

Quantitative methods [21–24] for automating Natural Language Processing (NLP) with the help of machine learning algorithms make up Machine Learning based Text Classification (MLTC). The following material delineates the preferred supervised learning methods for text categorization. Classification methods range from the Rocchio algorithm, which relies on feedback, to instance-based learning algorithms [25, 26], which use both newly-stored and previously-trained instances; decision trees, support vector machines, and artificial neural networks—which include genetic algorithms and supervised learning algorithms—to name a few.

16.3.2 Ontology-Based Text Classification

By providing a framework for the formal definition of ideas, their descriptions, and the semantic links between them, ontology offers a potential answer to the issues at hand. There are several types of ontology, which stand for the meaning of data, including: domain area's ontology is its collection of concepts and the relationships between them. A few of the most fundamental building blocks of ontology include classes, attributes, relations, function words, and rules.

16.3.3 Hybrid Approaches

The text categorization was accomplished using many classification approaches. The hybrid approach produces effective results in text mining classification by combining several classification algorithms.

16.4 Conclusion

Text mining involves sifting through vast volumes of unstructured data to find relevant information. Artificial intelligence and natural language processing are frequently seen as methods for sifting through massive amounts of text in search of hidden insights. This study focuses on two significant subfields of text mining that employ machine learning techniques: feature-based text summarization and text similarity identification. Possible future research paths include creating summary systems that imitate the signals of all assessment metrics and investigating stakeholder feedback on summary quality using satisfactory indicators. Improving the system's efficiency and quality might also entail developing new algorithms for large-scale summarization. Text summarization systems assessed utilizing extrinsic methodologies might be useful for applications such as information retrieval and question answering.

References

1. Sukanya, M. and Biruntha, S., Techniques on Text Mining. *IEEE International Conference on Advanced Communication Control and Computing Technologies (ICACCCT)*, pp. 269–271, 2012.
2. Gupta, A. and Yadav, D., Semantic similarity measure using information content approach with depth for similarity calculation. *Int. J. Sci. Technol. Res.*, 3, 2, 56–59, 2014.

3. Paul, C., Rettinger, A., Mogadala, A., Efficient Graph-based Document Similarity. *International Sematic web Conference, the semantic web and latest advances*, pp. 17–25, 2016.
4. Derrac, *et al.*, A practical tutorial on the use of nonparametric statistical tests as a methodology for comparing evolutionary and swarm intelligence algorithms. *Swarm Evol. Comput.*, 1, 1, 3–18, 2017.
5. Gambhir, M. and Gupta, V., Recent automatic text summarization techniques: a survey. *Artif. Intell. Rev.*, 47, 1, 1–66, 2017.
6. Thilagavathi, K. and Priya, VS., Survey on text mining techniques. *Int. J. Res. Comput. Appl. Rob.*, 2014.
7. Kaushik, A. and Naithani, S., A Comprehensive Study of Text Mining Approach. *Int. J. Comput. Sci. Netw. Secur. (IJCSNS)*, 16, 2, 69, 2016.
8. Jadhav, A.M. and Gadekar, D.P., A Survey on Text Mining and Its Techniques. *Int. J. Sci. Res. (IJSR)*, 2012.
9. Rajawat, A. S., Rawat, R., Barhanpurkar, K., Shaw, R. N., & Ghosh, A., Vulnerability analysis at industrial internet of things platform on dark web network using computational intelligence. *Computationally intelligent systems and their applications*, 39–51, 2021.
10. Patel, F.N. and Soni, N.R., Text mining: A Brief survey. *Int. J. Adv. Comput. Res.*, 2, 4, 243–248, 2012.
11. Kanya, N. and Geetha, S., Information Extraction: A Text Mining Approach. *IETUK International Conference on Information and Comm. Technology in Electrical Sciences*, Dr. M.G.R. University, Chennai, Tamil Nadu, India, pp. 1111–1118, IEEE, 2007.
12. Gupta, V. and Lehal, G.S., A survey of text summarization extractive techniques. *J. Emerg. Technol. Web Intell.*, 2, 3, 258–268, 2010.
13. Agrawal, R. and Batra, M., A Detailed Study on Text Mining Techniques. *Int. J. Soft Comput. Eng. (IJSCE)*, 2, 6, January 2013.
14. Mishra, A. K., Tyagi, A. K., Dananjayan, S., Rajavat, A., Rawat, H., Rawat, A., Revolutionizing Government Operations: The Impact of Artificial Intelligence in Public Administration, in: *Conversational Artificial Intelligence*, pp. 607–634, 2024.
15. Bijalwan, V., Kumar, V., Kumari, P., Pascual, J., KNN based Machine Learning Approach for Text and Document Mining. *Int. J. Database Theory Appl.*, 7, 1, 2014.
16. Ghareb, A.S., Bakar, A.A., Hamdan, A.R., Hybrid feature selection based on enhanced genetic algorithm for text categorization. *Expert Syst. Appl.*, 49, 2016.
17. Kudeliu, R., Konecki, M., Malekoviu, M., Mind Map Generator Software Model with Text Mining Algorithm. *33 Int. Conf. on Information Technology Interfaces*, Cavtat, Croatia, June 27–30, 2011.
18. Zhang, L., Li, Y., Sun, C., Nadee, W., Rough Set Based Approach to Text Classification. *IEEE/WIC/ACM International Conferences on Web Intelligence (WI) and Intelligent Agent Technology (IAT)*, 2013.

19. Nahar, S., Pithawa, D., Bhardwaj, V., Rawat, R., Rawat, A., Pachlasiya, K., Quantum technology for military applications, in: *Quantum Computing in Cybersecurity*, pp. 313–334, 2023.
20. Sikarwar, R., Shakya, H.K., Kumar, A., Rawat, A., Advanced Security Solutions for Conversational AI, in: *Conversational Artificial Intelligence*, pp. 287–301, 2024.
21. Rathi, M. and Rajavat, A., High Dimensional Data Processing in Privacy Preserving Data Mining, in: *2020 IEEE 9th International Conference on Communication Systems and Network Technologies (CSNT)*, pp. 212–217, IEEE, 2020, April.
22. Patsariya, M. and Rajavat, A., Network Path Capability Identification and Performance analysis of Mobile Ad hoc Network, in: *2020 IEEE 9th International Conference on Communication Systems and Network Technologies (CSNT)*, pp. 82–87, IEEE, 2020, April.
23. Dhar, S., Dhar, U., Rajavat, A., Factors and Attributes of Team Players: A Study of Engineering Students in India, in: *International Simulation and Gaming Association Conference*, pp. 53–60, Springer International Publishing, Cham, 2021, September.
24. Pithawa, D., Nahar, S., Bhardwaj, V., Rawat, R., Dronawat, R., Rawat, A., Quantum Computing Technological Design Along with Its Dark Side, in: *Quantum Computing in Cybersecurity*, pp. 295–312, 2023.
25. Shrivastava, M., Patil, R., Bhardwaj, V., Rawat, R., Telang, S., Rawat, A., Quantum Computing and Security Aspects of Attention-Based Visual Question Answering with Long Short-Term Memory, in: *Quantum Computing in Cybersecurity*, pp. 395–412, 2023.
26. Rawat, R., Chakrawarti, R.K., Raj, A.S.A., Mani, G., Chidambarathanu, K., Bhardwaj, R., Association rule learning for threat analysis using traffic analysis and packet filtering approach. *Int. J. Inf. Technol.*, *15*, 6, 3245–3255, 2023.

17

Automated Query Processing Using Natural Language Processing

Divyanshu Sinha[1*], G. Ravivarman[2], B. Rajalakshmi[3], V. Alekhya[4], Rajeev Sobti[5] and R. Udhayakumar[6]

[1]Department of Computer Science, MRIIRS Faridabad, India
[2]Department Of EEE, Karpagam Academy of Higher Education, Eachanari, Coimbatore, Tamil Nadu, India
[3]Department of Computer Science, New Horizon College of Engineering, Bangalore, India
[4]Institute of Aeronautical Engineering, Dundigal, Hyderabad, India
[5]Lovely Professional University, Phagwara, India
[6]Vel Tech Rangarajan Dr Sagunthala R&D Institute of Science and Technology, Avadi, Chennai, Tamil Nadu, India

Abstract

Electronic papers are more accessible on a daily basis. Efficient data retrieval techniques are crucial for users to extract valuable information from vast quantities of electronic data, which has experienced significant growth in recent years. This article seeks to get insights from a Natural Language (NL) text query by examining several study areas in Natural Language Processing (NLP). Natural language processing (NLP) has experienced significant expansion in recent years, establishing itself as one of the most extensively studied subfields in artificial intelligence (AI). The researcher possessed a comprehensive understanding of natural language processing (NLP) techniques and their many applications, such as information retrieval (IR) and natural language interface to database (NIDB) systems. The Automated Intelligent Query Processing System (AIQPS) can handle text queries expressed in natural language. By employing several levels of natural language processing to the query, this goal can be accomplished. One of the challenges in natural language processing (NLP) is extracting knowledge from natural language text.

**Corresponding author*: divv4u@gmail.com
R. Udhayakumar: ORCID: 0000-0002-2447-664X

Rajesh Kumar Chakrawarti, Ranjana Sikarwar, Sanjaya Kumar Sarangi, Samson Arun Raj Albert Raj, Shweta Gupta, Krishnan Sakthidasan Sankaran and Romil Rawat (eds.) Natural Language Processing for Software Engineering, (245–258) © 2025 Scrivener Publishing LLC

Keywords: Natural language processing, intelligent query processing, artificial intelligence, SQL, information retrieval

17.1 Introduction

The pursuit of automating human languages is a long-standing goal within the field of Artificial Intelligence (AI). Intelligent Query Processing is centered around the utilization of several knowledge-base approaches from the AI field to automatically handle natural language text inquiries. For an intelligent system to understand, it is essential to possess wisdom, information, reasoning, cognition, language acquisition, and other related ideas. Intelligence is characterized by the acquisition, comprehension, and application of knowledge, as well as the ability to engage in abstract reasoning. To achieve the automation of intelligence, it is necessary to develop a computer system capable of doing tasks that typically require a significant level of intellectual capacity. It is possible to extract information from natural language documents by transforming them into a format that computers can process. Previously, academics in the domain of natural language processing (NLP) have attempted to manually assemble this information. Knowledge acquisition is a significant obstacle in the field of natural language processing (NLP) due to the need to encode a substantial amount of information that is both incomplete and erroneous. An estimated annual volume of NL text type information reaches around 160 terabytes. Academics are now exploring the intricacies of syntactic and semantic processing to unlock the potential advantages of natural language processing (NLP), which is known to be a complex task [1].

17.1.1 Natural Language Processing

The fundamental components of every language consist of its principles for manipulating symbols (grammar) and the set of symbols themselves (phonemes) that facilitate the communication of novel information through speech. Natural language processing (NLP) is concerned with constructing computational models capable of processing language in a manner similar to humans. This area requires a significant level of intellectual capacity. A computer may do natural language processing (NLP) when it has the skills of natural language understanding (NLU) and natural language generation (NLG). Natural Language Processing (NLP) refers to the theoretical framework that underlies computing techniques used to analyze text in natural language at various linguistic levels. A natural language (NL) document passes through one or many stages of language analysis, which is a thriving area of research in the field of artificial intelligence (AI). When individuals desire to express their ideas and emotions, Natural Language (NL) is the most widely used and direct system of symbols to employ. Natural languages and formal languages, used by computers, are distinct. Investigating natural language understanding (NLU), commonly referred to as computational linguistics, is crucial for enabling communication between computers and people. The cornerstone for the advancement of natural language understanding (NLU) lies in determining the research technique and direction, as well as describing and modeling natural language (NL). There are two primary paradigms in natural language processing: the data-driven approach and the knowledge-driven approach. Most of the earliest systems were founded on statistical principles. Various techniques have been proposed by researchers to enhance the performance of NLP systems [2].

The Annual Review of Information Science and Technology (ARIST) presents several theoretical breakthroughs, offering a comprehensive overview of the area. These encompass many techniques in natural language processing (NLP), such as statistical and corpus-based methodologies, research utilizing WordNet, computationally efficient finite-state approaches to NLP, and collaborative endeavors to create grammar and NLP tools. Statistical methods have several uses in natural language processing (NLP), such as word sense disambiguation, grammar construction and parsing, and others. They recommend use WordNet to augment the results of statistical analyses performed on texts produced from natural language. WordNet, developed at Princeton University, is an exceptional natural language processing (NLP) tool that categorizes verbs, adjectives, and adverbs into synsets, which are the fundamental units of lexical notions. To obtain further details on WordNet, one has to go to [Fellbaum, 1998] or conduct an online search. WordNet has been included into several research and applications in the field of natural language processing. Euro WordNet was established in 1996, marking a significant use of WordNet in natural language processing throughout Europe. Euro WordNet is structured in a manner that is comparable to the English WordNet. It consists of WordNets for other European languages, such as Dutch, Italian, Spanish, German, French, Czech, and Estonian [3].

Natural Language Processing (NLP) is an interdisciplinary field that combines linguistics and computer science to investigate the interaction between humans and computers. Computational linguistics and other disciplines of artificial intelligence should have significant overlap with language processing systems. The study of natural language processing (NLP) is necessary to explore the cognitive abilities associated with language due to its direct link to human cognition. The human mind responds to events because of its ability to engage in symbolic thinking, which entails managing intricate relationships and dealing with ambiguity. Natural Language Processing (NLP) provides a significant opportunity to apply statistical and logical approaches of Artificial Intelligence (AI). This study demonstrates the application of knowledge extraction techniques to get valuable insights from written texts in natural language. Comprehending the surroundings and the language itself is crucial for constructing computer models with the ability to comprehend human language. This, in turn, requires a grasp of how people acquire, retain, and process language.

17.2 The Challenges of NLP

The complexity of natural language processing (NLP) is influenced by several factors related to representation and interpretation. Representing NL accurately is difficult because of its significant level of ambiguity and vagueness. It is impossible to completely capture the extensive range and profound comprehension of human cognition in language processing. Compositional semantics considers the different meanings of words. Words alone do not form a whole phrase, as is often acknowledged. A language undergoes continuous evolution as new vocabulary is regularly incorporated and existing terms are repurposed in other situations. The terrorist attack on the World Trade Center in 2004 is commonly known as 9/11 among the majority of media outlets and television networks. When we process spoken or written language, there is a mental image that we can access. In the absence of access to explicitly coded comprehensive global or specific subject knowledge, a computer may alone comprehend the significance of a word in a message by analyzing its surrounding context. The co-occurring word context includes every word and its preceding or following elements. Deciphering written information gets increasingly challenging when idioms, metaphors, and ellipses are employed. Consider the following sentence: A rolling stone is incapable of collecting moss. Due to the fact that NL users rely on both explicit and implicit sources of information, they often fail to detect the ambiguity of the language. Effective language communication necessitates the involvement of both the speaker's and the reader's brains. We do not encode any information that the receiver should be aware of. To get a precise interpretation, the recipient must complete the missing information using the available resources. To understand the speech of others, those who acquire language must consider both past and present cultural knowledge and traditions. The incorporation of context and global information is the most significant obstacle to language processing. While those from outside of India may not instantly connect the name "Taj" with a hotel, landmark, or tea brand, it is a familiar association among Indians. Natural language (NL) has several sources of ambiguity at both the word-level and sentence-level. There are two potential sources of ambiguity for a word: "its" part of speech (POS) and its meaning. The word "can" has an ambiguous connotation in the present tense, although the word "bat" lacks a distinct meaning as well. We must develop several models and algorithms to address this issue. To determine if "can" functions as a noun or a verb, we may employ part-of-speech (POS) tagging. Similarly, to ascertain whether "bank" refers to a "financial institution" or a "river bank," we can utilize word-sense-disambiguation (WSD). The structural validation of a sentence in any natural language provides its unique linguistic characteristics, even if all natural languages have some common features such as syntax, alphabets, and lexicon. The main goal of computational linguistics is to establish a formalized framework for the grammar of natural language processing.

17.3 Related Work

It was recommended by Aghmazadeh and Dillig [1] that SQLizer, a system that is type-based and driven by database content, be used to generate SQLs from NLS database files. The structure in question developed its very own syntax, which may be thought of as a form of relational algebra. After that, it constructed a set of rules for the production of logical expressions that represent predicate clauses, and it utilized deductive rules to turn these expressions into a well-defined program in Structured Query Language. Methods such as rewriting and transformations based on inference rules were utilized extensively during the course of this research. It is not possible to create nested sub-queries using the language that Navid and Dillig [1] give since it is inadequate. A simple recommendation is made to regard nested SQLs as a sub-sketch of the main sketch, and it is suggested that the methods that are used to produce the initial query be repeated to construct the sub-queries. It is necessary to expand the language to build a complicated WHERE clause, which may include nested WHERE clauses. To summarize, SQLizer just offers a high-level description of nested query synthesize as part of its broader scheme of synthesis. It suggests that nested inquiries may be constructed by simply repeating the operation of the primary query, but it does not include instructions on how to actually make nested SQLs.

When it comes to handling the dynamic rearrangement and pipelining that is required when merging sub-queries, using rule-based rewriting techniques is not a clear way to address the situation. For the purpose of rating the intermediate logical forms or the initial sketch completions, SQLizer implements an internal scoring algorithm known as confidence scoring. This function uses a set of pre-defined features to determine confidence scores. High-quality training sets are either difficult to come by or complex to design, which makes it challenging to deploy NL2SQL systems that are based on machine learning. Rather than producing conventional (logic-based) outputs for a range of inputs, Deep Learning and Neural Network-based approaches are unable to handle complicated scenarios that may require dynamic interventions for rewriting, extension, or repair. This is because of the "black-box" nature of these techniques, which makes them incapable of handling such scenarios. Another category of NL2SQL systems is dependent on regular user input, which can be troublesome when it exceeds an acceptable limit, particularly when constructing complex SQLs. This is especially true when the limits are exceeded. It is necessary to make use of functional programming methodologies to provide the flexibility and composition that are required for the construction of nested inquiries. The fact that it offers a realistic viewpoint on automating query creation, it is ideally suited to the extensive collection of program transformation techniques that are included in Bird-Meetan's [2] formalism. The SQLizer specifier-repair approach is maintained in this work; however, it is expanded upon and a more in-depth examination of nesting is carried out. By applying more advanced methods for translation automation, particularly with respect to nested query integration, it goes above and beyond what is expected of it.

Linq, which stands for language integrated query, and other similar technologies are able to translate sentences written in imperative programming languages into SQL queries. The extent to which these systems are comprehensive and the degree of detail that they are able to manage (for example, nesting) relies on how effectively they function [3]. It is possible to convert embedded query expressions in programming languages into SQL instructions. These instructions may then be injected into the database to obtain the results that correspond to the expression that was provided in the programming language. Language was included and other programming languages have an impedance mismatch, which makes it impossible to perform recursion and other conventional operations on statements that might have unexpected implications in query expressions. This is because the impedance mismatch is caused by the conflict between the two languages. It is possible for translation to fail during runtime for a variety of reasons, such as run-time problems or a phenomenon known as partiality. Partiality happens when the translation fails to completely turn the expression into a SQL query and instead creates just a partial sketch. Without even taking into consideration nested query structures, this is already a scenario that is problematic. Although it is well known that the FERRY [4] system offers a comprehensive translation, it is important to note that it does not offer any support for abstraction.

Examples of non-linear information databases (NLIDBs) that make use of ontologies in combination with an easy-to-use authoring module are provided in [5, 6]. When the DRS keywords are contained within a query context, the query context is a subgraph of the semantic graph. This particular subgraph is built on the foundation of associations between tables. The information that is obtained from NLQ/DRS is then turned into data items before being stored in the database. These data items include the names of tables and views, relations, attributes (column names), and values. To produce the final SQL query, the query context, select list, and relational constraint columns are employed. The select clause may contain any columns that are not part of a constraint and are indicated in the NL query. These columns are considered potential inclusions.

This is accomplished through the utilization of ontology-assisted programming paradigms, which allow natural language programming to make use of entities derived from natural language phrases. A natural-language user interface is yet another tool that is developed with the intention of simplifying the translation process for users. The process of automatically producing programs that are compliant with a predetermined collection of input-output examples has also been the subject of research. The implementation of tree transformations on Hierarchical Data Trees was also accomplished through the utilization of systems that generate path transformation functions in the intermediate language. The very first graphical query language was called Query-By-Example (QBE), and it was used to list and show database tables. It also gave the user the ability to input instructions, example items, and criteria that were centered on these tables to obtain data. One of the fundamental premises of QBE is that the input text is converted into DML instructions (like SQL) by utilizing parser. It is possible for skeleton tables in QBE to be connected to actual tables in the database. This means that whenever the user performs an action on the database, an example of a solution to that operation is filled in. SEQ2TREE [7] is a Neural Network model that transfers NL statements into their semantic representations. This translation is accomplished with the assistance of an additional attention layer. NL utterances are converted to vectors by SEQ2Tree, which then builds sequences or trees that reflect the logical forms of the vectors. This process is carried out by RNNs using LSTM units. It is necessary to encode the NL tokens at the beginning as a vector for the neural network to be able to process an NLQ initially. With regard to the majority of cases, attention models are also necessary to improve translation accuracy. In comparison to the SEQ2SEQ model, the SEQ2TREE model is superior in terms of performance since it clearly models the compositional structure of logical forms. This is accomplished by including a Hierarchical Tree (H-Tree) decoder. Within sequence-to-sequence decoders, the production of tokens is restricted because it is dependent on all tokens that were formed before it. In lieu of semantic parsing of aggregations and fundamental WHERE clause requirements that justify the development of nested predicate clauses, all Sequence-to-Sequence models disregard the possibility of producing nested Sub-Queries. This is the case regardless of whether or not Reinforcement Learning is utilized. In the event that an NL query and the schema of a database are provided, the Neural Network model SQLNet [8] is able to generate SQL queries. This is accomplished by utilizing the Seq2SQL architecture. The Initial Query Sketch is used by SQLNet to offer the dependency relationship of distinct slots in the sketch. This is done to guarantee that the predictions of each slot are in agreement with the forecasts of its dependent slots. SQLNet presents two new constructs—sequence-to-set and column attention—to put this concept into action. These constructions are derived from the attention map that is constructed by utilizing the properties of the NL questions and the names of the columns in the database table. Sequence-to-set eliminates the need for reinforcement learning and makes it possible to repair by rewriting predicate clauses. This is accomplished by eliminating the constraint that "order does not actually matter" from the generation of predicate clauses. Deep learning systems such as SEQ2SQL [8] and SQLNet [9] have only been examined on datasets that included simple NLQs. This is the only dataset that has been used for evaluation. As a result of the fact that SEQ2SQL and SQLNet are restricted to the creation of SQL queries over a single table, nested SQL queries are not a good fit for these two databases. For the purpose of integrating many tables through the utilization of JOIN clauses, neither SQLNet nor Seq2SQL performs exceptionally well, despite the fact that SQLNet offers greater accuracy.

In April of 2018, P. Utama and others released a paper with the title "DBPal: An End-to-end Neural Natural Language Interface for Databases" [10]. An auto-completion model that was learned was applied by the authors to compose complicated queries. Additionally, Deep Neural Networks, more especially a sequence-to-sequence Recurrent Neural Network model, were utilized to convert NLS to SQL. Utilizing the database structure in conjunction with a collection of basic templates and "Slot filling" dictionaries, DBPal generates a tedious training set consisting of one to two million pairings to acquire every possible NL-SQL pair. This is done to acquire every possible pair. Within the WHERE clause, DBPal only generates Sub-Queries that are not connected with one another. The Query Sketches that are developed for the purpose of conventional NL to SQL translation are enlarged for the building of nested queries, just as they are expanded for the development of non-nested queries. With regard to 'patients,' DBPal functions more effectively than Geo DB.

When Iyer *et al.* [11] were putting together their implementation of an interactive user-based feedback learning scheme, they were required to manually construct a training set for each and every database and schema. This was done to build NL to SQL pairings that were a match. The Neural Semantic Parser (NSP) that they have developed is a model that directly translates natural language queries (NL) into SQL queries by utilizing the capabilities of the target database. This encoder-decoder paradigm is powered by a bidirectional LSTM network, which is responsible for international attention. Following the receipt of binary input from users on its predictions to lower and the set of queries that require labeling, NSP makes use of paraphrasing to reduce the amount of annotation efforts, which ultimately leads to more efficient learning. When it comes to performance, this paradigm can only compete with systems that directly construct SQL from NLS or those that translate speech into logical representations and then synthesize SQLs. These are the only systems that can effectively compete with this paradigm because it depends on SQL templates to generate the final SQL query, NSP is not ideal for circumstances that need the development of nested or co-related sub-queries. This is because NSP is less dynamic than other SQL queries because it relies on SQL templates.

17.4 Natural Language Interfaces Systems

An interface allows any search engine (IR system) to receive a user's request. The search engine will employ it and convert it into requests. Typically, the translation will include a compilation of index phrases or keywords that succinctly explain the queries. Data retrieval systems search structured persistent storage for things that satisfy specific conditions, such as Regular Expressions (RE) and Relational Algebraic (RA) Expressions NL. The textual data that an information retrieval system operates on is inherently lacking in organization and may include uncertainty in its semantic interpretation. By accepting an NL query, this study can reveal the complexities of user interaction with the system. Figure 17.1 depicts the Natural Language Query Processing (NLQP) in both the Natural Language Processing (NLP) application areas. The user submits a natural language query to a question processing system to obtain keywords. The system will evaluate the query using natural language processing techniques. In the next step, the keywords are inputted into the information retrieval (IR) system as a query to obtain articles that are rated based on their relevance. When dealing with structured databases, natural language queries can be turned into relational algebra (RA) or relational expressions (RE), which can then be easily transformed into SQL queries. The outcomes will be delivered in a format that adheres to the principles of a relational database as shown in Figure 17.1: Natural language query processing.

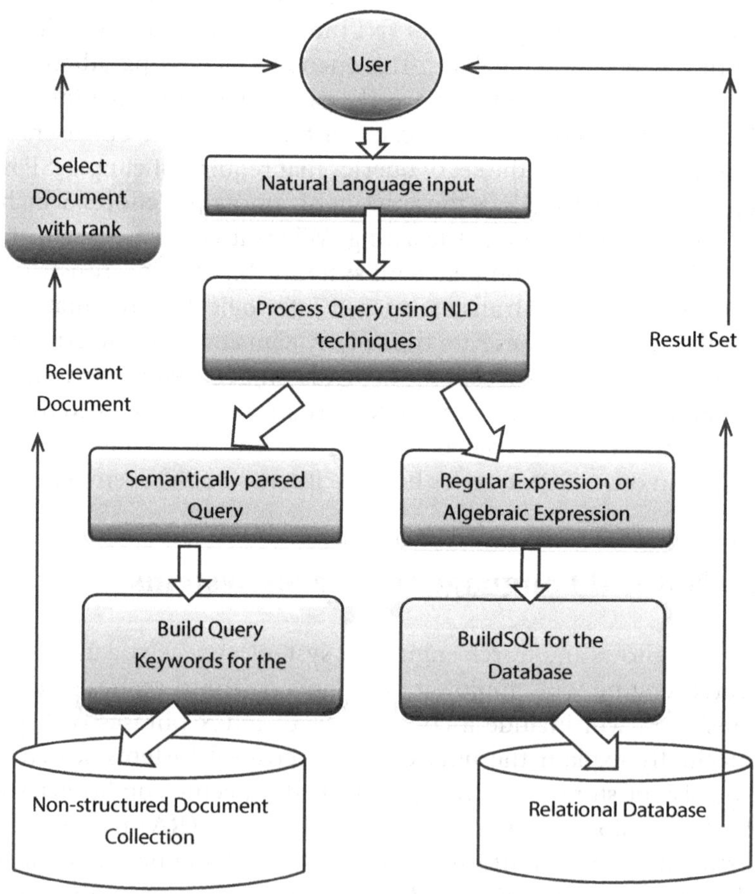

Figure 17.1 Natural language query processing.

Artificial intelligence researchers face a daunting task of developing systems that can accurately replicate human intelligence. The ability to engage in metaphorical thinking is fundamental to how the human mind processes different situations. Intelligence refers to the capacity to engage in cognitive processes such as thinking, reasoning, and comprehending intricate concepts. Individuals assimilate new information into their cognitive faculties as knowledge. The human mind [11–14] represents information as symbols, which may be altered through the process of thinking. AI [15–17] researchers face several challenges, one of which is the creation of a computer that can understand human knowledge. Knowledge representation is a crucial aspect of AI. Language may be used to convey human mind, especially complex and consciously inferred thoughts. The integration of artificially intelligent systems poses significant difficulties in the creation of NL-aware applications [15, 18]. Knowledge serves as the fundamental basis for many forms of logical thinking and behavior, encompassing problem-solving, task delineation, inference, and decision-making. Research on knowledge representation is propelling the advancement of the information age, transitioning it from its initial stage of data processing [16, 19, 20] to a more sophisticated stage of knowledge processing. However, there are currently alternative methods for encoding knowledge, including production rules, logic, script, semantic networks, and frames. An urgent concern in the field of artificial intelligence now revolves around the necessity to uncover more effective methods for representing knowledge. Fortunately, knowledge graphs are an innovative method that expands upon the methodology of knowledge representation. This approach utilizes principles from philosophy and psychology to construct a semantic representation model that elucidates the way in which humans perceive and process information. This thesis presents the author's research on natural language processing (NLP), intelligent query processing (IQP), and machine learning (ML). Both sectors have conducted thorough and comprehensive research; hence, merging them will enable us to use their individual capabilities.

17.5 Conclusion

It is the goal of this research to find a solution to the problem of intelligently processing a natural language text inquiry by utilizing natural language processing (NLP). Examining the many different query languages that a normal user may use to ask a question is done to determine the level of difficulty associated with query processing. This article presents a structured framework for the problem of inquiry processing, as well as a number of intelligent approaches from the literature on artificial intelligence that have the potential to manage inquiries. These methods include the Conceptual Graph, the Ontology, and the Frame techniques. The utilization of natural language is among the most ingenious methods of expressing one's expertise.

References

1. Mishra, A. K., Tyagi, A. K., Dananjayan, S., Rajavat, A., Rawat, H., Rawat, A., Revolutionizing Government Operations: The Impact of Artificial Intelligence in Public Administration, in: *Conversational Artificial Intelligence*, pp. 607–634, 2024.
2. Bird, R.S., An Introduction to the Theory of Lists, in: *Logic of Programming and Calculi of Design. NATO ASI Series*, vol. 36, M. Broy (Ed.), pp. 5–42, Springer Verlag, USA, 1987.
3. Bhalotia, G., Hulgeri, A., Nakhe, C., Chakrabarti, S., Sudarshan, S., Keyword searching and browsing in databases using BANKS, in: *ICDE*, 2002.
4. Grust, T., Mayr, M., Rittinger, J., Schreiber, T., FERRY: Database-supported program execution. *SIGMOD-PODS'09 – Proc. Int. Conf. Manag. Data 28th Symp. Princ. Database Syst*, pp. 1063–1065, 2009.
5. Lopez, V., Pasin, M., Motta, E., Aqualog: An ontology-portable question answering system for the semantic Web, in: *The Semantic Web: Research and Applications*, 1st ed., vol. 3532 of Lecture QNotes in Computer Science, A. Gómez-Pérez and J. Euzenat (Eds.), pp. 546–562, Springer-Verlag Berlin Heidelberg, Crete, Greece, 2005.
6. Bernstein, A., Kaufmann, E., Göhring, A., Kiefer, C., Querying ontologies: A controlledenglish interface for end-users, in: *The Semantic Web - International Semantic Web Conference*, vol. 3729 of Information Systems and Applications, Y. Gil, E. Motta, V.R. Benjamins, M. Musen (Eds.), pp. 112–126, Springer, Galway, Ireland, 2005.
7. Nahar, S., Pithawa, D., Bhardwaj, V., Rawat, R., Rawat, A., Pachlasiya, K., Quantum technology for military applications, in: *Quantum Computing in Cybersecurity*, pp. 313–334, 2023.
8. Sikarwar, R., Shakya, H. K., Kumar, A., Rawat, A., Advanced Security Solutions for Conversational AI, in: *Conversational Artificial Intelligence*, pp. 287–301, 2024.
9. Pithawa, D., Nahar, S., Bhardwaj, V., Rawat, R., Dronawat, R., Rawat, A., Quantum Computing Technological Design Along with Its Dark Side, in: *Quantum Computing in Cybersecurity*, pp. 295–312, 2023.
10. Namdev, A., Patni, D., Dhaliwal, B. K., Parihar, S., Telang, S., Rawat, A., Potential Threats and Ethical Risks of Quantum Computing, in: *Quantum Computing in Cybersecurity*, pp. 335–352, 2023.

11. Shrivastava, M., Patil, R., Bhardwaj, V., Rawat, R., Telang, S., Rawat, A., Quantum Computing and Security Aspects of Attention-Based Visual Question Answering with Long Short-Term Memory, in: *Quantum Computing in Cybersecurity*, pp. 395–412, 2023.
12. Rathi, M. and Rajavat, A., High Dimensional Data Processing in Privacy Preserving Data Mining, in: *2020 IEEE 9th International Conference on Communication Systems and Network Technologies (CSNT)*, pp. 212–217, IEEE, 2020, April.
13. Patsariya, M. and Rajavat, A., Network Path Capability Identification and Performance analysis of Mobile Ad hoc Network, in: *2020 IEEE 9th International Conference on Communication Systems and Network Technologies (CSNT)*, pp. 82–87, IEEE, 2020, April.
14. Dhar, S., Dhar, U., Rajavat, A., Factors and Attributes of Team Players: A Study of Engineering Students in India, in: *International Simulation and Gaming Association Conference*, pp. 53–60, Springer International Publishing, Cham, 2021, September.
15. Nahar, S., Pithawa, D., Bhardwaj, V., Rawat, R., Rawat, A., Pachlasiya, K., Quantum Technology for Military Applications, in: *Quantum Computing in Cybersecurity*, pp. 313–334, 2023.
16. Pithawa, D., Nahar, S., Bhardwaj, V., Rawat, R., Dronawat, R., Rawat, A., Quantum Computing Technological Design Along with Its Dark Side, in: *Quantum Computing in Cybersecurity*, pp. 295–312, 2023.
17. Chauhan, D., Singh, C., Rawat, R., Chouhan, M., Conversational AI Applications in Ed-Tech Industry: An Analysis of Its Impact and Potential in Education, in: *Conversational Artificial Intelligence*, pp. 411–433, 2024.
18. Chauhan, D., Singh, C., Rawat, R., Dhawan, M., Evaluating the Performance of Conversational AI Tools: A Comparative Analysis, in: *Conversational Artificial Intelligence*, pp. 385–409, 2024.
19. Shrivastava, M., Patil, R., Bhardwaj, V., Rawat, R., Telang, S., Rawat, A., Quantum Computing and Security Aspects of Attention-Based Visual Question Answering with Long Short-Term Memory, in: *Quantum Computing in Cybersecurity*, pp. 395–412, 2023.
20. Rawat, R., Chakrawarti, R.K., Raj, A.S.A., Mani, G., Chidambarathanu, K., Bhardwaj, R., Association rule learning for threat analysis using traffic analysis and packet filtering approach. *Int. J. Inf. Technol.*, *15*, 6, 3245–3255, 2023.

18

Data Mining Techniques for Web Usage Mining

Navdeep Kumar Chopra[1]*, Chinnem Rama Mohan[2], Snehal Dipak Chaudhary[3], Manisha Kasar[4], Trupti Suryawanshi[5] and Shikha Dubey[6]

[1]*Department of CSE, Seth Jai Parkash Mukand Lal Institute of Engineering and Technology, JMIT, Radaur, USA*

[2]*Department of Computer Science and Engineering, Narayana Engineering College, Nellore, Andhra Pradesh, India*

[3]*Information Technology, Bharati Vidyapeeth (Deemed to be University) College of Engineering Pune, Maharashtra, India*

[4]*Computer Engineering, Bharti Vidyapeeth (Deemed to be University) College of Engineering, Pune, Bharti Vidyapeeth Deemed to be University, Pune, Maharashtra, India*

[5]*Computer Science and Engineering, Bharati Vidyapeeth (Deemed to be University) College of Engineering, Pune, Bharati Deemed to be University, Pune, Maharashtra, India*

[6]*MCA, Dr. D. Y. Patil Institute of Management and Research, Pimpri, USA*

Abstract

Web use mining is the application of data mining and computational methods to analyze and understand web server logs, which provide insights on how individuals utilize the internet. The crucial data requirements of the computational methods are fulfilled by obtaining and converting web server logs. Computational algorithms aid in constructing learning models that enhance the online environment by efficiently detecting interesting patterns. The primary areas of emphasis in web research are web cache optimization and online customization. This research aims to optimize web caching and enhance web personalization by analyzing significant online trends, including user groups and categories that engage with interesting content at a later time. Improved web cache design may be achieved by

**Corresponding author*: navdeepkumar17@gmail.com; ORCID: 0000-0003-4751-0326
Chinnem Rama Mohan: ORCID: https://orcid.org/0000-0001-9209-3029

Rajesh Kumar Chakrawarti, Ranjana Sikarwar, Sanjaya Kumar Sarangi, Samson Arun Raj Albert Raj, Shweta Gupta, Krishnan Sakthidasan Sankaran and Romil Rawat (eds.) Natural Language Processing for Software Engineering, (259–270) © 2025 Scrivener Publishing LLC

using predictive algorithms that anticipate the categories of interesting pages that will be browsed next. Data about user interests obtained via the creation of groups may be used to customize the online experience for individual visitors. This paper extensively explores the subject of online content mining and web usage mining. In this chapter, we introduce decision tree techniques for web usage mining.

***Keywords*:** Web content mining, web usage mining, data mining, data preprocessing, decision tree, pattern analysis

18.1 Introduction

Web miners may efficiently and automatically extract useful information and discover interesting patterns by using information mining methods on data stored on the World Wide Web. Although web mining has its origins in the discipline of information mining, it is important to note that the two are separate and different. The unstructured nature of online data is an intrinsic characteristic that adds to the unpredictable nature of web mining. Web mining is the systematic extraction of extensive information on a user's interactions with a website via the analysis of their server logs, which are also referred to as web server logs. Almost all online projects may considerably benefit from the valuable information obtained via an analysis of server logs [1].

Web mining may be classified into three primary categories. One area is web content mining, which focuses on extracting information from internet sites, including both text and visuals. Web structure mining is the process of collecting data or information from the structures of web pages and analyzing how these structures impact navigation. This helps in comprehending the user's requirements and integrating them into online applications. Online use mining is the process of deriving valuable usage patterns from online data. It encompasses several crucial applications such as online customization, site design, e-commerce, advertising, marketing, fraud detection, transaction analysis, and educational data mining [2].

18.1.1 Web Usage Mining

The primary objective of web use mining is to get more insights on the behavior of online users and their interactions with websites. Web use mining seeks to efficiently and effectively identify patterns of user access from web log data. Web usage mining enables the retrieval of data pertaining to client access, including server logs, registration information, and other relevant details. Web mining steps are discussed as follows:

1) Data Collection

Various types of online log information document storage can be accessed to successfully retrieve log information.

A) Web server logs (server-side log data): The web server stores its logs internally. Web server logs may include various information, such an IP address, requested URL, time stamp, bytes, and the convention used. Typically, this data [15, 16] is presented in a certain manner. The Common Log Format (CLF) is widely used as one of the most common log record formats. A web server generates a standardized log design document to monitor and record the requests made on a website.

B) Proxy server logs (proxy side log data): The data that is saved on the intermediary server is referred to as proxy server logs. During periods of temporary unavailability of the main server, the intermediate servers take up the responsibility of handling client requests. Consequently, the intermediary servers create logs [17, 18]. Intermediate server logs provide further information related to the intermediary server, in contrast to web server log records.

C) Browser logs (client-side log data): The client's own computer, from which they access websites, has its browser records collected. Developers use Java or JavaScript to deploy remote agents that are then integrated into web sites to get client data, including a user's browsing history. Disregarding problems [19, 20] such as caching and IP misinterpretation, data obtained from clients are more reliable than data obtained from servers. Users must provide help to access these data. However, users often restrict the capability of Java and JavaScript apps due to security [18, 19, 21–23] concerns.

2) Data Pre-Processing

Data pre-processing is a crucial step in web use mining. After collecting vast amounts of data from various sources, the subsequent stage involves data preparation. Prior to proceeding to pattern identification, it is essential that the data be both consistent and integrated. Data preparation include information cleaning, client identification, session identification, and pathway completion [3].

3) Pattern discovery

A) Association: The technique relies on the establishment of a consistent pattern and the formulation of rules as its fundamental basis. Upon doing initial processing, the data extracted from the web log file uncovers several captivating insights, such as the ratio of URL visits to users. This information enables the identification of frequently visited websites; hence aiding in the comprehension of user preferences and wants. The main objective of the association rule is to identify relationships among web pages that have been seen by the user. An association rule may be used to link a user's most frequently visited landing page to their session. Association rule mining utilizes several techniques, including Apriorism, Eclat, Frequent Pattern tree, and others [4].

B) Clustering: Clustering is a technique used to group together persons or data elements that have similar features or characteristics. It has the potential to be a valuable advantage in the creation and execution of next marketing plans. Users may be clustered together based on their similar navigational behaviors to establish groups. Utilizing market dispersion in e-commerce operations or delivering personalized online content to targeted customers may be significantly enhanced by deducing user data. Internet search engines and Web service providers profit from page clustering since it enables them to identify groupings of pages that contain relevant material [5].

C) Sequential pattern: There are many techniques, such as Apriorism, SPADE, GSP, Prefix Span, and Spam, that may be used for sequential pattern analysis. The objective of this investigation is to ascertain the temporal gap between the visits of a suspected user to links X and Y. This research has the potential to enhance criminal detection by uncovering the suspected user psychology [6].

D) Classification: This technique allocates each data element to one of many pre-established categories, which then function as the foundational components for user profiles. Initially, a person will be required to extract and choose features that distinctly describe the attributes of a certain class or category. Grouping may be achieved by the use of directed inductive learning techniques such as Support Vector Machines, k-nearest neighbor classifiers, naïve Bayesian classifiers, and decision tree classifiers [7].

4) Pattern Analysis: During the pattern analysis phase, a valuable model or standard pattern is discovered for a certain internet use mining application. Pattern analysis employs several techniques such as visualization, online analytical processing (OLAP), data and knowledge querying, and usability analysis.

18.2 Web Mining

Web mining is a specialized kind of data mining that focuses on extracting valuable information from websites and other online data sets by analyzing user habits and structural components. A diagram (Figure 18.1) illustrating the categorization of web mining is available.

There are three methods which are relevant for web mining. Web Content Mining• Web Structure Mining• Web Usage Mining

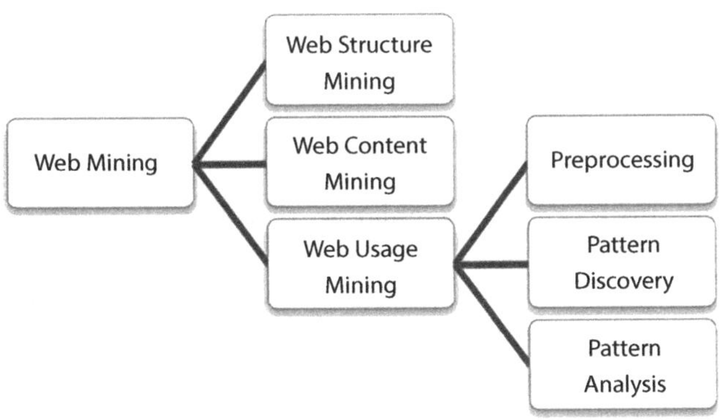

Figure 18.1 Steps involved in web mining.

18.2.1 Web Content Mining

In essence, web mining refers to the extraction of data from the internet. There are necessary procedures for retrieving the data saved on the internet. The activity is referred to as online content mining. The internet provides a vast amount of information, with many websites accessible to users. The web content includes activities such as information retrieval and accessing search engine sites. The content mining result pages provide the most recent and precise result [8]. The various contents of Web Content Mining are -

Web Page: A web page often contains a variety of information, including core content, advertisements, navigation panels, copyright notices, and more. For every particular job, only a portion of the data is useful and can be acted upon, while the rest is just irrelevant information.
Search Page: A frequent use of a search page is to do several searches inside a certain webpage of a website. A content database categorizes and groups web pages in a manner that facilitates easy navigation for both users and search engines.
Result page: Content mining result pages often include the search results, the visited websites, and an explanation of the most recent accurate result.

18.2.2 Web Structure Mining

It is feasible to define web structure mining using a graph-based approach. Web pages may be seen as nodes, while hyperlinks can be likened to edges in a network diagram [9]. The essential link between users and the web has been unveiled. The objective of web structure mining is to provide systematic synopses of material discovered on the internet. Below is a hyperlink that connects one website to another. The various contents of Web structure mining are -

Links Structure Mining: Link analysis is a well-established area of research. However, with the increasing popularity of Web mining, researchers delve further into structural analysis, giving rise to a new discipline known as link mining. Classification, clustering, connection type, link strength, and link cardinality are all components of it.
Internal Structure Mining: It enhances search results via the process of filtering. Additionally, it endeavors to reveal the underlying architecture of the internet's link structures and may provide insights into page ranking or authority. By using this methodology, the interconnections and resemblances across different websites can be analyzed.

URL Mining: A hyperlink is a fundamental element that allows for navigation across online pages, including the ability to redirect to a completely other web page.

18.2.3 Web Usage Mining

Web use mining [10] enhances overall speed for future accesses by facilitating the identification of essential links and prioritizing the search process via the recognition of users' frequent access habits. Web Usage Mining is the use of data mining techniques to identify trends in online data, with the goal of gaining a deeper understanding of web-based services and meeting their specific needs. Web Usage Mining is classified into three aspects,

- Preprocessing
- Pattern Discovery
- Pattern Analysis

The main focus of the Web Usage Mining technique is to analyze the data stored in log records. The registration folder of a website comprises logical data pertaining to consumer requirements. One potential objective of online use mining is to provide useful recommendations to website visitors or to enhance website organization. The main objective of internet use mining is to extract significant patterns from extensive datasets, including visually captivating or otherwise fascinating patterns.

18.2.3.1 Preprocessing

A custom tread that incorporates data breakdown from these use logs as well as integration with other use logs is a data-focused approach [11]. Finding out what kind of file includes a prohibition, such as a hyperlink with text, helps someone to finish this procedure. Data cleaning is the process of identifying and removing errors and inconsistencies to improve data quality.

18.2.3.2 Pattern Discovery

The analyst utilizes the obtained data to assist the organization in formulating marketing strategies, and one method to accomplish this is by identifying patterns. It is also important to understand the key vocabulary used in web mining. After session identification, the organization has the freedom to select any data mining technique, such as classification analysis, association rule discovery, sequential pattern discovery, clustering analysis, or statistical analysis, based on the analyst's needs. The utilization of classification analysis is performed to categorize customer profiles. The process of association rule discovery in web mining enables the identification of the most frequently accessed pages during user sessions. By analyzing data from a collection of records related to frequently visited web pages, it is feasible to enhance website design and predict customer behavior in connection to the most often seen sites. Sequential pattern identification is a significant advancement in the field of internet use mining. It may be used to predict client behavior by collecting data from web logs that record their surfing patterns. Offering personalized attention to clients is a strategy that organizations may employ to enhance connections with new customers and retain existing ones.

18.2.3.3 Pattern Analysis

Pattern analysis is the final stage in the process of extracting insights from online usage data. After the discovery of patterns, they undergo thorough evaluation to exclude any extraneous information from the gathered data. The organization highly prioritizes this phase since it enables them to easily comprehend client behavior. Pattern analysis employs several methodologies such as visualization, online analytical processing (OLAP), data and knowledge querying, and usability testing.

18.3 Web Usage Data Mining Techniques

The various techniques are used to acquire the hidden information in Web usage mining.

A. Decision trees

A decision tree is composed of rectangular forms that represent the core nodes and oval shapes that represent the leaf nodes. This structure gives the decision tree a resemblance to a flowchart. Each internal node has at least two child nodes. Split nodes, which assess the worth of an attribute expression, are found in every internal node. Every test result is linked to an arc that stretches from a parent node to its children. Each leaf node is assigned a class label. Decision trees are often used as a method for collecting data for making decisions. Each decision tree has a primary node where the user may execute actions. From this node, users iteratively partition each node according to the decision tree learning process. The final outcome is a decision tree, where each node represents a possible choice and its corresponding result. The ID3, CART, CHAID, and C4.5 decision tree learning algorithms are the four most often used ones [12].

THE ID3 DECISION TREE

The ID3 method, devised by J.R. Quinlan, selects successive attributes based on their associated information gain. The test characteristic for the current node is chosen based on the one that offers the most information gain or decrease in entropy. Ross Quinlan developed ID3, a direct method for acquiring decision trees. The ID3 approach is based on a top-down, greedy search that evaluates each characteristic at every node of the decision tree using the given sets. A metric called "information gain" is presented to determine the most beneficial attribute for classifying given datasets. To determine the optimal approach for classifying a collection of learning data, it is necessary to minimize the number of questions, also known as lowering the depth of the tree. A function that can identify which questions result in the most fair and balanced distribution of replies is needed. Illustrations of such functions encompass the information gain metric. The C4.5 approach, developed by Ross Quinlan, is a tool used to generate decision trees. C4.5 is the successor to ID3. C4.5 incorporated several improvements to the ID3 algorithm. The C4.5 algorithm use the gain ratio as a statistic to choose characteristics. C4.5 categorizes attributes as either discrete or continuous. Breiman's proposed CART (Classification and Regression Tree) method is almost indistinguishable from ID3. The Gini index is used as a measure of impurity when selecting a variable in CART. Classification trees are generated for categorical target variables, whereas regression trees are created for numerical objectives with continuous values. When constructing trees, CHAID (Chi-squared Automatic Interaction Detector) employs the Chi-square contingency test in two distinct approaches. The process begins by verifying the compatibility of the predictor levels for merging. Once each predictor level has been simplified to its most significant form, the algorithm identifies the most important predictor for distinguishing between the levels of the dependent variable.

B. Bayesian Classifier. For the purpose of computing the parameters, this approach requires just a minimal amount of data preparation, which makes it not only simple but also intuitive to use. The classifier is well-structured to handle both real and different data, and irrelevant attributes are also insensitive to the classification process. A Bayesian classifier is characterized by the presence of evident class conditional independencies among its subsets of variables. Using a graphical depiction of the causal linkages between events can make the learning process easier to understand.

C. Neural Networks The immense capability of neural networks resides in their ability to extract significance from complex data for the purpose of identifying patterns and revealing potentially hazardous tendencies. An important advantage of neural networks is its capacity to uncover novel tasks through the utilization of training data or early experience. The Neural Network is capable of discovering all potential interactions between variables and predictors. The main reason for utilizing neural networks in educational data mining is to get the desired outcome [13].

D. Clustering Techniques. The process involves constructing collections of interconnected abstract entities into collections of interconnected parallel elements. Cluster analysis is conducted on a partitioned data set, where groups are generated based on data comparison. Subsequently, the following task involves allocating distinct labels to each group. Similarly, the data objects are treated as separate entities in this scenario. One of the main advantages of clustering in classification is its flexibility and use of distinct positive criteria to distinguish across groupings. Clustering techniques primarily focus on many fields, including data analysis, pattern recognition, and image processing [14].

18.4 Conclusion

Web Usage Mining is the process of using data mining techniques to find trends in online data to obtain a better knowledge of web-based services and fulfil their unique requirements. The primary goal of the Web Usage Mining approach is to evaluate data saved in log files. The registration folder of a website contains logical data related to customer needs. One possible goal of online usage mining is to make relevant recommendations to website users or to improve website organization. This study attempts to improve web caching and personalization by analyzing key online patterns, such as user groups and categories that engage with intriguing information later. Improved web cache design may be accomplished by utilizing predictive algorithms that anticipate the categories of interesting sites that will be visited next. Data about user interests gathered through group formation may be utilized to personalize the internet experience for individual visitors. This study delves thoroughly into the topics of online content mining and web use mining. In this chapter, we will discuss decision tree algorithms for online usage mining.

References

1. Chauhan, D., Singh, C., Rawat, R., Dhawan, M., Evaluating the Performance of Conversational AI Tools: A Comparative Analysis, in: *Conversational Artificial Intelligence*, pp. 385–409, 2024.
2. Bhradwaj, B., Mining educational data to analyze students performance. *IJACSA*, 2, 6, 63–69, 2011.
3. Rawat, R., Chakrawarti, R.K., Sarangi, S.K., Choudhary, R., Gadwal, A.S., Bhardwaj, V., eds. *Robotic Process Automation*. John Wiley & Sons, 2023.
4. Shahiria, A.M., Husaina, W., Rashida, N.A., A Review on Predicting Students Performance using Data Mining Techniques. *The Third Information Systems International Conference, Procedia Computer Science*, vol. 72, 2015.
5. Rawat, R., Telang, S., William, P., Kaur, U., CU, O. K. (Eds.)., *Dark Web Pattern Recognition and Crime Analysis Using Machine Intelligence*. IGI Global, 2022.
6. Pandey, U.K. and Pal, S., A Data mining view on class room teaching language. *Int. J. Comput. Sci.*, 8, 2, 277–282, 2011, ISSN:1694-0814.
7. Rawat, R., Kaur, U., Khan, S. P., Sikarwar, R., Sankaran, K. (Eds.), *Using Computational Intelligence for the Dark Web and Illicit Behavior Detection*. IGI Global, 2022, https://doi.org/10.4018/978-1-6684-6444-1.
8. Rawat, R., Telang, S., William, P., Kaur, U., C.U., O. (Eds.)., *Dark Web Pattern Recognition and Crime Analysis Using Machine Intelligence*. IGI Global, 2022, https://doi.org/10.4018/978-1-6684-3942-5.
9. Rawat, R., Chakrawarti, R.K., Sarangi, S.K., Patel, J., Bhardwaj, V., Rawat, A., Rawat, H. eds, *Quantum Computing in Cybersecurity*. John Wiley & Sons, 2023, https://onlinelibrary.wiley.com/doi/book/10.1002/9781394167401.
10. Mishra, A.K., Tyagi, A.K., Dananjayan, S., Rajavat, A., Rawat, H., Rawat, A., Revolutionizing Government Operations: The Impact of Artificial Intelligence in Public Administration, in: *Conversational Artificial Intelligence*, pp. 607–634, 2024.
11. Srivastava, M., Garg, R., Mishra, P.K., Preprocessing Techniques in Web Usage Mining: A Survey. *Int. J. Comput. Appl.*, 97, 18, 0975–8887, July 2014.
12. Namdev, A., Patni, D., Dhaliwal, B.K., Parihar, S., Telang, S., Rawat, A., Potential Threats and Ethical Risks of Quantum Computing, in: *Quantum Computing in Cybersecurity*, pp. 335–352, 2023.
13. Nahar, S., Pithawa, D., Bhardwaj, V., Rawat, R., Rawat, A., Pachlasiya, K., Quantum technology for military applications, in: *Quantum Computing in Cybersecurity*, pp. 313–334, 2023.

14. Sikarwar, R., Shakya, H.K., Kumar, A., Rawat, A., Advanced Security Solutions for Conversational AI, in: *Conversational Artificial Intelligence*, pp. 287–301, 2024.
15. Rathi, M. and Rajavat, A., High Dimensional Data Processing in Privacy Preserving Data Mining, in: *2020 IEEE 9th International Conference on Communication Systems and Network Technologies (CSNT)*, pp. 212–217, IEEE, 2020, April.
16. Patsariya, M. and Rajavat, A., Network Path Capability Identification and Performance analysis of Mobile Ad hoc Network, in: *2020 IEEE 9th International Conference on Communication Systems and Network Technologies (CSNT)*, pp. 82–87, IEEE, 2020, April.
17. Dhar, S., Dhar, U., Rajavat, A., Factors and Attributes of Team Players: A Study of Engineering Students in India, in: *International Simulation and Gaming Association Conference*, pp. 53–60, Springer International Publishing, Cham, 2021, September.
18. Nahar, S., Pithawa, D., Bhardwaj, V., Rawat, R., Rawat, A., Pachlasiya, K., Quantum Technology for Military Applications, in: *Quantum Computing in Cybersecurity*, pp. 313–334, 2023.
19. Pithawa, D., Nahar, S., Bhardwaj, V., Rawat, R., Dronawat, R., Rawat, A., Quantum Computing Technological Design Along with Its Dark Side, in: *Quantum Computing in Cybersecurity*, pp. 295–312, 2023.
20. Chauhan, D., Singh, C., Rawat, R., Chouhan, M., Conversational AI Applications in Ed-Tech Industry: An Analysis of Its Impact and Potential in Education, in: *Conversational Artificial Intelligence*, pp. 411–433, 2024.
21. Chauhan, D., Singh, C., Rawat, R., Dhawan, M., Evaluating the Performance of Conversational AI Tools: A Comparative Analysis, in: *Conversational Artificial Intelligence*, pp. 385–409, 2024.
22. Shrivastava, M., Patil, R., Bhardwaj, V., Rawat, R., Telang, S., Rawat, A., Quantum Computing and Security Aspects of Attention-Based Visual Question Answering with Long Short-Term Memory, in: *Quantum Computing in Cybersecurity*, pp. 395–412, 2023.
23. Rawat, R., Chakrawarti, R.K., Raj, A.S.A., Mani, G., Chidambarathanu, K., Bhardwaj, R., Association rule learning for threat analysis using traffic analysis and packet filtering approach. *Int. J. Inf. Technol.*, *15*, 6, 3245–3255, 2023.

19

Natural Language Processing Using Soft Computing

M. Rajkumar[1*], Viswanathasarma Ch[2], Anandhi R. J.[3], D. Anandhasilambarasan[4], Om Prakash Yadav[5] and Joshuva Arockia Dhanraj[6]

[1]*School of Computer Science Engineering and Information Systems, Vellore Institute of Technology, Tamil Nadu, India*
[2]*AI & DS, VIIT, Visakhapatnam, Andhra Pradesh, India*
[3]*Department of Information Science Engineering, New Horizon College of Engineering, Bangalore, India*
[4]*Department of Computer Science and Engineering, Karpagam Academy of Higher Education Coimbatore, Eachanari, Coimbatore, Tamil Nadu, India*
[5]*School of Computer Science and Engineering, LPU, Punjab, India*
[6]*Department of Computer Science and Engineering (AI&ML), School of Engineering, Dayananda Sagar University, Devarakaggalahalli, Harohalli, Kanakapura Road, Ramanagara District, Bengaluru, Karnataka, India*

Abstract

The fields of text mining and information retrieval were the origins of natural language processing (NLP), which was first developed from those fields. Throughout the years, several applications that are based on artificial intelligence have developed out of its initial domain. Some examples of these applications include machine translation, query expansion, robotic command detection, and many more. The origins of natural language processing (NLP) may be traced back to a variety of disciplines, such as psychology, mathematics, computer science, linguistics, computer engineering, electrical and electronic engineering, artificial intelligence, robotics, and computer science and information. This paper provides a comprehensive analysis of a wide variety of soft computing techniques to natural language processing (NLP).

***Keywords*:** Natural language processing, soft computing, NLP challenges, support vector machine

**Corresponding author*: rajkumar.m@vit.ac.in
Joshuva Arockia Dhanraj: ORCID: 0000-0001-5048-7775

Rajesh Kumar Chakrawarti, Ranjana Sikarwar, Sanjaya Kumar Sarangi, Samson Arun Raj Albert Raj, Shweta Gupta, Krishnan Sakthidasan Sankaran and Romil Rawat (eds.) Natural Language Processing for Software Engineering, (271–282) © 2025 Scrivener Publishing LLC

19.1 Introduction

The study and development of practical applications for computers to interpret and analyze human spoken and written language is the focus of the discipline of Natural Language Processing (NLP), which includes both research and development. Researchers in the field of natural language processing (NLP) anticipate that one day they will be able to implement techniques and tools that will train computers to interpret and manipulate natural languages to carry out specified tasks [1, 2]. This will be accomplished by researching human language comprehension and usage. In the 1950s, when artificial intelligence (AI) and linguistics were just beginning to gain traction, the concept of natural language processing (NLP) started to take form. When it was first being developed, natural language processing (NLP) initially focused on text mining and information retrieval as its primary areas of interest. Throughout the years, several applications that are based on artificial intelligence have developed out of its initial domain. Some examples of these applications include machine translation, query expansion, robotic command detection, and many more. Natural language processing (NLP) is built on the foundation of a number of disciplines, including computer science, mathematics, psychology, linguistics, electrical and electronic engineering, artificial intelligence and robotics, and linguistics.

In recent years, natural language processing (NLP) has made significant progress in its development. Many of the activities that we do on a daily basis include the core applications of natural language processing. Amazon and Flipkart are two examples of online shops that make it simple to browse reviews that were made by genuine consumers. The "sentiment" that these evaluations communicate, that is, whether the product has a positive or negative review, is what decides how they are organized. Sentiment analysis, which is a job based on natural language processing, does all of this. A further excellent illustration is provided by search engines such as Google. The phrases that we type into the search engine determine whether or not it is able to offer results that are relevant to our query. In this case, natural language understanding (NLU) is the first stage, and then metadata retrieval comes next. It is vital that the search engine is able to "understand" the query that we have entered. Taking into consideration our previous searches, it ought to provide us with suggestions for relevant material whenever we key in terms such as "Match," for instance. The phrase "match" is, however, not entirely clear. This might refer to any sporting event; it is not limited to simply cricket or football. One further interpretation that may be given is the pairing process. Google will then employ query expansion to get the most accurate result possible. The use of natural language processing is also responsible for this accomplishment.

Some of the primary NLP applications are listed as follows:

- Information Retrieval
- Text Mining
- Query Expansion
- Sentiment Analysis
- Machine Translation
- Speech Recognition
- Question Answering
- Optical Character Recognition

Many have remarked that the presence of slang and polysemous terminology complicates natural language comprehension. Polysemous words may mean several things. Listeners and readers are asked to make an ongoing judgement on the appropriate interpretation depending on what is relevant to the current situation. Ambiguity is one of the most challenging aspects of natural language processing.

19.2 Related Work

Word-sense-detection (WSD) is the computational challenge of identifying the specific word-sense activation in a particular environment. The user should be able to input "That is Right," and the computer should properly determine the meaning of "right" in this context. "Correct" is one interpretation that might fit here. Human rights are another possible context here. Perhaps the "right direction" is another way of looking at it. When a term is ambiguous, its precise meaning is always deduced from its context. Word Sense Dilemma (WSD) is a well-known classic in natural language processing (NLP) that involves lexical ambiguity; several methods have been suggested to solve it [4, 5]. When thinking about ways to fix WSD, the Lesk algorithm was among the first revolutionary ideas. Words in the same "neighborhood" or "section of text" are presumed to have a similar "topic" according to the Lesk algorithm. Locating the "sense that overlaps the most between its dictionary definition and the given context" is how the Simplified Lesk algorithm determines each word's most relevant meaning. This approach takes a word-by-word approach to analyzing its meaning, rather than trying to determine the overall meaning of the text based on how other words in the same context are seen. Until recently, this algorithm was the best of its kind. In subsequent updated versions, it was further integrated. Adopted Lesk, one of the updated versions, had a 33.1% accuracy rate [5, 6].

It was tested using the SENSEVAL2 dataset. Unfortunately, this level of precision is obviously unsuitable for any real-world use. Another approach, Distributional Similarity, was suggested and explored in the literature to further enhance the accuracy. Its working hypothesis is that distributional similarity increases as the degree to which two words are "semantically similar" increases. This suggests that they are more likely to be found in comparable language circumstances. Correct contextual awareness was achieved by its utilization in several ways across different test settings [7–11]. On SENSEVAL2, this method achieved an accuracy of 39.54%. The main benefit of this method was that it introduced the concept of using semantics in WSD, which is a relatively new notion. Yet another drawback of this method was that it produced false expansions for most of the words that were evaluated.

The Translation-based Semantic Model is another method that has been published in articles. It depended on text that had been machine translated. Multiple levels of semantic analysis were used to these translations. The GOLD standard dataset was used for testing [12]. Various variants of this technique are also published in the literature [12–14]. The accuracy rates for the sports dataset are around 52.7% and the finance dataset is 58%. The main issue with this method was that it relied on translations, which weren't always accurate. An important thing to remember is that this method supported the idea of semantics in WSD [15–17].

As a result of the high levels of accuracy it achieved, WordNet graph-based approaches have grown in popularity among the aforementioned methods. Up to now, the state-of-the-art has been methods based on WordNet graphs. Numerous scholars from all around the world have delved into this area of study [17]. WordNet graphs are constructed by using a depth-first search strategy. In WordNet, the several definitions of a word serve as nodes. Semantic relations such as hypernymy, holonomy, and others form the margins. Over time, the researchers hone this technique. However, this approach has a logical flaw in that it disregards the relevance of all semantic relations. It gives each edge of the WordNet graph the same weight of 1 and assumes that all semantic relations are equal. In actuality, however, this is not the case. It appears, for example, that the hypernym "vehicle" should be given greater weight than the hyponym "sedan" when attempting to solve the "car" ambiguity. Currently available WordNet graph-based methods exclude all these factors.

Automatically constructing a summary for a given document using the main points of the original material is known as text summarization. Applying TS to a paragraph of material (10-12 lines) should result to a brief summary (3-4 lines) that provides a general overview of the full piece. All the unnecessary and superfluous details are removed. The user's reading time is preserved. Knowing the right meaning of a word is crucial for discovering the best phrases and keywords. Labeling topics is another benefit of accurate text/document summary. Generating headlines and analyzing social media and markets are two of the most common uses of text summary. Researchers have suggested Automatic Text Summarization (ATS) methods for a number of languages. As an example, the Arabic TS, or Textual Graph Model, was previously suggested in the literature and used as a standard for Arabic text summarization [18]. But this approach only managed a 28% accuracy rate when tested on 1651 papers. The lack of specification of the association factor for clustering was a drawback of this approach. Its primary value, however, is it effectively eliminated repetition from the provided text.

In addition, the LDA model was considered. The main idea was that for every paragraph of text, important subject labels could be retrieved, and then the sentences could be alphabetized. Its performance on the ROUGH2 dataset was subpar, according to the results [19]. Its main contribution, meanwhile, was elucidating the need of word frequency, phrase location, and sentence length in text sample summary. One such method that failed to handle complicated sentences was ATSSC, which used a soft computing strategy for sentence ranking [20]. Another significant method in this area that was evaluated on the ROUGH1 dataset is LexRank. For scholars, it was a watershed moment since it proposed the possibility of building text graphs based on semantics. The assessment revealed that the method's main flaw was that it just used degree centrality to choose the most important information nodes.

A large number of scholars from different parts of the world have taken an interest in studying short answer assessment. Automatic evaluation of students' brief responses is feasible. However, it is necessary to disambiguate all subject terms since students might use multiple phrases to describe the "ideal answer." Researchers have tried a number of different strategies in their quest to identify the best way to address this issue, but they have so far been unsuccessful. In [21–23], we may find descriptions of some of the major methods used in this field of study.

With optical character recognition (OCR), the goal is to make the image's text editable and machine-readable. The input might be an image file type. The picture is created by extracting the necessary text and pages from a large collection of relevant papers. OCR is useful in many aspects of daily life. After cars undergo Automated Number Plate Recognition (ANPR), traffic challans are created. Since OCR exists, this is now feasible. Using optical character recognition (OCR) software to digitize antique books and historical documents extends their storage life. It is to be expected that OCR, being a procedure that deals with images, is prone to many mistakes throughout the recording and conversion of images. Use of natural language processing methods fixes these mistakes. Disambiguation strategies are used to replace the incorrect term with the right one. Take this example: "I am going to the Aank of the river." It's rather clear that the term "Aank" is the wrong one. However, the WSD method may be required to substitute it with the proper term. Then, from the list of possibilities—"Bank," "Tank," etc.—we may choose the best term.

19.3 NLP Soft Computing Approaches

The following is a display of the typical supervised NLP machine learning algorithms that are derived from the categorized fundamental approaches

Support Vector Machine

The objective of a support vector machine, also known as an SVM, is to discover a hyperplane in a space that has N dimensions, where N is the number of features that identify the data points in a particularly distinctive manner. For the purpose of splitting the two sets of measurement data points, it is possible to investigate a number of different hyperplane concepts. Finding the best possible margin, which is defined as the biggest feasible distance between data points in both classes, is the goal of this endeavor. The ability to classify forthcoming data items is simplified by having a margin that is greater. Support vector machines, often known as SVMs, are able to classify data points based on their location on hyperplanes, which act as decision boundaries. The term "support vectors" refers to the data points that are less far from the hyperplane and have the potential to influence its positioning and orientation. The removal of these support vectors will result in a modification to the placement of the hyperplane. This is because these support vectors act as indicative points in the construction of the support vector machine (SVM), and their use will maximize the classifier margin.

Bayesian Networks

For the purpose of computing probabilities, Bayesian Networks make use of Bayesian inference, which is a kind of probabilistic graphical model. The primary purpose of this model is to illustrate, via the use of directed edges in the graph, the interdependencies and causal interactions that exist between the variables. Using these links allows for the systematic inference of factors based on the random variables that are represented by the graph. The distribution is factorized because Bayesian Networks provide a product of N components that are restricted to contingency. Naive Bayes is a well-known example that demonstrates how the most persuasive findings may be produced from the most straightforward explanations. The fact that it is simple, accurate, and consistent has allowed it to be used successfully in a variety of applications, particularly for natural language processing (NLP) challenges.

Maximum Entropy:

As a probabilistic classifier, the Max Entropy technique is related to models that use exponential functions or variables expressed as exponents. It is not presumptuous that the features must be autonomous. Using the "Principle of Maximum Entropy," the algorithm chooses the best-fitting model based on the entropy value relative to the training data. Language identification, topic classification, sentiment analysis, and other large-scale text classification problems often use the Max Entropy classifier. By modelling all known characteristics and making no assumptions about unknown ones, the maximum entropy classifier may employ dependent features to categorize texts. For each batch of training data, it takes into account all possible classifiers and chooses the one that maximizes entropy. Aspects of the text, such as unigrams and bigrams, may be mined for statistical and contextual information using this method. Classifications like "positive/neutral/negative" or "objective/subjective" are therefore used to these characteristics. Commonly used in Natural Language Processing and Knowledge Extraction is the Bag-of-Words Framework, which stores each document as a sparse array of 1s and 0s denoting the existence or absence of a particular word.

Conditional Random Fields

Conditional random fields are a kind of "Statistical Modelling Method" that sees widespread use in ML and pattern recognition. While a classifier predicts a tag for an individual image without considering "neighboring samples," a CRF may take context into consideration. It is built as a diagrammatic (graph-based) model to include interdependencies between many prognostic variables. Various kinds of graphs are used in practice, depending on their intended use. As an illustration, linear chains commonly utilized in natural language processing, CRFs are responsible for incorporating sequential dependencies into the predictions. For the purpose of developing consistent interpretations, CRFs—a form of unique directionless probabilistic graphical model—are used to discern the ensuing alliance between data. Common applications [33–37] include human word processing and other forms of linear and sequential data classification and interpretation. It is evident that CRF may be used to tasks such as point-of-sale tagging, shallow parsing, detecting entitled articles, studying genomes, and predicting important peptide portions. They are also often used in several fields where Hidden Markov Models (HMM) need to be enhanced or replaced in operation. Both "Object Recognition" and "Image Segmentation" are common applications of CRFs in computer visualization.

Artificial Neural Network

One subfield of machine learning is known as artificial neural networks (ANN), or just neural networks. To conduct the classification using ML, two sets of input data are required for the "Training" and "Testing" processes, which are derived from the way the human brain works. Neural networks are capable of identifying previously unseen patterns inside data. It is a valuable tool for data scientists that utilize Neural Network approaches to identify patterns in images, videos, audio, or text. Thanks to this approach of emotion-focused assessment, real text categorization is now within our reach. ANN can manage the relationship and correlation between input variables with the correct intricate design. Neural networks' precedence is defined by two theoretical features. Firstly, these methods are adaptable, fact-based, and capable of self-improvement. Second, every function may be correctly estimated by neural networks, thanks to a number of popular practical estimates. Typical "Recurrent Neural Networks" (RNN) were the backbone of this case. The capacity of the connected network to accept words in chronological sequence is used by vanilla RNN. Due to a simple relationship, one-dimensional Convolution Neural Networks (CNN) have outperformed RNN in terms of accuracy and may achieve a sizeable level. Summing up people's feelings on an item is what sentiment analysis is all about. As more and more technological tools become available, it is more important than ever to gauge public sentiment on goods, businesses, and personal preferences. One way to anticipate how to respond to anything on social media is to try to put oneself in the author's shoes. One may choose between social networks and online communities as their preferred kind of social media. Social networks are formed and maintained by individuals who have interacted with each other in the past; these people often seek out new connections to broaden their sphere of influence. Communities, on the other hand, consist of individuals from many walks of life and professions, with whom they often have nothing in common. One commonality among a community's members is their love of a well-known pastime.

19.4 Conclusion

It is possible to trace the origins of natural language processing (NLP) back to a wide range of disciplines, such as linguistics, computer science, mathematics, computer engineering, computer science and information, robotics, artificial intelligence, and computer and electrical engineering. The topic of natural language processing (NLP) is the primary emphasis of this article, which provides an in-depth analysis of a variety of soft computing methodologies. Support Vector Machines, Bayesian Networks, Maximum Entropy, Conditional Random Fields, and Artificial Neural Networks are some of the technologies that have shown to be useful in the processing of natural language. Within the scope of this chapter, natural language processing via the use of soft computing techniques is completely investigated.

References

1. Chowdhury, G.G., Natural language processing. *Annu. Rev. Inf. Sci. Technol.*, 37, 1, 51–89, 2003.
2. Agirre, E. and Edmonds, P. (Eds.), *Word sense disambiguation: Algorithms and applications*, vol. 33, pp. 1–12, Springer Science & Business Media, USA, 2007.
3. Namdev, A., Patni, D., Dhaliwal, B. K., Parihar, S., Telang, S., Rawat, A., Potential Threats and Ethical Risks of Quantum Computing, in: *Quantum Computing in Cybersecurity*, pp. 335–352, 2023.
4. Krovetz, R. and Croft, W.B., Lexical ambiguity and information retrieval. *ACM Trans. Inf. Syst. (TOIS)*, 10, 2, 115–141, 1992.
5. Hogaboam, T.W. and Perfetti, C.A., Lexical ambiguity and sentence comprehension. *J. Verbal Learn. Verbal Behav.*, 14, 3, 265–274, 1975.
6. Banerjee, S. and Pedersen, T., An adapted Lesk algorithm for word sense disambiguation using WordNet, in: *International conference on intelligent text processing and computational linguistics*, pp. 136–145, Springer, Berlin, Heidelberg, 2002.

7. Shrivastava, M., Patil, R., Bhardwaj, V., Rawat, R., Telang, S., Rawat, A., Quantum Computing and Security Aspects of Attention-Based Visual Question Answering with Long Short-Term Memory, in: *Quantum Computing in Cybersecurity*, pp. 395–412, 2023.
8. Noonia, A., Beg, R., Patidar, A., Bawaskar, B., Sharma, S., Rawat, H., Chatbot vs Intelligent Virtual Assistance (IVA), in: *Conversational Artificial Intelligence*, pp. 655–673, 2024.
9. Agirre, E., Alfonseca, E., Hall, K., Kravalova, J., Paşca, M., Soroa, A., A study on similarity and relatedness using distributional and WordNet-based approaches, in: *Proceedings of Human Language Technologies: The 2009 Annual Conference of the North American Chapter of the Association for Computational Linguistics*, pp. 19– 27, Association for Computational Linguistics, 2009.
10. Rapp, R., Word sense discovery based on sense descriptor dissimilarity, in: *Proceedings of the ninth machine translation summit*, pp. 315–322, 2003.
11. Miller, T., Biemann, C., Zesch, T., Gurevych, I., Using distributional similarity for lexical expansion in knowledge-based word sense disambiguation. *Proceedings of COLING*, vol. 2012, pp. 1781–1796, 2012.
12. Marcu, D. and Wong, D., A phrase-based, joint probability model for statistical machine translation, in: *Proceedings of the 2002 Conference on Empirical Methods in Natural Language Processing (EMNLP 2002)*, pp. 133–139, 2002.
13. Koehn, P., Statistical significance tests for machine translation evaluation, in: *Proceedings of the 2004 conference on empirical methods in natural language processing*, pp. 388–395, 2004.
14. Quirk, C., Brockett, C., Dolan, W., Monolingual machine translation for paraphrase generation, in: *Proceedings of the 2004 conference on empirical methods in natural language processing*, pp. 142–149, 2004.
15. Seemakurty, N., Chu, J., Von Ahn, L., Tomasic, A., Word sense disambiguation via human computation, in: *Proceedings of the acm sigkdd workshop on human*, pp. 60–63, ACM, computation, 2010.
16. Navigli, R., Faralli, S., Soroa, A., De Lacalle, O., Agirre, E., Two birds with one stone: learning semantic models for text categorization and word sense disambiguation, in: *Proceedings of the 20th ACM international conference on Information and knowledge management*, pp. 2317–2320, ACM, 2011.
17. Navigli, R. and Lapata, M., An experimental study of graph connectivity for unsupervised word sense disambiguation. *IEEE Trans. Pattern Anal. Mach. Intell.*, 32, 4, 678–692, 2009.
18. Alwan, M.A. and Onsi, H.M., A Proposed Textual Graph Based Model for Arabic Multidocument Summarization. *Int. J. Adv. Comput. Sci. Appl.*, 7, 6, 435–439, 2016.
19. Liu, N., Tang, X.J., Lu, Y., Li, M.X., Wang, H.W., Xiao, P., Topic-Sensitive Multi document Summarization Algorithm, in: *Parallel Architectures, Algorithms and Programming (PAAP), Sixth International Symposium*, pp. 69–74, IEEE, 2014.

20. Tayal, M.A., Raghuwanshi, M.M., Malik, L.G., ATSSC: Development of an approach based on soft computing for text summarization. *Comput. Speech Lang.*, 41, 214–235, 2017.
21. Suthar, H., Rawat, H., Gayathri, M., Chidambarathanu, K., Techno-Nationalism and Techno-Globalization: A Perspective from the National Security Act, in: *Quantum Computing in Cybersecurity*, pp. 137–164, 2023.
22. Bakharia, A. and Dawson, S., Using Sentence Compression to Develop Visual Analytics for Student Responses to Short Answer Questions, in: *VISLA@ LAK*, pp. 11–13, 2015.
23. Padó, U., Get Semantic With Me! The Usefulness of Different Feature Types for Short-Answer Grading, in: *COLING*, pp. 2186–2195, 2016.
24. Kouloumpis, E., Wilson, T., Moore, J., Twitter sentiment analysis: The good the bad and the omg!, in: *Fifth International AAAI conference on weblogs and social media*, pp. 1–5, 2011.
25. Pak, A. and Paroubek, P., Twitter as a corpus for sentiment analysis and opinion mining, in: *LREc*, vol. 10, no. 2010, pp. 1320–1326, 2010.
26. Agarwal, A., Xie, B., Vovsha, I., Rambow, O., Passonneau, R., Sentiment analysis of twitter data, in: *Proceedings of the Workshop on Language in Social Media (LSM 2011)*, pp. 30–38, 2011.
27. Saif, H., He, Y., Fernandez, M., Alani, H., Contextual semantics for sentiment analysis of Twitter. *Inf. Process. Manage.*, 52, 1, 5–19, 2016.
28. Taboada, M., Brooke, J., Tofiloski, M., Voll, K., Stede, M., Lexicon-based methods for sentiment analysis. *Comput. Ling.*, 37, 2, 267–307, 2011.
29. Zhang, L., Ghosh, R., Dekhil, M., Hsu, M., Liu, B., Combining lexicon-based and learning-based methods for Twitter sentiment analysis. HP Laboratories, Technical Report HPL- 2011, pp. 8–19, 2011.
30. Kanjanawattana, S. and Kimura, M., Novel Ontologies-based Optical Character Recognition-error Correction Cooperating with Graph Component Extraction. *BRAIN. Broad Res. Artif. Intell. Neurosci.*, 7, 4, 69–83, 2017.
31. Vinitha, V.S. and Jawahar, C.V., Error Detection in Indic OCRs. Document Analysis Systems (DAS). *2016 12th IAPR Workshop*, IEEE, pp. 180–185, 2016.
32. Darwish, K. and Magdy, W., Error correction vs. query garbling for Arabic OCR document retrieval. *ACM Trans. Inf. Syst. (TOIS)*, 26, 1, 5–15, 2007.
33. Pithawa, D., Nahar, S., Bhardwaj, V., Rawat, R., Dronawat, R., Rawat, A., Quantum Computing Technological Design Along with Its Dark Side, in: *Quantum Computing in Cybersecurity*, pp. 295–312, 2023.
34. Shrivastava, M., Patil, R., Bhardwaj, V., Rawat, R., Telang, S., Rawat, A., Quantum Computing and Security Aspects of Attention-Based Visual Question Answering with Long Short-Term Memory, in: *Quantum Computing in Cybersecurity*, pp. 395–412, 2023.
35. Rawat, R., Chakrawarti, R.K., Raj, A.S.A., Mani, G., Chidambarathanu, K., Bhardwaj, R., Association rule learning for threat analysis using traffic

analysis and packet filtering approach. *Int. J. Inf. Technol.*, *15*, 6, 3245–3255, 2023.

36. Rathi, M. and Rajavat, A., *Analysing Cryptographic and Random Data Sanitization Techniques in Privacy Preserving Data Mining*, vol. 83, Allied Publishers, New Delhi, India, 2023.
37. Dhar, S., Dhar, U., Rajavat, A., Factors and Attributes of Team Players: A Study of Engineering Students in India, in: *International Simulation and Gaming Association Conference*, pp. 53–60, Springer International Publishing, Cham, 2021, September.

20

Sentiment Analysis Using Natural Language Processing

Brijesh Goswami[1]*, Nidhi Bhavsar[2], Soleman Awad Alzobidy[3], B. Lavanya[4], R. Udhayakumar[4] and Rajapandian K.[5]

[1]*Institute of Business Management, GLA University, Mathura, UP, India*
[2]*Department Information Technology, Thakur College of Engineering and Technology, Mumbai, Maharashtra, India*
[3]*Department of English Language and Translation Studies, College of Sciences and Theoretical Studies, Saudi Electronic University, Riyadh, Kingdom of Saudi Arabia*
[4]*Vel Tech Rangarajan Dr Sagunthala R&D Institute of Science and Technology, Avadi, Chennai, Tamil Nadu, India*
[5]*SRM Kattankulathur Dental College, SRM Nagar Kattankulathur Chengalpattu, Tamil Nadu, India*

Abstract
Complex text mining techniques include text classification, topic discovery and summarization, concept extraction, document clustering, sentiment extraction, text conversion, natural language processing, and more. These techniques can then be used to extract non-trivial information from a set of text-based documents. Arguments, divergent points of view, and verbal altercations are all useful tools for presenting the facts around a current topic. Text mining, as used in natural language processing, is the process of gleaning sentiment from text that has been obtained through online networking web-based systems. This research outlines a strategy to enhance machine learning and natural language processing in an attempt to simplify and pinpoint the textual feelings that underlie information that is extracted from social media comments.

***Keywords*:** Sentiment analysis, text analysis, challenges, machine learning, preprocessing, tokenization

**Corresponding author*: brijesh.goswami@gla.ac.in
R. Udhayakumar: ORCID: 0000-0002-2447-664X

Rajesh Kumar Chakrawarti, Ranjana Sikarwar, Sanjaya Kumar Sarangi, Samson Arun Raj Albert Raj, Shweta Gupta, Krishnan Sakthidasan Sankaran and Romil Rawat (eds.) Natural Language Processing for Software Engineering, (283–294) © 2025 Scrivener Publishing LLC

20.1 Introduction

Sentiments are the feelings that a person expresses via their behavior, which influences the behavior of people around them. Sentiment analysis (SA), the study of computationally leveraging these emotions, is therefore continuing, and what counts are the outcomes. One significant natural language processing (NLP) application in this research that addresses the interplay between human and machine language is opinion mining [1]. The act of creating a system to gather and arrange data from various social media platforms, blogs, online forums, and web-based surveys is known as opinion mining. Because people base their judgements on the tools at their disposal, business establishments can gain insight into the buyer's mindset, evaluation, sentiment, and attitude through social media. Politicians and officials also make modifications while addressing public issues. Now is the moment to develop a new application using real-world data, emphasizing textual approaches for information discovery (especially on Twitter) for searching, organizing, or studying. Because Twitter is used to communicate messages via social media and blog sites, numerous unique elements in tweets also affect the different domains and methodology covered in sentiment analysis. This leads to the emergence of new difficulties [2].

Sentiment analysis provides organizations with important insights into customer sentiment, enabling them to better understand how customers respond to particular offerings. Sentiment analysis is now widely accepted by businesses, governments, and other organizations in addition to academics. Sentiment analysis is a potent technique because people's thoughts and sentiments about a certain subject can provide insightful information for a wide range of industries, including academics and business [3].

Organizations must prioritize understanding the attitudes of their customers towards their brand. Enhanced goods, in-the-moment issue detection, and distinguishing markers can all lead to happier customers. Sentiment analysis has applications across a wide range of disciplines. It gives us useful information in fields like sports, economics, politics, tourism, and healthcare and aids in our understanding of consumer behavior [4].

Sentiment analysis, a branch of natural language processing, is currently one of the most active areas in computer science study (NLP). Data extraction is made possible by genuine discourse Processing (NLP), which uses a range of machine learning algorithms to automatically examine and comprehend genuine human discourse. The authors of the survey have made recommendations for potential future improvements. They found problems with sentiment analysis and carried out a survey that could help a novice researcher tackle new tasks with remarkable accuracy. They discovered that sentiment analysis has a number of possible applications, such as predicting equity and market prices, assessing political opinion, and categorizing movie reviews to anticipate box office receipts. In conclusion, the authors feel that sentiment analysis holds great potential for further research. Sentiment analysis in social media content is a difficult undertaking because dialect articulation is diverse and varied. The difficulty of the endeavor lies not only in its complexity but also in the huge amount of real-time content available. Sentiment analysis cannot be done by hand; instead, a strong tool or intelligent system is needed [5].

20.2 Sentiment Analysis Levels

Sentiment analysis can take place at several levels, for instance, in a document or in a sentence.

20.2.1 Document Level

By employing document-level analysis, we are able to categorize the general sentiment of a reviewer after extracting it from the whole review. The main emphasis of this level is on documents that express viewpoints, whether they are positive or negative. The techniques employed for this approach yield a precision rate of 70 to 80% across several publications. This tool mostly serves the purposes of product reviews and film reviews. Sentiment analysis at the document level only considers a single entity. This strategy is unsuitable for comparing several objects or analyzing papers.

20.2.2 Sentence Level

At this stage, the initial step is to determine if a statement is subjective or objective. In this context, "personal interpretation" refers to the act of examining the statement from an individual's distinct perspective, whereas "from a distance" it implies analyzing it from the viewpoint of another person [6]. The main objective of the second task is to determine if the subjective sentence is positive, negative, or neutral. Unlike an objective sentence, which often conveys factual information, a subjective statement expresses one's personal views, beliefs, emotions, or values. To distinguish between the two, we utilize the Naive Bayesian Classifier technique. However, merely determining whether the sentence conveys a positive or negative attitude is inadequate. Since a subjective statement might contain subjective and factual components, as well as several views, this intermediary process is valuable for eliminating phrases that do not express any viewpoints.

20.2.3 Aspect Level

In fine-grained analysis, the prioritization of perspectives is done at the aspect level classification, which is also known as entity level, phase level, or document level. This is in contrast to language constructions such as documents, paragraphs, sentences, clauses, and phrases. By considering the positive and negative emotions expressed in a review, it enables the identification of the sentiments and characteristics associated with an object. Next, the system proceeds to detect and obtain the object attributes that have been expressed by the reviewer. The generation of the feature-based feedback summary occurs after the conclusion of synonym grouping. The principal purposes of this are to extract aspects and categorize aspect emotions [7].

20.3 Challenges in Sentiment Analysis

Ambiguity resolution, word sense disambiguation, handling out-of-vocabulary words, cultural and contextual adaptation, and domain specific challenges are some of the issues encountered at the Lexicon Level in Natural Language Processing. Addressing ambiguity necessitates mastering the nuances of words having many meanings and creating systems to accomplish accurate disambiguation in different settings at the level of the lexicon. The goal of word sense disambiguation is to resolve cases when a word might have more than one correct interpretation depending on the context. With the ever-changing nature of language and the introduction of new terms, it is essential to develop methods for dealing with words that do not appear in current dictionaries to effectively manage Out-of-Vocabulary Words. To make sure that NLP systems can understand a broad variety of expressions, it is necessary to adapt lexicons to account for cultural subtleties and contextual differences in language use. This process is called cultural and contextual adaptation. Overcoming obstacles in lexicon usage within certain domains or businesses is what "Navigating Domain-Specific Lexicon Challenges" is all about. Tailored solutions are necessary for precise processing due to the uniqueness, development, and specialization of terminology.

At the document level, Natural Language Processing has challenges such as detecting sarcasm and irony, dealing with contradictions and negations, and dealing with contextual complexity. Taking into account the larger context, such as word connections, the text's tone, and the development of emotion across a document or discussion, is an important part of contextual complexity. Understanding the many nuances of language in varied and ever-changing contexts is essential for natural language processing models when dealing with contextual complexity. Negation and contradiction are challenges that need to be overcome for sentiment analysis to be accurate in a text. These challenges might take the form of negative phrases, contradictory claims, or bad feelings. To correctly discern irony and sarcasm, one must be able to recognize and comprehend statements that reflect emotions contrary to their literal meaning. Conditional and comparative sentences, opinion word sharing, subjectivity identification and sentiment categorization, opinion source and target, handling negation, and other issues are encountered at the sentence level of natural language processing. Due to their subtle and context-dependent character, analyzing phrases that describe conditions or make comparisons requires nuanced sentiment interpretation. Identifying instances when the distribution of opinion terms among entities impacts the accuracy of sentiment analysis. When dealing with phrase level sentiment analysis, it might be difficult for natural language processors to detect subjectivity and categorize feelings. In natural language processing (NLP), knowing who expressed an opinion and where it came from, as well as how to deal with negation, are all vital parts of sentence-level sentiment analysis and opinion extraction.

Important obstacles in aspect-level sentiment analysis in NLP include aspect classification, aspect stemming, and aspect trimming. In aspect-based sentiment analysis, aspect pruning is the process of eliminating or downplaying less important or irrelevant features. Improving the analysis's efficiency and eliminating irrelevant or irrelevantly noisy data is the job of aspect trimming. Because different words might have the same root but different meanings, aspect-level analysis can be complicated due to stemming ambiguity. Operating at the aspect level presents a challenge for aspect classification in natural language processing. The challenge is in correctly classifying characteristics, making sure we comprehend subtleties in individual traits, and adjusting to the ever-changing language.

There are three tiers to these natural language processing problems: syntactic, semantic, and pragmatic. Much of the earlier work on sentiment analysis concentrated on solving problems at the syntactic layer, such as lemmatization, sentence boundary disambiguation, micro text normalization, and part of speech (POS) tagging. Problems including idea extraction, subjectivity detection, entity identification, and word meaning disambiguation are handled at the semantic layer. Practical considerations include tasks such as polarity identification, aspect level tasks, metaphor comprehension, personality recognition, and sarcasm detection.

20.4 Related Work

A number of different supervised machine learning algorithms were utilized by Pragya Juneja *et al.* (2017) to categorize the feelings that were expressed on Twitter as either positive or negative. It was the major objective of this project to make a prediction on the results of the elections for the Delhi Corporation. In the course of this work, the most effective categorization model for machine learning was also discovered. This research investigated the behavior of a number of classification models by making use of the Twitter dataset including information on various political parties. When compared to the other classifiers, the Multinomial Naive Bayes model performed much better in terms of the percentage of correct classifications. We are able to make this model even more refined to achieve even more favorable results [8].

Text analysis, natural language processing, text preparation, and stemming were some of the methods that Chhaya Chauhan *et al.* (2017) utilized in their research of the complex data. The process of deciphering human speech was accomplished via the use of a variety of computer software and methods. According to the findings of the research, the availability of natural language that is available on the internet allows for a variety of approaches to be utilized to ascertain the tone of a phrase or piece of writing. A wide range of algorithms and methods were utilized by the writers to extract [25–27] a comprehensive description of the product, item by item, to build a review that was authentic. After the system had excluded all other terms, the advice was to concentrate on higher-level natural language processing [28–30] jobs in the future. This would allow for the most efficient methods or tools to be utilized to extract more accurate results from datasets that comprised mainly keywords [9].

As a result of the growth of both persons and modern methods of communication, there has been a meteoric rise in the usage of social media websites, as stated by Jamil Hussain *et al.* (2017). It is now much simpler for individuals to convey their opinions through social media platforms such as Facebook, Blogs, Twitter, and others as a result of technological developments in CPU architectures and mobile phones. According to the findings of the study, it is possible to utilize emotion theories, machine learning techniques, and natural language processing algorithms to locate SA on a variety of social media sites. Phrase-level sentiment analysis was utilized by the authors to investigate SVM, ME, and NB, which are three of the currently available classifiers for the assessment of depression in the research. In the course of testing on Twitter and the 20 newsgroups dataset, they have included voting and feature selection algorithms. According to their findings, support vector machines (SVM) perform better than Naive Bayes in terms of accuracy [10].

Zahra Rezaei *et al.* (2017) utilized Twitter to get an understanding of the subject matter of the brief messages and the influence that they have on other people. In addition, users tweet often and swiftly. For the purpose of extracting the separation aspects of the data from Twitter, researchers utilized filtering and wrapping approaches which resulted in an improvement in SA's performance. When it came to Hoeffding trees and McDiarmid trees, they utilized the approaches that were applicable. Despite the fact that the McDiarmid tree strategy worked better than the others, SA had to work quickly to process all of the Twitter data [11].

The tweets have been further classified into seven separate emotion groups by the utilization of text-based binary and ternary classifications, as demonstrated by Mondher Bouazizi *et al.* (2017) and other organizations. To carry out the classification, they initially developed SENTA, a software that features an easy-to-use graphical user interface and provides users with the ability to select from a variety of criteria [12].

An opinion mining technique was utilized by Mondher Bouazizi *et al.* (2018) to examine Multiclass sentiment analysis when they were working on SA analysis. The purpose was not to determine the overall emotional polarity of the text message; rather, it was to determine the specific attitude of the intended recipient. They conducted an experiment using eleven distinct emotion classes, each of which was allocated to a separate internet article rather than a single tweet. The experiment was carried out utilizing the "quantification" approach and the SENTA tools. On the other hand, the data set to be used in this investigation was manually annotated, and the outcomes of the analysis were compared to those annotations [13].

Text mining and neural networks were utilized in the development of a hybrid model that was built by Mohammed H. Abd El-Jawad and colleagues (2018) to characterize sentiments. A number of deep learning and machine learning techniques were utilized in the development of the model. For this study, an analysis was performed on more than one million tweets that were collected from five distinct domains. After training with 75% of the dataset and testing with 25% of the dataset, this model exceeded the strategies that came before it with an accuracy rate of 83.7%. Additionally, the authors suggested conducting additional research, particularly in Arabic tweets, with a specific focus on the coupling of sentiment and text for the purpose of sentiment analysis. It is [14].

As stated by Mondher Bouazizi *et al.* (2019), the majority of research conducted on text SA has focused on binary and ternary data classification. The multi-class categorization of natural languages has proven to be a challenging endeavor, despite the fact that natural languages are both diverse and involved. Moreover, it is a great deal more challenging to "quantify" the manner in which individuals communicate their emotions using statistical methods. This model not only studied the difficulties associated with multi-class classification, but also discovered areas in which there is room for further development in terms of the accuracy of multi-class classification [15].

To determine whether or not a particular service or product could be appropriate for the consumer, Shahnawaz *et al.* (2017) relied on the writer's position on a particular issue. To make up for the lack of labeled data, the authors reasoned out that it would be straightforward to employ semi-supervised and unsupervised learning-based models provided that there would be sufficient unlabeled data available. This would allow them to make up for the lack of labeled data [16].

20.5 Machine Learning Techniques for Sentiment Analysis

The algorithms belong to an area of artificial intelligence called machine learning. These algorithms facilitate computer learning. Consequently, algorithms frequently acquire data sets and form assumptions on the data's quality based on their observations. This knowledge enhances the ability to forecast future data discoveries by increasing the probability of such discoveries. Given that most non-random data contain patterns that enable machines to make generalizations, it becomes very easy to forecast the hidden data [17]. A computer-trained model is employed to govern the crucial data points for the purpose of generalization. Sentiment analysis employs supervised and unsupervised machine learning methods to extract meaningful insights from both structured and unstructured textual data, with the aim of assisting decision-makers. The objective of this strategy is to tackle the distinctive challenges in sentence categorization that algorithms encounter by training a text classifier using a pre-existing dataset that has been labeled by humans. The fundamental principles of this approach are derived from both supervised and unsupervised learning [18].

Support Vector Machines:

Due to their renowned proficiency in recognizing conventional text, Support Vector Machines (SVMs) consistently outperform Naive Bayes (NB). The Support Vector Machine (SVM) is a probabilistic classifier, in contrast to Naive Bayes and MaxEnt, which prioritize accuracy. In the training phase of the two-category scenario, the primary objective is to identify a hyperplane, denoted by vector w, that effectively distinguishes the document vectors in each class, with a substantial separation or margin between them [18].

Random Forest (RF):

The computing system in issue is the outcome of combining several decision trees. These trees are built using an entropy metric. The purity level of a node is determined by using the value of this integer [19]. In this circumstance, classifier systems with minimal bias and significant variance are often trained since it simplifies the process of generating decision trees. There are several techniques available to enhance the efficiency of different decision trees. However, it is a frequent practice to employ the model average technique while also insuring a specific number of trees. This approach reduces the variability of the model while somewhat increasing the bias. Empirical evidence has shown that this approach enhances precision. It is crucial to randomize the construction of a feature set for each decision tree to generate diverse and impartial trees [20].

Logistic Regression:

Many individuals employ this technique to resolve binary classification problems. One of the several uses of logistic regression is in text mining, where it is used to convert tasks into binary classification. The fundamental concept underlying this approach is utilizing patterns identified in a vast dataset to forecast the level of positivity in a tweet. The model was named based on the logistic structure of the probability function [21].

Rule-based Classifiers:

A rule-based classifier employs a collection of rules to depict the data space. The left representation, denoted in standard form [22], signifies a location inside the feature set. Conversely, the right representation, denoted in class, indicates the reverse. The words are present on the page. We rarely utilize the term "absence" as it lacks significance in situations when there is a dearth of knowledge. Each rule in the training phase is derived from one of the several rules-generation criteria that are available. The two predominant criteria are confidence and support [23]. The support training data set comprises all cases that are pertinent to the rule. Confidence refers to the conditional likelihood of the right side being satisfied, given that the left side of the rule has been met. Vader is a widely-used model that operates based on a set of rules and incorporates several lexical characteristics. Unlike conventional approaches, this method focuses on doing sentiment analysis on data gathered from microblogs and delivers comprehensive and precise outcomes [24].

20.6 Conclusion

The way people express their feelings or emotions may have a big influence on how those around them behave. Sentiment analysis (SA), the study of harnessing these emotions digitally, is therefore continuous, and the outcomes are what really count. One important NLP application in this study that addresses the relationship between machine and human language is opinion mining. The aim of text mining in the context of natural language processing is to derive meaning from text gathered via online networks and web-based systems. This work proposes an approach to enhance machine learning and natural language processing by simplifying and identifying the underlying textual sentiments of data collected from social media comments.

References

1. Anagha, M. *et al.*, Fuzzy logic based hybrid approach for sentiment analysis of Malayalam movie reviews. *2015 IEEE International Conference on Signal Processing, Informatics, Communication and Energy Systems (SPICES)*, IEEE, 2015.
2. Shoukry, A. and Rafea, A., A hybrid approach for sentiment classification of Egyptian Dialect Tweets. *2015 First International Conference on Arabic Computational Linguistics (ACLing)*, IEEE, 2015.
3. Han, P., Li, S., Jia, Y., A topic-independent hybrid approach for sentiment analysis of chinese microblog. *2016 IEEE 17th International Conference on Information Reuse and Integration (IRI)*, IEEE, 2016.
4. Appel, O. *et al.*, A hybrid approach to sentiment analysis. *2016 IEEE Congress on Evolutionary Computation (CEC)*, IEEE, 2016.

5. Biltawi, M., Al-Naymat, G., Tedmori, S., Arabic sentiment classification: A hybrid approach. *2017 International Conference on New Trends in Computing Sciences (ICTCS)*, IEEE, 2017.
6. Jagdale, J. and Emmanuel, M., Hybrid Corrective Critic Neural Network for Sentiment Classification in Community Media. *2019 3rd International conference on Electronics, Communication and Aerospace Technology (ICECA)*, pp. 1236–1241, 2019.
7. Zouzou, A. and Azami, I.E., Text sentiment analysis with CNN & GRU model using GloVe. *2021 Fifth International Conference On Intelligent Computing in Data Sciences (ICDS)*, pp. 1–5, 2021.
8. Juneja, P. and Ojha, U., Casting online votes: to predict offline results using sentiment analysis by machine learning classifiers. *2017 8th International Conference on Computing, Communication and Networking Technologies (ICCCNT)*, IEEE, 2017.
9. Chauhan, C. and Sehgal, S., Sentiment analysis on product reviews. *2017 International Conference on Computing, Communication and Automation (ICCCA)*, IEEE, 2017.
10. Hassan, A.U. *et al.*, Sentiment analysis of social networking sites (SNS) data using machine learning approach for the measurement of depression. *2017 International Conference on Information and Communication Technology Convergence (ICTC)*, IEEE, 2017.
11. Rezaei, Z. and Jalali, M., Sentiment analysis on Twitter using McDiarmid tree algorithm. *2017 7th International Conference on Computer and Knowledge Engineering (ICCKE)*, IEEE, 2017.
12. Bouazizi, M. and Ohtsuki, T., A pattern-based approach for multi-class sentiment analysis in Twitter. *IEEE Access*, 5, 20617–20639, 2017.
13. Bouazizi, M. and Ohtsuki, T., Multi-class sentiment analysis in Twitter: What if classification is not the answer. *IEEE Access*, 6, 64486–64502, 2018.
14. El-Jawad, M.H.A., Hodhod, R., Omar, Y.M.K., Sentiment Analysis of Social Media Networks Using Machine Learning. *2018 14th International Computer Engineering Conference (ICENCO)*, IEEE, 2018.
15. Rathi, M. *et al.*, Sentiment Analysis of Tweets Using Machine Learning Approach. *2018 Eleventh International Conference on Contemporary Computing (IC3)*, IEEE, 2018.
16. Astya, P., Sentiment analysis: approaches and open issues. *2017 International Conference on Computing, Communication and Automation (ICCCA)*, IEEE, 2017.
17. Rabeya, T., Chakraborty, N.R., Ferdous, S., Dash, M., Al Marouf, A., Sentiment Analysis of Bangla Song Review- A Lexicon Based Backtracking Approach. *2019 IEEE International Conference on Electrical, Computer and Communication Technologies (ICECCT)*, pp. 1–7, 2019.
18. Yang, L., Li, Y., Wang, J., Sherratt, R.S., Sentiment Analysis for E-Commerce Product Reviews in Chinese Based on Sentiment Lexicon and Deep Learning. *IEEE Access*, 8, 23522–23530, 2020.

19. Koto, F. and Rahmaningtyas, G.Y., Inset lexicon: Evaluation of a word list for Indonesian sentiment analysis in microblogs. *2017 International Conference on Asian Language Processing (IALP)*, pp. 391–394, 2017.
20. Wu, X., Linghu, Y., Wang, T., Fan, Y., Sentiment Analysis of Weak-RuleText Based on the Combination of Sentiment Lexicon and Neural Network. *2021 IEEE 6th International Conference on Cloud Computing and Big Data Analytics (ICCCBDA)*, pp. 205–209, 2021.
21. Ding, Y., Li, B., Zhao, Y., Cheng, C., Scoring tourist attractions based on sentiment lexicon. *2017 IEEE 2nd Advanced Information Technology, Electronic and Automation Control Conference (IAEAC)*, pp. 1990–1993, 2017.
22. Mehto, A. and Indras, K., Data mining through sentiment analysis: Lexicon based sentiment analysis model using aspect catalogue. *2016 Symposium on Colossal Data Analysis and Networking (CDAN)*, pp. 1–7, 2016.
23. Thavareesan, S. and Mahesan, S., Sentiment Lexicon Expansion using Word2vec and fastText for Sentiment Prediction in Tamil texts. *2020 Moratuwa Engineering Research Conference (MERCon)*, pp. 272–276, 2020.
24. Liu, J., Yan, M., Luo, J., Research on the Construction of Sentiment Lexicon Based on Chinese Microblog. *2016 8th International Conference on Intelligent Human-Machine Systems and Cybernetics (IHMSC)*, pp. 56–59, 2016.
25. Pithawa, D., Nahar, S., Bhardwaj, V., Rawat, R., Dronawat, R., Rawat, A., Quantum Computing Technological Design Along with Its Dark Side, in: *Quantum Computing in Cybersecurity*, pp. 295–312, 2023.
26. Shrivastava, M., Patil, R., Bhardwaj, V., Rawat, R., Telang, S., Rawat, A., Quantum Computing and Security Aspects of Attention-Based Visual Question Answering with Long Short-Term Memory, in: *Quantum Computing in Cybersecurity*, pp. 395–412, 2023.
27. Rawat, R., Chakrawarti, R.K., Raj, A.S.A., Mani, G., Chidambarathanu, K., Bhardwaj, R., Association rule learning for threat analysis using traffic analysis and packet filtering approach. *Int. J. Inf. Technol.*, *15*, 6, 3245–3255, 2023.
28. Rathi, M. and Rajavat, A., High Dimensional Data Processing in Privacy Preserving Data Mining, in: *2020 IEEE 9th International Conference on Communication Systems and Network Technologies (CSNT)*, pp. 212–217, IEEE, 2020, April.
29. Patsariya, M. and Rajavat, A., Network Path Capability Identification and Performance analysis of Mobile Ad hoc Network, in: *2020 IEEE 9th International Conference on Communication Systems and Network Technologies (CSNT)*, pp. 82–87, IEEE, 2020, April.
30. Dhar, S., Dhar, U., Rajavat, A., Factors and Attributes of Team Players: A Study of Engineering Students in India, in: *International Simulation and Gaming Association Conference*, pp. 53–60, Springer International Publishing, Cham, 2021, September.

21

Web Data Mining: Exploring Hyperlinks, Contents, and Usage Data

C. V. Guru Rao[1*], Nagendra Prasad Krishnam[2], Akula Rajitha[3], Anandhi R. J.[4], Atul Singla[5] and Joshuva Arockia Dhanraj[6]

[1]School of CS & AI, SR University, Warangal, Telangana, India
[2]School of Management & Commerce (SoMC), Malla Reddy University, Hyderabad, Telangana, India
[3]Institute of Aeronautical Engineering, Dundigal, Hyderabad, India
[4]Department of Information Science Engineering, New Horizon College of Engineering, Bangalore, India
[5]Lovely Professional University, Phagwara, India
[6]Department of Computer Science and Engineering (AI&ML), School of Engineering, Dayananda Sagar University, Devarakaggalahalli, Harohalli, Kanakapura Road, Ramanagara District, Bengaluru, Karnataka, India

Abstract
Web structure mining aims to identify interesting patterns within the inter-document link structure. By classifying the web pages based on the link structure's topology, the authors may infer important details about the connections and similarities between them. Associations such as those between analogous entities, entities with similar content, or entities hosted on the same server can be extracted. The structure of a domain's hyperlink hierarchy may also be found using web structure mining. This is useful for efficiently modelling the databases connected to these websites. Another aspect of online mining is web content mining. It focuses on trying to extract interesting and non-trivial patterns from the content of the web pages. A web page may include many different kinds of data, some examples of which are text, images, music, video, metadata, and links. A portion of the data is highly organized and shown as tables and HTML pages created by databases, while another portion is more semi-structured and presented as HyperText

**Corresponding author*: guru_cv_rao@hotmail.com
Joshuva Arockia Dhanraj: ORCID: 0000-0001-5048-7775

Rajesh Kumar Chakrawarti, Ranjana Sikarwar, Sanjaya Kumar Sarangi, Samson Arun Raj Albert Raj, Shweta Gupta, Krishnan Sakthidasan Sankaran and Romil Rawat (eds.) Natural Language Processing for Software Engineering, (295–310) © 2025 Scrivener Publishing LLC

Markup Language (HTML). This study project provides a thorough analysis of web data mining by examining hyperlinks, use statistics, and web content mining.

Keywords: Web content mining, natural language processing, web structure mining, data mining techniques, www architecture, unstructured data

21.1 Introduction

This global computing network known as the Internet is shared by all of us. It allows all connected computers to communicate data globally. It is the cornerstone of the World Wide Web and other online services. The web is made up of all the webpages that are stored on different web servers. The amount of information and services available over the Internet is growing at an incredible pace. Every year, the number of web pages is thought to double. As the breadth and variety of the Web have increased, so too has the significance of search engines in the WWW's architecture [1].

It is a difficult effort to find and get relevant information from the Internet because of the data's extreme lack of organization. In search engines, keywords determine content. The exponential growth of WWW information sources makes it more crucial than ever for users to use automated tools to find, extract, filter, and evaluate the pertinent data and resources. Furthermore, because the Web has emerged as the primary tool for electronic commerce and because businesses have invested millions in intranet and Internet infrastructure, they also need to keep an eye on and evaluate user access habits. These factors make it imperative to create intelligent systems that, both on the client and server sides, can efficiently mine data throughout the Internet and in particular Web places [2] as shown in Figure 21.1: Web Data Mining Process.

On the internet, a number of businesses and organizations offer a wide variety of tools and applications, in addition to providing automated customer service and the ability to make purchases with the internet. The use of web-based applications and configurations for activities such as online news broadcasts, online collaboration, online education, electronic commerce, and other similar activities is rapidly becoming the general practice [3, 4]. From young children trading music files with their friends to grandparents receiving images and messages from grandchildren located all over the world, the internet is rapidly becoming an instrument that is considered to be normal for the activities that are performed by the general population on a daily basis. Even for classes that are taught in more traditional classroom settings, it is normal practice for websites that provide

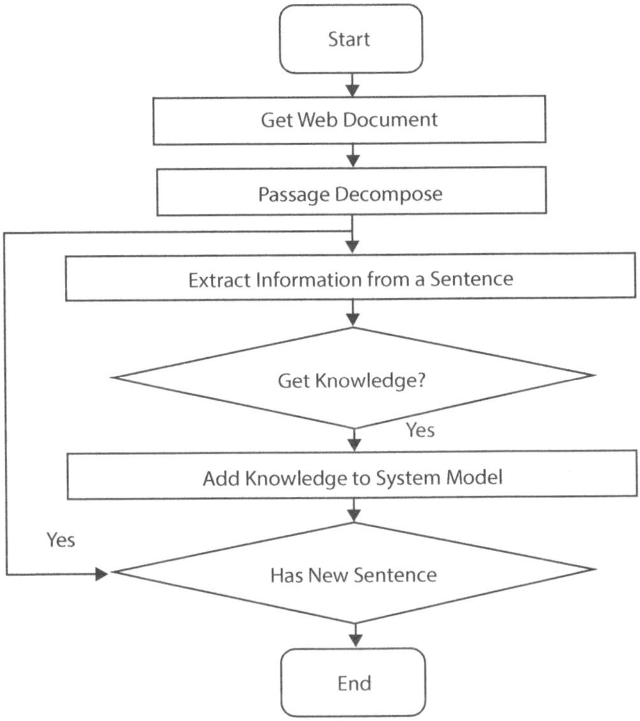

Figure 21.1 Web data mining process.

courses offered by universities and colleges to include course materials as well as extra materials. The fact that modern sophisticated distance education systems are created with the web in mind should not come as a surprise to anyone [5].

Researchers in the field of artificial intelligence, computer scientists, and information engineers who work in the field of natural language processing investigate how computers interact with human languages. More specifically, they investigate ways to teach computers to manage and comprehend large amounts of textual communication. In natural language processing (NLP), some of the most prevalent areas of difficulties are the recognition of spoken language, the comprehension of natural language, and the generation of new natural language [6]. The majority of natural language processing (NLP) systems were dependent on complex rule sets that were once constructed by hand. On the other hand, the late 1980s saw the beginning of a revolution in natural language processing brought about by the application of machine learning techniques to language processing. This development was made possible by the exponential growth of computing power as well as the diminishing influence of Chomskyan linguistic theories. The theoretical foundations of these theories have previously been a barrier to the kind of corpus linguistics that serves as the foundation for the approach that machine learning takes to language processing. In essence, the third Decision trees and other early machine learning algorithms created systems of rigorous if-then rules, which mimicked the effects of previously established rules that were already in existence. Hidden Markov models were first utilized for the purpose of part-of-speech tagging; however, statistical models have lately garnered a great deal of attention due to their capacity to make probabilistic and soft decisions by assigning real-valued weights to the features of the input data. One example of a statistical model is the cache language model, which is utilized by a significant number of voice recognition systems in the present day. These models have a tendency to be more trustworthy and more robust when given with unexpected data, particularly information that contains mistakes, when they are included into a larger system that is comprised of numerous subtasks. One of the first areas to see substantial success was machine translation, mostly as a consequence of research at IBM Research, which built more complicated statistical models. This was one of the first areas to see major development. These systems of government were able to make use of multilingual textual corpora that had been developed by the European Union and the Canadian Parliament as a result of laws that mandated the translation of all governmental proceedings into all official languages of the respective systems of government. The success of the majority of other systems, on the other hand, was and continues to be severely constrained due to the fact that these systems relied on corpora that were specifically constructed for the work that these systems intended to accomplish. The result of this is that a great deal of research has been done on techniques to learn more effectively with fewer data [7].

21.2 Web Mining

Data mining techniques are utilized in the process of web mining, which is the process of automatically locating and extracting information from documents and services that are located on the World Wide Web. This topic of study is now seeing a significant amount of growth, mostly as a result of the interest in online business. Due to the presence of this phenomenon, it is not always apparent what exactly is meant by the term "web mining" or how to compare research that pertain to this topic.

Similar to, suggest decomposing Web mining into these subtasks, namely

Data Accumulation
Gathering information from various sources, such as e-commerce websites, is the next phase. Data extraction from web documents is the primary objective. Emails, docs, newsgroups, online logs, and database transactions are all potential sources of data.

Data preprocessing
Employment and certainty are two common features of data that must be prepared. Preprocessing the collected data is essential for more efficient information mining. Accurate, succinct, and preprocessed data are necessary for data mining. Pre-processing of data includes cleaning the data, identifying users and their sessions, adding access pathways, and identifying transactions.

Pattern Discovery
Through the process of pattern identification and the use of mining algorithms, we may acquire significant and ultimately comprehensible knowledge. Several examples of such methodologies include clustering analysis, dependency modelling, classification analysis, association rule discovery, sequential pattern discovery, and so on.

Pattern Analysis
The fundamental goal of pattern analysis is to identify patterns among the patterns discovered by the model pattern discovery approach. The fundamental purpose is to identify a usable model, rules, and modes. One is capable of generating a user-friendly graphical user interface by using visualization approaches.

21.3 Taxonomy of Web Data Mining

The Web mining analysis relies on three general sets of information: previous usage patterns, degree of shared content, and inter-memory associative link structures corresponding to the three subsets in Web mining namely, as shown in Figure 21.2: Taxonomy of Web Data Mining:

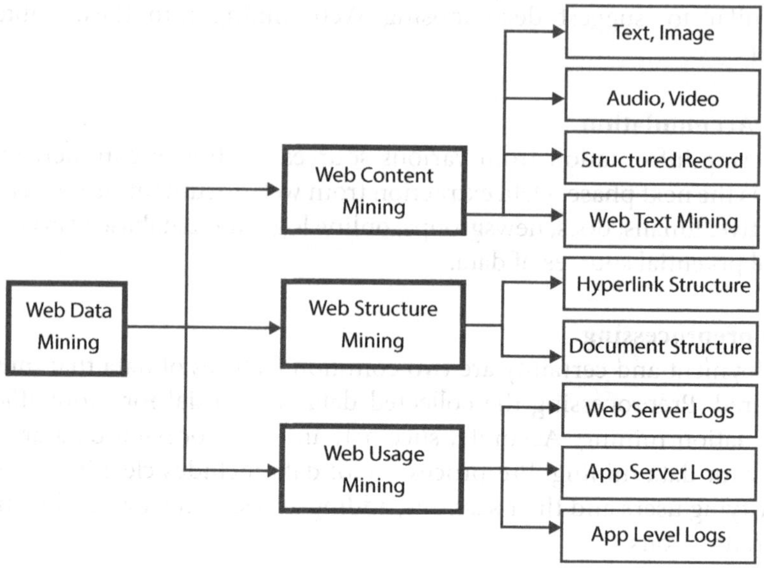

Figure 21.2 Taxonomy of web data mining.

- Web usage mining
- Web content mining
- Web structure mining

21.3.1 Web Usage Mining

The objective of web usage mining is to derive practical insights from secondary data obtained from customers' online activity. The main focus is on methods that can predict a person's behavior when visiting a website. Anticipating user behavior on the site, analyzing the differences between projected and actual usage, and customizing the site based on user preferences are all instances of mining objectives that encompass the potential strategic goals in each domain. Web use mining is same to the other two forms. Web use mining, web content mining, and web structure mining are interconnected. Clustering in pattern discovery acts as a bridge between usage mining and web content and structure mining. The web site topology will serve as the primary source of information for presenting data in web usage mining. The substantial research in the disciplines of information retrieval, databases, intelligent agents, and topology greatly enhances the benefits of web content and structure mining. Web use mining, a burgeoning topic of study, is attracting increasing attention from individuals [8].

21.3.2 Web Structure Mining

The vast majority of online information retrieval systems only use textual information, despite the fact that link data may be of great benefit. One of the goals of web structure mining is to generate a summary of the structural components that are present on the website and on each page. Web content mining is more concerned with the structure of individual documents, whereas web structure mining is more concerned with identifying the structure of the connections between documents. This is something that we can see when we break it down into its component pieces. Information such as links and similarities between websites may be generated via the use of web structure mining, which allows for the categorization of websites into different groups. Web structure mining may also result in the identification of the structure of the document, which is another potential conclusion. Using this method of structure mining, it is possible to uncover web page structures, also known as schemas. This is beneficial for navigational purposes and enables the comparison or integration of different web page schemes. Through the utilization of this structure mining technique, a reference schema will be generated, which will make it simpler to employ database techniques in order to get access to information on web pages [9].

There is a possibility that the structural information that is produced from it will be consulted for the study that is thorough on the issue. The following are elements that are included in web structure mining: the data that measures the frequency of internal and external connections in the tuples of a web table, including those that are included within the same document. This refers to the information that is used to measure the frequency of web tuples in a web table that includes both global links and linkages that span many websites. Assuming that web structure mining and web content mining are related to one another is a logical assumption to make, given that the majority of web papers have links and that both types of mining make use of main information that can be obtained on the internet. When applications are submitted, it is not unusual for these two mining occupations to be combined.

21.3.3 Web Content Mining

Data extraction from websites is the process that is known as web content mining. This technique involves automatically scanning through various online information resources. Web content mining is a branch of web mining that aims to uncover knowledge in the unstructured data that is contained inside internet pages. This is similar to the data mining methodologies that are utilized for relational databases. The most frequent types of data that may be found in online documents include text, photos, audio, video, metadata, and hyperlinks. You can also find metadata.

The majority of the data are in the form of unstructured text, although some of them are semi-structured, such as HTML pages or data in tables, or more structured, such as HTML websites created by a database. There is a need for increased complexity in web content mining due to the inherently unstructured nature of web data. The Information Retrieval View and the Database View are the two views that differentiate online content mining from other methods. For the purpose of expressing the semi-structured material, each of the works makes use of HTML structures inside the pages, and some of the works also make use of hyperlink structures between the papers. When it comes to the database viewpoint, mining is constantly trying to infer the structure of a website in order to turn it into a database. This enables better information management and querying on the web. Mining is also known as "data mining." The process of extracting useful information and insights from vast online multimedia databases is referred to as content mining. Multimedia data mining is a subset of content mining [10].

21.4 Web Content Mining Methods

Web content mining has the following approaches to mine data: Unstructured text mining, structured mining, Semi-structured text mining and Multimedia mining.

21.4.1 Unstructured Text Data Mining

The majority of the data found on the web is in the form of unstructured text. To effectively mine material, two methodologies are required: data mining and text mining. Research in the field known as text data mining, text mining, or KDT (Knowledge Discovery in Texts) focuses on applying data mining techniques to unstructured text. Some of the techniques used in text mining are

- Information Extraction
- Topic Tracking
- Summarization
- Categorization
- Clustering
- Information Visualization

21.4.2 Structured Data Mining

The Structured Data on the Web represents their host pages. Structured data is easier to extract when compared to unstructured texts. The techniques used for mining structured data are:

Web Crawler

A web crawler, often known as a spider, spiderbot, or simply crawler, is a type of Internet bot that routinely scans the whole World Wide Web, usually with the purpose of indexing it (web spidering). To keep the indexes of other sites' material up-to-date, web search engines and other websites employ web crawling or spidering software. Web crawlers save sites for further processing by search engines, which then index the pages for better user search results. Crawlers frequently access websites without permission and use system resources when they do so. When accessing huge collections of pages, issues with schedules, loads, and politeness arise. If a public website does not want to be crawled, there are ways to let the crawling agent know. For instance, by using a robots.txt file, one may instruct bots to index either certain pages or the whole website. Because there are so many sites on the Internet, not even the biggest crawlers can get them all. This is why, prior to the year 2000, search engines had a hard time providing relevant results when users entered search terms on the World Wide Web. Relevant results are provided very immediately nowadays. Humans may validate HTML code and hyperlinks using crawlers. You may use them to scrape websites as well.

Wrapper Generation

One piece of encouraging news is that the vast majority of websites that rely heavily on data make use of dynamic generation. In other words, when a user makes a request, a server script software retrieves data from a database that is located on the back end of the system and then fills it into a certain HTML template. In most cases, the pages in question include a large number of instances of data objects that adhere to a particular alignment and format. This particular kind of template is described by the wrapper.

21.4.3 Semi-Structured Data Mining

Semi-structured data has emerged as a solution to enable the accurate representation of complex real-world entities without imposing unnecessary constraints on application developers. This evolution has moved away from rigidly ordered relational databases that primarily store strings and numbers. HTML is the only language that has such a distinctive intra-document structure. The techniques utilized in semi-structured data mining encompass

21.5 Efficient Algorithms for Web Data Extraction

A genetic algorithm might be used to automatically eliminate the information that is deemed to be bad from a number of different websites. In the event that any extraneous components have been eliminated, the data are subsequently transmitted to the trinity structure.

Trinity is a method for gathering content from the internet in a process that is automated. Due to this particular reason, having connection to the internet is essential. The three basic methods that it uses to sort the data that it has gotten from the web are the prefix, the separator, and the suffix. Furthermore, it computes the estimation problem that the system is experiencing. Immediately following the retrieval of the material from a website, the stemming process is utilized to do an automated cleaning of the material. A technique known as "Ant Colony Optimization" is utilized in order to extract the content that is relevant from the webpage. Ant colony optimization produces accurate results when it is done correctly. An absence of the NP-Completeness property may be observed in it. There is a beneficial framework for data that are provided by its application. The authors' methodology allows for the detection of additional online contents that have been retrieved.

During the process of partial alignment, only the fields in a collection of data records that are capable of being aligned or matched with absolute confidence are aligned. All of the other fields in the data set are disregarded by it. It searches the internet for records of data and then extracts data from those records. The data records are separated by means of visual information, which allows for the identification of each record that is contained on a page. Following that, it inserts the data into a table that is stored in the database. With this method, the data records are initially gathered from a web page in order to facilitate the alignment process. To extract data, only records of data that have been officially acknowledged are utilized. Because there are k trees involved in the process, the complexity of the approach is O (K2).

This method, which is based on Hadoop MapReduce, is employed for the purpose of integrating, extracting, and traversing web pages on a massive scale. The procedures of navigation, extraction, and integration that are involved in the process of obtaining data from the web are all carried out without interruption. The data record set is compiled from a significantly large number of online articles that are similar to one another through the use of a loop arrangement. Through the use of the Hadoop Map Reduce framework, the three phases of the extraction model as well as the rules for regulating the loop are parallelized. The strategy of "divide and conquer" should be utilized. The implementation of a rule holder that is referred to as a page model will result in each and every web page having its own individual set of rules for the extraction of data and the navigation of the internet. Creating the Mapper class is done with the intention of making the execution of parallel extraction easier. A specific search page will serve as the beginning point for its navigation, retrieval, and integration of results.

21.6 Machine Learning Based Web Content Extraction Methods

In their 2017 study, Qingtang Liu and colleagues proposed an automated method for extracting the core content of web pages. As a means of identifying the characteristics of web page attributes, this method makes use of text density and hyperlink density as markers and indicators. An estimating approach may detect whether a node is content or noise by using the attributes of the node and its neighbors. This is done in accordance with a continuous distribution of page content. Using this strategy, we are able to filter out navigation that is irrelevant as well as ad nodes. The results of an experiment conducted on ten different news websites showed that this algorithm was successful in achieving an acceptance rate of 96.34% on average [11].

According to Vijay and Prasadh's description, a framework was developed for the processing of deep web pages in multi-data regions. The framework makes use of an enhanced co-citation approach that extracts the visual information of deep web pages directly from the web database. This is done rather than developing a separate set of application programming interfaces (APIs) [7, 15–17] for the purpose of visual information extraction. Empirical experiments with a broad range of databases demonstrate that the suggested vision-based technique (VBEC) may give high accuracy, enabling efficient and accurate recall value of comparable queries with improved time consumption, and outperform other approaches. This is demonstrated by comparing the VBEC to alternative extraction procedures [12].

The authors Narendra *et al.* proposed a method for the aggregation of information that involves the extraction of certain portions of the contents of web pages. The process of extracting paragraphs from web pages [18–22] is a work in progress. For this aim, one should make use of a parsing system that is capable of deciphering HTML pages and URL files. Java queries are those that are used as our data extraction and manipulation tools. To accomplish the task of gathering fragmented content from a number of different websites, a recommendation was made. The jsoup library is required to extract paragraphs from an HTML text that is not currently being accessed online. During the process of obtaining web pages, the approach that has been presented takes into consideration the queries that users have entered, and then separates those pages into partial pieces for each individual user [13].

The two-stage Map-Reduce strategy to data warehouse optimization that is known as Chabok was created by Barkhordari and Niamanesh [14]. In this method, the intermediate results are transmitted to the Reducer once the aggregation process has been completed on the Mappers. Omission may be joined by Chabok without the need to replicate data. For the purpose of benchmarking, the solution that was described was implemented on Hadoop, and TPC-DS queries were executed. In terms of the amount of time it takes to execute queries, Chabok fared better than other prominent big data solutions for data warehousing.

Mythili and Vetriselvi [7] constructed a DOM tree for a web content and utilized a Genetic algorithm (GA) to calculate fitness values in order to identify the optimal number of clusters in a dataset. This was done to find the optimal quantity of clusters. We have broadened the scope of our study to incorporate the WCOLT technique for classification and the COATES algorithm for clustering. Both of these methods are founded on the content of the web as well as auxiliary components. Because of the incorporation of these techniques into web mining, noisy blocks are eliminated, which results in significantly improved outcomes for online data mining. To train a machine learning model, Wu *et al.* [15] generated many features by making use of the properties of the nodes that make up a DOM tree. Afterwards, the learning model is utilized to ascertain the nodes that are contenders for the position. To choose possible nodes that are lacking data, one needs to develop a clustering method. After that, noisy data should be filtered out based on the idea that true content is frequently located in a geographically continuous block. By doing exhaustive testing on an actual dataset, you can demonstrate that the solution generates high-quality results and outperforms a number of baseline methodologies.

Nguyen-Hoang *et al.* proposed the Genre-Oriented Content Extraction (GOCE) framework as a novel approach to the process of content extraction. The first stage is the categorization of online genres, and the second stage is the development of algorithms for content extraction based on the detected genre. To assess the genre of a website based on an image that is presented, GOCE begins by employing cutting-edge models that are derived from convolutional neural networks. Following that, the content extraction algorithm is utilized in conjunction with the genre information to enhance the process of textual content extraction. GOCE has been shown to function effectively in trials, as seen by the results of the end-to-end content extraction task and the online genre classification [16].

21.7 Conclusion

One kind of data mining is known as online content mining, and its primary objective is to identify relevant patterns within the information posted on websites. A web page may contain a number of different kinds of data, including text, photographs, audio, video, metadata, and links, among other sorts of data. There are some data that are extremely well organized and presented in tables created by the database as well as HTML pages. On the other hand, there are some data that are more semi-structured and displayed in Hyper Text Markup Language (HTML). The purpose of this study project is to provide a complete analysis of web data mining by analyzing web content mining, use statistics, and connections.

References

1. Mishra, A.K., Tyagi, A.K., Dananjayan, S., Rajavat, A., Rawat, H., Rawat, A., Revolutionizing Government Operations: The Impact of Artificial Intelligence in Public Administration, in: *Conversational Artificial Intelligence*, pp. 607–634, 2024.
2. Al-asadi, T.A. and Obaid, A.J., Discovering similar user navigation behavior in web log data. *Int. J. Appl. Eng. Res.*, 1, 16, 8797–8805, 2016.
3. Munshi, A. and Tanna, S., An Improved Approach to Find Frequent Web Access Patterns from Web Logs. *Int. J. Adv. Res. Innov. Ideas Educ.*, 2, 3, 1183–1190, 2016.

4. Chitraa, V. and Thanamani, A.S., Clustering of navigation patterns using Bolzwano_Weierstrass theorem. *Indian J. Sci. Technol.*, 8, 12, 1–9, 2015.
5. Garcin, F., Dimitrakakis, C., Faltings, B., Personalized news recommendation with context trees. *Proceedings of the 7th ACM Conference on Recommender Systems*, pp. 105–112, 2013.
6. Hussain, T., Asghar, S., Masood, N., Web usage mining: A survey on preprocessing of web log file. *2010 International Conference on Information and Emerging Technologies (ICIET)*, pp. 1–6, 2010.
7. Mythili, S. and Vetriselvi, T., Analytics of Noisy Data in Web Documents Using a Dom Tree. *Int. J. Adv. Res. Comput. Sci. Softw. Eng.*, 5, 4, 1473–1480, 2015.
8. Nadee, W. and Prutsachainimmit, K., Towards data extraction of dynamic content from JavaScript Web applications, in: *2018 International Conference on Information Networking (ICOIN)*, pp. 750–754, IEEE, 2018.
9. Nagappan, V.K. and Elango, P., Agent-based weighted page ranking algorithm for Web content information retrieval. *International Conference on Computing and Communications Technologies (ICCCT)*, pp. 31–36, IEEE, 2015.
10. Nesi, P., Pantaleo, G. *et al.*, A Distributed Framework for NLP-Based Keyword and Keyphrase Extraction from Web Pages and Documents, in: *Proc. of 21st Int. Conf. on Distributed Multimedia Systems (DMS2015)*, 2015.
11. Liu, Q., Shao, M. *et al.*, Main Content Extraction from Web Pages Based on Node Characteristics. *J. Comput. Sci. Eng.*, 11, 2, 39–48, 2017.
12. Vijay, R. and Prasadh, K., A Vision-Based Approach for Web Data Extraction Using Vision-Based Approach for Web Data Extraction Using Enhanced Cocitation Algorithm. *Int. J. Comput. Sci. Issues*, 10, 5, 2, 1694–0784, 2013, ISSN (Print): 1694-0814 | ISSN (Online).
13. Jathe, N.M., Nayana, K., Netware B., *et al*, Comparative Analysis of Various Methodology to Detect Paragraph from Web Document. *Int. J. Eng. Dev. Res.*, 5, 2, 1437–1440, 2017.
14. Barkhordari, M. and Niamanesh, M., Chabok: a Map-Reduce based method to solve data warehouse problems. *J. Big Data*, 5, 1, 40, 2018.
15. Rathore, N. and Rajavat, A., Smart Farming Based on IOT-Edge Computing: Applying Machine Learning Models For Disease And Irrigation Water Requirement Prediction In Potato Crop Using Containerized Microservices, in: *Precision Agriculture for Sustainability*, pp. 399–424, Apple Academic Press, USA, 2024.
16. Patsariya, M. and Rajavat, A., A Progressive Design of MANET Security Protocol for Reliable and Secure Communication. *Int. J. Intell. Syst. Appl. Eng.*, *12*, 9s, 190–204, 2024.
17. Rathi, M. and Rajavat, A., Investigations and Design of Privacy-Preserving Data Mining Technique for Secure Data Publishing. *Int. J. Intell. Syst. Appl. Eng.*, *11*, 9s, 351–367, 2023.

18. Dubey, P. and Rajavat, A., Effective K-means clustering algorithm for efficient data mining, in: *2023 2nd International Conference on Vision Towards Emerging Trends in Communication and Networking Technologies (ViTECoN)*, pp. 1–6, IEEE, May, 2023.
19. Chauhan, D., Singh, C., Rawat, R., Chouhan, M., Conversational AI Applications in Ed-Tech Industry: An Analysis of Its Impact and Potential in Education, in: *Conversational Artificial Intelligence*, pp. 411–433, 2024.
20. Chauhan, D., Singh, C., Rawat, R., Dhawan, M., Evaluating the Performance of Conversational AI Tools: A Comparative Analysis, in: *Conversational Artificial Intelligence*, pp. 385–409, 2024.
21. Wu, S., Liu, J. *et al.*, Automatic web content extraction by a combination of learning and grouping, in: *Proceedings of the 24th international conference on World Wide Web, International World Wide Web Conferences Steering Committee*, pp. 1264–1274, 2015.
22. Nguyen-Hoang, B.D., Pham-Hong, B.T. *et al.*, Genre-Oriented Web Content Extraction with Deep Convolutional Neural Networks and Statistical Methods, in: *Proceedings of the 32nd Pacific Asia Conference on Language, Information, and Computation*, 2018.

22

Intelligent Pattern Discovery Using Web Data Mining

Vidyapati Jha[1]*, Chinnem Rama Mohan[2], T. Sampath Kumar[3], Anandhi R.J.[4], Bhimasen Moharana[5] and P. Pavankumar[6]

[1]*Department of Computer Applications, NIT Raipur, Chhattisgarh, India*
[2]*Department of Computer Science and Engineering, Narayana Engineering College, Nellore, Andhra Pradesh, India*
[3]*School of CS & AI, SR University, Warangal, Vijay, Telangana, India*
[4]*Department of Information Science Engineering, New Horizon College of Engineering, Bangalore, India*
[5]*School of Computer Science and Engineering, Lovely Professional University, Punjab, India*
[6]*Vardhaman College of Engineering, Hyderabad, India*

Abstract

Finding trends in people's internet activity and subsequently customizing their experiences is the aim of web usage mining. In online usage mining, the functional information derived from the data was employed. It gathers information from web log records to comprehend how users interact with websites. There are several approachable research projects and helpful resources available for certain purposes. The soon-to-be-collected data can be used for customization, structure enhancement, website modification, and industrial intelligence and usage characterization. A technique known as "web usage mining" is used to collect information from real users about how they navigate websites. Web usage mining, also known as web log mining, aims to identify intriguing and frequently occurring user access patterns from web browsing data stored in web server logs, proxy server logs, or browser logs. Personalization, system improvements, corporate intelligence, advertising, and design enhancement are just a few of the numerous applications for web usage mining. The goal of this research is to find intelligent patterns in web usage mining.

**Corresponding author*: vjha.phd2021.mca@nitrr.ac.in

Rajesh Kumar Chakrawarti, Ranjana Sikarwar, Sanjaya Kumar Sarangi, Samson Arun Raj Albert Raj, Shweta Gupta, Krishnan Sakthidasan Sankaran and Romil Rawat (eds.) Natural Language Processing for Software Engineering, (311–322) © 2025 Scrivener Publishing LLC

Keywords: Pattern discovery, web usage mining, machine learning, graph base methods

22.1 Introduction

A branch of data mining called "web mining" focuses on how far the field has advanced in terms of retrieving valuable information from the internet. Web mining focuses mostly on techniques for extracting insightful information from data that is stored on the internet. Data mining, the science of analyzing data from several perspectives to find novel and fascinating patterns, trends, correlations, and patterns of useful knowledge, is applied to web data. This thesis describes the study of using publicly accessible benchmark data to find interesting online patterns, such as web page navigation sequences, through the application of graph traversal and data mining techniques. An overview of web mining techniques is given at the beginning of this chapter, followed by a description of the datasets used and their application to online page navigation sequences. The structure of the remainder of the thesis is outlined in the section that follows. Driven by the exponential rise in internet users, a large number of researchers are exploring the web domain in an attempt to find interesting and non-trivial patterns. By identifying useful and engaging patterns, they may enhance the online user experience and draw in new visitors while maintaining existing ones. The technique of finding important information connected to various online pages is known as web mining. Web mining mostly targets websites that provide electronic services. "E-services" refers to a broad category of online activities, such as banking, government, advertising, education, and shopping [1].

Discovering interesting patterns in the inter-document link structure is the aim of web structure mining. By classifying web pages based on the structure of their link structures, important details about the connections and commonalities among them can be inferred. It is possible to infer relationships that are synonymous, have similar content, are hosted on the same server, and have other similar affiliations. Web structure mining can also be used to learn the details of a domain's link hierarchy. This is helpful in mimicking the functionality of the databases that these websites employ.

Another aspect of online mining is web content mining. Its objective is to extract meaningful and non-trivial patterns from the text of online pages. A web page can host various kinds of data including text, images, audio, videos, metadata, and hyperlinks. A fraction of this data is more formally arranged in tables and HTML pages produced by databases, and the remainder is provided in a semi-structured HTML style. On the other hand, most of the content on the websites are disorganized. The immense challenges presented by the need to manage such different data sources, in addition to unstructured data, call for sophisticated and intricate approaches [2].

Web mining also includes the analysis of user behavior on the internet. Here, the primary focus is on data mining techniques to discover useful patterns from secondary data that are gathered from customers' online activity. As a user browses the internet, an audit trail that lists every website they have visited is maintained. Furthermore, a substantial amount of other system-related data is also retained. The web servers log every request a user makes for a web page, no matter where they come from.

22.2 Pattern Discovery from Web Server Logs

An analysis of the web server logs uncovers fascinating patterns and a plethora of valuable insights into the web pages and user behavior. Analysis and processing of log entries can reveal valuable insights into highly desirable web pages, captivating websites, categories of intriguing web pages accessed thereafter, communities of users sharing common interests, identification of both fraudulent and legitimate sessions, patterns in web traffic behavior, consumer preferences in purchasing, and numerous other findings. Uncovering these fascinating patterns helps improve the online environment by personalizing it, optimizing web caching, boosting systems, making site changes, and providing business intelligence, among other methods.

Personalization refers to the practice of customizing a user's online experience based on their previous internet activities. Web cache optimization involves implementing modifications to web caches to minimize user latency to the greatest extent possible. To enhance the system, it is necessary to study the patterns of web traffic to determine appropriate rules for network transmission. This, in turn, enhances the quality of service in terms of speed and other performance measures. Site modification refers to the process of redesigning websites based on feedback from users and insights gained from studies on user behavior on the web. Business intelligence aims to improve the online environment by focusing on the increasing number of e-marketing sales. The patterns in which people travel through online pages are highly valuable data that may be collected from web server logs and utilized in the indicated fields. The identification of each user's sessions is achieved by preprocessing the data obtained from the web server logs [3].

Using the user ID in combination with the timestamp allows for determining the order of sessions, at a minimum. The scenario dictates the pre-established length of a session. The user's subsequent page visits during that session can be determined by aggregating all of the page requests made by the user inside that one-hour time frame, assuming the time duration is set to that specific period of time. One can acquire extensive knowledge regarding user groups, both fraudulent and genuine sessions, web traffic patterns, consumer purchasing preferences, following web page visits, highly interconnected and loosely interconnected web pages, as well as trends within these navigation sequences, among other things [4].

22.2.1 Subsequently Accessed Interesting Page Categories

In the future, intriguing page categories that online users are interested in can be found by analyzing and processing web page navigation sequences. Knowing which web page categories are most often requested, which ones aren't, and which ones ought to be given priority while building a web cache is made easier with the use of this data. Web cache has a limited amount of storage; thus, it should be used wisely by storing the most interesting content first. The removal of these pages ought to be a secondary priority. On the other hand, the least crucial documents should be thrown first when you're cleaning up the storage [5].

22.2.2 Subsequent Probable Page of Visit

The subsequent probable page of visit pattern provides information about the next page that the visitor may view based on his previous browsing behavior. This pattern is useful in a variety of applications, including web page recommendation systems, pre-fetching of potential visit pages, configurable page design, and others.

22.2.3 Strongly and Weakly Linked Web Pages

Reorganizing the website to draw in more visitors can be aided by the information offered by pages with strong and weak links. Web pages that are heavily connected or frequently browsed can be easily reached with the help of quick links. Conversely, poorly linked web pages can be improved or eliminated to increase their popularity within the website.

22.2.4 User Groups

Online communities that are comprised of individuals who share a common interest are extremely important from a variety of perspectives. The concept of "similar interest" is also multi-faceted in its own right. According to the general rule, people who use the internet have a tendency to congregate together based on the interests that they have in common. One further method for categorizing website users according to their interests is to scrutinize the manner in which they browse around a website. If one user browses websites about recopies and cleaning the house, while another user browses websites about kitchen appliance maintenance and space management, then the user's interest in home arranging and maintenance might be said to be shared. It is possible to improve this customer's online experience by advertising products and services such as house cleaning supplies, storage organizers, and online food delivery services, among other things [6].

22.2.5 Fraudulent and Genuine Sessions

A person may tell if a session was started by a real user or a fake one by looking at their click streams and the order in which they navigated the web pages. By limiting the ability to continue, detecting this pattern can help prevent many fraudulent online activities.

22.2.6 Web Traffic Behavior

Among the numerous useful insights gleaned from studying web traffic patterns are the peak request times of day, the times of day with relatively few requests, the average amount of time users spend online, and much more. It is also necessary to frame policies based on traffic to preserve customer service quality due to the deluge of data transfer and the fast growth of video on demand services.

22.2.7 Purchase Preference of Customers

Aligning with customer interests to increase company profitability is the goal of the pattern linked with consumer purchasing preferences. This pattern's principal goal is to supplement the website's business intelligence with the purpose of improving its marketing strategies. Based on their browsing habits and previous purchases, customers can be shown a wide variety of relevant products. Our objective is to ensure client retention and satisfaction by providing exceptional service. The customer lifetime value, the effectiveness of promotional activities, cross-marketing strategies, policies on targeted offers and coupons, and many other important pieces of information can be derived from this pattern [7, 8].

To extract these patterns from the navigation sequences of web pages, efficient procedures are something that is required. Providing assistance to the community of online researchers would be an excellent example of social service, and methodological approaches that are based on data mining and graph traversal would be ideal for this circumstance. An overview of the numerous approaches that may be utilized to extract knowledge patterns from web server logs is shown in the next section.

22.3 Data Mining Techniques for Web Server Log Analysis

The extraction process requires a variety of techniques for each pattern to be successful. A summary of the core extraction approach is presented here in few sentences. The three primary aspects of web usage mining are data pre-processing, pattern discovery, and pattern analysis. There are three key components. The navigation sequences of web pages are subjected to pre-processing before being uploaded into data mining algorithms for the purpose of identifying patterns [9].

A number of studies have demonstrated that data mining techniques are employed with the purpose of uncovering useful information that is concealed within the data that is provided. Both supervised and unsupervised learning models are the two primary categories of data mining learning models.

Association rule mining and categorization are two examples of models that can be used for supervised learning. For the purpose of classification, models are formed by making use of training data, for which the class labels are already known. Using these models, we are able to make an educated guess as to the category of data whose label was previously unknown. Decision trees are among the most frequent choices for displaying the categorization rules that are used as a result of the classification process. Because of this, analysis and interpretation of the data that are provided are made easier [10].

There are three different kinds of nodes that can be found in a decision tree: root nodes, internal nodes, and leaf nodes. When a decision tree is constructed, the internal nodes are used to represent the characteristics.

The branches are used to display the possible values of these attributes, and the leaf nodes are used to indicate the ultimate option or classification label. Typically, the root node and its recursive subdivisions are the building blocks from which the complete tree is constructed in a tree structure. To construct the decision tree, the attribute values of the data provided are utilized. The first step in the process of creating a decision tree is to identify the particular characteristic that is readily apparent in distinguishing the various scenarios [11].

The information gain, gain ratio, gain index, and several other assessment metrics are utilized to ascertain which attribute would be capable of performing the most effective discriminating performance. In the process of constructing the tree, we make use of the attribute that has the greatest or lowest assessment metric, depending on the metric that we select. If all the data instances in a particular category have the same class value for the attribute that was chosen, then the branch is terminated, and the class that was obtained is applied to the leaf node. In situations when this does not work, we select an additional characteristic that corresponds to the assessment measure that is either the best or the worst. This is something that we continue to do until either we discover the ideal mix of traits for a certain class or we exhaust all the attributes that we have. When we are still unable to arrive at a choice that is unambiguous based on the information that we have, we assign the branch to the class that has the greatest number of instances under it.

It is not necessary for unsupervised data mining systems to have the ground truth of training data for them to learn information. Researchers state that clustering is one of the most widely used unsupervised approaches among the many strategies. A similarity measure is used to divide the data into groups, and the objective is to achieve a low intra-cluster distance while simultaneously achieving a high inter-cluster distance. Clustering algorithms handle the number of groups in a variety of different ways; some of them decide on it while the grouping process is taking place, while others receive it as an input and maintain it at a constant value [12].

Association rule mining is a technique that can be applied in either a supervised or unsupervised manner, depending on whether or not a particular purpose is present. Association rule mining is a technique that is used in data mining. This technique presents an opportunity to discover interesting associations between the attributes of a dataset. During the process of rule evolution, a metric of interest is utilized. To begin, the learning model will generate candidates. After that, it will prune to locate groups of objects that are encountered frequently. During the process of pruning, it is a common practice to use the minimum support that must be addressed as a guidance. If somebody wants to proceed with the process of developing association rules, the next step is to make sure that the frequent item sets meet the minimum confidence level. To generate candidates, it is necessary to create each and every conceivable combination of the components. The count and support of an object are computed to locate collections of objects that are frequently encountered. Following that, association rules are developed by making use of the frequent item sets that satisfy the minimum confidence requirement. In the following step, candidates of the next greater size are generated by using the combinations that were left out and that satisfy the interestingness criterion. In this instance, candidates are eliminated when their levels of support and confidence are insufficient. The procedure is restarted whenever there are no combinations that satisfy the interestingness metrics [13].

As a result, the association rules are constructed using antecedents and consequents as their fundamental components. The antecedents are the sections that are on the left side of the sentence, and the consequents are the elements that are on the right side of the sentence. By doing an analysis [10–13] of the antecedents and the consequents either separately or in conjunction with one another, it is feasible to arrive at intriguing findings. Jaccard similarity coefficient is a method for determining the degree to which the groups are comparable to one another. Estimating the degree to which different groups are similar is the principal application of this tool. To put it succinctly, it is an intersection over the matter of union process. Comparing the sizes of the two sets or groups that are being investigated and then dividing that number by the cardinality of the intersection is the method that is used to determine the degree of similarity. The Jaccard similarity coefficient between any two groups has to be as low as is practically possible, taking into consideration how dissimilar the groups ought to be from each other. Through the use of pattern analysis, one can have a better understanding of the outcomes of the data mining method of pattern identification, which in turn assists in the process of drawing conclusions.

22.4 Graph Theory Techniques for Analysis of Web Server Logs

Pattern analysis, pattern discovery, and data pre-processing are all components of graph theory approaches to web server log data analysis [14–17]. Graph theory also includes pattern analysis. The pre-processing in this context includes a number of different tasks, including the cleaning of data, the identification of users and sessions, the creation of navigation sequences for web sites, and the visualization [14, 15] of these tasks in graphs. Following that, methods that are founded on graph theory are utilized to discover patterns. Following that, the patterns that were obtained are analyzed to ascertain the degree of interest the patterns possess [18, 19].

Before anything else, the sequences of the web page are subjected to the standard preparation methods. Next, a similarity calculation is performed to determine whether or not it is possible to group pages that are similar to be together, whether or not it can assist with trimming, and so on. It is possible to use either a weighted or binary adjacency matrix to represent the patterns of internet access or the attributes that are obtained from them. Because of this, it is possible to create graphs that are either directed or undirected. Through the process of traversing this graph, users who share a great deal of commonalities are subsequently grouped together.

The process of traversing a graph involves going to each and every node in the graph (West 2001). Depending on the sequence in which people are visited, graph traversal algorithms are typically utilized in two different ways and are commonly used. Breadth First Search (BFS) and Depth First Search (DFS) are two examples of traversal algorithms. In the process of conducting a depth-first search, the child nodes are visited before the sibling nodes. To put it in another way, the depth of the graph is what is utilized for exploration, not the breadth of the graph. Stack is the data structure that is utilized to put this traversal strategy into action. However, while utilizing breadth, the sister nodes are explored first rather than the child nodes. This is because the child nodes are not traversed. A data structure known as a queue is utilized to make this traverse function properly. After beginning with a queue or stack that is empty and continuing until the graph contains no more nodes that have not been visited, user groups can be constructed by making use of the nodes that are already present in the graph. Following the collection of the user groups, we proceed to investigate each one in greater depth to discover fascinating insights.

22.5 Conclusion

Online use mining gathers information from online log records to better understand how users behave on websites. One can select from a variety of doable research assignments and helpful resources, depending on his/her requirements. The soon-to-be-acquired data can be used for customizing, structuring better, modifying websites, and obtaining intelligence and industrial usage insights. Researchers can gain additional insight into the "web usage mining" behaviors of real people by watching how they interact with the internet. The aim of web usage mining, also known as web log mining, is to look for intriguing and frequently occurring user access patterns by searching through web server logs, proxy server logs, or browser logs. Applications for web usage mining are numerous and include advertising, corporate intelligence, system improvements, customization, and design optimization. Our goal in this investigation is to identify astute patterns in online usage mining.

References

1. Vakali, A., Pokorny, J., Dalamagas, T., An Overview of Web Data Clustering Practices, 2013.
2. Ananthi, J., A Survey Web Content Mining Methods and Applications for Information Extraction from Online Shopping Sites. *Int. J. Comput. Sci. Inf. Technol.*, 2014.
3. Singh, S. and Kaur, S., Web Log File Data Clustering Using K-Means and Decision Tree. *Int. J. Adv. Res. Comput. Sci. Software Eng.*, August 2013.
4. Rana, H. and Patel, M., A Study of Web Log Analysis Using Clustering Techniques. *Int. J. Innov. Res. Comput. Commun. Eng.*, June 2013.
5. Mehtaa, P., Parekh, B., Modi, K., Solanki, P., Web Personalization Using Web Mining: Concept and Research Issue. *Int. J. Inf. Educ. Technol.*, October 2012.
6. Suguna, R. and Sharmila, D., clustering web-log files-A review. *Int. J. Eng. Res. Technol.*, April 2013.
7. Singh, S. and Badhe, V., An Exclusive Survey on Web Usage Mining For User Identification. *Int. J. Innov. Res. Comput. Commun. Eng.*, 2014.
8. Adhvaryu, R. and Vidyapith, G., A Review Paper on Web Usage Mining and Pattern Discovery. *J. Inf. Knowl. Res. Comput. Eng.*, Nov 12 to Oct 13.
9. Aldekhail, M., Application and Significance of Web Usage Mining in the 21st Century: A Literature Review. *Int. J. Comput. Theory Eng.*, February 2016.
10. Patel, R. and Kansara, A., Web Usage Mining- A survey on User's Navigation pattern from Web Logs. *Int. J. Sci. Res. Dev.*, 2014.
11. Chirgaiya, S. and Rajavat, A., Tiny object detection model based on competitive multi-layer neural network (TOD-CMLNN). *Intell. Syst. Appl.*, 18, September 2022, 200217, 2023.
12. Rathi, M. and Rajavat, A., *Analysing Cryptographic and Random Data Sanitization Techniques in Privacy Preserving Data Mining*, vol. 83, Allied Publishers, New Delhi, India, 2023.

13. Dhar, S., Dhar, U., Rajavat, A., Factors and Attributes of Team Players: A Study of Engineering Students in India, in: *International Simulation and Gaming Association Conference*, 2021, September, Springer International Publishing, Cham, pp. 53–60.
14. Nahar, S., Pithawa, D., Bhardwaj, V., Rawat, R., Rawat, A., Pachlasiya, K., Quantum Technology for Military Applications, in: *Quantum Computing in Cybersecurity*, pp. 313–334, 2023.
15. Pithawa, D., Nahar, S., Bhardwaj, V., Rawat, R., Dronawat, R., Rawat, A., Quantum Computing Technological Design Along with Its Dark Side, in: *Quantum Computing in Cybersecurity*, pp. 295–312, 2023.
16. Chauhan, D., Singh, C., Rawat, R., Chouhan, M., Conversational AI Applications in Ed-Tech Industry: An Analysis of Its Impact and Potential in Education, in: *Conversational Artificial Intelligence*, pp. 411–433, 2024.
17. Chauhan, D., Singh, C., Rawat, R., Dhawan, M., Evaluating the Performance of Conversational AI Tools: A Comparative Analysis, in: *Conversational Artificial Intelligence*, pp. 385–409, 2024.
18. Shrivastava, M., Patil, R., Bhardwaj, V., Rawat, R., Telang, S., Rawat, A., Quantum Computing and Security Aspects of Attention-Based Visual Question Answering with Long Short-Term Memory, in: *Quantum Computing in Cybersecurity*, pp. 395–412, 2023.
19. Rawat, R., Chakrawarti, R.K., Raj, A.S.A., Mani, G., Chidambarathanu, K., Bhardwaj, R., Association rule learning for threat analysis using traffic analysis and packet filtering approach. *Int. J. Inf. Technol.*, *15*, 6, 3245–3255, 2023.

23

A Review of Security Features in Prominent Cloud Service Providers

Abhishek Mishra[1]*, Abhishek Sharma[2], Rajat Bhardwaj[3], Romil Rawat[4], T.M.Thiyagu[5] and Hitesh Rawat[6]

[1]STA, SVIIT, SVVV Indore, Indore, Madhya Pradesh, India
[2]SVIIT, SVVV Indore, Indore, Madhya Pradesh, India
[3]Department of Computer Science and Engineering, ASET, Amity University, Bengaluru, KA, India
[4]Department of CSE, Shri Vaishnav Vidyapeeth Vishwavidyalaya, Indore, India
[5]Computer Science and Engineering, Vel Tech Rangarajan Dr. Sagunthala R&D Institute of Science and Technology, Avadi, Chennai, India
[6]Department of Business Management and Economics, University of Extremadura, Badajoz, Spain

Abstract

Today, cloud storage has become an important part of the computing model because it provides resources that are cost-effective, flexible, and less likely to fail. On the other hand, safeguarding issues in the broader adoption industry face serious challenges. The diversity of the cloud and the multitude of places where data is stored further exacerbate these problems. The main points discussed about protection are; availability, recognition, integrity, authenticity and confidentiality. Encouraging more customers to move to the cloud will allow service providers to deliver secure data. Electronic forensic software, encryption methods and intrusion detection mechanisms are some of the guarantees of a reliable service in recovering and collecting evidence of intrusion activities. This article outlines some of the issues, pitfalls, and solutions associated with cloud platforms. It also includes the use of major cloud service providers for data storage and protection.

***Keywords*:** Cloud security, AWS, GCS, oracle, alibaba, sales force, IBM

**Corresponding author*: Abhishekmishra559@gmail.com

Rajesh Kumar Chakrawarti, Ranjana Sikarwar, Sanjaya Kumar Sarangi, Samson Arun Raj Albert Raj, Shweta Gupta, Krishnan Sakthidasan Sankaran and Romil Rawat (eds.) Natural Language Processing for Software Engineering, (323–334) © 2025 Scrivener Publishing LLC

23.1 Introduction

The term cloud is derived from the diagram where the Internet is represented as a cloud symbol [1]. Cloud Computing (CC) is a network that optimizes resources and services at lower cost [2]. CC is a standard that enables unified, simple, on demand network access to a shared set of computing resources (such as networks, servers, storage, usage, and services) accessible to a minimum of Management and/or administrator. The National Institute of Standards and Technology (NIST) [3] states that cloud computing is a shift in technology that uses the internet. Virtual Data Center (VDC) is efficient and provides the hardware, software and data needed to create CC services. The goal of the CC concept is to enable users to get all the work done without having to purchase hardware or software. Organizations using CC eliminate infrastructure costs by paying for the resources they use. Tools for privacy, access control, monitoring, encryption, and other capabilities are available on Amazon Web Services (AWS). It is known for its openness and flexibility in its joint security role. Confidentiality, data integrity and hardware security are the three key areas that Google Cloud Provider (GCP) focuses on. Azure gives the same priority to security management for hybrid cloud deployments [4]. Some security vulnerabilities in cloud computing still remain a major problem in the cloud environment. CC is growing as more and more companies embrace the use of the cloud, but it also brings with it many security features. Many companies are reluctant to entrust sensitive data to the cloud due to the various risks involved. The use of virtual machines brings with it many problems in terms of security and privacy of cloud services. Sending information over the Internet is another problem. Multiple users can share cloud resources using multiple strategies. Creating a secure architecture is also under the influence of this concept. Cloud service providers refuse to include access control or security monitoring and protection measures due to obvious problems. To protect important data and users from external or internal threats and ensure availability, integrity and confidentiality, some cloud service providers offer secure operation. There are always some security issues with major cloud service providers as shown in Table 23.1: Attack Breaches on cloud providers.

23.2 Cloud Computing Overview

CCs can be divided into different groups, for example, by deployment and service. These classifica-tions help understand the differences and concepts of cloud computing. The main categories of service examples are as follows:

Table 23.1 Attack breaches on cloud providers.

Cloud service provider	Security breach	Year
AWS	Data from 1 billion users was exposed by a misconfigured S3 bucket.	2019
IBM	The user's financial information is shared by the cloud server without security.	2019
Salesforce	Phishing attempts to obtain customer information by using user cre-dentials.	2018
Alibaba Cloud (ABC)	Marketing Cloud misconfiguration allowed unauthorized access.	2019
GCP	Nicknamed "Gooligan" - Malware exploited vulnerabilities on Android devices to steal Google account credentials. Not a direct GCP breach, but exposed access to GCP resources if leveraged.	2016
Azure	Azure Cosmos DB misconfiguration accidentally exposed customer support data (2.5 million records).	2022

Infrastructure as a Service (Iaas): Provide users with the ability to install and run software, including operation and use, as well as operation, storage, networking and other important financial services. The operating system, storage, installed applications, and possibly limited control of certain network components are entirely under the customer's control.

Platform as a Service (PaaS): Give users options to purchase or upload home inventory live directly to the property using approved providers, programming languages, and tools. The applications used and the configuration of the application hosting environment will be under the control of the customer; However, the networks, servers, operating systems and storages that make up the cloud infrastructure are not controlled and managed.

Software as a Service (Saas): allows users to access and use applications created by cloud service Providers. Web browsers and other user interfaces allow users to access applications from a variety of devices, such as webbased email. Except for some specific users choosing the application configuration option, customers have no control over the network, servers, operating systems, storage, or even the functionality of an application in the cloud architecture. For cloud architecture solutions, deployment methods have been discovered and are explained below:

Public cloud: Cloud infrastructure is owned by a company that provides cloud services and is publicly traded or available to large business groups.
Private Cloud: Cloud infrastructure provides more control, privacy, and customization because it is devoted to a single company.
Hybrid Cloud: integration of public and private clouds, enabling the sharing of apps and data between them.
Community Cloud: shared by multiple groups with related issues
Multi Cloud: This includes improving resilience, avoiding vendor lock-in, and utilizing services across several cloud providers.

23.3 Cloud Computing Model

CC Framework. Based on their involvement, as depicted in Figure 23.1, there are five main players in CC [3]. One who uses services from a cloud provider and pays for them according to usage is known as a cloud consumer, or cloud service consumer (CSC). Cloud services are supplied to the CSC by a cloud provider, often known as a cloud service provider (CSP). An unbiased evaluation of the performance, security, and information system operations of cloud deployments is carried out by a cloud auditor. To facilitate commercial transactions, the cloud broker works as a liaison between CSP and CSC. It is the cloud carrier who connects CSP and CSC to the cloud and offers cloud services. The cloud can be called private cloud, public cloud, community cloud and hybrid cloud. Our delivery models IaaS, PaaS and SaaS are widely accepted and legal as shown in Figure 23.1 CC Actors.

A collection of technologies, guidelines, regulations, and practices known as cloud security are used to safeguard cloud-based infrastructure, data, and

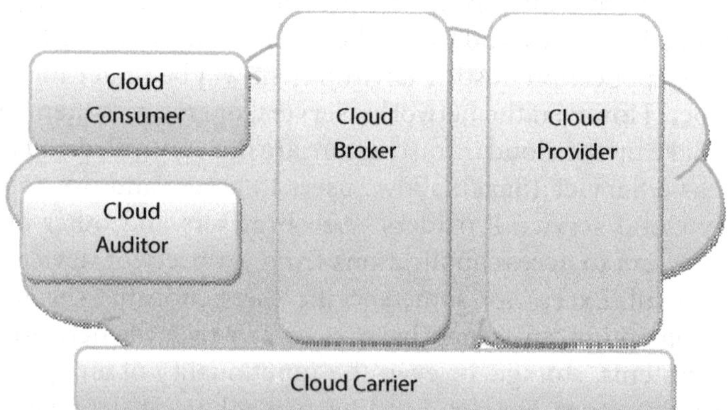

Figure 23.1 CC Actors.

Table 23.2 Features provided by service model.

Component	SaaS	PaaS	IaaS
Application Protection	CSP	CSC	CSC
Platform Protection	CSP	CSP	CSC
Services	CSP	CSC	CSP
Endpoint Protection	CSC	CSC	CSC
Data Protection	CSC	CSC	CSC
Network Protection	CSP	CSP	CSC
User Protection	CSC	CSC	CSC
Containers Workloads	CSC	CSC	CSC
APIs and Middleware	CSP	CSC	CSC
Code	CSC	CSC	CSC
Virtualization	CSP	CSP	CSC

systems. Ensuring the confidentiality, integrity, and availability of resources housed in the cloud requires a multi-layered approach. Both the consumer and the cloud service provider (CSP) share responsibility for cloud security, although their roles are different as shown in Table 23.2: Features provided by Service Model. The functions of CSP and CSC in the service delivery models are clearly defined in the Table 23.3- Various security issues in cloud.

23.4 Challenges with Cloud Security and Potential Solutions

Any system can experience security issues due to attacks, malfunctions, misconfigurations, vulnerabilities, or physical vulnerabilities. Many aspects of CC contribute to cloud security issues. An important aspect of computing today is cloud security, which deals with the protection of processes, data and applications in the cloud environment. While the cloud has many benefits, including cost-effectiveness, scalability, and flexibility, it also presents unique challenges and security issues that companies must address to protect their assets. Various issues in CC security and their solutions are listed in Table 23.3 below.

Table 23.3 Various security issues in cloud.

Cloud security problem	Description	Challenges	Mitigation strategies
Data Breaches and Loss of Data Control	Unauthorized access or leakage of sensitive data.	Lack of control over data storage and processing in the cloud, shared responsibility model.	Encrypt sensitive data, implement access controls, conduct regular audits, and educate users on security best practices.
Insecure Interfaces and APIs	Vulnerabilities in cloud service interfaces and APIs.	Lack of standardization, poor implementation, and inadequate security controls.	Update your API regularly, use secure coding practices, and use good authentication and authorization processes.
Inadequate Identity, Credential, and Access Management	Insufficient control over user identities, credentials, and access.	Weak authentication, compromised credentials, and improper access controls.	Implement robust identity and access management (IAM), enforce strong authentication, and regularly review and revoke unnecessary permissions.
Insecure Configuration of Cloud Services	Improperly configured cloud resources leading to vulnerabilities.	Complexity of cloud configurations, lack of expertise, and misconfigurations.	Regularly audit and monitor configurations, employ automation for security compliance, and follow security best practices for each cloud service.
Insider Threats	Security risks posed by employees, contractors, or business partners.	Malicious or unintentional actions by authorized users.	Implement least privilege access, conduct regular employee training, monitor user activities, and enforce strong insider threat detection measures.
Compliance and Legal Issues	Violation of regulatory requirements and legal obligations.	Varying regulatory landscapes, lack of transparency, and evolving compliance requirements.	Stay informed about regulatory requirements, conduct regular compliance assessments, and work with legal and compliance experts.

(Continued)

Table 23.3 Various security issues in cloud. (*Continued*)

Cloud security problem	Description	Challenges	Mitigation strategies
Data Loss Prevention (DLP)	Measures to prevent unauthorized access, sharing, or theft of sensitive data.	Ensuring data privacy and compliance, dealing with different data types, and preventing accidental data loss.	Use encryption, classify and label sensitive data, implement robust DLP solutions, and monitor data access and transfers.
Multi-tenancy Risks	Shared infrastructure and resources among multiple users or tenants.	Isolation concerns, resource contention, and potential for cross-tenant attacks.	Implement strong isolation mechanisms, conduct regular security assessments, and choose cloud providers with robust multi-tenancy security measures.
Denial of Service (DoS) and Distributed Denial of Service (DDoS)	Disruption of services by overwhelming resources.	High-profile targets, resource limitations, and evolving attack methods.	Implement DDoS mitigation solutions, use Content Delivery Networks (CDNs), and design scalable architectures with redundancy.
Lack of Transparency and Visibility	Limited insight into the security controls and processes implemented by the cloud provider.	Uncertainty about security practices, monitoring capabilities, and incident response procedures.	Choose cloud providers with transparent security practices, use third-party security tools, and conduct regular audits and assessments.

Table 23.4 Various Security measures used by major cloud providers.

Security aspect	AWS	Azure	GCP [8]	Alibaba cloud [7]	Sales force	IBM cloud
Identity and Access Management (IAM)	Robust IAM with fine-grained access control	Azure Active Directory for identity management	Cloud IAM for access control	Resource Access Management (RAM)	Salesforce Identity	IBM Cloud IAM
Network Security	Virtual Private Cloud (VPC), Network ACLs	Virtual Network (VNet), Network Security Groups (NSGs)	VPC, Firewall Rules	VPC, Security Groups	Salesforce Shield	VPC, Security Groups
Data Encryption	Encryption at rest and in transit	Azure Disk Encryption, SSL/TLS for data in transit	Encryption at rest and in transit	Data Encryption Service	Platform Encryption	Encryption at rest and in transit
Compliance and Certifications	ISO 27001, SOC 2, HIPAA, GDPR, etc.	ISO 27001, SOC 2, HIPAA, GDPR, etc.	ISO 27001, SOC 2, HIPAA, GDPR, etc.	ISO 27001, SOC 2, HIPAA, GDPR, etc.	ISO 27001, SOC 2, HIPAA, GDPR, etc.	ISO 27001, SOC 2, HIPAA, GDPR, etc.
Security Monitoring and Logging	AWS CloudWatch, AWS Config, AWS CloudTrail	Azure Monitor, Azure Security Center, Azure Log Analytics	Cloud Monitoring, Cloud Audit Logging	CloudMonitor, Log Service	Event Monitoring, Salesforce Shield	IBM Cloud Monitoring and IBM Cloud Activity Tracker
Distributed Denial of Service (DDoS) Protection	AWS Shield	Azure DDoS Protection	Cloud Armor	Anti-DDoS	Not specified	DDoS Protection
Incident Response	AWS Incident Response, AWS WAF	Azure Security Center	Google Cloud Security Command Center	Not specified	Incident Response	Not specified

(Continued)

Table 23.4 Various Security measures used by major cloud providers. *(Continued)*

Security aspect	AWS	Azure	GCP [8]	Alibaba cloud [7]	Sales force	IBM cloud
Container Security	AWS ECR, AWS Fargate, AWS App Mesh	Azure Kubernetes Service (AKS), Azure Container Registry (ACR)	Google Kubernetes Engine (GKE), Container Registry	Container Service, Security Center	Salesforce Functions, Heroku	IBM Cloud Kubernetes Service (IKS), Container Registry
Serverless Security	AWS Lambda, AWS Step Functions	Azure Functions, Azure Logic Apps	Cloud Functions, Cloud Run	Function Compute, Serverless Workflow	Salesforce Functions	IBM Cloud Functions, IBM Cloud Code Engine
Threat Detection and Prevention	Amazon Guard Duty	Azure Security Center	Cloud Security Scanner	Alibaba Cloud Threat Detection Service	Not specified	IBM Cloud Security Advisor

23.5 Comparative Analysis

The cloud security [9–13] includes threats, security issues and possible attack preventions [5]. The shift towards zero trust architecture is an important trend in cloud security, driven by the need for stronger access controls and more effective protection against advanced threats [6, 12–15]. The comparative analysis of several aspects provided by different service providers that completely satisfy customers' high demand for cloud services [16, 17] is displayed as below in Table 23.4: Various Security measures used by major cloud providers.

23.6 Conclusion

CC has advantages such as fast use, money saving, large storage capacity and easy access to the system anytime, anywhere. It strives to support users by providing a seamless and complete experience, regardless of resources. Cloud computing appears to be a very fast technology and global computing environment. The main issues regarding CC are data security and privacy. Businesses that are aware of security threats and attacks are rapidly using the cloud. This comparative analysis with the help of forums will help users understand and choose better services according to their needs and help them get better social decisions, scalability, implementation, connectivity, distribution and support. Since the CC is a very fast changing engine, many new features have been added. The framework needs to be improved by adding more features but for now the comparison is based on the features and technologies provided by the open source here.

References

1. Zissis, D. and Lekkas, D., Addressing Cloud Computing Security Issues. *Future Gener. Comput. Syst.*, 28, 3, 583–592, 2012.
2. Ali, M., Khan, S.U., Vasilakos, A.V., Security in cloud computing: Opportunities and challenges. *Inf. Sci.*, *305*, 357–383, 2015.
3. Hogan, M. and Sokol, A., NIST Cloud Computing Standards Roadmap Version 2. NIST Cloud Computing Standards Roadmap Working Group, NIST Special Publications 500-291, NIST, Gaithersburg, MD, pp. 1–113, 2013.

4. Guptha, A., Murali, H., Subbulakshmi, T., *Proceedings of the Fifth International Conference on Intelligent Computing and Control Systems (ICICCS 2021)*, 2021, ISBN: 978-0-7381-1327-2.
5. Mishra, A., Gupta, N., Gupta, B.B., Security Threats and Recent Countermeasures in Cloud Computing, in: *Modern Principles Practices and Algorithms for Cloud Security*, pp. 145–161, IGI Global, USA, 2020.
6. Olaoye, G. and Luz, A., Future trends and emerging technologies in cloud security, 2024.
7. Luqman, A., Mahesh, R., Chattopadhyay, A., Privacy and Security Implications of Cloud-Based AI Services: A Survey. arXiv preprint arXiv:2402.00896, 2024.
8. Manthiramoorthy, C. and Khan, K.M.S., Comparing several encrypted cloud storage platforms. *Int. J. Math. Stat. Comput. Sci.*, *2*, 44–62, 2024.
9. Chirgaiya, S. and Rajavat, A., Tiny object detection model based on competitive multi-layer neural network (TOD-CMLNN). *Intell. Syst. Appl.*, 18, September 2022, 200217, 2023.
10. Rathi, M. and Rajavat, A., *Analysing Cryptographic and Random Data Sanitization Techniques in Privacy Preserving Data Mining*, vol. 83, Allied Publishers, New Delhi, India, 2023.
11. Dhar, S., Dhar, U., Rajavat, A., Factors and Attributes of Team Players: A Study of Engineering Students in India, in: *International Simulation and Gaming Association Conference*, 2021, September, Springer International Publishing, Cham, pp. 53–60.
12. Nahar, S., Pithawa, D., Bhardwaj, V., Rawat, R., Rawat, A., Pachlasiya, K., Quantum Technology for Military Applications, in: *Quantum Computing in Cybersecurity*, pp. 313–334, 2023.
13. Pithawa, D., Nahar, S., Bhardwaj, V., Rawat, R., Dronawat, R., Rawat, A., Quantum Computing Technological Design Along with Its Dark Side, in: *Quantum Computing in Cybersecurity*, pp. 295–312, 2023.
14. Chauhan, D., Singh, C., Rawat, R., Chouhan, M., Conversational AI Applications in Ed-Tech Industry: An Analysis of Its Impact and Potential in Education, in: *Conversational Artificial Intelligence*, pp. 411–433, 2024.
15. Chauhan, D., Singh, C., Rawat, R., Dhawan, M., Evaluating the Performance of Conversational AI Tools: A Comparative Analysis, in: *Conversational Artificial Intelligence*, pp. 385–409, 2024.
16. Shrivastava, M., Patil, R., Bhardwaj, V., Rawat, R., Telang, S., Rawat, A., Quantum Computing and Security Aspects of Attention-Based Visual Question Answering with Long Short-Term Memory, in: *Quantum Computing in Cybersecurity*, pp. 395–412, 2023.
17. Rawat, R., Chakrawarti, R.K., Raj, A.S.A., Mani, G., Chidambarathanu, K., Bhardwaj, R., Association rule learning for threat analysis using traffic analysis and packet filtering approach. *Int. J. Inf. Technol.*, *15*, 6, 3245–3255, 2023.

24

Prioritization of Security Vulnerabilities under Cloud Infrastructure Using AHP

Abhishek Sharma[1]* and Umesh Kumar Singh[2]

[1]*Shri Vaishnav Vidyapeeth Vishwavidyalaya, Indore, India*
[2]*Institute of Computer Sciences, Vikram University, Ujjain, India*

Abstract

In an ideal world, cyber security and IT experts would aggressively find and patch every possible vulnerability, ensuring that their enterprises would be safe across all known attack vectors. Conventional vulnerability management solutions just aren't up to the task in this fast-paced world. Despite this, cybersecurity and IT professionals are always under pressure to keep the business secure from the avalanche of vulnerabilities. The CVSS system is used by most businesses to prioritize vulnerability control operations. It's a free, open-source methodology for determining the severity of vulnerabilities. CVSS, on the other hand, fails as a prioritizing metric because it lacks the specificity to discern between the highest levels of severity — how can anything be "critical" if everything is? The majority of businesses understand the importance of having a priority strategy. In the absence of any strategy, the organizations will be faced with an overwhelming volume of effort and will have to make near-random decisions on what to mitigate first. Hence, to mitigate all the vulnerabilities in the system is practically not feasible. So, there is a strong research scope for a framework or model which is capable of prioritizing the security vulnerability which will be further helpful for the mitigation. The objective here is to propose novel security attributes matrix which can be used as input for proposed method. A novel approach and model is introduced for prioritization of security vulnerabilities for Cloud computing environments using Analytical Hierarchical Process (AHP).

***Keywords*:** Cloud computing, vulnerabilities assessment, cloud security, prioritization, mitigation plan, Machine Learning Model (MLM), Artificial Intelligence (AI), Analytical Hierarchical Process (AHP)

**Corresponding author*: abhiujn9@gmail.com

Rajesh Kumar Chakrawarti, Ranjana Sikarwar, Sanjaya Kumar Sarangi, Samson Arun Raj Albert Raj, Shweta Gupta, Krishnan Sakthidasan Sankaran and Romil Rawat (eds.) Natural Language Processing for Software Engineering, (335–356) © 2025 Scrivener Publishing LLC

24.1 Introduction

The delivery of IT resources is becoming dominated by the business model known as "cloud computing," which is an evolution of information technology. With cloud computing, people and businesses may access managed, scalable IT resources like servers, storage, and apps on demand [1]. The majority of cloud users erroneously believe that cloud providers would handle "entirely" cloud security. That kind of complacency is flawed. Certain aspects of the cloud (referred to as "cloud security") are within the control of cloud providers, while other aspects (referred to as "cloud security") are the responsibility of cloud users. According to reports, Cloud Providers were not technically at fault in the great majority of data breaches; rather, the breaches were caused by security or access misconfigurations that Cloud Users had made. The [2], describes the shared responsibility matrix between Cloud Providers and various types of Cloud Users. By modelling the suggested SRM-based Cloud Computing security framework in their own or other cloud systems, cloud actors may assess security features and compliance. The author of [3] examined the worries and difficulties with the cloud computing architecture at several levels, such as application, network, host, and data. Maintaining the security of cloud computing is important, especially for the infrastructure. Several research works have been conducted in the cloud infrastructure security area; however, some gaps have not been completely addressed, while new challenges continue to arise. However, digital transformation has created new economic potential, it has also generated additional risk areas. The corporate cyber-attack surface now includes cloud infrastructures, mobile devices, DevOps, IoTs/IIoTs and key assets.

In [4], the author describes how to build an experimental setup using open-source cloud service provider. Open stack platform is one of them which has to be evaluated through the study. To investigate the security issues following open-source platforms are used for building a cloud based experimental setup, the list of OSS are as follows. It is required to set up some application over the cloud experimental setup like LMS, CRM, CMS, etc. The authors also describe how they used the cloud computing architecture to model and build an online learning solution. It focuses on how all stakeholders may be included in the teaching-learning process and how to build and implement a fully managed learning management system (LMS) using open-source on a cloud computing platform. There are numerous security and protection concerns as a result of the ongoing growth in the number of established Cloud Service Providers (CSPs).

In [5], the author discusses the security purposes and difficulties of Cyber Physical Systems, analyses the security risks and assaults on three layers of Cyber Physical Systems, and describes these issues. A wide range of security flaws, from network-level to application-level, can affect cloud technologies. Cloud service security outlines the many types of current cloud assaults as well as the successfully implemented measures to reduce the risks.

In [6], the author looks into some of the significant security problems and difficulties associated with the cloud computing environment. The reasons behind the vulnerabilities that are exceptional to the cloud are discussed, which helps with security risk analysis and identification. In the future, risk analysis and evaluation could be carried out using vulnerabilities to safeguard cloud data from hackers. The authors of [7] discuss the significant security threats and difficulties connected to cloud, which are existing in this study. Additionally, causes of cloud-specific vulnerabilities are discussed, which facilitates identification & evaluation of safety threats. Also provided is a taxonomy of protection-related dangers and challenges. Authors in [8] established that cloud environments, including virtualization and SOA, are to blame for various security flaws. Additionally, the author compares and investigates the main security problems and difficulties between in-house datacenter-based deployment and public cloud computing environments like AWS and GCP.

The authors' main goal in [9] is to create an experimental model to reduce characteristics, achieve the best accuracy on the test data set, and identify the best existing schemes used to the dataset. The behavior of different machine-learning algorithms is examined to show a danger factor related to cloud computing. By arbitrarily dividing the sub dataset into four different groups, the influence of the testing and training subsets of the information is described. The results of the experiment show that partitioning the dataset into 95% - 5% yields the highest yield of all the remaining partitions. They also show that the Decision Tree Classifier algorithm, which is used in cloud computing, performs better than randomizable filter classifier across all data sets.

To solve these problems, the author of [10] proposes an artificial intelligence-enabled access control mechanism (AI-ACM) including vehicle nodes and roadside units (RSUs). For V2I deployment, roadside units (RSUs), which are regularly fixed, are necessary to gather information on the current state of local traffic. As a result, to raise automotive environmental consciousness, V2I requires a wide coverage of RSUs.

A concerning 312% rise, or 20173 new Common Vulnerabilities and Exposures (CVEs), were published in 2021 compared to 6454 in 2016 [11]. 16,500 new CVEs were discovered in 2018. Patching every vulnerability is just not possible because the typical organization discovers 870 CVEs across 960 IT assets every single day (according to the report published in tenable). The problem set must be scaled down by organizations. The Common Vulnerability Scoring System (CVSS) is used by many businesses to rank what needs to be fixed. However, CVSS cannot significantly improve operational effectiveness on its own. Instead, companies must distinguish between vulnerabilities that pose hypothetical risks and those that actually pose risks, and then, they must order those vulnerabilities according to the level of risk they pose.

24.2 Related Work

According to Gartner (June 4–7, 2018), "Through 2021, reducing vulnerabilities will be the single most important enterprise effort to improve security." But vulnerability mitigation is more difficult than ever. In addition to traditional IT-managed assets, the cyberattack surface has grown to include cloud, DevOps, mobile, and web infrastructure, as well as newly linked hardware like IP-enabled operational technology and IoT devices. The issue of vulnerability overload is made worse by this increase in assets. To prioritize software vulnerabilities, the authors in [12] utilized a hybrid Fuzzy best-worst approach (FBWM) that took decision-makers' complexity and subjectivity into account. The author also discovered that the most serious vulnerabilities, Information Gain (IG), SQL Injection (SQLI), and Gain of Privileges, need to be fixed as soon as they are feasible. However, it is only applicable to software flaws like SQL injection, etc. In [13], the author's primary goal in developing the cost model is to determine the ideal discovery and patch release time so that the overall developer cost can be reduced while taking risk considerations into account. A high exploitability reported vulnerability in Google Chrome has been explored at the source level to demonstrate the suggested methodology.

In [14], the authors give a synopsis of robust ICS characteristics as well as an ICS cyber resilience evaluation tool. The methods for creating cyber resilience measures are shown in the end, along with an example of how to calculate pliability metrics using the Analytical Hierarchy Process (AHP). A multi-criteria decision support system may be built upon the resilience framework, which can also help technical experts identify areas of unmet research [30–34] need in the field of ICS resilience. In [15], the authors present a strategy for evaluating effectiveness metrics using two decision theory approaches. Analytical Hierarchy Process (AHP) and Analytical Network Process were the MCDM techniques chosen (ANP). Both models make use of numerical scales within an eigenvector-based prioritization technique [35–37].

A security risk assessment is carried out using both qualitative and quantitative methods. All the steps in the risk analysis process were given numerical values in the quantitative cybersecurity risk analysis that was published. To calculate the risk, the analysis is factored into the calculation. This kind of risk assessment is exceedingly intricate, costly, time-consuming, and uses a qualitative approach. The qualitative technique evaluates countermeasures by going through many scenarios for risk probability and threat levels. The qualitative evaluation technique incorporates the assessor's opinions and expertise. The risk is graded on a hierarchical scale, such as critical, high, medium, and low, rather than having numerical numbers in qualitative risk analysis. The focus in this study is on the application of qualitative and quantitative risk assessment approaches [16]. The analytic hierarchy process is also described in [17] as a solution to the problem of accounting information system risk assessment. AHP can, for example, determine the relevance of each option and rank them in order of priority. This is accomplished by placing an overall item on the top level, which is designated by the criteria in the intermediate level. The author suggests an accounting information systems risk assessment algorithm using an analytical hierarchy method. This paper's index is divided into two tiers. Technical risk, operational risk, managerial risk, and emergency risk are the four first-level risk categories.

In [18], the authors used a vulnerability's description to determine priority instead of assigning software flaws a severity level. Convolution neural networks and word embedding are used in this study (CNN). To enable it to recognize distinguishing words and characteristics for the classification job, the CNN is qualified through adequate samples of vulnerability categories across all categories. The authors of [19] propose a technique that predicts the features of software vulnerabilities and then uses those predictions to determine vulnerability severity scores. A dataset of 99,091 records from a sizable, publicly accessible vulnerability database was used to carry out this assignment. In this approach, text analysis and multiple-target classification methods are combined.

Modern enabling methodologies and various computational resources utilized for partitioning and offloading are presented by the authors [20]. Also, they look into applicable paradigms and mobile cloud computing from the standpoint of partitioning and offloading enabling technologies.

After that, they examine a few well-known offloading frameworks and provide a taxonomy for these partitioning and offloading strategies. In hierarchical wireless sensor networks, the authors [21] suggested a brand-new password-based user authentication system, comparing the security and effectiveness of our proposed technique to those of other password-based methods now in use. The authors [22] create LAM-CIoT, a brand-new, lightweight authentication technique for cloud-based IoT environments. An authorized user can remotely view the data from IoT sensors by utilizing LAM-CIoT. LAM-CIoT uses effective "bitwise XOR operations" and "one-way cryptographic hash algorithms. The authors [23] show that the attacker may compute previously established session keys and that the usage of a constant pseudo-identity allows the scheme's user to be traced. Moreover, it presents a unique authentication mechanism for multi-gateway based WSNs rather than attempting to improve a flawed scheme.

Actually, the goal of the Analytic Hierarchy Process (AHP) is to address unstructured issues in management, social sciences, and economics [24]. By using the Analytic Hierarchy procedure (AHP) technique, the decision maker may organize the problem and deconstruct it into a top-down, hierarchical procedure. After that, he or she uses a [25] scale to do a pairwise matrix comparison of the criteria. Eigen vectors or a condensed form with weighted sum (SAW) are used to determine the priorities after normalization.

In contrast, the Evolutionary Optimization Algorithm for Cloud Based Image Retrieval System (EOA-CIRS) approach is introduced by the authors in [26]. During the exhaustive literature review and study of previous related work, it was observed that the prioritization was performed for various data like software vulnerability, accounting information etc. But the ranking of security risk issues and network specific vulnerabilities for Cloud Computing environment is still left. So, there is a need to develop an integrated and dynamic prioritization model which include Cloud Customer interaction, opinions, and reviews. The authors [27, 30] suggested a brand-new user authentication and key management approach. A user and personal server linked to WBAN via the healthcare server housed in the cloud are able to establish a secret session key for their future communication; thanks to the suggested scheme's support for mutual authentication.

Comparing the suggested technique by the authors [21, 28, 29] to other password-based approaches in use, it delivers more security and efficiency. Also, the technique has the advantage of changing the user's password locally and dynamically without the assistance of the base station or gateway node.

24.3 Proposed Method

The Analytical Hierarchy Process is a Multi-Criteria Decision Making (MCDM) process that aggregates criteria specified by the cloud customer using similar and numerical data through the use of normalizing procedures. To arrive at the final ratings or scores for prioritizing Cloud environment vulnerabilities, AHP uses a pairwise technique to evaluate the options in light of a set of criteria. Prioritizing a collection of vulnerabilities that best meet a specified set of requirements in accordance with the needs of cloud consumers is the goal of AHP approaches. A set of standards or independent qualities known as criteria must be met by a number of options that have been accepted via discussion and communication with cloud consumers.

It is necessary to do a security risk assessment that considers to the implementation of academic applications for eLearning universities that are cloud and CC based. IT professionals create specific business processes using the SPI model to fulfil business demands. The ICS-E-Educational deployed University cloud was tested in real time using the suggested technique on 3 distinct platforms: GCP, AWS, and the deployed University's Cloud developed for this work, to identify its weaknesses [8]. 18325 vulnerabilities were found in 2020, and 8350 were found up to the first week of June in 2021. In addition to those, NIST-NVD has currently disclosed more than 34700 vulnerabilities that are unique to the cloud. Among the top CSPs that have revealed their vulnerabilities are GCP-6034, AWS-112&IBM-5142.

Here, the proposed approach is the Analytical Hierarchical Process Model (AHP). In this approach a model is developed based on the priority matrix, which is generated through the Cloud Customer interaction, opinions and reviews. The pairwise matrix comparison of the criteria is performed iteratively using an AHP algorithm. Then on the basis of results of AHP, a new priority matrix is generated which helps the Cloud Security Administrator to analyze and prepare mitigation plans.

Before the implementation of the proposed approach, the authors considered the system having n no. of vulnerabilities as represented by a vulnerability vector $[V_1, V_2, V_3 \ldots\ldots V_n]$. These vulnerabilities were taken as input called Alternatives for the proposed algorithm. There are eight Primary Security Criteria based on CVSS are $[C_1, C_2 \ldots C_8]$ and five Proposed Security Criteria based on threat intelligence as $[C_9, C_{10} \ldots C_{13}]$. The details of these criteria are represented in following Table 24.1:

Table 24.1 Primary & proposed security criteria.

Primary security criteria (PSC)	Proposed security criteria (PRSC)
AV: Attack vector	ACC: Number of assets compromised/ critical at all layers.
CA: Complexity of Attack	ATI: Attack Incidents which includes Past threat Patterns, Past threat sources, etc.
RP: Required Privileges	PFD: Patch fixation duration.
UI: User Interaction	DoD: How old/duration of discovery.
SC: Scope	FAI: Frequency of attack incidents.
C: Confidentiality Impact	
I: Integrity impact	
A: Availability Impact	

The vulnerability vector and Primary & Proposed Security Criteria are taken as inputs to the proposed approach based on AHP algorithm. The steps of proposed approach & implementation are as follows:

Step 1: Developing a hierarchical structure with an objective/goal at the top level, the attributes or criteria at the second level and the alternatives at the third Level.

Here, the objective is prioritization of vulnerability which is at the top level of proposed hierarchical structure. The Primary security criteria and Proposed Security Criteria are taken together to develop a single criteria vector as [C1....C13], and placed at second level. The vulnerabilities are represented as alternatives at the third level. The proposed hierarchical structure is represented in the Figure 24.1 as follows:

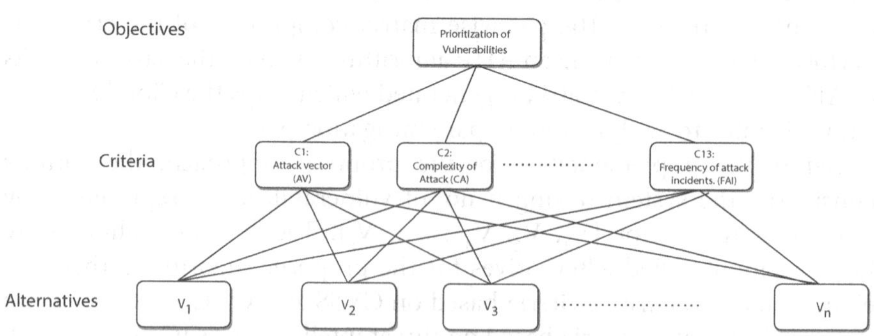

Figure 24.1 Hierarchical structure of proposed approach based on AHP.

Each vulnerability has its own value of all the 13 criteria, and the objective is to prioritize the vulnerabilities represented in the form of vulnerability matrix based on the criteria matrix represented as C1, C2....C13.

Step 2: Determine the relative importance of different attributes or criteria with respect to the goal or objective through creation of a pairwise comparison matrix.

The pairwise comparison matrix represents the relative importance of various attributes or criteria with respect to the objective. One by one criteria pairs are taken and compared based on the relative scale represented in Table 24.2 as follows:

Table 24.2 Scale of relative importance.

1	Equal importance
3	moderate importance
5	strong importance
7	very strong importance
9	extreme importance
2,4,6,8	intermediate values

The pairwise comparison matrix is of size 13x13, which include all 13 criteria and their relative importance. For example, C_1 - C_2 is n12, it means n12 is their relative importance and C_2 - C_1 will be its reciprocal, that is, 1/n12. Similarly, all the values of relative importance can be filled as shown in Table 24.3:

Table 24.3 Pairwise comparison matrix for security criteria.

Criteria	C_1	C_2	C_3	C_4	C_5	C_6	C_7	C_8	C_9	C_{10}	C_{11}	C_{12}	C_{13}
C_1	1	n_{12}	n_{13}	n_{14}	n_{15}	n_{16}	n_{17}	n_{18}	n_{19}	n_{110}	n_{111}	n_{112}	n_{113}
C_2	$1/n_{12}$	1	n_{23}	n_{24}	n_{25}	n_{26}	n_{27}	n_{28}	n_{29}	n_{210}	n_{211}	n_{212}	n_{213}
C_3	$1/n_{13}$	$1/n_{23}$	1	n_{34}	n_{35}	n_{36}	n_{37}	n_{38}	n_{39}	n_{310}	n_{311}	n_{312}	n_{313}
C_4	$1/n_{14}$	$1/n_{24}$	$1/n_{34}$	1	n_{45}	n_{46}	n_{47}	n_{48}	n_{49}	n_{410}	n_{411}	n_{412}	n_{413}
C_5	$1/n_{15}$	$1/n_{25}$	$1/n_{35}$	$1/n_{45}$	1	n_{56}	n_{57}	n_{58}	n_{59}	n_{510}	n_{511}	n_{512}	n_{513}
C_6	$1/n_{16}$	$1/n_{26}$	$1/n_{36}$	$1/n_{46}$	$1/n_{56}$	1	n_{67}	n_{68}	n_{69}	n_{610}	n_{611}	n_{612}	n_{613}
C_7	$1/n_{17}$	$1/n_{27}$	$1/n_{37}$	$1/n_{47}$	$1/n_{57}$	$1/n_{67}$	1	n_{78}	n_{79}	n_{710}	n_{711}	n_{712}	n_{713}
C_8	$1/n_{18}$	$1/n_{28}$	$1/n_{38}$	$1/n_{48}$	$1/n_{58}$	$1/n_{68}$	$1/n_{78}$	1	n_{89}	n_{810}	n_{811}	n_{812}	n_{813}
C_9	$1/n_{19}$	$1/n_{29}$	$1/n_{39}$	$1/n_{49}$	$1/n_{59}$	$1/n_{69}$	$1/n_{79}$	$1/n_{89}$	1	n_{910}	n_{911}	n_{912}	n_{913}
C_{10}	$1/n_{110}$	$1/n_{210}$	$1/n_{310}$	$1/n_{410}$	$1/n_{510}$	$1/n_{610}$	$1/n_{710}$	$1/n_{810}$	$1/n_{910}$	1	n_{1011}	n_{1012}	n_{1013}
C_{11}	$1/n_{111}$	$1/n_{211}$	$1/n_{311}$	$1/n_{411}$	$1/n_{511}$	$1/n_{611}$	$1/n_{711}$	$1/n_{811}$	$1/n_{911}$	$1/n_{1011}$	1	n_{1112}	n_{1113}
C_{12}	$1/n_{112}$	$1/n_{212}$	$1/n_{312}$	$1/n_{412}$	$1/n_{512}$	$1/n_{612}$	$1/n_{712}$	$1/n_{812}$	$1/n_{912}$	$1/n_{1012}$	$1/n_{1112}$	1	n_{1213}
C_{13}	$1/n_{113}$	$1/n_{213}$	$1/n_{313}$	$1/n_{413}$	$1/n_{513}$	$1/n_{613}$	$1/n_{713}$	$1/n_{813}$	$1/n_{913}$	$1/n_{1013}$	$1/n_{1113}$	$1/n_{1213}$	1

Step 3: Calculate the Sum of column of attribute in pairwise comparison matrix.

Let C_{ij} representing the value of ith row and j^{th} column then the sum of column attribute can be calculated iteratively for each column by using following formula:

$$\text{for } i=1 \text{ to } 13 \quad \{\, \text{Sum}[i] = 1 + \Sigma_{j=1}^{13}\, Cji \,\} \tag{24.1}$$

Step 4: Normalized pairwise matrix is calculated.

To calculate the normalized pairwise matrix, each value of the matrix will be divided by its respective sum of attributes. It can be given as:

$$\begin{gathered} \text{for } i=1 \text{ to } 13 \\ \text{for } j=1 \text{ to } 13 \\ \{\, C_{ij} = C_{ij} / \text{Sum}[i] \,\} \end{gathered} \tag{24.2}$$

Step 5: Calculate the criteria weight by averaging the row values in pair-wise comparison matrix.

Updated value of matrix row elements which are evaluated through equation no. (24.2) are considered for evaluation of average criteria weight. It can be evaluated for each row by:

$$\text{for i=1 to 13} \quad \{ CW[i] = \Sigma_{j=1}^{13} Cij \} \tag{24.3}$$

Step 6: Calculate the consistency matrix, again calculate the weighted sum value by summation of each criterion now ratio of weighted sum value with criteria weight. Now calculate λ_{max} through average of this ratio.

Now, to verify the relative importance considered in the step 2 for generation of pairwise comparison matrix, it is required to calculate the consistency matrix, weighted sum and λ_{max} using following formula:

a) Consistency matrix = $CW[i] * C_{ij}$ (24.4)
b) weighted sum of each row $= CW[i] = \Sigma_{j=1}^{13} Cij$ (24.5)
c) for each row Calculate Ratio, R[i] = weighted sum Sum [i]/ criteria weight CW[i]
d) λ_{max} = average of R[i]
e) Consistency Index (CI) = λ_{max} - n/n-1
f) Consistency Ratio = CI/Random Index (RI)

Where, Random index (RI) is the standard index and as per the following Table 24.4, it is 1.56 for 13 criteria:

Table 24.4 Random index (RI).

n	1	2	3	4	5	6	7	8	9	10	11	12	13	14	15
RI	0.00	0.00	0.58	0.9	0.12	0.24	1.32	1.41	1.45	1.49	1.51	1.48	1.56	1.57	1.58

Now, check Consistency Ratio with the maximum permissible inconsistency (value = 0.1). If it is under or equal to 0.1, it means the priority matrix is reasonably consistent. Hence, the criteria weights which are generated in step 5 are utilized for prioritization of vulnerabilities. The criteria weight CW[i] will be converted into the weighted percentage and then will be multiplied by the respective value of the criteria of vulnerability for ranking. The final outcome of this approach will be a Priority matrix which will further help the system and security administrator for preparation of mitigation plan.

24.4 Result and Discussion

The following security criteria are taken as input for the proposed AHP as given in Table 24.5: Security Criteria for AHP and in Table 24.6: Pairwise comparison matrix for Security criteria:

Table 24.5 Security criteria for AHP.

id	Security criteria
C_1	AV: Attack vector
C_2	CA: Complexity-of-Attack
C_3	RP: Required-Privileges
C_4	UI: User-Interaction
C_5	SC: Scope
C_6	C: Confidentiality-Impact
C_7	I: Integrity-impact
C_8	A: Availability-Impact
C_9	ACC: Number of assets compromised/critical at all layers.
C_{10}	ATI: Attack Incidents which includes Past threat Patterns, Past threat sources, etc.
C_{11}	PFD: Patch fixation duration.
C_{12}	DoD: How old/duration of discovery.
C_{13}	FAI: Frequency of attack incidents.

Now, as per step 2 and Table no. 24.3, the pairwise comparison matrix will be:

After implementation of step 3 & 4, normalized pairwise comparison matrix will be generated as represented in Table 24.7:

Calculating the criteria weights and percentage according to step 5, the weighted priority matrix will be generated as shown in Table 24.8:

Table 24.6 Pairwise comparison matrix for security criteria.

Criteria	AV	CA	RP	UI	SC	C	I	A	ACC	ATI	PFD	DoD	FAI
AV	1.00	3.00	7.00	3.00	3.00	0.33	0.20	0.20	0.20	0.20	0.14	0.14	0.33
CA	0.33	1.00	7.00	5.00	3.00	0.33	0.20	0.20	0.33	0.20	0.14	0.14	0.14
RP	0.14	0.14	1.00	3.00	3.00	0.33	0.20	0.33	0.20	0.20	0.14	0.14	0.14
UI	0.33	0.20	0.33	1.00	5.00	0.33	0.33	0.33	0.33	0.33	0.14	0.14	0.14
SC	0.33	0.33	0.33	0.20	1.00	0.33	3.00	3.00	0.20	0.33	0.14	0.14	0.14
C	3.00	3.00	3.00	3.00	3.00	1.00	3.00	3.00	3.00	3.00	3.00	3.00	3.00
I	5.00	5.00	5.00	3.00	0.33	0.33	1.00	3.00	3.00	3.00	3.00	3.00	3.00
A	5.00	5.00	3.00	3.00	0.33	0.33	0.33	1.00	3.00	0.20	0.20	0.20	0.20
ACC	5.00	3.00	5.00	3.00	5.00	0.33	0.33	0.33	1.00	0.11	0.14	0.14	0.20
ATI	5.00	5.00	5.00	3.00	3.00	0.33	0.33	5.00	9.00	1.00	0.33	0.33	0.20
PFD	7.00	7.00	7.00	7.00	7.00	0.33	0.33	5.00	7.00	3.00	1.00	3.00	0.33
DoD	7.00	7.00	7.00	7.00	7.00	0.33	0.33	5.00	7.00	3.00	0.33	1.00	0.33
FAI	3.00	7.00	7.00	7.00	7.00	0.33	0.33	5.00	5.00	5.00	3.00	3.00	1.00

Table 24.7 Normalized pairwise comparison matrix.

Criteria	AV	CA	RP	UI	SC	C	I	A	ACC	ATI	PFD	DoD	FAI
AV	0.023	0.047	0.048	0.051	0.050	0.082	0.023	0.008	0.008	0.011	0.022	0.013	0.021
CA	0.012	0.024	0.071	0.051	0.050	0.055	0.029	0.011	0.013	0.011	0.018	0.013	0.021
RP	0.012	0.008	0.024	0.051	0.050	0.082	0.023	0.014	0.008	0.011	0.027	0.019	0.021
UI	0.012	0.012	0.012	0.025	0.075	0.055	0.039	0.014	0.013	0.019	0.022	0.019	0.018
SC	0.012	0.012	0.012	0.008	0.025	0.041	0.231	0.085	0.008	0.019	0.022	0.019	0.018
C	0.047	0.071	0.048	0.076	0.100	0.164	0.231	0.085	0.076	0.170	0.217	0.189	0.373
I	0.116	0.094	0.119	0.076	0.013	0.082	0.116	0.085	0.114	0.170	0.217	0.189	0.248
A	0.116	0.094	0.071	0.076	0.013	0.082	0.058	0.042	0.076	0.014	0.022	0.019	0.025
ACC	0.116	0.071	0.119	0.076	0.125	0.082	0.039	0.021	0.038	0.006	0.018	0.016	0.025
ATI	0.116	0.118	0.119	0.076	0.075	0.055	0.039	0.127	0.190	0.057	0.036	0.031	0.025
PFD	0.116	0.142	0.095	0.127	0.125	0.082	0.058	0.169	0.152	0.170	0.108	0.189	0.041
DoD	0.163	0.165	0.119	0.127	0.125	0.082	0.058	0.169	0.190	0.170	0.054	0.094	0.041
FAI	0.140	0.142	0.143	0.178	0.175	0.055	0.058	0.169	0.114	0.170	0.217	0.189	0.124

Table 24.8 Weighted priority matrix for security criteria.

Criteria	AV	CA	RP	UI	SC	C	I	A	ACC	ATI	PFD	DoD	FAI
%	3.14	2.91	2.69	2.56	3.93	14.20	12.61	5.45	5.79	8.19	12.12	11.99	14.41

According to step 6, λ_{max} is calculated for each criterion and with the help of which consistency matrix, consistency index and consistency ratio are also calculated. The value of consistency ratio is 0.1 which is found to be a satisfactory value when compared with the maximum permissible inconsistency value (0.1).

Now, using priority Matrix for security criteria represented in Table 24.8 the priority of the vulnerability represented in Table 24.1 is regenerated. The results are represented in Figure 24.2, shows that

The results of proposed method-1 used for prioritization of vulnerabilities shows that the percentage of critical level is 7.6% and high level is 11.08% for cloud network vulnerability, which was 77% and 2% in previous case. Similarly, the percentage of critical level is 9.41% and high level is 15.13% in case of cloud server vulnerabilities, which was 74% and 6% in previous case. So, after analyzing the result of proposed Method-1 it can be concluded that the percentage of critical level vulnerabilities are reduced up to the acceptable level so that the network and security administrator can successfully design a plan and policy for their mitigation. The following table represents the results in Table 24.9: Comparison of results of Proposed and previous method:

Table 24.9 shows that the percentage of cloud network vulnerabilities was 77% previously and it reduced to 7.64%. Similarly, critical cloud server

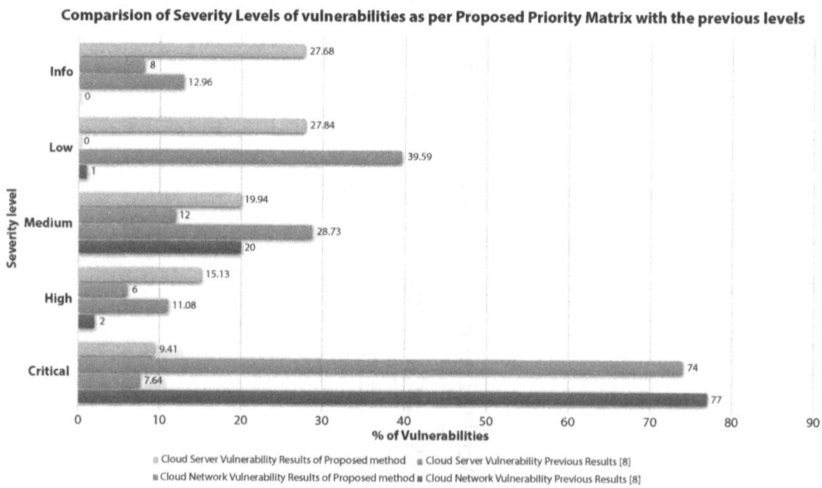

Figure 24.2 Comparison of severity level of vulnerabilities according to the proposed priority matrix with the previous level.

Table 24.9 Comparison of results of proposed and previous method.

Method / Severity		**Critical**	**High**	**Medium**	**Low**	**Info**
Cloud Network Vulnerability	Previous Results [8]	77 %	2 %	20 %	1 %	0 %
	Results of Proposed method	7.64 %	11.08 %	28.73 %	39.59 %	12.96 %
Cloud Server Vulnerability	Previous Results [8]	74 %	6 %	12 %	0 %	8 %
	Results of Proposed method	9.41 %	15.13 %	19.94 %	27.84 %	27.68 %

vulnerabilities was 74% previously and was reduced to 15.13%. Hence, it helps the Cloud security administrator to decide which vulnerabilities are required to mitigate first and also assist them to develop mitigation plan accordingly.

24.5 Conclusion

It is practically not feasible to resolve every system vulnerability. Therefore, a unique approach and model are proposed for combining AI and machine learning to prioritize security vulnerabilities for Cloud computing environment to achieve the goal. In this work, risk vectors are enhanced by adding more risk variables, and then AI and machine learning techniques are implemented. Five novel characteristics are identified in this research work, and they are combined with the CVSS score to create an enhanced and annotated risk vector. A new risk matrix is then created utilizing this enhanced and updated risk vector system, which will be used as input for both of the suggested options. This work employed the Analytical Hierarchical Process Model (AHP). In this method, a model is created based on the priority matrix that is produced by cloud customer interaction, feedback, and reviews. The AHP technique is used iteratively to compare the criteria in a pairwise matrix. A new priority matrix is then created based on the AHP results, which further will be helpful to the Cloud Security Administrator in the analysis and mitigation plan preparation.

References

1. Sunyaev, A., Cloud Computing, in: *Internet Computing*, Springer, Cham, 2020, https://doi.org/10.1007/978-3-030-34957-8_7.
2. Singh, U.K. and Sharma, A., Cloud computing security framework based on shared responsibility models, in: *Cyber-physical, IoT and autonomous systems in industry 4.0*, 1st ed, V. Bali (Ed.), pp. 39–55, CRC Press Taylor & Francis Group, USA, 2021, https://doi.org/10.1201/9781003146711-3.
3. Alghofaili, Y., Albattah, A., Alrajeh, N., Rassam, M.A., Al-rimy, B.A.S., Secure Cloud Infrastructure: A Survey on Issues, Current Solutions, and Open Challenges. *Appl. Sci.*, 11, 9005, 2021, https://doi.org/10.3390/ app11199005.
4. Sharma, A. and Singh, U.K., Deployment model of e-educational cloud for departmental academic automation using open source. *HTL J.*, 27, 5, 36, 2021, ISSN 1006-6748, https://doi.org/10.37896/HTL27.5/3535.
5. Singh, U.K. *et al.*, Security and Privacy aspect of Cyber-Physical Systems, in: *Cyber physical System: Concept and Application*, 1st ed., CRC press Taylor &

francis group, Chapman and Hall/CRC, USA, 2023, https://doi.org/10.1201/9781003220664-9.
6. Sharma, A. and Singh, U.K., Investigation of Cloud Computing Security Issues & Challenges. *3rd International Conference on Integrated Intelligent Computing Communication & Security (ICIIC), 2021*, 2021, doi: https://doi.org/10.2991/ahis.k.210913.055.
7. Sharma, A., Singh, U.K. *et al.*, An investigation of security risk & taxonomy of Cloud Computing environment. *2021 2nd International Conference on Smart Electronics and Communication (ICOSEC)*, pp. 1056–1063, 2021, doi: 10.1109/ICOSEC51865.2021.9591954.
8. Sharma, A., Singh, U.K. *et al.*, A Comparative analysis of security issues & vulnerabilities of leading Cloud Service Providers and in-house University Cloud platform for hosting E-Educational applications. *IEEE Mysore Sub Section International Conference (MysuruCon)*, 2021, ISBN: 978-0-7381-4662-1.
9. Mishra, A. K., Tyagi, A. K., Dananjayan, S., Rajavat, A., Rawat, H., Rawat, A. (2024). Revolutionizing Government Operations: The Impact of Artificial Intelligence in Public Administration, in: *Conversational Artificial Intelligence*, pp. 607–634, 2024.
10. Silvia Priscila, S. *et al.*, Risk-Based Access Control Mechanism for Internet of Vehicles Using Artificial Intelligence. *Secur. Commun. Netw.*, 2022, 13, 2022, Article ID 3379843, https://doi.org/10.1155/2022/3379843.
11. Current CVSS Score Distribution For All Vulnerabilities, cvedetails.com, https://www.cvedetails.com/ (accessed Sep. 5, 2022).
12. Anjum, M., Kapur, P.K., Agarwal, V., Khatri, S.K., A Framework for Prioritizing Software Vulnerabilities Using Fuzzy Best-Worst Method, pp. 311–316, 2020, 10.1109/ICRITO48877.2020.9197854.
13. Kansal, Y., Kapur, P.K., Kumar, U., Kumar, D., Prioritising vulnerabilities using ANP and evaluating their optimal discovery and patch release time. *Int. J. Math. Oper. Res.*, 14, 236, 2019, 10.1504/IJMOR.2019.097758.
14. Haque, M.A., De Teyou, G.K., Shetty, S., Krishnappa, B., Cyber Resilience Framework for Industrial Control Systems: Concepts, Metrics, and Insights. *2018 IEEE International Conference on Intelligence and Security Informatics (ISI)*, pp. 25–30, 2018, doi: 10.1109/ISI.2018.8587398.
15. Nahar, S., Pithawa, D., Bhardwaj, V., Rawat, R., Rawat, A., Pachlasiya, K., Quantum technology for military applications, in: *Quantum Computing in Cybersecurity*, pp. 313–334, 2023.
16. Petrova, V., The Hierarchical Decision Model of cybersecurity risk assessment. *2021 12th National Conference with International Participation (ELECTRONICA)*, pp. 1–4, 2021, doi: 10.1109/ELECTRONICA52725.2021.9513722.
17. Li-Sheng, Y. and Ru-Ping, D., A Novel Risk Assessment Algorithm for Accounting Information System Using Analytic Hierarchy Process. *2015*

8th International Conference on Intelligent Computation Technology and Automation (ICICTA), pp. 61–64, 2015, doi: 10.1109/ICICTA.2015.24.
18. Sharma, R., Sibal, R., Sabharwal, S., Software vulnerability prioritization using vulnerability description. *Int. J. Syst. Assur. Eng. Manag.*, 12, 58–64, 2021, https://doi.org/10.1007/s13198-020-01021-7.
19. Georgios Spanos, A. and Angelis, L., A multi-target approach to estimate software vulnerability characteristics and severity scores. *J. Syst. Software*, 146, 152–166, 2018, ISSN 0164-1212, https://doi.org/10.1016/j.jss.2018.09.039.
20. Gu, F., Niu, J., Qi, Z., Atiquzzaman, M., Partitioning and offloading in smart mobile devices for mobile cloud computing: State of the art and future directions. *J. Network Comput. Appl.*, 119, 83–96, 2018.
21. Das, A.K., Sharma, P., Chatterjee, S., Sin, J.K., A dynamic password-based user authentication scheme for hierarchical wireless sensor networks. *J. Network Comput. Appl.*, 35, 5, 1646–1656, 2012.
22. Wazid, M., Das, A.K., Vivekananda Bhat, K., Vasilakos, A.V., LAM-CIoT: Lightweight authentication mechanism in cloud-based IoT environment. *J. Network Comput. Appl.*, 150, 102496, 2020, ISSN 1084-8045, https://doi.org/10.1016/j.jnca.2019.102496.
23. Wu, F., Xu, L., Kumari, S., Li, X., Shen, J., Raymond Choo, K.-K., Wazid, M., Das, A.K., An efficient authentication and key agreement scheme for multi-gateway wireless sensor networks in IoT deployment. *J. Network Comput. Appl.*, 89, 72–85, 2017, ISSN 1084-8045, https://doi.org/10.1016/j.jnca.2016.12.008.
24. AVafaei, N., Ribeiro, R.A., Camarinha-Matos, L.M., Normalization Techniques for Multi-Criteria Decision Making: Analytical Hierarchy Process Case Study, in: *Technological Innovation for Cyber-Physical Systems. DoCEIS 2016.* IFIP Advances in Information and Communication Technology, vol. 470, L.M. Camarinha-Matos, A.J. Falcão, N. Vafaei, S. Najdi, (Eds.), Springer, Cham, 2016, https://doi.org/10.1007/978-3-319-31165-4_26.
25. Camarinha-Matos, L.M. and Afsarmanesh, H., Collaborative systems for smart environments: trends and challenges. *Collab. Syst. Smart Networked Environ.*, vol. 434, pp. 3–14, 2014.
26. Vijayakumar, T., Ramalakshmi, K., Priyadharsini, C., Vasanthakumar, S., Sharma, A., Bio-Inspired Optimization Algorithm on Cloud based Image Retrieval System using Deep Features. *2022 International Conference on Augmented Intelligence and Sustainable Systems (ICAISS)*, Trichy, India, pp. 871–876, 2022, doi: 10.1109/ICAISS55157.2022.10010739.
27. Wazid, M., Das, A.K., Vasilakos, A.V., Authenticated key management protocol for cloud-assisted body area sensor networks. *J. Network Comput. Appl.*, 123, 112–126, 2018, ISSN 1084-8045, https://doi.org/10.1016/j.jnca.2018.09.008.
28. Zekrifa, D.M.S., Sharma, A., Satyam, Patankar, A.J., Bamane, K.D., Data Analyzing with Cloud Computing Including Related Tools and Techniques.

Int. J. Intell. Syst. Appl. Eng., 11, 9s, 233–238, 2023, Retrieved from https://ijisae.org/index.php/IJISAE/article/view/3112.

29. Dixit, V. *et al.*, A Survey on Reliability of Cloud Applications. *Int'l Conf. Emerging Trends and Developments in Science, Management and Technology (ICETDSMT '13)*, pp. 476–481, 2013, ISBN: 978-81-924342-2-3.
30. Zekrifa, D., Sharma, A., Sharma, D., Sharma, R., Rai, S., Pillai, A., A System Based on AI and M1 Enhanced to Investigate Physiological Markers for User Forecasting Decision-Making, pp. 2487–2490, 2023, 10.1109/IC3I59117.2023.10398037.
31. Chirgaiya, S. and Rajavat, A., Tiny object detection model based on competitive multi-layer neural network (TOD-CMLNN). *Intell. Syst. Appl.*, 18, September 2022, 200217, 2023.
32. Rathi, M. and Rajavat, A., *Analysing Cryptographic and Random Data Sanitization Techniques in Privacy Preserving Data Mining*, vol. 83, Allied Publishers, New Delhi, India, 2023.
33. Dhar, S., Dhar, U., Rajavat, A., Factors and Attributes of Team Players: A Study of Engineering Students in India, in: *International Simulation and Gaming Association Conference*, 2021, September, Springer International Publishing, Cham, pp. 53–60.
34. Chirgaiya, S. and Rajavat, A., Comprehensive Analysis of State-of-the-Art Techniques for VQA, in: *Proceedings of International Conference on Advances in Computer Engineering and Communication Systems: ICACECS 2020*, Springer Singapore, pp. 107–115, 2021.
35. Nahar, S., Pithawa, D., Bhardwaj, V., Rawat, R., Rawat, A., Pachlasiya, K., Quantum Technology for Military Applications, in: *Quantum Computing in Cybersecurity*, pp. 313–334, 2023.
36. Pithawa, D., Nahar, S., Bhardwaj, V., Rawat, R., Dronawat, R., Rawat, A., Quantum Computing Technological Design Along with Its Dark Side, in: *Quantum Computing in Cybersecurity*, pp. 295–312, 2023.
37. Chauhan, D., Singh, C., Rawat, R., Chouhan, M., Conversational AI Applications in Ed-Tech Industry: An Analysis of Its Impact and Potential in Education, in: *Conversational Artificial Intelligence*, pp. 411–433, 2024.

25

Cloud Computing Security Through Detection & Mitigation of Zero-Day Attack Using Machine Learning Techniques

Abhishek Sharma[1]* and Umesh Kumar Singh[2]

[1]Shri Vaishnav Vidyapeeth Vishwavidyalaya, Indore, India
[2]Institute of Computer Sciences, Vikram University, Ujjain, India

Abstract

With the extensive use of Cloud computing in areas such as e-government, e-commerce, internet payments, health care, and other daily necessities, the danger of being exposed to numerous threats has grown exponentially. Several businesses are investing in this domain either for their own benefit or as utility to anyone else. The creation of numerous security risks for both producers and society are among the consequences of Cloud-based solutions. The recent global increase in cybercrime and cloud threats has increased the requirements and opportunities for better intrusion detection and prevention systems. The technique used here for enhancing the protection of the cloud computing environment is machine learning (ML). Machine learning techniques have been used in a number of ways on the Cloud to prevent or detect attacks and security issues. But after exhaustive literature review, it was observed that the stand-alone ML model is not sufficient in the current emerging attack techniques. To achieve greater prediction results than would be attained from any of the constituent learning algorithms alone, this work proposes an integrated strategy leveraging ensemble approaches through several learning algorithms and AI technique. Nonmonotonous methodology is also implemented with an ensemble model for enhancing continuous adaptive capabilities of ML model which is further helpful to develop a method for detecting unknown malicious activities on a cloud network for predicting a zero-day attack.

***Keywords*:** Cloud computing, security, machine learning, zero-day attacks, cyber threats, ensemble learning, artificial intelligence

**Corresponding author*: abhiujn9@gmail.com

Rajesh Kumar Chakrawarti, Ranjana Sikarwar, Sanjaya Kumar Sarangi, Samson Arun Raj Albert Raj, Shweta Gupta, Krishnan Sakthidasan Sankaran and Romil Rawat (eds.) Natural Language Processing for Software Engineering, (357–388) © 2025 Scrivener Publishing LLC

25.1 Introduction

The ongoing advancement and sustainable use of the Cloud benefits a multitude of Cloud users in different ways. But as more people utilize the Internet, cloud security becomes more and more important. Cloud security aims to stop unauthorized access and alteration by being closely connected to apps, networking, infrastructure, and diversified data. But as the number of Cloud-connected systems in the financial, e-commerce, e-government, and military domains increases, so does their vulnerability to network attacks, which presents a serious danger and potential for harm. Basically, effective methods for spotting, thwarting, and maintaining security against Cloud attacks are needed. Additionally, different attacks typically require different approaches. How to identify different kinds of cloud attacks raises a fundamental issue with cloud security that needs to be resolved, especially with regard to zero-day attacks, or assaults that have never been seen before. Researchers utilized various types of machine learning approaches to categorize network assaults without existing understanding of their precise features for numerous years. On the other hand, traditional ML methods, are incapable to provide unique features extracted to address the challenge of cloud attack discovery due to model complication/restrictions. Cloud computing presents various issues, including cloud user administration, multi-tenancy support, and application security [1]. The security framework will notify together cloud users and CSPs about clear boundaries and shared duties at every level because security is a key priority in the cloud-based computing systems. By modelling the suggested SRM-based Cloud Computing security framework in their own or other cloud systems, cloud actors may assess security features and compliance [2]. Because of fast technological advancements, many phishing operations have evolved from specific incidents of theft or damage to well-organized and economically sponsored individuals seeking massive gains. In this arena, organized crime's goals vary from economic benefit to attaining diplomatic interests. It shifts forces businesses to explore advanced and complicated methods to remain with evolution of attacks. As an outcome, a newly in demand wave of security solutions, known as Cyber Threat Intelligence is evolving and gaining increasing attention from researchers and protection professionals. It is a cyber-threat information system that delivers substantial proof-based information. Companies can make cyber security decisions based on the information they've gathered, such as identifying, preventing, and healing from breaches [3].

Currently, during COVID-19 pandemic, the frequency of data security assaults has risen considerably since the epidemic has caused enterprises throughout the world to implement work-at-home policies despite implementing necessary and effective countermeasures [4, 12]. Another element of COVID-19 is that hacker groups are seeing an upsurge in discussions about leveraging the epidemic as a new chance for assaults, most prominently assaults hitting distant work tools and outright fraud targeting individuals seeking for employment or knowledge concerning COVID-19 [5]. On the Deep and Dark Webs, social networking sites are seen as vital resources for attackers seeking technical information and honing their abilities. Individuals exchange information, interact with one another, and trade hacking-related products including compromised data and stolen identities over these networks like card numbers, and system vulnerabilities [6]. The number of established Cloud Service Providers (CSPs) is continuously increasing, raising a slew of protection and safety issues. This study [7] examines the security threats and attacks of three tiers of Cyber Physical Systems, explains the security aims and challenges of Cyber Physical Systems, and explains the security objectives and challenges of Cyber Physical Systems. Cloud technology is vulnerable to a variety of security vulnerabilities, ranging from network-level to application-level. Cloud service security identifies the numerous forms of cloud attacks that have happened recently, as well as the effectively adopted ways to limit the risks [8–10].

Cloud computing has evolved into a foundation of the IT industry in recent years, enhancing the capability of virtualization, storing, hosting, and other internet services. However, cyber assaults can compromise the cloud infrastructure. Forty percent of businesses disclosed cloud security vulnerabilities in 2021. Accenture was hit by the LockBit ransomware outbreak in August of 2021. The perpetrators reported to have stolen 6Terabytes of data and demanded a $50 million ransom in exchange. Kaseya, a supplier of IT solutions, discovered an assault on their integrated remote monitoring and trusted network protection application in July 2021. The intruders wanted to take control of Kaseya services from managed service providers to downstream clients. Cognyte, a cyber-analytics business, left a database unencrypted and without authentication mechanisms in May of 2021. As a result, hackers were able to get access to 5 billion records. Names, email addresses, passwords, and vulnerability data points from their system were all compromised. Search engines have even indexed the data. In April 2021, Facebook announced a data breach impacting there were exposed tens of billions of user records publicly on AWS. Two third-party Facebook app development businesses sparked the issue by posting the records in plain sight. The database contained personal data that social engineers may use in targeted attacks or hacking attempts. Online chat software Raychat managed to evade a significant cyberattack in February 2021. After that a cloud database setting was compromised, 267 million usernames, emails, passwords, files, and encrypted chats were exposed to intruders. A targeted bot assault deleted the whole data of the company shortly after that. According to sources, the data was revealed due to a Mongo-DB misconfiguration. This assault proved how bot threat actors may possibly use NoSQL databases as straightforward aims [11].

During April–May 2022, US Federal agencies have been instructed to either immediately patch or temporarily deactivate a set of enterprise products from VMware in response to "active and expected exploitation of multiple vulnerabilities". At the same time, two flaws in the IT monitoring system Icinga's web control interface allowed even unauthorized attackers to execute arbitrary PHP code and take over servers. According to recent research from the DevOps Institute, enterprise IT people believe that cyber security skills are the most crucial technical talents for their teams. Security proficiencies are either "critical" or "important" to the performance of their team's tasks, according to 92% of respondents to the "Upskilling IT 2022" poll. In Feb 2022, a significant cyberattack that interrupted satellite internet in Ukraine and "helped enable President Vladimir Putin's invasion of the nation" was attributed to Russia by the EU. One hour before Russia's invasion of Ukraine on February 24, 2022, an attack on the KA-SAT network knocked down thousands of devices.

The major research objective here is to create a system/model for detecting one or more unknown harmful behaviors on a cloud network to forecast a zero-day assault, which includes a route, a physical layer, or a storage system, among other components.

25.2 Related Work

According to Symantec's 2016 Internet Threat Report [13], targeted assaults have increased by 125 percent over the previous year. In addition, on average, a new zero-day vulnerability was discovered every week in 2015. With 8 zero-day vulnerabilities revealed in 2011, 14 zero-day vulnerabilities reported in 2012, and 23 zero-day vulnerabilities reported in 2013, the number of zero-day vulnerabilities has doubled over the previous year. In 2014, the figure remained stable at 24. However, an increase in zero-day vulnerabilities in 2015 underscores the importance of zero-day assaults.

Up till October 2016, 82 zero-day vulnerabilities had been revealed. Attacks against undiscovered system defects with no patch or repair are known as zero-day attacks [14]. Standard defenses have a hard time detecting zero-day attacks because the conventional security measures depend on malware signs, which are unidentified for zero-day assaults. Invaders are very adept, and its malware may remain undiscovered on systems for many days or may years, giving them enough opportunity to wreak irreversible damage. Trading with unidentified vulnerabilities is obviously a difficult challenge. Even though there are numerous efficient ways for combating known attacks, including as IDS/IPS, firewalls, antivirus, software upgrades, and patching, zero-day assaults are notoriously difficult to defend owing to lack of knowledge. Uncovering unforeseen flaws and determining how to exploit them is clearly a difficult undertaking. The most dangerous of all the threats to an organization's IT infrastructure are zero-day vulnerabilities. They made the faults in the system known to the intruders before a fix was offered. Though zero-day vulnerabilities are unidentified, Software (s/w) vendors may be aware of a defect but have yet to publish a cure. According to a FireEye analysis [15], thieves uncover vulnerabilities that are undisclosed to the community, together with makers, for an average of more than 300 days.

Distributed attack detection is contrasted with centralized detection, and the deep learning model [16] is contrasted with conventional machine learning methods. Our distributed attack detection method beats centralized deep learning-based detection techniques, according to tests. The DL model has also been shown to be more successful at detecting attacks than its shallow counterparts. According to [17], the automobile sector is in the forefront of implementing machine learning algorithms for risk assessment. The most widely used machine learning approach for engineering risk assessment is artificial neural networks. This page also includes additional conclusions from the review process. The authors of [18] create a Honey Net based on Docker technology that collects data to detect and analyze adversary attack patterns. The data is subsequently transformed into pictures, which are then utilized as examples to train a deep learning model. Finally, the AIoT deploys the trained model to identify threats and give situational awareness. The authors of [19] incorporated a dynamic safety risk monitoring, control, and management platform into a building information modeling (BIM) management platform. Finally, the processing and analysis of massive data collected from 3S methods and sensors offer excellent prospects for developing an integrated excavation technology system. According to the professional procedures and standards described in [20], the author used several analytical techniques to generate information based on those standards. The dataset includes about 1940 occurrences of each of the 18 input characteristics. Additionally, it looked at how different machine-learning algorithms behaved to show potential dangers associated with cloud computing. This study describes the impact of testing and training subsets of data by randomly dividing the sub dataset into four different groups. Because the service provider is in charge of ensuring that numerous services are accessible and available, maintenance is inexpensive, and consumers are exempt from issues with resources planning and upkeep on the supplier's side. Cloud Computing has been dubbed "IT on Demand" or "Utility Computing" because of these traits. Scalability is a key element of Cloud Computing, which is achieved by the virtualization of servers [21, 37].

A software fault discovered by attackers before it is discovered by the provider is known as a zero-day vulnerability (ZDVs). Since there is no known fix for ZDVs and no protections are in place on user computers, attacks are extremely likely to be successful. A zero-day incident is a tactic methodology used by threat actors to target organizations with undiscovered vulnerabilities. Zero-day malware, for example, is a malicious software designed by attackers to exploit a ZDVs. ZDAs are harmful acts that entail exploiting an undiscovered product or software vulnerability. Hackers take advantage of them until the manufacturer releases a fix over all affected systems. The programmers distribute applications with known flaws and vulnerabilities initially. The black-hat community finds technology flaws or weaknesses and afterwards runs a 0-day exploit against them. When the developers become aware of such exploits, they create a patch to address the flaws. They distributed a fix to all users to prevent additional attacks because of the issue [22].

The authors of [23] present a robust intelligent technique for detecting ZA signatures. The suggested work is partitioned into two modules: (a) HVA, which uses heavy hitter to produce high volume ZAs, and (b) LVA, which uses graph approach to develop signatures for low volume ZAs. The information is gathered by creating a virtual scenario with ten actual, high-volume attack nodes and three low-volume attack nodes. The binary classification accuracy for real-time assault data is 91.33 percent for binary classification and 90.35 percent for multi-class classification. On the other hand, binary and multi-class classification accuracy for the CICIDS18 benchmark data set is 91.62 percent and 88.98 percent, respectively. In [24], the authors show that in comparison to other attacks, malware attacks have the greatest percentage rate. Malware has become more prevalent, posing a long-term and significant danger to the security of computer systems and the internet. The well-known WannaCry ransomware assault, for example, damaged millions of devices and generated billions of dollars in losses. Every year, the quantity of malware specimens has grown dramatically, with a new malware specimen emerging every 4.6 seconds in 2018. Other forms of attacks and threats discussed in [25, 26] include SQL injection, drive-by attacks, password assaults, man-in-the-middle attacks, authentication attacks, wrapping attacks, watering hole attacks, and web shell attacks. In [27], the author integrates DNN with PCA and introduces IDS to enhance security level and detection latency.

The purpose of the systematic literature review (SLR) presented by the authors in [28] is to give future scholars access to a research resource on the different approaches, strategies, ML, and DL algorithms that have been employed in the detection of zero-day attacks. Since security is a crucial component of systems, the authors in [29] provide systematic instructions as to how businesses can adopt and audit their security. They also give an agile, up-to-date, and state-of-the-art evaluation of intrusion detection systems and their guiding principles. Concrete items used in operational systems are taken into consideration, along with functionalities and development methodologies for these defense mechanisms.

A framework developed by the authors of the current study [30] has the ability to reduce the possibility of zero-click and zero-day attacks on digital transactions. This review is unusual because of its thorough examination of academic sources and creation of a theoretical framework to guard against Zero-Click and Zero-Day attacks on online banks. By lowering the likelihood of these kinds of assaults, the possible application of this framework might greatly increase the security of digital transactions.

A survey of current Intrusion Detection Systems (IDS) for identifying zero-day vulnerabilities is presented by the authors of [31] and is based on the following factors: the sorts of cyberattacks that are employed, the datasets that are used, and the types of network detection systems. Based on the argument that cyberthreats are a public health concern rather than just a competitive factor, the authors of [32] analyze the relationship between the incidence of malware infections in a population of systems and system vulnerabilities. This paper derives structural recommendations for resilience response and policy requirements.

The techniques for identifying zero-day attacks are described by the authors in [33] as Random Forest (RF) and Extreme Gradient Boosting (XGB). The compute architecture that was applied produced better results than earlier techniques that were reported in the IDS literature.

This highlights the need for protecting critical infrastructures from security threats and intrusions. The authors of [33] examined DDoS attacks in SDN-IoT Networks. This article examined several Software-Defined Networking (SDN)-based DDoS attack mitigation techniques to identify the best one for a given set of network needs.

In [34], the author provides a thorough taxonomy and looks at potential ways to detect and prevent intrusions in cloud computing systems. This allows the author to scan, explore, and educate academicians about the most recent IDPSs and alert management techniques. A set of pertinent needs is created, taking into account the intended features of cloud computing and IDPS systems. To meet these requirements, four concepts—fuzzy theory, risk management, ontology, and autonomic computing self-management—are used.

The authors of [35] show notable gains in malware detection rates, with the system effectively seeing new threats that conventional protection methods frequently overlook. The suggested system is a workable and expandable approach that makes use of containerized apps and is easily implementable by small and medium-sized businesses that are eyeing to strengthen their cyber-defense capabilities.

Authors in [36]. The use of container-based security mechanisms for combating zero-day attacks in cloud infrastructures is investigated in this article, which focuses on containerization. The study evaluates how containerization strategies reduce attack surfaces and improve application separation from one another. To forecast and identify key risks as well as threats, the authors of [37–41] conducted risk-based experiments, data analysis, and investigations on IOT and cloud platforms for the purpose of creating mitigation strategies by the security administrator. The model's accuracy rate was 98%. The author of [42] proposed a deep learning approach for detecting and preventing zero-day attacks in the cloud. The HMM model was used in this model to identify attacks, while k-medoids clustering was used to refine attack datasets. In the case of the NSL-KDD dataset, the greatest accuracy was 94%, while in the case of the CIDD dataset, it was 95%.

25.2.1 Analysis of Zero-Day Exploits and Traditional Methods

Before performing actual threat detection in real time, it is advisable to analyze the Zero Day exploits (ZDEs) and how it can be done. Figure 25.1 describes the workflow of ZDEs:

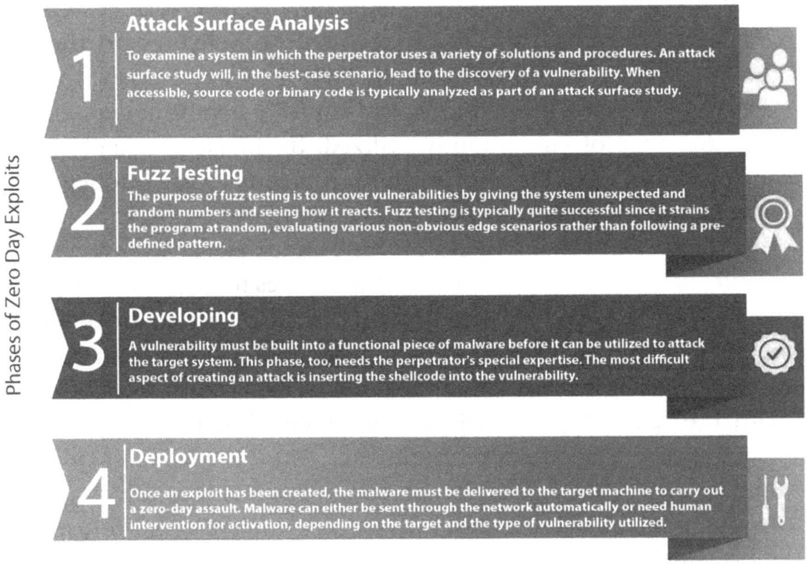

Figure 25.1 Phases of zero day exploits.

Four phases of ZDEs are represented in Figure 25.1. In the first phase, analysis of the attack surface is performed to get the vulnerabilities. During the second phase fuzz testing is performed for uncovered vulnerabilities of the previous phase. During the third phase, development is done. The quantity of storage that is accessible on the exposed stack on the victim machine determines how challenging this assignment is. Code that enables the program to go to the whole executable code should be introduced if there isn't enough free RAM. It's also crucial to have the ability to conceal utilized code and protect it from detection. Recent zero-day assaults involve cutting-edge countermeasures that may be divided into two groups:

- Metamorphic: Falsification is used to make malware code hard for humans to understand, creating software that is absolutely equivalent but structurally different from the initial.
- Polymorphic: Encryption methods are employed to encode the source data and bundle that one into encryption algorithm in the payload. Here, Polymorphic zero-day malware is incredibly sophisticated and hard to spot.

During the fifth and last phase deployment is performed. Once an exploit has been created, the malware must be delivered to the target machine to carry out a zero-day assault. Malware can be sent through the web repeatedly or need human intervention for activation, dependent on the target and type of vulnerability utilized. In the latter situation, social engineering techniques like phishing and spam emails are frequently used for persuading customers to copy and execute malware. Mystification and additional techniques to subtly modify the attack sign with every successive assault are utilized by a lot of recent malwares to prevent it from being discovered when used several times. Such measures, which are often taken by offenders when designing malwares, along with the truth that the virus is aiming an undiscovered vulnerability and lacks recognized attack sign to start with, create this type of malware extremely difficult to identify.

Statistics-based detection techniques rely on knowledge of previously identified system vulnerabilities. To compile statistical information on prior assaults and provide a baseline for safe system behavior, machine learning is widely employed in statistics-based detection systems. The primary benefit of these systems is that the more precise they get, the more data they gather. During the course of its operation in a system, a statistics-based solution gathers more data regarding fresh zero-day vulnerabilities, expanding its dataset and creating a more thorough profile for a potential new attack [44].

Though, depending on the standards used, a resolution like this might result in a lot of FP and FN. It might be difficult for programmer developers to strike an appropriate equilibrium with the standards because false negatives must be avoided to prevent missing a zero-day assault, but false positives must be limited to avoid disrupting the company's regular operations. Overall, statistics-based approaches' usefulness in detecting zero-day exploits is restricted. It also has poor detection abilities for malware that is substantially scrambled and disguised. Statistics-based strategies, on the other hand, can be useful for a hybrid solution.

When antivirus software detects malware, it generally uses *signature-based detection* algorithms. The approach, as the name indicates, is based on present malware signature records that are utilized as a guidebook for checking for malware on a system. If often revised, signature repositories are unable to spot new zero-day attacks since by definition, zero-day vulnerabilities lack a verified signature. Therefore, its only way to protect from zero-day assaults using signature-based detection is to use machine learning and related models to create real-time signatures that may meet a virus which is currently unidentified and thus identify it. The following methods can be used to create three different sorts of signatures:

- ➢ Content-based
- ➢ Semantic-based
- ➢ Vulnerability-based signature

Behavior-based detection methods check for malware's features based on how it communicates with the intended system. According to this, a behavior-based approach looks at how incoming files interact with current software rather than the code of those files to determine if such interactions are the result of malicious activity. Building baseline behavior based on information from prior and ongoing system interactions is typically done using machine learning. Similar to statistics-based detection methods, this identification becomes more reliable when more data are provided. A behavior-based detection method which runs for long period on a single target system might be highly good in predicting the outcomes of present operations and detecting malicious software [44].

Hybrid detection approaches are designed to use various capabilities of the three techniques outlined above while preventing their flaws. Hybrid detection systems typically combine 2 or 3 approaches to generate more precise findings. A statistics-based method, for example, may be used to reinforce a behavior-based standard for common behavior and accelerate learning method, while signature-based technique can be applied to filter false positives and improve detection accuracy.

Through the presented and exhaustive work done, it is observed that any single approach, technique or model is unable to work properly or may be less effective because it will not include various Cloud exploit scenarios. Hence, the authors strongly propose an integrated and smart model or framework to perform analysis and detection of Zero-day exploits. It is also recommended that a specific mitigation plan or policy be proposed to reduce the effect of attacks.

25.3 Proposed Methodology

To develop a method for detecting unknown malicious activities on a cloud network in its ability to forecast a zero-day attack, as well as to analyze and mitigate potential losses in cloud platforms and security of an enterprise-wide cloud in terms of operational, informational, and security networks, proper security risk investigation is required. An integrated strategy is created utilizing different machine learning algorithms simultaneously to investigate security threats in terms of threads and identify intrusion or detection of assaults during the runtime. It is necessary to collect data from memory dumps and log files and prepare various data sets prior to deployment. The data sets are then preprocessed using a variety of ways to avoid under and over fitting. The connection between the various attributes must be discovered during the preprocessing of the Data set [51–53] for it to be free of outliers. Before implementation of the proposed method, it is required to define Security objectives and requirements for zero-day protection and design ensemble learning and predictive models on the basis of them. Figure 25.2 presents the Road map for training algorithms and classification of new customer connection:

The following steps show the proposed approach and methodology:

Step 1: Data retrieval, Collection & Preprocessing
Data retrieval and data collection is the backbone of any machine learning model, that's why in this step, six different datasets are taken as an input based on various threats and risks. After data collection from various sources, the dump files and system files are examined and then csv files are prepared with respective Features [54–56]. During data preprocessing, data cleaning, integration, transformation, reduction are performed. Then preprocessed data sets are digitized, so that they will reduce the size of dataset file and time complexity during the implementation of next level machine learning algorithms. The process will be described as shown below:

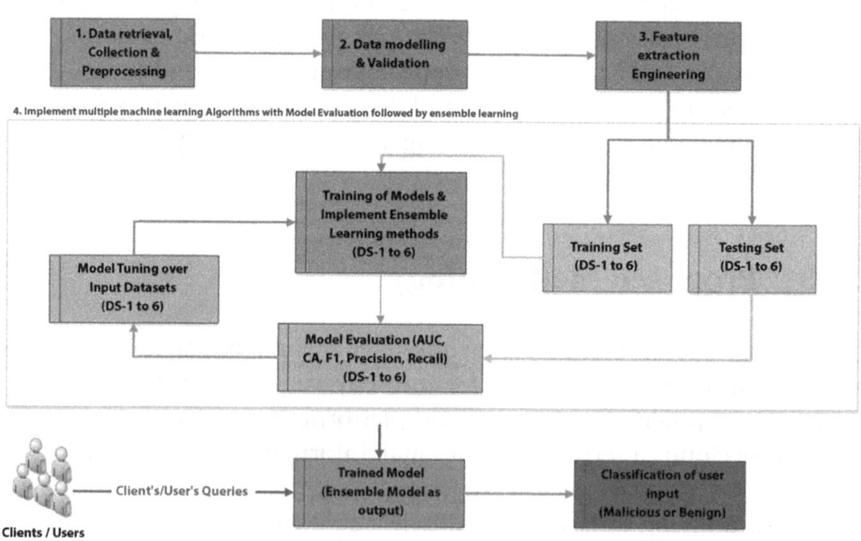

Figure 25.2 System flow for training and classification of cloud network traffic.

a) Collect Data from log files, memory dump files, and miscellaneous files.
b) Present the gathered data into csv format.
c) Digitize all the features of the dataset using numeric values.
d) Define and declare the target feature within the proposed dataset.
e) Fill up the missing parameters of the dataset by finding 'mode' of the respective feature.

Based on the various datasets six different models will be constructed for the ensemble machine learning model. The following data sets are collected as given in Table 25.1: Specification of Data Sets used and their respective threats/risk:

Results: The outcome of this step is Six Data set csv files, which are used as input to the next step.

Step 2: Data modelling and Validation

The following are the steps performed to get the desired dataset csv file before the implementation of feature extraction and selection:

a) Import the processed datasets within the experimental setup built on GCP using Jupyter Notebook.
b) Visualize the finalized digital dataset having no missing values and outliers for each dataset.
c) Define and declare target features in each dataset.

Result: Finalized digital dataset is imported.

Step 3: Feature extraction Engineering

After visualization of the datasets received from the previous step, it is observed that they all are derived from random sampling methods and the parameters are continuous and normally distributed, so during the feature extraction engineering, it is recommended that Pearson Correlation coefficient be used following this sequence:

a) Find the Pearson Correlation coefficient of all the pairs of features for each dataset using following expression:

$$R = \frac{n(\Sigma\alpha\beta) - (\Sigma\alpha)(\Sigma\beta)}{\sqrt{(n\Sigma\alpha^2 - (\Sigma\alpha)^2)(n\Sigma\beta^2 - (\Sigma\beta)^2)}} \quad (25.1)$$

Table 25.1 Specification of Data Sets used and their respective threats/risk.

Data set	Distribution of data set	Threat/risk	Reference
Malware Memory Analysis (CIC-MalMem-2022)	Spyware: 10020 Ransomware: 9791 Trojan Horse: 9487 Benign:29298	Malware (Spyware, Ransomware, Trojan Horse)	[43]
Malicious Domains using DNS Traffic Analysis (CIC-Bell-DNS 2021)	Spam: 4337 Phishing: 5001 Malware: 5001 Benign:500001	Spam, phishing, and malware	[44]
Darknet traffic classification (CIC-Darknet2020)	Darknet: 24311 Benign: 134348	TOR, VPN	[45, 46]
DDoS attack (CICDDo S2019)	Portmap:186950 BENIGN: 4734	PortMap; NetBIOS; LDAP; MSSQL; UDP; UDP-Lag, SYN; NTP; DNS; SNMP; SSDP;WebDDoS; TFTP	[47]
IDS (CSE-CIC-IDS2018)	Benign:13484755 DDoS:1263902 DoS:654352 Brute force:380988 Botnet:286188 Infiltration:161843 Web attack:974	Brute-force, Heartbleed; Botnet; DoS; DDoS; Web attacks; infiltration of the network from inside;	[48]
ISOT -2020	Benign: 25076703 Malicious: 11862282	HTTP Flood DOS; Dictionary/Brute Force login attacks; NetworkScanning;DNS Amplification DOS;Synflood DOS; UDP Flood DOS;Probing; Backdoor (reverse shell); Remote-to-Local (R2L);Network Scanning; Trojan Horse; Unclassified (unsolicited traffic);	[49, 50]

b) Identify the features on the basis of correlation threshold value for each dataset.
c) Find the outliers and discard them in each dataset.

Result: Final data set with selected features in csv files.

Step 4: Implementation of multiple machine learning Algorithms with Model Evaluation and tuning over all six datasets followed by ensemble learning

Before the implementation of multiple machine learning algorithms over all six datasets parallelly using experimental setup prepared through Jupyter notebook over GCP, splitting the data set is performed and training and test datasets are identified in the ratio of 75-25 %. Following are the steps:

a) Implementation of K-nearest neighbor (kNN):
The kNN classifier often starts with the Euclidean distance for test and chosen training samples. Let x_a be an input sample with f features (a=1to n), p:no. of features (b=1 to f), and x_{a1}, x_{a2}, ..., x_{af} be the no. of input samples. The following equation describes the Euclidean distance for sample x_a and x_c (c=1to n):

$$d(x_a, x_c) = \sqrt{(x_{a1} + x_{c1})^2 + (x_{a2} + x_{c2})^2 + \cdots .. + (x_{af} + x_{cf})^2} \quad (25.2)$$

If the dependent variable and one or more independent variables are present, the 1-nearest neighbor rule sets the test piece x's projected class to be identical to the true class I of closest neighbor of them, where I is x's closest neighbor:

$$d(\alpha_i, x) = \min_b\{d(m_b, x)\} \quad (25.3)$$

Model parameters used:
Number of neighbors: 5; Metric: Euclidean; Weight: Uniform;

b) Implementation of Support vector machine (SVM):
It is the most suitable supervised ML technique. Both classification and regression might be accomplished using SVM. The method may be trained using labeled data, and it can produce a hyperplane-based classification of the data into classes that optimizes margin across all attack classes. The SVM, which functions as a binary classifier, can also conduct multi-class

categorization in a cascade-style fashion. SVM mostly depends on the settings and types of kernels utilized. The Gaussian kernel calculated using a support vector (SV) is an exponentially declining function in the source feature space having highest value at the SV and uniform decay in all dimensions around the SV, resulting in hyper-spherical edges of the kernel function. The Gaussian or RBF kernel is:

$$K(\alpha,\beta) = EXP(-\frac{||\alpha-\beta||^2}{2\sigma^2}) \tag{25.4}$$

Here, $||\alpha\text{-}\beta||$ represents the Euclidean distance. The linear weighted arrangement of the kernel function generated within a data point and every SV is the SVM classifier having Gaussian kernel. The importance of SV in data point categorization is tempered by the SV's global prediction utility, and K (α, β), the SV's local influence on prediction at a specific data point. The Model parameters used are:

- SVM type: - SVM, C=1.0, ε=0.1;
- Kernel: - Sigmoid, tanh (auto $\alpha \cdot \beta$ + 1.0);
- Tolerance (Numerical): 0.001;
- limit of Iteration: 100;

c) Implementation of Random Forest (RF):
It is a sophisticated non-linear supervised method employed for regression and classification. This will create several decision trees while training the model, since results of predictions from each tree is combined to produce single conclusion This is referred to as an ensemble approach. The way RF classifiers operate is as observed: the more trees in the model, the greater the accuracy and less likely the model is to be overfit. A collection of decision trees with controlled variance is also made with it. Random forest builds multiple decision trees instead of just one to predict the final output activity class of mobile phone users based on their phone log data. By generating many decision trees for a given dataset, it mitigates the over-fitting problem caused by the one decision tree that was initially supplied. The model parameters that are employed are:

- Number of trees: 10
- Maximal number of considered features: unlimited
- Replicable training: No

- Maximal tree depth: unlimited
- Stop splitting nodes with maximum instances: 5

d) Implementation of logistic Regression (LR):
To examine the distinct collection of classes, LR is a supervised machine learning (ML) classification technique. The cost function, often known as the sigmoid function, is used by the logistic function. Predictions are converted to probabilities using this function. It is also suggested that the likelihood of an event occurring may be anticipated by fitting data to the logistic function. Logistic regression computes probabilities by utilizing a logistic function, which is also referred to as a sigmoid function. The function is often restricted to a range of 0 to 1, according to the logistic regression hypothesis. This classifier evaluates the relationship between several independent variables and the category dependent variable for a given dataset. Model parameters used for Regularization: Ridge (L2), C=1, class weights=False.

e) Implementation of Naive Bayes (NB) algorithms:
This model is based on a probability of set of Bayesian equations:

$$P(\alpha|\beta)=P(\beta|\alpha)*P(\alpha)/P(\beta) \quad (25.5)$$

This presupposes feature independence and the capacity to consider multiple attributes. Where $P(\alpha)$ is the chances that event α will occur, $P(\beta)$ is the chances that incidentβ will happen, $P(\alpha|\beta)$ is the chances that α will happen given β, $P(\beta|\alpha)$ is the chances that β will happen given α, and $P(\alpha\beta)$ is the chances that α and β will happen. It is assumed that the Naive Bayes properties are not related to each other. The classifier then determines the likelihood of every class until selecting the one with the greatest probability.

f) Implementation of Neural Network (NN):
NN is a type of distributed computing with biological inspiration. It is made up of connections between basic processing units, or nodes. Any two units that are connected have random weights, and they are used to estimate the degree to which one unit will impact the other. The unit serves as input nodes and output nodes, respectively, performing summing and thresholding. The over-6tting issue is typically solved by an early halting method. The early halting technique uses a different validation set to monitor network performance. As the network learns the data, the errors in the

validation set frequently decrease, then increase as the network discovers the peculiarities in the training data. A forward pass and a backward pass are the two steps of a feed-forward neural network. In the forward pass, the network is given a sample input and activations are allowed to flow until the output layer is reached. The linear sum, sigmoid function, and Gaussian function, ReLu, are 3 activation functions that are often used. During the backward pass, the network's actual output (from the forward pass) is contrasted with the desired output, and inaccuracy assessments are computed for the output nodes. To lessen the inaccuracies, one might change the weights that are attached to the output units. The Model Parameters used are:

- Hidden layers: 100;
- Activation: ReLu;
- Alpha: 0.0001;
- Max iterations: 200;
- Replicable training: True;
- ReLU (Rectified Linear Units) function, h(α) = Max (α, 0);

g) Evaluation of all the supervised classification algorithms or models with respective performance matrix:

Five performance metrics are developed in this research work using the confusion matrix: AUC, Accuracy, F1, Precision, and Recall. AUC stands for Area under the receiver operating characteristic curve (ROC). The accuracy metric is determined by dividing all true forecasts by all projected values, which includes all accurate predictions.

$$Accuracy\ (CA) = \frac{(TP_i + TN_i)}{(TP_i + TN_i + FP_i + FN_i)} \tag{25.6}$$

where the instances of the result data designated as TP, TN, FP, and FN are, respectively, true positive, true negative, false positive, and false negative. By dividing the true positive values between the genuine positive values and the false positive values, the accuracy measure is derived.

$$\text{Precision} = \frac{(TP_i)}{(TP_i + FP_i)} \tag{25.7}$$

where TP and FP stand for the result data's true positive and false positive cases, respectively. The recall measure is computed in a manner similar to how the accuracy measure is obtained.

$$Recall = \frac{(TP_i)}{(TP_i + FN_i)} \tag{25.8}$$

where TP and FN stand for the result data's true positive and false negative situations, respectively. F1 will be evaluated as:

$$\text{F1Score} = \frac{2 * (Precision_i * Recall_i)}{(Precision_i + Recall_i)} \tag{25.9}$$

The classification outcomes of the variations utilized in this article will be evaluated using these five-performance metrics. A new measure that will be covered in the following part will be made using the entire set of these five-performance metrics.

Results: Performance Matrix content AUC, accuracy, F1, Precision and recall.

This machine learning model (MLM) approach mixes many models with various datasets to get the best prediction model. The primary concept underlying the ensemble technique is to combine all weak learners into one strong learner, increasing the model's accuracy. Bagging, Boosting, and Stacking are a few methods of frequent ensemble technique types. The bagging ensemble approach uses the partial decision tree algorithm (PART), Adaptive Boost, and Naive Bayes to figure out the trail. It demonstrated that the ensemble technique outperforms PART, Naive Bayes, and Adaptive Boost.

Step 5: Update predictive Set of belief using non monotonic reasoning (AI technique)

According to the performance matrix received from the previous step as output, the model was built for deployment for real time prediction. When the proposed model will be deployed over the Cloud Computing environment, the cloud network traffic will be monitored, then this data will be considered as input for prediction.

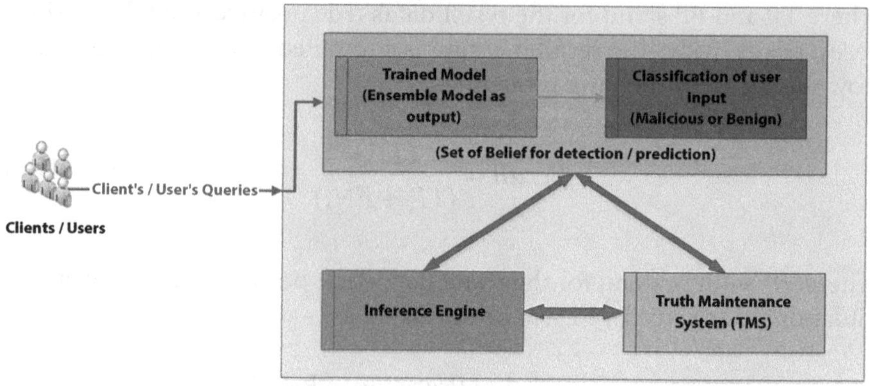

Figure 25.3 Adaptive Predictive Ensemble Machine Learning (APEML) system.

The outcome of prediction is then taken as input for maintaining a set of beliefs or knowledge base, which will be further used for enabling adaptive and predictive ensemble machine learning models (APEML model) to implement AI techniques like non-monotonous reasoning. Figure 25.3 will present the process as given below.

In Figure 25.3, the set of beliefs represents knowledge base as input to the proposed model. The set of beliefs will adaptively update itself with the arrival of new Cloud Computing environment network information through large numbers of new user's queries. Then the results of newly prediction values will also be included in the adaptive set of beliefs in the form of a knowledge base using non monotonous reasoning. The Truth Maintenance system is supposed to update the set of beliefs on the basis of previous prediction and the new client's queries.

25.4 Results and Discussion

Table 25.2 encapsulates the performance parameters of all six datasets in terms of AUC, Accuracy, F1, Precision and recall achieved by each algorithm. It is evident that from the confusion matrix shown in Table 25.2, the maximum accuracy (CA) achieved on DS-1 is 1 in case of RF, NN and second highest is .99 in case of kNN, NB and LR. The average area under ROC curve (AUC) and average accuracy (CA) is 0.986. Whereas average F1, precision and recall value is 0.983. The confusion matrix of all six datasets is given in Table 25.2:

Table 25.2 Confusion matrix of all six datasets with six algorithms/classifiers.

Dataset/ model	Method/ algorithm	Evaluation of results: confusion matrix				
		AUC	**CA**	**F1**	**Precision**	**Recall**
DS-1	kNN	0.99	0.99	0.99	0.99	0.98
	SVM	0.98	0.97	0.79	0.82	0.76
	RF	1	1	1	1	1
	NN	1	1	0.99	0.99	0.99
	NB	0.99	0.99	0.97	0.93	1
	LR	0.99	0.99	0.991	0.996	0.97
DS-2	kNN	0.995	0.997	0.998	0.997	1
	SVM	0.936	0.891	0.941	0.914	0.969
	RF	1	1	1	1	1
	NN	1	1	1	1	1
	NB	0.999	0.986	0.992	0.998	0.986
	LR	1	1	1	1	1
DS-3	kNN	0.92	0.97	0.98	0.98	0.99
	SVM	0.97	0.97	0.98	0.98	0.98
	RF	1	1	1	1	1
	NN	1	1	1	1	1
	NB	0.99	0.98	0.99	0.99	0.99
	LR	0.98	0.97	0.98	0.99	0.98
DS-4	kNN	0.99	0.99	0.99	0.99	0.99
	SVM	0.97	0.95	0.95	0.95	0.95
	RF	1	1	1	1	1
	NN	1	1	1	1	1
	NB	0.99	0.96	0.96	0.97	0.96
	LR	0.99	0.99	0.99	0.99	0.99
DS-5	kNN	1	1	1	1	1
	SVM	0.96	0.94	0.94	0.94	0.94
	RF	1	1	1	1	1
	NN	1	1	1	1	1
	NB	0.99	0.99	0.99	0.99	0.99
	LR	0.99	0.99	0.99	0.99	0.99

(Continued)

Table 25.2 Confusion matrix of all six datasets with six algorithms/classifiers. (*Continued*)

Dataset/ model	Method/ algorithm	Evaluation of results: confusion matrix				
		AUC	CA	F1	Precision	Recall
DS-6	kNN	1	1	1	1	1
	SVM	0.887	0.998	0.998	0.998	0.998
	RF	1	1	1	1	1
	NN	1	1	1	1	1
	NB	1	0.99	0.99	0.99	0.99
	LR	1	1	1	1	1

In Figure 25.4, A comparative analysis of performance of machine learning algorithms for each input data set in terms of accuracy is presented. The graph presents the variation of accuracy level of the kNN algorithm from 99 - 100% with respect to the data set used. Similarly, the accuracy level of SPM is observed from 89.1% to 99.8%. Accuracy of Random Forest and neural network is observed as hundred percent in all cases is given in Figure 25.4.

In Naive Bayes (NB) algorithm, the accuracy level is from 96% to 99%. But in case of Logistic regression the accuracy level is almost hundred percent in every case indicated in Figure 25.4.

Figure 25.5 depicts the trade-off between sensitivity (or TP) and specificity using the ROC curve (1 – FP). Classifiers that give curves that are

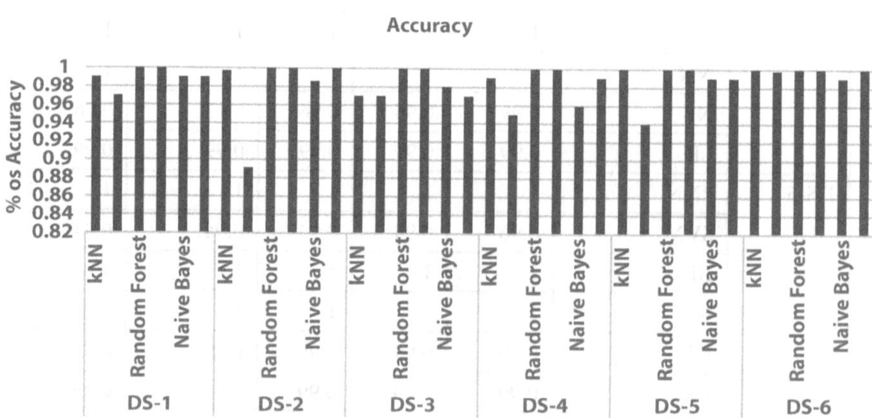

Figure 25.4 Comparative analysis of accuracy for ML algorithms for input datasets.

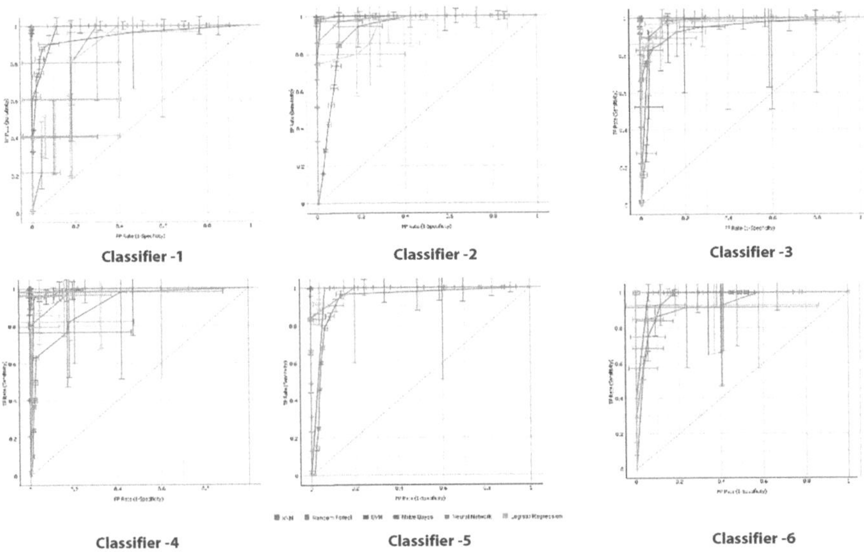

Figure 25.5 Area under ROC curve for classifier 1 to 6.

nearer to the top-left corner exhibit superior performance. It expects a random classifier to provide diagonal points (FP = TP) as a starting point. An AUC of 0.5 often indicates no classification, whereas values between 0.7 and 0.8 are regarded as acceptable, between 0.8 and 0.9 as outstanding, and values beyond 0.9 as remarkable. The target probability for target class 1 is 89% in case of DS-1, 90% for DS-2, 93% for DS-3, 94% for DS-4, 91% for DS-5 and 91% for DS-6 as shown in Figure 25.6. High-dimensional data are analyzed using the principal component analysis (PCA) in the framework of DS-1 to DS-6. Finding a smaller set of features that accurately represents the original data in a lower-dimensional subspace with little information loss is the purpose of PCA usage here.

In Figure 25.6, the result of PCA for classifier 1 to 6 is presented. The results show the portion of variance with the principal component which includes cumulative variance and component variance for each data set. The explained variance for DS-1 to DS6 is 71%, 53%, 60%, 44%, 45%, and 83% respectively.

The proposed methodology is able to identify 12 different kinds of attacks including frequently used attacks like Malware, ransomware, DDOS etc. The percentage of attack detection using proposed methodology is shown in Table 25.3.

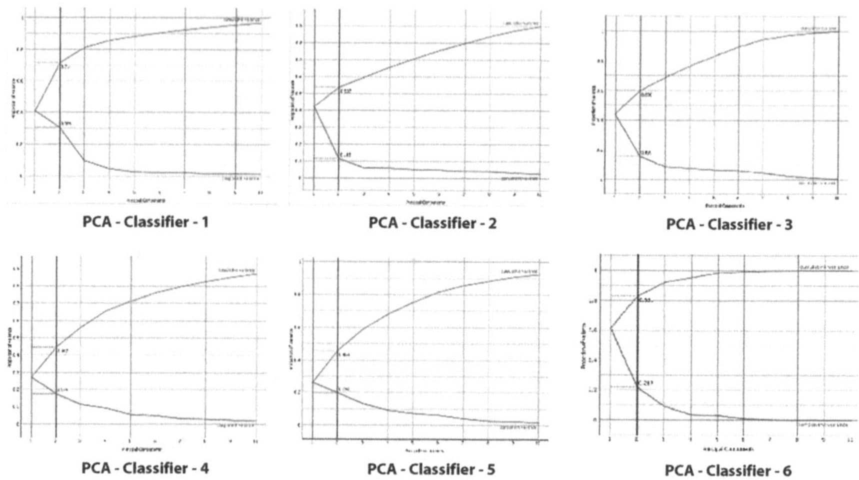

Figure 25.6 Principal component analysis for classifier 1 to 6.

Table 25.3 Detection of top 12 attacks/risk using proposed methodology

S. no.	Attack type	Accuracy/ detection (%)
1	Botnet attack	94%
2	Brute force Attack	94%
3	DoS/DDoS + PortScan	99%
4	Infiltration attack	97%
5	Malware	97%
6	Phishing	98%
7	Ransomware	97%
8	Spam	97%
9	Spyware	98%
10	Trojan Horse	97%
11	VPN and Tor (Darknet)	98%
12	Web attack	96%

Table 25.4 Comparison of performance of proposed model & previous methods/models.

S. no.	Method/model	Accuracy (%)	References
1.	Signature Extraction method	91.33	[23]
2.	HMM	94.00	[42]
3.	CNN for Darknet traffic	86.00	[46]
4.	Proposed APEML Model	99.99	Proposed

During the comparison of performance in terms of Accuracy (CA) of proposed APEML Model and existing methods, it is found that the average CA of the proposed Model is the best among the previous methods. The details are as shown below in Table 25.4.

25.4.1 Prevention & Mitigation of Zero Day Attacks (ZDAs)

Zero-day vulnerabilities and their accompanying assaults will grow indefinitely. If human error and supply chain attack surfaces continue, businesses should set up and meticulously monitor the tools, procedures, and policies to reduce the risk. Figure 25.7 depicts ten such techniques that can aid in the management of zero-day risk.

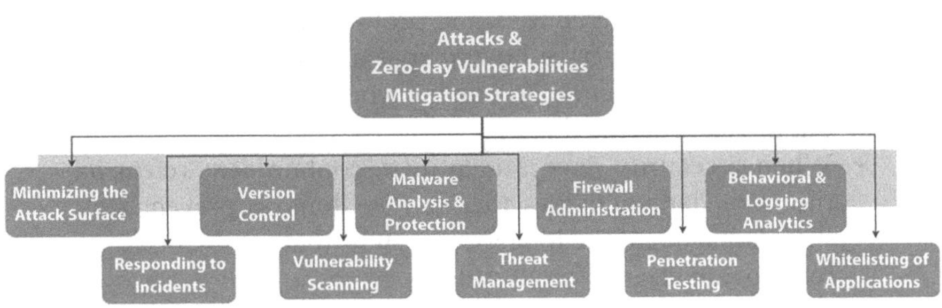

Figure 25.7 Top 10 zero day mitigation strategies.

- Attack Surface Reduction (ASR), which prevents malware from infecting computers by blocking attacks that come from scripts, Office files, and emails. ASR can provide favorable conditions while stopping the underlying actions of dangerous documents. It can identify and terminate malicious PowerShell scripts, JavaScript, VBScript, and macro code. It can also prevent the execution of executable email content and payloads downloaded from the Internet.
- Exploit Guard's network security prevents malware from connecting to a command-and-control server by blocking all outbound links before they are used. Outbound network traffic is analyzed using hostname and IP reputation, and connections to unreliable locations are severed.
- Controlled folder access keeps track of the modifications that programs the data in secured directories. Important directories may be secured, and only approved applications are given access. It could stop ransomware from encrypting data.

The Best Practices for Defense Against Zero-Day Attacks are as follows:

a) Implement Patch Management
b) Incident Response Plan should be ready.

The strategy should also include the following:

- The following should also be part of the plan: ✚ Prepare by doing a risk analysis and identifying the most critical assets, which the security team should focus on. Write a document describing the roles, duties, and protocols.
- Identification: describe how to spot a possible ZDA, verify that it's an occurrence, and define what else has to be found out to deal with the threat.
- When a security flaw is identified, containment refers to the immediate activities that can be done to prevent further damage and the longer-term steps that can be taken to rebuild and clean affected systems.
- Eradication: identifying the main cause of the attack and taking steps to prevent it from happening again.

- ➢ Recovery: how to restart, inspect, and monitor production systems to ensure that everything is running normally.
- ➢ Learnings: No later than two weeks following the attack, do a retrospective to review organizational policies and tooling and figure out how to be suitably prepared for the next attack.

Protection from dangers including 0-day assaults, advanced persistent threats (APT), sophisticated malware & trojans that could avoid conventional signature-based security procedures is provided by the advanced threat detection and response platform. Continuously monitoring of the Vulnerability scanning reports, Patch management, Input validation and sanitization should also be performed for prevention and mitigation of Zero-day Attacks.

25.5 Conclusion and Future Work

The proposed and current methodologies and outcomes are compared in this paper along with a thorough analysis. Each dataset's preparation step's data cleaning procedure was described. To lower the size of the dataset for effective analysis, the dimension reduction is also carried out via correlation. Each dataset is then subjected to an application of ensemble ML algorithms, and the outcomes are examined. The efficacy of identifying intrusions using the suggested dataset and ensemble ML algorithm is 99%, which is superior to the previous findings, according to the trials carried out and assessment results. The accuracy is nearly 100% when utilizing the kNN, RF, and NN techniques, which is highly acceptable. The contributions of this work are as follows:

- ➢ This article presents a detailed analysis and comparisons of various Datasets with 12 different categories of attacks/risk.
- ➢ This article also presents a detailed implementation of proposed method for evaluation of five performance parameter like Accuracy, AUC, F1, precision and recall.
- ➢ This article details how to develop a method for detecting unknown malicious activities using ensemble ML algorithm on a cloud network which adaptively evolve from the proposed system using non-monotonous reasoning for predicting a zero-day attack.

- This article also analyzes and mitigates business risks in cloud network and security of an enterprise-wide cloud with respect to Operational and Security networks to maintain a high level of integrity and security.

References

1. Karthiban, K. and Smys, S., Privacy preserving approaches in cloud computing, in: *2018 2nd International Conference on Inventive Systems and Control (ICISC)*, pp. 462–467, 2018.
2. Singh, U.K. and Sharma, A., Cloud computing security framework based on shared responsibility models, in: *Cyber-physical, IoT and autonomous systems in industry 4.0*, 1st ed, V. Bali (Ed.), pp. 39–55, CRC Press Taylor & Francis Group, USA, 2021, https://doi.org/10.1201/9781003146711-3.
3. Tounsi, W., What is cyber threat intelligence and how is it evolving?, in: *Cyber-Vigilance and Digital Trust: Cyber Security in the Era of Cloud Computing and IoT*, W. Tounsi (Ed.), ISTE Ltd, Washington, NJ, USA, 2019.
4. Dutta, A. and Kant, S., An overview of cyber threat intelligence platform and role of artificial intelligence and machine learning, in: *Proceedings of the 16th International Conference, ICISS 2020*, Lecture Notes in Computer Science book series (LNCS), pp. 81–86, Jammu, India, December 2020.
5. Mador, Z., Keep the dark web close and your cyber security tighter. *Comput. Fraud Secur.*, 2021, 1, 6–8, 2021.
6. Queiroz, A.L. and Keegan, B., Challenges of using machine learning algorithms for cybersecurity: a study of threatclassification models applied to social media communication data, in: *Cyber Influence and Cognitive 'reats*, J.M. Vladlena Benson (Eds.), Academic Press, Elsevier Inc., Cambride, MA, USA, 2020.
7. Sharma, A., Singh, U.K. *et al.*, Security and Privacy aspect of Cyber-Physical Systems, in: *Cyber Physical system: Concept and application*, A. Baliyan (Ed.), CRC Press Taylor & Francis Group, USA, 2022.
8. Sharma, A. and Singh, U.K., Investigation of Cloud Computing Security Issues & Challenges. *3rd International Conference on Integrated Intelligent Computing Communication & Security (ICIIC), 2021*, 2021, doi: https://doi.org/10.2991/ahis.k.210913.055.
9. Sharma, A., Singh, U.K. *et al.*, An investigation of security risk & taxonomy of Cloud Computing environment. *2021 2nd International Conference on Smart Electronics and Communication (ICOSEC)*, pp. 1056–1063, 2021, doi: 10.1109/ICOSEC51865.2021.9591954.
10. Sharma, A., Singh, U.K. *et al.*, A Comparative analysis of security issues & vulnerabilities ofleading Cloud Service Providers and in-house University Cloud

platform for hosting E-Educational applications. *IEEE Mysore Sub Section International Conference (MysuruCon)*, 2021, ISBN: 978-0-7381-4662-1.
11. Top 5 cloud security breaches, https://www.cybertalk.org/2022/04/26/top-5-cloud-security-breaches-and-lessons/.
12. Latest cloud security news, https://portswigger.net/daily-swig/cloud-security.
13. Internet Security Threat Report, Internet Report, vol. 21, APRIL 2016.
14. Kaur, R. and Singh, M., Automatic Evaluation and Signature Generation Technique for Thwarting ZeroDay Attacks. *Second International Conference, SNDS 2014*, India, March 13-14, 2014, pp. 298–309.
15. White Paper, —ZERO-DAY DANGER: A Survey of Zero-Day Attacks and What They Say About the Traditional Security Model, FireEye Security Raimagined, 2015.
16. Diro, A.A. and Chilamkurti, N., Distributed attack detection scheme using deep learning approach for Internet of Things. *Future Gener. Comput. Syst.*, 82, 761–768, 2018, ISSN 0167-739X, https://doi.org/10.1016/j.future.2017.08.043.
17. Hegde, J. and Rokseth, B., Applications of machine learning methods for engineering risk assessment – A review. *Saf. Sci.*, 122, 104492, 2020, ISSN 0925-7535, https://doi.org/10.1016/j.ssci.2019.09.015.
18. Tan, L., Yu, K., Ming, F., Cheng, X., Srivastava, G., Secure and Resilient Artificial Intelligence of Things: A HoneyNet Approach for Threat Detection and Situational Awareness. *IEEE Consum. Electron. Mag.*, 11, 3, 69–78, 1 May 2022, doi: 10.1109/MCE.2021.3081874.
19. Lin, S.-S., Shen, S.-L., Zhou, A., Xu, Y.-S., Risk assessment and management of excavation system based on fuzzy set theory and machine learning methods. *Autom. Constr.*, 122, 103490, 2021, ISSN 0926-5805, https://doi.org/10.1016/j.autcon.2020.103490.
20. Mishra, A. K., Tyagi, A. K., Dananjayan, S., Rajavat, A., Rawat, H., Rawat, A., Revolutionizing Government Operations: The Impact of Artificial Intelligence in Public Administration, in: *Conversational Artificial Intelligence*, pp. 607–634, 2024.
21. Sharma, A. and Singh, U.K., Deployment model of e-educational cloud for departmental academics automation using open source. *HTL J.*, 27, 5, 36, 2021, ISSN 1006-6748. https://doi.org/10.37896/HTL27.5/3535.
22. Olzak, T., Mitigating Zero Day Attacks with a Detection, Prevention and Response Strategy, 2021, [online], Available: https://www.toolbox.com/it-security/vulnerability-management/articles/mitigating-zero-day-attacks/. [Accessed: 16-03-2022].
23. Nahar, S., Pithawa, D., Bhardwaj, V., Rawat, R., Rawat, A., Pachlasiya, K., Quantum technology for military applications, in: *Quantum Computing in Cybersecurity*, pp. 313–334, 2023.
24. Narayan, V. and Shaju, B., Malware and Anomaly Detection Using Machine Learning and Deep Learning Methods, in: *Handbook of Research on Machine*

and Deep Learning Applications for Cyber Security, 2020, DOI: 10.4018/978-1-5225-9611-0.ch006.
25. Namdev, A., Patni, D., Dhaliwal, B. K., Parihar, S., Telang, S., Rawat, A., Potential Threats and Ethical Risks of Quantum Computing, in: *Quantum Computing in Cybersecurity*, pp. 335–352, 2023.
26. Shrivastava, M., Patil, R., Bhardwaj, V., Rawat, R., Telang, S., Rawat, A., Quantum Computing and Security Aspects of Attention-Based Visual Question Answering with Long Short-Term Memory, in: *Quantum Computing in Cybersecurity*, pp. 395–412, 2023.
27. Sikarwar, R., Shakya, H. K., Kumar, A., Rawat, A., Advanced Security Solutions for Conversational AI, in: *Conversational Artificial Intelligence*, pp. 287–301, 2024.
28. Ahmad, R., Alsmadi, I., Alhamdani, W. *et al.*, Zero-day attack detection: a systematic literature review. *Artif. Intell. Rev.*, **56**, 10733–10811, 2023, https://doi.org/10.1007/s10462-023-10437-z.
29. Chang, V., Golightly, L., Modesti, P., Xu, Q.A., Doan, L.M.T., Hall, K., Boddu, S., Kobusińska, A., A Survey on Intrusion Detection Systems for Fog and Cloud Computing. *Future Internet*, 14, 3, 89, 2022, https://doi.org/10.3390/fi14030089.
30. Yasmeen, K. and Adnan, M., Zero-day and zero-click attacks on digital banking: a comprehensive review of double trouble. *Risk Manage.*, 25, 25, 2023, https://doi.org/10.1057/s41283-023-00130-4.
31. Nair, D. and Mhavan, N., Augmenting Cybersecurity: A Survey of Intrusion Detection Systems in Combating Zero-day Vulnerabilities, in: *Smart Analytics, Artificial Intelligence and Sustainable Performance Management in a Global Digitalised Economy (Contemporary Studies in Economic and Financial Analysis, vol. 110A)*, P. Tyagi, S. Grima, K. Sood, B. Balamurugan, E. Özen, T. Eleftherios, (Eds.), pp. 129–153, Emerald Publishing Limited, Leeds, 2023, https://doi.org/10.1108/S1569-37592023000110A007.
32. Sepúlveda Estay, D.A., A system dynamics, epidemiological approach for high-level cyber-resilience to zero-day vulnerabilities. *J. Simul., 17*, 1, 1–16, 2023, https://doi.org/10.1080/17477778.2021.1890533.
33. Nkongolo, M. and Tokmak, M., Zero-Day Threats Detection for Critical Infrastructures, in: *South African Institute of Computer Scientists and Information Technologists*. SAICSIT 2023. Communications in Computer and Information Science, vol. 1878, A. Gerber, and M. Coetzee, (Eds.), Springer, Cham, 2023, https://doi.org/10.1007/978-3-031-39652-6_3.
34. Singh, C. and Jain, A.K., A comprehensive survey on DDoS attacks detection & mitigation in SDN-IoT network. *e-Prime Adv. Electr. Eng. Electron. Energy*, 8, 100543, 2024, ISSN 2772-6711, https://doi.org/10.1016/j.prime.2024.100543.
35. Noonia, A., Beg, R., Patidar, A., Bawaskar, B., Sharma, S., Rawat, H., Chatbot vs Intelligent Virtual Assistance (IVA), in: *Conversational Artificial Intelligence*, pp. 655–673, 2024.

36. Ilca, L.F., Lucian, O.P., Balan, T.C., Enhancing Cyber-Resilience for Small and Medium-Sized Organizations with Prescriptive Malware Analysis, Detection and Response. *Sensors*, 23, 15, 6757, 2023, https://doi.org/10.3390/s23156757.
37. Silvia Priscila, S., Sharma, A., Vanithamani, S., Ahmad, F., Mahaveerakannan, R., Alrubaie, A.J., Jagota, V., Singh, B.K., [Retracted] Risk-Based Access Control Mechanism for Internet of Vehicles Using Artificial Intelligence. *Secur. Commun. Netw.*, 2022, Article ID 3379843, 13, 2022, https://doi.org/10.1155/2022/3379843.
38. Zekrifa, D.M.S., Sharma, A., Satyam, Patankar, A.J., Bamane, K.D., Data Analyzing with Cloud Computing Including Related Tools and Techniques. *Int. J. Intell. Syst. Appl. Eng.*, 11, 9s, 233–238, 2023, Retrieved from https://ijisae.org/index.php/IJISAE/article/view/3112.
39. Sharma, A. and Dixit, V., A Survey on Reliability of Cloud Applications. *Int'l Conf. Emerging Trends and Developments in Science, Management and Technology (ICETDSMT '13)*, pp. 476–481, 2013/3, ISBN: 978-81-924342-2-3.
40. Zekrifa, D., Sharma, A., Sharma, D., Sharma, R., Rai, S., Pillai, A., A System Based on AI and M1 Enhanced to Investigate Physiological Markers for User Forecasting Decision-Making, pp. 2487–2490, 2023, 10.1109/IC3I59117.2023.10398037.
41. Vijayakumar, T., Ramalakshmi, K., Priyadharsini, C., Vasanthakumar, S., Shaina, Sharma, A., Bio-Inspired Optimization Algorithm on Cloud based Image Retrieval System using Deep Features. *2022 International Conference on Augmented Intelligence and Sustainable Systems (ICAISS)*, Trichy, India, pp. 871–876, 2022, doi: 10.1109/ICAISS55157.2022.10010739.
42. Pithawa, D., Nahar, S., Bhardwaj, V., Rawat, R., Dronawat, R., Rawat, A., Quantum Computing Technological Design Along with Its Dark Side, in: *Quantum Computing in Cybersecurity*, pp. 295–312, 2023.
43. Carrier, T., Victor, P., Tekeoglu, A., Lashkari, A.H., Detecting Obfuscated Malware using Memory Feature Engineering. *The 8th International Conference on Information Systems Security and Privacy (ICISSP)*, 2022.
44. Mahdavifar, A.S., Maleki, N., Lashkari, A.H., Broda, M., Razavi, A.H., Classifying Malicious Domains using DNS Traffic Analysis. *The 19th IEEE International Conference on Dependable, Autonomic, and Secure Computing (DASC)*, Calgary, Canada, Oct. 25-28, 2021.
45. Apriorit, Zero-day Attacks Detection and Prevention Methods, 2022, [online]. Available: https://www.apriorit.com/dev-blog/450-zero-day-attack-detection. [Accessed: 20-4-2022].
46. Lashkari, A.H., Kaur, G., Rahali, A., DIDarknet: A Contemporary Approach to Detect and Characterize the Darknet Traffic using Deep Image Learning (https://dl.acm.org/doi/10.1145/3442520.3442521). *10th International Conference on Communication and Network Security*, Tokyo, Japan, November 2020.
47. Sharafaldin, I., Lashkari, A.H., Hakak, S., Ghorbani, A.A., Developing Realistic Distributed Denial of Service (DDoS) Attack Dataset and

Taxonomy (https://ieeexplore.ieee.org/abstract/document/8888419). *IEEE 53rd International Carnahan Conference on Security Technology*, Chennai, India, 2019.
48. Sharafaldin, I., Lashkari, A.H., Ghorbani, A.A., Toward Generating a New Intrusion Detection Dataset and Intrusion Traffic Characterization. *4th International Conference on Information Systems Security and Privacy (ICISSP)*, Portugal, January 2018.
49. Aldribi, A., Traore, I., Moa, B., Data Sources and Datasets for Cloud Intrusion Detection Modeling and Evaluation, in: *Cloud Computing for Optimization: Foundations, Applications, and Challenges*. Studies in Big Data, vol. 39, B. Mishra, H. Das, S. Dehuri, A. Jagadev (Eds.), pp. 333–366, Springer, USA, 2018.
50. Aldribi, A., Traore, I., Moa, B., Nwamuo, O., Hypervisor-Based Cloud Intrusion Detection through Online Multivariate Statistical Change Tracking, in: *Computers & Security*, vol. 88, Elsevier, USA, 2023, January 2020.
51. Rathore, N. and Rajavat, A., Smart Farming Based on IOT-Edge Computing: Applying Machine Learning Models For Disease And Irrigation Water Requirement Prediction In Potato Crop Using Containerized Microservices, in: *Precision Agriculture for Sustainability*, pp. 399–424, Apple Academic Press, USA, 2024.
52. Patsariya, M. and Rajavat, A., A Progressive Design of MANET Security Protocol for Reliable and Secure Communication. *Int. J. Intell. Syst. Appl. Eng.*, *12*, 9s, 190–204, 2024.
53. Rathi, M. and Rajavat, A., Investigations and Design of Privacy-Preserving Data Mining Technique for Secure Data Publishing. *Int. J. Intell. Syst. Appl. Eng.*, *11*, 9s, 351–367, 2023.
54. Dubey, P. and Rajavat, A., Effective K-means clustering algorithm for efficient data mining, in: *2023 2nd International Conference on Vision Towards Emerging Trends in Communication and Networking Technologies (ViTECoN)*, pp. 1–6, IEEE, 2023, May.
55. Chauhan, D., Singh, C., Rawat, R., Chouhan, M., Conversational AI Applications in Ed-Tech Industry: An Analysis of Its Impact and Potential in Education, in: *Conversational Artificial Intelligence*, pp. 411–433, 2024.
56. Chauhan, D., Singh, C., Rawat, R., Dhawan, M., Evaluating the Performance of Conversational AI Tools: A Comparative Analysis, in: *Conversational Artificial Intelligence*, pp. 385–409, 2024.

26

Predicting Rumors Spread Using Textual and Social Context in Propagation Graph with Graph Neural Network

Siddharath Kumar Arjaria[1], Hardik Sachan[1], Satyam Dubey[1], Ayush Pandey[1], Mansi Gautam[1], Nikita Gupta[1] and Abhishek Singh Rathore[2]*

[1]Department of Information Technology, Rajkiya Engineering College, Banda (U.P.), India

[2]Department of Computer Science & Engineering, Shri Vaishnav Vidyapeeth Vishwavidyalaya, Indore, India

Abstract

In today's age of digital advancement, it has become very easy for people to share their opinions on the internet. Social media platform like Twitter, Facebook, etc. connects people to share the latest news in the world. Rumor is a term used to describe unsubstantiated information or rumors that are widely shared by users but not verified by reliable sources. With this freedom of sharing tweets and opinions, it becomes very easy to spread a rumor. Rumors can create chaos in the public domain that can trigger fear, damage a person's image, and can also affect other sectors like the economy, etc. To control the damage, a strong rumor detection system is needed so that it can detect rumors with better accuracy. Previous models only consider the tweep profile and authenticity of the profile while this paper aims to develop a rumor detection system that uses the previous history of users, propagating pattern of tweets, and semantic relation of text content. At last, attention mechanism is also used to enhance the accuracy of the model. This comprehensive methodology harnesses the strengths of graph-based and textual analysis for nuanced and accurate rumor detection model on social media, particularly Twitter.

Keywords: Rumors detection, graph neural network, social media network, twitter, bert, word2vec, representation learning

**Corresponding author*: abhishekatujjain@gmail.com

Rajesh Kumar Chakrawarti, Ranjana Sikarwar, Sanjaya Kumar Sarangi, Samson Arun Raj Albert Raj, Shweta Gupta, Krishnan Sakthidasan Sankaran and Romil Rawat (eds.) Natural Language Processing for Software Engineering, (389–402)

26.1 Introduction

In today's digital age, where social media like Twitter and Facebook have become integral parts of our daily lives, the dependency on these platforms to disseminate information has skyrocketed. However, this increased reliance also brings with it the risk of the rapid spread of rumors, capable of causing significant disruptions in individuals' lives. The pervasive nature of social media makes it a fertile ground for the propagation of misinformation, necessitating a critical examination of the impact rumors can have on society.

The potential for rumors to bring about massive changes in the lives of individuals cannot be understated. False information, once unleashed on social media, can quickly gain traction, leading to widespread panic, confusion, and damage to reputations. Recognizing the urgency of the situation, the need for a robust rumor detection system has become increasingly apparent. As rumors can have far-reaching consequences, from affecting personal relationships to influencing political climates, the development of effective detection mechanisms has become a pressing concern.

Mitigating the effects of rumors is not only essential for safeguarding individual integrity but also for maintaining the stability of communities and societies at large. The destructive potential of false information necessitates proactive measures to identify and counteract rumors before they can cause irreparable harm. As a result, the focus on rumor detection has intensified in recent years, with researchers and technologists exploring various techniques to address this burgeoning issue.

The proposed methodology integrates multiple stages to form a comprehensive framework for rumor detection. Firstly, a hybrid data collection strategy combining API interfaces and third-party crawler programs is employed to extract Twitter rumors information from the Twitter public page. Feature extraction encompasses both content and context analysis, incorporating textual content and social context features of users involved in the tweet, such as followers, interests, and verified accounts.

Textual embeddings are generated using advanced models like Word2Vec [1] and Bidirectional Encoder Representations from Transformers (BERT) [2], enabling the system to understand the semantic relationships within tweet text. A unique contribution lies in the construction of a propagation graph, where the tweet serves as the root node and involved users as leaf nodes. Graph Neural Networks (GNNs) [3] are then applied to extract features capturing the influence and engagement of users. This involves message passing, node updating, and iterative refinement processes, allowing complex relationships within the network to be captured effectively.

Furthermore, an attention-based mechanism [4] combines textual embeddings with GNN-derived user involvement embeddings to obtain a precise and less redundant tweet representation. Finally, a neural classifier is trained on the integrated embeddings to predict the probability of a tweet being a rumor. This comprehensive methodology offers an advanced and adaptive solution, leveraging the strengths of both graph-based and textual analysis for more accurate and nuanced rumor detection on social media platforms, particularly Twitter.

The paper is organized as follows. Section 26.2 presents a review of the literature done for rumor identification. Section 26.3 discusses the proposed methodology, followed by section 26.4. Section 26.4 discusses the results of the proposed work.

26.2 Literature Review

This section covers the work done by different authors to detect rumors using machine learning techniques. Despite extensive research from various viewpoints, the dissemination mechanism of rumors has not been properly examined. In terms of monitoring, it is difficult to concretely define propagation patterns.

Ma *et al.* [5] applied recurrent neural networks to extract rumors sequentially. Yang *et al.* [6] extracted location and client-based [7] features to identify the rumors.

Kipf and Welling [8] presented a semi-supervised approach to graphical data. First-order approximations are applied on convolutional neural networks (CNN) for layer-wise propagation. Li *et al.* [9] added gate recurrent units [10] to update the output sequence of GNNs [3]. Xu *et al.* [11] combined GNNs with hierarchical analysis of text and propagation structure. The text-granularity and word-granularity features were integrated to provide hierarchically fused features that reflect word nodes in source text graphs.

Chen *et al.* [12] proposed a soft attention-based recurrent neural network that focuses on selective attributes and learns hidden representations of social posts over time. Gao *et al.* [13] used uncertainty semantics with event context to generate rumor representation using attention networks. Kwon *et al.* [14] identified three feature sets. Temporal and structural feature sets are extracted through time series which are later combined with linguistic feature sets to identify rumors in comparison with standard features. Later Kwon *et al.* [15] identified rumors spreading patterns using a three to two months window. Constraints have been proposed to remove options for using subject information as features, to make preconceived notions about the nature of the network, or to make preliminary assumptions about user characteristics about the information signal [16].

Song *et al.* [17] identified reposting sequences on microblogs to find detection points for early rumors detection. A convolutional neural network is proposed to identify the rumors spreading behavior of a person focusing on the past posts of the users, his reactions, and reposting the rumors [18]. Wang *et al.* [19] used a partition-based approach to identify rumors propagation structure and learn through a temporal attention network. The content and temporal structures are then fused to predict rumors in the network. Zhang and Hara [20] proposed a probabilistic model to classify malicious users, as the source of rumors. Rumors traceability under incomplete information is a real issue. A symmetric difference between the contaminated set at the final layer of the social network and the recently tainted set is identified to trace the sources of rumors [21].

Wei *et al.* [22] proposed a transformer-based learning model to capture deep rumor sequences and their semantic relationships. Zhu *et al.* [23] studied rumor propagation by analyzing the behavior of users through the reaction-diffusion dynamic model. Wang *et al.* [24] proposed an unsupervised model based on neighborhood information transmission. A generation-based improvement strategy is used to improve the results of the unsupervised model.

Patel *et al.* [25] tackle the class imbalance challenge in rumor detection through a combination of contextualized data augmentation, and novel GNN models. The oversampling technique creates synthetic examples for underrepresented classes in the dataset by utilizing contextualized data augmentation. The basic notion uses a thread's tweet selection for augmentation, which is made feasible by giving a non-random selection criterion that directs the augmentation process to relevant tweets.

Huang *et al.* [26] developed a tweet-word-user heterogeneous graph based on the text content and source tweet propagation of rumors. It captures the global semantic relations of text contents, as well as the global structural information of source tweet propagations, to identify rumors. Han *et al.* [27] suggested a classifier that provides balanced performance on both current and new datasets by employing continuous learning approaches to gradually train GNNs.

Wu *et al.* [28], created a gated propagation network based on the structure of Twitter postings. The propagation network constantly adjusts the weights of each node by integrating attention methods for improved classification tasks. Ali and Malik [29] employed Word2Vec and BERT to add contextual information in rumor identification.

Furthermore, past research employed emotional and conversational characteristics to identify rumors without taking into account distinct emotions, as well as effective PoS elements in content-based techniques. Similarly, the bulk of previous studies employed content-based techniques to feature development, while contemporary context-based approaches were not investigated. In addition, semantic and social characteristics are also not fully utilized for rumor identification.

26.3 Proposed Methodology

The proposed framework, TTRD (Tweep Tendency-aware Rumors News Detection), tackles the challenge of identifying rumors within news content. TTRD operates in three key stages:

a. Unveiling Tweep Tendencies: Analyze the historical social media activity (e.g., tweets) of tweeps who interacted with a news item to uncover their preexisting inclinations and tendencies. Text representation techniques like word2vec and BERT process their past posts to glean these insights. The news textual content is similarly encoded.
b. Capturing Network Dynamics: Moving beyond individual tendencies, Harness the "social fingerprint" of the news by constructing a network reflecting its propagation on social media platforms (e.g., retweet relationships on Twitter). This network analysis captures the broader context surrounding the news and its resonance with different tweep groups.
c. Integrating Tweep and Network Signals: The final stage seamlessly combines these insights through a multi-layered information fusion process. Leverage Graph Neural Networks (GNNs) to analyze the social network and extract an "involvement embedding" reflecting tweep interaction within it. This embedding is then combined with the encoded textual content of the news to create a comprehensive representation. Subsequent sections delve deeper into each component, detailing how to extract tweep tendencies, capture network dynamics, and ultimately fuse these elements by applying attention mechanisms to identify rumors within news content.

The proposed framework aims to detect tendencies in tweep-generated rumors news. By analyzing the news content alongside the interactions of active users on social media platforms, we construct a news propagation graph to capture the broader context. The intrinsic details are gleaned from tweeps' historical posts and the content of the news articles. These diverse sources of information are integrated using a GNN encoder. The resulting news representation combines user engagement features with textual attributes, which are then inputted into a neural classifier to assess the credibility of the news piece as shown in Figure 26.1: The proposed TTRD framework.

26.3.1 Tweep Tendency Encoding

Accurately modeling tweep tendencies solely from their social network data poses a significant challenge. Following prior work that infers personality, sentiment, and stance based on historical posts, propose an implicit

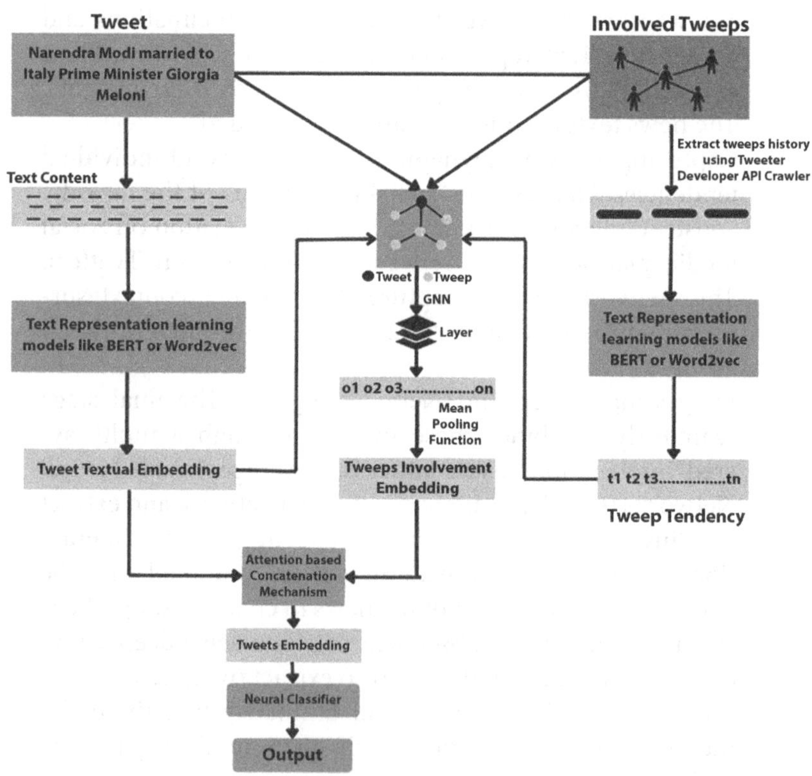

Figure 26.1 The proposed TTRD framework.

approach leveraging tweet analysis. However, existing rumors news datasets lack such tendency information.

To address this gap, the researchers utilize the Rumours News Net dataset, which provides news content and corresponding Twitter involvement data. By harnessing the Twitter Developer API, they retrieve the most recent 200 tweets (approximately 20 million in total) from accounts that retweeted each news item. To account for inaccessible accounts (e.g., suspended or deleted), they substitute random tweets with tweeps sharing the same news, ensuring the integrity of the news propagation cascade for effective context analysis.

Before using text representation learning methods, the data are preprocessed by removing special characters like "@" mentions and URLs. To capture both news content and tweep tendencies, two pre-trained language models are employed, and we follow these:

a. Word2vec: Leverage spaCy's pre-trained vectors for 680k words to encode semantic relationships between words and respective sentences. For each tweep, obtain their tendency representation by averaging the vectors of existing words in their combined 200 recent tweets. Similarly, create a news text embedding following the same process.
b. BERT: Use the cased BERT-Large model to encode news and tweep information as sequences. While the news content can be directly fed into BERT (max length 512 tokens), individual tweet encoding is required due to length limitations. Encode each tweet separately and average their resulting vectors to represent a tweep's tendency. To optimize encoding speed for shorter tweets compared to news text, empirically set the maximum tweet length to 16 tokens.

Combining these pre-trained models and carefully handling inaccessible accounts, creates a robust approach to encode tweep tendencies implicitly from their tweet history. This paves the way for further analysis and applications aimed at detecting rumors within news content.

26.3.2 Network Dynamics Extraction

The social fingerprint of a news piece on social media is influenced by the collective interactions of all users engaging with it. One has to delve into this fingerprint by constructing a news propagation graph. He/She has to imagine this graph like a branching tree (refer to Figure 26.1): the root represents the news, and each branch signifies a tweep who shared it. This paper focuses on rumor detection on Twitter, using this approach as a proof of concept.

To build these Twitter networks, one has to follow established methods. He/She has to consider a news item as node v_1 and tweeps who retweeted it as nodes v_2 to v_n, listed chronologically. Two rules guide how to establish the news propagation path:

Rule 1: Following the Trend: If tweep v_i retweets the news after any previous retweeter in the sequence (v_1 to v_n), assume the news spread from the later tweep to v_i. This logic stems from the assumption that recent tweets are more likely to be seen and retweeted.
Rule 2: Leveraging Influence: If v_i doesn't follow any previous retweeters, conservatively assume the news spread from the tweeps with the highest follower count. This reflects the higher visibility of tweets from these tweeps based on Twitter's content distribution mechanisms.

Utilize these guidelines to create news dissemination graphs on Twitter. This method can also be expanded to other social networking sites [33–35] such as Facebook [29–32].

26.3.3 Extracted Information Integration

Previous research has shown that combining tweep features with news propagation graphs can significantly enhance fake news detection accuracy. Graph Neural Networks (GNNs) excel at this task due to their ability to seamlessly integrate node features and graph structure within a unified learning framework. Propose a hierarchical information fusion approach that leverages this strength, further refined by an attention mechanism for a more precise and robust representation.

Stage 1: GNN-based tweep tendency and network dynamics Information Integration:

1. Node Feature Preparation: Represent the news content using its textual embedding and each tweep's tendency using their embedding derived from historical tweets. These embeddings serve as node features in the news propagation graph.
2. GNN Feature Aggregation: Employing a GNN, aggregate the features of a node's neighbors to refine its representation.

This process captures the collective influence of related tweeps and the underlying network structure.

3. Pooling Function: Similar to graph classification models using GNNs, apply a pooling function (e.g., mean pooling) overall node embeddings to obtain a single embedding for the entire news propagation graph, effectively summarizing the collective "tweep involvement embedding."

Stage 2: Attention-based Refinement of Tweep Involvement Embedding: To further refine the tweep involvement embedding obtained from the GNN, introduce an attention mechanism that focuses on the most relevant aspects of each tweep's involvement:

1. Dot Product Attention: Employ a dot-product attention mechanism that calculates the similarity between the tweep involvement embedding and each tweep's embedding, considering various factors:
   - Tweep Tendency: Accounts with tendencies similar to the news content are assigned higher weights, reflecting their potential bias or alignment.
   - Tweep Profile Features: Verified accounts with more followers typically indicate greater credibility and receive higher weights.
   - Tweep Belief: Tweeps who express positive sentiments or beliefs aligned with the news content gain higher weights, reflecting potential agreement or support.
2. Weighted Combination: Based on these attention weights, create a weighted combination of the tweep involvement embedding and each tweep's embedding, highlighting the most relevant information for this particular news item.

Stage 3: Final News Embedding and Classification:

1. Concatenation: Enrich the news embedding by concatenating the refined tweep involvement embedding with the original news textual embedding. This combined representation captures both the content itself and the surrounding social context.
2. Multilayer Perceptron (MLP): The fused news embedding is fed into a two-layer MLP with two output neurons, predicting the probabilities of the news being fake or real.

3. Training and Optimization: The model is trained using a binary cross-entropy loss function and optimized with stochastic gradient descent (SGD).

26.4 Results and Discussion

Dataset: To explore the dissemination of rumors on social media, we have selected the Rumors dataset, which comprises information on both rumor and non-rumor tweets. This dataset includes data from two fact-checking websites as well as the corresponding social engagement on Twitter. By analyzing the tweet tendency and the involvement of Twitter users, we aim to gain insights into the propagation of rumors as shown in Table 26.1: Dataset and graph statistics.

For extracting the tweep information use an API crawler that extracts information of all the tweeps which are related to the tweet. Upon evaluation, observe that the TTRD model has a better performance compared to all other models. The experimental results of TTRD show that Social Context significantly improves the result, and the Tweet Tendency and attention mechanism could help when the text content of the tweet is limited. The attention mechanism gives importance to only those attributes that play a considerable role in spreading the rumors as given in Table 26.2: Performance Evaluation.

Second, all other models encode the text content (tweet) without considering the tweep history, which can tell that leveraging the tweep history could improve the Rumor detection performance. The TTRD with the best performance on both datasets uses BERT as the text encoder as shown in Table 26.3: Rumor detection model performance with different node features models and types.

Table 26.1 Dataset and graph statistics.

Dataset	#Graphs (#Rumour)	#Total Nodes	#Total Edge	#Avg. Nodes per Graph
PolitiFact (POL)	360 (148)	41,054	42,740	135
Gossip cop (GOS)	5556 (2830)	314,262	305,457	62

Table 26.2 Performance evaluation.

	Model	POL		GOS	
		ACC	F1	ACC	F1
Tweets Only	BERT+MLP	72.06	72.03	85.05	85.35
	word2vec+MLP	77.47	76.86	85.61	85.9
Tweets+ Tweeps Involved	GNN-CL	63.90	63.25	95.28	95.34
	GCNFN	84.16	84.56	96.58	96.46
	TTRD (ours)	84.82%	84.85%	97.23%	97.22%

Table 26.3 Rumor detection model performance with different node features models and types.

Feature	POL				GOS			
	Graph SAGE		GCNFN		Graph SAGE		GCNFN	
	Accuracy	F1	Accuracy	F1	Accuracy	F1	Accuracy	F1
ProRile	77.58	77.42	77.04	76.92	92.69	92.56	89.10	89.06
word2vec	80.64	80.71	80.74	80.81	96.91	96.89	95.07	95.05
BERT	84.82	84.73	83.86	83.54	97.43	97.22	96.18	96.17

26.5 Conclusion

Rumors can spread quickly and unpredictably on social media platforms, making automatic rumor detection technology a necessity. In this paper, we developed a deep attention-based rumor detection model. The model is divided into 3 stages. Initially, news contents and tweeps are extracted for news propagation network. Tweeps are used to identify social fingerprints. Then a propagation network is constructed. The graph neural network is used to fuse the news contents and graphical structure. It provides the unified learning framework. An attention-based refinement is applied to GNN to find news embedding.

At present, images and videos are major sources of rumors and fake news. And such contents increase when a country faces national elections. Future work of this article is to extract features that are suspicious and integrate them to our proposed propagation network.

References

1. Mishra, A. K., Tyagi, A. K., Dananjayan, S., Rajavat, A., Rawat, H., Rawat, A., Revolutionizing Government Operations: The Impact of Artificial Intelligence in Public Administration, in: *Conversational Artificial Intelligence*, pp. 607–634, 2024
2. Nahar, S., Pithawa, D., Bhardwaj, V., Rawat, R., Rawat, A., Pachlasiya, K., Quantum technology for military applications, in: *Quantum Computing in Cybersecurity*, pp. 313–334, 2023.
3. Scarselli, F., Gori, M., Tsoi, A.C., Hagenbuchner, M., Monfardini, G., The Graph Neural Network Model. *IEEE Trans. Neural Networks,* 20, 1, 61–80, Jan. 2009, doi: 10.1109/TNN.2008.2005605.
4. Bahdanau, D., Cho, K., Bengio, Y., Neural Machine Translation by Jointly Learning to Align and Translate. Sep. 2014, [Online]. Available: http://arxiv.org/abs/1409.0473.
5. Ma, J. *et al.*, Detecting rumours from microblogs with recurrent neural networks, in: *IJCAI International Joint Conference on Artificial Intelligence*, vol. 2016-January, pp. 3818–3824, 2016.
6. Yang, F., Liu, Y., Yu, X., Yang, M., Automatic detection of rumour on Sina Weibo, in: *Proceedings of the ACM SIGKDD Workshop on Mining Data Semantics*, Aug. 2012, pp. 1–7, doi: 10.1145/2350190.2350203.
7. Rawat, R., Telang, S., William, P., Kaur, U., CU, O. K. (Eds.)., *Dark Web Pattern Recognition and Crime Analysis Using Machine Intelligence*. IGI Global, 2022.
8. Sikarwar, R., Shakya, H.K., Kumar, A., Rawat, A., Advanced Security Solutions for Conversational AI, in: *Conversational Artificial Intelligence*, pp. 287–301, 2024.
9. Pithawa, D., Nahar, S., Bhardwaj, V., Rawat, R., Dronawat, R., Rawat, A., Quantum Computing Technological Design Along with Its Dark Side, in: *Quantum Computing in Cybersecurity*, pp. 295–312, 2023.
10. Namdev, A., Patni, D., Dhaliwal, B.K., Parihar, S., Telang, S., Rawat, A., Potential Threats and Ethical Risks of Quantum Computing, in: *Quantum Computing in Cybersecurity*, pp. 335–352, 2023.
11. Xu, S. *et al.*, Rumour detection on social media using hierarchically aggregated feature via graph neural networks. *Appl. Intell.*, 53, 3, 3136–3149, Feb. 2023, doi: 10.1007/s10489-022-03592-3.
12. Shrivastava, M., Patil, R., Bhardwaj, V., Rawat, R., Telang, S., Rawat, A., Quantum Computing and Security Aspects of Attention-Based Visual Question Answering with Long Short-Term Memory, in: *Quantum Computing in Cybersecurity*, pp. 395–412, 2023
13. Gao, Y., Han, X., Li, B., A Neural Rumour Detection Framework by Incorporating Uncertainty Attention on Social Media Texts, in: *Cognitive Computing – ICCC 2019*, pp. 91–101, 2019.

14. Noonia, A., Beg, R., Patidar, A., Bawaskar, B., Sharma, S., Rawat, H., Chatbot vs Intelligent Virtual Assistance (IVA), in: *Conversational Artificial Intelligence*, pp. 655–673, 2024
15. Rawat, R., Kaur, U., Khan, S. P., Sikarwar, R., Sankaran, K. (Eds.), *Using Computational Intelligence for the Dark Web and Illicit Behavior Detection*. IGI Global, 2022, https://doi.org/10.4018/978-1-6684-6444-1
16. Rawat, R., Telang, S., William, P., Kaur, U., C.U., O. (Eds.), *Dark Web Pattern Recognition and Crime Analysis Using Machine Intelligence*. IGI Global, 2022, https://doi.org/10.4018/978-1-6684-3942-5
17. Song, C., Yang, C., Chen, H., Tu, C., Liu, Z., Sun, M., CED: Credible Early Detection of Social Media Rumours. *IEEE Trans. Knowl. Data Eng.*, 33, 8, 3035–3047, Aug. 2021, doi: 10.1109/TKDE.2019.2961675.
18. Rawat, R., Chakrawarti, R.K., Sarangi, S.K., Patel, J., Bhardwaj, V., Rawat, A., Rawat, H. (eds.), in: *Quantum Computing in Cybersecurity*. John Wiley & Sons, 2023. https://onlinelibrary.wiley.com/doi/book/10.1002/9781394167401
19. Suthar, H., Rawat, H., Gayathri, M., Chidambarathanu, K., Techno-Nationalism and Techno-Globalization: A Perspective from the National Security Act, in: *Quantum Computing in Cybersecurity*, pp. 137–164, 2023
20. Zhang, Y. and Hara, T., A probabilistic model for malicious user and rumour detection on social media, in: *Proceedings of the Annual Hawaii International Conference on System Sciences*, vol. 2020-January, 2020, doi: 10.24251/hicss.2020.309.
21. Li, Y., Zhu, J., Wang, G., Huang, J., Rumour source identification under incomplete information in dynamic social network. *Xitong Gongcheng Lilun yu Shijian/Syst. Eng. Theory Pract.*, 43, 4, 1132–1144, Apr. 2023, doi: 10.12011/SETP2022-0262.
22. Singh, R., and Rajavat, A., Short-Lived Social Vehicular Network, in: *2024 International Conference on Electronics, Computing, Communication and Control Technology (ICECCC)*, pp. 1–9, IEEE, 2024, May
23. Singh, R., and Rajavat, A., VANET Security Using Blockchain, in: *Fostering Multidisciplinary Research for Sustainability*, p. 159, 2024
24. Vyas, G., Vyas, P., Muzumdar, P., Chennamaneni, A., Rajavat, A., Rawat, R., Extracting and Analyzing Factors to Identify the Malicious Conversational AI Bots on Twitter, in: *Conversational Artificial Intelligence*, pp. 71–83, 2024
25. Rawat, R., and Rajavat, A., Perceptual Operating Systems for the Trade Associations of Cyber Criminals to Scrutinize Hazardous Content. *Int. J. Cyber Warf. Terror. (IJCWT)*, 14, 1, 1–19, 2024.
26. Chauhan, D., Singh, C., Rawat, R., Dhawan, M., Evaluating the Performance of Conversational AI Tools: A Comparative Analysis, in: *Conversational Artificial Intelligence*, pp. 385–409, 2024.
27. Rawat, R., Chakrawarti, R.K., Sarangi, S.K., Choudhary, R., Gadwal, A.S., Bhardwaj, V. (eds.), *Robotic Process Automation*. John Wiley & Sons, 2023.
28. Manmadhan, S., and Kovoor, B.C., Visual question answering: a state-of-the-art review. *Artif. Intell. Rev.*, 53, 8, 5705–5745, 2020.

29. Ali, G. and Malik, M.S.I., Rumour identification on Twitter as a function of novel textual and language-context features. *Multimed. Tools Appl.*, 82, 5, 7017–7038, Feb. 2023, doi: 10.1007/s11042-022-13595-4.
30. Rathore, N. and Rajavat, A., Smart Farming Based on IOT-Edge Computing: Applying Machine Learning Models For Disease And Irrigation Water Requirement Prediction In Potato Crop Using Containerized Microservices, in: *Precision Agriculture for Sustainability*, pp. 399–424, Apple Academic Press, USA, 2024.
31. Patsariya, M. and Rajavat, A., A Progressive Design of MANET Security Protocol for Reliable and Secure Communication. *Int. J. Intell. Syst. Appl. Eng.*, *12*, 9s, 190–204, 2024.
32. Rathi, M. and Rajavat, A., Investigations and Design of Privacy-Preserving Data Mining Technique for Secure Data Publishing. *Int. J. Intell. Syst. Appl. Eng.*, *11*, 9s, 351–367, 2023.
33. Dubey, P. and Rajavat, A., Effective K-means clustering algorithm for efficient data mining, in: *2023 2nd International Conference on Vision Towards Emerging Trends in Communication and Networking Technologies (ViTECoN)*, pp. 1–6, IEEE, 2023, May.
34. Chauhan, D., Singh, C., Rawat, R., Chouhan, M., Conversational AI Applications in Ed-Tech Industry: An Analysis of Its Impact and Potential in Education, in: *Conversational Artificial Intelligence*, pp. 411–433, 2024.
35. Chauhan, D., Singh, C., Rawat, R., Dhawan, M., Evaluating the Performance of Conversational AI Tools: A Comparative Analysis, in: *Conversational Artificial Intelligence*, pp. 385–409, 2024.

27

Implications, Opportunities, and Challenges of Blockchain in Natural Language Processing

Neha Agrawal[1*], Balwinder Kaur Dhaliwal[2], Shilpa Sharma[3], Neha Yadav[4] and Ranjana Sikarwar[5]

[1]*Department of Computer Science Engineering, Shri Vaishnav Vidyapeeth Vishwavidyalaya, Indore, India*
[2]*Department of Computer Science and Engineering, Lovely Professional University, Jalandhar, Punjab, India*
[3]*Master of Computer Applications Department, IPS Academy, Sanwer Campus, Indore, MP, India*
[4]*Institute of Engineering and Science, IPS Academy, Indore, MP, India*
[5]*Amity University, Gwalior, MP, India*

Abstract

Blockchain technology is becoming a game-changer in sectors including healthcare, banking, and supply chain management. Its possible influence on Natural Language Processing (NLP) is still mainly untapped, nevertheless. The goal of natural language processing (NLP), a branch of artificial intelligence, is to make text resources comprehensible, interpreted, and producible by computers. This article examines how blockchain and natural language processing might work together, emphasizing the possible advantages for enhancing data security, trust, and transparency. NLP is challenged by unstructured text data, which includes problems with data quality and origin verifiability. The blockchain's decentralized and unchangeable properties offer a remedy by fostering confidence and guaranteeing the authenticity of textual materials. The article explores the use of blockchain technology in copyright protection, plagiarism detection, and content verification, emphasizing its capacity to verify material and stop intellectual property theft. Furthermore, decentralized, and cooperative textual data annotation and categorization are made easier by the combination of blockchain technology and natural language processing, which raises

**Corresponding author*: agrawal.na@gmail.com

Rajesh Kumar Chakrawarti, Ranjana Sikarwar, Sanjaya Kumar Sarangi, Samson Arun Raj Albert Raj, Shweta Gupta, Krishnan Sakthidasan Sankaran and Romil Rawat (eds.) Natural Language Processing for Software Engineering, (403–424) © 2025 Scrivener Publishing LLC

the Caliber and accessibility of annotated datasets. But to properly utilize the potential of this integration, issues with scalability, privacy, and transparency need to be resolved. This paper advances the development of secure, dependable, and effective NLP systems through a thorough study of the body of existing literature, use case analysis, discussion of challenges, and suggestion of future research areas.

Keywords: Natural language processing, blockchain, artificial intelligence, decentralization, security

27.1 Introduction

Blockchain technology is becoming more and more potent, revolutionizing a wide range of sectors, including supply chain management, healthcare, and finance. By combining with Blockchain technology, AI applications become more powerful and address issues with trust and data integrity. Blockchain technology and artificial intelligence together create a safe foundation for innovation in a time when industries are becoming more and more reliant on data-driven decision-making [1, 2]. Blockchain and AI work together to create a strong coalition that addresses problems with efficiency, transparency, and data security. As a result, the market for blockchain and AI technologies is expected to grow at a compound annual growth rate (CAGR) of 25.3% from 2020 to 2025, surpassing $703 million as shown in Figure 27.1 [3].

Natural language processing (NLP) is a subfield of artificial intelligence (AI) that aims to enable computer devices and applications to comprehend, interpret, and produce organized and accessible corpora in human

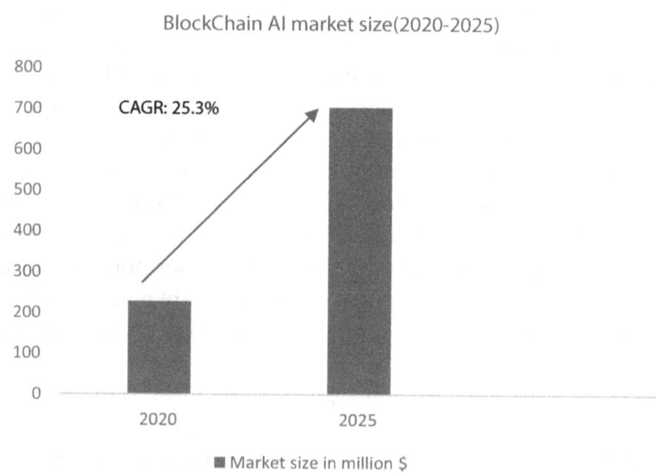

Figure 27.1 Blockchain AI market size.

languages [4]. The combination of blockchain technology and natural language processing has great promise for enhancing data security, fostering trust, and increasing transparency. Its possible influence on Natural Language Processing (NLP) is still largely unknown, though.

NLP researchers face many difficulties when dealing with unstructured textual data that may be found on the Internet, such as news stories, social media posts, and scientific publications. Data confidentiality, data quality, and data origin reliability are a few possible problems. By ensuring confidence and integrity of textual resources, blockchain technology—with its decentralized and immutable register—offers a solution. Blockchain technology can help NLP researchers and developers address important problems like secure data sharing, copyright protection, plagiarism detection, and locating data references.

Blockchain technology is being applied in NLP for the purposes of copyright protection and content verification, or authentication. This is achieved by keeping the original text's distinct hash values on the blockchain. This creates a decentralized, tamper-proof block that makes it possible to verify the text's integrity and authorship. Additionally, by comparing hashes of suspected material with those blocks on the blockchain, blockchain technology can help detect plagiarism [5] more effectively while guaranteeing authenticity and avoiding intellectual property (IP) infringement.

Additionally, the combination of blockchain technology and natural language processing creates new avenues for collaborative and decentralized textual data annotation and classification. Blockchain-based systems can improve the availability and quality of annotated datasets, which will help NLP research and model development, by incentivizing contributors through tokenization and intelligent categorization.

But despite its enormous potential, there are obstacles to overcome before blockchain technology can be applied to NLP. This involves worries about scalability as Blockchain networks facing large-scale NLP applications face scalability challenges. Blockchain's intrinsic immutability and transparency raise privacy issues, especially when handling sensitive text data. Private information may be revealed in NLP applications due to the decentralized and publicly accessible nature of blockchain technology. Transparency and trust are fostered by blockchain technology, but there may be trade-offs between the two. Furthermore, not all data can be made public within NLP applications, and it might be difficult to strike a balance between openness and the security of private information.

Our research study reviews the literature, looks at used examples, and analyses obstacles to give readers a thorough grasp of how blockchain technology affects NLP. In the end, this study's unique contribution will be to advance the state of the art in blockchain technology and NLP research, creating chances for cutting-edge applications and encouraging cooperative, safe, and reliable NLP systems.

The integration of NLP with blockchain technologies is examined in the remaining study. The second section gives a general review of NLP and blockchain technology, highlighting both of their key features and range of uses. After that, Section 3 delves into the topic of fusing blockchain technology with natural language processing, examining the possible advantages of doing so. We will examine a range of used cases and applications of blockchain in NLP, such as enhancing text authentication and plagiarism detection, enhancing the origin and validity of data, and providing decentralized translation services. Scalability, privacy, and transparency issues related to this integration will also be looked at, with an emphasis on suggested fixes and future paths. Section four concludes with a list of future projects and conclusions.

27.2 Related Work

The potential for combining blockchain and NLP has been extensively studied in a variety of domains. The authors of [6] proposed a system to improve the security and reliability of event data by taking advantage of blockchain technology's immutability and decentralization features as well as the precision and effectiveness of NLP and RNN algorithms for processing and analyzing natural language data. To guarantee accurate and reliable evaluations, a reputation-based review evaluation system is presented in [7] and is constructed on top of the blockchain system. The reviewers' reputations are then modified depending on this evaluation.

The authors of [8] describe a computational model that uses blockchain technology and natural language processing (NLP) to create intelligent codes from the analysis of legislation. The prototype and preliminary testing of the model are presented, and the results are promising; they demonstrate the applicability of the research topic. Using social media platforms as a key component, the authors of [9] developed a solution for managing disasters and emergency response that focuses on text analysis techniques to enhance the emergency response process of authorities and filter information using automatically gathered data to support relief efforts.

In [10], the research highlights the need for high-quality abstract summaries in handling textual and multimedia content, explaining the difficulties and methods involved. The paper focuses on detecting false media utilizing natural language processing and blockchain technology. The author of [11] presented a system for evaluating employee performance that combines blockchain technology with natural language processing (NLP) to extract characteristics from text input and store them on blockchain, which improves accuracy and transparency. The author of [12] suggested using blockchain technology to securely retain patient records and facilitate quick and easy claims processing. A tabular description of some related research is shown in Table 27.1.

Table 27.1 Various research work on NLP with blockchain.

S. no.	Paper	Authors	Proposed work
1	Blockchain based Secure Event Management System using NLP and RNN Algorithm [6]	Jayakumar D, Haripriya G	This paper, besides using the accuracy and efficiency of NLP and RNN algorithms to process and analyze event data, also uses Blockchain to improve event security by storing validated data in a decentralized, safe manner.
2	Maintaining Review Credibility Using NLP, Reputation, and Blockchain [7]	Zachary Zaccagni; Ram Dantu	Blockchain is used with NLP to preserve review credibility by securely storing reviewers' reputations and evaluation results, thus ensuring reliable evaluations in a decentralized system.
3	Combining Natural Language Processing and Blockchain for Smart Contract Generation in the Accounting and Legal Field [8]	Emiliano Monteiro, Rodrigo Righi	This paper combines NLP and Blockchain for the creation of smart contracts in legal operations. This improves code accuracy and automates the process of interpreting legislation.

(Continued)

Table 27.1 Various research work on NLP with blockchain. (*Continued*)

S. no.	Paper	Authors	Proposed work
4	Blockchain-Based Event Detection and Trust Verification Using Natural Language Processing and Machine Learning [9]	Zeinab Shahbazi; Yung-Cheol Byun	In this paper, Blockchain is used in disaster management to verify confidence in event detection through Natural Language Processing. By removing a single point of authority, it improves security and openness and guarantees accurate information sharing on social media.
5	Fake Media Detection Based on Natural Language Processing and Blockchain Approaches [10]	Zeinab Shahbazi; Yung-Cheol Byun	The paper suggests an approach to combine NLP and blockchain with machine learning methods to detect fraudulent accounts and news.
6	Using Natural Language Processing and Blockchain for Employee Performance Evaluation [11]	Umesh Prasad, Soumitro Chakravarty	It combines blockchain and NLP, with the aim to provide a more reliable and accurate way of evaluating employee performance.
7	Smart Patient Records using NLP and Blockchain [12].	Akash Dubey, Kartik Jain	The paper suggests how blockchain can be used to securely keep health records and facilitate quick claim processing.

27.3 Overview on Blockchain Technology and NLP

Due to the potential for influence in various domains, including finance, blockchain technology and natural language processing (NLP) are two emerging technologies. Consequently, investigating the potentially transformational potential of blockchain technology requires an understanding of its foundations and how it intersects with NLP.

27.3.1 Blockchain Technology, Features, and Applications

Blockchain technology, which is a distributed, decentralized ledger that safely records and validates transactions over a network of computers, is frequently linked to cryptocurrencies. It uses cryptographic concepts to guarantee data storage stability, transparency, and trustworthiness. Every transaction or bit of data is included in a "block" that is connected to other blocks to create a chain of information. Due to its numerous distinctive qualities, blockchain technology is becoming more and more popular and widely used in a variety of industries. The features and advantages of blockchain technology are discussed in the following sections.

- **Decentralization**
  One of the fundamental characteristics of the blockchain is decentralization. Blockchain operates on a distributed network of computers, also known as nodes, which collaboratively maintain and verify the integrity of the system and data, in contrast to previous centralized systems [5]. Decentralization also guarantees that no one party has total control over the data, enhancing transparency and lowering the possibility of manipulation. Popular blockchain-based cryptocurrency Bitcoin is operated by a global decentralized network of nodes. Peer-to-peer transactions can be safe and transparent without the need for middlemen when there is no central authority.

- **Transparency and Immutable Records**
  Blockchain keeps an unchangeable, transparent record of all network-stored transactions and data. There is a high level of data integrity and trust since once a transaction or piece of information is recorded in a block, it is nearly hard to change or tamper with. We mention Ethereum (https://ethereum.

org/en/), the second biggest blockchain platform, in this context since it makes smart contract formulation and execution possible. These self-executing agreements are openly documented on the blockchain, guaranteeing the conditions of the agreement's immutability, and fostering mutual confidence amongst the involved parties.

- **Security**
  Blockchain protects data and transactions with cutting-edge encryption technologies. Information is shielded against unwanted access and manipulation by encryption, which also guarantees the information's authenticity, integrity, and confidentiality. To ensure that only authorized parties may access and edit data, a blockchain architecture for business applications, for example, can use encryption techniques to safeguard and validate transactions.

- **Traceability and Audibility**
  Blockchain offers a thorough audit trail of every activity and transaction registered on the network. This traceability feature encourages accountability and transparency by allowing tracking and verification of the ownership, movement, and provenance of assets. In fact, the supply chain sector has improved traceability by utilizing blockchain technology. To trace and validate the provenance and path of food goods, for instance, several food companies employ blockchain technology. This gives customers access to comprehensive details regarding the provenance, ingredients, and processing of a product. The aforementioned features of blockchain technology have the power to transform industries by enhancing efficiency, security, traceability, and transparency. The development of blockchain technology is creating new avenues for innovation and disruption in several industries, including finance, supply chains, healthcare, and government.

27.3.2 Natural Language Processing

The main goal of natural language processing (NLP) is to make computer programs and devices able to communicate with humans through language translation, sentiment analysis, speech recognition, Chabot interactions, and other tasks. For the interpretation, processing, and creation of human language, it combines several technologies, such as rule-based systems, machine learning, deep learning, and language analysis. While these security concerns are rapidly growing, several academics are unaware of the critical role that natural language processing (NLP) approaches play in applications that try to detect spam in mailboxes, intrusion detection, and cyber threats identification. Considering this, we provide a brief description of how NLP approaches are used in spam identification. Spam emails are always changing and no longer fit for old methods of detection. Cybercriminals bypass spam filters by manipulating material and employing social engineering techniques. To detect possible spam, natural language processing (NLP) algorithms examine text patterns, language traits, and email metadata. But to stay put with the latest spams, NLP-based spam detection systems need to upgrade their algorithms frequently.

27.3.3 Challenges in NLP

NLP has numerous difficulties because of the intricacy and ambiguity of human language as well as the rise in data production in the digital age. It is evident that the language used by humans is ambiguous, with words and phrases having several meanings that can be clarified depending on the situation. For NLP systems to accurately comprehend and interpret human language, resolving linguistic ambiguity appears to be a necessary first step. When comprehending a language, knowledge of its syntactic structure and grammatical rules is crucial. It is challenging to capture and represent the intricate syntax and grammar of a natural language because of its variances, exceptions, and informal expressions [19]. Furthermore, the most challenging issue in NLP is determining the semantic meaning of the linguistic components. This implies that a word's meaning might vary depending on the context in which it is used, and that deciphering the intended meaning necessitates a thorough comprehension and study of the context given the precision of that analysis. Large volumes of textual data are needed for NLP systems to train their models and generate predictions. Therefore, maintaining data integrity is crucial to avoiding biases and errors that may result from erroneous, incomplete, or deceptive data gathering. Robust NLP applications require high-quality, properly annotated data sets with data source and validation techniques.

27.3.4 Data Integration and Accuracy in NLP

Because they guarantee dependable outcomes, lessen biases, provide high-quality annotations to data, and create dependable tools, data accuracy and integrity are crucial to NLP. These two elements contribute to the enhanced functionality and efficacy of natural language processing (NLP) systems in various domains, including the healthcare industry, where NLP technologies are essential for processing patient data, including medical reports, health records, etc. In [20] the authors propose an intelligent data integration approach that combines ontology learning, automated mapping, and statistical methods to effectively integrate data and knowledge from diverse sources. Through the use of NLP techniques and semantic analysis, this approach attempts to bridge the gap between disparate data formats and facilitate the integration of valuable information into the knowledge framework.

Since users must have faith in the systems' ability to accurately comprehend and interpret their language input, data accuracy is another essential component in the successful adoption of NLP systems. Moreover, reproducible outcomes, ethical biases or issues that may surface during language processing, and transparent and interpretive natural language processing (NLP) models are all important ways to foster data accuracy. To raise the strength and dependability of NLP datasets, researchers are constantly creating methods for data standardization, cleansing, and annotation. Large numbers of labeled sentences or phrases (related to statistical techniques) are typically included in these datasets, which enable researchers to assess and compare performance.

In NLP, suggested applications and tools must raise the bar for accuracy, data integrity, and cooperation amongst well-established language processing programs. We therefore want to investigate how blockchain and NLP interact. This convergence might offer a viable route for creating innovative solutions that bring together the strength of blockchain technology and natural language processing skills to achieve reliable and safe language processing in the modern digital era.

27.4 Integration of Blockchain into NLP

Combining blockchain technology with natural language processing is a potential field of study and application. NLP researchers can solve numerous issues in this discipline, including data integrity, accuracy, and privacy, by utilizing blockchain technology [21]. Moreover, the decentralized and unchangeable characteristics of Blockchain enable data provenance tracking, guarantee copyright protection, expedite plagiarism detection, and provide safe data exchange among NLP applications.

NLP can validate content originality and safeguard intellectual property (IP) rights by integrating blockchain. Then, because hash values—unique identifiers of the original content—are stored on the blockchain, it is feasible to verify again the authorship and integrity of the textual material. Consequently, this aids in avoiding both plagiarism and infringement of copyright.

Additionally, the blockchain can provide collaborative, decentralized annotation and labeling of textual material, increasing the number of annotated datasets available and enhancing their quality for usage in NLP research projects. Furthermore, Blockchain-based solutions can offer a transparent and safe framework for exchanging NLP data, ensuring that all parties involved may manage their data, giving specific parties access while maintaining data security and privacy. Users can safely exchange resources and language models, for instance, on a blockchain-based data marketplace. One such marketplace would enable businesses and researchers to access and utilize NLP data while retaining ownership and control over their contributions. Furthermore, the construction of reliable linguistic paradigms may be aided by the integration of blockchain technology with natural language processing.

Therefore, users can get increased confidence in the output of NLP models based on the transparency and auditability that blockchain technology provides. Suppose that a blockchain-based language model enables users to track the entire lifecycle of the model, including the used training data and updates this level of transparency ensures that users have visibility into the factors that influence form behavior as shown in Figure 27.2.

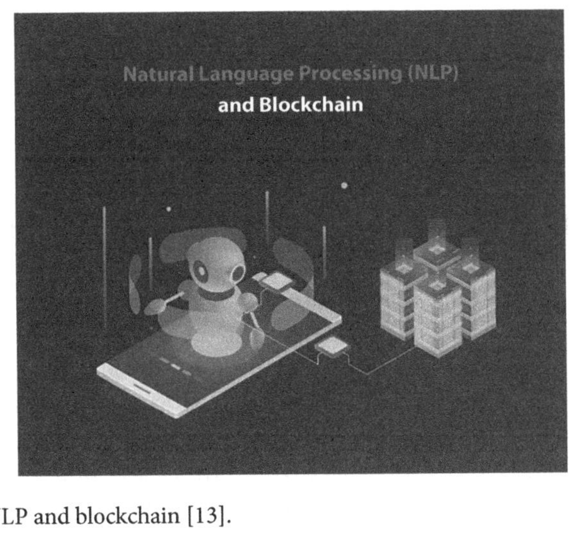

Figure 27.2 NLP and blockchain [13].

27.5 Applications of Blockchain in NLP

There are several opportunities for combining blockchain solutions with NLP. Here are a few examples:

- **Data Source and Authenticity**
  To guarantee that the data used in models and algorithms are dependable and trustworthy, it would be fantastic if Blockchain could be utilized to ascertain the source and credibility of NLP data. We can confirm the accuracy and dependability of the data we work with by logging the source, date of update, and ownership information of the resources on the blockchain. This used case can foster confidence and transparency among the NLP community and aid in the prevention of problems like data tampering, spoofing, and quality concerns. Assume that in order to train AI models, a research team creates a sizable NLP dataset. As a result, they document the steps involved in gathering the data set, such as data sources, pre-processing techniques, and blockchain updates. Blockchain records offer a transparent audit trail that ensures the validity and integrity of datasets shared with other academia or organizations. In this instance, employing blockchain lowers the possibility of using altered or illegal data while enhancing the repeatability and legitimacy of NLP research. It encourages the development of a more reliable and responsible environment for projects involving languages.

- **Distributed Language Resource Sharing**
  Decentralized systems for exchanging linguistic resources, such lexicons and annotated data sets, can be established; thanks to blockchain technology. Through the distributed ledger of a blockchain, NLP researchers can establish a peer-to-peer network that is safe for the exchange of language-related resources. The terms and conditions for resource sharing, such as equity distributions, license agreements, and access rights, can be specified using smart contracts. In this sense, linguists and NLP researchers might establish a blockchain-based platform where they can publish and distribute their multilingual dictionary with other academics

if they collaborate to construct one. Again, in the event that the dictionary is utilized for commercial purposes, smart contracts automatically pay contributors royalties and oversee terms of use and acknowledgement. Collaborating and exchanging knowledge among linguists within the NLP community is facilitated by the sharing of decentralized linguistic resources, which in turn fosters empowerment. In addition, it expedites the creation of more extensive textual materials and lessens reliance on centralized repositories.

- **Enhanced plagiarism detection and text authentication**
  Blockchain technology, which offers an unchangeable record of content that has been timestamped, can improve text authentication and plagiarism detection systems. A document or text becomes nearly impossible to alter or influence covertly when it is stored on a blockchain. This feature can be applied to stop intellectual property theft, identify plagiarism, and confirm the legitimacy of textual content. Taking into consideration a publishing platform that uses blockchain integration to date and store articles that authors submit; in this scenario, each article's hash is recorded on the blockchain, creating an unchangeable record of its existence. By leveraging blockchain for textual resource authentication and plagiarism detection, content providers may firmly ensure the uniqueness and integrity of their written work. As a result, there are more trustworthy publication references, which deters plagiarism and safeguards intellectual property rights.

- **Decentralized Translation Services for Languages**
  Blockchain technology can be used to create decentralized translation services that do not require middlemen and let clients interact directly with qualified translators. Smart contracts can employ user ratings and reputation systems to guarantee quality control [18] if a self-employed translator decides to work as a service provider on a blockchain-based translation platform. Subsequently, they need to make a profile detailing their languages, experience, and previous projects. As a result, clients seeking translation services can check through the translator profiles on the website, evaluate the translators' ratings and testimonials from prior

clients, and select the best translator for their needs. As a result, the platform makes it possible for the client and translator to communicate directly, fostering productive teamwork. Payment settlements will be managed by smart contracts according to predetermined criteria, including word count or project completion benchmarks. The application of Blockchain will have a significant impact on decentralized language translation services, removing the need for middlemen and lowering prices while enhancing process transparency. Additionally, it gives independent translators a stage on which to showcase their abilities and promote themselves to a larger audience. Additionally, user reviews and reputation systems foster trust and assist clients in choosing translators with confidence.

- **Secure and Private Communication:**
  Communication channels that are private and secure can be established with the usage of blockchain technology. Unauthorized access to communications between individuals or organizations can be prevented by encrypting them and storing them on a decentralized network. NLP can be used to preserve communication privacy while analyzing texts and extracting insights like mood or intent.

- **Identity Verification:**
  While natural language processing (NLP) can be used to examine and validate identity information in papers written in natural language, such passports, driver's licenses, and other official documents, blockchain technology can be used to store and authenticate personal identity information. This might contribute to the development of a decentralized, safe identity verification system that is independent of any one government or group.

- **Fraud Detection:**
  While NLP can be used to analyze transactional data and find patterns of fraud or other questionable activity, blockchain development services can be utilized to establish a tamper-proof record of transactions. By doing so, fraud may be avoided, and financial transaction security may be enhanced.

27.6 Blockchain Solutions for NLP

Blockchain technology can be applied to Natural Language Processing (NLP) in many ways. The technologies that can be used to implement blockchain in NLP technologies as shown in Figure 27.2 [13] can be-

Smart contracts: Smart contracts are those that are programmed to run automatically, with lines of code to set parameters of the agreement between the seller and the buyer [16]. They can be used to build decentralized applications that perform functions like voice or text data authentication automatically.
Tokenization: The process of converting data into a digital token that can be traded and transferred on a blockchain is known as tokenization. Tokenization can be used in natural language processing (NLP) to create digital tokens that represent words or phrases that can be kept on a blockchain.
Decentralized storage: Data can be validated and kept on a distributed network by using decentralized storage solutions made possible by blockchain technology. Text or voice recordings, among other types of NLP data, might be safely and impenetrably stored in this way.
Consensus algorithm: Consensus algorithms are employed in blockchain technology to validate transactions and ensure network reliability and security. They could be used in NLP applications to verify the accuracy and legitimacy of data.
Interoperability: The ability of different blockchain networks to exchange data and communicate with one another is referred to as interoperability. For NLP applications that need to transfer data between different networks or systems, this could be helpful as shown in Figure 27.3 and Figure 27.4.

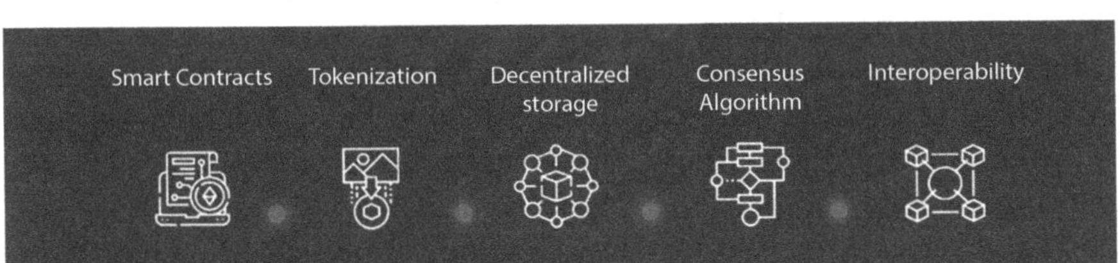

Figure 27.3 Various blockchain solutions.

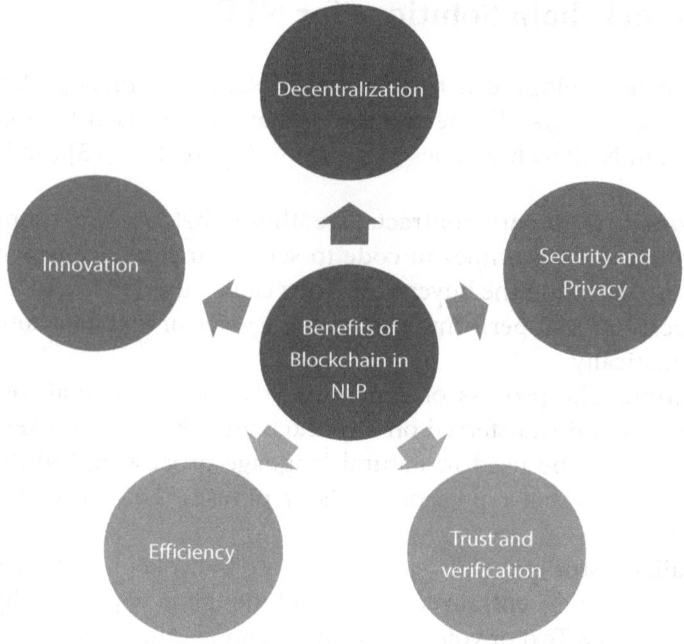

Figure 27.4 Implications of blockchain on NLP.

27.7 Implications of Blockchain Development Solutions in NLP

Blockchain has major implications for NLP and can completely change the way linguistic data is analyzed and handled. The following are some ways that blockchain technology affects NLP:

Decentralization: As blockchain technology lacks a single point of failure, it is inherently decentralized [17]. Because the data is not governed by a centralized authority, NLP systems may be more transparent, safe, and impervious to manipulation.

Security and privacy: To protect language data against compromise, blockchain techniques can be utilized. Sensitive data can be securely and impenetrably maintained on the blockchain, preserving people's privacy and confidentiality.

Trust and verification: Blockchain technology can be used to confirm language data's authenticity and make sure it hasn't been altered. This can help build trust in linguistic data and improve the accuracy and reliability of NLP systems.

Efficiency: Data can be transferred and stored more quickly and securely with blockchain technology, which opens the door to more efficient language processing systems. As a result, processing linguistic data can be completed faster and for less money, with improved accuracy.
Innovation: Blockchain technology and natural language processing (NLP) have the ability to produce novel and creative answers to persistent problems in language processing. By merging the advantages of both technologies, researchers and developers can produce NLP systems that are more precise, effective, safe, and better fit the needs of companies and organizations.

27.8 Sectors That can be Benified from Blockchain and NLP Integration

The integration of blockchain technology with natural language processing has numerous prospects for enhancing a wide array of businesses through the provision of fresh and inventive resolutions to enduring issues [14]. The following are a few sectors that stand to gain from the integration of natural language processing and blockchain technology:

Healthcare: Sensitive patient data can be securely stored using blockchain technology, and insights can be gleaned from the data via analysis and natural language processing. Personalized healthcare solutions that are more successful and efficient could be created using this combination.
Finance: Financial data can be analyzed and interpreted using natural language processing, and financial transactions can be secured by blockchain technology. This combination has the potential to produce financial systems that are more accurate and efficient.
Legal: Legal documents can be securely stored using blockchain technology, and their content can be analyzed, and insights extracted using natural language processing. This combination may be used to produce legal solutions that are more accurate and successful.
Marketing: Natural language processing can be used to evaluate and comprehend client feedback, and blockchain can be used to track and validate the success of marketing campaigns. This could be utilized to develop marketing strategies that are more focused and successful.
Education: Education data may be interpreted using natural language processing (NLP), and educational credentials can be safely stored and verified

using blockchain services. With this combination, educational systems could be developed that are more accurate and productive.
Supply Chain Management: Blockchain is useful for tracking the movement of commodities and ensuring the legitimacy of products while NLP is useful for analyzing and interpreting data from product descriptions, reviews, and user feedback. By combining these two strategies, organizations may establish supply chains that are more responsive to market demands and more transparent and efficient.
Social media and News Analysis: Blockchain technology can be used to confirm the legitimacy of news sources and social media posts While NLP can be used to evaluate and glean insights from the information. This could enhance the information's accuracy and dependability while assisting in the fight against false information and fake news. Thus, businesses and organizations may design more accurate, efficient, and secure systems that better fit their needs by leveraging the characteristics of both technologies.

27.9 Challenges

There can be many challenges to consider when integrating blockchain technology into NLP. Some major challenges are-

- **Scalability and performance:**
  Blockchain technology has scalability issues by nature, particularly public and permission-less blockchains. There is a limit to the number of transactions that can be processed by these blockchains because of the consensus procedures that need nodes to verify and retain every transaction. Scalability becomes an important consideration since NLP [22–25] activities sometimes require processing enormous volumes of data [15]. Complex NLP algorithms can place a strain on the blockchain network [26, 27] due to their increased processing demands, which could result in longer transaction confirmation times and higher transaction fees. Researchers and developers are investigating a range of ways to address scalability difficulties, including layer-two scaling (e.g., off-chain transactions, sidechains), breaking the blockchain up into smaller components, and using more scalable blockchain topologies. By lowering latency and

increasing transaction throughput, these strategies hope to make blockchain-based NLP applications more capable of managing heavier workloads.

- **Implications for privacy and data protection:** Privacy and data protection in NLP applications are challenged by the blockchain's transparency and immutability. Transparency can help foster a sense of trust and accountability, but it can also jeopardize the privacy of sensitive information, particularly in situations where privacy is a top priority (such as the healthcare industry). Various techniques, including differential privacy, zero-knowledge proofs, and encryption, can be employed to tackle privacy problems. Privacy can be improved by encrypting data before storing it on the blockchain or by employing zero-knowledge proofs to confirm the legitimacy of data without disclosing its true content. To further address privacy concerns while taking advantage of blockchain technology, privacy-preserving smart contracts can be used, as can private or consortium blockchains.

- **Transparency and Privacy in Blockchain:** Integration of NLP Integrating NLP with blockchain presents a significant challenge: striking a balance between privacy and transparency. While every transaction is recorded and verified on the blockchain, which promotes openness, some NLP applications may have privacy concerns that the blockchain cannot address. Techniques like permissioned blockchains and selective disclosure can be utilized to determine a balance. Through selective disclosure, people can share certain information while keeping the rest private. Authorized blockchains give users more control over data exposure and privacy by limiting access to only those who are permitted. The application of blockchain technology to NLP still has a lot of potential to advance data integrity, credibility, and cooperation in this field—despite the obstacles that need to be addressed. Blockchain solutions that are scalable and maintain privacy will be developed through continued study and innovation.

27.10 Conclusion

This study offers a thorough investigation of the combination of NLP with blockchain technologies. This paper advances the fields of blockchain technology and natural language processing by examining use scenarios, evaluating advantages and disadvantages, and outlining potential future research avenues. The findings of this study open new possibilities for creative applications that encourage the use of dependable, safe, and cooperative NLP systems. The future of NLP could be shaped by the combination of both technologies, which could lead to breakthroughs in a variety of industries, such as business, education, and health, as blockchain continues to develop and NLP's capabilities grow.

The field should be advanced, and the issues indicated should be addressed in future work on the blockchain technology and NLP integration. Research might be focused on creating blockchain systems that are scalable and ideal for NLP applications. To ensure that large-scale NLP activities are processed efficiently, this entails investigating alternate techniques and improving transaction throughput. To strike a balance between data privacy and transparency, more research must be done on privacy techniques. The processing of sensitive textual data in blockchain-NLP systems can be done securely and privately because of the developments in privacy-enhancing technologies like differential privacy and secure computing. Additionally, to promote cooperation and integration between various blockchain platforms and NLP systems, efforts should be made to develop interoperability and standards protocols. The promise of blockchain technology to improve natural language processing (NLP) can be further exploited by addressing future research paths, which could lead to revolutionary applications across multiple domains.

References

1. Alphonse Inbaraj, X. and Rama Chaitanya, T., Need to know about combined technologies of Blockchain and machine learning, in: *Handbook of Research on Blockchain Technology*, DOI: https://doi.org/10.1016/B978-0-12-819816-2.00017-4.
2. Salah, K., Rehman, M.H.U., Nizamuddin, N., Al Fuqaha, A., Blockchain for AI: review and open research challenges. *IEEE Access*, 7, 10127–10149, 2019.
3. Integration of AI and Blockchain: All you need to know, https://appinventiv.com/blog/ai-in-blockchain/. (accessed Mar. 18, 2024).

4. Khurana, D., Koli, A., Khatter, K., Singh, S., Natural language processing: State of the art, current trends, and challenges. *Multimed. Tools Appl.*, 82, 3, 3713–3744, 2023.
5. Palmisano, T. and Convertini, V.N., Notarization and Anti-Plagiarism: A New Blockchain Approach. *Appl. Sci.*, 12, 243, 2022, https://doi.org/10.3390/app12010243.
6. Jayakumar, D., Haripriya, G., Ramkumar, M.O., Manjula, S., Blockchain based Secure Event Management System using NLP and RNN Algorithm. *2023 2nd International Conference on Applied Artificial Intelligence and Computing (ICAAIC)*, 2019, doi: 10.1109/ICAAIC56838.2023.10140877.
7. Zaccagni, Z., Dantu, R., Morozov, K., Maintaining Review Credibility Using NLP, Reputation, and Blockchain. *2022 IEEE 4th International Conference on Trust, Privacy and Security in Intelligent Systems, and Applications (TPS-ISA)*, DOI: 10.1109/TPS-ISA56441.2022.00018.
8. Monteiro, E., Righi, R., Kunst, R., da Costa, C., Combining Natural Language Processing and Blockchain for Smart Contract Generation in the Accounting and Legal Field. *2020 International Conference on Intelligent Human Computer Interaction.*
9. Mishra, A.K., Tyagi, A.K., Dananjayan, S., Rajavat, A., Rawat, H., Rawat, A., Revolutionizing Government Operations: The Impact of Artificial Intelligence in Public Administration, in: *Conversational Artificial Intelligence*, pp. 607–634, 2024
10. Nahar, S., Pithawa, D., Bhardwaj, V., Rawat, R., Rawat, A., Pachlasiya, K., Quantum technology for military applications, in: *Quantum Computing in Cybersecurity*, pp. 313–334, 2023
11. Prasad, U., Chakravarty, S., Bisht, Y., Using Natural Language Processing and Blockchain for Employee Performance Evaluation. *2023 3rd International Conference on Advance Computing and Innovative Technologies in Engineering (ICACITE).*
12. Dubey, A., Jain, K., Kalaiselvi, K., Smart Patient Records using NLP and Blockchain. *Proceedings of the 5th International Conference on Smart Systems and Inventive Technology (ICSSIT 2023).*
13. https://www.lcx.com/natural-language-processing-nlp-and-blockchain/. (accessed Mar. 20, 2024).
14. https://www.oodlestechnologies.com/blogs/blockchain-and-nlp:-uncovering-the-possibilities-and-benefits/.(accessed Mar. 20, 2024).
15. Sikarwar, R., Shakya, H.K., Kumar, A., Rawat, A., Advanced Security Solutions for Conversational AI, in: *Conversational Artificial Intelligence*, pp. 287–301, 2024
16. Song, Z., Shen, P., Liu, C., Liu, C., A Survey on the Integration of Blockchain Smart Contracts and Natural Language Processing. *Proceedings of the 13th International Conference on Computer Engineering and Networks*, 2024.

17. Deshmukh, A., Mishra, A.K., Balamurugan, G., Tyagi, A.K., *Blockchain-Empowered Decentralized Applications Current Trends and Challenges*, chapter 19, Wiley, USA, 2021, https://doi.org/10.1002/9781394213726.ch19.
18. Harris, J.D. and Waggoner, B., Decentralized and collaborative ai on blockchain, in: *Proceedings of the IEEE International Conference on Blockchain (Blockchain)*, 14-17 July 2019, IEEE, Atlanta, GA, USA, pp. 368–375.
19. Pithawa, D., Nahar, S., Bhardwaj, V., Rawat, R., Dronawat, R., Rawat, A., Quantum Computing Technological Design Along with Its Dark Side, in: *Quantum Computing in Cybersecurity*, pp. 295–312, 2023.
20. Kumar, N. and Aggarwal, D., LEARNING-based focused WEB crawler. *IETE J. Res.*, 69, 4, 2037–2045, 2023.
21. Namdev, A., Patni, D., Dhaliwal, B.K., Parihar, S., Telang, S., Rawat, A., Potential Threats and Ethical Risks of Quantum Computing, in: *Quantum Computing in Cybersecurity*, pp. 335–352, 2023.
22. Chirgaiya, S. and Rajavat, A., Tiny object detection model based on competitive multi-layer neural network (TOD-CMLNN). *Intell. Syst. Appl.*, 18, September 2022, 200217, 2023.
23. Rathi, M. and Rajavat, A., *Analysing Cryptographic and Random Data Sanitization Techniques in Privacy Preserving Data Mining*, vol. 83, Allied Publishers, New Delhi, India, 2023.
24. Dhar, S., Dhar, U., Rajavat, A., Factors and Attributes of Team Players: A Study of Engineering Students in India, in: *International Simulation and Gaming Association Conference*, 2021, September, Springer International Publishing, Cham, pp. 53–60.
25. Pithawa, D., Nahar, S., Bhardwaj, V., Rawat, R., Dronawat, R., Rawat, A., Quantum Computing Technological Design Along with Its Dark Side, in: *Quantum Computing in Cybersecurity*, pp. 295–312, 2023.
26. Chauhan, D., Singh, C., Rawat, R., Chouhan, M., Conversational AI Applications in Ed-Tech Industry: An Analysis of Its Impact and Potential in Education, in: *Conversational Artificial Intelligence*, pp. 411–433, 2024.
27. Chauhan, D., Singh, C., Rawat, R., Dhawan, M., Evaluating the Performance of Conversational AI Tools: A Comparative Analysis, in: *Conversational Artificial Intelligence*, pp. 385–409, 2024.

28

Emotion Detection Using Natural Language Processing by Text Classification

Jyoti Jayal[1]*, Vijay Kumar[2], Paramita Sarkar[3] and Sudipta Kumar Dutta[3]

[1]*Department of English, SHSS Sharda University, Noida, India*
[2]*Department of English SOLE, Galgotias University, Noida, India*
[3]*Department of C.S.E JIS UNIVERSITY, Nilgunj Road, Agarpara, Kolkata, India*

Abstract

Emotion recognition is one of the branches within the field of emotion analysis. Advanced emotion analysis is required to identify a sentence as positive, negative, or neutral. Our emotions get more profound as we comprehend the positive or negative tone of the statements or ideas. People communicate their emotions using various methods, such as facial expressions, written language, verbal communication, and bodily movements. Opinions and perspectives form the foundation of individuals' emotions, actions, and the impact of those emotions on their speech and actions. Linguistics and machine learning are broad areas that include subfields like computational linguistics, natural language processing (NLP), and artificial intelligence (AI). Thanks to Natural Language Processing (NLP), computers are now capable of comprehending, analyzing, and interpreting spoken language. Natural language processing (NLP) has become an essential component of our daily lives due to the widespread adoption of machine translation programs, voice assistants, and search engines. This article examines various machine learning and deep learning techniques to the task of emotion recognition through text classification utilizing natural language processing.

***Keywords*:** Emotion detection, natural language processing, machine learning, deep learning, ensemble learning, text classification

**Corresponding author*: jyoti.jayal@sharda.ac.in

Rajesh Kumar Chakrawarti, Ranjana Sikarwar, Sanjaya Kumar Sarangi, Samson Arun Raj Albert Raj, Shweta Gupta, Krishnan Sakthidasan Sankaran and Romil Rawat (eds.) Natural Language Processing for Software Engineering, (425–442) © 2025 Scrivener Publishing LLC

28.1 Introduction

Emotional expression is a fundamental and intrinsic component of human behavior. Essentially, they are embodiments of the distinct feelings and experiences influenced by both internal and external causes. Emotions can be represented through several means, such as facial expressions, nonverbal indications during conversations, body posture and language, physiological responses, and written words. The importance of text as a means of communication has significantly increased as a result of the widespread use of social media applications and platforms. In contemporary times, the majority of individuals engage in communication through various digital platforms such as text messaging, tweets, online posts, blogs, and so on. Consequently, we now have access to a vast amount of social data, which presents numerous intriguing opportunities for a variety of applications [1].

Analyzing the emotional state of content shared on social media sites has various potential applications, including the development of affect-aware human-computer interfaces. Additional possible applications involve monitoring corporate reputation and brand management. Psychologists could employ an emotion detection system to enhance their comprehension of how to assist individuals when they articulate their concern orally, or to ascertain the intended tone of an email prior to its transmission. By employing emotion recognition on textual data extracted from popular social media platforms, candidates running for public office can effectively customize their political agenda to align with the desires and preferences of the voting population.

Precise and methodical emotion recognition aids in closing the communication divisibility between computers, which have difficulty understanding emotions, and individuals who are very expressive. The primary objective of affective computing is to develop computational systems that adapt their response according on the user's emotional state. For a system interface to effectively respond to users' different emotional states, it is essential for it to reliably recognize their affective or emotional states. Therefore, the detection of these states is of utmost importance. Enhancing the computer-user interaction can be achieved by automatic emotion recognition, which enables an interface to respond to the emotional states of the user. Interfaces that are sensitive to users' emotions can considerably enhance both human-computer interaction (HCI) and computer-mediated communication (CMC). Research into emotion analysis is necessary for the development of text-to-speech (TTS) synthesis systems [2].

Emotion-aware text-to-speech systems possess the capability to detect nuances in textual content and enhance the translation to get a more authentic and genuine sound. Various disciplines are currently engaged in the development of affect-sensitive interfaces, including educational technology, mental health, and gaming. Developers can utilize emotion recognition to customize their systems according to the user's emotional state and establish automated responses based on this data. Recent advancements in AI and ML have opened up new opportunities to include emotional sensitivity and expressiveness into HCI interfaces.

Emotions are impacted by multiple factors and have their roots in cognition. Individuals convey their emotions by means of their facial expressions and spoken or written communication. Our approach solely focuses on recognizing the emotional orientation of textual utterances made on different social networking platforms. The subjective human appraisal determines the emotional content and the character of the exhibited emotion. It is widely recognized that, just as there are multiple ways to convey emotions, different readers may interpret the same expression in various ways. The approaches given here were tested using data that had an emotional orientation and was rated as identical by at least two persons. The main objective of affect detection research has been to determine the positive, negative, or neutral polarity of sentiments. This study specifically examines one aspect of affect identification that has received less attention: the ability to recognize emotions that are relevant to a certain domain. Through acquiring the skill to discern the emotions conveyed in written material, readers can enhance their understanding of the author's objectives, attitude, and the content of the text.

28.2 Natural Language Processing

Computational linguistics, natural language processing (NLP), and artificial intelligence (AI) are subdisciplines that fall within the broader sciences of machine learning (ML) and linguistics. Natural Language Processing (NLP) enables computers to understand, analyze, and interpret spoken language. Natural language processing (NLP) has become an essential component of our daily lives due to the widespread use of machine translation programs, voice assistants, and search engines. Identifying the semantic context of words and managing their diverse interpretations within different sentences in a document or corpus are just two of the numerous challenges in natural language processing. Some of the challenging tasks include: recognizing sardonic or caustic phrases; identifying words with contradictory information; and understanding statements with several interpretations. Different NLP approaches are presented in Figure 28.1.

Rule-based Approaches - Patterns are frequently analyzed or compared using rule-based methods. Generally speaking, these approaches can be quite effective for certain jobs. However, they deteriorate when employed on a worldwide level.

Traditional machine learning Approaches - Conventional machine learning relies on training models and deriving conclusions from test sets as its primary methods. By employing this approach, it is possible to achieve many natural language processing tasks, such as sequence tagging. Models are utilized to derive meaningful inferences from the data.

Neural network Approaches - Word embeddings, which are word vector representations, serve as inputs for training neural networks. Various alternative neural network architectures, such as Convolutional Neural Networks (CNNs), Recurrent Neural Networks (RNNs), and Long Short-Term Memory (LSTM) networks, have been extensively researched. Additionally, there have been encouraging advancements in integrating deep learning with natural language processing.

The significance of unstructured data in processing, analysis, and decision-making is being demonstrated by the rapid increase in their abundance. When managing vast quantities of significant content such as biographies, photographs, videos, and tweets, natural language processing (NLP) is the optimal choice. Advanced AI systems often incorporate Natural Language Processing (NLP) and Machine Learning (ML) methods to enhance their ability to perform tasks [3]. Siri and Alexa, two AI-based virtual assistants, utilize natural language processing (NLP) techniques and

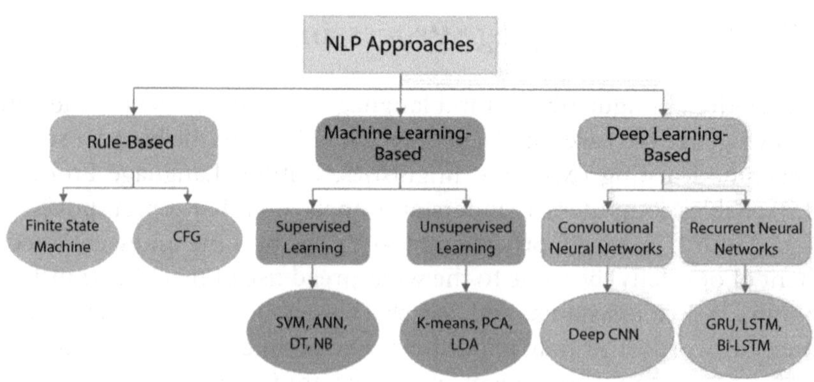

Figure 28.1 Different NLP approaches.

voice recognition to comprehend human speech. They leverage machine learning algorithms to analyze patterns learned from previous interactions.

Some of the applications of NLP are listed below:

- Language Translation
- Social Media Monitoring
- Chat bots and Virtual assistants
- Survey Analysis
- Voice Assistants
- Grammar check
- E-mail Filtering
- Market Intelligence
- Speech Recognition
- Text Extraction
- Text Classification
- Text Summarization
- Web Sampling
- Face Recognition
- Pattern Recognition

28.3 Emotion Recognition

Emotion analysis includes various subfields, and one of them is emotion recognition [6]. Advanced emotion analysis can only go as far as classifying a statement as positive, negative, or indifferent. Once we comprehend the negative or good nature of the statements or thoughts, our emotions delve into a more profound level. Facial expressions, written words, verbal communication, and physical gestures are all means through which individuals express their emotions. sentiments, behaviors, and the consequences of those sentiments on people's words and actions are all based on personal opinions and perspectives [4].

The main purpose of this tool is to assist businesses in assessing the sentiment of their customers towards their brand or product. Within the medical domain, it possesses the capacity to mitigate patients' requirements for medication. One possible use in the field of automation is the ability to understand human emotions. When a driver experiences drowsiness, an emotion recognition system can alert them. Emotion analysis and recognition is a broad field of research that offers useful understanding of spoken and written language. Plutchik's proposed approach of mood swings allows for the differentiation of several emotions, including rage, fear, melancholy, disgust, surprise, desire, optimism, and joy.

Investigating human emotions poses significant challenges. Many corporations and groups utilize it due of its immense power. The surge in popularity of micro-blogs in recent years has led to the emergence of a new area of research that focuses on automatically recognizing emotions in these entries. Micro-blog postings, due to their brevity and lack of structure, cannot be readily processed like longer texts often used in text mining studies. Microblogs use several symbols, conventions, and unique usages that can greatly influence the impact of the text. Psychologists and behavioral scientists have dedicated significant time and effort to studying emotions due to their fundamental importance in the human experience. Computer scientists specializing in human-computer interaction have also shown a keen interest in emotion analysis. They conduct studies on facial expressions, speech recognition, and emotion recognition using various methodologies [5].

28.4 Related Work

28.4.1 Emotion Detection Using Machine Learning

A novel proposition has been put out to categorize emotions with machine learning methodologies that rely on physiological attributes. Jang *et al.* [6] employed four machine learning methods, namely LDA, CART, SOM, and SVM, to categorize the emotions of 200 college students, specifically boredom, pain, and surprise. Physiological signals, such as electrodermal activity (EDA), electrocardiogram (ECG), photoplethysmography (PPG), and skin temperature (SKT), were measured for one minute before the emotional test. The differential values of each attribute were subtracted from the baseline to categorize emotions. Emotions served as the fundamental basis for machine learning algorithms. Based on the findings, SVM classification yielded the most optimal results, and emotional accuracy is of utmost importance. Many human emotions can be inferred from physiological indicators.

Psychologists have been intrigued by research in neuroscience, linguistics, and human-computer interaction systems that focus on autonomous face recognition and facial emotion recognition.

Jaikrishnan [7] developed a recognition system called AFERS, which consists of three steps: face recognition, feature extraction, and detection of facial expressions. The YCbCr color scheme was used to ascertain an individual's skin tone. Lighting compensation was used to establish consistency in the face, while morphological operations were employed to preserve the desired appearance. The data extraction process utilized the outcome of the initial step. The Active Augmentation Method (AAM) was used to augment the eyes, nose, and mouth. The Appearance Model was utilized to calculate an individual's physical appearance. The final stage involved automated facial recognition.

The intensity of textual emotions can be determined by assessing them, as stated by Mohammad and Bravo-Marquez [8]. The tweets, when analyzed with annotations, displayed intense emotions such as anger, fear, joy, and sadness. The writers enhanced annotation consistency and provided reliable fine-grained scores by implementing best-worst scaling (BWS).

Tsai and Chang [9] developed a three-stage support vector machine (SVM) to detect facial expressions. Each of the twenty-one support vector machines (SVMs) used in the initial phase consisted of a binary amalgamation of seven phrases. The initial phase would suffice if there were just two phrases; the subsequent step would be utilized if there were three; and the final stage would be utilized if there were all three.

Healy *et al.* [10] has published a full account of their novel method for identifying emotions in real-time video. The work showcased the implementation of a distinct machine learning support vector machine (SVM) for rapid and precise classification, utilizing 68-point facial features. Through a regulated laboratory environment, the application has acquired the ability to recognize six distinct emotional states. The tracking of changes in facial expressions was beneficial in assessing individuals' emotional states in the given settings.

Tsai and Chang [9] proposed a FERS approach that utilized SQI filters to extract Haar-like characteristics from images. There was an enhancement in the rate of face detection. SQI filters are renowned for their exceptional effectiveness in various lighting conditions. The discrete cosine transform (2D-DCT) and Gabor filtering have been chosen to represent the features. Finally, support vector machines (SVMs) were used as the classifiers to assign various categories to the facial expressions. Schneider *et al.* [11] utilized the Wall Street Journal (WSJ) test set to showcase a novel application of wav2vec in unsupervised pre-training for speech recognition. Their approach yielded an impressive Word Error Rate of 2.43%. Baevski and colleagues [12] developed Vq-wav2vec as a means to examine discrete representations of audio samples using the Timit corpus as a benchmark. This approach utilizes a self-supervised prediction task that leverages BERT pre-training archives.

Deshmukh *et al.* [13] used feature extraction and classifier training to recognize emotions from audio data. The feature vector encompasses the elements that characterize the audio signal. When evaluating a speaker, it is important to consider their intensity, pitch, and tone. Hence, it is crucial to instruct the classifier model in recognizing the emotional expression of a certain object. The process of segregating the source dataset from the training and testing datasets was performed manually. Anger, despair, and joy were recovered as Mel-Frequency Cepstral Coefficients (MFCC) from the audio.

Deng and Ren [14] proposed a Multi-Label Emotion Detection Architecture (MEDA) to accurately identify all the emotions expressed in a given text. The fundamental components of MEDA consist of the Emotion Correlation Learner (ECorL) and the MultiChannel Emotion-Specific Feature Extractor (MC-ESFE). By utilizing its MC-ESFE module, which consists of several ESFE networks for each channel, the system successfully extracted certain features related to underlying emotions.

Uddin and Nilsson [15] proposed a dependable method for emotion recognition by utilizing audio speech as a dataset for machine learning. The computation of Mel-frequency cepstral coefficients (MFCC) was used as a feature to train emotion recognition algorithms that are not dependent on individuals. Audio data is necessary for this purpose. It is crucial to acknowledge and distinguish the following emotions: sadness, wrath, scorn, contempt, surprise, and terror. [16] created a surveillance system to identify these emotions in video recordings. The target demographic of the product was the elderly.

Tafreshi and colleagues [17] conducted research that investigated the impact of news-based essays on collaborative tasks related to empathy and emotion prediction. The combination of features extracted from transformer models with concurrent learning problems allows for strong modelling of empathy, discomfort, and emotion inside a transformer language model. Despite extracting lexical features from sentiment, opinion, and emotion lexicons, these resilient contextualized aspects have a significant impact on empathy, distress, and emotion models.

28.4.2 Emotion Detection Using Deep Learning

The advancement of efficient classifiers for speech emotion recognition has predominantly depended on models that utilize audio data. To enhance comprehension of voice data, Yoon and colleagues [18] developed a novel deep dual recurrent encoder model that concurrently utilized both textual data and audio inputs. This model employed dual recurrent neural networks (RNNs) to capture information from both audio and text sequences to predict the emotion category, taking into account the auditory and linguistic aspects of emotional speech. This architecture differs from models that solely focus on auditory elements by thoroughly analyzing speech data at all levels, encompassing signals and languages. As a result, it effectively utilizes the intrinsic information included in the data. The efficacy and attributes of the proposed model were evaluated through extensive experiments. When tested on the IEMOCAP dataset, this model demonstrated accuracies ranging from 68.8% to 71.8% in accurately categorizing data into four emotion categories: angry, joyful, sad, and neutral. This outperformed prior cutting-edge methods.

Yang *et al.* [19] introduced a face recognition-based method to assess a student's understanding of distant learning. The researchers proposed a three-step methodology for constructing emotion identification models: feature extraction, subset feature selection, and emotion classification. The input image depicted a human face, which was identified using a Haar Cascades methodology. The eyes and lips were isolated using Sobel edge detection. Subsequently, the distinctive value was acquired. The training of a Neural Network classifier resulted in the identification of six unique emotional groups. The JAFF database experiments confirmed the method's exceptional classification performance. Experimental results indicate that students' expressions in virtual learning settings align with this approach. This study demonstrates the practicality of employing facial expression-based emotion identification to identify a student's real-time learning state in remote education. Hence, instructors should modify their instructional approaches in online classrooms according to the emotional states of their pupils, which can be beneficial.

Ortis, Farinalla, and Battiato [20] offer a thorough examination of the current body of research on image sentiment analysis by discussing various methodologies, datasets, and challenges that new researchers may face. The article states that emotional models, Image Sentiment Analysis datasets, and feature design are the three fundamental elements for constructing ISA systems. They provided comprehensive explanations for each of these choices, utilizing cutting-edge research to support their assertions. Social networking platforms, which users frequently utilize to upload and share photographs, offer convenient access to datasets like VSO and others. Recent discoveries in picture sentiment analysis indicate that models for this particular type of analysis experience advantages when employing learning approaches such as multi-modal embedding and convolutional neural networks. The discussed topics encompassed picture popularity and virality prediction, relative attributes, sentiment and ideograms, as well as the challenges faced by academics.

[21] developed a multimodal emotion recognition model that utilizes both text and speech as inputs. Haryadi and Kusuma [22] employed deep learning techniques, specifically Long Short-Term Memory (LSTM) and Nested Long Short-Term Memory, to classify seven emotions (angry, fear, joy, love, sadness, surprise, and thankfulness) in text. They trained a Bi-LSTM (bidirectional long short-term memory) network that utilizes captured textual features as fusion features. Utilizing the Twitter API, a dataset was generated, subjected to pre-processing, and subsequently evaluated by comparing the results with Support Vector Machines (SVM). SVM utilized TF-IDF as features for classification. After training the LSTM and Nested LSTM models, we collected the accuracy and loss outputs from the checkpoints. Nested LSTM demonstrates superior performance compared to the other two approaches, with an accuracy rate of 99.167 percent.

[23] presented a classification of expressions based on the emotions of joy, fury, fear, and melancholy. A deep Convolutional Neural Network (CNN) has been employed, utilizing learned word vectors, to categorize the provided dataset. This approach suggests four unique categories, namely joy, anger, fear, and sadness, to streamline the process of classifying emotions in Arabic tweets. Their proposed approach for sentence classification problems employed deep Convolutional Neural Networks (CNNs) that were trained using dataset-specific word vectors. To evaluate the EI-oc aim, they assessed the effectiveness of their proposed deep learning approach by conducting experiments on the SemEval Arabic tweets dataset. The primary procedures involved in this task were the vectorization of words, phrases, documents, and classification. This study investigated the performance of three different models: CNN-static, CNN-non-static, and CNN-rand. The outcome was compared using three additional machine learning algorithms: Support Vector Machines (SVM), Naive Bayes (NB), and Multilayer Perceptron (MLP). Three different Arabic stemmers, namely Light stemmer, ISRI, and Snowball, were used to implement these methodologies. In addition, two primary feature variables were utilized: Count and TF-IDF.

Lopez and Ivan [24] conducted a study in the United States to investigate public sentiment towards the COVID-19 vaccination. A total of 2,000 tweets were extracted from Twitter for the dataset between February 3, 2021, and February 10, 2021. The data was categorized based on factors such as location, description, sentiment, number of followers, number of likes, and other relevant criteria. A preliminary analysis of the collected tweets using vaccine-related keywords was performed and a sentiment score ranging from -2 to +2 was employed to reflect the sentiment. A statement was deemed positive if its value above zero, and negative if its value fell below zero. Before evaluating tweets based on their creation date and location, the dataset was organized based on the tweets with the highest number of favorites. There was a mixture of positive and negative comments about vaccination, with somewhat more positive tweets than negative ones.

28.4.3 Emotion Detection Using Ensemble Learning

Perikos and Hatzilygeroudis [25] implemented a classifier ensemble strategy utilizing bagging and boosting methods to successfully identify emotional material from social media. The experiments made use of two datasets: the International Survey on Emotion Antecedents and Reactions (ISEAR) and the Affective text dataset. The two datasets underwent analysis using machine learning classifiers known as Naive Bayes and Maximum Entropy. The results demonstrated that the proposed classifier significantly improved Twitter's ability to recognize emotions.

Po-Yuan Shih and Chia-Ping Chen [26] proposed a model that utilizes ensemble learning techniques with neural networks to enhance the accuracy of voice emotion identification tests. This model employs an imbalanced dataset to train subsets that are balanced, and subsequently merges them to generate predictions. By utilizing the FAU-Aibo database, experiments were conducted and determined that a recall rate of 45.5% produced the most optimal outcomes. This yielded innovative results in comparison to the old model. Rather than using a large, unbalanced dataset, this result was achieved by using smaller, more balanced subsets of the data.

Aribisala and colleagues [27] developed a model for emotion recognition using EEG data. To ascertain emotions, our model utilized a publicly available EEG dataset. Data from participants were gathered by assessing four emotional states: arousal, dominance, valence, and preference. The dataset yielded three features: energy, wavelet entropy, and standard deviation. Regarding sensitivity, specificity, and accuracy, this model demonstrated superior performance with scores of 97.54%, 99.21%, and 97.80%, respectively.

[28] suggested a method for face expression regression employing multilevel features in a Convolutional network. The researchers attributed certain emotions such as surprise, neutrality, sadness, fear, anger, happiness, and disgust to distinct face regions in the photos. The FER2013 dataset was used to conduct the experiments. In comparison to the most advanced methods, their model demonstrated promising outcomes.

Mishra *et al.* [29] proposed a method for classifying emotions based on EEG patterns. Their approach involved combining a support vector machine with an ensemble Convolutional network. The process entailed utilizing deep learning models to extract features, followed by employing a support vector machine classifier to accurately categorize EEG patterns into their respective emotion classifications. The emotional state of the subject was determined by employing a Support Vector Machine classifier that considered both single and multiple emotional characteristics. In this experiment, physiological signals (DEAP) were utilized to assess emotions using the most renowned convolutional networks, namely AlexNet and GoogleNet. while categorizing a single attribute (valence), the accuracy achieved using AlexNet and SVM was 87.5%. However, while classifying two attributes (arousal and valence), the accuracy rate dropped to 62.5%.

Youngquist [30] developed a novel neural network architecture for classifying emotions based on short sentences. In this approach, a combination of recurrent, convolutional, and pooling layers was employed to effectively capture the emotional context of the text. Emotions were extracted from the text by conducting experiments utilizing five separate data sets. Compared to the historical models and all data sets, this technique produced an average enhancement rate of 8.31% based on the experimental findings. This ensemble recurrent convolutional network utilized only few sentences as the sole input for emotion classification.

Salama *et al.* [31] proposed the design of a 3D-Conventional Neural Network to extract spatio-temporal properties and video data from human faces. The final fusion productions were decided by integrating data augmentation with ensemble learning methodologies. The system employed RCNN object detection techniques in combination with the OpenCV libraries to precisely extract the facial characteristics related to emotional content. Two fusion approaches, bagging and stacking, were employed in the conducted experiments. The stacking technique resulted in the highest recognition accuracy rate of 96.3 percent and valence accuracy of 96.7 percent. The utilization of the grid search ensemble learning technique facilitated the achievement of this degree of precision.

(Sun *et al.*) Modified iterations of gradient-based explanation techniques and Layer-wise Relevance Propagation (LRP) were employed to incorporate attention mechanisms into photo captioning models. The focus of the study was to analyze the predictions made by these models, surpassing mere attention visualization. This study thoroughly compared the interpretability of attention heat maps using methods such as LRP, Grad-CAM, and Guided Gradient-weighted Class Activation Mapping (G-GAM).

Robots can derive advantages from Wisha Zehra *et al.*'s [32] ensemble learning-based cross-corpus multilingual speech recognition system, which enables them to provide more efficient and emotionally expressive responses. This model compared ensemble learning with more traditional machine learning methods. Through experimental research, it was discovered that several classifiers achieved the highest level of accuracy across different corpora. Ensemble learning was employed to amalgamate many classifiers. The trials revealed a 13% enhancement in accuracy for the Urdu corpus, an 8% enhancement for the German corpus, an 11% enhancement for the Italian corpus, and a 5% enhancement for the English corpus. The experimental results repeatedly showed that the innovative ensemble learning strategy considerably enhanced accuracy in comparison to state-of-the-art methods.

28.5 Machine Learning Techniques for Emotion Detection

Regarding data mining, the KNN algorithm is the most straightforward approach for managing classification tasks and regression problems. It utilizes a non-parametric approach to arrange newly acquired data by comparing it to similar data in the training set. The KNN approach, being a collaborative learning strategy, bypasses the process of constructing models prior to testing them. Understanding the correlation between the attributes and the outcomes is not a prerequisite for the effectiveness of this technique; it is highly flexible. During a traffic gridlock, the nearest neighbor value can replicate the current condition by recreating the corresponding historical data. A KNN-based forecasting approach can be constructed using three primary components: a monitoring database, a nearest-neighbor finding procedure, and a forecasting task. The conventional approach to identifying similarities across records involves calculating the edit distance (ED). The KNN method can be employed to estimate the speed and flow of data based on the inputs of density, with density being the desired result. This approach is used to identify nearby and essential input data. This function retrieves the closest objects by calculating their Euclidean distance whenever a data point is given. It is possible to calculate, provided that there is a sufficient amount of data available.

The CNN technique primarily focuses on managing 2D data, such as photographs. The model consists of several concealed layers, such as convolution layers, fully linked layers, and pooling, along with an input and output layer. A convolutional layer is capable of retaining features by applying filters that modify the input value according to a predetermined pattern. The next phase involves utilizing a minimum or maximum matrix to combine the clustering outcomes from the previous stage into distinct sections at the subsequent level. The pooling layer simultaneously decreases dimensionality to assist the overall model and imparts knowledge of abstract level data.

The Artificial Neural Network (ANN) is widely recognized as the prominent model for predicting traffic flow. Some of its strengths include multidimensional value management, adaptability, learning, and increased generalization. This artificial neural network (ANN) technique excels at dealing with input values that are noisy or absent, and it eliminates the need for data estimation. Typically, it is defined by employing three types of identifiers and constructed as a multilayer network system. The parameters encompass the arrangement of communication between the layers, the mechanism for initiating input-output, and the frequency at which the layers' weights are updated. Artificial Neural Networks (ANN) are considered the fundamental basis of Artificial Intelligence (AI). They are a non-parametric approach to solving problems. Neural networks (NN) are trained to execute a pre-established task by regulating the weights of the connections between the various units. These units operate in coordination. "Neurons" refer to the individual components responsible for processing information. The regulation of neuron relevance is necessary for training the neural network. Each individual neuron utilizes a link to communicate a scalar value p for intake. We have to compute the product of the input value and its weight, add the bias data, and subsequently use a transfer mechanism to derive the target value. The function f takes this value as input and produces the result as output. To achieve the desired result, adjustments are made to the bias value (b) and the weights (w). The neuron's output is the input value that is considered by other neurons, and this process is iterated for each data point. Sigmoid, purelin, hardlim, and other transmission mechanisms are available options for function f, depending on the specific condition needed.

The multilayer perceptron is a type of artificial neural network that utilizes feed-forward connections. The primary strengths of this model lie in its numerous layers and its capacity to effectively process non-linear input. The input layer, consisting of seven nodes, receives data from the user and transmits it to the maximum likelihood prediction (MLP) algorithm. This is achieved by performing the dot function on each layer and combining it with the weight value of the layer below. Except for the output type layer, the activation method is employed to transmit output using the dot function in all other layers. Once the output type layer contains only one node, the process is iterated for all layers. The anticipated velocity corresponds to the value obtained from a single node. Every layer in this paradigm relies on and is influenced by every layer that is positioned beneath it. During the training process, the error value is calculated by comparing the real value with the output values. The erroneous data is inputted into the Rprop method, which specifically aims to reduce the magnitude of the partial derivative. The magnitude of the weight is influenced by its new value, whereas the sign of the derivative function indicates the specific direction of the weight.

28.6 Conclusion

To attain a more genuine and realistic tone, text-to-speech algorithms that are capable of detecting emotions should be able to perceive nuances in the text and enhance the output accordingly. Currently, various industries such as educational technology, mental health, and gaming are actively developing interfaces that are capable of detecting and responding to human emotions. Emotion detection enables programmers to customize their systems based on the individual user's distinct emotional state and establish automated responses accordingly. Recent advancements in machine learning (ML) and artificial intelligence (AI) have opened up new opportunities to integrate emotional sensitivity and expressiveness into human-computer interaction (HCI) interfaces. This article discusses various machine learning and deep learning strategies for emotion recognition via text classification using natural language processing.

References

1. Kawade, O. and Oza, K., Sentiment Analysis: Machine Leaming Approach. *Int. J. Eng. Technol.*, 9, 2183–2186, 2017, I 0.21817/ijel/2017/v9i3/l 709030151.
2. Mishra, A.K., Tyagi, A.K., Dananjayan, S., Rajavat, A., Rawat, H., Rawat, A., Revolutionizing Government Operations: The Impact of Artificial Intelligence in Public Administration, in: *Conversational Artificial Intelligence*, pp. 607–634 , 2024.
3. Drus, Z. and Khalid, H., Sentiment Analysis in Social Media and Its Application: Systematic Literature Review. *Procedia Comput. Sci.*, 161, 707–714, 2019, 10.1016/j.procs.2019.11.174.

4. Nahar, S., Pithawa, D., Bhardwaj, V., Rawat, R., Rawat, A., Pachlasiya, K., Quantum technology for military applications, in: *Quantum Computing in Cybersecurity*, pp. 313–334, 2023.
5. Raghuvanshi, A., Veluri, R. *et al.*, Learning analytics using deep learning techniques for efficiently managing educational institutes. *Mater. Today: Proc.*, 51, 2317–2320, 2022, Available: 10.1016/j.matpr.2021.11.416.
6. Jang, E., Park, B., Kim, S., Sohn, J., Emotion classification by machine learning algorithm using physiological signals. *Proc. Comput. Sci. Inf.*, vol. 25, pp. 1–5, 2012, [Online].Available http://www.icmlc.org/icmlc2012/00I_icmlc2012.pdf.
7. Jaikrishnan, V., Emotion Detection Using Machine Learning. *Int. J. Recent Trends Eng. Res.*, 3, 6, 28–32, 2017, https://doi .org/10.23883/ijrter.2017.3267.lovl p.
8. Mohammad, S. and Bravo-Marquez, F., Emotion Intensities in Tweets, pp. 65–77, 2017, 10.18653/v1/$17-1007.
9. Tsai, H.H. and Chang, Y.C., Facial expression recognition using a combination of multiple facial features and support vector machine. *Soft Comput.*, 22, 13, 4389–4405, 2018, doi: 10.1007/s00500-017-2634-3.
10. Healy, M., Donovan, R., Walsh, P., Zheng, H., A Machine Leaming Emotion Detection Platform to Support Affective Well Being. *Proc. - 2018 IEEE Int. Conf. Bioinforma. Biomed. B1BM 2018*, vol. I, pp. 2694–2700, 2019, doi: IO.1109/B1BM.2018.8621562.
11. Schneider, S., Baevski, A., Collobert, R., Auli, M., WAV2vee: Unsupervised pre-training for speech recognition. *Proceedings of the Annual Conference of the International Speech Communication Association, INTERSPEECH*, 2019-Septe, pp. 3465–3469, 2019, https://doi.org/10.21437/ Interspeech.2019-1873.
12. Baevski, A., Schneider, S., Auli, M., vq-wav2vec: Self-Supervised Learning of Discrete Speech Representations, pp. 1–12, 2019, http://arxiv.org/abs/1910.05453.
13. Deshmukh, G., Gaonkar, A., Golwalkar, G., Kulkarni, S., Speech based emotion recognition using machine learning. *Proceedings of the 3rd International Conference on Computing Methodologies and Communication, ICCMC 20/9*, Jccmc, pp. 8 I 2–8 I 7, 2019, https://doi.org'I 0.1I09/ICCMC.2019.88 I 9858.
14. Deng, J. and Ren, F., Multi-label Emotion Detection via EmotionSpecified Feature Extraction and Emotion Correlation Leaming. *IEEE Trans. Affective Comput.*, 3045, 0, 1–12, 2020, https://doi.org/10.1109/TAFFC.2020.3034215.
15. Uddin, M.Z. and Nilsson, E.G., Emotion recognition using speech and neural structured learning to facilitate edge intelligence. *Eng. Appl. Artif. Intell.*, 94, September, 103775, 2020, https://doi.org/10.1016/j.engappai.2020.103775.

16. Shrivastava, M., Patil, R., Bhardwaj, V., Rawat, R., Telang, S., Rawat, A., Quantum Computing and Security Aspects of Attention-Based Visual Question Answering with Long Short-Term Memory, in: *Quantum Computing in Cybersecurity*, pp. 395–412, 2023.
17. Tafreshi, S., De Clereq, O., Barriere, V., Buechel, S., Sedoc, J., Balahur, A., W ASSA 2021 Shared Task: Predicting Empathy and Emotion in Reaction to News Stories. *Proceedings of the Eleventh Workshop on Computational Approaches to Subjectivity, Sentiment and Social Media Analysis*, pp. 92–104, 2021, https://aclanthology.org/2021. wassa-1.10.
18. Yoon, S., Byun, S., Jung, K., Multimodal Speech Emotion Recognition Using Audio and Text, 2018, I 0.1109/SLT.2018.8639583.
19. Yang, D., Alsadoon, A., Prasad, P.W.C., Singh, A.K., Elchouemi, A., An Emotion Recognition Model Based on Facial Recognition in Virtual Leaming Environment. *Procedia Comput. Sci.*, 125, 2009, 2–10, 2018, https://doi.org/10.1016/j.procs.2017.12.003.
20. Ortis, A., Farinella, G.M., Battiato, S., An overview on image sentiment analysis: Methods, datasets and current challenges. *ICETE 2019 Proceedings of the I6th International Joint Conference on e-Business and Telecommunications*, 2019.
21. Sikarwar, R., Shakya, H. K., Kumar, A., Rawat, A., Advanced Security Solutions for Conversational AI, in: *Conversational Artificial Intelligence*, pp. 287–301, 2024.
22. Haryadi, D. and Kusuma, G.P., Emotion detection in text using nested Long Short-Term Memory. *Int. J. Adv. Comput. Sci. Appl.*, 10, 6, 351–357, 2019, https://doi.org/10.14569/ijacsa.2019.0100645.
23. Pithawa, D., Nahar, S., Bhardwaj, V., Rawat, R., Dronawat, R., Rawat, A., Quantum Computing Technological Design Along with Its Dark Side, in: *Quantum Computing in Cybersecurity*, pp. 295–312, 2023.
24. Lopez, T.I., Twitter-Vaccine Sentiment Analysis, doi:10.2139/ssrn.3942987. PPR:PPR422888.
25. Perikos, I. and Hatzilygeroudis, I., Recognizing emotions in text using ensemble of classifiers. *Eng. Appl. Artif. Intell.*, 51, 191–201, 2016, https://doi.org/10.1016/j.engappai.2016.01.012.
26. Shih, P.-Y. and Chen, C.-P., Computer Science and Engineering Kaohsiung, Taiwan ROC National Chung Kung Univerisity Computer Science and Information Engineering. *IEEE International Conference 011 Acoustics, Speech, and Signal Processing (ICASSP)*, pp. 2756–2760, 2017.
27. Aribisala, B., Olori, O., Owate, P., Emotion Recognition Using Ensemble Bagged Tree Classifier and Electroencephalogram Signals. *J. Res. Rev. Sci.*, 5, 1, 106–111, 2018, https://doi.org/10.36108/jrrslasu/8102/50(0141).
28. Namdev, A., Patni, D., Dhaliwal, B. K., Parihar, S., Telang, S., Rawat, A., Potential Threats and Ethical Risks of Quantum Computing. *Quantum Computing in Cybersecurity*, pp. 335–352, 2023.

29. Mishra, A., Singh, A., Ranjan, P., Ujlayan, A., Emotion classification using ensemble of convolutional neural networks and support vector machine. *2020 7th International Conference on Signal Processing and Integrated Networks, SPIN 2020*, pp. 1006–1010, 2020, https://doi.org/10.1109/SPIN48934.2020.9071399.
30. Youngquist, O., An ensemble neural network for the emotional classification of text. *Proceedings of the 33rd International Florida Artificial Intelligence Research Society Conference, FLAIRS 2020*, pp. 270–275, 2020.
31. Salama, E.S., EI-Khoribi, R.A., Shoman, M.E., Wahby Shalaby, M.A., A 3D-convolutional neural network framework with ensemble learning techniques for multi-modal emotion recognition. *Egypt. Inf. J.*, 22, 2, 167–176, 2021, https://doi.org/lO.1016/j.eij.2020.07.005.
32. Zehra, W., Javed, A.R., Jalil, Z., Khan, H.U., Gadekallu, T.R., Cross corpus multi-lingual speech emotion recognition using ensemble learning. *Complex Intell. Syst.*, 7, 4, 1845–1854, 2021, https://doi.org/10.1007/s40747020-00250-4.

29

Alzheimer Disease Detection Using Machine Learning Techniques

M. Prabavathy[1]*, Paramita Sarkar[2], Abhrendu Bhattacharya[2] and Anil Kumar Behera[3]

[1]*Centre for Differently Abled Persons, Bharathidasan University, Tiruchirapalli, Tamil Nadu, India*
[2]*Department of C.S.E, JIS University, Agarpara, West Bengal, India*
[3]*Doctorate in National Board, Neurology, DNB Medicine, MBBS, Hyderabad, Telangana, India*

Abstract
Alzheimer's disease is a progressive neurological condition that gradually diminishes cognitive function, affects task performance, and disrupts normal behavior. In the absence of regular surveillance, numerous diseases, such as Alzheimer's, remain unnoticed until they have already advanced to a severe stage. Alzheimer's disease is considered a leading cause of death in many countries. The initial phase of Alzheimer's disease is referred to as preclinical sickness, which is followed by stages characterized by mild cognitive and/or behavioral impairment. For the prediction of medical illnesses, a machine learning model is one of the most efficient choices. Most machine learning algorithms are not appropriate for high-dimensional data because to the sparsity problem. As a result, they can only detect Alzheimer's disease using a limited feature space and dimensionality. This study's technique focuses on various machine learning, deep learning, and transfer learning models to enable early diagnosis of Alzheimer's disease.

Keywords: Alzheimer disease detection, machine learning, deep learning, feature selection, classification

**Corresponding author*: cdapraba@bdu.ac.in

Rajesh Kumar Chakrawarti, Ranjana Sikarwar, Sanjaya Kumar Sarangi, Samson Arun Raj Albert Raj, Shweta Gupta, Krishnan Sakthidasan Sankaran and Romil Rawat (eds.) Natural Language Processing for Software Engineering, (443–456) © 2025 Scrivener Publishing LLC

29.1 Introduction

3D scans of the human body, typically taken using a computed tomography (CT) or magnetic resonance imaging (MRI) scanner, are now being used in medical image processing for research, diagnosis, and guiding medical operations like surgery planning. Additionally, medical image processing helps specialists like radiologists, engineers, and physicians to better understand the anatomy of both individual and group patients. The main benefit of medical image processing is that it allows for a thorough evaluation of interior anatomy without intrusive procedures. Better patient treatment outcomes, improved medical equipment and drug delivery systems, and more precise diagnoses are all possible outcomes of building and studying 3D models of relevant anatomy. Chronic diseases, or illnesses that continue for a longer duration, are defined as conditions that last three months or more, according to the US national center for health statistics. In addition to not going away on their own, vaccinations are unable to prevent or cure chronic illnesses. In 1998, 88% of Americans 65 and older were dealing with a chronic condition. Most prevalent chronic illnesses have three main causes: tobacco use, insufficient physical exercise, and poor eating habits. Asthma, cancer, obesity, cardiovascular disease, diabetes, and Alzheimer's disease are just a few examples of the many chronic illnesses that exist. These chronic illnesses are presently affecting the majority of the population. Machine learning (ML) algorithms for early illness prediction are proliferating along with other advances in information and communication technology [1].

For example, Alzheimer's disease (AD) is one of such conditions that, without routine monitoring, would go undetected until it has already developed a significant amount. While advancing age is the leading cause of this cognitive disease, other variables including a serious brain damage can also play a role in the onset of this concerning illness [2]. The capacity to remember and accurately represent information is profoundly affected by the presence of AD. German doctor Dr. Alois Alzheimer found Alzheimer's disease in the brain of a 56-year-old lady after she passed away in 1906. A lady with a history of mental illness and suspicious conduct had her brain altered by Alzheimer's disease. Early onset, moderate, and advanced phases are used to categorize this condition, which is characterized by behavioral and functional dysfunction. Mild Alzheimer's disease patients in the initial stage may seem well on the outside, but they are actually becoming more confused about what's going on in their lives. In contrast, patients in the second stage of Alzheimer's disease require more constant monitoring and care, and those in the last stage are completely reliant on others for their survival [3].

One of the top killers in a lot of nations is Alzheimer's disease. Memory loss is the initial symptom of Alzheimer's disease. Declining physical and cognitive capacities exacerbate patients' already substantial challenges with day-to-day functioning. They will eventually need other people to help them take care of themselves. As a result, caring for people with Alzheimer's has become a major economic and social concern. A correct identification of the illness is crucial for prompt treatment. Mild cognitive impairment (MCI) is the first stage of Alzheimer's disease dementia; those who have it have an increased risk of 10% year for getting the condition. As of now, there is no pharmacological treatment that can restore cognitive function to those who have suffered from Alzheimer's disease or mild cognitive impairment (MCI) [4]. Nonetheless, detecting AD early enough to halt its growth is extremely challenging. Consequently, determining if a patient has AD or MCI becomes an extremely difficult assignment for the clinic. There is ongoing dispute on the primary benefit of early diagnosis of this illness. During the mild dementia stage, loved ones and medical professionals see that a person is experiencing significant memory and cognitive issues that are impacting their ability to carry out daily tasks. This is the hallmark of mild Alzheimer's disease. Over time, the individual and their loved ones may start to notice that something is off. Memory loss, poor judgement leading to poor decisions, lack of initiative and impulsivity, prolonged completion of everyday chores, question repetition, disorientation, roaming, and misplacing items in unusual locations are all possible issues [5].

29.2 Machine Learning Techniques to Detect Alzheimer's Disease

Out of the several medical sickness prediction models, a machine learning model is considered one of the most superior. Due to the sparsity problem, the majority of machine learning algorithms can only detect AD using data and feature spaces that have a minimal number of dimensions. Figure 29.1 depicts it. Several recent suggestions have emerged for predicting AD automatically utilizing advanced clustering and classification techniques that handle high-dimensional data. Current research efforts are focused on developing an enhanced machine learning model to diagnose Alzheimer's disease with greater speed and accuracy [6]. By employing either supervised or unsupervised learning techniques, one may successfully diagnose Alzheimer's disease and forecast its severity. The initial stage in supervised

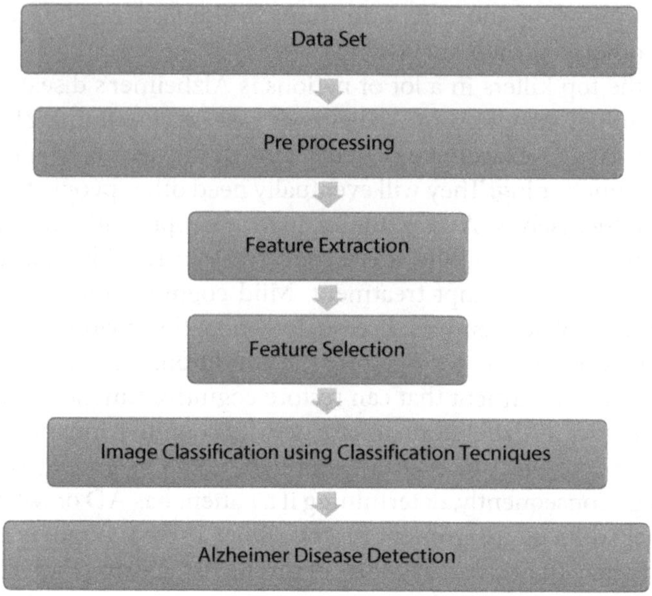

Figure 29.1 Framework to detect Alzheimer's disease using machine learning techniques.

learning involves partitioning the data into a training set and a test set. The training dataset is used to train the classifier, while the test dataset is used to evaluate the performance of the trained classifier model. Typically, the training dataset consists of 70% to 80% of the total data, whereas the testing dataset comprises the remaining 20%. Preprocessing entails examining the dataset for abnormalities, such as missing values or noisy data, once the training dataset has been established. Subsequently, to consistently and distinctly differentiate between the classes, feature extraction is performed. Feature selection is the subsequent stage in improving performance. Ultimately, the process of learning for AD detection is conducted utilizing supervised models such as decision trees (DT), random forests (RF), and support vector machines (SVM). Similarly, the testing dataset is used to assess the performance of the trained classifier.

29.3 Pre-Processing Techniques for Alzheimer's Disease Detection

Prior to utilizing a machine learning model with unprocessed data, it is imperative to do data pre-processing. Semi-automatic and fully-automatic methods have been employed for processing and categorizing AD data on several occasions. Researchers also observed that there are several techniques available for diagnosing AD. Active research is now focused on the discovery of biomarkers that can predict the start of cognitive decline, particularly in the early stages of Alzheimer's disease. Typical in real-world circumstances is the presence of complex, cacophonous, and erratic data. The occurrence of anomalies or inaccuracies in data gathering can be attributed to the rapid increase in data volume and the widespread availability of varied data sources. The capacity to generate dependable models and, consequently, dependable forecasts, relies on the caliber of the data utilized. Hence, it is imperative to process data for best quality. The process of information pre-processing has four main steps: cleaning, integration, transformation, and reduction. Data cleaning is the process of improving the quality of data by filling in missing values and reducing outliers. Integrating several sources of data offers users a consolidated perspective. Data transformation involves modifying the structure, values, or format of data to enhance its use. However, the computing expenses were decreased by implementing data reduction techniques to minimize the dimensions [7].

Data cleaning techniques are employed to rectify mistakes, identify anomalies, and impute missing values, while simultaneously reducing the impact of noise. Filters are essential as they effectively remove noise from the visual data. The Gaussian, mean, median, and bilateral filters are the most often employed filters for image processing, despite the availability of several other options [8]. The process of reducing visual noise is accomplished by utilizing a Gaussian filter. On the other hand, a mean filter, which is essentially a sliding window, calculates the average of all the pixels within the window and assigns it as the central value. A median filter, in contrast to a mean filter, selects the middle value from all the pixels inside the window and assigns it as the central value. Nevertheless, a bilateral filter, which is a non-linear smoothing filter, can effectively decrease noise while preserving edges. Authors propose a method that replaces the intensity of each pixel with a weighted average of intensity values from neighboring pixels. Due to the inherent characteristics of data integrations and transformations, their utilization in medical image processing is limited.

While there are several techniques available for decreasing data, only a limited number are commonly employed to enhance the accuracy of machine learning models. Data reduction solutions utilize the integrity of the original data to generate a smaller dataset while preserving its integrity. Alternatively, one may argue that it serves as a means to decrease the dimensionality of a dataset while preserving the integrity of the data. Data reduction strategies encompass several techniques such as data aggregation into cubes, dimensionality reduction, data compression, elimination of redundancy, data discretization, and creation of a concept hierarchy. Dimensionality reduction techniques are widely employed in machine learning to enhance the accuracy of prediction models for data classification and clustering [9].

29.4 Feature Extraction Techniques for Alzheimer's Disease Detection

Features are essential in image processing. Before extracting features, the sampled image goes through many image pre-processing procedures, including binarization, thresholding, scaling, and normalization. Subsequently, feature extraction approaches are employed to obtain features that may be applied for picture categorization and recognition [10]. The method of feature extraction may be used to divide a large dataset into smaller, more manageable parts. Processing will be simplified as a result. There is a vast array of variables in these extensive databases. Significant computational resources are required to manage these variables. Feature extraction is a process that identifies and selects the most relevant characteristics from large datasets [11]. It involves calculating the number of features in the dataset and creating new features, thereby lowering the amount of data. These properties also uniquely and easily describe the real dataset. Feature extraction is commonly used when raw data is very variable and not useful for machine learning models, and it becomes necessary to convert it into a more suitable format. Potential sources of data that may be analyzed for valuable attributes including text, images, geographic data, web information, audio recordings, and sensor data, among other possibilities. This study attempt incorporates the analysis of both image and audio data. To enhance the diagnosis and classification of Alzheimer's disease, it is customary to search for distinct characteristics in medical imaging [13].

Authors assert that forms play a crucial role in characterizing an object based on its most significant features, hence minimizing the volume of data that has to be stored. The region-based strategy utilizes the method of clustering and assigning labels to all pixels that are associated with objects, considering them as part of a unified region. The image is divided into distinct parts based on certain criteria, and each zone is assigned a unique set of pixels. A contour is a line that connects all the areas along the boundaries of an image that have the same level of brightness [14].

The field of audio analysis is now seeing significant expansion in the use of artificial intelligence and deep learning. Prior to training any statistical or machine learning model, it is necessary to extract the pertinent features of the audio stream. One of the stages involved in the processing of audio signals is the extraction of audio characteristics. The primary emphasis is on the manipulation or alteration of audio signals. It achieves equalization of time-frequency ranges and reduction of undesirable noise by converting both digital and analogue signals [15]. The focus of this topic revolves around the use of computational techniques to manipulate sounds. Audio features refer to descriptions of sounds or audio signals that may be utilized to train statistical or machine learning models for the development of intelligent audio systems. Several audio applications that utilize these characteristics include speech recognition, audio segmentation, source separation, automated music tagging, and audio categorization [16]. Various characteristics capture distinct components of sound that may be heard. Generally, musical signals may be categorized into three levels of abstraction: high-level, medium-level, and low-level. This is grounded in the auditory characteristics. Next, we will discuss the temporal properties of instantaneous, segmental, and global scales. The subsequent musical elements are rhythm, pitch, melody, harmony, timbre (the tonal quality of sound), and beat. Furthermore, the signal domains can encompass both temporal and spectral information, together with automatically retrieved characteristics from deep learning models or features chosen by machine learning models [17].

29.5 Feature Selection Techniques for Diagnosis of Alzheimer's Disease

The use of the labels provided in supervised feature selection aims to improve the ensuing classification process. Unsupervised feature selection aims to improve the clustering of data samples without using the labels of the data samples. There are three primary types of feature selection techniques based on the mechanism used: filter approaches, wrapper approaches, and intrinsic approaches. Filter techniques evaluate properties by examining their statistical characteristics of occurrences. Feature assessment in wrapper approaches relies on the prediction error of a learning algorithm [18]. Wrapper techniques utilize an iterative process of applying a learning algorithm to a specific subset of characteristics and data. This allows them to choose the subsets that yield the most accurate prediction errors. Feature selection is an integral component of the modeling process in intrinsic approaches [19].

Typically, feature selection strategies are organized based on the interaction between machine learning algorithms and feature assessment procedures. The popularity of the feature selection filter approach is driven by the advantages it offers in terms of computing costs and learner independence. Filter techniques for feature selection are constructed without considering any specific machine learning algorithms. The qualities, however, are chosen based on the outcomes of several statistical tests. A set of univariate measurements is employed to rank all the characteristics, and the ones that score highest are chosen. Instead of measuring the error rate, the filter approaches evaluate the feature subset using a surrogate quantity. We chose this quantity because it effectively encompasses the feature set and its usefulness without requiring excessive processing resources [20].

Wrapper techniques employ a novel prediction model to evaluate the feature subsets. The model is trained using individual, newly created subsets and then assessed against a separate control set. A new score is generated for this subgroup by including the actual errors made on a separate set. Wrapper techniques often yield the most optimum feature set for a given model, but they are computationally expensive due to the need to train new models for each subset. To choose the optimal subset, we employ an internal cross-validation approach and a focused classification algorithm to evaluate the true quality of the features. The intrinsic feature selection technique utilizes decision trees to pick features based on metrics. Unsupervised learning depends on correlation to choose features [21].

Significant feature selection procedures include domain knowledge, handling missing data, assessing correlation with the target class, evaluating correlation between features, using principal component analysis, employing forward feature selection, and considering feature significance. A proficient data scientist or machine learning engineer will greatly enhance any case study by effectively identifying characteristics. Real datasets frequently have missing values as a result of data manipulation or oversight in capturing them. Regarding missing values, there are several imputation techniques, albeit their effectiveness is not always guaranteed. Models trained on incomplete data characteristics may not consistently yield higher outcomes. The correlation coefficient is used to assess the degree of connection between each variable and references to the target class. It is a measure of the correlation between the label and attributes of the target class [22]. Two variables are said to be related only if their correlation coefficients are high. Therefore, each modification to a particular characteristic results in changes to associated variables. Matrix factorization preserves variance while reducing the dimensionality of the dataset. It defines a specific group of the most successful characteristics for the machine learning model, while also considering the process of selecting those characteristics. The model's ranking of characteristics is outlined in the feature relevance section. A significance score is awarded to each variable. The filter-based entropy technique was utilized in this work to choose features for AD detection.

29.6 Machine Learning Models Used for Alzheimer's Disease Detection

Machine learning is utilized in several fields such as biomedical systems, digital image processing, knowledge engineering, bioinformatics, and biomedical engineering. The three primary classifications of machine learning methodologies are reinforcement learning, supervised learning, and unsupervised learning. In supervised learning, the training step involves utilizing a large dataset to train the classifier. The testing phase, on the other hand, involves evaluating the performance of the classifier using a different dataset that was not used for training. However, there are instances where the distribution of classes in the training data is uneven. The scarcity of real-time medical data examples hinders the training and testing of classifiers. Common supervised learning models utilized for AD detection encompass Naive Bayes, Support Vector Machines (SVM), logistic regression, K-Nearest Neighbors (KNN), decision trees, neural networks, and random forests [23]. Unsupervised learning does not require data training. Unsupervised learning is a distinct approach from supervised learning, which aims to identify concealed patterns within data for the purpose of grouping related data types [24]. These models can also be utilized in the AD prediction procedure. Common unsupervised learning methods utilized for anomaly detection (AD) encompass hierarchical clustering, C-means clustering, and k-means clustering. Reinforcement learning is a machine learning approach that enables intelligent agents to acquire knowledge by interacting with their surroundings. On the other hand, reinforcement learning is an approach to instructing machine learning that employs rewards for desirable behavior and penalties for subpar performance [25]. An agent that learns by experiential learning possesses the ability to perceive and comprehend its surroundings, execute actions, and acquire knowledge from its errors. The model utilizes reinforcement learning (RL) in combination with domain knowledge and differential equations to simulate the progression of Alzheimer's disease (AD). Specific aspects associated to Alzheimer's disease can be represented by differential equations. To include the missing connections into the model, it is necessary for them to conform to fundamental rules governing brain functionality, such as maximizing cognitive performance while limiting the resources required to sustain cognition [26].

Authors assert that the model may restore the lost connections by optimizing an objective (reward) function that satisfies the aforementioned constraints. The study utilized decision trees, convolutional neural networks, support vector machines (SVMs), and a pre-trained visual geometry group (VGG16) model as supervised models to accurately classify AD classes [27].

Deep learning (DL) is a very innovative advancement in current artificial intelligence (AI) that is also known as hierarchical learning or deep structured learning. Until the 1990s, conventional machine learning methods were used to draw conclusions and make forecasts based on data. However, it had certain flaws. For instance, it depended on manually crafted features and had restrictions because it could only achieve precision at the level of human capability. Within the larger field of artificial intelligence (AI), deep learning (DL) specifically refers to a type of learning algorithm or model that is built upon artificial neural networks (ANN). On the other hand, deep learning has the advantage of extracting features from data during training rather than depending on manually designed feature engineering. Furthermore, Deep Learning has the capability to enhance its predictive and classification abilities by using extensive datasets, state-of-the-art computational power, and creative techniques. The inherent characteristics of DL models, such as their capacity to extract distinctive attributes, non-linear behavior, and extensive parallel processing, have significantly contributed to their efficacy and extensive adoption. Currently, there are several deep learning models accessible, such as convolutional neural networks, recurrent neural networks, long short-term memory networks, and various others. Several more deep learning models have been suggested for computer vision problems following the triumph of AlexNet, a model based on convolutional neural networks (CNNs), including VGGNet, GooglNet, ResNet, DenseNet, and various others. Like in machine learning (ML), the first stage of the framework in deep learning (DL) will include the pre-processing of pictures. To increase the number of samples, augmentation is performed following pre-processing. Subsequently, a deep learning model such as a Convolutional Neural Network (CNN), Recurrent Neural Network (RNN), Long Short-Term Memory (LSTM), or similar, would be employed to facilitate the learning process. Finally, the identical model is employed as a classifier to ascertain the different categories of Alzheimer's disease.

Given the alarming worldwide transmission [12] of the illness, it is imperative to now prioritize the screening, isolation, and treatment of AD patients [28]. Regrettably, the extended duration required to get MRI images results in infrequent utilization of testing facilities in hospitals or community health centers. Researchers in this field are dedicating significant time and effort to develop many viable deep transfer learning (DTL) models that utilize Mel spectrogram, derived from audio data gathered from patients, to address this issue. Transfer learning is a technique that can significantly decrease the time and effort required to train and fine-tune a model for a new task. Deep learning (DL) needs a substantially larger quantity of training data compared to standard machine learning methods. Creating extensive, well-annotated medical datasets is difficult and costly, which poses a significant barrier to accomplishing certain crucial domain-specific tasks due to the need for a substantial volume of labeled data. This holds particularly true in the context of medical applications. Despite the diligent work of academics, the traditional deep learning model still needs a substantial amount of computer resources, such as a server equipped with GPU capabilities. DTL, or Domain Transfer Learning, can significantly decrease the training data and time needed for a given job in a target domain. This can be achieved by utilizing a pre-trained model as either a fixed feature extractor or by further fine-tuning.

29.7 Conclusion

Alzheimer's disease, the prevalent kind of dementia in older individuals, is a progressive neurological disorder that imitates many of the brain's activities while gradually diminishing brain capability as a result of neuronal cell demise and tissue deterioration. While there is presently no proven remedy for Alzheimer's disease, there are several medications available that can assist in symptom management, as well as coping strategies to aid with behavioral regulation. Scientists embarked on a quest to identify methods for early detection and prevention of Alzheimer's disease, as an early and precise diagnosis is advantageous for managing the condition. Efficient automated techniques are necessary for the timely detection of Alzheimer's disease. Researchers have proposed several innovative methods to categorize Alzheimer's disease.

To enhance our learning strategies, however, we require a more profound understanding of Alzheimer's research. The current models for forecasting the start of Alzheimer's disease are insufficient.

References

1. Chauhan, D., Singh, C., Rawat, R., & Chouhan, M., Conversational AI Applications in Ed-Tech Industry: An Analysis of Its Impact and Potential in Education. *Conversational Artificial Intelligence*, 411–433, 2024.
2. Durga Prasad Jasti, V., Zamani, A.S., Arumugam, K., Naved, M., Pallathadka, H., Sammy, F., Raghuvanshi, A., Kaliyaperumal, K., Computational Technique Based on Machine Learning and Image Processing for Medical Image Analysis of Breast Cancer Diagnosis. *Secur. Commun. Netw.*, 2022, Article ID 1918379, 7, 2022, https://doi.org/10.1155/2022/1918379.
3. Wen, J., *et al.*, Convolutional neural networks for classifcation of Alzheimer's disease: overview and reproducible evaluation. *Med. Image Anal.*, 63, 101694, 2020.
4. Mishra, A. K., Tyagi, A. K., Dananjayan, S., Rajavat, A., Rawat, H., & Rawat, A., Revolutionizing Government Operations: The Impact of Artificial Intelligence in Public Administration. *Conversational Artificial Intelligence*, 607–634, 2024.
5. Physicians PC, Alzheimer's disease facts and figures. *Alzheimers Dement.*, 16, 3, 391–460, 2020.
6. Yang, Y., Li, X., Wang, P., Xia, Y., Ye, Q., Multi-Source transfer learning via ensemble approach for initial diagnosis of Alzheimer's disease. *IEEE J. Transl. Eng. Health Med.*, 1, 1–10, 2020.
7. Adelina, C., The costs of dementia: advocacy, media, and stigma. *Alzheimer's Dis. Int. World Alzheimer Rep.*, 2019, 100–1, 2019.
8. Suthar, H., Rawat, H., Gayathri, M., & Chidambarathanu, K., Techno-Nationalism and Techno-Globalization: A Perspective from the National Security Act. *Quantum Computing in Cybersecurity*, 137–164, 2023.
9. Noonia, A., Beg, R., Patidar, A., Bawaskar, B., Sharma, S., & Rawat, H., Chatbot vs Intelligent Virtual Assistance (IVA). *Conversational Artificial Intelligence*, 655–673, 2024.
10. Simon, A., Deo, M., Selvam, V., Babu, R., An overview of machine learning and its applications. *Int. J. Electr. Sci. Eng.*, 1, 22–24, 2016.
11. Priyanka and Balwinder, S., An Improvement In Brain Tumor Detection Using Segmentation And Bounding Box. *Int. J. Comput. Sci. Mob. Comput. (IJCSMC)*, 2, 239–246, 2013.

12. Yousuf, M.A. and Nobi, M.N., A new method to remove noise in magnetic resonance and ultrasound images. *J. Sci. Res.*, 3, 1, 81–89, 2010.
13. Ramalakshmi, C. and Chandran, A.J., Automatic brain tumor detection in MR images using neural network based classification. *Biom. Bioinf.*, 5, 6, 221–225, 2013.
14. George, E.B. and Karnan, M., MRI Brain Image enhancement using filtering techniques. *Int. J. Comput. Sci. Eng. Technol. (IJCSET)*, 3, 399–403, 2012.
15. Manjón, J.V., Carbonell-Caballero, J., Lull, J.J., García-Martí, G., MartíBonmatí, L., Robles, M., MRI denoising using non-local means. *Med. Image Anal.*, 12, 4, 514–523, 2008.
16. Sakthivel, K., Jayanthiladevi, A., Kavitha, C., Automatic detection of lung cancer nodules by employing intelligent fuzzy c means and support vector machine. *Biomed. Res.*, 27, 123–127, 2016.
17. Seixas, F.L., Zadrozny, B., Laks, J., Conci, A., Saade, D.C.M., A Bayesian network decision model for supporting the diagnosis of dementia, Alzheimer's disease and mild cognitive impairment. *Comput. Biol. Med.*, 51, 140–158, 2014.
18. Chauhan, D., Singh, C., Rawat, R., & Dhawan, M., Evaluating the Performance of Conversational AI Tools: A Comparative Analysis. *Conversational Artificial Intelligence*, 385-409, 2024.
19. Vemuri, P., Gunter, J.L., Senjem, M.L., Whitwell, J.L., Kantarci, K., Knopman, D.S., Jack, C.R., Alzheimer's disease diagnosis in individual subjects using structural MR images: validation studies. *Neuroimage*, 39, 3, 1186–1197, 2008.
20. Gad, A.R., Hassan, N.H., Seoud, R.A.A., Nassef, T.M., Automatic Machine Learning Classification of Alzheimer's Disease Based on Selected Slices from 3D Magnetic Resonance Imagining. *Age*, 67, 10–15, 2016.
21. Siddiqui, M.F., Mujtaba, G., Reza, A.W., Shuib, L., Multi-Class Disease Classification in Brain MRIs Using a Computer-Aided Diagnostic System. *Symmetry*, 9, 3, 1–37, 2017.
22. Beheshti, I. and Demirel, H., Feature-ranking-based Alzheimer's disease classification from structural MRI. *Magn. Reson. Imaging*, 34, 3, 252–263, 2016.
23. Xiao, Z., Ding, Y., Lan, T., Zhang, C., Luo, C., Qin, Z., Brain MR Image Classification for Alzheimer's Disease Diagnosis Based on Multi feature Fusion. *Comput. Math. Methods Med.*, 1, 1–14, 2017.
24. Bhateja, V., Rastogi, K., Verma, A., Malhotra, C., A non-iterative adaptive median filter for image denoising. *International Conference on Signal Processing and Integrated Networks (SPIN)*, pp. 113–118, 2014.
25. Kaplan, I., Applying the Haar wavelet transform to time series information, pp. 1–176, 2001.
26. Zhao, W. and Wang, J., A new method of the forest dynamic inspection color image sharpening process. *2010 3rd International Conference on Advanced*

Computer Theory and Engineering (ICACTE), pp. V4–211-V4-214, 2010, doi: 10.1109/ICACTE.2010.5579715.

27. Rawat, R., Mahor, V., Rawat, A., Garg, B., & Telang, S. Digital transformation of cyber crime for chip-enabled hacking. In *Handbook of research on advancing cybersecurity for digital transformation* (pp. 227-243), IGI Global, 2021.
28. Ibrahim, I. and Abdulazeez, A., The Role of Machine Learning Algorithms for Diagnosing Diseases. *J. Appl. Sci. Technol. Trends*, 2, 01, 10–19, 2021, Available: 10.38094/jastt20179.

30

Netnographic Literature Review and Research Methodology for Maritime Business and Potential Cyber Threats

Hitesh Rawat[1]*, Anjali Rawat[2] and Romil Rawat[3]

[1]Department of Business Management and Economics, University of Extremadura, Badajoz, Spain
[2]Department of Computer and Communication Technology, University of Extremadura, Badajoz, Spain
[3]Department of Computer Science and Engineering, Shri Vaishnav Vidyapeeth Vishwavidyalaya, Indore, India

Abstract
Worldwide apprehension over transnational organized crime at sea is growing. People are focusing on cyberthreats and crime-related convergences as a result of this uncertainty, which is impeding the development of a unified foreign policy response (ocean and maritime criminology and protection). The work focuses on the comprehension gap by conveying a compositional conceptualization and examinination of cross-border organized crime in the Pacific. The proposed work represents information, including observations of cyberthreats to the marine industry. A netnographic analysis is conducted on the OSN channels, where vulnerabilities are analyzed and disseminated. The method involves conducting a netnographic study on the digital platform, and entails making long-term descriptive observations and interpretations of online social networks and platforms. The framework for a promising investigation into the various types of oceanic crime committed by malicious actors to map their unique characteristics is also discussed in the work.

***Keywords*:** Ocean crime, maritime, cyber security, illicit trafficking, cyber attack, business threat

**Corresponding author*: hrawat88@gmail.com

Rajesh Kumar Chakrawarti, Ranjana Sikarwar, Sanjaya Kumar Sarangi, Samson Arun Raj Albert Raj, Shweta Gupta, Krishnan Sakthidasan Sankaran and Romil Rawat (eds.) Natural Language Processing for Software Engineering, (457–474) © 2025 Scrivener Publishing LLC

30.1 Introduction

A qualitative research approach called ethnographic [34] research uses in-person observation to examine individuals in their natural settings. It is a fundamental approach in feminist geography, development studies, cultural ecology, and the social and behavioral sciences and is frequently employed in these fields. This may involve researching all facets of human communication, including tone of voice, body language, and netnography—all of which are research methodologies.

Netnography [34] is a research approach that focusses on online communities and digital cultures. It is characterized as participant-observational research based on OSN that incorporates methods of data gathering such as in-depth interviews conducted on virtual platforms and participant observation.

Ocean piracy, human trafficking [22, 23], drug trafficking [24, 25], weapons trafficking, and waste trafficking by the ocean, as well as environmental crimes, are all becoming important aspects of ocean monitoring [18] and governance, oceanic security, and law enforcement. Such violations take various forms throughout the world's oceans, causing political, social, national, and economic disruptions, ranging from the effects on foreign shipping to Dedicated channels and timely web links created for clients and actors involved in illicit activities who like to trade across nations [19–22].

At the highest levels of foreign policymaking, oceanic piracy is getting more recognition. In February 2019, the United Nations Security Discussion on the subject was titled "Transnational Organised Crime in the Ocean as a Challenge to International Peace and [1] Security." The topic of debate was the effects of the oceanic dark web trade and crime. One of the reasons for this was the widespread misunderstanding and illegal practices in the diverse nature of oceanic cybercrime [17] and [18]. We begin with a review of current concepts of cross-border organized crime in the ocean related to international law, especially the UN Convention on Transnational Organised Crime (UNTOC) [3]. Perhaps such offences, such as piracy, are politically prioritized and reasonably well researched, whereas some are not. Others, such as cocaine abuse, are well recorded and known in some areas but not in others. Conducting more in-depth research on the content and scope of available evidence on any oceanic crime is thus a critical challenge for ocean criminology and police responses.

Business disruptions [2] and cyber events are sometimes referred to as assaults or significant problems. The most troublesome attacks might actually be those that are most localized. Email phishing tactics do indeed still rule the world of cybercrime [3]. While concerns like WannaCry, crypto-currency mining, and state-sponsored assaults [4] are in the news, lower-level cyberattacks are having a much greater impact, and cargo is by no means immune. A phishing campaign is when a cybercriminal uses a compromised email account to deceive victims into disclosing sensitive or confidential data. Phishing scams and corporate email hack assaults aim to scam companies at all levels [5]. The shipboard [6] equipment of today is well integrated, yet poorly protected. These dangers are high. Key systems, particularly navigation devices, might be jeopardized if attacked or if a virus was unintentionally downloaded, as ships rely more and more on automation [7] and remote monitoring.

Social engineering [8] is combined with phishing, since the originator attempts to make the receiver believe they are someone, they are not. But effective phishing [9] attempts can also be attributed to inadequate online safety. It describes the procedures and actions computer users take to maintain system health and enhance internet privacy. A vessel that had been the victim of a cyberattack has been sailed on by over half (49%) of commercial seamen. There are no signs that cyberpiracy will decrease as a result of improving technology and rising freight values. In a marine poll, 45% [13] of participants revealed that their only cyber security measure was a simple firewall. Figure 30.1 shows the crime increase rate in marine territory.

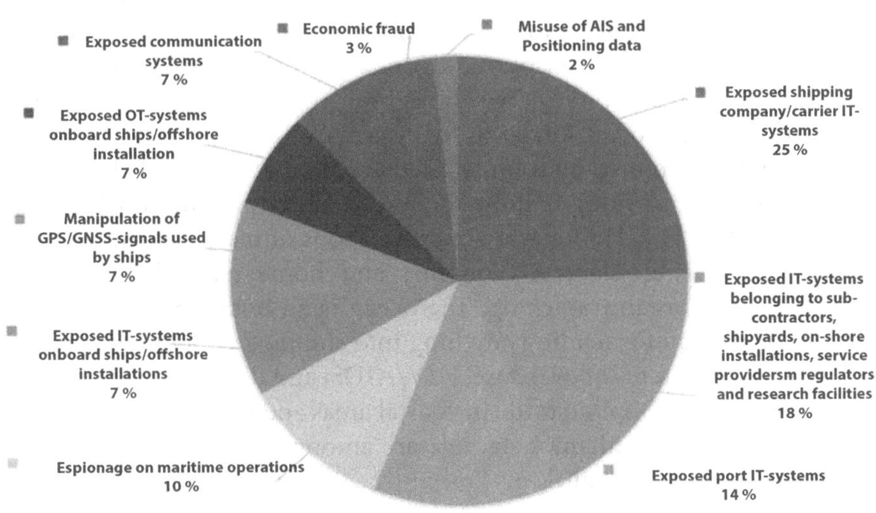

Figure 30.1 Crime increase rate at marine territory [23, 28].

The International Maritime Organization (IMO) [11, 12], which advises that cyber security is a crucial component of risk mitigation, is at odds with this. Internet piracy [14] lacks the passion and excitement of traditional piracy. Because modern piracy is carried out behind locked doors hundreds of kilometers [15] away, faster ships and greater weapons will not be able to prevent cyberattacks or keep sailors safe. The maritime industry [16, 17] is confronting an additional challenge as a result of the fast digitization of its operations and information, as is the case for many other businesses [18] throughout the world. This digital [19] transition has numerous implications and advantages, but if the proper precautions are not taken to maintain the security of ships, it might easily be used by bad actors.

The rest of the paper is organized as follows: Section 30.2. Shows the Criminal Flows Framework, Section 30.3. Describes Oceanic Crime Exchange and categorization, Section 30.4. It is about fishing crimes, mobility crimes, and finally, Section 30.5. This concludes the paper with a discussion in Section 30.6.

30.2 Criminal Flows Framework

The division is classified into four categories, namely: (1) Crime Mutation; (2) Forced Crimes; (3) Military Activities; and (4) Atmosphere-Disturbing. The categorization is further discussed and presented in Table 30.1: Oceanic Crimes Categorization.

The majority of global smuggling and trafficking activities are tied to oceanic space. Different types of illegal flows in the ocean can be differentiated based on what is transported. Human trafficking, organ trafficking rackets [3, 15, 16] and piracy are serious problems in many oceanic countries, with refugees often forced to fly in precarious boats. Such practices are frequently promoted by sophisticated criminal networks [12]. Human smuggling and trafficking is done for forced labor, prostitution [12, 13], arms smuggling [14, 17] for war zones, weapons of mass destruction and testing, kidnapping, slavery, economic and home instability, narcotic trafficking, and organ trafficking. The ocean is an open and well-known illegal activity hub for loading anything into shipping containers for concealment. Higher rates of overdose, HIV/AIDS, and domestic abuse are all consequences of the opioid trade in coastal areas and beyond [14]. Heroin, opium, hemp, and methamphetamine are among the narcotics trafficked by Ocean [13]. Arm trafficking [28, 29] has the potential to destabilize nations by causing hidden wars among nationals. The movement of war

Table 30.1 Oceanic crimes categorization [3, 4].

Sub categories	Crime mutation	Forced crimes	Military activities	Atmosphere disturbing
Ocean Relation and Area of Vulnerability.	Within the Ocean Territory	Across the Ocean	Under and across the Ocean	Under the Ocean
Crime Classes.	Ship and Cargo capturing, Drug trafficking, National Security Threat, Illicit Trade, Tax Evasion	Fisheries Crimes, Blackmailing, Organ Trafficking, Unauthorized Entry	Disastrous Weapons Showcasing and Testing.	Plants and Animal Trafficking, industrial Waste Pollution and Discharging, Illicit Mining, Violence at Ship Attack by Missile
Affecting Objects and Organizations.	Cargo ,Marine and Shipping Industry	Healthcare, Food Industry, Destroying Cultural Heritage	Border Enhancement and Capturing.	Biodiversity Disturbance.
Crime Categories.	Slavery and Illegal Entry into Countries	Child and Human Trafficking, Ancient Antiques Trafficking.	International Law and Treaty Dissolution	Natural Resources Disturbance, myths about missing of ships
Reasons of Crime and Inability of Security agencies to Track and Stop the Vulnerable Events.	Unchecked Power and Support by Terrorist Groups, Trained Pirate Attacks	Passing from Criminal Zones, To hide Militant from International Security Agencies by Continuously moving over Ocean	Supremacy and Superpower Competency Across the Global.	Coastal Locations Limitation for Checked and Controlled Law Enforcement
Automated Crime	Control System Hacking by Unidentified Hackers (Cyber Criminals).	Malware Injection and Security Penetration.	Secure Location Coordinates Tracing and Automated Attack Installation.	Online Bidding at illicit Forums and Transaction.

groups and materials or precursors could jeopardize national and international security. Regulated or banned items such as counterfeit merchandise, antiquities, animals, hardwood lumber, or waste, among others, can be trafficked at Ocean [2]. Illicit trade [30–32] in goods will jeopardize environmental efforts, encourage ecosystem loss, and endanger biodiversity [16]. Finally, licit products like gold, charcoal, gasoline, tobacco, and sugar can be diverted to circumvent taxes, customs duties, and foreign sanctions [11]. Avoiding taxes and customs fees increases the amount of money associated with illegal trade and activities.

30.3 Oceanic Crime Exchange and Categorization

The research suggests that more research is needed to better grasp how various actors and organizations participating in the battle against oceanic crime [5] exchange knowledge with one another and with the general public. This is partly due to questions over accountability, confidence, and the availability of effective data-sharing networks. It does, however, raise methodological concerns, such as the degree to which data can be compared or obtained using standard categories and meanings. The relationship between how oceanic crimes are conceptualized, interpreted, security-focused responses, law enforcement and social justice interventions, underlying causes of crime, community growth, or capacity-building programs is unlikely to be successful, and attention must be given to how different solutions can work together.

The transport of goods and oceanic shipping are the targets of crimes against mobility. Crimes occur on the water or in close proximity to the shore. Movements in the ocean are the subject of crimes against mobility. The ship and the port are the primary targets of damage, with the harmed items being not only vehicles, goods, and their crews, and supply chain destruction is a major offense. Different criminal movements exist. Across the ocean, illegal acts are taking place. Although the damage is done on shore, the ocean provides an outlet for criminals. These offenses have a negative impact on families and cultures. The main crime in this group is smuggling in all sorts of goods. Environmental violations occur in the ocean and are directed at the oceanic environment, including natural resources, installations, and artifacts. The main practices included in this group are illegal mineral trafficking and offenses against oceanic resources. Table 30.1 shows a summary of each division.

A. **Crime Mutation**

A major type of oceanic crime involves crimes in which the ocean is mainly used as a medium for illegal activity rather than the primary location of the crime. The high oceans still have looser and more ambiguous regulatory regimes than those jurisdictions of individual nations, reducing the chance of being apprehended and prosecuted for drug trafficking.

There are frequently associated violent crimes with fishing or recreational boating in general with the courage and desire to use violence with guns or light firearms in war communities with gun cultures. For example, an illegal vessel may engage in lawful fishing, fishery violations, different types of trafficking, or even piracy [9]. Because of these power synergies, oceanic law enforcement can find it difficult to discriminate between legal users of the ocean and those involved in oceanic crime. This may be because such roads, such as those in Djibouti, Somalia, and Yemen, are of vital geo-economic significance for oceanic traffic and are targeted by criminals to commit crime [7]. These areas will serve as chokepoints for oceanic traffic, causing ships to slow down to navigate safely and increase their susceptibility to attack [16].

Criminals often use informal trade networks to transport various illegal goods, such as weapons, people, and drugs. The Western Indian Ocean's show trading network, for example, has been frequently connected to smuggling activities [7]. Overlap may occur through common modes of criminal enterprise or commercial activities that aid in the commission of crimes. For illegal markets, banking, tax fraud, money exchanges, and laundering networks are among them. Traditional activities like bribery or forgery, slave labor, or unethical bribes to ministers, private workers, and criminals may participate in the legal economy in a variety of ways. Table 30.2 depicts the increase in crime rate [26, 27] over the previous four years.

Table 30.3 shows the marine threat generated targeting [23, 26] (port, ocean business, military activities, and trafficking). Table 30.4 represents the Comparative Work Analysis.

Figure 30.2 and Figure 30.3 shows the comparative study of cybercrime that penetrated the security infrastructure of the ocean in Year 2022 and in 2024 respectively, and caused millions of losses towards security organizations and trade.

Table 30.2 Increased in crime rate chart [7, 8].

Ref.	Crime categorization/ identified cases(year) in percentage	2018(in %)	2019(in %)	2020(in %)	2021(in %)	2022(in %)	2024(in %)
[2, 8]	Ocean Relation and Area of Vulnerability.	18	25	48	51	59	63
[3, 9]	Crime Classes	36	41	46	57	63	68
[4, 10]	Affecting Objects and Organizations.	43	56	67	74	77	82
[5, 11]	Crime Categories.	53	68	77	82	87	91
[6, 12]	Reasons of Crime and Inability of Security agencies to Track and Stop the Vulnerable Events.	44	51	67	87	91	93
[7, 13]	Automated Crime	59	69	78	82	87	89

Table 30.3 Generated marine threats [32–34].

Crime	**2024 (Crime-increased rate) (in %)**
Capturing , Drug trafficking , National Security Threat, Illicit Trade, Tax Evasion	83
Fisheries Crimes, Blackmailing, Organ Trafficking, Unauthorized Entry	77
Healthcare, Food Industry, Destroying Cultural Heritage	91
Child and Human Trafficking, Ancient Antiques Trafficking, Slavery and Illegal Entry into Countries	95
Passing from Criminal Zones ,To hide Militant from International Security Agencies by Continuously moving over Ocean	75
Unchecked Power and Support by Terrorist Groups, Trained Pirate Attacks	77
Malware Injection and Security Penetration, Control System Hacking by Unidentified Hackers (illicit agents and Criminals).	87

Table 30.4 Comparative work analysis.

Reference	**Approach**
[22]	Cyberthreats to the water transport industry are explored.
[23]	Based on the pertinent area of international law, the paper elaborates on the legality of eavesdropping on underwater communications cable networks.
[24]	This paper contrasts the development of cyberspace as a man-made realm with the history of the creation of maritime laws, conventions, customs, and standards of conduct.
[25]	Cyberthreat case patterns involving international crime are addressed.
[26]	The topic of the discussion is the economics, safety, and security of the oceans for the ensuing decades, as well as current civilian and military foresight reports, studies, and articles from five continents.
[27]	For new paths spanning digital and green criminology, academics are encouraged to create reflective interactions with post-anthropocentric criticisms.
Proposed Work	Structural and conceptualization study of cross-border organized crime in the ocean are discussed

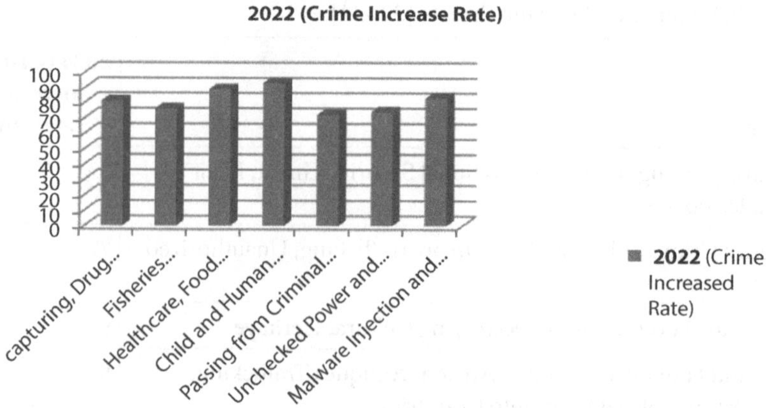

Figure 30.2 Crime increase rate at marine territory (2022).

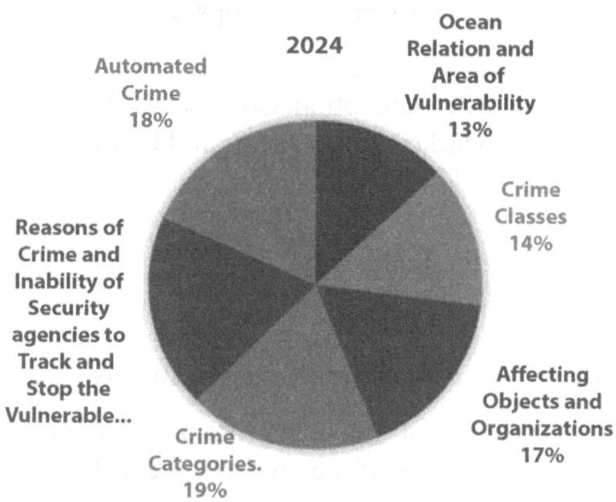

Figure 30.3 Crime increase rate at marine territory (2024).

B. **Atmosphere Disturbing Crime**

Environmental offenses apply to actions that have a direct negative impact on the aquatic environment, with humans being only a secondary victim. Such offenses happen in water, in the context of destruction or depletion of the ocean's fauna, wealth, cultural history, and infrastructure. Anthropocene offenses occur in the form of human actions that communicate and interfere with the ocean's ecosystem [14]. This suggests a greater view of "the climate," acknowledging that it is impossible to separate nature and society in the Anthropocene [3]. Human-made artifacts, shipwrecks, pipelines, wind turbines, and oil platforms are all so intertwined with nature that it's impossible to set them apart. Such environmental violations are often significant and occur with differing levels of organization. They primarily consist of financial gain-oriented breaches of environmental regulations, such as intentional contamination and waste disposal at Ocean, ship ballast water discharge and unchecked breakage operations [8], or the illegal exploitation of natural resources at Ocean [2].

Offshore platforms and vital facilities, such as pipelines and underwater data cables, are all used in the oceanic world. They are vulnerable to illegal activity, such as accidental harm or intentional threat of criminal intent [9]. Crimes against cultural heritage are also included here for related reasons. Treasure searching, pillaging antiquities, and war graves, such as the plundering of sunken warships for scrapping purposes, are examples. Such offenses can have an environmental effect, releasing pesticides or fuels within water bodies that have new biodiversity hotspots [4].

Offenses in the ocean have a wide range of pathological consequences, and illegal fishing puts species in jeopardy. Coral reefs and other underwater habitats are harmed by destructive fishing techniques. Waste disposal and other polluting practices may have disastrous consequences for wildlife and ocean health. Such activities will reduce the productivity and profitability of fishing grounds for legal fishermen, their livelihoods, and fragile coastal areas [6].

Figure 30.4 describes the marine activities [15] that have increased so much in recent years.

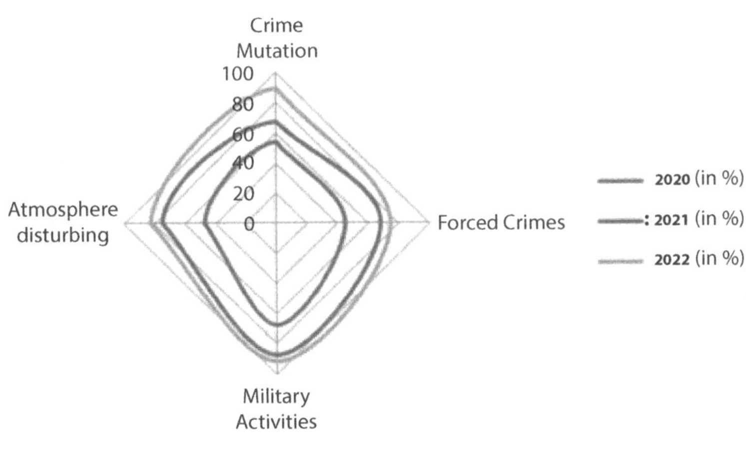

Figure 30.4 Increased marine activities.

C. **Forced Crimes**

Oceanic crime is adaptable and complex. Criminals that are involved in one kind of crime may also be involved in another at the same time or move from one to the other [8]. Motivations resulting from unintended outcomes are the reasons for the transformation and adaptation of oceanic crime and the criminal market, motivated by risk and reward equations, according to criminologists [11]. When the chances of committing a specific type of crime in a specific location become too high, law enforcement action, defensive strategies, criminal justice practices, and offenders are more likely to turn to fewer countermeasures and more favorable risk-reward balances [12]. Piracy coast of Somalia is a good example of the establishment of an effective court prison system, incarceration of pirate suspects for prosecution, oceanic patrolling, and usage of protective armed guards on submarines [13]. It's assumed that the major pirate organizational frameworks are still in place, and that their leaders are still on the loose [4]. Since these organizations are no longer as heavily involved in piracy, they have also broadened their scope to include the transfer of illegal piracy proceeds into legal businesses on the Somali coast, and their networks expertise adapted skills, such as weapons and people trafficking [7].

Countermeasure-driven adaptation often coexists with opportunity-driven motives. When such crimes become more dangerous, new opportunities can arise as a result of geopolitics or criminal creativity to replace them. Changing geopolitical circumstances frequently constrain such opportunities. A rise in war or insecurity in a given nation or area, for example, may result in new armament demands or an influx of refugees fleeing violence or deprivation. For example, the outbreak of Yemen's war in 2015 provided new possibilities for trafficking operations both to and from the country through [3].

Similarly, the destabilization of more developed roads by Russia and the Balkans (Western Indian Ocean) resulted in the advent of a crucial outlet for the transport of Afghani heroin (Northern and Balkan routes). Since 2014, European sanctions against Russia have increased border protection in Eastern Europe and blocked trafficking along the northern pathway. The Balkan route was disrupted by significantly improved border control between Turkey and Iran as a result of the Syrian conflict [5]. On the other hand, global wars, such as the one in Syria, will make operations more complex. Such conditions pose risks to those operating in or passing through them [7].

D. **Military Activities**

Interconnections between oceanic crime and the broader security system include conflict, chaos, and state vulnerability, among others, but it's also worth noting that oceanic crime is linked to geopolitics and terrorism. In the South China Sea [9], illicit fishing interacts with inter-state tensions and geopolitical rivalry. Solid evidence indicates that some of these organizations may participate in oceanic crime to fund their operations. Smuggling of sugar and charcoal in Somalia is linked to the Al Shabab group [16], as is kidnapping and killing for ransom in the Sulu and Celebes Seas, which is linked to the Abu Sayyaf group [5].

30.4 Fisheries Crimes and Mobility Crimes

Following that, Landing endangered animals or using prohibited methods (cyanide or dynamite fishing) are examples of illegal fishing linked to a slew of fishing industry issues, including forgery of documents or tax evasion, trafficking of crew members on board ships, forced labor and slavery [12], collectively termed as "fisheries crimes" [13]. Illegal fishing is expected to cost the fishing industry up to USD 23.5 billion a year, with other fishing-related offenses causing far more financial harm [13]. Artisanal fishermen in restricted areas on a habitual basis may engage in illegal fishing at a low level. However, it is frequently a highly complex and organized crime, involving cross-border criminal networks operated by shell corporations and using several flags of convenience.

The UNCLOS [3] concept has been criticized for its inflexibility and failure to catch certain forms of criminality, particularly referred to as contemporary oceanic piracy [1]. It is a complex phenomenon encompassing a wide range of business structures, which are regionally unique and classified as crime in sovereign waters. Crime in the Gulf of Guinea is focused on the region's oil economy and occurs in the territorial waters of countries like Nigeria [13]. Stealing of cargo or kidnapping of crews is a common crime in the Malacca Straits and Southeast Asia. The bulk of such events, as in the Gulf of Guinea, occur in territorial waters [4]. The guidelines for preventing crime in the maritime industry use a broad term that includes "the use of violence against the ship using digital autonomy, its passengers, crew, or cargo, or any attempt to use violence" [5]. Theft at sea is the result of fraud, and offenses against vehicles are possible at port facilities [9]. Data breaches caused by malware (ransomware) are an emerging criminal practice and have proven difficult to quantify due to concerns about reputational harm for targets [12]. They are frequently well-organized, costing the oceanic industry a lot of money in terms of disembarkation-repatriation conditions and possible penalties for ship owners [13].

30.5 Conclusion

The concept of cross-border organized digital crime in the ocean has made it to the United Nations Security Council and is constantly being designed for discussion on oceanic security and governance. This paper has taken the argument a step further by outlining the essential categories. This lays the groundwork for understanding not just the differences between different forms of crime but also how they connect and bind together. The UNODC and Interpol emerged as the main global organizations tackling oceanic crime by forming governance structures focusing on crimes against the mobility of shipping and port regulations. Border and customs agencies are all focused on criminal movements. Environmental offenses are handled by environmental bodies such as the UNEP (United Nations Environment Program) and the FAO (Food and Agriculture Organization), which lack experience in dealing with violence. Crimes against utilities get very little attention. The international approach to oceanic crimes would have to include rethinking mechanisms and tackling structural instability on both a regional and global basis.

30.6 Discussion

The world community is becoming increasingly concerned about cross-border organized crime in the ocean. This ambiguity has impeded a coordinated foreign policy response by forcing individuals to focus on specific digital risks that intersect with other crimes (ocean and maritime criminology and protection). We fill this gap in our knowledge by presenting a structural conceptualization and study of cross-border organized crime in this article.

References

1. Tachie-Menson, E.A., Investigating the Intersection of Maritime and Cyber Crime in the Gulf of Guinea. *Sci. Mil. S. Afr. J. Mil. Stud.*, *51*, 3, 89–112, 2023.
2. Manhas, N.S., Maritime Security Cooperation Between India and ASEAN, in: *India and ASEAN in the Indo Pacific: Pathways and Perils*, pp. 43–64, Springer Nature Singapore, Singapore, 2024.
3. Rawat, R., Mahor, V., Rawat, A., Garg, B., Telang, S., Digital Transformation of Cyber Crime for Chip-Enabled Hacking, in: *Handbook of Research on*

Advancing Cybersecurity for Digital Transformation, pp. 227–243, IGI Global, USA, 2021.
4. Vrancken, P., State jurisdiction to investigate and try fisheries crime at sea. *Mar. Policy*, 105, 129–139, 2019.
5. Guilfoyle, D., Prosecuting pirates: a critical evaluation of the options. *J. Int. Crim. Justice*, 10, 4, 767–796, 2012.
6. Ford, J.H. and Wilcox, C., Shedding light on the dark side of maritime trade – a new approach for identifying countries as flags of convenience. *Mar. Policy*, 99, 298–303, 2019.
7. Miller, D.D. and Sumaila, U.R., Flag use behaviour and IUU activity within the international fishing fleet: definitions and identifying areas of concern. *Mar. Policy*, 44, 204–211, 2013.
8. Makarenko, T., The crime-terror continuum: tracking the interplay between transnational organised crime and terrorism. *Glob. Crime*, 6, 1, 129–145, 2004.
9. Ekici, B. and Coban, A., Afghan heroin and Turkey: ramifications of an international security threat. *Turk. Stud.*, 15, 2, 341–364, 2014.
10. Gunavathi, R. and Bharathi, K.M., Cybercrimes in the Associated World, in: *Artificial Intelligence for Cyber Defense and Smart Policing*, pp. 21–31, Chapman and Hall/CRC, USA, 2023.
11. Wyatt, T., The local context of wildlife trafficking: the heathrow animal reception centre, in: *Emerging Issues in Green Criminology: Exploring Power, Justice, and Harm*, D. Westerhuis, R. Walters, T. Wyatt (Eds.), pp. 108–126, Palgrave Macmillan, Basingstoke, 2013.
12. Wyatt, T., *Wildlife Trafficking: A Deconstruction of the Crime, the Victims, and the Offenders*, Palgrave Macmillan, Basingstoke, 2013.
13. Gikonyo, C., The Jeddah amendment and the fight against wildlife trafficking. *Crim. Law Forum*, 30, 2, 181–200, 2019.
14. Rawat, R., Mahor, V., Chirgaiya, S., Rathore, A.S., Applications of Social Network Analysis to Managing the Investigation of Suspicious Activities in Social Media Platforms, in: *Advances in Cybersecurity Management*, pp. 315–335, Springer, Cham, 2021.
15. Rawat, R., Mahor, V., Chirgaiya, S., Shaw, R.N., Ghosh, A., Sentiment Analysis at Online Social Network for Cyber-Malicious Post Reviews Using Machine Learning Techniques, in: *Computationally Intelligent Systems and their Applications*, pp. 113–130, 2021.
16. Rasmussen, J., Sweet Secrets: Sugar Smuggling and State Formation in the Kenya-Somalia Borderlands, 2017, DIIS Working Paper 11.
17. UNODC, United Nations Office on Drugs and Crime, Transnational Organized Crime in the Fishing Industry, 2011, Available at, http://www.unodc.org/documents/human-trafficking/Issue_Paper_-_TOC_in_the_Fishing_Industry.pdf.
18. Chalk, P., *The Maritime Dimension of International Security: Terrorism, Piracy, and Challenges for the United States*, RAND Corporation, USA, 2008.

19. Maritime Cyber-Attacks Increase by 900% in Three Years, Available online: https://www.marineinsight.com/shipping-news/maritime-cyber-attacks-increase-by-900-in-three-years/# (accessed on 20 July 2020).
20. https://www.unodc.org/unodc/en/piracy/index.html
21. Senarak, C., Port cybersecurity and threat: A structural model for prevention and policy development. *Asian J. Shipp. Logist.*, *37*, 1, 20–36, 2021.
22. Caponi, S.L. and Belmont, K.B., Maritime cybersecurity: a growing threat goes unanswered. *Intell. Prop. Tech. L. J.*, *27*, 1, 16, 2015.
23. [22] Alekseenkov, A., Klyuchnikova, D., Dedova, N., Sokolov, S., Cyberattacks in the Water Transport Industry: Types and Diversity, in: *International Scientific Siberian Transport Forum TransSiberia-2021: Volume 2*, 2022, March, Springer International Publishing, Cham, pp. 1532–1540.
24. Botua, H.L., Dewi, C.T.I., Siswandi, R.A.G.C., WIRETAPPING ON SUBMARINE COMMUNICATIONS CABLE: QUESTIONING ITS LEGALITY AMIDST LONG STANDING PRACTICE. *Padjadjaran J. Int. Law*, *6*, 1, 20–42, 2022.
25. Howard, L.C.T.D. and da Cruz, J.D.A., Like the Sea, So Cyberspace: A Brief Exploration of Establishing Cyberspace Norms through a Maritime Lens. *J. Adv. Mil. Stud.*, *13*, 2, 142–153, 2022.
26. Rawat, R., Logical concept mapping and social media analytics relating to cyber criminal activities for ontology creation. *Int. J. Inf. Technol.*, *15*, 2, 893–903, 2023.
27. Fita, G.A., Ismira, A., Khaldun, R.I., Fatra, D., Patterns of Transnational Crime in The Border of Sulawesi Sea-Sulu Sea and Threats to Indonesia's Maritime. *Resolusi: J. Sos. Polit.*, *5*, 2, 133–142, 2022.
28. Lauro, A. and Corrêa, C.R., Futures for the Maritime Domain: Signs and Trends That Shape Scenarios, in: *Power and the Maritime Domain*, pp. 286–301, Routledge, USA, 2023.
29. Rawat, R., Gupta, S., Sivaranjani, S., Cu, O.K., Kuliha, M., Sankaran, K.S., Malevolent Information Crawling Mechanism for Forming Structured Illegal Organisations in Hidden Networks. *Int. J. Cyber Warf. Terror. (IJCWT)*, *12*, 1, 1–14, 2022.
30. Bedford, L., Mann, M., Foth, M., Walters, R., A post-capitalocentric critique of digital technology and environmental harm: New directions at the intersection of digital and green criminology. *Int. J. Crime Justice Soc. Democr.*, *11*, 1, 167–181, 2022.
31. Rawat, R., Chakrawarti, R.K., Vyas, P., Gonzáles, J.L.A., Sikarwar, R., Bhardwaj, R., Intelligent Fog Computing Surveillance System for Crime and Vulnerability Identification and Tracing. *Int. J. Inf. Secur. Priv. (IJISP)*, *17*, 1, 1–25, 2023.
32. Meland, P.H., Bernsmed, K., Wille, E., Rødseth, Ø.J., Nesheim, D.A., A retrospective analysis of maritime cyber security incidents. *TransNav: Int. J. Mar. Navig. Saf. Sea Transp.*, *15*, 123–139, 2021.

33. Rawat, R., Oki, O.A., Sankaran, K.S., Olasupo, O., Ebong, G.N., Ajagbe, S.A., A New Solution for Cyber Security in Big Data Using Machine Learning Approach, in: *Mobile Computing and Sustainable Informatics: Proceedings of ICMCSI 2023*, Springer Nature Singapore, Singapore, pp. 495–505, 2023.
34. Kozinets, R.V., *Netnography*, Wiley Online Library, USA, 2015.

31

Review of Research Methodology and IT for Business and Threat Management

Hitesh Rawat[1]*, Anjali Rawat[2], Sunday Adeola Ajagbe[3,4] and Yagyanath Rimal[5]

[1]Department of Business Management and Economics, University of Extremadura, Badajoz, Spain
[2]Department of Computer and Communication Technology, University of Extremadura, Badajoz, Spain
[3]Department of Computer Science, University of Zululand, Kwadlangezwa, South Africa
[4]Department of Computer Engineering, Abiola Ajimobi Technical University, Ibadan, Nigeria
[5]Department of Computer Science, Pokhara University, Pokhara, Nepal

Abstract

Technology is used to improve and streamline the research process, from data collection and analysis to reporting and distribution, through the combination of research methodology (REM) and IT. To enhance accuracy and efficiency, speed up data analysis, and simplify and automate activities, specialized software such as statistical analysis programs, data visualization tools, and collaboration platforms can be used. Furthermore, handling huge amounts of information and identifying intricate patterns may be facilitated by the use of cloud computing, big data analytics, and machine learning (ML). This enables Analysts to obtain fresh perspectives and draw more defensible conclusions. An organized REM for IT and threat management is represented by the work and focuses on methodical planning of data analysis and gathering strategies. Businesses may successfully discover possible risks, vulnerabilities, and security breaches by adhering to a well-defined research process. Businesses may proactively address security risks and safeguard their digital assets by putting in place a strong research and maintenance agreement (REM).

***Keywords*:** Research methodology, IT, business, threat management, data collection

**Corresponding author*: hrawat88@gmail.com

Rajesh Kumar Chakrawarti, Ranjana Sikarwar, Sanjaya Kumar Sarangi, Samson Arun Raj Albert Raj, Shweta Gupta, Krishnan Sakthidasan Sankaran and Romil Rawat (eds.) Natural Language Processing for Software Engineering, (475–486) © 2025 Scrivener Publishing LLC

Abbreviation Used

REM	Research Methodology
IT	Information Technology
ML	Machine Learning
QLR	Qualitative Research
QTR	Quantitative Research
MMR	Mixed Methods Research
NLR	Narrative Literature Review
SLR	Systematic Literature Review
MAR	Meta-Analysis Review
SLR	Scoping Literature Review
BM	Business Management

Table 31.1 REM framework [3].

Methods	Description
Qualitative research (QLR)	• collects and analyzes data regarding lived experiences, feelings, behaviors, and the meanings people ascribe to them using non-numeric techniques. • Analyst can get a deeper understanding of intricate ideas, interpersonal relationships, or cultural phenomena with the use of this kind of study.
Quantitative research (QTR)	• Measures variables and confirms preexisting theories or hypotheses using numerical data to produce numerical statistics. • Analyst typically use exams, databases, questionnaires, surveys, and organizational records to gather information from a significant sample of individuals. • comparisons and statistical analysis to examine the data.
Mixed methods research (MMR)	• integrates QTR and QLR. • To use QLR to investigate a scenario and create a conceptual framework, Analyst may employ QTR techniques to test the model experimentally. • Using a combination of closed-ended and open-ended surveys is an additional strategy where participants can create their own responses to certain questions and use pre-written answers for others.

31.1 Introduction

A strategy framework [1] called REM [2] describes the steps Analysts take to gather, evaluate, and analyze data. It serves as a roadmap for the whole investigation, guaranteeing the accuracy and authenticity of the results. Table 31.1 provides information about the REM framework.

- **Sampling designs in REM**

A key component of a REM is sampling, which is choosing a representative sample [4] of the population to research, drawing statistical conclusions about them, and estimating the features of the entire population from these conclusions. In REM, there are two different kinds of sampling designs: nonprobability and probability. The sampling design approaches are displayed in Table 31.2.

- **Data Gathering**

During research, data [6] are collected using various methods depending on the REM being followed and the research methods being undertaken.

Table 31.2 Sampling designs methods [5].

Method	Details
Probability sampling	• A sample is taken at random from a larger population. • Methodical sample members are selected on a regular basis and necessitate choosing a sample and sample size calculation beginning point that can be performed on a regular basis. • Clusters focus-population is separated using (age, sex, geography, demographic characteristics.)
Non-probability sampling	• The convenience approach uses this method to choose subjects who are most convenient for the Analyst to reach out based on factors like time of day, location, etc. • The purpose of the Analyst is to choose who gets to participate. • Analysts take into account the target audience's comprehension as well as the study's goal. • The snowball effect relates to the individuals who have previously been selected using their social networks to suggest new possible volunteers to the Analyst. • The number of participants in the study and their characteristics are determined by the Analyst during the design phase.

Table 31.3 Data gathering methods [7].

Method	Details
QLR	▪ 1- to-1 interviews: assist in comprehending a respondent's subjective viewpoint and experience on a certain subject or incident. ▪ Analyst examine pre-existing written resources, including reports, research papers, guidelines, official documents, and so on. ▪ For Learning the participants opinions on a particular issue, a moderator and a small sample of around 8–12 people generally participate in constructive conversations. ▪ QLR observation focusses on the five senses (sight, smell, touch, taste, and hearing) that are used by Analyst to gather data.
QTR	▪ Probability sampling most frequently used. ▪ Interviews - phone or in person. ▪ Observations -Analyzing people behavior in defined surroundings. ▪ Analyzing published papers. ▪ Includes questions and surveys- can be conducted via platforms (online or offline), based on the needs and size of the sample.

Both QLR and QTR have different data Gathering methods. Table 31.3 shows the Data Gathering Methods.

- **Data Analysis Methods**

For QLR and QTR, the data gathered [8, 11–13] using the different techniques must be analyzed to produce insightful findings. Between QTR and QLR, these data analysis techniques also vary. Table 31.4 provides information on data analysis techniques.

- **Literature Review**

The classifications of the literature reviews are displayed in Table 31.5.

- **Dataset**

A dataset in REM is a group of data that's used for modeling, analysis, or ML algorithm training. Although spreadsheets, tables, and databases are frequently used to organize datasets, they might simply include notes from QLR or photos or videos that were shot for a research project.

Table 31.4 Data analysis methods [8].

Methods	Details
QTR	• Incorporates a deductive approach to data analysis. • descriptive and inferential, uses statistical analysis software to examine numerical data. • descriptive analysis is used to characterize data types. • descriptive analysis methods: frequency measurements, central tendency measurements. • dispersion or variation measurements, • Position measurement (percentile and quartile rankings).
Inferential analysis	• It is employed to forecast the behavior of a broader group by analyzing data gathered from a smaller one. • The purpose of this analysis is to examine the connections between various variables. • To comprehend the link between two or more variables, use correlation. Examine the association between several variables using a cross-tabulation method. • Analyze the effects of independent factors on the dependent variable using regression analysis. • Frequency tables: To comprehend data frequency. • The purpose of variance analysis is to determine how much two or more variables differ from one another in an experiment.
QLR	• It uses an inductive approach to data analysis, in which theories are generated subsequent to data gathering. • Content analysis: This involves looking for certain words or concepts in texts to analyze recorded information from text and pictures. • Analyzing material from sources like surveys, field observations, and interviews is possible with narrative analysis. • Research issues are addressed by means of the narratives and viewpoints that individuals communicate. • Discourse analysis: This method examines social context, or the surroundings and way of life in which a conversation takes place, while analyzing interactions with individuals. • Grounded theory: formulates theories by gathering and evaluating facts in order to explain why a thing happened. • Thematic analysis is the process of finding significant themes or patterns in data and using them to solve problems.

Table 31.5 Literature review classifications [10].

Method	Details
Narrative Literature review (NLR)	• One type of research approach called a narrative review is a comprehensive summary of primary studies on a certain subject. • The review may be used to make methodical findings since it is grounded in the Analyst 's personal experience and current beliefs.
Systematic Literature review (SLR)	• Research is used to guide practice and decision-making based on evidence. • It entails looking for, assessing, and combining research findings. The methods used in systematic reviews might differ, and they are frequently study-specific.
Meta-analysis review (MAR)	• a statistically based systematic review that synthesizes the findings of separate investigations. • It can offer more accurate health care impact estimates than those obtained from the individual research included.
Scoping Literature Review (SLR)	• focuses on big research problems to gauge the amount of research that has been done. • It offers a first estimation of the possible volume and range of the body of research literature that is now accessible. • Key ideas, features of the literature, and research gaps may all be found with the use of scoping reviews.

Table 31.6 Datasets [6, 7].

Methods	Details
Numerical	• include numerals and are employed in QTR.
Text	• include documents, text messages, and postings.
Multimedia	• include music, video, and picture files
Time-series	• hold information gathered over time for trend and pattern analysis.
Spatial	• Include data that is spatially related, like GPS information.
Correlation	• include interrelated variables, meaning that altering one will affect all of the others.
Bivariate	• include a pair of variables that convey a connection between the information. • To illustrate how temperature variations relate to the time of day. • A dataset can comprise a temperature variable and a time variable.

Text, numbers, pictures, audio files, and even simple item descriptions can all be found in datasets. The details of the datasets are displayed in Table 31.6.

- **REM for Business Management**

REM is a fundamental framework [5, 6] for investigating and understanding various phenomena, with significant implications for business management. Its purpose lies in facilitating informed decision making, problem-solving, performance evaluation, and fostering innovation. Within the dynamic landscape of business management, REM shows about the evidence-based decision making, risk mitigation, strategic planning, and continuous improvement.

In the dynamic and increasingly complex landscape of business management, the importance of REM cannot be overstated. The Table 31.7 shows about the RM in BM.

- **Threat management**

Threat management [4–7] is an all-encompassing strategy that guards against cyber threats to an organization's networks, data, and systems

Table 31.7 RM in BM [8].

Method	Details
Evidence-Based Decision Making	• REM offers a paradigm for deriving actionable insights from large datasets in an era of abundant data. • empowering organizations to make well-informed decisions based on factual information rather than conjecture or gut feelings.
Risk Mitigation	• Businesses may reduce the risks associated with market instability, competitive challenges, and disruptive technologies by carrying out in-depth research and analysis. • By detecting possible risks and opportunities, REM facilitates proactive risk management, allowing companies to create backup plans and calculate reactions.
Strategic Planning	• Strategic planning is aided by REM's insightful analysis of consumer behavior, market trends, and competitive dynamics. • Businesses may achieve sustained development and competitive advantage by formulating strategic objectives. • outlining executable plans and allocating resources efficiently by utilizing strong research approaches.
Continuous Improvement	• REM encourages companies to embrace innovation, experimentation, and learning to promote a culture of continuous improvement. • Businesses are able to accommodate changing client wants and preferences by improving product and service offerings, streamlining operations, and refining strategy through iterative research cycles.

using a range of technologies and procedures. It entails locating, evaluating, ranking, and reacting to threats to lessen the effect of possible security events. Table 31.8 provides information on threat management systems.

- **REM tools**

Analysts [4] can get assistance from REM tools [6, 7] and software for activities like organizing references, doing data analysis, and creating data visualizations. Software for managing references: It facilitates the gathering,

Table 31.8 Threat management systems [7, 8].

Method	Details
Risk assessment	• To assist teams in understanding the state of their systems and creating a strategy to remedy vulnerabilities. • Threat intelligence is correlated with asset inventories and existing vulnerability profiles.
STRIDE model	• Identifying all ecosystem assets that may be attacked is part of the STRIDE attack [2, 3] strategy. • The rapid pace of digital change on a worldwide scale has hampered this process.
Asset identification	• Examine attack patterns and behaviors to find instances of them. • Expert systems, ML, and statistical techniques are frequently used in this discipline.
Attack detection	• a proactive strategy to reduce risk that aids security teams by charting. • the network's weak points so they can evaluate risk, find weaknesses, and take preventative action to safeguard important assets.
Attack path modeling	• a threat modeling reference model (REM) that aids in the identification and classification of possible security risks to software systems by developers and security experts. • This aids in their ability to identify possible security threats to a system and to prioritize security measures appropriately.
Threat analysis	• explains how possible enemies might make use of system flaws to further their objectives. • It recognizes risks and establishes a policy for mitigating them for a particular architecture, feature set, and configuration.

sharing, and organization of research. Table 31.9 provides information about the RM Tools.

Tools for statistical analysis and data visualization [1, 10] that assist Analyst in analyzing data aid in data visualization for academics. Details on the visualization tools are displayed in Table 31.10.

Table 31.9 RM tools [8, 9].

Tool	Details
Zotero:	• A free, browser-integrated application that assists Analyst in storing papers, publications, and research projects. • It features an organizing system for classifying, labeling, and labeling data.
Mendeley:	• It has the ability to import articles from other research applications and automatically create bibliographies.
EndNote:	• A single, comprehensive tool for organizing citations and references. • Analyst to format and construct bibliographies, track adjustments and changes, and exchange references with teams.

Table 31.10 Visualization tools [9, 10].

Tool	Details
SPSS	• It provides data analysis for descriptive and bivariate statistics, predictions, and numerical result forecasts. • Facilitates data processing, direct marketing, and graphing.
Tableau and Excel	• A data visualization tool

31.2 Conclusion

For business and threat management in IT, REM is essential. It entails gathering information, analyzing it, and drawing conclusions using methodical procedures. Businesses may recognize possible dangers, make well-informed choices, and create efficient risk-mitigation plans by utilizing a clearly defined REM. This method guarantees that IT expenditures are optimized for security and performance and are in line with business objectives. Data gathering and analysis in threat management research may be improved by implementing cutting-edge IT technologies. Analyst can more quickly spot patterns and trends by utilizing advanced techniques. This may result in improved threat mitigation and response plans. When combined with IT solutions, REM may offer insightful information and enhance decision-making procedures for companies dealing with a range of security issues.

References

1. Paul, J. and Criado, A.R., The art of writing literature review: What do we know and what do we need to know? *Int. Bus. Rev.*, *29*, 4, 101717, 2020.
2. Wohlin, C. and Runeson, P., Guiding the selection of research methodology in industry–academia collaboration in software engineering. *Inf. Softw. Technol.*, *140*, 106678, 2021.
3. Staron, M. and Staron, M., Action research as research methodology in software engineering, in: *Action Research in Software Engineering: Theory and Applications*, pp. 15–36, 2020.
4. Seniv, M.M., Kovtoniuk, A.M., Yakovyna, V.S., Tools for selecting a software development methodology taking into account project characteristics. *Radio Electron. Comput. Sci. Control*, 2, 1, 175–175, 2022.
5. Brachle, B.J., McElravy, L.J., Matkin, G.S., Hastings, L.J., Preparing leadership scholars in PhD programs: A review of research methodology training. *J. Leadersh. Educ.*, *20*, 3, 108–122, 2021.
6. Girard, N., Cardona, A., Fiorelli, C., Learning how to develop a research question throughout the PhD process: training challenges, objectives, and scaffolds drawn from doctoral programs for students and their supervisors, in: *Higher Education*, pp. 1–20, 2024.
7. Taekema, S. and van Klink, B., Progress in Legal Methodology–A Methodological Assessment of Six PhD Theses, in: *Law and Method*, pp. 1–24, 2023.
8. Mishra, A.K., Tyagi, A.K., Dananjayan, S., Rajavat, A., Rawat, H., Rawat, A., Revolutionizing Government Operations: The Impact of Artificial Intelligence in Public Administration, in: *Conversational Artificial Intelligence*, pp. 607–634, 2024.
9. Noonia, A., Beg, R., Patidar, A., Bawaskar, B., Sharma, S., Rawat, H., Chatbot vs Intelligent Virtual Assistance (IVA), in: *Conversational Artificial Intelligence*, pp. 655–673, 2024.
10. Rawat, R. and Rajavat, A., Perceptual Operating Systems for the Trade Associations of Cyber Criminals to Scrutinize Hazardous Content. *Int. J. Cyber Warf. Terror. (IJCWT)*, *14*, 1, 1–19, 2024, http://doi.org/10.4018/IJCWT.343314.
11. Nahar, S., Pithawa, D., Bhardwaj, V., Rawat, R., Rawat, A., Pachlasiya, K., Quantum technology for military applications, in: *Quantum Computing in Cybersecurity*, pp. 313–334, 2023.

12. Sikarwar, R., Shakya, H.K., Kumar, A., Rawat, A., Advanced Security Solutions for Conversational AI, in: *Conversational Artificial Intelligence*, pp. 287–301, 2024.
13. Pithawa, D., Nahar, S., Bhardwaj, V., Rawat, R., Dronawat, R., Rawat, A., Quantum Computing Technological Design Along with Its Dark Side, in: *Quantum Computing in Cybersecurity*, pp. 295–312, 2023.

About the Editors

Rajesh Kumar Chakrawarti, PhD is a dean and professor in the Department of Computer Science and Engineering, Sushila Devi Bansal College, Bansal Group of Institutions, India. He has over 20 years of professional experience in academia and industry. Additionally, has organized and attended over 200 seminars, workshops, and conferences and has published over 100 research papers and book chapters in nationally and internationally revered publications.

Ranjana Sikarwar is currently pursuing a PhD from Amity University, Gwalior. She competed her Bachelor of Engineering in 2006 and Master of Technology in Computer Science and Engineering in 2015. Her research interests include social network analysis, graph mining, machine learning, Internet of Things, and deep learning.

Sanjaya Kumar Sarangi, PhD is an adjunct professor and coordinator at Utkal University with over 23 years of experience in the academic, research, and industry sectors. He has a number of publications in journals and conferences, has authored many textbooks and book chapters, and has more than 30 national and international patents. He is an active member and life member of many associations, as well as an editor, technical program committee member, and reviewer in reputed journals and conferences. He has dedicated his career to taking care of Information and Communication Technology to enhance and optimize the information and worldwide research that can lead to improved student learning and teaching methods.

Samson Arun Raj Albert Raj, PhD is an assistant professor and placement coordinator in the Division of Computer Science and Engineering, School of Computer Science and Technology, Karunya Institute of Technology and Sciences, Tamil Nadu, India. His research is focused on smart city development using drone networks and energy grids with various applications, and his areas of expertise include wireless sensor networks, vehicular ad-hoc networks, and intelligent transportation systems.

Shweta Gupta, Assistant Professor, Computer Science and Engineering Department, Medicaps University, Indore (M.P.), India. I am Shweta Gupta work as an assistant professor of computer science and engineering at Medicaps University, with a focus on Natural Language Processing, Data mining, machine learning. I want to close the knowledge gap between theory and real-world applications in the tech sector through my love of research and teaching. My approach is centred on encouraging creativity and motivating students to strive for technological excellence.

Krishnan Sakthidasan Sankaran, PhD is a professor in the Department of Electronics and Communication Engineering at Hindustan Institute of Technology and Science, India. He has been a senior member of the Institute of Electrical and Electronics Engineers for the past ten years and has published more than 70 papers in referred journals and international conferences. He has also published three books to his credit. His research interests include image processing, wireless networks, cloud computing, and antenna design.

Romil Rawat has attended several research programs and received research grants from the United States, Germany, Italy, and the United Kingdom. He has chaired international conferences and hosted several research events, in addition to publishing several research patents. His research interests include cyber security, Internet of Things, dark web crime analysis and investigation techniques, and working towards tracing illicit anonymous contents of cyber terrorism and criminal activities.

Index

Also of Interest

From the same editors

Online Social Networks in Business Frameworks, Edited by Sudhir Kumar Rathi, Bright Keswani, Rakesh Kumar Saxena, Sumit Kumar Kapoor, Sangita Gupta, and Romil Rawat, ISBN: 9781394231096. This book presents a vital method for companies to connect with potential clients and consumers in the digital era of Online Social Networks (OSNs), utilizing the strength of well-known social networks and AI to achieve success through fostering brand supporters, generating leads, and enhancing customer interactions.

Quantum Computing in Cybersecurity, Edited by Romil Rawat, Rajesh Kumar Chakrawarti, Sanjaya Kumar Sarangi, Jaideep Patel, and Vivek Bhardwaj, ISBN: 9781394166336. This cutting-edge new volume provides a comprehensive exploration of emerging technologies and trends in quantum computing and how it is used in cybersecurity, covering everything from artificial intelligence to how quantum computing can be used to secure networks and prevent cyber crime.

ROBOTIC PROCESS AUTOMATION, Edited by Romil Rawat, Rajesh Kumar Chakrawarti, Sanjaya Kumar Sarangi, Rahul Choudhary, Anand Singh Gadwal, and Vivek Bhardwaj, ISBN: 9781394166183. Presenting the latest technologies and practices in this ever-changing field, this groundbreaking new volume covers the theoretical challenges and practical solutions for using robotics across a variety of industries, encompassing many disciplines, including mathematics, computer science, electrical engineering, information technology, mechatronics, electronics, bioengineering, and command and software engineering.

AUTONOMOUS VEHICLES VOLUME 1: Using Machine Intelligence, Edited by Romil Rawat, A. Mary Sowjanya, Syed Imran Patel, Varshali Jaiswal, Imran Khan, and Allam Balaram. ISBN: 9781119871958. Addressing the current challenges, approaches and applications relating to autonomous vehicles, this groundbreaking new volume presents the research and techniques in this growing area, using Internet of Things, Machine Learning, Deep Learning, and Artificial Intelligence.

AUTONOMOUS VEHICLES VOLUME 2: Smart Vehicles for Communication, Edited by Romil Rawat, Purvee Bhardwaj, Upinder Kaur, Shrikant Telang, Mukesh Chouhan, and K. Sakthidasan Sankaran, ISBN: 9781394152254. The companion to *Autonomous Vehicles Volume 1: Using Machine Intelligence*, this second volume in the two-volume set covers intelligent techniques utilized for designing, controlling and managing vehicular systems based on advanced algorithms of computing like machine learning, artificial Intelligence, data analytics, and Internet of Things with prediction approaches to avoid accidental damages, security threats, and theft.

Check out these other related titles from Scrivener Publishing

FACTORIES OF THE FUTURE: Technological Advances in the Manufacturing Industry, Edited by Chandan Deep Singh and Harleen Kaur, ISBN: 9781119864943. The book provides insight into various technologies adopted and to be adopted in the future by industries and measures the impact of these technologies on manufacturing performance and their sustainability.

AI AND IOT-BASED INTELLIGENT AUTOMATION IN ROBOTICS, Edited by Ashutosh Kumar Dubey, Abhishek Kumar, S. Rakesh Kumar, N. Gayathri, Prasenjit Das, ISBN: 9781119711209. The 24 chapters in this book provide a deep overview of robotics and the application of AI and IoT in robotics across several industries such as healthcare, defense, education, etc.

SMART GRIDS FOR SMART CITIES VOLUME 1, Edited by O.V. Gnana Swathika, K. Karthikeyan, and Sanjeevikumar Padmanaban, ISBN: 9781119872078. Written and edited by a team of experts in the field, this first volume in a two-volume set focuses on an interdisciplinary perspective on the financial, environmental, and other benefits of smart grid technologies and solutions for smart cities.

SMART GRIDS FOR SMART CITIES VOLUME 2: Real-Time Applications in Smart Cities, Edited by O.V. Gnana Swathika, K. Karthikeyan, and Sanjeevikumar Padmanaban, ISBN: 9781394215874. Written and edited by a team of experts in the field, this second volume in a two-volume set focuses on an interdisciplinary perspective on the financial, environmental, and other benefits of smart grid technologies and solutions for smart cities.

SMART GRIDS AND INTERNET OF THINGS, Edited by Sanjeevikumar Padmanaban, Jens Bo Holm-Nielsen, Rajesh Kumar Dhanaraj, Malathy Sathyamoorthy, and Balamurugan Balusamy, ISBN: 9781119812449. Written and edited by a team of international professionals, this groundbreaking new volume covers the latest technologies in automation, tracking, energy distribution and consumption of Internet of Things (IoT) devices with smart grids.

DESIGN AND DEVELOPMENT OF EFFICIENT ENERGY SYSTEMS, edited by Suman Lata Tripathi, Dushyant Kumar Singh, Sanjeevikumar Padmanaban, and P. Raja, ISBN 9781119761631. Covering the concepts and fundamentals of efficient energy systems, this volume, written and edited by a global team of experts, also goes into the practical applications that can be utilized across multiple industries, for both the engineer and the student.

INTELLIGENT RENEWABLE ENERGY SYSTEMS: Integrating Artificial Intelligence Techniques and Optimization Algorithms, edited by Neeraj Priyadarshi, Akash Kumar Bhoi, Sanjeevikumar Padmanaban, S. Balamurugan, and Jens Bo Holm-Nielsen, ISBN 9781119786276. This collection of papers on artificial intelligence and other methods for improving renewable energy systems, written by industry experts, is a reflection of the state of the art, a must-have for engineers, maintenance personnel, students, and anyone else wanting to stay abreast with current energy systems concepts and technology.

SMART CHARGING SOLUTIONS FOR HYBRID AND ELECTRIC VEHICLES, edited by Sulabh Sachan, Sanjeevikumar Padmanaban, and Sanchari Deb, ISBN 9781119768951. Written and edited by a team of experts in the field, this is the most comprehensive and up to date study of smart charging solutions for hybrid and electric vehicles for engineers, scientists, students, and other professionals.

Printed in the USA/Agawam, MA
September 16, 2026

910661.159